W9-CEF-147

#60538-1/2

CANADA'S 1960s:
THE IRONIES OF IDENTITY IN A REBELLIOUS ERA

Rebellious youth, the Cold War, New Left radicalism, Pierre Trudeau, Red Power, Quebec's call for Revolution, Marshall McLuhan – these are just some of the forces and figures that come to mind at the mere mention of the 1960s in Canada. Focusing on the major movements and personalities of the time, as well as the lasting influence of the period, *Canada's 1960s* examines the legacy of this rebellious decade's impact on contemporary notions of Canadian identity. Bryan Palmer demonstrates how, after massive postwar immigration, new political movements, and at times violent protest, Canada could no longer be viewed in the old ways. National identity, long rooted in notions of Canada as a white settler Dominion of the North and profoundly marked by the country's origins as part of the British Empire, had become unsettled.

Concerned with how Canadians entered the 1960s relatively secure in their national identities, Palmer explores the forces that contributed to the post-1970 uncertainty about what it was to be Canadian. Tracing the significance of dissent and upheaval among youth, trade unionists, university students, Native peoples, and Québécois, Palmer shows how the Sixties ended the entrenched, nineteenth-century notions of Canada. The irony of this rebellious era, however, was that while it promised so much in the way of change, it failed to provide a new understanding of Canadian national identity.

A compelling and highly accessible work of interpretive history, *Canada's 1960s* is the book of the decade about an era many regard as the most turbulent and significant since the years of the Great Depression and the Second World War.

BRYAN D. PALMER is a professor and Canada Research Chair in the Department of Canadian Studies at Trent University.

Canada's 1960s

The Ironies of Identity
in a Rebellious Era

BRYAN D. PALMER

UNIVERSITY OF TORONTO PRESS
Toronto Buffalo London

© University of Toronto Press Incorporated 2009
Toronto Buffalo London
www.utppublishing.com
Printed in Canada

ISBN 978-08020-9954-9 (cloth)
ISBN 978-08020-9659-3 (paper)

Printed on acid-free paper

Library and Archives Canada Cataloguing in Publication

Palmer, Bryan D., 1951–
Canada's 1960s : the ironies of identity in a rebellious era / Bryan D. Palmer.

Includes bibliographical references and index.
ISBN 978-0-8020-9954-9 (bound) ISBN 978-0-8020-9659-3 (pbk.)

1. Canada – History – 1963–. 2. Canada – Social conditions – 1945–1971.
3. Nineteen sixties. 4. National characteristics, Canadian. I. Title.

FC625.P34 2009   971.064'3   C2008-907729-6

University of Toronto Press acknowledges the financial assistance to its publishing program of the Canada Council for the Arts and the Ontario Arts Council.

University of Toronto Press acknowledges the financial support for its publishing activities of the Government of Canada through the Book Publishing Industry Development Program (BPIDP).

This book has been published with the help of a grant from the Canadian Federation for the Humanities and Social Sciences, through the Aid to Scholarly Publications Programme, using funds provided by the Social Sciences and Humanities Research Council of Canada.

*For Alvin and all of those who keep
a part of the flame of 1968 burning brightly*

Contents

Acknowledgments

I owe a great debt to the Canada Research Chairs program, which for the past seven years has funded my research and allowed me to pursue it without inhibition. At Trent University I have been favoured with a supportive administration that has always done what it could to advance my scholarship. I am particularly grateful to James Parker, Associate Vice-President Research; Susan Apostle-Clark, Vice-President Academic; and two Deans of Arts and Science, Colin Taylor and Christine McKinnon. My colleagues in Canadian Studies are a wonderful group, always ready to read a chapter or discuss a project. The Frost Centre for Canadian and Indigenous Studies at Trent University, headed in the recent past by Joan Sangster and James Struthers, has provided a congenial and helpful environment in which to undertake research and participate in graduate teaching. Students in my undergraduate lecture course, Canadian Studies 228H (Canada in the 1960s), heard me talk this book in lectures before anyone else read its words on a page. It was from this course that this book took flight. Trent-inspired, it has been Trent-supported ever since.

I am deeply grateful for the rigorous reading the manuscript as a whole received from four critical, if divergent, thinkers. I sent a long first draft to these colleagues, asking that they spare me nothing. Ramsay Cook, Alvin Finkel, Cy Gonick, and Mel Watkins took the original manuscript seriously enough to pull it apart here and there, to prod me to rethink almost every chapter, and to let me know where I was off track or what I had failed to include in my coverage. Each of these readers was, in various ways, present at the creation of something associated with the 1960s, and all of them brought different sensibilities and sympathies to their scrutiny of my account. None agree with me in everything I have written. As sensitive readers will know well, Ramsay, in particular, is especially distanced from much of the interpretation and argument that follow. And yet he was able to be fair-minded and to push me in directions where I needed to go. Each of these original readers, then, made this book better, although none can be held accountable for my ideas or the shortcomings that continue to exist in my presentation of Canada's 1960s.

Others, too, read chapters for me and improved them greatly. Among those who provided me much food for thought are Dimitry Anastakis, Gillian Balfour, Joanne Chuvalo, Mike Davis, Greg Kealey, John Milloy, Dimitri Roussopoulos, Joan Sangster, and John Wadland. Len Husband at the University of Toronto Press was always an advocate of this book from the moment he read, and commented perceptively on, the chapter on George Chuvalo. Since then he has done everything an author could imagine to help this book see the light of day. I owe him much. I am grateful to Frances Mundy for guiding this book expertly through the production process and to Jim Leahy for his sensitive copy editing. A first draft of the chapter on Red Power received a highly critical peer review from two scholars, both of whom saw many flaws in the analysis. While I disagree with much of the criticism received, I have benefited greatly from it, and the chapter is now seriously amended and its arguments, I hope, stated more clearly and more convincingly. I received particularly good guidance from two anonymous peer reviews commissioned by the University of Toronto Press.

For research aid I was truly blessed with some marvellous assistance. I thank in particular Donica Belisle, Caroline Langill, and Kevin Plummer. A current student and two former students – Ted McCoy, Todd McCallum, and Sean Purdy – have given me direction and provided me with sources for which I am grateful. Portions of the manuscript were presented at various public lectures, workshops, and conferences at the Munk Centre, University of Toronto; Queen's University; Trent University's Seventh Annual Rooke Lectures; and the Society for Socialist Studies. I thank the audiences for their stimulations and challenges.

As I was trying to finish this book I faced a particularly trying ordeal associated with an attempt to see justice done in the Trent University Faculty Association. What some of us tried to do was, I would suggest, very much 'a Sixties thing.' As such, it proved to be, every step of the way, an uphill battle. And, as was so often the case in that decade of tumult, what was fought for was not, in the end, achieved. But it was not for lack of trying; perhaps some good was done. I did manage to see, for instance, that some people are indeed made of 'the right stuff.' I would like to thank Gillian Balfour and Peter Dawson for their efforts and, especially, Mary-Jo Nadeau and Joan Sangster, who, in their different ways, never let me down and were always there, knowing what to do and why it was important to do it.

Joan, who has given me everything a loving partner could, makes so much possible that I cannot begin to even list the ways she keeps me going. I depend on her warmth, affection, and tenderness, as well as her capacity to challenge and push me in so many ways. I could not imagine either my intellectual life or my social being without her. Our love is both a product of the intersections of our politics and a measure of the ways in which our mutual attractions and regards can thrive amid difference.

Those closest to me who were not born until decades after the 1960s – Beth, Kate, Laura, and Rob – will, I hope, read this book and appreciate how it was that their parents' pasts formed something of their lives, even if this was not entirely, as Marx would have said, of their own choosing. Their causes will always, at least in part, be mine as well. Yet, undoubtedly, they will strike out on their own roads. This is as it should be.

This book is dedicated to all of those who keep something of the flame of 1968 burning brightly. In particular, I offer it to my friend Alvin. He knows how important it is to stand up and be counted and to speak his mind in the face of injustice and wrong. No one tells a better story.

CANADA'S 1960s:
THE IRONIES OF IDENTITY IN A REBELLIOUS ERA

Prologue

Canada in the 1960s: Looking Backward

Any real change involves the breakup of the world as one has always known it, the loss of all that gave one an identity, the end of safety.

James Baldwin

In late May 2006, as I was envisioning (prematurely as it turned out) the completion of this book, tensions peaked in the southern Ontario town of Caledonia. A land claims dispute, pitting two developers and the apparatus of the state and capitalist notions of 'progress' against the Six Nations Confederacy, had grown increasingly rancorous over the course of four months. On Victoria Day, Aboriginal protesters and white townspeople clashed across barricades. A roadway blockade had been set up by Native people tired of governing authority's complacency in the face of their insistence that the land ceded to them in a nineteenth-century treaty was being sold to build a subdivision of 600 houses. Bread and cheese were dropped off at the site. But the ritual, now a century-and-a-half old, of the British monarch providing the Six Nations and other 'Indian' subjects with the offerings of Empire's Victoria Day table as an expression of paternal goodwill had become rather tired. On 22 May 2006, in Caledonia, the plastic-wrapped slabs of cheddar and loaves of sliced white bread were perhaps regarded as much as an insult

Donald Fleming, John G. Diefenbaker, and E. Davie Fulton, Progressive Conservative Party Convention, Ottawa, Ontario, December 1956 (Library and Archives Canada/Duncan Cameron/PA-112695).

as an invocation of peaceable coexistence. They were thrown back at
those who brought the symbolic sustenance to their Aboriginal neighbours. Victoria Day's gifts became yet another projectile in the guerilla
war of Canada's white colonizers and First Nations peoples.[1]

More than a year later, with frustrations growing among Canada's
Indigenous populations, a National Day of Action was organized on 29 June
2007. It brought together established Native leaders, such as Phil
Fontaine, Grand Chief of the Assembly of First Nations, as well as Liberal
Party opposition leader Stéphane Dion, Canadian Auto Workers president Buzz Hargrove, and the New Democratic Party's Jack Layton, all of
whom committed themselves to march with thousands of others – Aboriginal and white – to protest treaty violations, land claims that remained
unresolved, and the poverty and living conditions of Canada's Native
men, women, and children. The National Day of Action, which promised
Aboriginal-led marches and actions across the country, also pitted those
who advocated peaceful, lawful demonstrations against a more radical
and militant minority, among them a Mohawk warrior named Shawn
Brant. Brant helped to orchestrate disruptive blockades and direct action
tactics that brought central Canada's rail and highway arteries to a grinding halt. As cheese became a missile in 2006, and as the National Day of
Action approached at the end of June 2007, not a few Canadians pondered the meaning of national identity, or wondered aloud if something
of the 1960s and its protest traditions had lived on into a new century.[2]

Many Canadians were undoubtedly puzzled by the image of Native
people tossing packaged dairy products and bread across a land claims
barrier. Victoria Day traditions are poorly understood in present-day
Canada. More common is appreciation of the politics of Aboriginal protest. What follows attempts to convey both how Victoria Day changed in
the 1960s, and how Indigenous peoples, who have a long and varied history of political interaction with white settlers and the structured relations of colonizing power in Canada, also shifted their stance in the
same decade, adopting more militant tactics. In this they were not
unlike dissident counterparts in Quebec and youthful radicals in the
unions and the universities, who raised the banners of revolutionary
resistance, wildcat strikes, and New Left thought and action in particularly unruly ways. All of this, as is well known, is associated with the
decade known as 'the Sixties.'

Much more happened in the 1960s, however. The country's long-
standing self-image of itself as a settler dominion, an empire of the
north, a British colony that marched progressively and valiantly to its

particular version of nationhood, was dealt a series of decisive blows in this critical decade. Canada as it had been known ceased, for all practical purposes, to exist in the 1960s. What once had been, was now gone.[3] What might replace it remained to be determined and, arguably, is still very much up for grabs to this day. The legacy of the 1960s, I suggest, is not unrelated to this contemporary ambiguity of Canadian identity. The decade's developments are thus more far-reaching than many might today concede, although this heritage is also less clear-cut than some might want to claim.

Too often the Sixties are seen as *sui generis*. I try to look at the decade differently, reaching back in time to explore how it was that this era came to unfold as it did. However much the 1960s were about new developments and abrupt change, these were also times that existed in the shadows of what had gone before. It is necessary to dig rather deeply into Canada's history to understand how and why the politics and culture associated with a decade known for its departures 'happened' as it did and what this meant in terms of the nation and its identity.

It is for these reasons that this book charts the 1960s in a new way, outlining both its sense of rupture from the past, proclaimed with vigour at the time, *and* how it produced a future that could never merely go back to what had once been. The 1960s was a pivotal decade, then, not only because it was stamped with dissent, protest, and change. Canadians may have been forced to decisively shift their self-conception away from an age-old attachment to empire, in which much comfort could be taken in prideful understanding of keeping alive European traditions by sustaining a unique dominion of the north.[4] The irony of Canadian identity in the 1960s was that as the old attachment to British Canada was finally and decisively shed, it was replaced only with uncertainty. The ambivalences of the decade fuelled recognition of the crisis of Canada, admittedly a phenomenon overripe for its recognized emergence. After the 1960s, Canadians faced their futures liberated from many shackles of the past at the same time that they were puzzled by what it meant, exactly, to be Canadian.[5]

Nationalism/Nation – Identity/Irony

This phrasing – to be Canadian – is of course fraught with difficulty. All nations, according to Benedict Anderson, are 'imagined communities.' Narratives of nationhood are poured on to the representational page of everyday life, where they become the imagery of a collective self. Often this happens in the prose and hardening concoction of a forced identity that does considerable violence to the lived experience of 'millions of anonymous human beings of whom the last question asked is their nationality.'[6] Yet this insight is a relatively recent phenomenon. For much of the twentieth-century past the nineteenth-century birth of the nation-state and the ideas, principles, and commitments that either brought it into being or sustained the longing for its birth – nationalism – assumed the stature of the 'natural.'[7] All of this seemed a set of givens no more to be interrogated than other seemingly inevitable 'states': bodies, places, climates, social spaces, timeless relations.

Nations are defiantly difficult to define. They are constructs of geography, of institutions, and of the mind. Different than states, which can contain more than one nation, nations are nevertheless intimately paired with structures of governance, as the coupling 'nation-state' suggests. At their most basic, nations are rooted in material space (a common territory or homeland), rest on the historically repetitious elaboration of common memories and mythologies, develop a relatively shared mass public culture, and evolve a set of recognized legal-political-economic relations.[8] Nationalism is equally challenging to judge discerningly and define precisely, so wildly wide-ranging is its practical activity and intellectual arsenal. This encompasses, in the last two centuries, the reasonable and restrained as well as the irrational and the terrifyingly extreme.[9] As a politics of advocacy, nationalism holds that there should be a congruence between the institutions central to civil society and the collective group that is judged the legitimate heir to citizenship's rights and responsibilities. Such an ensemble is judged, in its collective being, to be the nation. It is useful, then, to appreciate how much lies in the proverbial eye of the beholder, commencing with some clarifications about beginnings.

As Gellner suggests, 'nations as a natural, God-given way of classifying men, as an inherent though long-delayed political destiny, are a myth.' But the nationalisms that brought them into being are quite real. So, too, is the apparatus of the state. It has, in relatively recent times, come to be the embodiment of aspirations forged in the belief that ostensible commonalities of culture, language, and 'race'/ethnicity dictate a superstructure of institutions, laws, and bureaucracies, all of which order life and situate it within spatial boundaries. The social metaphysic of this process of nation-building and state formation draws selectively and partially on an inherited and historically always proliferating cultural capital. Its cartography may well be an arbitrary mapping of seemingly rightful place, but the engineering agenda of nationalism registers not so much as illusion as a dominant hegemonic drive in the histories of the nineteenth and twentieth centuries. 'Nationalism,' as Gellner concludes, 'is not what it seems, and above all it is not what it seems to itself.' It revives what is often dead, invents what it needs to survive, suppresses the 'other' that complicates its need for essentialism, and fictions pristine purities out of dirtied complexities. Nationalism and the nation are thus the triumph of will over experience, of hope over actuality.[10]

The individual subjects that are made in this process, and that are pressured in so many ways to conform to it, remain, however, the ultimate articulations of this will to power and authority. To the extent that they can be made to identify with nationalist mythologies and *the* nation as the site of a significant part of their being, nationalism negotiates a part of its way through the minefield of forces competing in the struggle to secure hegemony. As Hobsbawm has argued, we can never assume that 'for most people national identification – when it exists – excludes or is always or ever superior to, the remainder of the set of identifications which constitute the social being. In fact, it is always combined with identifications of another kind, even when it is felt to be superior to them.' Moreover, he continues, 'national identification and what it is believed to imply, can change and shift in time, even in the course of quite short periods.'[11]

It is because of this that I have structured this book around identity, a term that is, admittedly, amorphously unsatisfying in its conceptual and political clarity.[12] Identity means many things to many people, and it has come to mean even more as an age of so-called 'identity politics' has elevated subjectivity to a decisive category in analytic and political practice. In what follows identity is not invested with this weighty meaning. Instead, it designates a dual process: on the one hand identity is a semantic shorthand conveying a consciousness of collectivity, a subjective understanding of attachment to the nation that is shared broadly, not quite as an essential *sameness*, and not necessarily with the fervour characteristic of deeply committed nationalism; on the other it is a social construction, often purposefully and forcefully ideological, conveyed through powerful agencies in order to foster and deepen belief in what is being proclaimed. This, I am well aware, is a less than precise formulation and, as such, it is not out of step with the indiscriminate way in which identity has come to be utilized in intellectual and political circles.[13]

National identity invariably entails historicizing a dehistoricizing endeavour. Unevenly forged on the ahistorical back of fuzzy commonalities that have been manufactured into concrete pillars of identity (language, culture, ethnicity, 'race'), national identity makes and remakes men and women in the image of such ambiguous markers. Eventually, such identity formation crashes under the burden of a long-overdue historical accounting. This introduces a final term of reference, that of irony.

Irony has a long pedigree as an analytic aid. But it also leads in many, and indeed conflicting, interpretive directions, depending on the historical, disciplinary, and political context in which it is embedded. There are pre-modern, modern, and postmodern kinds of irony,[14] stable and unstable ones.[15] Once perceived as out of fashion in traditional literary criticism, irony experienced something of a comeback in the mid- to late 1980s with the stimulations of postmodernism. Irony moved, as a trope, from being a reflection of pessimism and apolitical detachment, a condition of accommodation associated with the cynical, the absurd, and the satirical, to a rhetorical strategy, ostensibly oppositional and resisting. Much was made of playful embrace of risky subversions, adopted to destabilize the conventional and the traditional.[16]

My use of irony is more modernist than postmodernist, more historicized than textualist, and more attuned to Marxist sensibilities than it is to the reification of discursive destabilization characteristic of current theoretically fashionable premises, which in my judgment veer in a pseudo-anarchistic direction.[17] It is thus attentive to the dialectic of development, in which historical possibility emerges, finally, out of the contending oppositions that make movement possible, but also obscure and hold it back. Decisive ruptures occur, not as cataclysmic spontaneous explosion, but as a historically conditioned articulation of past determinations. Many have been in the making for some time, so much so that they may well have turned into their opposite. This historicized, Marxist sense of irony is thus classically double-visioned, as is all irony: it is critically poised to appreciate the salience of disjuncture and crisis in the social order.[18] Such a perspective highlights the capacity of objective phenomenon, pressured by the social relations of production and power, to become what they once were not; to be framed by a range of ideological constructions in ways that obscure their actual meanings; and to implode rather than to fade away, giving rise to new and different contentions, seemingly benign, even banal, but pregnant with the ongoing charge of change.

There is thus a substantial gulf separating a historicized and Marxist appreciation of irony from a postmodern embrace of irony. For the latter is perhaps too willing to collapse the program of politics and the strategic charting of change into a stimulating, provocative, but always limiting, fixation on discourse. However important this may be, it is an end, to perhaps parody the Canadian literary theorist of irony, Linda Hutcheon,[19] lacking the kind of socially transformative edge that Marxism has always seen less in words and more in actions, paced not so much by rhetorical flourish and playful double-talking as by programmatic direction.[20]

Whereas postmodernists may revel in 'irony in *use*, in discourse,' then, I focus attention on practices that unfolded ironically, producing outcomes that were socially and politically ironic.[21] Less inclined to adopt irony as a means to destabilize, my approach is to highlight the ironic destabilizations that arise out of the logic of the capitalist regime of accumulation. These invariably highlight the social relations of class antagonism (exploitation) and the debilitating inevitability of inequality (oppression). Given that nationalism, the nation-state, and national identity are all situated within the totalizing and seamless web of these capitalist relations, it follows that in their making, as well, irony will inevitably unburden itself.[22]

As Terry Eagleton, arguably the single Marxist literary critic whose oeuvre rests most transparently on the use of irony, has suggested of Marx:

> The image which Marxism offers of capitalism is that of a system frozen in its fixed modes of representation, yet mobilizing a desire which overturns all representation; which gives birth to a great carnival of difference, inversion, transgression, while never ceasing to be rigidly self-identical; which reproduces itself by a rigorously quantified exchange of commodities which are spectral and elusive, incarnate conundrums of presence and absence; which constantly conjures material inequality out of abstract equality; which is in need of an authority it continually flouts, and of immutable foundations it threatens to kick away; and which ceaselessly presses up against its own limits and nourishes its own antagonists. It is no wonder that irony was one of Marx's most treasured tropes.[23]

Reading Marx – such as the brilliantly ironic *The Eighteenth Brumaire of Louis Bonaparte* – is often an education in the value of irony as a literary *and* interpretive device, a point not wasted on one of the few, and long disparaged, historical examinations of the unequal union of Canadian Confederation.[24]

The Peculiarities of the Canadians: Place and Provenance

Canada has always been an ongoing production, a creation in transit: demographic movements – 'arrivals' and 'assimilations' – people vast expanses of land. Armies of newcomers build the arteries of nationhood, and those who end their global migrations as Canadians further the projects of colonization and Confederation. One group, dominantly Anglo-European and/or Anglo-American in origin, has generally managed to come out of this process bettering others: 'nationality' is rooted in inequalities and unfairness as broad as the country itself and as deep as its layered settlements.

A young Sandor Hunyadi, the protagonist in John Marlyn's 1957 novel of immigrant alienation, *Under the Ribs of Death*, put it well in words supposedly uttered in 1913. He struggles to explain to his father how often he has been made the object of ridicule and how he longs to 'be like other people.' Mr Hunyadi asks in innocence, 'Who are these people?' Sandor answers in a whisper: 'The English ... Their fathers got all the best jobs. They're the only ones nobody ever calls foreigners. Nobody ever makes fun of their names or calls them "bologny-eaters," or laughs at the way they dress or talk ... cause when you're English it's the same as bein' Canadian.'[25] Such expansive Canadianness as emerged in the 1920–60 years, when the myth-symbol complex of identity congealed representationally in the wilderness aesthetic of the Group of Seven or the decorous order conveyed by the Royal Canadian Mounted Police and its scarlet tunic, occurred precisely because this equation of Canadian = English had involved so much erasure, subordination, and displacement.[26]

Those who have 'spoken' *Canadian*, then, have always suppressed 'Others' in their midst. Native peoples on and off reserves, including many whose isolation in the far north placed them well beyond the horizons of 'national' vision,[27] as well as other peoples of colour, such as the residents of Africville in Halifax[28] or Asians on the west coast,[29] were simply invisible until they became a 'problem' to address. Then came the ugliness of riotous street confrontations or the coercions of the state. Results might include the disciplines and punishments associated with the seemingly civilizing benevolence of the 'residential school'; levying a prohibitive 'head tax' on prospective immigrants or deporting 'dangerous foreigners'; and herding people into internment camps.[30] There was even an Order-in-Council drafted by the federal government in 1911 prohibiting immigration to Canada by anyone 'belonging to the Negro race,' but it was never declared to be in force.[31] And Canada was of course differentiated historically by two 'official' linguistic, European groups. One was admittedly more equal than the other, a stature secured within a general colonization and by a particular 'conquest.'[32]

Finally, beyond these social constructions, geological boundaries divided the country into regions by river and lake, mountain and plain, seashore and woodlot. Canada was, for a century and more, mapped as a problem to be transcended, a project whose patchwork political-economic order could only be sustained by a unique congealing of the symbolic and the substantive. This endeavour, heralded as a 'new nationality,' was, in the language of the late nineteenth and early twenti-eth centuries, *imperialist*, as Carl Berger has shown. The term designated a close connection of Canada and the 'mother country.' The young dominion's economic, military, and political development paralleled its integration, influence, and loyalty to the ideals and character of the Brit-ish Empire.[33] As Harold Adams Innis, architect of arguably Canada's most impressive interpretive contribution to political economy, put the matter in 1930, situating ideas and ideals in their material context: 'Canada remained British in spite of free trade and chiefly because she continued as an exporter of staples to a progressively industrialized mother country.'[34]

The elaboration of Canadian nationhood was thus a complicated historical process, one that unfolded at the interface of worlds old and new. It reached across the expanse of Canada's nineteenth and twentieth centuries, through two world wars and multiple moments of independence-making. A colony came to see itself as a nation. On the eve of Confederation, George Brown's Toronto *Globe* looked longingly at the expanse of the western territories, our 'national' newspaper waxing eloquent on the prospects of a provincial colony undertaking its own acts of colonization. 'If Canada acquires this territory it will rise in a few years from a position of a small and weak province to the greatest colony any country has ever possessed, able to take its place among the empires of the earth.'[35] As Canada's prime minister, Sir Wilfrid Laurier, proclaimed in a speech in London, England, in 1897: 'A colony, yet a nation – words never before in the history of the world associated together.'[36]

This history of place/provenance registers indistinctly in perhaps the major literary and sociocultural constructions of Canada predominat-ing up to the mid-1960s. Best known among these, perhaps, is Northrop

Frye's 1965 attempt to frame the pluralities of Canadian identity in a
sense of place that idealized unity as a regionalized respect for difference that stood in stark contrast to what he dubbed a strained uniformity. Frye's 'garrison mentality' was in some senses a summation of what
seemed to be reflected in the poetry and prose of nation prior to the
1960s, in which the accent had been on the frontiers – physical and psychological – that separate Canadians from one another, as well as from
their American and British cultural legacies.[37] In this reading, wilderness and nature figure centrally in the consciousness of being Canadian.
It is a theme pursued as well by a range of multidisciplinary cultural critics who allude to art and history as well as the printed word. Their lineage extends as far back in 'Canadian' letters as publications of the first
half of the nineteenth century. In what stands as one of the lyrical pin-
nacles of the homogenizing and mythologizing essentialism of a particular strain of the pre-1960s social construction of Canadian identity,
historian-turned-nationalist W.L. Morton wrote of 'the wilderness ven-
ture now sublimated for most of us to the summer holiday or the
autumn shoot; the greatest of joys, the return from the lonely savagery
of the wilderness to the peace of the home; the puritanical restraint
which masks the psychological tensions set up by the contrast of wilderness roughness and home discipline. The line which marks off the frontier from the farmstead, the wilderness from the baseland, the
hinterland from the metropolis,' concluded Morton with a passionate
innocence that masked the troublingly unstated coercive moulding of
all to a fabricated norm, 'runs through every Canadian psyche.' For
Morton there was but 'one narrative line in Canadian history.'[38]

   In this mythic oneness of experiences and communities, isolated and
always dwarfed by nature's many threatening challenges, Canada
emerged as a distinctly human undertaking. It was supposedly characterized by 'a great respect for the law and order that holds [it]
together, [confronting] a huge, unthinking, menacing, and formidable
physical setting.' Frye echoed the thoughts of Morton, whose 1961
reflections on identity concluded that however often and in whatever
diverse ways Canadians had succumbed to various forces, 'what is
important is not to have triumphed, but to have endured.' Margaret
Atwood's later popularization of Frye's Canadian questioning of
'Where is here?' gestured more explicitly to the difference that
scratched itself into this accent on survival. Her sense of survival highlighted Indigenous perspectives, immigrant reluctance, the peculiarities of Quebec, and the presence of troublemakers. It largely turned

the mirror darkly to Frye's light representation, reflecting not so much a repudiation of his idealization of unity as an understanding of its costs. Frye, of course, celebrated *the* tradition of Canadian literature, proclaiming with moral certainty that 'what one owes one's loyalty to is an ideal of unity, and a distrust of such a loyalty is rooted in a distrust of life itself.' Atwood, very much a product of a different epoch, clasped this same tradition in order to discover new departures. This relationship of the old and the new, and the ways they could emerge out of the crucible of difference that was the 1960s, signals something of the irony of Canadian identity in this decade of movement and change.[39]

Historicizing Identity: An Arduous Achievement

Morton's certainties of Canadian sameness, for instance, were soon judged inadequate. His embrace of a hegemonic constitutionalism that reified the British monarchical tradition appeared antiquated. It was soon superseded by Frank Underhill's attempts to revive an idealized understanding of Confederation as a project of French–English cooperation. Acknowledging the claims of Quebec nationalists as just, Underhill's 1963 Massey Lectures pleaded that they be posed in a moderate language of reciprocity and mutuality, accenting what had been and what could be accomplished in the *togetherness* of the two linguistic groups. A century before the gay and lesbian movement and the politics of alternative coalition took the rainbow sign as their symbol of diversity, Underhill hearkened back to the 1865 proposal of an urbane francophone, Henri Joly de Lotbinière, to make this many-coloured refraction the emblem of Canadian nationality. Underhill worried that Canadians were entering their second century 'without feeling very confident about the nature of our identity.'[40]

The reigning historian of liberalism had cause for concern. Over the course of the next five years few Canadians could take for granted understandings of their country as a meeting place for French–English unity. Pierre Vallières, author of arguably the most powerful statement of Québécois resentment, *White Niggers of America* (1968), delivered a message as explosive as the tactics of the underground Front de Libération du Québec (FLQ) cells that were demanding the freedom of French Canadians. Canada could no longer be politely and complacently presented as, in the 1961 words of W.L. Morton, 'one common response to land and history expressed in many strong variants' that were nevertheless 'still one in central substance.'[41] By 1968, the 'vari-

ants' were refusing to have their histories, crippled by hidden injuries
and deformed by decades of exploitation, collapsed into subordination.
Montreal streets in the years 1963–8 echoed the shouts and slogans of
the dispossessed, as Leonard Cohen's fictionalized *Beautiful Losers*
(1966) chronicled: 'History they shouted. Give us back our History!
The English have stolen our History! ... Give us our blood. We demand
our History!'[42]

Vallières's book, a New Left manifesto as well as a clarion call to action
in the name of the FLQ, was so troubling because its radicalism confirmed a good part of what the liberal-conservative mainstream had
been fretting about during the same period. *White Niggers of America*
shouted the need for national liberation in an *internationalist* idiom that
found inspiration in the struggles of the oppressed and mobilizations of
radical, oppositional youth, its companion volumes being Frantz
Fanon's *The Wretched of the Earth* (1961), *The Autobiography of Malcolm X*
(1965), and *Soul on Ice* (1968), by Black Panther spokesman Eldridge
Cleaver.[43] It was one of the ironies of an ironic decade that Quebec's
struggle for *independence* seemed, to some, *dependent* on the exhilarating
example of those very others – United States anti-war protesters, anti-
colonial guerillas, and a vanguard of African-American revolutionaries –
marked as doubly dangerous to a long-standing 'loyalist' enclave of
English-Canadian cultural nationalists. To such traditionalists the virtues
of the southern republic had always been suspect and the extremes of
those galvanized to armed rebellion especially disconcerting.[44]

Historians such as Morton and Underhill offered warnings. The philosopher George Grant acknowledged defeat. Grant would later confess
that his poignant 1965 lament for what he understood as the final,
undeniable, and inevitable failure of Canada was 'written too much
from anger and too little from irony.' He recalled the memory and tradition of a conservative project of nation-building in defiance of U.S.
domination that he saw sacrificed on the altar of capitalist accommodation to accumulation. It had proven a remaking of Canada into little
more than 'a northern extension of the continental economy.'[45] Ironically, Vallières and Grant, so obviously separable on almost all political
and intellectual planes, met at a certain juncture in obvious agreement.
The mid-1960s was, for them, one of those historical moments in bourgeois society when, in the words of Marx and Engels, 'all fixed, fast-
frozen relations, with their trail of ancient and venerable prejudices and
opinions, are swept away, all new formed ones become antiquated
before they can ossify.'[46]

To appreciate how truly unsettling the 1960s would be in terms of destabilizing notions of Canadian national identity, it is first necessary to look backward and appreciate what had been built in the aftermath of Confederation. Against all odds, it often seemed, the mythologies of nationhood had been planted and nurtured. The environment of this 'new nationality' was not always hospitable. Capitalist industrialization, economic depression, unfolding regional and 'racial' resentments such as the first and second Riel uprisings in the west, and consequent French–English tensions, all threatened the idea of nationhood and raised the spectre of annexation to the powerful republic to the south. War and the unsettled relations of the sexes, as well as the labour upheaval associated with working-class revolt in the 1917–25 period and the rallying cry of 'white Canada forever' that greeted migrants not only from Asia and India but from southern and eastern Europe as well, offered further challenges.[47] To be sure, a staple in the first wave of elite and state response was carved in the bedrock of political economy. The material imprint of nationality registered in railroads and tariff protections for native Canadian industry, dual pillars of the post-Confederation National Policy.[48] This program of development was also supplemented with an ongoing ideological construction of a Canadian identity reverential and retrospective in its historicized grasp of the canon of Canadianness. Canada was presented as peopled by a sturdy loyalist stock, attached to empire and its greatness, rooted in a northern environment of orderly advance and routinized progress.

Late nineteenth-century movements such as 'Canada First,' born of colonial elitism, first propounded the fusion of climate and character in articulating a racialized understanding of nordicity. In conjunction with a retrospective loyalism, this fashioned Canadian identity in the image of '*the Northmen of the New World.*' It was perhaps not surprising that as these northmen (and women/children) were experiencing the harsh discipline of a recently consolidated industrial-capitalist order, the 'new nationality' was framed as escaping the limiting confines of material subordination:

> Unless we intend to be mere hewers of wood and drawers of water until the end, we should in right earnest set about strengthening the foundation of our identity … It is not by mimicking the formalities of the Old World, or aping time-worn solemnities which have ceased to be solemn, that dignity is to be acquired, nor is it by pantomime or burlesque that the thews of our nationality are to be strengthened. Periwigs and Gold-sticks have had their

day, and it is not well for us to attempt to set up the mummied idols of a
buried past as objects of worship, or graft on our simple Canadian maple
the gaudy outgrowth of a luxuriant tropical vegetation. Here every man is
the son of his own works, and we need no antique code of etiquette nor the
musty rules of the Heralds' office to tell us whom or what to honour.[49]

In extolling the virtues of labour, and embracing a 'producer ideology,'
the 'new nationality' obscured the ravages and conflictual relations of
class at the historical moment of their often quite contentious birth.[50]

Canada, as a dominion of works, was to be different from the United
States or Great Britain, a solid building block of empire resting firmly
on the resources of 'the rugged Canadian character.' 'Let us fear to
become a nation where the vast wealth of a few individuals will develop
that extreme luxury which is now the disgrace of the United States,'
wrote New Brunswick's W. Frank Hatheway in a 1906 book that also
wanted no sycophantic mimicking of either the glory or dishonour of
Ireland, Scotland, or England. Hatheway's treatise was appropriately
titled *Canadian Nationality: The Cry of Labor.* 'We wear no rose, thistle or
shamrock,' Hatheway noted, Canada's 'new nationality' having been
created by 'labor,' which 'lays the foundation of every art, of all trades
and professions.' National character was not forged in texts and past
attachments, but in what people 'see, feel, and have to do.'[51]

Unlike other dominions, none of which lay north of the forty-ninth
parallel, moreover, Canada was ostensibly a natural home to a superior
'racial stock' not given to the indolence of 'coloured' southern peoples.
In conjunction with tried and true attachments to liberty and progress,
this assured the country a pride of place, even exalted station, within the
British Empire. Tramps and vagabonds were repelled by the brisk northern climate, assuring further the creation of a 'homogeneous Race' peo-
pling a 'most virile nation.'[52] When Canadians contributed that 'virility'
to sustain the empire in the Boer War[53] and in the First and Second
World Wars,[54] they tied tighter the imperialist knot of the 'new nationality' that was increasingly evident not only in Canadian arts and letters,
but also in such commonplace phenomena as mass consumption.[55]

Mid-Century Myopias

The construction of Canada's national identity, reaching from the nineteenth century into the Second World War era, was thus an arduous
achievement. Like most nationalist projects, it was an undertaking

always at odds with a mix of defiant realities, even, perhaps, with itself. Nonetheless, the settled understanding of 'being Canadian' seemed to characterize something of the tone of life in the northern dominion well into the 1950s.

This was evident in Arthur Irwin's February 1950 article in *Maclean's*, 'What It Means to Be a Canadian.' A Canadian, Irwin insisted, in the gendered language of the time, was both a Geography Man and a History Man: 'a man who has had to build a way of life suited to a stern and difficult land, in the face of great obstacles both physical and political ... a man who has responded and still responds to the pull of history ... driven by a deep intuitive response to the traditional values enshrined in his heritage overseas.' Inevitably such a man was 'skilled in the art of bringing opposites together ... a moderate, a Man of the Middle ... a conservative but not a reactionary.' Walking with tradition even as he marched with change, the Canadian could embrace socialism, but only in its mildest forms. He was invariably 'of two worlds, the Old and the New, drawing spiritual sustenance from one and finding inspiration in the challenge of the other.' But this Canadian faced, by mid-century, newly vigorous threats. As the Cold War pressured Canadians, Irwin wondered if the archetypal Canadian Man in the Middle might become 'the ham in the sandwich between the Russian colossus and the American leviathan – minced ham, that is.' How would the Canadian dominion achievement fare? Could the demonstrated, and much vaunted and valued, national independence of Canada continue to 'capture freedom to live its own unique life ... under a sovereignty not unlimited, but a sovereignty limited by organic association with other nations for a common purpose?' Irwin thought Canada by 1950 faced its greatest of many historical and geographical tests, and in the outcome lay the fate of national identity.[56]

By this late date Canadian identity of the settled imperialist, nationalist type was caught in a web of compromise and contradiction. Historian Arthur R.M. Lower was one of the first to sound the alarm bell. In what was a pioneering, if flawed, effort to write a social history of Canada, Lower pieced together a popular, late-1950s, narrative of nationality. It sketched the rise of Canadian nationhood, and its parallel of identity formation, in which the independent yeomanry and a nascent culture of nationality were schooled in imperialism and the values of rural and, of course, northern productive labours. But a clash of peoples and pleasures marked the changing face of Canada in the interwar years, and the post-1945 countenance of Canadian identity was wracked with change. For Lower, the perilous erosions of Canadian identity were evident in malignant urbanism; a social landscape altered forever by 'lesser breeds' of new immigrants (whom he had publicly opposed since 1930); the march of secularism (even paganism!) and its socio-economic incubator, the suburb; a worship of technology, consumption, and crude entertainments that signalled the rise of mass culture and, indeed, what Lower dubbed *mass-man*, who was, by definition, both *average* and *common*. 'To-day, with the five-room bungalow as the object of life and every woman in sight pregnant,' wailed Lower, the '"average man" ... and his average wife, glued to the television screen, and his average daughter, with her lipstick and her chewing gum,' were the 'fine and final product' of debased civilization. Alien ideals of equality and social justice bespoke a rampant assault on class (and gender) distinctions that the irreverent nationalist associated with the United States. The material basis for this *dilution* was the piecemeal purchase of the country by American business.[57] A symbolic marker of this economic dominance and cultural devastation was 'the great god,' the automobile. Hearkening back to the sacred land that had for so long defined the 'new nationality' of Canada, Lower bemoaned the plight of 'God's earth: rightly used, it was not only "valuable," in the sense that even the dull English Canadian could grasp, but *freedom.*' This cherished pillar of Lower's liberal order was now under assault.[58] 'Think for a moment,' he admonished, 'while the endless lines of cars sent their carbon monoxide fumes into the city streets, of what stretched on and on into the silent North!' Silent, *and* suffering, he might have added. Cars troubled Lower almost as much as the thought of students and faculty in universities using the same washroom. For they wheeled across the land, a crass reminder of an ongoing Americanization – both commercial and cultural – that reduced Canadians to the identity of 'half-way' men and women aware of being '"American" in the continental sense without being American in the national sense.' Lower located in all of this 'a new variant of imperialism.'[59]

This shrill cry of anguished, ironic defeat, in which a material and unashamedly capitalist imperialism from the American republic to the south overtook an idealist, seemingly sociocultural, imperialism of age-old attachment to a different, British, empire, would be reproduced in George Grant's mid-1960s *Lament for a Nation*. It is easy to suggest, as did Carl Berger in the conclusion to his study of the imperialist nationalist idea in the 1867–1914 years, that Grant's book was little more than a depressing footnote to the long and slow death of a particular variant of Canadian identity. For Berger, in 1970, this original imperialism belonged to 'the remote past.'[60] Certainly the 1940s witnessed many important developments in an expanding understanding of citizenship, just as the 1920s had, previously, given rise to constitutionalist crises, expanding federal authority, and, at the margins, a consolidating sense of Canadian nationhood attuned to regional diversity and the 'rights' it entailed.[61] These were part of the long process of Canadian identity's evolution, and its distancing itself from the limitations of the idea of 'new nationality' as it had been scripted by Victorian imperialists. Yet for all of this, the final curtain had not lowered on the imperial vision of Canada. To understate the significance of Grant's book erases a sense that the 1960s were not only the final, but also a decisive, nail in the coffin of entrenched understandings of a particular kind of national identity. That is what is suggested in this book.

For as late as the 1950s, however much the writing was on the crumbling wall of an antiquated, imperialistic understanding of nationhood, the values and attachments of and to this particular identity were still vigorously in evidence throughout Canada. They were on display in specific quarters of metropolitan centres, throughout small-town Ontario, within anglophone Quebec, across wide swaths of the Maritimes, dotting the Prairies and reaching into *British* Columbia.[62] 'Newer' Canadians and modern developments seemed, at times, to swamp long-established traditions. But in Ottawa's Honey-Dew Restaurant or Victoria's Empress Hotel, not to mention Toronto's Canadian National Exhibition or Montreal's Ritz Carlton Bar, the older imperialism was often on display.[63] Vincent Massey reflected this continuity as well as its waning force. His 1948 *On Being Canadian* clung to something of the imperialist 'new nationality' past and its implicit reluctance to concede much to twentieth-century Canada's Woodsworthian immigrant 'strangers within our gates' in ways that his 1961 *Canadians and Their Commonwealth* would find easier to relinquish.[64]

This survival of the old alongside the challenge of the new was one important strain in a 1954 collection of essays, *Our Sense of Identity: A Book of Canadian Essays*, edited by Malcolm Ross. It would prefigure the 1960s, if only weakly, at the same time that it hearkened back to earlier 'latent loyalties' of the sort that permeated Sara Jeannette Duncan's *The Imperialist* (1904).[65] It had room between its covers for anger and contentment, complacency and surprise, antiquated attachments and fresh, innovative convictions.[66]

Indeed, Ross's compilation, which included Northrop Frye and Marshall McLuhan, Lower, Underhill, and Harold Innis, J.S. Woodsworth, and

Barker Fairley, as well as Duncan, Susanna Moodie, Goldwin Smith, and
Joseph Howe, hinted at the future. Yet it remained dominantly rooted in
the past. 'Our Canadianism,' declared Ross in what was a mid-twentieth-
century articulation of the old coupling of colony-nation, 'is a baffling,
illogical but compulsive athleticism – a fence-leaping which is also, and
necessarily, a fence keeping.' Ambivalence and irony figured centrally in
this understanding of identity, an idealization, again, of unity in the face
of diversity: 'a deepening of the properly Canadian *feel*, an awareness of
an imaginative sympathy for the life that is to be found on the other side
of the fence.'[67] On the one hand, this was an *old* narrative of heroic
French–English coexistence, but, on the other, it tried, in Ross's construction, to open out into a larger multiculturalism, welcoming to racialized
'others' such as Montreal Jews or Winnipeg Ukrainians. Ross posited
within Canadian identity a 'movement from the dual irony to the multiple
irony, from the expansive open thrust of the French–English tension to
the many-coloured but miraculously coherent, if restless, pattern of the
authentically Canadian nationhood.'[68]

Lower was not really buying it, his brief contribution a put-down of the
colonialism of one old Tory imperialist, former prime minister R.B.
Bennett. Having 'made it' in Canada, Bennett then abandoned his nation
and, seemingly, his identity, to adopt patrician pretensions in his newly
acquired English country manor house. 'Mr. Bennett talks the traditional
language of United Empire Toryism,' Lower fumed, 'but he has had to
find room also for a new concept, Canada.' But this concept seemed to
rest uneasily on the shoulders of a national leader who, having vaulted
over 'the centuries at true pioneer speed, from poverty to prime minister,'
then leaped across the Atlantic to 'continue the process by playing at being
[an] aristocrat.' Lower found Bennett's willingness to do 'his turn of duty,'
only to set it all aside for the more congenial life of the patrician anglo-
phile, unsettling to the very notion of Canadian identity. 'Is there not a saying about deeds and words,' the historian wondered. 'Have perchance our
French co-citizens some reason for saying that we English-speaking Canadians are not Canadians at all, merely Englishmen overseas?' Lower, writing in the 1950s, was at least spared the new millennium's version of
Bennett's jettisoning of Canadian identity to take up a lordly British residence: the later spectacle of Lord Black of Crossharbour.[69]

In the 1950s this contested proclamation of Canada that emerged in
the polite sparring of Ross and Lower was highly volatile inasmuch as it
was a twisting of arms past *and* present. It was an identity tug-of-war
that alluded to what once was, and could not continue, as well as a

summoning up of what was wanted but could not yet be accepted. For Ross this *was* Canadian identity, an amalgam of resilient prudence, discursive loyalties, and endless contest with beloved 'natural' constraint:

> This prudence of ours is *not* a negative virtue. It lies in us coiled like a spring ... *Prudence is thus central to our experience without being typical of it.* For we have been relentlessly (and self-critically) in motion ... We kick against the pricks of necessity. Yet, strangely, we are in love with necessity. Our natural mode is therefore not compromise but 'irony' – the inescapable response to the presence and pressures of *opposites in tension.* Irony is the key to our identity.[70]

The point of departure for the book of suggestion that follows is that the ultimate irony lay just around the mid-1950s corner. Canadian identity was to be forged decisively anew in a truly ironic clash of the breakup of what was once thought to be and the development of an ongoing anxiety over what it was that indeed could be labelled Canada.

Canada as it had been understood to exist for centuries, however conflicted, fractured and came apart in the 1960s. This implosion was not necessarily a single, sudden event, and it drew on and grew out of many different happenings, both inside and outside of Canada. But when the Humpty Dumpty of Canadian identity came to be put back together again, in the aftermath of the shakes, rattles, and rolls of the 1960s, it bore little resemblance to the Canada that many of the pre-1950 years thought they knew so well.[71]

Suggestions and Specifics

What follows builds on the view that the 1960s wrote *finis* to the safety of being Canadian. As the decade's developments unfolded they did so in ways that ended forever the possibility of championing *one Canada*, with its Britishness a settled agreement. This was not a purposeful destruction, but it happened nonetheless. Along the way, a decade became a historical happening, riveting in its rebellious uniqueness.

Research on this period is underdeveloped, and there are so many areas where so much more needs to be explored and written about that this book can provide no complete picture of the 1960s. What I offer is not so much synthesis as suggestion, rooted in some specifics.

First, I point to the antecedents of the decade by beginning with chapters on money and the crisis-ridden years of the Cold War. It is necessary to historicize largely because such forays into the late 1950s and very early 1960s reveal the critically important material context of a capitalist global order fraught with instabilities and inherent tensions. Canada's British past was soon overshadowed by its relations with its powerful imperialist neighbour, the United States, which loomed especially large in the post–Second World War era. Second, I then follow the politics and culture of the early to mid-1960s through some detailed discussions of particular events and developments, exploring how conventional wisdoms relating to sex and gender, race and ethnicity, and ideas and governance were in the throes of destabilizing change. I use the specifics of undoubtedly atypical occurrences to highlight more general patterns. The momentum of significant sociological shifts is highlighted by examination of the Munsinger affair, the Ali–Chuvalo Maple Leaf Gardens fight of 1966, and the celebrity accorded two of Canada's most heralded figures of the 1960s, Marshall McLuhan and Pierre Elliott Trudeau. In the treatment of Trudeau, which largely ends with the furor of his 1968 electoral victory and his attaining the office of prime minister, I seek not so much to outline constitutional and legislative politics; rather I appreciate Trudeau in terms of how he offers insight into the mood of the period. Change was very much in the air, and Trudeau seemed to capture the possibilities inherent in the moment at the level of mainstream politics.

Substantive transformations were, however, taking place in other ways as well. A politics of radical, at times revolutionary, challenge, building throughout the decade, reached something of a peak in 1968–9. This is the substance of the final sections of this book. Part 3, for instance, looks at the little-studied upheavals in the streets of the mid-1960s. One chapter focuses on youthful rebels in largely working-class neighbourhoods, whose Victoria Day riots brought to the fore fears of rampaging juvenile delinquents. Another addresses young trade union dissidents, whose violent opposition to employers, the state, and trade union officialdom resulted in a wave of wildcat strikes that struck fear into the growingly complacent bosom of bourgeois authority. These mid-1960s indications that order's reign would not go unopposed were in some ways prefaces to the radical agendas of the later 1960s. They would be articulated in the rise of the New Left; the breakdown of Quebec's Quiet Revolution in the loud demand for Revolution Now! that animated a new politics of insurgent nationalism; and the emergence of Red Power militancy among Canada's Native peoples.

For some, especially those concerned with the left, the 1960s do not begin until the mid-decade teach-ins and anti–Vietnam War protests, and they carry through into the late 1970s, when many of the Marxist (especially Maoist and Trotskyist) organizations that had their origins in the later 1960s imploded.[72] As Barbara L. Tischler has noted in her introduction to a United States collection of essays, *Sights on the Sixties* (1992), there are a plethora of chronologies that could be utilized to define the decade and extend its reach both backwards and forwards in time.[73] In one of the most sophisticated attempts at periodizing the Sixties, Fredric Jameson accents the decisive breaks of 1967 and 1972–4 in an attempt to locate the politics and aesthetics of the period within a particular international conjuncture framed by Third World beginnings and global conclusions.[74]

The same approach could be taken in Canada, but I have opted, instead, for a different, seemingly more conventional setting of decadal boundaries. Admittedly, my account gestures towards the past and the future, but it tries to keep the focus on the actual years of the decade. I do this for three reasons, none of which deny the extent to which Canada's 1960s were always a mix of international and national influences. First, inasmuch as the early 1960s are critically important in setting the stage for later, more tumultuous, developments, it is crucial to understand something of how the conventionalities of the first half of the decade contained the seeds of change that would sprout with such vehemence in the post-1965 years. Trudeau's early aura, I suggest, is more explainable when we appreciate what Gerda Munsinger symbolized. We cannot understand the Canadian New Left of 1968 if we do not look seriously at initiatives and mobilizations such as the Combined Universities Campaign for Nuclear Disarmament and the Student Union for Peace Action, as well as what was happening in China, Cuba, and California. Second, those who insist that Canada's 1960s extends into the 1970s, largely because of the New Left reach of revolutionary youth in various nascent party formations, may well be right. A historical understanding of these organizations and their meaning remains underdeveloped, however, and in my view represents a different chapter in the politics and culture of dissent. One central reason for this relates to Quebec and what happened to the project of revolutionary nationalism as the decade ended in a tragic closure of possibility. This constitutes my third reason for largely ending my narrative of the 1960s in 1970. For Canada, at least, a large part of the 1960s was pushed on to entirely new terrain with the October Crisis of 1970.

Placards and slogans and youthful radical zeal were replaced by tanks and troops: the demand for revolution weakened as the costs in human life were made more visible and the march of the gendarmes grew both louder and more determined.

Canadian youth schooled in these developments would live into the late twentieth century in ways that made it difficult to forget or bypass what had happened in the course of their 1960s coming of age. They imagined a world differently. If they failed to achieve the realization of this brave new world, their Canada could never quite lapse into the comfort of the seeming fixities of a once-thought-to-be settled identity that previous generations had so often assumed as the core of their nationality. The greatest of ironies of Canada's Sixties was that in its failure to secure a truly different national identity, it nevertheless brought crashing down an understanding of nation that had lasted almost a century. To be sure, that conception of place had been eroded from within for decades, but it was surely no accident that a period as controversial, contentious, and change-ridden as was the 1960s managed, in spite of itself, to finally extricate Canadians from a national identity that so many voices had come to proclaim outmoded. If the Canada that survived the 1960s remained an uncertain and unsettled place, still very much in need of definition and consolidation four decades later, we can at least thank this momentous period for refusing to stand pat on some formulaic script, written in the hand of a tired past.

PART I

Money and Madness in the Shadow of Fear

Chapter One

When the Buck Was *Bad* : The Dollar and Canadian Identity Entering the 1960s

Money makes the world go round. Money talks, while more base entities walk. Show me the money, screams a celebrity-conscious society that knows well the final arbiter of worth. To put money in your pocket, where it is yours, even if only for a fleeting instant, is a good thing; to 'lose' money pleases no one. Like everything of value, however, money must be earned, then, with appropriate bourgeois deferment of gratification, it must be saved. It doesn't, after all, grow on trees. Money matters.

On Money

Everyone in modern Canadian society, from a toddler grasping a penny to retirees living on 'fixed'-dollar incomes, knows what money is. Scholars nevertheless have a difficult time offering concise definitions. Money has many incarnations, all of them embedded in particular political economies. It has generally been identified with its functions as a medium of exchange, a store of value, and a unit of account.[1] In past societies money was often a commodity, which meant that its value actually coincided with the material out of which it was made, gold or silver being the most common precious metals that circulated as tokens of their intrinsic worth. As the modern world of exchange was emerging, however, and as such commodity currencies proved cumbersome and were subject to rapid change or fluctuations in their value – through physical filing, wear, and inflation/depreciation, especially as

Diefen-Doller (Elsie Scott, Peterborough, Ontario).

sources of gold and silver increased with the expansion of empire into the Americas – various forms of abstract accounting were developing. In the last two centuries, the predominant of these has come to be known as fiduciary money, a set of low-denomination coins made of base metals (copper or brass) and paper bills that have a designated value unrelated to the materials from which they are fashioned.

Until the financial collapse of the Great Depression plunged the advanced capitalist nations of the world into economic uncertainty and fiscal chaos, most modern nineteenth- and twentieth-century currencies were issued in ways that related to what came to be known as the international gold standard. Under this system, national states tied their circulating money to a guarantee to buy and sell gold at a fixed price. This supposedly ensured a measure of stability in the value of money, facilitating the liberal movement of capital. There thus apparently existed a strict proportionality between money in circulation and a country's gold reserves. The latter could be depleted due to gold outflow attendant upon international balance of payments deficits, resulting in currency deflation and other economic consequences, few of them positive. This gold standard was abandoned in 1933, replaced by the gold exchange standard established at the Bretton Woods World Monetary Conference in July 1944. Some forty-four governments participated in the discussions at Bretton Woods, conducted as the hot war of the Allies against the Axis powers wound down and the nuclear age Cold War against communism commenced. One state stood pre-eminent among parties that were anything but equals. The United States was the guiding force in an institutional apparatus of a global monetary order that consolidated in the International Monetary Fund (IMF) and the World Bank. These bodies seemingly oversaw a system whereby the U.S. dollar assumed the role of a convertible currency, exchangeable for gold and to which all other currencies were related. Alone among the advanced capitalist economies of the West, the United States had both the economic authority and the imperial ambition to dictate the strategic direction of financial and defence policy in the post–Second World War world. Its dollars propped up sagging, war-torn European economies, and its military arm contained the seemingly insatiable Soviets. With the rise to global hegemony of the American superpower, money moved increasingly freely in what seemed to be a new epoch of unambiguous U.S. economic dominance. This worked as long as Cold War fears and postwar reconstruction conditioned a climate in which the dollar was sought after and held contentedly, deemed as good as gold.

For almost two decades nation-states around the world kept their currencies valued at artificially low levels in comparison with the U.S. dollar, which was the symbolic money of the 'free world colossus.' America thrived on cheap imports and low interest rates. Eventually, however, the U.S. gold reserves were dwarfed by foreign states' dollar holdings. By the end of the 1950s it was clear that as Europe and Japan recovered, trade became more balanced, and rampant and ongoing U.S. military expenditure soared, there was growing doubt of the credibility of the United States to redeem its dollars for gold. Further complications arose as American multinational corporate investment climbed overseas. Fear escalated that the United States would witness a 'run' on its reserves. Over the course of the 1960s things worsened. Having suffered a series of setbacks to its imperialist project with the rise of Castro's 'socialist' Cuba barely ninety miles offshore, the challenging superpower status attainments of the Soviet Union, and a demoralizing defeat in Vietnam, the United States took on the status of an increasingly precarious bank, poised for collapse. Its domestic scene – replete with assassinations, ghetto rebellions, and increasingly rancorous internal dissent – only added to the instability.

Money, of course, was merely the messenger of bad news. Capitalism's falling rate of profit and the global glutting of markets with overproduction ushered in an era of 'stagflation' as economic growth ground to a halt, unemployment rose to double-digit levels, and the declining purchasing power of the world's major currencies led to rising prices for goods and services. Capitalism appeared to be falling on tough times.

A superficial fix for the obviously troubled U.S. economy lay in revoking the gold-exchange standard, devaluing the dollar, and thus monetarily staving off the inevitable, at least for the immediate moment. President Richard Nixon, before his departure from the White House in disgrace, unilaterally ended the convertibility of the dollar into gold in 1971, hoping to buy some time for the rebuilding of American hegemony. Watering down the national currency eased the potential push against United States gold reserves and reinvigorated the possibility of capital movements. The 1960s thus stand as a decade signalling the beginning of the end of capitalism's long post–Second World War boom, a preface to the equally long downturn that would commence with the recession of the 1970s. Currency destabilization and significant fluctuations, devaluations, and revaluations in the early 1970s helped to usher in an era of globalization and unrestricted flow of investment that capitalism's generalized crisis demanded. Ideologically rationalized by neoliberalism and its commitment to 'market freedoms,' this destabilizing restructuring unleashed a heightened economic uncertainty unprecedented since the crash of 1929.[2]

Money is thus not only a medium of exchange. It is also a political, social, and cultural solvent, with the capacity to reconfigure people's sense of themselves, especially in an epoch of capitalism's rise and its increasingly troubled demise. Classical sociology, from Georg Simmel to Max Weber, addressed money's meanings, as have playwrights and psychoanalysts.[3] But it was Marx who perhaps explored most acutely the symbolic meaning of money within capitalist political economies. A 'visible Godhead,' money in capitalism is for Marx an intrinsic component of human alienation. All natural human warmth and sociability, all human character, is obliterated as money becomes, under capitalism, the bond binding man to man and, ultimately, man to society. But this exchange tie is destructive in its illusoriness, in its inversions. For money is the antithesis of man: it places an object above humanity, reducing humanity to its inanimate properties at the same time as it proclaims its value 'the supreme good.' Money buys what is wanted and needed and, in the process, turns desire into debt, and sustenance into separation. Its creativity is craven; its promise a distortion. Confounding and confusing all things, money *makes* man, rather than the other way around, and in the process it turns everything into its opposite:

> Money's properties are my – the possessor's – properties and essential powers. Thus, what I *am* and *am capable of* is by no means determined by my individuality ... That which I am unable to do as a *man* ... I am able to do by means of *money* ... It transforms fidelity into infidelity, love into hate, hate into love, virtue into vice, vice into virtue, servant into master, master into servant, idiocy into intelligence, and intelligence into idiocy ... As money is not exchanged for any one specific quality, for any one specific thing, or for any particular human essential power, but for the entire objective world of man and nature, from the standpoint of its possessor it therefore serves to exchange every quality for every other, even contradictory, quality and object: it is the fraternization of impossibilities. It makes contradictions embrace.

Marx concluded that money, under capitalism, is little more than 'the common procurer of people and nations.'[4]

Canadian Identity and the Dollar

Does money have a country? Convention dictates not. Studies of the invention of national traditions and nation-state formation in the nineteenth century often allude in passing to the parallel nationalization of currencies and states, but the connective tissues of identity and money are thinly developed, at best, in contemporary scholarship.[5]

As Eric Helleiner suggests, however, money historically often greased the wheels of national development, driving the emergence of national identity. Money was not just a medium of exchange, but also a language of common communication, part of a policy of emergence, as in the case of Canada's movement from colony to nation. Control over national currency was a means of exercising 'popular sovereignty,' out of which came understandings of political citizenship and entitlements.[6] As early as 1880, one advocate of currency reform proclaimed, 'What we want in this country is a money of the people, by the people, for the people, not money of the people, by the people, for the bankers.' Isaac Buchanan, an idiosyncratic Tory merchant influential in central Canadian political circles, rephrased a picturesque Francis Bacon dictum, stating in 1875 that 'money is like manure; it's only valuable when spread around.'[7]

It took the Canadian nation-state the better part of a century to get its money spreading perfected. The first Bank of Canada–issued notes appeared in 1935. In form, they were an expression of imperial connection, all of the bills adorned with portraits of the royal family, the reverse celebrating agriculture, transportation, electrical power, and modern invention. The content of this new currency, as a product of a centralized national bank, owed much to socialist demand that the onset of a debilitating economic depression be met head on by an activist, federal monetary policy. But this new national currency was rivalled, for two more decades, by other notes, issued privately by banks. The iconography of this national paper money was recognizable in its promotion of empire, for only the restricted-circulation $500 and $1,000 denominations depicted architects of Canadian nationality, former prime ministers Sir John A. Macdonald and Sir Wilfrid Laurier. It was not until 1954 that a single national, Bank of Canada–issued currency prevailed, the right of banks to issue notes being finally rescinded. This new currency reiterated the traditional understanding of landscape and nature in Canada's diverse, regionalized northern identity. Canadian money, in Emily Gilbert's words, was now 'a daily affirmation of the nation-state,' a 'medium through which social consensus, social integration and territorial borders [were] produced and reproduced.'[8]

The Postwar World of the Dollar

Yet money, like national identity, is a precarious foundation on which to build, as Canada would witness directly in the early 1960s. The Canadian dollar may well have carried representations of the kind the nation-state wanted to promote as intrinsically civic minded, but its value was also a matter of materiality. What was it worth? In the first six months of 1962 Canada experienced a dollar crisis. Its currency's value fell. As in all things monetary, more was at stake than a few cents.

Throughout the twentieth century, Canada's economy was characterized by its openness, which meant that exports and imports figured decisively in its gross national product (GNP), these two dimensions of international trade comprising fully 56 per cent of GNP in the mid-1950s. By this period, the United States had emerged as Canada's pre-eminent trading partner, overtaking Great Britain in dramatic fashion. The percentage of Canadian exports flowing to the United Kingdom declined from 38 per cent in 1937 to 18 per cent in 1955. Comparable figures for the United States were 36 and 60 per cent. In addition, whole sectors of the Canadian economy had, by 1954, come under the control of foreign capital, the bulk of it American (fully $441 million of a total of $488 million in direct foreign investment in Canada in the years 1946–50 originated in the United States). In specific Canadian economic sectors such as automobiles, chemical, rubber, electrical, pulp and paper, petroleum and natural gas, and mining, the percentage of investment associated with foreign capital was anywhere from 51 to 95 per cent. By the 1950s Canada had certainly become the single most important national outlet for U.S. direct investment, replacing Latin America as a whole and rivalling Europe. Approximately one out of every three United States foreign investment dollars came to its northern neighbour.[9]

This substitution of American economic influence for an older British domination would of course have many ramifications, not the least being those that would register in the realm of identity. As Canadians were drawn more and more into the sphere of influence of an increasingly powerful U.S. economy, the dollar would in some ways be the measure of the northern nation's sovereignty.

Under the regulations of the International Monetary Fund, member states were expected to adhere to the basic premises of the gold-exchange standard, maintaining a fixed rate of exchange for their currencies relative to the American dollar. A spread of two percentage points was allowed, one below and one above the fixed rate. Any variation beyond this was only conceded if the IMF was consulted and agreed that a serious disequilibrium had developed in a country's international trade balance of payments, its holdings of U.S. dollars, or other measures of fiscal health. Instabilities occasioned by war and postwar inflation exacerbated Canada's always exposed position as a nation unduly reliant on trade and increasingly subject to external pressures associated with its economic dependency on the United States. Canadian loans to the United Kingdom in the immediate postwar period, as well as the unleashing of pent-up consumer demand for American goods, made for volatility in its reserves as surpluses gave way to deficits within a short span of one or two years. Its holdings of U.S. dollars and gold soared at war's close, dropped in the later 1940s, and began to climb again from 1948 to 1950. In order to address this situation, and to offset the influences of inflation in the United States (where consumer and wholesale price indexes climbed 25–45 per cent from mid-1946 to the end of 1947, outstripping Canadian inflation considerably), Canada undertook a series of monetary revaluations in the late 1940s.

Throughout the Second World War years, the Canadian dollar had been pegged at 90.9 cents U.S. It was revalued to parity with the U.S. currency in July 1946, with IMF permission, but Canadian gold and U.S. dollar reserves were subject to an alarming drain in 1947, occasioning efforts to suppress American imports through a series of 'controls.' A relatively quick recovery of reserves was effected, but the global monetary markets were reacting to the U.S. dollar with universal and large devaluations (from 30 to 9 per cent), and in 1949 the Canadian dollar was devalued to Second World War levels.

By 1950 short-term capital was rushing the border as U.S. investment soared. The flood of American dollars into Canadian reserves, and the resulting speculative mania fed by the view that the Canadian dollar had been pegged too low, impaled the state on a particular dilemma. American investment capital was short-term and fickle. It could flee the country if conditions – domestically or internationally – changed. Speculators who were buying Canadian dollars could also sell them if circumstances changed. A national economy that seemed buoyant might spiral downward quite quickly. What external forces gave, they could take away. Whatever the Canadian state did, moreover, was likely to worsen the situation, and perhaps blacken its eye on the domestic political front. And so the decision was made to do nothing, to opt out of the IMF fixed-exchange protocols, and allow the Canadian dollar to float freely in the monetary marketplace. Snubbing the IMF seemed the safest of economic and political options, and Canada, reverting back to the dollar regime of the 1930s, became the sole Western capitalist nation in the world with a freely floating currency.[10]

From 1950 to 1962 Canada thus operated within the IMF, but in defiance of its regulation that all member states have a fixed exchange rate vis-à-vis the American dollar. How this state of affairs, which was intended as a temporary exception, managed to continue for over a decade was, in retrospect, something of a mystery, even to officials of considerable authority, such as Canada's minister of finance in the late 1950s and early 1960s, Donald M. Fleming. Canada in fact rode the American wave of postwar prosperity. As an initial, Korean War–induced inflationary surge of the early 1950s settled down, the years of mid-decade were ones of relative prosperity, with high employment, steady prices, and moderate policies of monetary restraint keeping the economy on an even, and seemingly upward, keel. With the winding down of postwar reconstruction spending and the ending of the Korean War, however, the costs of a creeping inflation and a slowing of production began to be apparent by 1957: the unemployment rate doubled from a monthly average of just over 3 per cent in 1956 to approximately 7 per cent by the end of 1957; the price of American domination of certain sectors of the economy registered in dividend and interest payments flowing out of the country, a drain that grew from $424 million in 1954 to $1.5 billion in 1957; as consumer expenditure faltered and raw materials exports dipped, prices rose, and the economy was caught in the scissors-effect of employment reduction and income restriction on the one hand, and steadily increasing inflation on the other.

To make matters worse, the governor of the Bank of Canada, James Elliot Coyne, a Liberal appointee who followed tighter money proscriptions than were fashionable in many Keynesian-influenced circles, was distrusted by the recently elected Conservatives, led by a western populist, John Diefenbaker. The Tories came to power in 1957 with a minority government and then swept to a resounding majority in a 1958 election that saw Diefenbaker almost double his seat count to an astounding 208, wiping out the Liberals in six of the ten provinces.[11] The dollar and its value, increasingly politicized, were poised to be markers of national identity.

Throughout the 1950s, the key factor affecting the dollar's value was that Canada's trade deficit (it was importing more than it was exporting) was offset by the significant flow of capital into the country in direct investment. Coyne's late-1950s Bank of Canada policies aimed to moderately restrain domestic credit and spending to keep inflation in check. An unintended consequence of such restrictive monetary policy was to encourage this external capital and the consequent Americanization of the Canadian economy by propping up domestic interest rates. The situation was nevertheless pregnant with contradiction. Canada's currency reflected this. Its value had been anything but constant throughout the 1950s, and its fluctuations revealed the inherent instabilities in the Canadian economy. The upward trajectory of the Canadian dollar was, overall, startling: from 90.9 U.S. cents in September 1950, it climbed to 95 cents by the end of November. Two years later, it had topped out at $1.04 U.S., crossing the $1.05 threshold in the third quarter of 1957, after dropping to par with the American dollar in 1956, and then rising again to as high as $1.06. Diefenbaker's first years as prime minister saw continued fluctuations, and constant wrangling with the head of the Bank of Canada, but the dollar remained well above par. In the eyes of the Conservative government this hurt exports, particularly in the sagging mining and wheat sectors, stifled tourism, and limited possibilities for domestic producers.[12]

The Buck Goes from *Bad* to Just Plain Bad

As Canada entered the 1960s, its economy seemed to contain mixed messages. From the doldrums of the later 1950s, to be sure, a number of economic indicators were on the rise. Yet unemployment clearly compromised economic well-being. Having improved somewhat from the late 1950s official rate of 8 per cent, it slipped back to that level in 1960 before beginning a new climb that was much commented on in 1961–2, having broken the 10 per cent level. Whatever peace existed on the employment front, as inadequate as it was, had been purchased with considerable (and chaotic) government spending on winter and other public works, housing grants, regional aid, vocational training, and infrastructure funding for universities. The government did not help matters with its statistical ineptitude, reporting in the same February 1960 political breath that there were 500,000 Canadians looking for work but 800,000 collecting unemployment insurance. Other economic sectors, however, could be made grounds for optimism: exports had rebounded, the trade deficit transformed into a surplus; industrial production was booming, and grew over the course of a year some 9 per cent, fuelling a jump in the gross national product; and inflation had seemingly been brought under control.

The problem was that the Diefenbaker Tories were hardly of one mind on economic policy. Diefenbaker's primary concern in this realm often seemed to be to deflect 'the old cry that Tory times are hard times.' He was desperate to bury the view that Conservatives had led Canadians into the Great Depression and that only Liberals could rescue the nation from impending economic collapse. Suspicious of central Canadian banking and financial interests, and always wary of the powerful United States capitalist colossus to the south, 'the Chief' adhered to traditional populist 'soft money' maxims. He was, in many ways, a pre-Keynesian whose instincts to spend money freely on government programs was a comfortable, if superficial, fit with post–Second World War conventional wisdoms. In contrast, many in his cabinet inner circle, including influential figures such as Fleming, adhered to more orthodox conservative principles in which, contrary to the fashions of economic thought, fiscal restraint and balanced budgets were not to be dismissed out of hand. Prudence was valued in such circles, especially when some of the forecasts of national material well-being were anything but rosy. To further complicate matters, by the mid- to late 1950s and early 1960s Coyne, as head of the Bank of Canada, was treading ground no previous governor had even approached, clashing publicly with the minister of finance, issuing statements that many economists questioned and challenged, and facing an onslaught of allegations that the central bank's *Annual Reports* misinformed and obfuscated fundamental matters, including basic data relating to the money supply. Many thought Coyne had simply dug in his 'hard money' heels and was promoting policies far in excess of what Fleming thought appropriate or the sages of Canada's Keynesian corps of academic and civil service economists considered well advised.[13] Battles brewed on many fronts.

As the reigning Diefenbaker Conservatives offered budget after budget that promised tax cuts *and* increased government expenditure, the deficit inched upwards. The state was putting out more than $1.5 million a day in excess of what it took in through various revenues.[14] To be sure, this was not necessarily cause for panic, given the big picture of the economy's overall health, but it did undoubtedly stoke the ideological fires that burned hottest in the growing and complicated rifts dividing

Diefenbaker, Fleming, and Coyne. If the former worried about the political fallout of the rising numbers of workless Canadians, and wanted to spend his way to contentment and prosperity, the latter, as head of the country's central bank, became fixated on stabilizing prices, beating back inflation, and curbing the inflow of American capital. Coyne, given to almost puritanical public statements about profligate spending (on the part of individuals *and* governments), gave little indication that he saw job creation and the increase in the ranks of the unemployed as anything to be overly concerned with. All of this put the dour finance minister, Donald Fleming, between a rock and a hard place.[15]

As Coyne ran headlong into Diefenbaker and Fleming in the 1958–61 years, it was apparent that his days were numbered. He stretched them out about as long as it was possible to imagine that any figure in his position could. Demands for the Bank of Canada official's resignation initially got Coyne's back up in stubborn refusal, but eventually the financial governor was forced out in June 1961. Coyne's departure proved a highly publicized and controversial conflict that, however much it was inevitable, also besmirched the Conservatives, then ruling with the largest majority of seats in the history of the House of Commons.[16]

Louis Rasminsky succeeded Coyne as governor of the Bank of Canada. His main task was to smooth some of the old rocky fiscal ground that had proven difficult terrain for his predecessor and the Diefenbaker Tories to negotiate. The new money man would find himself facing an awkward dilemma, little of which was of his own making.

Canadians had experienced twelve years of the dollar's value fluctuations on the international monetary markets, and they had perhaps been lulled into a sense that a bouncing currency was of little consequence in their day-to-day lives. Coyne's 1950s tight money regime at the Bank of Canada had inadvertently and ironically kept the state and investors reliant on American sources for capital, maintaining the premium of the Canadian dollar, but deepening developing continentalist dependencies. These increased as American imports rose steadily throughout the early 1960s, and in 1962 imports outstripped exports. Combined with Rasminsky's loosening of the restraints on domestic borrowing and investment, as well as developments in the United States that curbed capital flow internationally, the result was a growing Canadian deficit in the balance of payments. Discounting the Canadian dollar helped ease the strain, but this currency manipulation was a two-edged sword and, if not monitored judiciously, would result in a free fall of the Canadian dollar that was unprecedented in the post–Second World War experience.

This is exactly what happened. The Diefenbaker government opened the Pandora's box of currency change gingerly at first, beginning what it hoped would be a slow and incremental devaluation of the over-priced Canadian dollar. It saw in this move a surefire way to shore up its export economy and bring down higher domestic interest rates. By buy-ing foreign currencies and supplying Canadian dollars, the Canadian state hoarded international money and dumped its own, thereby changing the supply–demand balance and cheapening its dollar. In a matter of months the exchange premium that had long characterized Canadian–U.S. dollar relations had evaporated and the Canadian dol-lar was declining fast. From rough parity in June 1961, the exchange rate on the Canadian dollar slipped to 96 and then 95 cents by April 1962. In order to stop the currency bleeding, and offset the impact of international speculators, who now knew that the Canadian govern-ment was backing devaluation and thus moved to liquidate their hold-ings in the falling dollar, Canada's foreign reserves were being rapidly depleted. In January and February 1962 almost $310 million in U.S. dollar reserves had been sold by Canada's Exchange Fund to prevent too sharp a fall in the exchange rate. By late April and early May 1962, the Exchange Fund was sometimes selling $35 million a day in order to keep the dollar from falling below the psychological breakpoint of 95 cents U.S. Canada had spent almost half a billion dollars of its reserves, 25 per cent of its total holdings, between October 1961 and May 1962, to keep the sagging dollar afloat. The 1962 balance of pay-ments deficit was looking like it might top out at $1.25 billion, a figure some Tory cabinet ministers regarded as menacing.

All of this began to register with an increasingly irate IMF, and above all with the powerful Americans. *Barron's* and *The Economist* wagged their disapproving fingers at a Canadian state that refused to follow the rules and establish a fixed rate of exchange all the while running defi-cits and manipulating the value of its currency. Robert Roosa, undersec-retary of the U.S. treasury, pounded the pulpit of responsible monetary policy. He warned Canadian manufacturers of the price to be paid for defying the godhead of sound money. Especially vehement were his attacks on those rogue countries that were creating escape hatches through which they effected 'temporary refuge from balance of payment disciplines by juggling [exchange rates] – beggaring [neigh-bours] and disrupting the orderly processes of cost and price adjust-ment.' Around the world foreign investors, wary of a rise in Canadian nationalism that had just registered in the nationalization of the British

Columbia Electric Company, were getting cold feet as far as the Canadian dollar was concerned. Fearing that the Conservatives did not have a firm enough grip on the economic reins of the country, a concern exacerbated by a rising Liberal chorus of critique and opposition, such investors pulled the plug on their Canadian holdings, worsening the dollar's place internationally. Money had become a 'national question' in an arena decidedly international.[17]

Indeed, astute observers might well have predicted that the dollar would prove a symbolic marker of national identity's differences in the mid- to late 1950s. Diefenbaker, on the one hand, and Coyne on the other, reflected competing understandings of nationhood and, particularly critical at this juncture, those forces threatening to it. The former, for instance, hearkened back to the co-mingling of patrician and plebeian reform interests of the 1870s, proclaiming himself an advocate of 'Canada First,' a politician committed to the northern country's destiny of greatness. On the hustings, Diefenbaker's rhetoric reached back to the familiar, if often empty, promises of older campaigns, ordered by the likes of Macdonald and Laurier. It spoke loudly of the promise of 'One Canada, One Nation,' and the potential for greatness. Small wonder, as well, that Diefenbaker championed the producer ideology of a long-gone era, embracing its anathema to 'tight money.' The Conservatives railed against restricting the people's access to currency in the 1957 and 1958 elections, taking credit for bringing interest rates down at the same time that their policies and programs would eventually again drive them up. But in the political arena, Dief's jowled promise was that tight money would disappear as Conservatives governed, freeing the producers (farmers, fishermen, and small businesses) from their crucifixion on the Liberal government's cross of currency restraint. If Diefenbaker might resent personally the slight of Americans of authority, from Eleanor Roosevelt to John F. Kennedy, displacing him, he was less concerned, in his national identity, with U.S. dominance of the economy.[18]

Coyne, in contrast, was far more focused on the substance of the ongoing Americanization of Canadian economic life and, ultimately, became the architect of the very monetary policies that Diefenbaker and the Conservatives abhorred. A nationalist of a different kind, Coyne saw the need to practise tight money policies the better to limit the influence of the United States in Canada. As most subsequent commentators agree, however, Coyne's understanding of international monetary mechanisms was flawed and his policies perversely ineffectual.

In charting a Bank of Canada regime of restraint in the late-1950s climate of recession, for instance, Coyne intended to curb inflation, keep the costs of production in Canada competitive internationally, and discourage the flow of American investment capital north of the forty-ninth parallel. Yet Coyne's restrictive 'tight money' approach to the problems of the period exacerbated a worsening situation: Canadian interest rates were pushed up; American capital was attracted to the high returns it could secure in Canadian markets; the Canadian dollar remained artificially elevated; imports were encouraged, exports discouraged; and unemployment rates climbed.[19]

Coyne's nationalism, premised as it was on a puritan's illusion that self-sacrifice and virtuous restraint would pull the nation out of its economic doldrums, flew not only in the face of Keynesianism, but seemed rigidly and mechanically naive in its grasp of the complexities of the international workings of modern capitalism. Coyne was not about to be moved, however. He wore his patrician superiority as comfortably as Diefenbaker draped himself in a plebeian populism. Aloof and arrogant, the governor was known unaffectionately among journalists as 'Jesus E. Coyne,' and his Bank of Canada staff once toyed with the idea – on reflection they thought better of it – of presenting their boss with a Christmas present of an icicle tied with a blue ribbon. Coyne's instinctual parsimoniousness translated into his brand of nationalism and his policies. By the end of the 1950s, Coyne was convinced that Canada had for too long lived beyond its means. He recoiled from the possibility that it could only continue its perilous path of depending on U.S. imports and financing their purchase through selling more and more of its natural resource industries, which fuelled the economy's lucrative export sector, to Americans at the cost of Canadian independence. 'If we do not effectively change the trends of the past,' he asserted unequivocally, 'we shall drift into an irreversible form of integration with a very much more powerful neighbour.' For Coyne this meant surrendering 'the very idea of Canadianism, the dream of Canada.'[20]

Coyne and Diefenbaker, then, both spoke the language of national identity, but in an entirely different idiom. On the stage of fiscal politics, money proved the parlance of two contradictory scripts. If Diefenbaker wrote the decisive lines, Coyne would perhaps have the last laugh. The economy, however, was not a comedy.

The ultimate act in this theatre of the dollar curtained down on 2 May 1962, with Fleming announcing that the Canadian dollar would now be pegged at 92.5 cents U.S. The minister of finance reversed his position of less than a month previously, when he declared in a 10 April 1962 budget speech that the government's monetary policies had been a success and it would not be appropriate to fix the dollar relative to its U.S. counterpart.[21] But this had neither assured nor appeased the critics of Diefenbaker's Conservatives, who, if they were part of the parliamentary opposition, howled of fiscal incompetence, or if they were players in the international monetary and investment markets, continued their run on the Canadian dollar. The *Wall Street Journal* declared that 'the Canadian dollar has been the victim of one of the largest speculative raids of any currency in history.' To defend the exchange rate the Conservative government eventually mobilized external financial support from the Bank of England, the IMF, and various U.S. sources – totalling over $1 billion – as well as slashing its budgetary expenditures by $250 million, raising interest rates from 4 to 6 per cent, and imposing $200 million in surcharges on a wide array of imported goods.[22] Devaluation was poised to bring a governing party to its knees.

Money Goes to the Polls: The Election of 1962

Diefenbaker's Conservatives had been in power for five years when the Canadian dollar started to tank visibly in 1962, and they had been in office four years from the date of their last victory, the 31 March 1958 romp that left them in total command of Parliament. They chose to go to the people once more, but Diefenbaker and his colleagues entertained no idea, in late April 1962, how bad the timing of their call for an election would be. They thought the dollar crisis had been handled, placed at bay by strategic expenditures from the reserves. Diefenbaker preferred to call the spring 1962 election without tabling a budget from his finance minister, knowing that this gave him more spending leeway. Fleming prevailed, however, and managed to both cook enough books and restrain his leader's spending impulses sufficiently to propose a modest $745 million deficit in a period he foresaw as one of 'rapid economic growth.' A week after the budget speech, Diefenbaker announced an 18 June 1962 election. He stood in the Orpheum Theatre of his Prince Albert, Saskatchewan, hometown on a Saturday night and basked in the limelight of leadership. Warming to the forthcoming campaign, he overreached himself in solicitous appeal and exaggerated humility. Playing up the importance of his modest origins and the attractions of familiarity, he thanked the crowd for welcoming him on a first-name basis: 'I tell you,' he concluded sycophantically, 'this is something that money can't buy.'[23]

Money may not have bought that, but it paid Diefenbaker back. The devaluation of the Canadian dollar figured forcefully in the 1962 election, where other issues – unemployment, nuclear weapons, relations with the United States, the Cold War and anti-communism, and shifting electoral demographics[24] – also eroded faith in the Tories and whittled down the votes that would be cast for them. When the ballots were counted, Diefenbaker clung tenaciously to office, but his authority, so decisive in the 1958 victory, was gone. The Conservatives won 116 of 265 seats, a devastating loss of 92 seats that allowed Lester B. Pearson and the Liberals, reduced to 48 MPs in Diefenbaker's charismatic carnage of 1958, to come back into the parliamentary game, topping 98 of the 1962 polls. Social Credit won a surprising 30 seats, campaigning largely on a program of saying 'no' to the old-line parties, while the recently renamed New Democratic Party secured 19 seats for social democracy.

Diefenbaker tried to work the old populist magic, appealing to what he called the 'average people of this country,' those who were not 'living in castles.' In some places, at some times, it worked. The old 'Chief' got considerable mileage out of an off-the-cuff quip, delivered at a Trail, BC, gathering, as three Doukhobor women stripped naked and walked toward him to protest his policies. Diefenbaker remarked, with a head gesture toward the women's breasts, 'I know what those things are.' But too often this homespun populism had worn thin, and Conservative rallies featuring the party leader saw breakdowns of the usual electoral decorousness in rude heckling that occasionally turned acrimonious to the point of riot.

From east to west, Diefenbaker met resistance. On the benign side, the prime minister's cavalcade was pelted with eggs after he addressed an overflow crowd at a Sydney, Nova Scotia, auditorium in early June. Less than a week before, things were particularly ugly at a Wednesday night rally. Two hundred Vancouver protesters marched into a 7,000-strong Diefenbaker crowd waving banners proclaiming, 'Hello John, Where Are Our Jobs?' The boisterous, workless demonstrators disrupted the prime minister's speech, reducing Diefenbaker to plea for a hearing while cabinet ministers sat mute on the podium. Fighting erupted throughout the crowd, with one reporter describing the event as 'the biggest, noisiest and most unruly rally in Vancouver's political history.' With 'blood all over the place,' fists flying, matronly Tory ladies tore the signs from the hands of the unkempt unemployed. One war veteran, with his miniature medals clanking, led a charge of Young Progressive Conservatives to block the way of an advancing contingent of 'hoodlums' moving menac-ingly toward the podium, roaring against the demonstrators: 'It's just like Dieppe. Let's give 'em hell.' From the dais an outraged Diefenbaker, per-spiration raining off of his formidable face, looked out at the human sea of chaos, defiant in defence of his right to speak, his voice pitched against the din of what he referred to as 'organized anarchists.' 'Heads were bruised, clothing ripped, spectators knocked from their seats in the melee.' Two days later, 'the Chief' and his entourage faced a similar scene in Chelmsford, Ontario, near Sudbury, as the antagonisms of a tense labour environment spilled over into the campaign. Diefenbaker, his aides, and his wife, had to run a gauntlet of shoving and pushing pro-testers, who surrounded a schoolhouse talk by the prime minister, clubs and signs much in evidence. A local Conservative candidate was bullied and bruised, and during Diefenbaker's speech the building was pelted with stones and debris. The Tories' exit proved anything but prime min-isterial. After Olive Diefenbaker elbowed one Liberal demonstrator in the stomach, the Diefenbakers made it to the car, but not without 'the Chief' being struck in the head, leaving an egg-sized swelling that lasted for days. They then found themselves prisoners unable to escape, their automobile rocked, and Diefenbaker's riding nominee subjected to fur-ther physical abuse.[25]

The decline of the dollar was never far from this political turmoil.[26] In Winnipeg Diefenbaker was met with a crescendo of fiscal critique: 'We want our dollar back ... Coyne! Coyne! Coyne!' By the end of the cam-paign the *Free Press* had dubbed the 1962 vote 'the dollar election.'[27] The *Calgary Herald* reported in mid-June 1962 that the dollar had 'emerged as the most-talked about piece of green paper in Canada's history,' not-ing that it now had wide-reaching symbolic meaning.[28] Political Tory insiders, as Peter Stursberg found in countless interviews, regarded the devaluation of the dollar as economically sound, but a disastrous elec-toral blunder. The timing of the dollar's demise cost Diefenbaker greatly, including all but one of the many seats bordering the United States. '*Nationalist pride was hurt*,' concluded Stursberg.[29] Newfoundland's pre-mier, Joey Smallwood, dubbed the dollar 'the hottest political topic in Canada today,' as he lashed out at the Rotary Club for offering Fleming a luncheon platform to talk on the subject. Smallwood earned national notoriety for lambasting the Rotarians, threatening them with with-drawal of the provincial government's host support at a future conven-tion event if the finance minister was allowed to 'use the Club as a tool for his Tory propaganda.'[30] Most press coverage of the slumping dollar placed the accent on how it would materially affect Canadians, raising the cost of basic necessities such as foodstuffs, as well as bumping higher the prices of so many consumer goods. Everything from a loaf of bread, to a cup of coffee, to automobiles, to meat, to air fares to a bottle of imported whisky or French wine was said to be rising in price as a consequence of the dollar's drop.[31]

There was also comment on the sagging currency's sociopolitical consequences. Charles Lynch suggested a class divide. He argued that the business and manufacturing 'community' understood the advantages of devaluation, but 'the average citizen' had a more difficult time in coming to grips with the decline of the dollar. The man and woman on the street 'tended to take pride in the fact that the Canadian dollar was worth more than that of the U.S.'[32] A letter to the editor published in *The Vancouver Sun*, and signed 'Critical,' stressed that Canada was internationally embarrassed by the plummeting dollar, and that monetary stability had been achieved by 'lesser and poorer countries … Why not Canada?' Canadians, according to this writer, were 'ashamed of our dollar's weakness' and longed for a return to a past when their currency was strong and they 'enjoyed considerable prestige.' To the east, Halifax's 'Realist,' bemoaned the 'humiliation' that the dollar's decline had imposed on all Canadians.[33] From the *Globe and Mail* came editorial assurance that 'Canada is not a pauper among nations. She still has great wealth, great resources of materials, brains and skills, and a host of customers who still value our goods and services.'[34] A voice of dissident (and conspiratorial) nationalism emerged in Toronto, where Tim Buck, national chairman of the Communist Party of Canada, declared that the Diefenbaker government had been forced by an external triumvirate of President John F. Kennedy, the United States Federal Treasury Board, and the International Monetary Fund, to drop the value of the dollar. Lowering the value of the country's currency, Buck claimed, eased Canada into its role as 'an economic and political satellite of the United States.'[35] From the Liberal mainstream, Pearson declared himself hopeful in late May 1962 that Diefenbaker could successfully stave off another run on the dollar, threatening to erode it and force its value below the pegged level of 92.5 cents U.S. 'I am a Canadian before I am a Liberal,' Pearson opined. He was quick to add, however, that whatever Diefenbaker and the Tories could accomplish in shoring up the free fall of Canadian currency, they had left the country in a mess. Saving the dollar was Pearson's stated political, and national, priority.[36]

Diefenbaker and the Conservatives found the dollar's dive, the rising fear of inflation coupled with persistent unemployment, which in some blighted districts was said to be soaring to 16 per cent (a jobless picture one Halifax resident described as 'the shame of the western world'),[37] and their own hapless political incapacity to convey to the electorate that the government had monetary policy under its control, to be their downfall. Matters worsened throughout the late spring campaign. It was revealed that within cabinet there was no agreed-upon rate at which to peg the dollar and that some ministers had indeed favoured a lower level of 90 cents. When word leaked that Fleming merely set the rate midway between two figures bandied about within government discussions at the highest ministerial levels, pundits had a field day with this kind of tic-tac-toe decision making.[38] The dollar, meanwhile, continued to slide.[39] Diefenbaker's shrill cries that he would deal harshly with those profiting from devaluation through unfair price gouging fell on cauliflower ears.[40] Inflation increased. As Social Credit began to pillory the Tories for their embrace of 'funny money,' the politics of the dollar slid from tragedy for the ruling Conservatives into the realm of farce.[41]

Capping the whole dollar fiasco was the proliferation of Diefendollars or Diefenbucks. Representations of the dollar's decline and its meanings appeared on editorial pages of Canadian newspapers and then springboarded into public prominence. A Manitoba publisher in The Pas printed tens of thousands of imaginary 92.5-cent dollar bills. Adorned with the prime minister's eminently caricatured visage, they carried the words 'Bank of Kuch,' celebrating a Winnipeg cartoonist who supposedly popularized the idea of the Diefendollar. Handed out at campaign rallies by Liberals, New Democrats, Socreds, and independents antagonistic to the Tories, the popular bills were indeed political money: a unit of account that spelled defeat for the reigning Conservatives.[42]

Canada thus entered the 1960s in a peculiarly ironic political way. The Conservative Party of the late 1950s had been catapulted to power on a promise to end tight money only to find itself impaled on the consequences of riding into the decade on the contradictory consequences of a dollar that had become all too loose. Old understandings of national identity, summed up in Diefenbaker's commitment to a British constitutional monarchy and the appeal of 'One Canada, One Nation,' failed, in the end, to adequately address the new reality of continentalism.[43] A rhetoric of national identity rooted in a past that had long been superseded was no substitute for confronting an epoch of change. Diefenbaker's understanding of Canadian national identity on the eve of the 1960s was thus sadly dated. He made the mistake of addressing national identity in the language of previous generations while failing to speak in the dialect of his present, where the words and grammar of his time were those of money. The hegemonic place of the American economy, and the dollar that symbolized its rising world power, were to Diefenbaker and the Conservatives something easily passed over with vague assurances, a national matter of importance that they dealt with complacently.

Money had been underestimated. It was a fatal error. As Canada's currency slipped, national identity was rocked, its material underpinnings eroded by the twinned assaults of unemployment and inflation. Michael Barkway, writing in the *Calgary Herald* as Diefenbaker's 208-seat House of Commons majority was frittered away on the campaign trail of late May 1962, understood well that the dollar symbolized not so much what was right with Canada but what could go very wrong. 'The ghostly voice of James E. Coyne, now living in seclusion in Toronto, still dominates the sound and fury of the election campaign,' Barkway concluded.[44]

Money never ceases to talk.[45] Its babble, however, often shouts down the truth. For the Canadian dollar crisis of the early 1960s merely foreshadowed global capitalism's coming downturn; not until the decade had run its course did the recession of the early to mid-1970s make it bluntly obvious that the long boom of the postwar era had finally ended. Yet the signs of a growing instability in Canadian economic life, situated as they were in an increasing dependency on the United States, were already apparent as the 1960s commenced, predictors of what was to come.

Few in Canada read these disturbing economic tea leaves. Instead, they followed the money. And as Diefenbaker and the Tories learned to their disappointment in 1962, the dollar's words were not always soothing. After years of Canada's dollar drifting downward, we might think, from the vantage point of 2009, that the 1962 devaluation to 92.5 cents U.S. was a small matter. After all, most Canadians today can remember our dollar plunging in a *fin-de-siècle* free fall that saw it crash the 65-cent U.S. barrier. An 85-cent dollar is something we have come to live with quite comfortably. Indeed, as the Canadian dollar reached parity with its U.S. equivalent by the close of 2007, and then actually soared to roughly $1.10 before falling again, many observers were wringing their hands in worry. A rising Canadian dollar, they thought, had all kinds of unintended, negative consequences.

This was not, however, how things looked as Canadians entered the 1960s. At that point, within the living memory of all adults, the dollar had crested at $1.06, only to be pegged at 92.5 cents, threatening to fall further to 80–85 cents.[46] The buck had been, like Canada itself, *bad*, which is to say it had been perceived, in terms of mid-century national identity but in the wording of our current times, as quite good. Then it became, like the country, uncertain and lost in the wilderness of threatening international pressures, just plain bad. The dollar in 1962 thus prefigured the ambiguities of identity that Canadians would grapple with over the course of a decade of decisive change.[47]

Chapter Two

Shelter from the Storm:
The Cold War and the Making
of Early 1960s Canada

A website with the innocent moniker 'KiCanada' carries the more telling, but still cryptic, subtitle, 'To the Limits of Safety.' It is about bomb shelters. There is an elaborate, photo-laden spread on the bunker to beat all bunkers, the Bomb Shelter Supreme. Known as Ark II, the biblically canonized subterranean shelter is a truly awesome articulation of the terrors of war in the nuclear age. Decades in the making, the Ark II was built and designed by owner Bruce Beach, who has spared no expense and left little to the imagination in his survivalist creation. Ark II's spatial material base is a hulking collection of forty-two school bus frames. It now contains seven bunk rooms, each with twenty-four beds. Slept in through designated adult and children's shifts, the staggered bunking system supposedly allows this wild structure to house hundreds of people. Each person has a cubicle for 'personals': toothbrush, towel, and the obligatory change of underwear. Five-thousand-gallon stainless steel milk tankers hold the immense water supply. Fire stations keep the terror of incineration at bay, and two kitchens outfitted with industrial-sized ovens provide for cooking. For those who fetishize maintenance of the body in the aftermath of a thermonuclear blast, workout and gym areas have been developed. Who would ever want to come back to station earth?

'Don't even think of trying to build another one like this,' Mr Beach wisely counsels those contemplating reproducing Ark II. In his expert opinion the better investment in the family future is a two-bus shelter

Protest/fallout shelter, 5 August 1960 (York University, *Toronto Telegram* Fonds, FO433, 1974-001/168 [1147]).

for twenty-four people that he claims can be thrown together in ten days for less than $5,000 Canadian. A bargain, no doubt, and Bruce might even be taking orders.[1]

To understand the origins of Bruce Beach's survival and safety compulsions and the making of Ark II, we have to step back to another time, when Canada and the world it was a part of stared nuclear holocaust in the face.

Cold War: The Continuation of Politics by Other Means

The capitalist nations of the 1950s 'free world' worshipped at the altar of money, albeit in ways that often unleashed unseemly competitions and combative currency wars. If their God in the postwar period was a voracious, acquisitive individualism, their Devil was the socio-economic order that seemed the very antithesis of this political economy of accumulation: communism and the Marxist ideas that supposedly brought it into being.

Reaching across the international history of the twentieth century, this confrontation of rival systems of thought and governance translated into a titanic clash of worlds, in which two superpowers, the United States and the Soviet Union, became national repositories of opposition encompassing capitalism and socialism, freedom and autocracy, markets and bureaucracy, even good and evil. Known as the Cold War, this disfiguring battle of ideas and territories left a frozen burn scorching the politics and cultures of diverse moments, scarring East and West in ways different but reciprocal. Central to the clash of oppositional world systems was the arming of their two leading nation-states with potentially globally destructive nuclear weapons. The United States demonstrated the capacity of its destructive atomic bomb arsenal in the Second World War, while the Soviet Union developed its nuclear weaponry in the years 1949–53, waging an impressive catch-up arms race. More than a brief interlude associated with the 1950s campaigns of Senator Joseph McCarthy, the anti-communism central to the century's politics was a practice of containment that began with the making of the first revolutionary Soviet Union workers' state in 1917 and continued well after the implosion of actually existing socialism at the end of the 1980s. The Cold War associated with this long history threatened to go hottest in the 1950s and early 1960s, the possible annihilation of nuclear war dominating the politics of the period.[2]

Canada has cherished the illusion that it was somehow immune from the political and cultural fallout of this Cold War blowback. But this is national myth.[3] Anti-communism affected Canadian institutions in this period, just as it did in the United States, structuring relations within the labour movement and scapegoating those who leaned decidedly left.[4] Jobs were lost, careers destroyed, and lives left in shambles.[5] Spy scandals, such as the 1945–6 Igor Gouzenko affair, and the 1957 suicide of E.H. Norman, a sensitive scholar of Japanese feudalism and a Canadian diplomat hounded by McCarthyite forces who claimed that his links to communism in the 1930s posed a security risk, framed a decade of political ugliness.[6] The culture of the conventional was in some ways rewritten, with film, pulp fiction, and understandings of what constituted normal Canadian behaviour all deeply affected.[7] Tensions in Canadian–American relations, while by no means acute, brought to the forefront issues of Canada's independence in an era when U.S. influence in the world was both growing and taking on a more ideologically bellicose character.

The Northmen as Peacekeepers

Canadian identity in the late nineteenth and early twentieth centuries was unabashedly related to soldiering in international conflicts. Nationhood in the northern dominion seemed confirmed as it was militarized.[8] In this history, Canada's connection to, and eventual separation from, Great Britain was replaced by a tightening link to the rising world power of the United States,[9] a process that was, as well, deeply gendered and decisively racialized. As Sherene H. Razack suggests, the militarization of nationhood had its origins in the colonization and armed suppression of Native peoples, manhood and whiteness supposedly being first tested in the struggle for Canadian national identity that unfolded in the Riel Rebellion of 1885–6.[10]

In the epoch of the heightened tensions of the Cold War, with the path from colony to nation having been successfully negotiated, the national question posed for Canada was what kind of role it would play internationally. Older mythologies of nordic hardiness and communal helpfulness as central to a peculiarly Canadian capacity for survival in a harsh environment helped to define an emerging understanding of the dominion as a 'middle power.' As a nation Canada was supposedly well suited to play a peacekeeping role in the modern world, replete as it was inevitably going to be with regional conflict and outbreaks of war.[11] Coinciding with the establishment of the United Nations in 1945, Canada's evolving understanding of itself as a middle power with international peacekeeping responsibilities consolidated over the course of the late 1940s, 1950s, and 1960s, sustained by the commitments of Lester B. [Mike] Pearson, George Ignatieff, Escott Reid, John Holmes, and others in the External Affairs bureaucracy.[12]

Ad hoc peacekeeping forces were dispatched by Canada to Kashmir, Korea, Indochina, Suez, the Congo, and Cyprus in these years. The Canadian state made much of its foreign relations independence, rejecting outright allegations that it was little more than a U.S. satellite. There was nevertheless stark recognition that Canada as a middle-power nation was ·unquestioningly aligned with the Americans, who were judged to be 'first' among equals in the 'free world.'[13] Pearson, head of External Affairs in 1948, and later prime minister, thought it inconceivable that the United States would ever initiate an aggressive war. Only the Soviets were capable of undertaking such violations of international peace. Under Diefenbaker's Conservatives, who governed in the late 1950s and early 1960s, there would be some rocking of this boat of Canadian accommodation to U.S. strategic interests. On the whole, however, national identity in Canada, inasmuch as it was tied to middle-power peacekeeping, was a Cold War project of continental integration dressed in the narcissisms of small difference and dependent on considerations of international trade and the dollars it garnered. This would be increasingly apparent in the 1960s, with Canada's complicity in the U.S. war in Vietnam.[14]

As the Cold War heated up in the late 1950s and early 1960s, a number of issues in the growing subordination of Canada to the United States surfaced, raising yet again the ironic banners of identity. Planes that did not fly and missiles armed with sandbags, like the dollar devaluation of 1962 to which they were not unrelated, as well as bomb shelters from the coming storm of war, proved to be further symbols of Canadianism on the eve of the 1960s.

As Straight (Down) as an Arrow

For some Canadians peacekeeping paid handsome dividends. The Cold War gave birth, in the United States, to an impressive economic arm, the military-industrial complex. Billions of dollars were at stake. A single U.S. missile development project in the 1950s could involve a score of contractors, hundreds of subcontractors, and a workforce of tens of thousands. Between 1952 and 1956, the U.S. Department of Defense owned more than 60 per cent of all aeronautics plants and equipment.[15] In Canada one firm, A.V. Roe, became what Michael Bliss termed 'a single-company Canadian military-industrial complex.'

Diefenbaker later referred to the firm as having 'lived and grown rich on Canadian defence contracts ... not accustomed to doing business in a "normal commercial way." ... They apparently had no intention of even trying to do so,' huffed 'the Chief.'[16]

A.V. Roe Company of Canada was first chartered in 1945. Within twelve years it grew from a single aircraft firm, producing warplanes for the Pacific theatre, into a diversified complex of almost forty companies, employing 41,000 workers, controlling assets of $300 million, and commanding net sales of $380 million in 1958. A.V. Roe made a bold bid to dominate aircraft design by putting in place one of the world's first jet-propelled passenger planes, the C-102 Jetliner. But this venturesome entrée into a new field foundered as commercial airlines judged the new plane unsuitable for their uses. Heavily bankrolled by the Canadian state, and especially C.D. Howe's Department of Reconstruction and Supply,[17] A.V. Roe was pulled out of the Jetliner doldrums by the Korean War, which drove new demand for military aircraft. The company produced some 700 CF-100 Canuck fighter planes after 1951, as well as their Orenda engines, becoming the industrial arm of the Royal Canadian Air Force (RCAF). Seemingly in the forefront of North American aviation technology, A.V. Roe pioneered a successor to the Canuck, the CF-105, a supersonic, all-weather jet interceptor colloquially known as the Arrow, distinguished by its tailless, delta-winged airframe.[18]

Arrow prototypes were brought off the assembly line and put into the air from 1953 to 1958. The idea was originally to produce the planes in Canada, but to import their engines and control systems. A combination of nationalist exuberance, corporate cajoling, and the enthusiasm of a wide array of engineers, designers, and promoters managed to swing the decision makers in Brooke Claxton's Ministry of National Defence to back the Arrow as a patriotic play and sanction the production of an all-Canadian plane. Howe told Claxton as early as 1952 that the Arrow scheme had him worried on a number of levels, but his recalcitrance barely dented the machinery of A.V. Roe's advancing juggernaut of expansion and experimentation. Cost-plus defence contracting financed the company's frenzied acquisition of other concerns, from foundries to wheel manufacturers. This economic mushrooming had a high-technology counterpart, as the Arrow was joined by Roe's development of the Avrocar, a flying saucer–like craft capable of vertical take-off and landing. Earmarked for use and purchase by the U.S. Department of Defense, the doughnut-shaped space-age product was a dud and never made it to the final stages of production. It was nothing if not a prime example of the chutzpah that A.V. Roe's Canadian president, the abrasively hard-drinking and always belligerent Crawford Gordon, displayed to good effect through the mid-1950s.

Gordon, once one of C.D. Howe's cronies, blustered his way through mounds of Liberal-dispensed money in this period. Wild optimism, freely flowing taxpayer dollars, the manipulation of the media, and a seeming need to show the Americans that Canada, too, could produce almost any-thing, ensured that the Arrow had the breathing space of birth. But soar-ing costs and Russian refusals to stand pat in the arms and space races eventually choked the production process, leaving the plane stillborn.

A 1953 cabinet-approved order for a large number of Arrows, possi-bly 500–600 being earmarked for the RCAF, had been premised on a delivery date of 1957 and a cost per plane, estimated in March 1955, to be approximately $1.25 million. In almost no time the projected price of the planes soared, possibly to as much as eight times the original esti-mate. The numbers needed dropped to one hundred. C.D. Howe reported to the House of Commons in June 1955 that 'we have now started on a program of development that gives me the shudders.'

Things worsened as the Diefenbaker minority government took the helm from the Liberals in June 1957. The new government was increas-ingly jittery at how the planes were to be armed. A wider politics of Canadian–American relations also complicated matters. Consideration of Canada's involvement in the U.S.-pushed North American Air Defense Agreement (NORAD) had just been postponed, and three Arctic radar detection networks built on American initiative between 1954 and 1957 were the basis of growing tension. Concerned that no one other than the RCAF wanted to buy the Arrows, now priced at six times the cost of a comparable U.S. interceptor, the governing Tories were having second thoughts about bankrolling A.V. Roe and its CF-105. Conscious of the need to trim its losses, Diefenbaker's minority govern-ment proposed backtracking on non-Arrow purchases from Roe, for sav-ings of $66 million. The company, knowing that the government was in a precarious political position, blackmailed the state, threatening mas-sive layoffs of 3,200 centred at its Malton works. This would have directly affected three Conservative MPs who had been elected on a program of maintaining jobs. Furthermore, Roe executives warned, if the Arrow contracts were compromised, companies would close, parts producers would suffocate, and possibly as many as 15,000–25,000 workers would be thrown onto the street. Diefenbaker's cabinet was brought to its knees, the company appeased, and more dollars and commitments were pumped into its coffers.[19]

For the Tories, the fortunes of electoral war improved their position significantly in 1958. Handed an overwhelming parliamentary majority, Diefenbaker was now in the driver's seat and able to bring the escalating costs of producing the Arrow to a halt. By this time, moreover, it was clear that the Arrow was an albatross around the state's neck. One estimate from the summer of 1958 suggested a surging price tag of over $14 million a plane. Strategic doubts were increasingly voiced about the Arrow's obsolescence. With the launching of Sputnik, 4 October 1957 (the same poorly timed day that the Arrow was officially rolled out of its hangar for a flag-waving celebratory public debut), the Soviet military threat had to be reassessed and the role of long-range bombers such as the CF-105 reconsidered.[20] The importance of a large and sophisticated Canadian aircraft industry, especially one so integrated into the military-industrial complex, necessarily began to be rethought. Finally, American influence on the shape and specifics of Canadian defence policy was becoming an increasingly volatile matter, one that called into question Canadian sovereignty and identity. In a January 1959 article in the *Globe and Mail*, George Bain predicted a number of difficulties with which the new Diefenbaker government would have to grapple. Citing the extent to which defence policy had been in a muddle for months, Bain rapped specifically 'the controversy and uncertainty over the Arrow jet fighter' as 'the most dramatic example of the problem.'[21]

Five weeks later Diefenbaker pulled the plug on the plane. Wanting no monument to the Avro Arrow fiasco, Diefenbaker ordered the five completed planes unceremoniously blowtorched into scrap and the half-completed craft dumped. This gave generations of nationalist dissidents grievous resentment that 'no museum of science and technology would ever be able to show what [Canadians] could design and produce.' A.V. Roe's almost 14,000 Malton workforce had more prosaic concerns, the shutting down of the Arrow production resulting in their en masse sacking. Newspapers bemoaned the collapse of Canada's aeronautics industry and 'the town that died' as a consequence. Some of those pink-slipped found work at other Roe operations, especially employees with engineering and other transportable credentials. Many went to the booming military-industrial complex and space-age research sectors in the United States, particularly the beckoning possibilities of California. Others were taken on by Canadian firms such as de Havilland and Canadair. The Arrow, the plane that didn't fly (except in test runs), became a symbol of Canada's capacity to turn success into failure, a myth born of Cold War excess and a stubborn pride of country that needed the pyrotechnics of a plane bloated by defence dollars to bolster national identity.[22]

Cold War's Cost Efficiencies: Nuclear Warheads
Look for a Canadian Home

One of the Avro Arrow's downfalls was that it could not compete, in bang for the buck, with Bomarc missiles. The Cold War of the late 1940s and 1950s existed under the ominous shadow of the atomic bomb, first developed in the United States and dropped on the Japanese cities of Hiroshima and Nagasaki in August 1945. Within five years the death toll from this horrendous pair of bombings climbed to over 350,000. From that point on, the world has never been the same, its security and, indeed, the continuity of humanity, clouded by the existence of weapons of immense apocalyptic import, and an arms race that threatens mutually assured destruction if taken to its limits.

Amid glowing postwar reports of American and Canadian affluence, the A-bomb highlighted modernity's ultimate fear, the danger of atomic annihilation.[23] Moreover, the aggressive rush to develop and stockpile nuclear and other weaponry drove both the United States and the Soviet Union to channel immense resources into the technologies of warfare, which were in a constant state of production, development, refinement, and deployment testing.[24] The death of the Arrow was a footnote in the making of this narrative. By the late 1950s it was evident to all within the North American strategic hierarchy that interceptor bombers of the Arrow type, manned with nuclear warheads, were now grossly inferior to ground-to-air missiles outfitted with atomic weapons, not to mention considerably more expensive.

Bomarc missiles were named because of their joint development by the Boeing corporation and the Michigan Aerospace Research Center (MARC). They were pilotless, ramjet-powered, nuclear-armed, long-range surface-to-air guided missiles. First tested in the early 1950s, the prototypes evolved until, by 1957, they seemed perfected. At least that was somebody's story, and they were sticking to it. Boeing received the first production contract for its Bomarc interceptor missiles at the end of the year, and, in September 1957, the first squadron was operational. Housed in semi-hardened shelters (coffins or silos), the missiles could be launched and guided on command from a ground system whose long-range radar tracked enemy aircraft and interceptors. Once it was within ten miles of its target, the Bomarc's own system guided it to the target. Originally designed to be armed with either conventional high-explosive charges or a nuclear fission warhead, the missile had a maximum range of 250 miles. To be truly effective it had to be deployed throughout the continental United States and also in Canada, where bases in Quebec and Ontario proved necessary if critical strategic sites inside the American border but congruent to its northern neighbour were to be protected from Soviet bombers flying over the North Pole.

Canada had agreed as early as December 1957 to the introduction of tactical nuclear weapons as part of its commitment to the North Atlantic Treaty Organization (NATO) and European defence. In the period when the Diefenbaker government was considering abandonment of the Arrow's production, the United States Defense Department sweetened the Canadian state's acceptance of the inevitable by committing itself to cost-sharing for both Bomarc missile bases and radar installations. It all seemed, in Diefenbaker's biographer's words, 'deceptively simple.' Canada would accept the Bomarc as a cost-efficient replacement of the Arrow, and 'the accompanying implication that the weapon might be armed with atomic warheads was noted' by cabinet without 'apparent concern.' North Bay, Ontario, was the site of the country's first Bomarc missile base, construction of which began in the spring of 1960. La Macaza, Quebec, would house the second launch site. The Cold War was heating up with the shooting down of an American U-2 intelligence aircraft over Siberia (and the capture of its parachuting pilot, Francis Gary Powers), an international outrage that resulted in the cancellation of a Parisian great powers summit in which disarmament talks were scheduled to take place.

By this point, however, a new Bomarc missile, labelled B, was in production. It could not handle conventional high explosives and thus was restricted in its armaments to atomic warheads. There were open turf wars within competing sections of the military-industrial complex, as the U.S. Army badmouthed the Air Force–backed Bomarcs and lobbied for an alternative system, the Nike-Hercules short-range missile. From other quarters came arms race voices carping that the manned bombers the Bomarcs were designed to repel had been displaced by intercontinental ballistic missiles (ICBMs), making the missiles scheduled to be deployed in Canada rather less effective than they might have been a few years before. 'About as useful as a pump gun,' as one Diefenbaker loyalist would later quip.

One problem with the arms race was that technologies overtook themselves. The proliferation of nuclear arms was thus necessarily paced by a pseudo-scientific rhetoric of weaponry's infinite capacity to spawn further and deeper developments in the escalating rush to Armageddon. To safeguard itself against charges of unpreparedness –

the supreme faux pas in the state's ideological defence arsenal –
Diefenbaker's Tory government kept apace with the Bomarc missile
project *and* purchased 66 F-101 Voodoo interceptor aircraft to patrol
the northern skies and monitor the increasing numbers of unidentified
planes entering Canadian airspace by 1961. But to appease critics, a
decision to arm the Bomarcs (and Voodoos) with nuclear warheads was
postponed, and instead the missiles carried deadweights, sacks of dirt.
The Bomarcs were, in any case, looking to be a bit of a defence turkey,
a series of spectacular test failures marring their Cape Canaveral,
Florida, dry runs. *Toronto Daily Star* cartoonist Duncan Macpherson
pictured Diefenbaker's minister of defence, George Pearkes, as a feath-
ered, prancing 'white-crested Bomarc booster.'[25]

Indeed, Canadians offered a significant challenge to the prospects of
nuclear proliferation, and one that registered with Diefenbaker's populist sentiments. Issues of Canadian sovereignty and national identity in
the face of powerful American encroachments were never far from the
Tory leader's concerns. Organizations such as the Combined Universities Campaign for Nuclear Disarmament (CUCND) and the Voice of
Women (VOW) linked arms with international bodies like Britain's
Campaign for Nuclear Disarmament and the American Committee for a
Sane Nuclear Policy to call for a halt to the arms race and the abolition
of nuclear weapons. They were supplemented by a host of similar mobilizations, some of them drawing on roots in an older communist-
socialist left: Canadian Campaign for Nuclear Disarmament, Peace
Research Institute, Canadian Peace Congress, and Youth Campaign for
Nuclear Disarmament. Out of the growing anti-nuclear weapons campaign came publications like *Sanity* and the Montreal CUCND publication, *Our Generation against Nuclear War,* its self-proclaimed purpose to
'create a theory of peace' by historicizing the nuclear disarmament
movement and philosophizing about its purposes and practices. By
1961, Christmas and Thanksgiving 'peace gatherings' and disciplined
marches heralded a new politics of public demonstration; a large seventy-
two-hour Parliament Hill protest brought the cause of nuclear proliferation into the homes of virtually all Canadians via newspaper, magazine,
radio, and televised reports. CUCND and VOW managed to bring journalists, churches, trade unionists, even the New Democratic Party, on to
their side. They gathered almost 150,000 signatures on a petition presented to government officials. Such voices of protest would soon face
events that made abundantly clear how ominous the politics of the
nuclear age could become.[26]

Revolution in a Cold War Climate

The Cold War was about counter-revolution. But it could not derail revolutions unleashed by the contradictions inherent in parts of the world where suffering seemed endemic and alternatives posed themselves as acute need. Prior to the 1960s, Cuba had long been an outpost of American imperialism, a decadent playground for the rich and a resource to be tapped by U.S. monopoly capital (United Fruit Company, Continental Can Company, Cuban-American Sugar Company, Cuban Telephone Company). The party ended late in 1958. President Fulgencio Batista, whose excesses had alienated even his fair-weather, cash-grubbing, supportive Yankee interlopers was forced to flee Havana. 'The bearded ones,' as Fidel Castro's guerilla forces came to be known, assumed governing control of Cuba in January 1959.

Cuba was quickly viewed by the Americans as communistic, and the U.S. structured its relations and policies around the need to destabilize and overthrow Castro. John F. Kennedy, the youthful and seemingly reform-oriented American president, sanctioned a clandestine, if abortive, CIA-orchestrated 'invasion' of Cuba by exiles trained and outfitted by the U.S. from a base in Guatemala. A total U.S. trade embargo was declared and rigorously enforced, and Castro grew increasingly dependent on Soviet trade and aid. The recipient of the USSR Lenin Peace Prize, Castro proclaimed himself 'a Marxist-Leninist' and looked to the Soviets to support his plans for Cuban industrialization. But it would be Soviet bombs, not the bounty of factory production, that emerged as the tip of a Cold War iceberg now threatening to move ballistic.[27]

Cuba, Canadian Identity, and the U.S.–Soviet Standoff, 1962

For Canadians the Cold War's home front was a Gulf Stream storm originating ninety miles off the Florida coast. Castro and Soviet leader Nikita Khrushchev increasingly saw eye to eye on trimming the sails of the Americas. U.S. global power-brokering assumed menacingly interventionist stands with nuclear warhead missiles aimed at the Soviet Union based in Turkey and Italy, Polaris-armed submarines prowling ocean and sea waters, and American intentions toward the Cubans clearly governed by a no-holds-barred commitment to starve them into submission. The Russians proposed to take a part of their immense stockpile of effective, but increasingly obsolete, medium-range missiles and surreptitiously install them on Cuban launching pads, shoring up their new Caribbean theatre with the atomic firepower of some Soviet submarines. Castro and his Cuban inner circle were not convinced by the Soviet ideological tub-thumping that they needed Russian warheads to protect the revolution from the imperialists. Cuban opposition to Khrushchev's plan melted away, however, with Soviet promises to assume the entire cost of the atomic enterprise, to ship a requested arsenal of other defensive weapons for free, and to forgive all prior debts that the Castro regime had incurred with the USSR.

The Soviets used the summer of 1962 to assemble a fleet of innocuous cargo ships, loaded them to the decks with missiles, warheads, launchers, and other nuclear paraphernalia, and sent them on their way to the Caribbean. Khrushchev bested Kennedy in a series of discussions over Berlin, where the Cuban card was played to good effect by the Russian leader. The United States was intent on avoiding U-2 surveillance plane affairs (two such craft had compromised Soviet and Chinese airspace in September 1962, one of them shot down) that might provoke an international incident. To placate the Soviets, the Kennedy administration cancelled the regular twice-monthly island-long Cuban flyovers that, by the end of August 1962, were revealing the making of a new, if undesignated, Soviet arsenal. All told, some 85 Russian vessels made 150 trips, carrying a total of 40,000 Soviet soldiers and technicians, 40 launchers, and 60 nuclear missiles, the warheads of each promising explosive yields ten to forty times that of the bomb which devastated Hiroshima. A sophisticated surface-to-air missile system was to surround Cuba, capable of guarding it from high-flying American spy planes. Imagined to be camouflaged by palm trees (a risible illusion), the launch silos were to be constructed by Soviets (no Cubans were allowed to be involved, not even in unloading the missiles and their accompanying cargo) utilizing equipment and materials shipped from Russia. Among the boatloads of supplies were to be 120 dump trucks; 20 bulldozers; 30 mobile cranes, graders, and excavators; 2,000 tons of cement and a half dozen mixers; hundreds of tents; twenty prefabricated barracks; ten wooden houses; seven warehouses; and three hospitals. In transporting a self-sufficient nuclear army and its medics, building tradesmen, engineers, and outfittings across the world, and establishing this atomic city under the noses of the Americans, Operation Anadyr, as the Soviets dubbed it, was undoubtedly the Cold War's most grandiose undertaking.[28]

With the nuclear arms ships en route from the USSR in July, the first missiles reached the port of Mariel in mid-September. Soon cumbersome trucks transporting seventy-foot-long tubes meandered through the Cuban night, the United States receiving odd intelligence reports as the summer of 1962 wound down. Hawks in the Republican party insisted that an arms buildup in Cuba was endangering American security; extremists demanded a U.S. invasion to put the menace to rest.[29] Late-September reports had CIA analysts scratching their heads until U-2 surveillance was resumed in mid-October. A routine spy flight over western Cuba revealed that nuclear weapons were now being installed at two and possibly three sites. Kennedy awoke on 16 October 1962 to a confirmation of his worst nuclear nightmare, as well as a prescient *New York Times* headline, 'Eisenhower Calls President Weak on Foreign Policy.'[30]

The U.S. supreme commander toughened his stand. Defense Condition 3 was put into effect: instead of the usual twelve nuclear-armed bombers dispatched on flight paths to the USSR, sixty-six were put in the air, readied for further orders; army divisions were diverted to Georgia and Florida; the navy inundated Caribbean waters with 180 ships, eight of them aircraft carriers involved in a broad plan of sea blockade and air attack that was ready to launch 1,000 bomber flights within twenty-four hours; 2,500 women and children were hastily evacuated from the United States base at Cuba's Guantanamo Bay. Polaris-armed nuclear subs sallied forth from their Holy Loch, Scotland, base, while roughly 260 short-range European nuclear missiles and American intercontinental ballistic missiles were poised to deliver the nuclear equivalent of 30 billion tons of TNT in a massive pre-emptive atomic strike against the USSR.[31]

Having prepared his offence, Kennedy took to the public airwaves. The largest television audience in American history was glued to their sets as the president addressed 100 million listeners, hundreds of thousands of them Canadian, on Monday, 22 October 1962, at 7 p.m. They saw a solemn Kennedy denounce the Cuban arms buildup as a clandestine violation of Soviet assurances of peaceful world intentions, nothing less than a 'deliberately provocative and unjustified change in the status quo.' The aggressive move could not be tolerated by the United States 'if our courage and our commitments are ever to be trusted again by either friend or foe,' Kennedy proclaimed. The weapons would be withdrawn or they would be eliminated, promised the president. While loath to 'risk the costs of worldwide nuclear war in which even the fruits of victory would be ashes in our mouth,' Kennedy nevertheless stood defiant in his refusal to 'shrink from that risk at any time it must be faced.' Amid the

bluster and bullying, the United States also offered more quiet suggestion, balancing ultimatum with prudent diplomacy. For now, while
America was on ultra alert, only an unbreakable naval blockade – euphemistically dubbed a 'quarantine' – would be imposed, to ensure that no
more Soviet weapons reached Cuban soil. Kennedy further requested an
urgent meeting of the United Nations Security Council to consider a
U.S. resolution calling for the removal of the missiles and all other
'offensive' weaponry, as well as the dismantling of the bases, the undertaking to be supervised by international forces. Closing with a plea for
his fellow citizens to accept 'the sacrifice and self-discipline' that lay
ahead, Kennedy insisted that 'the cost of freedom is always high, but that
Americans have always paid it.'[32]

The White House had little time for Canada, or any other country, as
it prepared for an ultimate, nuclear, war. Diefenbaker was briefed two
hours before Kennedy went to the American people. The Tory chief was
noticeably irritable when confronted by the Kennedy administration's
emissary, irked at not being given more notice and at first reluctant to
believe the worse-case scenario presented by the United States. Rising to
the middle-power occasion, Diefenbaker posed Canada's duty in this
hour of threat to world peace as one of not fanning 'the flames of fear,
but to do our part to bring about relief from the ... great tensions' of
the moment. It was not what the White House was expecting. In
Washington there was 'surprise and disappointment' that the Canadians
were not jumping onside. When Diefenbaker called on the UN to verify
what was happening in Cuba it seemed a rude slap in the Kennedy
administration's face.[33]

To make matters worse, Diefenbaker refused to place Canada's armed
forces, including its NORAD units that were stationed to act in concert
with their U.S. counterparts, on a war alert. Pressured by his minister of
defence, Douglass Harkness, to go along with the Kennedy administration, Diefenbaker balked. Harkness did an end run around his prime
minister's inaction. He and his chiefs of staff mobilized Canada's military
'in as quiet and as unobtrusive way as possible.' (The defence minister
would resign in February 1963, refusing to follow what he regarded
as Diefenbaker's unacceptable indecision any further.) Meanwhile,
Kennedy and Diefenbaker had a heated telephone conversation in
which the U.S. president informed the Canadian prime minister, in a
brusque and perfunctory manner, that while Canada had not been consulted about war readiness, it was expected to fall in line. Within days
Diefenbaker did just this, and Canada's NORAD and other forces joined

their American allies in preparation for 'immediate enemy attack.' As Soviet ships approached the U.S. blockade an American U-2 spy plane was shot down over Cuba. Khrushchev and Kennedy were locked in desperate and often despairing negotiations. The situation appeared grim.[34]

Armageddon did not come. It was no thanks to the major Cold War players. In the poker-faced standoff of Kennedy and Khrushchev it was the latter who blinked first. The Soviets turned their ships back when they ran into the American naval blockade, and Khrushchev offered Kennedy his promise to agree to withdraw the Cuban missiles under UN supervision. The United States had to commit not to invade their adversary's socialist island in the Caribbean Sea. The American chip, cradled cautiously and thrown on the table with as little fanfare as possible, was the removal of U.S. Jupiter nuclear-warhead missiles from Italy and Turkey. Castro felt abandoned, knowing full well that the promise of U.S. non-aggression was as empty and dead as his missile coffins were about to become. But the world breathed something of a sigh of relief, having spent six days perched on the edge of the abyss. The Kennedy mystique consolidated, and although JFK's presidential term would be cut short by his 22 November 1963 assassination, his handling of the Cuban missile crisis was lauded as his finest hour. Arthur Schlesinger, Jr, wrote in 1965 that John F. Kennedy had 'dazzled the world' in October 1962, 'displaying the ripening of an American leadership unsurpassed in the responsible management of power.'[35]

Diefenbaker, in contrast, would live to see his political demise, a direct consequence of his refusal to jump when American power cracked its whip. Nothing loomed larger in the upper reaches of the Canadian state in the months following the Cuban missile crisis than the governing party's disarray on the question of nuclear arms. For the Conservatives the fallout was not quite nuclear, but for all the destructiveness it might as well have been. The Tory record seemed one of lurching ambivalence, and the stage was set for 'the Chief's' inevitable electoral defeat. The Cuban missile crisis had highlighted that Canada's commitment to an American-waged Cold War was uncertain and its apparent embrace of nuclear arms in defence of North America against Soviet aggression hesitant at best. Canada under Diefenbaker had acquired a missile and bomber arsenal centred around the Bomarc, only to refuse to arm it with nuclear warheads. To Diefenbaker it was an act of Canadian sovereignty, an honourable policy decision of an independent Canada not to contribute to the proliferation of atomic weaponry. The bottom line was that Canadians had spent $685 million to acquire, in Peter Newman's words, 'the most impressive collection of blank cartridges in the history of military science.' To many in the Tory caucus this was sheer madness; they began to plot against 'the Chief' in an effort to topple his now shaky regime.[36]

In January 1963 matters came to a head, and, after a cabinet review of Canada's arms policy, there appeared a consensus that the Conservatives had to commit the state to a nuclear role in NORAD. Diefenbaker truculently scotched the proposal. Defiantly declaring he would have none of it, he nonetheless promptly integrated much of this new concessionary content into a speech before Parliament. At the same time, he struck a declarative note that no one 'visiting our country' was going to push the government around with respect to its foreign policy decisions or its ongoing negotiations with the United States relating to its taking on an atomic arsenal. Few knew what was happening or, even, exactly what the Canadian government's position was. The Americans had had enough. At the end of the month the Kennedy administration offered up a blistering attack on the Canadian government's indecision, which had led to nothing approximating an adequate arrangement that might 'contribute effectively to North American defense.' In the end Diefenbaker raged, like a lunatic according to some, and tried to cajole his colleagues into moving dissolution of Parliament and standing with him against the meddling Kennedy administration. The conspiratorial Conservative knives came out, and Diefenbaker was pressured to step down as prime minister, the one act that might supposedly keep the Tory governing ship afloat. He told his colleagues to go to hell. On 5 February 1962, word of the revolt in the Conservative cabinet having reached the Liberals and the Socreds, the Diefenbaker government was brought down, but 'the Chief' beat back his party opponents and led the Tories in the 8 April 1963 election. The result was a foregone conclusion. Pearson and the Liberals won a minority government, their 129 seats besting the Conservatives' 95, and the Socreds and the NDP held the balance of power with 24 and 17 seats respectively.[37]

The election was fought out in the populist idiom of an anti-American national identity, its appeal directed at the 'common man' rather than the well-heeled and the scions of the business community, who had long since abandoned 'the Chief.' Ridiculing Liberal Party public relations acts and questionable campaign tactics as something lifted from a Madison Avenue advertising manual gone bad, Diefenbaker chastised the reduction of the Canadian electorate to 'juveniles.' He took to the hustings declaring, 'I want Canada to be in control on Canadian soil. Now if that's an offence, I want the people of Canada to say so.' Extolling the accomplishment of his 'One Canada,' open to all immigrant peoples, Diefenbaker campaigned on giving 'Canadians as a whole the pride of being Canadians, [removing] that stigma that in the past existed that blood count constituted something in the nature of citizenship.' The *Toronto Daily Star* thought the prime minister was sounding 'like some alcoholic patriot in a tavern.'

The nuclear arms question was undoubtedly central. 'We shall not have Canada used as a storage dump for nuclear weapons,' thundered 'the Chief.' One Diefenbaker loyalist raged at a Montreal press conference: 'They don't even know we're a sovereign country up here. They think we're Guatemala or something.' Diefenbaker was handed a fortuitous campaign issue by the U.S. Defense Department. Secretary Robert McNamara allowed that Bomarc missile bases in general were now costly and obsolete. He added that they might as well be maintained, however, if only to draw Soviet firepower. McNamara had not meant to imply that the two Canadian Bomarc bases in North Bay and La Macaza were useful only to divert Soviet attack away from the United States, but this was certainly one way to interpret his words. 'The Liberal Party would have us put nuclear warheads on something that's hardly worth scrapping,' Diefenbaker snipped. 'What's it for? To attract the fire of the intercontinental missiles ... The Liberal policy is to make Canada a decoy.'

Pierre Berton, reflecting on the crash of the Conservatives, thought sadly that the electoral contest was indicative of national sovereignty's waning authority. Diefenbaker, meanwhile, promoted a highly conspiratorial understanding of Canada–U.S. relations. According to 'the Chief,' the Pentagon was directing the RCAF and his ministers of defence, while the U.S. ambassador used his embassy's basement to advise journalists on how the Canadian press could best topple the Tories. National identity had never seemed more precarious, more strained, or more shrill.[38]

Shelter from the Storm

For Diefenbaker and the internally wracked Conservative Party there was no defence from the harsh blasts of transformation that blew across the political spectrum as Canada entered the 1960s. 'The Chief' governed, but he did so against the winds of change. In the Cold War's nuclear winter of 1958–63, shelter from the political storm was nowhere to be found.[39]

Against the possibility of nuclear apocalypse, some prepared to go underground. The state itself constructed an immense subterranean emergency government centre located outside of Ottawa, just north and east of Almonte in what is now Carp, Ontario. Buried deep under a hillside, the 'Diefenbunker,' as it was colloquially known, was a four-storeyed, 100,000-square-foot facility housing a prime minister's suite, war cabinet room, CBC radio studio, Bank of Canada vault, emergency government situation centre, living quarters for top state officials and military personnel, and cryptographic areas. Built between 1959 and 1961, supposedly on the sly (Diefenbaker referred to it as 'probably one of the worst kept secrets ever'), the bunker lives on as a monument to the Cold War era, its illusions and its mindset of captivating fear.[40] It was complemented by a more modest private prime ministerial bunker built at 24 Sussex Drive. For a paltry $450, Canadians supposedly provided the nation's leader and his wife with protection from atomic bombs.[41]

Diefenbaker recommended to all Canadians that they protect their families by constructing basement fallout shelters, as Kennedy had done in a 26 July 1961 television address.[42] A 1961 Canadian government publication called *Your Basement Fallout Shelter: Blueprint for Survival No. 1* advised building bomb bunkers out of cement blocks, mortar, and framing studs to shield citizens from the radiation fallout. With clear instructions on how to construct a basement shelter housing from five to eight people, the booklet declared innocently that ventilation would not prove a problem. Assurances were given that radioactive dust could be kept out of the basement area merely by adjusting a canvas curtain to seal off any passageway to the main floor of the house.[43]

This kind of naive promotionalism perhaps reached its zenith in the United States, where former Atomic Energy Commission chairman Willard Libby opposed public funding for shelters. He countered that they could be constructed on the cheap by almost anyone with a will to find the survivalist way. In a fifteen-part newspaper series, Libby outlined how to build a poor man's shelter for $30. The West Los Angeles Libby bunker used railroad ties, old tires, and bags of dirt to give the down-and-out their supposedly fallout-free refuge. But the bottom-of-the-line bunker took a dive in its ratings when, at the inopportune height of the Cuban missile crisis, it was reduced to ashes in a brush fire. Former Libby colleague, physicist Leo Szilard, greeted the news that Libby's welfare hotel bunker had burned with the wry statement that this not only proved the existence of God, 'but that He has a sense of humor.' Was anyone laughing, however, when the U.S. Department of

Agriculture issued a pamphlet advising the country's farmers how to build a *Bunker-Type Fallout Shelter for Beef Cattle*?

In Canada, *Your Basement Fallout Shelter: Blueprint for Survival No. 1* did offer brief statements on heating and cooking, lighting, food and water, radios, fire precautions, medical supplies, the layout of space, and sanitation. The bunker brochure left little doubt that survival in the nuclear age was merely a matter of following basic guidelines. 'Cleanliness is the keynote,' lectured the pamphlet, adding for good measure: 'For reasons of hygiene, and in order to reduce shelter odour, you should provide a number of changes of underclothing for all occupants of your shelter.' The state's survival blueprint prompted all Canadians to invest in their nuclear-age futures: 'You can accomplish a great deal at little cost, with little effort and a little forethought. What is important, however, is to build the shelter NOW.' Neighbours and friends were encouraged to talk things over among themselves, to consider constructing safe basement spots for those unable to do the work on their own: 'Perhaps you can all get together and build your shelters as a team – it could be a real community project.' Necessary supplies were listed, canned food provisions for two weeks catalogued, and extensive diagramming outlined the sequence of building stages. Simple and authoritative, *Your Basement Fallout Shelter: Blueprint for Survival No. 1* was the decisive word from the Canadian state that there was indeed shelter from the nuclear storm. To sweeten the pitch, preparedness was even promoted as enhancing property values. Bunkers, after all, were easily turned to purposes other than protection in the event that nuclear war did not necessitate their use. Fallout shelters could double as cold storage cellars, fire-protection rooms, a spare bedroom, even a wine cellar.[44] It was all win-win in Cold War constructions. Suburban investments remained secure. Despair was dispensed with.

As the Cuban missile crisis unfolded, Canada's Emergency Measures Organization (EMO), established to address civilian mobilization and preparedness in the event of a nuclear attack, came under considerable criticism. Many claimed it had failed to promote and coordinate an adequate body of institutions and procedures that could reasonably be expected to safeguard the country and its citizens.[45] EMO federal director R.B. Curry explained that over 10 million survival booklets had been distributed by his department since 1959. His assistant director, Jack Wallace, estimated that $50 million had been spent on civil defence. But critics thought there was little to show for such efforts. An alert system of 1,328 sirens across the country was poorly understood. Few residents in most locales were aware of its existence or of how much warning it might provide. In Lindsay, Ontario, air-raid sirens installed six months prior to the Cuban events had never been publicly announced or their workings explained. When Oakville's fire alarm system was triggered by a smouldering mattress and a faulty sprinkler system the day after Kennedy's televised Cuban missile broadcast, residents thought it a war siren and some began a panicked search for fallout shelters they could not find. Federal plans were in place to take over communication and transportation networks as well as a centralized food pricing and distribution system. But groceries themselves had not, unlike medical supplies, been stockpiled. Key initiatives had clearly been focused on the Diefenbunker and other Ottawa-area locations readied for government evacuation. 'Apart from a bomb shelter for the Prime Minister and his key men,' one commentator noted, 'no provision has been made for the safety of the rest of Canada's people.' They were, announced a *Toronto Daily Star* headline, 'still sitting ducks.'[46]

Local EMO committees found themselves caught flat-footed in October 1962. Rush plans were made to step up shelter creation in the Oshawa area, a 'crash program' instituted to structurally modify an airport building to assure its functionality in the event of a nuclear attack. Public school trustees in Ottawa heard a report from their representative to an EMO meeting, deciding they could not provide every teacher with a radio, but did spring for transistors to be given to all school principals. Sending the children home if an alert was sounded was a plan most could agree on, but not before they debated the merits of various systems of communicating the nature of the crisis to classrooms. Out of the discussion came views reaching back to methods tried and true. From one quarter came the suggestion that 'a runner ... be sent from room to room spreading the word. Another proposed reverting back to the old-fashioned school gong.' One sage soul wondered aloud what could be done 'if the enemy is not gentlemanly enough to let us know.'[47] No one, at least, proposed that school children be tattooed or issued dog tags, procedures placed on the table and, in the case of the tags, implemented, in New York, San Francisco, and Seattle. Tattooing was rejected, according to a Milwaukee administrator, 'because of its associations' (holocaust or hell-raising?) and the problem of impermanence in the event of severe burns. In Canada, it seems, school officials worried about communications, but in the United States the concern was with the more extreme scenario of problems of identification should masses of children be lost, wounded, or dead.[48]

The biggest disappointment in both Canada and the United States was that the fallout shelter had not exactly become a household fixture. In 1961, forty U.S. state governors reported that there were 60,000 fallout bunkers already built or under construction, and by 1965 the number had possibly more than tripled, to 200,000. Statistics on shelters were in fact notoriously unreliable. They ranged from a 1960 low, outlined in a House Military Operations Subcommittee report, of only 1,565 units in thirty-five states and sixty-six cities, to the higher, and undoubtedly exaggerated, claim of civil defence officials in the same year that over one million families had built fallout bunkers. Even taking this latter grossly inflated figure at its word still meant that barely 1 per cent of the population had direct access to a shelter. Kenneth D. Rose thus notes that the bunker movement was a bust, precisely because Americans rightly knew what their leaders did not: that life could not be preserved in the aftermath of nuclear war, at least not the kind of living that the freedom-loving, consuming public of the United States wanted. The overwhelming majority of Americans – 97 per cent – admitted in the early 1960s to making no provision for protection from atomic war. Companies trading in Cold War fear and marketing basement bunkers usually went belly-up. Fallout shelters 'cast a pall over suburban life.' And it was in the suburbs, of course, where America marketed its image of capitalist, familialist contentment *and* the selling of the ideas of shelters, which were fundamentally dependent on basements and backyards, structures and spaces hardly associated with the inner city.[49]

In Canada the situation for shelter-making was, if anything, grimmer. Mere months before the Kennedy–Khrushchev standoff over Cuba, *Chatelaine*'s Christina McCall deflated the bunker balloon with a deft prick of objective scepticism. Admitting that 'even the most ostrich-like optimists' had to now 'come face to face with that horrific nightmare of this age of anxiety: the possibility of nuclear attack,' McCall provided her readers with instructions on how to build and stock a fallout shelter. But she refused to embellish the presentation of life after the bomb, recognizing that the level of destruction in the aftermath of nuclear warheads dropping on Canada was bound to be horrendous, and prospects for civilized existence considerably diminished: 'Assuming that you were lucky enough to escape these immediate effects of the bomb and reached the relative safety of a fallout or blast shelter, it's no use deluding yourself that life inside ... would be anything approaching normal, or indeed that life once you emerged would ever be the same again.' Deploring the 'unrealistic tendency' evident in the shelter promotion literature to make bunkers 'look like underground picnic areas,' McCall rubbed her readers' noses in a needed dose of nuclear dirt reality. Shelters, she insisted, would be 'cramped, stuffy, stinking, cages.' They offered little in the way of upbeat alternative to the very depressing reality of anyone faced with inhabiting them: 'the nerve tearing suspense of not knowing whether you and your family will emerge alive.'[50]

According to the EMO, between 2,000 and 3,000 Canadian families had built fallout structures. *Your Basement Fallout Shelter*'s admonition to make the bunker a communal undertaking had fallen prey to a secretive culture of privatized protectionism. Estimates were that as many as 3,000 more domestic units had built basement shelters but were not putting the word out in their neighbourhoods that they alone were in readiness. Not all survivalists, apparently, wanted company coming unannounced when the bombs started dropping. Still, even at an outside number of 6,000, basement bunkers were not a thriving undertaking. Their construction lagged significantly behind even the tepid mobilization to make shelters commonplace in the United States. The week of the Cuban missile crisis, Ottawa's Allied Builders Supplies, the capital city's sole commercial builder of fallout shelters, reported only two new orders for basement units, although there had been an increase in calls of interest.[51]

Money was certainly a large part of the problem. Diefenbaker's government refused to shell out the $4–5 billion that a works project of public fallout shelter construction demanded. The voluntarist alternative of nuclear families building their own nuclear shelters – an appropriately entrepreneurial option in a Cold War pitting individualist West against collectivist East – was simply not gaining mass support. It had, in the words of the *Ottawa Citizen*'s Hyman Solomon, 'simply fallen flat.'[52]

This outraged University of Toronto professor J.G. Eayrs, who appeared on the television show *Toronto File* on 24 October 1962. He blasted the federal government for doing 'next to nothing' as nuclear war approached, leaving Canada 'almost defenceless.' Dr Eayrs urged the immediate adoption of a comprehensive civil defence program that included mandatory building of private fallout bunkers. Citizens must be 'made [to] put shelters in their basements,' Eayrs fumed, and 'a survival force' established, 'even if it means conscriptive service.' The Cold War was clearly confusing the totalitarianisms of East and West. Eayrs sympathized with the EMO, admiring the good work it had done with 'altogether inadequate resources,' and he understood that the state was reluctant to proceed in certain directions with respect to civil defence. But the Cuban crisis, and the seeming inevitability of other such threatening developments in the next decades, necessitated preparative measures long overdue. Also on the program was John Pollard, Metro Toronto's EMO director. He thought Eayrs's commentary put the situation 'quite reasonably,' although off the air he placed more emphasis on the need for the Tories to start setting up public shelters. But Diefenbaker's government was not all that accommodating. It turned thumbs down on a request from Pollard to help fund the conversion of Toronto subway stations and the City Hall underground parking garage into fallout shelters that would be open to city residents. The plan, starved for cash, had to be shelved. In the event of a nuclear weapon detonating on Toronto, Pollard advised urban dwellers to be prepared: know your signals (a steady note or whine was an alert or warning, but a wobbling signal, pulsing as it rose and fell, was an indication that a bomb blast was imminent); lay in two week's supply of food; and at the eleventh hour 'take cover as best you can.'[53]

Assessing the Ironies of the Diefenbaker Interregnum

'Take cover as best you can.' The EMO official had been speaking directly to Torontonians facing the immediate threat of a nuclear explosion. His words were prophetic in their general applicability to Canada and its national identity in 1962–3. There was to be no shelter from the nuclear storm of this period, just as there would be no refuge from the turbulence of the next ten years.[54]

George Grant's *Lament for a Nation: The Defeat of Canadian Nationalism* makes the bold statement that 'the 1957 election was the Canadian people's last gasp of nationalism.' During what might be called the Diefenbaker interregnum, stretching from 1957 to 1963, the possibilities of populism, regionalism, conservatism, and a mild socialism melded in the struggle for a Tory Canadianism that could actually resist the Americanizing assault on the country's northern sovereignty. For Grant it was too late. Diefenbaker's 'confusions and inconsistencies' proved essential to a Canadian fate that was, by 1957, inevitable. 'The impossibility of conservatism in our era,' Grant proclaimed, 'is the impossibility of Canada.' By 1965 it was evident to Grant that 'Canada had ceased to be a nation.' While he eschewed predicting the future, he ventured a wry prophecy in conclusion: 'The formal end of Canada may be prefaced by a period during which the government of the

United States has to resist the strong desire of English-speaking Canadians to be annexed.'⁵⁵

Grant's hyperbole notwithstanding, and acknowledging that the
Dalhousie/McMaster University philosopher was decidedly premature
in his declaration of the death of Canadian nationalism, which would
indeed rise again, *Lament for a Nation* captures brilliantly the ironies of
the 1957–63 years. For the Diefenbaker interregnum was indeed a last
confused stand of an old Canada, of an identity long cherished but gone
forever. In the final, anguished gasp of refusal that itself denied renewal,
the interregnum was a preface to the changed context of the 1960s that
was in the making. It was of course ironic that a curmudgeonly conservative, a regional populist, and an idiosyncratic idealist should carry the
torch of Canadianism. Diefenbaker cherished British constitutionalism
and the pride of dominion over bowing and scraping in prostrate abjec-
tion to a rising American empire. He adopted an *almost* class-ordered
reverence of 'the people' and a consistent distrust of 'the interests.'⁵⁶ As
prime minister, he seemed to listen less to a military-industrial complex
establishment than to the Voice of Women letter writers who flooded his
desk with protest petitions. The irony of Diefenbaker's years of governance was that they birthed the melding of socialist and conservative
sensibilities in opposition to the faceless, alienating, dehumanizing,
unprincipled liberalism that measured everything by the standard of the
ledger sheet and that would concede all, even nuclear annihilation, to
continental capitalism's shrine of acquisitive individualism.⁵⁷

The Diefenbaker interregnum thus linked what was with what was to
come, historicizing a connection – Red Toryism and socialism – that
believed in the value, as Grant would have put it, of 'protect[ing] the
public good against private freedom.'⁵⁸ For Grant knew that there was
no shelter from the storm, that 'taking cover as best you can' was a risky
business as likely, in dire circumstances, to end in death as it was to sustain life. He had been lucky once, in years past, but his good fortune
embedded in his consciousness and his conscience the folly of retreating to something as illusory as a bomb shelter. For in the Second World
War, while a Rhodes Scholar at Balliol College at Oxford, Grant, a
Christian pacifist, had negotiated his way through a conservative
dilemma of how best to serve king and country. Like a true son of the
dominion, he helped to start a university ambulance unit and then
engaged in rescue and other work as an air raid precautions officer.
He lived in a bomb shelter; in February 1941 it suffered a direct hit.
Three hundred people died. Grant was left mentally broken, physically

exhausted. His obviously guilt-ridden efforts to join the navy and partic-ipate directly in the war effort were thwarted by failure to pass the requi-site medical examination. Vanishing into war-torn London, out of touch with his family for months, Grant finally resurfaced in Canada, conva-lescing until the end of the war.[59]

This was undoubtedly the interregnum's dark side, and it condi-tioned Grant's pessimistic view of Canadian national identity in the 1957–63 period. Yet there were also immense changes afoot, especially in understandings of sex and gender and ethnicity. New ideas were struggling to be born in this moment of lament and defeat as well, and personalities were emerging who would stamp the Sixties in Canada with images less dour than that of Grant. All of this would, for a new generation, offer fresh possibilities for Canada and open the doors wider to the ironies of identity.

PART II

National Identity and the Challenge of Change:
From Munsinger to Trudeau

Chapter Three

Scandalous Sex: A Cold (War) Case

Pierre Elliott Trudeau exemplified the 1960s for many Canadians. Of all the decade's politicians he is undeniably the best known and, arguably, the most controversial. His rise from 1965 to 1968 was astonishing, and once ensconced in the prime minister's office, his influence prodigious. One part of his appeal, which will be explored in a later chapter, was that he was downright sexy. Canada's leading gonzo journalist, Larry Zolf, would later comment: 'What could be more Canadian and ironic than the anointing, in the year of Our Lord 1968, of a shy, short, introverted, Jesuit-trained, single-combat warrior Québécois, as Canada's biggest sex symbol?' Without 'the politics of sex,' Zolf suggested, 'there never would have been Trudeau the prime minister, Trudeau the man of War Measures and Trudeau the world peace missionary.' Charismatic politics, driven by the libidinal charge of Trudeau's youthful appeal, fused in 'orgiastic celebration' in 1968, providing an even more potent mix than the Kennedy brothers in the United States in the period 1962 to 1967. Trudeau's bold move of taking the state out of the bedrooms of the nation, Zolf notes in further irony, could not quite keep the nation out of the prime minister's boudoir.[1]

Trudeau's 1971 marriage to Margaret Sinclair, twenty-nine years his junior, was merely the endnote to this politics of eroticized public life. At first the match-up simply confirmed Trudeau's sex appeal. Marshall McLuhan (who will also be commented on in a subsequent chapter that

Coles Bookstore promotion of Munsinger Report, 1 October 1966 (York University, *Toronto Telegram* Fonds, FO433, 1974-001/613 [4067]).

addresses Trudeau) regarded the prime ministerial wedding as a kind of wizardry. The political scene was transformed into 'a marriage feast,' and Canadians were proud of their publicly virile leader's conquest. It made the Americans sit up and take notice, especially when Margaret managed to deliver Trudeau sons on Christmas day. Trudeau no doubt orchestrated the relationship, and its immediate child-bearing years of the early 1970s, to good political effect, but when the Maggie and Pierre train went off the rails it was not a pretty picture. And as Zolf pointed out, in his characteristically understated way, with the sex gone so too was much of Trudeau's attraction to Canadians:

> The married Trudeau, in Hollywood parlance, had kissed away his political box-office for a mess of matrimonial dotage. Besides, it was not a well kept secret that Pierre was no longer amused by the passion of the politics of sex. In 1972 he decided to run on the bright pure reason of bureaucratic excellence. Trudeau told the press he was the best business manager in the country and that his cabinet was the best management team in Canada. In the campaign, Trudeau's second greatest political disaster, not a gasp, squeal or giggle could be heard in the land; charisma was out, and business-cum-usual was the political staple of Trudeau's garrison mentality ... as inevitable as was the demise of Trudeau's sexual politics, so too was the inevitability that it would have a dark, down side. That dark, down side was a nasty marriage breakdown, the real or Margaret-fancied cuckolding of the prime minister, the bitterness, frustration and public humiliation of Trudeau – a confluence of circumstances that forever ruled out the playful pyrotechnics of charisma politics for P.E.T.

As Trudeau's political carcass lay exposed to the moral majority right, critics lashed away at what was left of the man who had banished the state from the bedrooms of the nation. Such ideologues often suggested that Trudeau had never been anything more than someone whose life of the bed was dubious (i.e., homosexual) at best. Sex made Trudeau, and the wrong kind of sex, reputed or real, could go a long way in unmaking him. Trudeau became the first prime minister in Canada 'to be crucified by sexual McCarthyism.'[2]

The Trudeau phenomenon was not a unique illustration of the significance of sexuality in politics. It merely confirmed that a massively important sociocultural force had been unleashed and was marching more forcefully into the public arena. Sex was no longer kept underneath the cloistered sheets of seemingly private life. In this, it was part and parcel of the 1960s, when eroticized dress (the mini-skirt), the widespread dissemination of effective, female-controlled contraception (the pill), and the revamping of popular culture in ways that placed a decided accent on sexuality (from Elvis to the Rolling Stones in music to the reading public's taste for *Playboy* or the once-banned paperback, *Fanny Hill*) helped sustain a sexual revolution. It altered ideas and behaviours, moralities and norms, among all Canadians.

The group most emphatically affected was the youthful 15–25-year-old cohort that would soon prove a potent vanguard of consumer capitalism. Concentrated in the later 1960s, the effects of this societal transformation registered demographically in declining birth rates and delays in the age at which women conceived. Culturally it unleashed a pent-up domain of sexual life in ways that altered commerce and civil society, the arts, and attitudes. A study of sexuality and family planning among lower-income married couples in Quebec noted that prior to the late 1960s two-thirds of pregnancies were unplanned and only one-fourth of all couples used contraceptives after marriage or subsequent to having their first child. As the 1960s gave way to the 1970s, however, fully 86 per cent of couples practised birth control. Almost 50 per cent of women were taking oral contraceptives. This was a seismic shift in the meaning and practice of everyday (and night) life.[3]

Sex, and the sociocultural and historicized process of gender construction with which it is closely associated, has not traditionally been appreciated as central to understandings of national identity. The nation-state has, until quite recently, been structured within an almost nature-like association between governance and masculinity: the meanings and understandings of nationality, identity, and the practice of politics are draped in garb gendered unquestioningly male. Undoubtedly this has much to do with the close proximities of late eighteenth- and early nineteenth-century states and patriarchal relations, the family and its rule a comfortable metaphor for civil society and its hierarchical order. Modern bourgeois state power and the national identities with which it is associated, however, have increasingly been understood to shed this patriarchal skin. With this act of ostensibly discarding women's subordination to men the gender neutrality of both governance and nationalism, as well as their meanings, has supposedly been valorized and entrenched politically, socially, and culturally.

It has not played out, however, with this simple elegance. Feminist historians in Canada have quite assiduously uncovered the male trappings

in which state power has been layered since Confederation. The continuity of power as a male prerogative often sustained a dichotomization
of private and public life that reached forward from the nineteenth
century[4] and into the 1960s, when this separation began to be bridged
and resisted. Sex, which can both reproduce power relations and undermine them,[5] was never far from this unfolding narrative of the relations
of dominance/subordination.

As a host of recent studies, many of them concentrating on twentieth-
century Canada, have shown, the nation is indeed gendered. This
emerges with especial obviousness, even vehemence, in the Cold War
period. Attacks on communism and the defence of the nation and of
true Canadian identity easily slipped into assaults on so-called 'deviant'
sexuality that supposedly undermined the narrow familialist order that
was, ironically, judged the foundation of an expansive free society and
its broad northern vision of the good life. If the Cold War was primarily
and ostensibly about capitalism in combat with a threatening communism, 'promiscuous' women and homosexual 'perverts' were no less
dangerous. In their capacity to entice male power they could well be the
conduit through which a blackmailed personnel of governance passed
on secrets of state to the ever-nefarious Soviets.[6]

Woman as Displaced Person/Political Catalyst

Women coming to Canada and the United States from war-torn Europe
often arrived with tortured legacies. The innocence of their hopes and
dreams had been shattered on the hard and ugly realities of military conquest, labour camps, the Cold War's traumatizing confusions, and dis-
placements that ruptured ties to family and nation. To add insult to the
many injuries, they were unlikely to escape the watchful eye of the increasingly vigilant 'intelligence' forces, which saw in them a danger to national
security in an age of Cold War insecurities. But the starved 'domestic
labour' market needed these bodies: well-to-do Canadian housewives
were distraught that they could not find 'maids' and 'servants' for wages
of $75–$100 a month. Complaints lessened when 15,000 female displaced persons were brought to Canada between 1947 and 1953, their
'prevailing rate' of remuneration officially declared to be a modest $35 a
month.[7] Displaced women were seldom in a position to demand more.
They were often refugees from an environment of brutalizing coercion in
which their sexuality had been demanded as *both* the cost to be paid for
military defeat and the price of subsequent 'liberation.' They played a

role in reconfiguring understandings of gender relations within a generation of women who survived the Second World War and its immediate
aftermath in ways that are only beginning to be fully appreciated.[8]

Gerda Munsinger, née Heseler [Hessler], was one such woman. She
would bring into public view the private sexual underside of Canadian
politics before the wave of Trudeaumania hit the country in 1968.
Munsinger, it might be argued, prepared the way for Trudeau, the
'affair' that bore her name introducing sex and its political meaning
into discourses of national identity. The unfolding of these events, as
they were purposefully brought to light in 1966, revealed many a ludicrous association frozen in Cold War irrationalities. They also exposed
the petty and personalized nature of Liberal-Conservative conflict in the
House of Commons. Consequently, the sex/spy scandal that erupted
with the revelations of Munsinger's relations with Conservative cabinet
ministers in 1959–60 paved the road to the realization that a different
kind of Canadian politics was both desirable and struggling to be born.
Everyone knew in 1968 that Trudeau's phenomenal rise to power owed
much to women. But few have grasped that his metaphorical first lady
may well have been a German immigrant playgirl whose tastes in men
tended to the Tory.

From Occupied Germany to Canada, 1943–1957

There is a long history of what might be called sexual slumming. Men of
high social standing frequent 'low' places, attracted to sexual contacts
that step outside the boundaries of respectability.[9] Gerda Heseler, also
known as Olga Schmidt, Gerda/Ricky Munsinger, and Gerda Merkt,
found herself in the lowest and most threatening of places during the
1940s. She was born in what was then Koenigsberg, East Prussia (subsequently Kaliningrad, Russia), most likely on 10 September 1929, her
identity shrouded in obscurity, uncertainty, and conflicting reports.[10]
Whatever the actual truth, there is no doubt that the Heseler family, like
many others in Central Europe, did not weather well the social storms of
the late 1940s.[11]

Conflicting accounts of the Heseler family's postwar travails
exist,[12] but in Gerda's rendition, personal tragedy was emphasized.
Munsinger's father, later rumoured to have been a socialist and identified by the Royal Canadian Mounted Police (RCMP) as a communist, was apparently killed in 1943. In the tense and violent context
of the later war years, with Germany under siege, relations among

surviving family members were strained to the breaking point. Drafted for labour duty by the armed forces of the Nazi state in 1944, the adolescent Gerda was on increasingly poor terms with her mother and sister. A younger brother left home one day to get milk, never to be heard from again. Gerda became separated from her mother and sister shortly thereafter. 'I was 16 and I was a farmer's girl,' Munsinger told CBC newsman Norman DePoe in March 1966, 'With my figure, I was well-built, long, blond pigtails, and you know what was going on over there.' Later, less cryptically, Munsinger would tell the Cologne tabloid *Neue Illustrierte* (New Illustrated) what she had suffered at the hands of Russian soldiers, who treated her body as one of the spoils of war. As she stressed to Depoe, 'they did to me what they felt like it for two years ... I have had to have some operations, quite a few of them. My whole life has been ruined with it.'[13]

According to Munsinger, she escaped from the East German zone in the early 1950s. As a stateless person struggling to make precarious ends meet, Gerda pursued an often subterranean life, traversing borders that were simultaneously political and moral, socio-sexual, economically marginal, and gendered. From 1947 to 1949, Gerda Heseler slipped in and out of the German zones where Russian, American, French, and British troops were visible reminders of military defeat. Her scrapes with these armies of occupation were commonplace. She faced charges of petty thievery, faulty documentation, and there were allusions to prostitution as well. Living by her wits, and undoubtedly with the aid of her body, eighteen-year-old Gerda met a Russian major connected to intelligence services in Berlin, possibly setting up house with him for a while. In her 'work' on this man's behalf – pilfering passes, lifting wallets, and raising money and transferring currency, often through networks of sexual barter and casual prostitution – Gerda had her first, and apparently only, serious brush with the American West German border police. They extracted from her a confession of being involved in what was rather grandiosely labelled 'espionage.' Burdened with a counter-intelligence file, Heseler was now branded as a potential security risk. She apparently opted for less risky means of procuring subsistence, finding her way into a labour camp with other women, forced to work in order to secure ration tickets. But such women longed for some semblance of freedom, and Gerda, in concert with a dozen others, affected a break from the camp, determined to make her way to the western zone. Upon her arrival there, she not surprisingly neglected to follow the proper procedures in alerting the authorities of her presence and circumstances.

Instead, she concentrated on setting herself up as a waitress in a Bad Nauheim café near Frankfurt.[14]

It was there that she met the American serviceman and baseball player, Mike Munsinger, ostensibly the first love of her life. After dating for a year, Munsinger asked Gerda to marry him, secured a discharge, returned to the United States, and then went back to Germany to finalize his marriage. The couple thought that Munsinger's emigration to the United States would be secured by their wedding vows, but it was not to be. Gerda was denied entry to the United States in May 1953 on grounds of 'moral turpitude' and because she supposedly presented a 'security risk.' The decision was based on American Central Intelligence Agency files that could also have been used to bar her from Canada, to which Heseler had apparently applied for admission under her maiden name in 1952. A security report from Germany, dated 31 [*sic*] September 1952, supposedly informed the Royal Canadian Mounted Police that there was no evidence Gerda Heseler had been involved in any espionage activity subsequent to her 1949 arrest. It was impossible to prove or disprove any statements about her identity because she was, like so many persons displaced by the war, incapable of producing sufficient documentation to verify her claims. Later it would surface that European security forces had no information connecting Munsinger to espionage activity. This did her no good in seeking admission to Canada and the United States.[15]

Mike and Gerda later annulled their marriage, determining that if they could not live together in the United States there was little likelihood of a successful relationship. Gerda Munsinger then bounced from one job to another, working at American hotels in alpine resorts, winning a 'beauty contest,' and even securing a hostess position in an exclusive NATO officers' mess in Fontainebleau near Paris.[16] Her last position was in Pertisau, Austria, where she found employment at the Hotel Zur Post, her meagre pay of 130 marks a month supplemented by free meals and a room. Working long hours and living in an unheated garret, Gerda longed to leave Europe. Directed to the Canadian embassy in Munich, Munsinger promptly signed up for the transatlantic voyage. The Canadian state paid her $175 fare, extracting a commitment from her to toil as a domestic servant for one year, her earnings to be used to reimburse the government for the costs of her passage.[17]

Had Gerda pulled the wool over Canadian national security's eyes simply by changing her name from Heseler to Munsinger?[18] She did not lie to the state, declaring herself a divorcée, and no forms asked for her maiden name. All seemed to be going her way. With 173 marks in her pocket as she boarded the *Arosa Star* in July 1955, Gerda could not have imagined the men in high places who would be seeking her company in the years to come.[19]

Montreal: Sexual Adventure and the Lure of Upward Mobility

On her arrival in Canada in August 1955, Gerda Munsinger immediately got to work to settle her financial obligations to the government. She was assigned as a domestic to a doctor living 20 kilometres from Montreal, cleaning a bungalow for him and his wife. But Gerda was not to be denied her dreams of 'beautiful clothes, of jewelry, of elegant men, of romantic nights.' Had she not suffered enough? With her fare almost paid and her indentured servitude at an end, she moved to Montreal, securing apartments in the west end on Fort and Towers Streets, a short stroll to the neon-signed nightclubs that would soon be a mainstay of her life. Some neighbours knew her as quiet and unobtrusive, others remembering her as 'a happy, fun-loving girl who was always running out of money.'

Employed at first as a waitress and hostess in a St Catherine Street eatery, the Chick-n-Coop, a favourite with the baseball players who drew her interest, Munsinger had her eye on flashier pursuits, aiming at a career in modelling. She paid a photographic studio to prepare a portfolio, the glossy glamour shots retouched to accent a fuller bosom and a more slender waist. *Midnight*, a Montreal sex and sensation weekly, published one of the shots to give Gerda some publicity. Nothing grandiose came of Mrs Munsinger's modelling aspirations; she managed to make ends meet from month to month, paying her rent on a furnished apartment and absorbing the costs of lunches and other meals, likely cadging the odd dress from a manufacturer at a discounted price. She definitely toiled at the lower end of the scene, largely freelancing in downtown Montreal.

Munsinger referred to herself as a 'little mannequin who did not always know where to get the money for the rent.' Generous with what she had, Munsinger apparently lived life to the fullest. Female friends recalled that she never failed to pay her own way when she was on nights out with 'the girls.' Gerda managed, as well, to become a noticeable fixture at the downtown bars and lounges where doormen at burlesque and jazz clubs such as *Chez Parée* and *El Morocco* knew her as 'a high-class chick ... sharp and smart. She knew all the playboys.' The RCMP would stress that in her work as a hostess and cashier at some Montreal night-clubs, she worked on premises operated by racketeers and those involved in narcotics. One 'well-known Ottawa gambler and nightclub habitué' recalled Munsinger as a talkative woman with a tendency to drop names.[20]

Gerda's luck ran in the direction of survival. It did not extend to her relations with men. Her first Canadian lover, whom she took before com-pleting her indenture, was the maitre d' at the well-known restaurant Ruby Foo's. He arranged his work schedule so that his days off coincided with Gerda's, and they were able to spend some time together. Sex, for Gerda, was an instruction in the English language. And for her, this man *was* Canada: 'Rough and hard and, in the evenings, when the cold wind blew from the mountains, as tender as the strings of the guitars of the lumberjacks.' The archetypal Canadian romance ended badly, however. When another attractive blonde appeared in Ruby Foo's, Gerda was unceremoniously replaced. Longing to return to Europe, she still owed the government $43.35. And so she stayed, and adapted to her circum-stances and her new country.

In 1956–7 she relived her love affair with Mike Munsinger, setting up house for the baseball season with George 'Shotgun' Shuba, a pitching ace with the Montreal Royals. Munsinger's lifestyle may now have taken on some 'playgirl' dimensions, in which her trips to the United States, linking up with Shuba at Vero Beach spring training and games in Memphis, Tennessee, and elsewhere, were supplemented by 'partying' excursions off the Florida coast, at Boston greyhound tracks, in the clubs of New York, and among 'the rich nightclub hyenas of Las Vegas.' There were rumours of vacation jaunts to Panama, Colombia, and Mexico in the period stretching from late 1958 into the summer of 1959. Some of these stories were likely fabricated. Munsinger made fantastic claims to have been a party companion of shoe magnate and future husband of Debbie Reynolds, Harry Karl, and to have been wooed by Nat King Cole, whom her *Neue Illustrierte* handlers later had her describe as 'a coffee-brown troubadour' with a 'silky voice' that made Gerda 'shiver at [their] first meeting.' Developments of this period would later congeal into rep-resentations of jet-setting with Pierre Sévigny in the late 1950s and early 1960s that were most unlikely, if not impossible. But there was no deny-ing that Gerda had moved beyond domestic service and into a new stage in her life. It is entirely possible that her path crossed those of figures in Montreal's underworld. Yet Munsinger had her eye trained on more respectable, as opposed to mobbed up, money, if such a distinction can indeed be drawn. One lucrative dalliance supposedly led to her membership in an exclusive Lachute golf and country club.[21]

As Munsinger settled into the fast lane of freewheeling Montreal, she made friends easily, often with men of high social standing for whom discreet sexual encounters seemed to be commonplace. Her closest female companion was Jacqueline 'The Duchess' Delorme, a woman linked to corporate circles and the fashion industry. Munsinger and Delorme were introduced by Liberal Party insider Hubert Ducharme, counsel to the influential Grit power broker John C. Doyle,[22] a millionaire with interests in Central and South America. They knew Gerda by her nickname, Ricky, or as Olga, and also by the last name Monseignor.[23] Gerda Munsinger thus worked her way out of Ruby Foo's and into a network of fashionable establishments. They included the Hunt Club of the Sheraton Mount Royal Hotel, a favoured lunch spot for Montreal's high society and one of the city's finest cocktail bars, and the upscale dinner club, La Reserve of the Windsor Hotel.

It was in this context, in August 1959, that she first became associated, in a quasi-public way,[24] with Joseph Pierre Albert Sévigny, a rising francophone star in the Diefenbaker government. Sévigny's business success, war record, and distinguished family background in Quebec politics placed him well up the social pecking order. A friend who had escorted Gerda to a social reunion introduced the blonde German and the politician. Mrs Munsinger seemed 'charming,' 'very lovely,' 'dignified,' and 'reserved,' accepted and justifiably 'courted' and 'admired' by 'prominent people.' Sévigny and Munsinger developed what the former considered an 'occasional relationship,' one that he claimed lasted for a few months, then dragged out for another year. The Tory politician offered no apologies for his attraction to Munsinger. At its best moments, the relationship was undeniably characterized by considerable tenderness, although Sévigny would reveal the problematic chauvinism of the era in his reduction of women to adornments: 'It has been my good fortune in life to know and admire beautiful women,' he said, 'I love beautiful things – beautiful women, beautiful paintings, beautiful music. It's high time to recognize beauty and the nice things of life.'

Gerda, however, clearly wanted the liaison to become something more than a brief fling. This may have spurred her to travel to Ottawa,[25] where Sévigny, a decorated war hero who had lost his leg in combat, was about to enter the Conservatives' governing cabinet as an associate minister of defence. But it was another prominent Tory that she was destined to attract. Sitting alone in the restaurant of Ottawa's Château Laurier hotel, Munsinger was approached by George Hees, the athletic and vain heir-apparent to the Diefenbaker throne, and a member of cabinet who would hold significant portfolios in the Conservative government, including Transport and Trade and Commerce. 'He examined me the way a man musters a woman when he is already sure of his prey,' recalled Munsinger, adding that 'perhaps on this particular day I really looked as though I would have nothing against a little adventure.' And so it went, a few more elegantly outfitted and increasingly discreet lunch-time assignations culminating, according to Munsinger, in rather routine sex in a Château Laurier suite mere steps away from Parliament. Along the way, Gerda wrangled an invitation to the Montreal social event of the year, the St Andrew's Ball, in which she had an obligatory dance with Hees, her ego bolstered from flirtations directed her way by him and Sévigny. As 'two love-hungry ministers followed [her] with their eyes,' Gerda said to herself: 'now you have made it. You are up, very high up.' Her calculation was almost unnervingly mercenary: 'The St Andrew's Ball is the biggest social event in Canada. A charity ball for the two thousand topmost hats. Who is invited there, has it made for herself.' It was Sévigny (whom she knew would be attending the event, 'in tails and with orders on his breast, and with the woman to whom he has given his name') who captivated her, however, and she attended a huge public dinner in his honour at the end of September, some 3,500 guests fêting the recent appointment of a francophone Quebecker to cabinet.[26]

Munsinger claimed that she was both 'unsuspecting' and immediately appreciative of Hees's instrumental designs. She added that, 'meeting him did not disturb me because I already had a feeling: It could never be too serious with this man. A little flirting, perhaps. Even, maybe, an adventure. But more? Absolutely not.' Gerda then explained her attractiveness to powerful men:

If a woman wants to make a career for herself, she must learn to listen. Important and interesting men always feel, for whatever reason, that they are not understood. They are thankful when they find a woman who listens to them. I am no Loren, nor a Bardot ... When men want to talk I let them talk. When they want to make themselves admirable, then I admire them. And when they are telling tales, then I act as if I believed all the stories. No wonder, therefore, that also the trade minister found me exciting.

After securing her invitation to the St Andrew's Ball, Munsinger claimed that the low price of her admission was a brief sexual tryst with Hees. Once this obligation was fulfilled, the Munsinger-Hees exchange was over.[27]

Munsinger's attraction to Sévigny was not so easily ended, in large part because Gerda clearly romanticized a relationship that was deformed by the traumas of her adolescence and the ways her life had subsequently been structured around a base, often instinctual, struggle to survive. Drawn to the older man's gentleness, Munsinger perhaps saw in him 'a father, the great protector, for whom I felt the want,' adding, 'It was not the physical love I was searching for. It was simply love for which I had always been in want.' In a letter to her friend 'The Duchess,' written after she had left Canada, Munsinger asked after her close companion's routines, and whether she still went to Mount Royal's The Hunt, wanting to be remembered to the luncheon staff and wondering if Delorme had recently seen 'Daddy.' And she certainly enjoyed 'the excitement caused by the fact that I had made the top ten thousand people through Pierre Sévigny.' In Sévigny's view, Gerda's main fault was a tendency to 'embellish a situation with words of her own, to add romance to the simplest situations and to somewhat exaggerate, shall we say.' Such a judgment of course covered the associate minister of defence's flank, maintaining a 'gentleman's discretion' at the same time as it skirted the truth about the Sévigny-Munsinger relationship. From September through December 1959 Sévigny and Munsinger apparently met discreetly, often socializing with Jacqueline Delorme, lunching at the Hunt Club, dining at La Reserve, and, in Munsinger's remembrance, spending affectionate evenings together. It all clearly meant much more to Munsinger than to Sévigny, but she claimed to have vowed to be content with the moments she might have with him, confined, approximately, to twice a month.[28]

Costly Citizenship Charade: An Innocent's Naming of Names

What ultimately unhinged the Munsinger-Sévigny coupling was a displaced woman's need for some measure of security and what this meant for the secret state within the state, Canada's RCMP national security apparatus, described by one historian as suspended in a 'cult-like isolation.' Given Gerda's background and her lover's place at the pinnacle of the state's defence structure, in conjunction with the bad timing of their

illicit relationship at the height of the Cold War, it was a foregone conclusion that matters would get worse rather than better.[29]

In January 1960 Sévigny learned from Jacqueline Delorme that
Gerda was somewhat loose-lipped in her references to him, dropping
his name in conversations. 'The Duchess' made every effort to impress
upon her German friend that it was indiscreet to mention people she
knew in high places in casual talk. Gerda replied nonchalantly and with
some innocence that she was proud of her friends and considered that
there could be no harm in talking about them with other people.
Delorme expressed surprise 'that she would not realize the bearing of
her words.' Apprised of the situation, Sévigny tried to slowly extricate
himself from the relationship with Munsinger: his contact with her lessened; he instructed his Ottawa parliamentary staff to deflect her calls.
He saw Gerda, he later insisted, only by chance a few times between
January and November 1960, and talked with her on the telephone
rarely and reluctantly.[30]

It was at this point, from mid-January 1960 until she left Canada in
February 1961, that Gerda Munsinger's life totally unravelled. Jilted by
Sévigny, Munsinger suddenly had to face the end of her rollercoaster
ride through Montreal high society. Things worsened for her economically. By the fall of 1960, Munsinger was in a nightmarish free fall, her
life cascading from bad to worse. Health problems were catching up
with her. Doctors ostensibly feared an onslaught of leukemia; a gum
disease required hospitalization in Montreal and the removal of her
upper teeth. With her body and her face undergoing changes that
undermined her looks, Munsinger's modelling career stalled, sput-
tered, and then abruptly stopped. Reduced to a $45 weekly paycheque
for doing accounting work associated with her apartment building,
Gerda suffered another blow in October when she was burglarized and
many personal belongings stolen. (Could this have been a precursor of
subsequent RCMP 'dirty tricks,' directed against the Parti Québécois
and the Canadian left?)[31] Clearly at loose ends, she returned to
Germany in February 1960, hoping to rekindle an old relationship.
But she was back in Canada seventeen days later. Four months later,
Munsinger travelled outside the country for three weeks, and again in
December-January 1960–1. Possibly she was attending to medical problems in the United States, visiting West Germany and Austria, and
almost certainly accumulating debts that would have to be repaid in
one way or another.[32]

As a landed immigrant with official German papers, Munsinger was especially vulnerable as her situation skidded out of control, for her passport was due to expire sometime in the summer of that year. Possibly anticipating the problems this would pose for her, Munsinger applied for Canadian citizenship in June 1960. In what was a very un-spy-like move, she named George Hees and Pierre Sévigny as references. And then her real troubles began.[33]

In order to extricate herself from these worsening economic pressures, Munsinger may well have relied on connections to organized crime figures whom she had either known during the late 1950s or, possibly, come into contact with through her relations with Pierre Sévigny. Both Munsinger and Delorme (as well as John Diefenbaker) maintained that Sévigny had been linked to an underworld figure, William 'Willie Obie' Obront, in the late 1950s and early 1960s. A notorious racketeer who would eventually be indicted and convicted on drug-related charges, Obront was born to Jewish parents in Montreal in 1924. He managed to climb the ladder of the city's Italian-dominated Mafia. Obrant was a man Gerda feared, and rightly so, thinking of him chillingly and haunted by remembrance of this 'bull-necked, short 180-pounder' who 'laughed when he was called the chief of the Mafia in Montreal ... laughed when it was said that he was bribing politicians.' With his 'finger everywhere, in every business in which the police had an interest,' the gangster's 'arm reache[d] far,' including into the Munsinger-Sévigny liaison. In 1959–60 Obront's trusted chauffeur, Leo Robidoux, would apparently double as Sévigny's driver when he and Munsinger wanted to take a discreet automobile trip out of town. He knew their conversations and their intimacies like no other person. Munsinger may have been drawn to figures such as these in a moment of financial panic, and they could well have introduced her to the possibilities of profit that could be garnered by prostitution. Throughout the summer and fall of 1960, Munsinger may have turned, likely in desperation, to such avenues of sex trade work. On one occasion in August 1960 she reportedly ran afoul of the Montreal morality squad. Mysteriously, there was no record in police files.

More ominously, however, her movements (and those of Sévigny) were now closely monitored by the RCMP, which was also, by late November 1960, tapping her phone. Even the then minister of justice, Davie Fulton, would later concede that the RCMP had 'followed every usual, and some unusual, methods to obtain information.' There were rumours, circulating later, of RCMP photographs taken of Munsinger and Sévigny, referred to in the parlance of the times as 'in a compromising position' (although other reference was made to a picture of Gerda merely dancing with a cabinet minister). They were supposedly secured with an infra-red camera installed by the Mounties in the chandelier of a Montreal hotel bedroom. All very Cold War cloak-and-daggeresque.[34]

By innocently naming Hees and Sévigny on her citizenship application, Munsinger had unleashed the hounds or, as it were, the horsemen. The RCMP began an investigation into Munsinger, who had the temerity to cite not one but *two* cabinet ministers as references. It was not long before the RCMP uncovered her not-so-well-hidden paper trail that led back to the morals and security risk allegations of 1949 occupied Germany. Convinced, as higher-level 'intelligence' forces in the Mounties were wont to be, that spies existed under every politician's bed, and all the more so if someone other than a man's wife was to be found there, the security forces easily fell into the view that Munsinger was the classic femme fatale of a Canadian Mata Hari scene. A report from Germany's chief visa control officer indicated that Gerda had not 'come to our notice since 1949.' While there was no evidence of espionage, a point accented in one report by a Montreal RCMP investigator, the coincidences that surrounded Munsinger's life were too tantalizing to ignore. She had a past tarnished by allegation, even confession. Most ominously, Munsinger was linked to the infamous Russians, categorized as a woman of low reputation, engaged in the barter of sexual commerce and apparently linked to mobsters and narcotics smuggling. Much was made of a Soviet trading agency having an office in her apartment building and a supposed Russian agent working out of it.

As a later RCMP commissioner would sum it up, Munsinger presented a 'textbook' case of how sex would be used by the Soviets to foster an intelligence network inside Canada:

> To go back to the beginning, if I were writing a text book of instruction on espionage cases and I wanted to dream up a classical case – one which, unless you were very fortunate, as an intelligence officer you would likely encounter – we were faced with a situation in which a woman who was known to us from reliable sources to have been an agent of the Soviet Intelligence Service, who had been turned down for entry into our country under her maiden name and had, in some manner unclear to us, managed to get into the country under another name and had achieved an

association with the associate Minister of one of our most vital departments, the Department of National Defence; now, those were the circumstances and it is a classical type of case.

Munsinger was, in other words, what Deborah Van Seters labels 'the iconic female agent.'[35]

Sadly for Gerda, her life in Canada was now at an end. In November 1960 she was questioned by the RCMP, setting her head spinning with fears. Through her friend Jacqueline Delorme, Sévigny, who was refusing Gerda's calls, was prevailed upon to meet Munsinger at her apartment on 26–7 November 1960. No doubt the Tory cabinet minister simply wanted Munsinger to leave the country. Her German passport needed an extension, she was financially destitute, and Sévigny promised to help out. The Quebec politician was startled by how she looked: 'She had lost a great deal of weight ... really looked awful.' Sévigny apparently did not know that the RCMP had Munsinger's phone bugged and that surveillance on her building the evening of his late-night/early-morning visit was poised to reveal unusual traffic in and out of Gerda's apartment. The claim would be made that three other men had been to see Munsinger prior to Sévigny's arrival, all of them apparently paying for 'services.' There were later statements by the security forces that Munsinger was 'engaged in an active career in prostitution and had as her companions, and apparent confidantes, other women in Montreal who were engaged in the same practice.'[36] RCMP Commissioner Clifford Walter Harvison eventually met with Diefenbaker's minister of justice, Edmund Davie Fulton, and on 7 December 1960 instructions were forwarded to the Department of Citizenship and Immigration to cease and desist from any proceedings relating to Gerda Munsinger's application for Canadian citizenship. Aided by a friend (not Sévigny) who paid her airfare, Munsinger returned to Germany in December, came back to Canada, finalized her affairs, and prepared to leave her adopted country for good.

A few days before her departure, Gerda was arrested in a Montreal department store, ostensibly in the company of a woman known to be a prostitute, charged with trying to cash a cheque off an account with insufficient funds. She spent a night in jail and was then released. Diefenbaker would later pen a private memo in which he indicated that Sévigny provided Munsinger with $500, using Willie Obront, largely through the 'hot-tempered, nervous' Leo Robidoux as a go-between. The department store was convinced to drop the charges against the 'two prostitutes' lest it compromise government officials; a $50 fine was paid on the understanding that Munsinger would be leaving the country not to return (which apparently cleared her from police records); a one-way ticket to Germany was purchased for Gerda, who was also slipped some pocket money; and the ailing and undoubtedly frightened woman was driven to Dorval Airport on 5 February 1961.[37]

The only question that remained was the identity of the two men who later appeared in the Towers Street apartment complex questioning neighbours about Munsinger. They carried with them a picture of the woman and a letter bearing the ostensible return address of an aunt in Austria. Their claim was that she had died of leukemia. Were these men Obront and Robidoux, as Munsinger herself later suggested? Or were they an RCMP security service team, likely thinking that it was closing out a file on what would, five years later, become Canada's most celebrated 'sex and spy' scandal case? Or might the inquisitive duo have been the Liberal Party fixers, Ducharme and Doyle?[38]

The Resurrection of Gerda Munsinger

Early in 1961 it would have seemed that the Munsinger affair was over. Sévigny and Hees must have breathed a sigh of relief. So, too, did Prime Minister John G. Diefenbaker. He had been informed by Fulton of the RCMP's concerns that the Sévigny-Munsinger liaison presented a potential security risk on 12–13 December 1960, the minister of justice handing the prime minister a short security brief and outlining the situation to him orally. Diefenbaker was aghast and immediately summoned Sévigny to his office, informing him that he was aware of his relationship with Munsinger, that there was evidence of prostitution and underworld connections and concerns about an ostensible espionage past. Sévigny did a bit of a dance when hauled on the carpet, not quite coming clean as to the nature of his relations with Munsinger, but the 'Chief' was having none of it: 'This must end between you and this woman forthwith, period.' Sévigny was also asked if there had been any security breach or any attempted blackmail, to which he replied decisively in the negative. It was left open-ended as to whether Sévigny would remain in his cabinet position or if he should resign. The prime minister instructed his associate minister of defence not to be in touch with Munsinger in any way under any circumstances and, in a few subsequent encounters with Sévigny in December asked pointedly, 'Has this ended?' Sévigny assured the prime minister that he had terminated relations with the woman and that she was leaving the country. Fulton met twice with the RCMP's Harvison in the last weeks of December and regularly thereafter, being kept somewhat apprised of the situation. The final such meeting took place 16 February 1961, with Harvison informing Fulton of the details of Munsinger's sorry last days in Canada. Diefenbaker was then briefed and, as it was determined that there had been no breach of security, Sévigny was not formally disciplined or asked to resign. Somehow the prime minister got wind of how Willie Obront became involved as Sévigny's emissary, but with Munsinger out of the country 'this very much lessened the concern about the whole matter.' Sleeping dogs were let lie, and one low woman, sometimes referred to as 'the girl,' forgotten about.[39]

In Montreal, Jackie Delorme received a letter from her friend Gerda at the end of April 1961, letting her know that she was happily established in Munich, working as a secretary in the personnel branch of the American forces. 'The life I had in Montreal made me blue and miserable,' she confessed, adding that she no longer understood how she stood 'it that long.' For a year, the women corresponded, and towards the end of the summer Gerda let 'The Duchess' know that she was quite ill, suffering from leukemia, and that she required hospitalization. January 1962 brought word that Munsinger was recovering, but thereafter Delorme's letters to Gerda went unanswered. She thought her old friend must have died and told others who had known Gerda, including Sévigny, the bad news that Munsinger had likely succumbed to the blood disorder. Two such 'friends,' the Montreal wire-pulling duo, Hubert Ducharme and John Doyle, asked after Munsinger in November 1964, referring to her as 'Olga Monseignor.' They were informed that she had died some time ago of leukemia.[40]

On Parliament Hill, among Tories primarily, but possibly in other circles as well, the affair may well have become the stuff of insider gossip and male jocularity.[41] There were those who enjoyed a risqué joke at the puritanical Diefenbaker's expense, and Sévigny, although a reputed figure of authority in Quebec, was never regarded that highly in Ottawa. The rumours of Sévigny's affair with an East German playgirl no doubt found their way to many a wine-soaked dinner or cocktail-hour table, the laughter level rising as stories circulated of the suave French Canadian convincing the straight-laced prairie populist that Munsinger was purely a sexual conquest not a Cold War concubine in search of military secrets and classified plans for deploying Bomarc missiles.[42]

By the mid-1960s such jokes could never be told in mixed political company. Liberals and Conservatives were engaged in bitterly partisan warfare, often wallowing in a sea of scandal the likes of which had seldom been seen in modern Canada. Larry Zolf called it 'the Gunfight at the Pearson-Diefenbaker Corral,' a politics of 'mere survival of the law of the day,'[43] less Darwinian in its inspirations than it was Al Capone-ish in its plot lines. The St Valentine's Day Massacre was coming; the only question was when, who would first open fire on whom, and what, in the Canadian political tradition, would be left standing. John G. Diefenbaker and Lester B. Pearson were like rival gang bosses: they despised each other.

In 1965 Diefenbaker was holding on tenuously to his leadership of the Conservative Party, and Lester B. Pearson occupied the prime minister's office in an equally tentative manner. The November election of that year confirmed only one thing: Canadians were uncomfortable with both leaders and would refuse either of them a majority. Quebec kept Pearson in power; the west refused to let Diefenbaker go down to a totally humiliating defeat. The cities were Liberal, the countryside Conservative. The more things changed, the more they remained the same. In terms of popular vote, the Liberals had a lock on 40 per cent, the Conservatives 32, and the New Democratic Party 18. The major party seat totals stood at 131 and 97, leaving Pearson two shy of a majority. Whatever problems the Liberals might encounter in Quebec, and they would be many, Pearson needed French Canada to keep his house keys to 24 Sussex Drive.[44]

Since the last election in 1963, Tories and Grits had been throwing the mud of scandal at each other in the House of Commons. The Lucien Rivard affair, involving an imprisoned mobster serving time for narcotics convictions, raised questions of bribery in the office of the minister of immigration, with the alleged involvement of the prime minister's parliamentary secretary Guy Rouleau. A secretary of state and member of Pearson's inner circle, Maurice Lamontagne, was raked over the parliamentary coals for failure to pay for furniture that he had received from a firm owned by two Montreal gamblers who had gone missing in the wake of a provincial government probe into bankruptcies. Another Quebec minister, Yvon Dupuis, was charged with being on the 'sweet' end of influence peddling with respect to a race track charter. The toll of all of this Quebec upheaval was considerable. Pearson's minister of justice, Guy Favreau, was forced to resign as a consequence of such developments, placed under official scrutiny by an inquiry headed by former Conservative MP and chief justice of the Superior Court of Quebec, Frederic Dorion. Dupuis and Rouleau were fired and Lamontagne and another francophone minister, René Tremblay, could never quite escape the taint of wrongdoing. The Liberals were under constant attack, and Diefenbaker and the Conservatives were enjoying it, the assault led by Diefenbaker's irrepressible Yukon lieutenant, Erik Nielsen.[45]

The election results of 1965 changed little, and the scandal mongering continued. Nothing could be thrown with more venom than the dirt of Cold War spy allegations, and the parliamentary chaos of 1966 commenced with the case of George Victor Spencer, a Vancouver postal worker who undertook some low-level espionage assignments for the Soviets. At least the subject was not francophone and the locale of allegation was other than Quebec. Spencer knew no secrets of state but passed on to his Russian comrades some details of the post office security system, offering up as well commonplace information that might have been useful in creating effective covers for communist agents. The RCMP had Spencer contained and probably considered him non-threatening, but he was nonetheless fired from his job and placed on a permanent surveillance list. Apparently dying of cancer, Spencer was never brought to trial. When cobalt treatment lengthened his life beyond expectations, losing his job and his pension without having actually been convicted of any crime suddenly raised justifiable cries that his civil liberties had been handled too cavalierly. The new Liberal minister of justice, Lucien Cardin, generally perceived to be in a cabinet position much over his head, was soon hounded by television and print journalists, placed roughly in the parliamentary stocks by Diefenbaker, Nielsen, and company.[46]

Pearson's role in all of this was hardly exemplary. He had let his popular Quebec minister of justice, Guy Favreau, be hung out to dry, and many in his caucus were justifiably upset. More tellingly, driven to anger by the Conservative scandal mongering, and prompted by Liberal Party insider Jack Pickersgill, Pearson had requested from the RCMP all available security files on members of Parliament dating back to 1954. As Denis Smith concludes, 'this fishing expedition was a violation of cabinet convention and political decency unprecedented in Canadian history.' It brought to light the Sévigny-Munsinger file and prompted Pearson, then under Conservative assault in the House of Commons for the Liberal government's handling of the Rivard affair, to write a personal letter to Diefenbaker on 4 December 1964, inquiring as to how the case had been handled by him in his capacity as prime minister. Pearson rather innocently suggested in his memoirs that he was merely writing as one Privy Councillor to another. Diefenbaker interpreted the private communication as a more sinister 'attempt to blackmail His Majesty's Loyal Opposition into silence on the scandals rocking his government.' Davie Fulton thought the same, having been visited by Guy Favreau and given the impression that if the Tories would not tone down their attacks, a Liberal 'outburst' might trigger a security scandal in the House of Commons. This was a veiled threat to 'expose the Munsinger thing,' according to the former Conservative minister of justice. As George Bain would later write in the *Globe and Mail*, the Munsinger case was 'a pailful of slops' held by the Liberals 'over the heads of its chief political opponents.'[47]

In essence the Liberals were looking for a quid pro quo, albeit in ways that were decidedly unprincipled and underhanded. Diefenbaker, clearly at the end of his career, his hatred of Mike Pearson, Lucien Cardin, and other Liberal 'enemies' quite venomous, was in no mood to lighten up. One of the potential Quebec Liberal scandals that had somehow not managed to break, but that the Conservatives were threatening to move on, was the push for a parliamentary inquiry into the way six Social Credit MPs switched to the Liberals in 1963. It was widely rumoured that Liberal Party bagmen Hubert Ducharme and John Doyle had been involved in pay-offs to the Créditistes who crossed the floor and helped shore up Pearson in his unsuccessful quest for a majority government. Sévigny, well connected socially to Ducharme and Doyle, would later claim that his Montreal friends, very much of the fair-weather kind, had in fact successfully pressured the governing Liberals to call the 1965 election. The Liberal Party duo, Sévigny suggested, were anxious to defuse a situation in which a parliamentary investigation might have compromised both the party and its powerful backroom brokers in Montreal. With Sévigny no longer in politics and the election of 1965 seemingly unsuccessful in damming the floodgates of Conservative criticism, Ducharme and Doyle remained concerned that their actions in the *affaire des six* would inevitably come to light unless the Diefenbaker scandal juggernaut could be halted. They ostensibly plotted to expose the Sévigny-Munsinger 'sex/spy' imbroglio through Doyle's control of reporters at *Le Journal de Montréal*. According to a Sévigny informant, 'they were going to build up something similar to the Profumo–Christine Keeler story' in order to divert attention from 'the misdemeanours of the Liberals to scandals under the Diefenbaker administration.' With the 1963 British case of John D. Profumo – a secretary of state for war in the Harold Macmillan Conservative government – fresh in the minds of Canadians, it all seemed a good strategy. Profumo, who slept with Christine Keeler, a nineteen-year-old showgirl who had also had sexual relations with a naval attaché in the Russian embassy, lied to the House of Commons about the affair and then, no longer in a position to deny the sexual impropriety, resigned in silent shame. Front-page news around the world, the scandal almost brought down the government and led to the resignation of Macmillan, who cited ill health, in October 1963. Whether or not Pearson and his cabinet members were influenced or pressured by Ducharme and Doyle with respect to the Sévigny-Munsinger affair and Diefenbaker's closed-quarters handling of it, there is no doubt that there was discussion of the file among select cabinet ministers in the Liberal government between January and March 1966. Favreau had certainly been in the know for some time. Having been forced to resign, he had plenty of reason to be personally miffed at Diefenbaker and his parliamentary guard of scandal-pushing henchmen. Ducharme and Doyle may well have let it be known that 'Olga Monseignor,' the principal in the case, was conveniently dead. Pressed as to the human costs to Sévigny and his family that exposure of the old story would cause, Doyle replied: 'It's his skin, let him take care of himself.' All was fair, in love, war, money, and politics in 1966. Indeed, on the other side of the House, Cardin would publicly declare that 'there is a working arrangement not only between the Prime Minister, myself, and the members of the Cabinet, but also all the MPs, and what we are going to do is fight and fight hard, and, if we have to, use the same methods that are being used and have been used against us for the past three years.'[48]

From late January and throughout February 1966, Pearson and Cardin made veiled allusions to the Munsinger case in their response to Conservatives assailing their handling of security issues.[49] On 4 March 1966, Diefenbaker and Cardin exchanged harsh words in the House of Commons, and each sentence led to another more heated one. Goaded by the more experienced Conservative, the minister of justice was almost beside himself with rage and, shaking his fist across the parliamentary aisle, stated that the former prime minister was 'the very last person in the House who can afford to give advice on the handling of security cases.' Diefenbaker kept up a heckling prattle until Cardin, possibly prompted by Favreau, blurted out, 'I want the Right Honourable Gentleman to tell the House about his participation in the Monseignor case when he was Prime Minister of the country.' The Munsinger cat was now out of the political bag, and Cardin, pressed by journalists outside the house in days following, was forced to try to clarify the issue. He only muddied the waters. Correcting the spelling to Munsinger, Cardin mistakenly referred to Gerda as Olga. He indicated that Conservative cabinet ministers in the plural had been associated with her (romantically or not, he would not say); noted that the woman in question had a background in spying for the Russians before her arrival in Canada in the 1950s; pointed out that Diefenbaker and Fulton had known of the security risks created when Munsinger associated with high-ranking parliamentarians, but had neglected to proceed in appropriate legal ways; and claimed that Munsinger had left Canada and died in East Berlin in 1961. Cardin refused to discount the possibility that national security could have been compromised and concluded that the whole affair may well have been worse than the Profumo scandal. As the House of Commons turned into a Munsinger mudslinging match, thousands lined up outside of the Parliament buildings hoping to gain access to the galleries and hear word of the unfolding scandal or even catch a glimpse of some of the principals. In a later interview Cardin insisted that he had never seen the Munsinger file and that he would not 'say what my source of information was.' What he said, the way he said it, and the facts that he claimed to know were, however, entirely consistent with the understandings of the situation possessed by Hubert Ducharme and John Doyle.[50]

Journalists had their sources of information as well. Martin Goodman, the *Toronto Daily Star*'s Ottawa bureau chief, had been on the track of a story involving Sévigny and a mysterious blonde since 1963, following trails of gossip that led to and from Ottawa, Montreal, and Washington. His managing editor disappointingly concluded that it was nothing more than 'an ordinary bedroom scandal,' and the word was that whatever the affair had been, the woman was now dead.[51] When Cardin dropped his House of Commons bombshell on 4 March 1966, Goodman rushed to phone his editor, Ralph Allen, who quickly assigned investigative journalist Bob Reguly to the Munsinger case. Reguly's stock as a journalist had soared in 1964 when he had managed to find Hal Banks, the on-the-run racketeer-union boss, lounging on a yacht moored at the Seamen's Union Brooklyn piers, his Quebec-plated Cadillac parked near the docks. It was yet again a mid-1960s instance of the Liberals looking inept, and a Quebec minister, Justice's Guy Favreau, wearing egg on his face.[52]

Reguly wasted no time in dropping an omelet in the Pearson government's lap, one that looked like it had cracked a few Tory shells as well. As Cardin was holding a press conference in which he continued to maintain that Munsinger was dead, Reguly was well on his way to discovering that she was very much alive. Within a matter of days, the journalist confirmed that Gerda was among the living and likely working at a Munich café. Hopping a flight to Germany, Reguly questioned wait staff, secured an address, and hung around until a blonde woman entered the building and answered his knock at her door. 'I suppose you want to ask about Sévigny,' she said matter-of-factly. On Friday 11 March 1966, the *Star*'s fat second edition carried the large-print 'scoop' headline, 'Star Man Finds Gerda Munsinger.'[53] The Liberals had been upstaged, and some Tories worried that the final curtain was about to drop.

The Marketing of a Mannequin

From this point on, Munsinger was marketed by various forces. The Canadian print and electronic media set the buzz going, descending on Munich to track her down and secure interviews. Newsmen plastered their newspapers, magazines, radio airwaves, and television screens with sex and scandal narratives that drew the usually staid estates of journalism closer and closer to the tabloid sheets.

The mid-March 1966 frenzy of newspaper journalism gave way to the more illustrative poses of Munsinger in an April *Star Weekly* feature that included the German's face on the cover, glamour shots of Gerda's nights as an upscale club hostess, silhouette poses of a sporty woman holidaying on a Florida or Mexico beach, and 'mature' shots of the 'blonde and shapely' 36-year-old stretched out on a divan in her Munich apartment. The Montreal tabloid *Le Nouveau Samedi* was quick off the mark. It sported a headshot ménage-à-trois sequence of Gerda, Pierre, and Mme Sévigny on the cover of its 19 March 1966 issue. 'J'aime les femmes, c'est vrai,' shouted the headline, supposedly quoting Sévigny. Cabinet ministers (one photograph of George Hees was titled 'Body Beautiful') found themselves pictured next to contrasting images of the now-infamous blonde, her pictures labelled 'toute belle en 1959' and 'fatigué' in 1966. More highbrow publications, such as *Maclean's*, got into the act, occasionally lowering its tone, as when the magazine sponsored a limerick contest, won by the following entry:

There was a young lady from Munich
Whose bosom distended her tunic.
Her main undertaking
Was cabinet making
In fashions bilingue et unique.

But the newsstand favourite also ran a seven-page, profusely illustrated
interview with Pierre Sévigny and his wife, prefaced by a long description of the couple's tasteful Montreal house and its cultured atmosphere. The conversation represented the former cabinet minister as a
suave and sophisticated, albeit unfaithful, husband. He was supported
unquestioningly by his devoted and accomplished wife. The Sévignys
were understandably angered by the despicable behaviour of the RCMP
and the Liberal Party. Gerda was portrayed as an innocent in the entire
event, one who had, like the Sévignys, been harmed. The Montreal
businessman-politician was less repentant than he was irate. 'Forget the
sex,' he would later say. 'A man meets a woman and a woman meets a
man ... She was a pleasant, beautiful girl. How many men would have
done the same as I did?' Shocked that he would be questioned about
whether or not he and Munsinger engaged in intercourse, Sévigny
replied with an outraged sense of privacy: 'These men should be
ashamed of themselves ... whether a man or a woman has intercourse
with one person or another is their own business.'

Sévigny lashed out at Lucien Cardin, Pearson's minister of justice,
whom he saw as responsible for the public airing of his dirty linen.
Cardin's sin was not carnal, but the far more serious breach of a masculine political code, a defiling of the unspoken understanding of the limits to honourable behaviour among parliamentary combatants: 'It has
always been the rule in the House that private lives are never discussed.
That's one thing that Cardin will never live down – he broke the silence
rule that gentlemen don't break.'54

Munsinger would undoubtedly have preferred to concur, had she
been left alone. 'I knew Pierre as a man,' she said. 'He knew me as a
woman. That's all there was to it.'55 Yet once it was apparent that she was
a woman of international notoriety, sought after by journalists who
hounded her with offers of cash gifts, Munsinger availed herself of the
obvious opportunities. She secured the services of a rather indefatigable
'literary agent,' the debonair Josef Von Ferenczy. Munsinger's stock rose
astronomically, her identity signature price of $1,000 leading to $5,000

and $10,000 offers for her story. Higher and higher bidders clamoured for the much-sought-after 'exclusive,' which usually carried the cost of lower and lower standards of reporting.[56]

The Cologne *Neue Illustrierte* eventually won the war for rights, having long since lost the battle for some measure of journalistic integrity. It shelled out $45,000 and staged the Munsinger story on a foundation of fact and fiction, partial truth and embellished error. The tabloid published a five-part series appearing weekly in March and April 1966. Something of Munsinger's history appeared, but it was written within scripted boundaries of formulaic melodrama, accenting equal parts romantic sentimentalism, strained stories of gangsters, intrigue and danger, and unbelievable allusions to Gerda's almost mythical connection to the rich, the famous, and the notorious. Finally, it was served with cheesecake. Munsinger was pictured in white panties and sweater, supposedly dressing for a quick escape, or tightly corseted in black bustier and garter belt, preparing for an evening of her patented nightclubbing. The market had triumphed. Munsinger had sold herself, allowing a more mass commercialism to be mounted by corporate interests.[57]

It seemed difficult for even the most staid of Canadian journalists to get past this cashing in on Munsinger.[58] Norman DePoe introduced his famous 12 March 1966 CBC interview with Munsinger by outlining the clandestine, espionage-like arrangements that had been followed to link up with the now-notorious Gerda. He added an opening description of the femme fatale's 'blue eyes, carefully shaded with make-up and heavy false eyelashes.' To tart up his presentation of Munsinger to a Canadian television audience, he paused to add, 'And let it be said, a run in her left stocking.'[59] Mainstream historians would subsequently revel in uncritical reproduction of this crude trade in representation, quoting Gerda 'breathlessly telling' the tabloids of her sexual exploits, describing her as 'garrulous and "working" in a Munich bar,' the quotation marks around 'working' suggestive of an illicit 1966 present corresponding to her ostensibly lewd 1960 past.[60]

In actual fact, Munsinger was indeed employed in a Munich café, the Scotch Casino, making a modest living in a quite conventional, respectable, and unassuming way. She 'had found peace.' About to embark on marriage to her long-time companion, a tobacco manufacturer, Walter Wagner, Munsinger was a woman approaching middle age who merely wanted a quiet family life. Incredulous at the allegations that she was a Russian agent, Gerda replied: 'If I was a spy would I be working for a living?' Remembering her past, she added for good measure: 'I would have no reasons to do a favor for the Russians.'[61]

The political marketing of Munsinger would fly in the face of such mundane realities. It awaited the Pearson government's 14 March 1966 Order-in-Council establishing a commission of inquiry into matters relating to the Munsinger affair, as it had been referred to in the House of Commons and in various statements and communications by Lucien Cardin in the first and second week of March 1966.[62] Headed by Justice Wishart Flett Spence of the Supreme Court of Canada, the Spence Commission, as it became known, was a blank cheque to be cashed at the expense of Diefenbaker's handling of the original Sévigny-Munsinger file.[63] It owed its origin to Pearson's request that the RCMP deliver to him all damaging files relating to MPs and security issues. New Democratic Party leader Tommy Douglas likened it to 'the first step toward establishing a police state in this country.' The *Globe and Mail* voiced concern that 'the terms of reference which the Cabinet had approved for the inquiry were vague, vengeful, and prosecutory.' [Read Prosecute-a-Tory.] It wondered aloud what would come of striking commissions of inquiry to investigate prime ministerial decisions, however wrong-headed. The RCMP was allowed a free hand to provide evidence as it saw fit, much of which remained classified and thus closed to those whom it could potentially damage. There seemed no constraint on the security state's capacity to construct and deposit evidence that could not be properly interrogated or even adequately ascertained to have been legitimately developed out of the events of 1960–1, as opposed to pieced together afterwards. Summaries of such RCMP documents were released, but the original, ostensibly more substantial, evidence remained, for the most part, unavailable. The commission, which convened in May 1966, ended up concluding on a predictable note: Diefenbaker and Fulton had been remiss in allowing Sévigny to remain in his cabinet post after finding out about his indiscretions, and in not ordering further investigations charged with determining whether or not a security breach had occurred in 1959–60. Spence confirmed Cardin's positions, including the rather wild allegation that the Munsinger affair may well have given the Profumo case a run for its money in terms of its status as a scandal threatening to the state. The *Globe and Mail* capped the political careers of Diefenbaker, Fulton, and Sévigny with a terse concluding judgment on the commission of inquiry. 'The handling of the Munsinger affair' by these three Tories had served Canadians 'wretchedly.'[64]

Be that as it may, the Spence Commission had settled its vendetta on a particular marketing of Gerda Munsinger. Against the representation of her friend Jacqueline Delorme and her occasional lover Pierre Sévigny stood the relentless disparagement of Munsinger. Delorme had insisted that Gerda was 'the most wonderful person. A lot of charm. Witty. Amusing ... So very good to be with her. She had poise. She was very distinguished looking. Reserved. She didn't smoke. She was a light drinker and she was most attractive.' Sévigny concurred: 'Mrs. Munsinger was certainly not the despicable person that she is being represented to be in recent weeks. She was a very charming person. She was very lovely. She dressed well. Conducted herself with poise and even dignity ... neither a prostitute nor a call girl, and certainly not a thief.' Munsinger was 'a lady of distinction,' 'a good conversationalist,' and a woman who dressed 'conservatively and always in fine taste.' The former associate minister of defence thus reiterated before the commission of inquiry into the concerns around Mrs Munsinger what he had said when the scandal first surfaced in March.[65] If such assessments did indeed come from parties with an interest in portraying Munsinger in a good light, a former employer would have no need to touch up his recollection of the woman who worked in his west-end Montreal establishment. Yet his judgment was not unlike that of Sévigny and Delorme: 'She had a good appearance – wasn't flashy or anything like that – but gave the impression that she had good breeding. She was a good waitress and very intelligent.'[66]

To counteract this positive image, the Spence Commission unleashed a torrent of RCMP evidence that, through the inquiry's bullying legal inquisitors, was publicly translated into 'truths' passed through the sieve of a truncated summary report. It targeted Munsinger as a prostitute, a categorization based on selective and overstated evidence, never adequately open to public scrutiny, and drawn from an abbreviated and financially pressured period in the immigrant woman's life. For all intents and purposes, this 'evidence' boiled down to a few hard months at most and, possibly, one evening in late November 1960 that may or may not have been helped into being by security state agents. No trial had taken place, no conviction was secured, and Munsinger never had access to legal counsel. From this the commission lawyers reduced Gerda Munsinger to a woman of low character whose vile acts revealed, supposedly through phone tap records, 'the deportment and language of a common harlot.' Mere association with such a woman, even in a period predating Munsinger's 'fall,' cast aspersions on anyone associating with her. 'Mr. Sévigny and Miss Delorme attempted to paint Mrs. Munsinger with a veneer of apparent culture,' sneered Spence Commission counsel John L. O'Brien, 'but I suggest their appraisal can only be judged in view of their own choice of companions.' It was but a short step to Peter C. Newman's callous and unsubstantiated characterization of the Munsinger affair as little more than 'the lurid misadventures of a $15-a-trick prostitute.' The model was marketed as moral refuse.[67]

The Ironies of Sex Appeal

Oddly enough, Canadian national identity seemed to get a boost from the marketing of Munsinger. Canada was now front-page news, and nowhere did Munsinger figure more prominently than in New York's newspapers. It did not seem to matter much that the headlines screamed, 'Canada: Smear, Slander, Smut.' What registered was that the country itself had finally achieved some recognition. The United States humorist Art Buchwald made the point lightly in a Washington column entitled 'Sex and the Single Government': 'Canada can now be considered a major power,' he wrote with caustic wit. 'She rates it because she has a major sex scandal. This means more in the world of power politics than the highest stockpile of hydrogen bombs.' Buchwald, no doubt pondering the sudden attractiveness of Parliament, thronged by people who craved a look at the cast of characters engaged in mortal political combat over the meaning of Gerda Munsinger, predicted head-spinning times for the United States' once-subdued northern neighbour. The Canadian dollar would climb in value, the land of the Maple Leaf would demand a new veto status in the United Nations, and people would be swarming into the streets, slapping each other on the back, and gathering in front of television shop windows to follow the breathtaking events as they unfolded. The syndicated columnist characterized the country's newfound mood as one of festive celebration. Speculation from other quarters was that attendance at the nation's centennial celebration, Expo 67, was bound to rise. Who knew that the Diefenbaker years, long assumed to have been grey and dull, were really 'one long champagne bash.' As Dennis Braithwaite concluded in the *Globe and Mail*, 'However it turns out politically, *l'affaire Pierre* is a grand story. It provides, if only the Canada Council could recognize it, the ideal libretto for a great Canadian comic opera, offering besides such boffo ingredients as romance, mystery and international intrigue, the indispensable flavor of biculturalism.'

Canada was finding a part of its emerging identity in the ironies of a scandal that had a little something for almost everyone.[68]

Whatever Gerda Munsinger was and whatever she became as her life imploded in the latter half of 1960, it had never been entirely of her own making. And it would not quite be publicly marketed in 1966 in ways that she was single-handedly responsible for either. Munsinger had indeed made a part of her history, as the *Neue Illustrierte* images and imaginings confirmed, but it was not all done in ways exactly of her choosing. Moreover, there were many, from Sévigny and Hees, to Obrant and Havrison, and, further, to Spence and O'Brien, even possibly Ducharme and Doyle, who undoubtedly had much to do with constructing Munsinger and marketing her for their own ends.

When the Munsinger affair is placed in the context of the 1960s, what is striking is how much the decade contained within itself the politics of fundamental transformation rooted in a clash of oppositions. The politics of sex as the 1960s opened made it possible for Sévigny to undertake a liaison with Munsinger and feel confident that the parliamentary code of gentlemen's honour would shield him from scrutiny and scandal. It was the Cold War that ultimately brought him down, for sex that might be linked to national security was a forceful shibboleth as the 1950s gave way to the 1960s. It fuelled the engine of the RCMP's security state within the state, a powerful motor driving the undemocratic and irrational scapegoating of all dissidents and 'deviants,' be they self-defined communists, closeted homosexuals, or seemingly sexually predatory female agents.[69] It was surely ironic that Sévigny, a decorated war hero who had sacrificed a leg in the Second World War, a Conservative member of Parliament, a strong federalist and believer in the principle of 'One Canada,' and an associate minister of defence, would come to voice criticisms of the Canadian security state that would anticipate similar rumblings of discontent in the left and in the Parti Québécois a few years later. 'What are the RCMP doing apart from having their musical rides and ruining people's lives?' he asked in disgust in August 1966.[70]

Munsinger was marketed as a possible spy because her actions were supposedly entirely consistent with what the Soviets would do to bring Western nations into disrepute. The infamous Russian Embassy clerk, Igor Gouzenko, who had told Canadians of the dangers posed by Soviet espionage agents in the late 1940s, told *This Hour Has Seven Days* as much in a March 1966 airing of the popular television show.[71] Those heading the security forces and the Spence Commission in 1966 thought exactly the same way. Justice Spence, wading through the RCMP exhibits, could never extricate himself from the ideology of the security state, which refused to relinquish the thought that a promiscuous and compromised woman being deployed as an agent was too ideal a type not to be investigated and, ultimately, invested in the 'bank' of national security. Evidence indicating that Munsinger could not possibly have engaged in espionage while residing in Canada was copious and convincing. Few Canadians outside the inner ring of the Mounties' special services believed that she was actually a spy.[72] Yet RCMP Commissioner George Brinton McClellan conjured up worst-case scenarios. Munsinger, he insisted, might well have been dispatched by the Russians to carry out espionage assignments. Just because nothing could be proven, and no facts had been uncovered that even suggested she was a spy, did not mean that it had not happened, or that her spying had not been serious. Even if she had come to Canada of her own volition, unaffiliated with the octopus-like Soviet intelligence network, her past connection with Russians in the Eastern Zone made her a likely recruit for the resumption of spying duties once she was set up in Montreal. Moreover, Munsinger's low character – which involved prostitution and association with criminal underworld mobsters – made her and those with whom she associated subject to blackmail by communist agents. Given this mindset, Munsinger's die was cast: she was a national security risk because it was impossible that she was *not* one.[73] Ironically, however, the more those on high – RCMP commissioners, politicians in the House of Commons, or justices sitting on benches of the official inquiry – insisted on placing the security fetishes of the secret state in the bedrooms of the nation, the less believable were the supposed threats to the national interest. In the eyes of ordinary Canadians, little of this archaic Cold War Munsinger scaremongering seemed real.

The poisoned atmosphere of the House of Commons in the mid-1960s of course contributed to the inability of sectors of the Canadian state to grasp how exaggerated the Cold War fears of Munsinger had become. A gendered politics of masculine verbal pugilism kept alive the atavistic politics of an earlier era. If Pearson and Diefenbaker's political antagonism had not been so rancorously personal and ugly, it is unlikely that the Munsinger-Sévigny file would ever have come to light. 'The denizens of the Parliamentary Press Gallery had wallowed in a sea of scandal, growing fat off the avails of Rivard-Munsinger-Spencer,' wrote Larry Zolf in 1973. 'Journalistic careers were made by finding bail-jumping labour leaders or bed-hopping courtesans or by proving that the Mounties were terrorizing a cancer-ridden old Commie.'[74] As reporters revelled, parliamentarians shuddered. One of the recently arrived Quebec wise men, Gerard Pelletier, expressed dismay at the 'absurd nightmare' that Parliament had become, 'a Kafkaesque sort of labyrinth without any exit.' Judy LaMarsh referred to the 'uncontained violence' that animated the House of Commons as the scandals broke, seemingly above everyone's head. 'I have never felt anything like the atmosphere of raw emotion engendered by the Munsinger debate, and the anger, fear, and revulsion of members on all sides,' LaMarsh recalled. 'Members scuttled from the House heads down, even though the drama lured them back to their seats as the lethal verbal slashing went on. They were sick, Parliament was sick, but the press had a field day.' Pearson agreed. The effect of the Munsinger events, piggy-backed as they were on a series of other scandals, dirtied 'the reputation of Parliament.'[75] Sex and politics had indeed made for strange bedfellows, bringing Canada's most revered political institution, the House of Commons, into disrespect.

The Munsinger affair, then, originated in the particularities of a period that reached from the late 1950s into the mid-1960s. As such, it illustrated how central the mid-decade years were in illuminating shifts in social and cultural life. Sex appeal, in 1966, looked backwards to a politics of restraint, even repression. The Munsinger affair was certainly about that. It also revealed, on quite another level, different sensibilities, ones that looked forward to a sexual politics in which the erotic might have a different, more open, political content.

The world was changing. By 1968 sex appeal would be a respectable, marketable political commodity, as Trudeaumania made abundantly clear. Even 'the Old Chief' seemed to sense this reluctantly. As the Munsinger revelations broke in 1966, and rumours flew fast and furious of Tories bedding the blonde spy, Diefenbaker phoned Dorothy Downing, the Women's National Director of the Conservative Party, to inquire as to what the mood was in Toronto and among his women supporters. Downing thought the 71-year-old leader was concerned that he might be suspected of improprieties, and she rushed to respond: 'Nobody around Toronto would ever entertain the slightest thought that you might have been involved with her – you of all people!' There was a long pause as Diefenbaker considered the meaning of her words, and then a gruff rejoinder: 'I don't know whether I like the implications of that or not.'[76]

Even that paragon of propriety, Dief, knew that sex appeal was not something to be underestimated. But he had come to that recognition slowly and uncertainly, as had the country as a whole. His prompting had been the revelation that a low woman had consorted with men in high places, and had done so in ways that were interpreted in some rather extreme quarters as potentially threatening to the nation. Gerda Munsinger, a Canadian for a mere six years, and a woman whose private affairs were meant to be kept out of public view, perhaps managed, in spite of herself, to bring into the open matters that had a long history of being suppressed. In the process, something of a thaw in the deforming iciness of political life had been achieved, albeit almost by accident, and a Cold War whose time had long past was dealt a hard, if ironic, credibility blow.

Chapter Four

Canada's Great White Hope: George Chuvalo vs. Muhammad Ali

The distinguished social critic, socialism advocate, and early Pan-Africanist, C.L.R. James, once wrote knowingly, in what is possibly the best book ever published on cricket, 'What do they know of cricket who only cricket know?'[1] Of the so-called 'sweet science,' in which there is little that is scientific and less that is sweet, the same can be said: 'What do they know of boxing who only boxing know?' For I start from the premise that 'the fight game,' perhaps more than most sports, holds a mirror to the face of society. In it is reflected an image, however bruised and battered, that tells us as much about nations, cultures, and identities as it does about pugilism.[2]

Sporting events can serve as important markers of national identity, as is evident in the significance of soccer in a number of Latin American and European countries, or baseball in the United States and Cuba. In Canada it is possible to go back to the nineteenth century to explore how sport and a mix of class and regional values emerged in new understandings of nationhood. Over the course of the twentieth century, however, it is hockey that has generally been understood to be pre-eminent in the relationship of sport and nation, whether in the complicated relations of French vs. English, or in the generalized importance of a game that epitomizes the northern national identity and that Canucks supposedly take to as a birthright.[3]

George Chuvalo, 1958 (York University, *Toronto Telegram* Fonds, FO433, 1974-002/338).

In 1972, Paul Henderson scored a series-winning goal 'for Canada' against the Russians in a hockey summit that is remembered and celebrated to this day. Although the Canada–Russia contest unfolded at a time when the Cold War was ostensibly over, anti-Soviet prejudices died hard. The long-standing global arm-twisting, ritualized in its pitting of stereotypical opposites – capitalism vs. socialism, freedom vs. totalitarianism, the United States vs. the Soviet Union – nonetheless relaxed. New international points of crisis were emerging in the Middle East and were on the verge of overwhelming old antagonisms. In this political thaw, the symbolic defeat of the Soviet Union was played out in the world arena of Canada's 'national' pastime. If Canadians were second-tier peacekeepers in the postwar order, in the 1972 hockey faceoff they were the ultimate players in the humbling of 'socialism,' Soviet-style. It was enough to make a small world power puff itself up with pride.[4]

Less well remembered, perhaps, is the compromised 1966 World Heavyweight title fight between Muhammad Ali (a.k.a. Cassius Clay) and George Chuvalo that took place at Toronto's Maple Leaf Gardens on a Friday night, 29 March 1966. In that encounter within the roped ring unfolded a significant moment in Canadian identity, for it spoke to an old Canada forever gone and a new Canada struggling to be born. It also articulated subtle connections to a past that would not die and gestured toward a future whose pathways were never quite as smooth as the promises of the 1960s suggested they would be. As the Ali-Chuvalo matchup revelled in representing Canada as different, indeed better, than the United States, it nevertheless carried some of the same troubled baggage, especially in the large arena of race,[5] where the history of twentieth-century boxing so often fought out its contradictions.

Almost obliterated in a swirl of controversy, the bout, billed as 'The Heavyweight Showdown,' was eventually promoted in the face of the fight fraternity's nay-saying. Few in the know were willing to acknowledge that it was anything more than a sad reminder of how low boxing had sunk. The odds, if you could get them, were 7-1 against Chuvalo. Vegas bookmakers were refusing to take bets on Ali, and the sportscasters preferred to stay in Florida and cover baseball's spring training than make the trek to Toronto. Yet the Ali-Chuvalo fight, a bloody endurance test in which Ali emerged the victor, ironically dressed a pummelled George Chuvalo in the garb of national symbolism.

Canadian national identity has always been closely, and defensively, constructed out of relations with our more powerful neighbour, the

United States. In the famous quip of Pierre Elliott Trudeau, living next to the United States was like a mouse sharing its bed with an elephant. 'No matter how friendly and even tempered is the beast, if I can call it that,' Trudeau suggested, 'one is affected by every twitch and grunt.'[6] The Ali-Chuvalo boxing match took Canadian-American relations and metaphorically placed them inside a roped ring, where elephant and mouse were brought together on a different footing: the combatants were now at least comparable species. Still, no one expected the lesser Chuvalo Canadian mouse to come close to successfully fending off the twitches and grunts, let alone the deft dance and staccato-like blows, of the superior Ali American elephant. In courageous defeat, in going the distance with the larger-than-life United States, in standing to the end in a posture, however slouched, of resilient difference, Chuvalo seemed to speak for Canada in ways that Canadians understood.

As Stephen Brunt has written about the Chuvalo-Ali fight: 'Chuvalo the courageous; Chuvalo the hard rock; Chuvalo the toughest man in Canada. Chuvalo who in 1966 stood up to the great Muhammad Ali for fifteen rounds and never took a backwards step, defining a national stereotype: the plucky underdog; the gritty competitor, unfazed by long odds or the overwhelming Goliath to the south, undefeated even if, technically, truthfully, that fight in 1966 was a loss ... That night in Toronto at Maple Leaf Gardens in 1966 is, for Canadians, a cultural point of demarcation.' For Chuvalo, the loss was nothing to boast about, but he was able to see into the mirror of wider national reaction: 'In a crazy kind of way it made Canadians feel good. When I see people and they talk about the fight, I hear them say it made them feel good. Kind of proud. I made my fellow Canadians feel proud about being Canadian.'[7] What was it that made George Chuvalo so Canadian in 1966?

The Junction and Canada in the 1960s

George Chuvalo was not born on the wrong side of the tracks; he was brought up *on* them. The Junction, where the Chuvalo family settled after immigrating to Canada from Bosnia-Herzegovenia, was a Toronto working-class neighbourhood in the west end, bordered by Bloor/ St Clair and Jane/Weston Road. Its defining feature was a conjuncture of railroad lines, and the locale took its name from where the Canadian Pacific east-west mainline crossed the tracks of the Canadian National.

The economic lifeblood of the Junction in the mid-twentieth century was the abattoirs of Canada Packers, Ltd. Born of a 1927 merger of four major enterprises in the Canadian meat-packing industry, Canada Packers sprawled along St Clair Avenue West, a monument to the consolidated capitalism of the first three decades of the twentieth century. The millions of pigs that were herded from rail cars, through its doors, squealing on to the slaughterhouse killing floors, confirmed Toronto's early nineteenth-century designation as 'Hogtown.'

The Chuvalos were part of a wave of southern, eastern, and central European immigration that transformed Canada, and Toronto. Their coming preceded the peak influx in the immediate post–Second World War years, the family living through the rough times of the Great Depression. George was born in Toronto as the economic crisis showed some signs of abating in 1937. Over 1.5 million new non-British Canadians arrived between 1946 and 1962, a massive movement of peoples representing more than 10 per cent of the country's entire population.[8] 'Toronto the Good' had, seemingly, been the archetypal British-Canadian city prior to the Second World War, but postwar immigration changed that forever. The city's Lower Ward, studied by W.E. Mann, was typical of the demographic shift. Almost entirely Anglo-Saxon up to the end of the 1930s, by 1960 the lower-class area south of Queen Street and west of University Avenue was described as transformed by 'successive waves of Ukrainians, Poles, and Italians.'[9] To be Canadian in the 1960s was finally to come to grips with the challenges posed by ethnic diversity to a mythological, but materially structured, anglophone homogeneity.

The country had of course always depended on the labour and varied contributions of 'outcast' minorities: former American slaves who escaped north to establish precarious footholds of African-Canadian community in Nova Scotia, Ontario, and British Columbia; impoverished 'famine Irish' in the 1840s; the Chinese who built the transcontinental railroad and found their way to British Columbia mines in the 1860s and 1870s; European Jews in the late nineteenth century, some of whom ended up farming in Saskatchewan, others working in the sweated trades of urban garment districts; stalwart peasants 'in sheepskin coats' in the years of Clifford Sifton's 'open door' to western settlement. There nevertheless persisted the powerful image of Canada as a loyalist enclave of the British Empire. Such was the complacent construction of 'being Canadian' for much of the nineteenth and twentieth centuries that 'whiteness' and 'foreign' were mutually exclusive categories. Canada was Empire's last outpost, a socially constructed national project of 'racial purity' in which certain Europeans – Scandinavians for instance – might be allowed in, but others – 'Bohunks,' 'Douks,' 'Galicians,' 'Dagos,' or 'Hunkies,' not to mention 'Chinks' or 'Hindoos' – were denied true citizenship. '"A White Man's Country" has found an echo as a slogan in the hearts of most Canadians,' wrote one worker-instructor for Frontier College in a study of 'the bunkhouse man' first published in 1928. A contractor explained: 'We distinguish white men. Austrians and Italians we don't call them white men. I don't know that it's hardly fair but its customary.' 'Strangers within our gates' was the more benign, but equally racialized, phrasing of Methodist social worker and future Co-operative Commonwealth Federation founder, J.S. Woodsworth.[10]

Against the chauvinisms of 'white Canada' were arrayed the immigrant dreams of socio-economic advance and political equality. They were lived out, increasingly, in neighbourhoods like the Junction, where Old World ways adapted to New World settings. In the process, the cultures of difference blurred into one another, change registering in the shifting ground of everyday life. Subtle and profound, this movement altered Canada forever in the 1960s. Undoubtedly, it can be measured in the achievements of assimilation and toleration for diversity, promoted by the well-oiled machinery of the state and, in the view of many, linked to the accomplishments of Pierre Elliott Trudeau's liberal policies, which ostensibly created the first official 'multicultural country.'[11] It was also, however, an acculturation of violence, pain, and psychic trauma.

George Chuvalo saw his mother come home from her daily job of plucking chickens at the poultry plant, hands cracked and scarred with open wounds, her work apron a Jackson Pollock–like pastiche of blood, membranes, and feathers. His father, desperate in the fear that he might lose his Canada Packers butchering job, spent his annual two-week summer vacation hanging around outside the company fence, watching closely the man who replaced him. He was keeping an eye on the job that he worried would be given to someone else. George worked with his father at Canada Packers in 1953. The young Chuvalo was a mere fifteen years old, and he did not at the time understand what haunted the Chuvalo family throughout the decade of their decisive climb into a version of settled 'Canadianness.' It was only when an old friend of his dad's told the fighter a story of how an immigrant worker spent his summer vacations in the 1940s and 1950s that George appreciated the insecurity that dogged his father throughout his working life.[12]

George Chuvalo found his way out of Canada Packers through boxing. At age seventeen he was the amateur heavyweight champion of Canada. He was a bit of a rough customer, known to police as connected to a youth gang whose members sometimes found themselves battling rivals in the streets or being hauled before the magistrate. Poverty forced Chuvalo to forgo an Olympics appearance in November 1956, and he turned professional instead, his first purse of $500 earned at Maple Leaf Gardens, where he knocked out four opponents in less than thirteen minutes during a 'Jack Dempsey Tournament.'

Over the next decade Chuvalo battled incompetent managers as much as he did opponents. He struggled with the knowledge that his trainers were not the best and his backers interested in him only for the money he could get them. Leaving Toronto, he set up in Detroit and, for a time, managed himself. But he could not fight, train, promote, and handle finances all at the same time. He won fights, and he lost fights; even the Canadian heavyweight professional title, which he first won in 1958, passed from his hands twice in 1960–1. Ranked in *Ring Magazine*'s top ten one year, he would be dropped from the list the next. By the end of 1963, Chuvalo's ride to recognition in boxing had definitely stalled. There was not much more to be gained by fighting weak competition in Maple Leaf Gardens, and beyond this few in the boxing world saw him as worth taking on. It was an often-told Canadian tale: one of promise and potential compromised by underdevelopment.

Then, when Ernie Terrell pulled out of a fight with a European contender, Mike DeJohn, scheduled for Louisville, Kentucky, Chuvalo was brought in as a last-minute substitute. The fight was televised, billed as something of a lead into a later, and more critical, contest: the winner was supposed to take on a brash, if largely unknown, Louisville slugger backed by a consortium of well-heeled local businessmen, Cassius Clay. Chuvalo won the fight handily. Knocked down twice in the second round, DeJohn ended up draped over the ropes with the Canadian thrashing away, his arms pumping up and down as if he were working a scrub board. Clay wanted nothing to do with Chuvalo, whom he dubbed 'the washerwoman.' 'George Chuvalo fights rough and tough like a washerwoman,' Clay opined, 'I ain't going to fight him.' Months later, with Chuvalo hounding Clay at press conferences, gimmicking and shaming the outspoken Louisville fighter to get in the ring with him by donning a wig and the gaudy print dress of a tawdry laundress, the quip was predictably perfunctory: 'Georgie fights even worse than he dresses.'[13]

The Strange Fruit of the Sweet Science:
The Racialization of American Boxing

That American sport, like the society from which it emerges, is racialized is a truism that few would question. In boxing, the intensity of this reality was especially marked. W.E.B. Du Bois declared, on the 1903 publication of his monumental *The Souls of Black Folk*, that 'the problem of the twentieth century is the problem of the color line.' Boxing in the decisive heavyweight division was, as far as title fights were concerned, a property right of whites. Blacks boxed, of course, but they did so with each other, to entertain whites in southern 'battles royal,' in which money would be thrown to the winner. They might fight champions, even become world titleholders in the lighter weight categories (George Dizon, a Canadian black boxer, was the reigning feather and bantam weight world champion in the 1890s), but they were basically barred from fighting for serious recognition in the premier heavyweight category.

Early in the twentieth century Galveston's Jack Johnson, the son of a former slave, emerged as the heavyweight champion of 'Negro' boxing. Jim Jeffries, the reigning world champion, refused to fight Johnson because he was black. Not until Tommy Burns, the diminutive former resident of Hanover, Ontario, became the only Canadian to ever hold the heavyweight championship of the world, was Johnson allowed in the same ring with a white titleholder. Burns, who fought Johnson in Australia on 26 December 1908, pocketing $30,000 to Johnson's $5,000, was an incorrigible racist. No doubt he believed the supremacist creed that a black could be no match for a white. But in 1908 there were no overseers and slave codes to enforce this maxim. Burns's racial blindspot cost him more than he could have imagined. Johnson destroyed the Canadian in the ring. The outcome was a foregone conclusion from the first round, and Johnson ended up toying with Burns, seemingly for the sheer pleasure of punishing him physically and mocking him verbally. All Burns could sputter, through a mangled mouth, was the sad rejoinder, 'Come and fight, nigger. Fight like a white man.' The match was called off by the police in the fourteenth round, the smaller Canadian judged incapable of continuing.

Johnson's Australian victory unsettled racists around the world, who reviled Burns for losing to a black, tarnishing a cherished symbol of the superiority of white manhood. Jack London, one of American socialism's favoured authors, joined a journalistic chorus demanding a race rematch. Burns supposedly coined the phrase 'Great White Hope' and for a time roamed the world in search of a Caucasian contender who could put Papa Jack in his place. His quest to re-establish white supremacy in the ring was unsuccessful. In the 1940s Tommy Burns had an out-of-body experience that reversed his bodily beating at the hands of Johnson. Born again, he was transformed into an Apostle of Universal Love and preached against all forms of hatred, including the race bile that he had espoused for decades. He died in Vancouver in 1955 after delivering one of his evangelical sermons, a few months before George Chuvalo would first enter the professional ring. Little did he know that Chuvalo was to become Canada's belated Great White Hope.[14]

Johnson was denied the actual heavyweight championship of the world until 1910, when he finally fought Jeffries, who was goaded out of retirement, and won. As was his practice, Johnson jeered and taunted his lesser opponent, retaining control of the fight for fifteen rounds and then, having scored more than his point, dispatched the exhausted Jeffries with a knockout. An African American now claimed the title of heavyweight champion of the world. Black pride echoed in the verse of the streets:

> The Yankees hold the play
> The white man pulls the trigger;
> But it makes no difference what the man say
> The world champion's still a nigger.[15]

Whites, however, were not rhyming.

Race riots, which in the parlance of the time often meant anti-black pogroms, resulted, scarring some fifty cities and leaving eight dead. Blacks who cheered Johnson too loudly were fired at with pistols, threatened with the lynch noose, had their throats slashed, and suffered beatings in parks and on the street. Religious groups and right-wing zealots called for boxing to be banned. Legislation restricted the commercial distribution of films showing Johnson's victories, lest they spark black–white conflagrations. The editor of the *Chattanooga Times* openly voiced the fear generated by the unfathomable spectacle of 'a powerful negro knocking a white man about the ring,' a sight that could well 'inspire the ignorant negro with false and pernicious ideas as to the physical prowess of the race.'

A defiant transgressor, Johnson did more than 'steal' the heavyweight championship of the world from its rightful white owners; he also committed the ultimate race 'crime': he took white women into his bed, even marrying them, three all told. When he trained he wrapped his penis in gauze, the better to enhance its proportions, which were accentuated by tight shorts. Fond of outlandish display, Johnson dressed flamboyantly, drove automobiles conspicuous in their size and expense, sipped vintage wines through a straw, and maintained an air of cultural superiority. He was defiant and brazen in his sexualized blackness. It was all too much, and it brought down on Johnson the revulsion of an era not known for its tolerance of those who stepped outside the containments of race place. In 1913 Johnson was charged under the Mann Act, which outlawed the transportation of women across state lines for the purposes of illicit sex. Johnson and his fiancée had driven from one state to another.

Forced into exile, Johnson avoided jail by living and fighting anywhere but in the United States. Jess Willard, one in a long line of white antagonists, eventually dethroned the defiant Johnson (who later claimed he had taken a dive) in Cuba in 1915. Returning to the United States in 1920, Johnson was sentenced to Leavenworth and, upon his release, boxed only in exhibition matches. He ended his days as a dime museum entertainer living off the interest generated by his outrageous past.[16]

Johnson had not so much cracked the colour bar that protected white heavyweight titleholders from facing black challengers as he had reinforced it. There was no taste in an America hardening in its racial animosities for crowning another Johnson, and from 1915 well into the 1930s a string of white heavyweight champions steadfastly refused to step into the ring with black boxers.

Not until Joe Louis appeared on the scene in the 1930s – a moment of ambivalence in which dual racisms fused in one of boxing's Great White Hopes, Max Schmeling – was it possible for an African-American to aspire to the heavyweight championship of the world. With the possibility that the march of the Great White Hope might continue with Schmeling at the head of the parade, U.S. boxing's apartheid was hoisted on competing and conflicting chauvinisms. Schmeling, on the eve of the Second World War, symbolized not only American racist commitment to white supremacy but also the troubling spectre of Nazism's Aryan 'superman' and his promise of world domination.[17]

Consciously adopting the demeanour of a Southern black male who knew his place, Louis shook no race boats. His astute handlers did not let Louis be photographed with white women, kept him on a protective leash in all of his public activity, especially in nightclubs, and tutored him on the do's and don'ts of the fight game: suffer your pain and defeat stoically; be gracious and understated in your victories; meet your opponents with respect; honour them as they fall. Louis, who ironically would end his days in battles with destitution, drugs, and dementia, was the embodiment of the fighter who lived and boxed clean. He was the antidote to Jack Johnson. If Schmeling was to be stopped he was perhaps the last hope, albeit not a white one. He was as close to that as a black man could be in 1930s America, the racist southern press christening him a 'good nigger.' Northern boxing columnists like Jimmy Cannon proclaimed Louis a 'credit to his race – the human race.'

Louis would lose to Schmeling in 1936 but defeat the reigning heavyweight champion of the world, Jim Braddock, the next year, and, in a rematch with the German on 22 June 1938, scored a first-round knockout. 'The brown bomber' was deified in black America, where a subterranean desire to wreak vengeance on whites, and settle the score for centuries of racism and oppression, seemed fulfilled as Joe Louis quietly manhandled his white opponents in the ring. Louis held the heavyweight championship of the world from 1937 until he first retired in 1948. Sweet indeed was the strange fruit born of American ring racism. White racists were disarmed by Louis assuming the role they demanded: his deference and seemingly unassailable character merely masked his appeal to black America, where his devastating dominance in the ring struck a blow against assumptions of racial superiority.[18]

In spite of future comeback attempts in the 1950s, Louis was never able to regain his stature of the late 1930s and 1940s. And the fight game took on some of the trappings that would tarnish its image forever. In the postwar period, mobsters moved in, led by the 'boss of boxing,' Frankie Carbo, and control over the lucrative promotional side of the sport was now undeniably in the hands of organized crime. Television and then closed-circuit broadcasting upped the financial ante beyond the stadium gate, and boxing was becoming big business with an underworld tone to it. Fighters were routinely compromised and manipulated: bribes were offered and taken, fixes were engineered, and boxers went down when they were told to. 'The game' was no longer Joe Louis clean.

In this climate, white contenders battled blacks, and boxing was seemingly less and less about any colour other than green. Blacks could now meet whites in the ring, but ironically they could do so only in a kind of stereotypical 'black face.' By the early 1960s, with black fighters dominating the rankings in the prized heavyweight category, African-American fighters were designated 'good' and 'white,' such as Floyd

Patterson, or 'bad' and 'nigger,' such as Sonny Liston. None came close to Joe Louis in the largesse of their skills; black fighters were contenders, but they were generally regarded, in the early 1960s, as the best of a rather poor boxing lot. Moreover, history weighed heavily on the sweet science's present, and, indeed, African-American fighters remained locked into the paradigms of the past. The strange fruit of boxing's racialization, so evident in 1964, was that if blacks now fought each other for the heavyweight championship of the world, they did so in the structured and typecast roles whites assigned them, and profited from.[19] Enter Cassius Marcellus Clay.

From Cassius Clay to Muhammad Ali: A 1960s Odyssey

What did black Americans think of all of this? When asked in 1963, some replied in ways that shocked white counterparts: 'They'll always give us an opportunity to act like animals.'[20] The fight game was not what was on their minds.

This was the year that James Baldwin published *The Fire Next Time*. It had been preceded by almost a decade of civil rights agitation that commenced with the widespread revulsion at the murder of a 14-year-old black boy, Emmet Till, in Money, Mississippi, in August 1955; Rosa Parks's refusal to surrender her bus seat to a white in Montgomery, Alabama, four months later; and the subsequent municipal transit boycott led by Martin Luther King, Jr. School segregation battles, student sit-ins, freedom rides, retaliatory church bombings, and marches on Washington followed. Malcolm X was emerging as a spokesman of Elijah Muhammad's Nation of Islam, only to come to champion genuinely radical views that would see him driven from the sect. In the years to come both King and Malcolm X would fall to assassins' bullets; the fires of ghetto rebellion would burn in hundreds of riot-torn American cities; the Black Panther party would be founded in Oakland, California, in 1966; and the League of Revolutionary Black Workers would emerge out of Michigan's auto plants in 1969. Baldwin's *next time* had arrived. Black America was in a state of upheaval, and the reverberations paralleled a growing youth revolt that erupted in campus rebellion, spilled into the discontents and alienations of factory workers fresh out of high school, and unsettled gender relations. Drafted to fight in what they perceived as a war of imperialist aggression in Vietnam, young Americans, black and white, opted out of acquiescence and into a questioning of all authority. Some wanted to bring the war home, and they did their best to make the streets of Chicago and Washington places where there would be no more business as usual.

Cassius Clay was nothing close to an architect of any of this; he stood back from activism. He understood well the trials and tribulations of being black in America and knew there were those, in 1963, who would hate him as his stock climbed in the heavyweight division. Yet he was a promoter of self not of social change. Sonny Liston, nobody's role model in the early 1960s, was far more cognizant of the civil rights struggle than the young Clay and insisted on contractual clauses barring segregated movie theatres from showing his title fights on closed-circuit television. As Clay became Muhammad Ali he was drawn into the spirit of the 1960s. 'The Greatest' came to symbolize some of its rebelliousness. In turn, he discovered its promise. Frederick Douglass once observed that 'a man is worked on by what he works on. He may carve out his circumstances, but his circumstances will carve him out as well.'[21] Karl Marx said much the same thing when he noted that men and women make their own history, 'but they do not make it just as they please; they do not make it under circumstances chosen by themselves, but under circumstances directly encountered, given and transmitted from the past.'[22] Ali made history in the cauldron of the 1960s, and how he made it was a unique blend of experiences individual and collective.

The young Cassius Clay, a child of southern segregation and the modest security of the postwar respectable black working class, was the unlikeliest of graduates into professional boxing. Lacking school smarts, he nevertheless had none of the toughness of the street and trained as a youth with a Bible in his gym bag. Respectful towards his 'superiors,' he was brash and confident in approaching ring opponents, most of whom he dazzled with his footwork and then, having exhausted them, cut them up with his boxing. But Clay knew next to nothing of life and needed the seasoning that a 1960 Olympic gold medal and trips out of Louisville provided. Originally backed by a syndicate of paternalist white businessmen, Clay soon gravitated to trainers such as Archie Moore and Angelo Dundee, continued to work on his body, and, influenced by Sugar Ray Robinson and the wrestler Gorgeous George, cultivated a fast-talking, rhyming trickster image.[23] In quick succession he dispatched eighteen often lacklustre opponents in the years 1961–3, including a humiliating two-round public sparring defeat of Swedish contender Ingemar Johannson. Clay was climbing the boxing ladder, and he was doing it with bravado, often accurately predicting the round when his opponent would go down. He wanted a crack at the heavyweight championship of the world, claiming he was 'the greatest' and that he would take the title away from Sonny Liston if only 'the ugly bear' would give him a shot.

Liston saw the potential money that could be made through Clay's mouth – the rising contender was known as the Louisville Lip – and agreed to a 25 February 1964 Miami fight. Clay was now in the spotlight, and he used it to good effect, mugging with the Beatles, mocking Liston with a band of merry pranksters he assembled around him, and hyping his way into the press with a blend of bombast and his trademark doggerel verse. The fight columnists, for the most part, hated it. Jimmy Cannon wrote that Clay represented all that was wrong with the rebellious Sixties. 'Clay is part of the Beatle movement,' wrote Cannon, his prose running ahead of his antagonism:

> He fits in with the famous singers no one can hear and the punks riding motorcycles with iron crosses pinned to their leather jackets and Batman and the boys with their long dirty hair and the girls with the unwashed look and the college kids dancing naked at secret proms held in apartments and the revolt of students who get a check from Dad every first of the month and the painters who copy the labels off soup cans and the surf bums who refuse to work and the whole pampered style-making cult of the bored young.[24]

The book on Clay, in early 1964, was thus easily read. He was all flash and no bash. Fast footwork, hands held low, a defence that leaned back, bobbing and weaving, defied the odds of the ring as the old guard understood them. That was the 'professional' judgment, and it dictated that Clay would get the beating he deserved from Liston. But there was more to it. Clay seemed to give little respect to the curmudgeonly white journalists who remembered when Joe Louis had called them 'Sir.' They didn't much care for a 'black boy' who prattled on about his prettiness (a cardinal sin in the boxing world, an antiquated enclave of hyper-masculinity),[25] who turned the weigh-in into a carnivalesque cacophony of performative insult, and who didn't have an ounce of deference in him. As much as Liston was regarded as a sullen black animal, the illiterate son of a sharecropper, a dangerous man impossible to control and hence often in trouble with the law, he could be condescended to by a complacent, racialized authority. It was as though Liston's awesome physical dominance inside the ring was proof of his racial inferiority outside of it. And this was the safe ground of his being the heavyweight champion of the world. Cassius Clay threatened that. As early as March 1963 *Ebony* was declaring Clay 'a blast furnace of racial pride.'[26] Those who publicized and patronized the fight game wanted Clay 'whupped' because to do so would be to whip a certain kind of African American back into line. On the eve of the Liston-Clay contest Jackie Gleason wrote in the *New York Post*: 'I predict Sonny Liston will win in eighteen seconds of the first round, and my estimate includes the three seconds Blabber Mouth will bring into the ring with him.' Murray Kempton commented: 'Liston used to be a hoodlum; now he was our cop; he was the big Negro we pay to keep sassy Negroes in line and he was just waiting until his boss told him to throw this kid out.'[27]

It did not work out that way. Clay wore down the overly confident, undertrained Liston, cut him badly, and worked on his head until it was bloody and puffy. Liston had his corner juice his gloves with a stinging lineament that, once it came in contact with his opponents' eyes, left Clay blinded for much of two rounds. Clay could have quit, but he didn't; he yardsticked Liston, keeping the aged and quickly tiring fighter at a distance. When his eyesight returned, Clay finished Liston off. The beaten champion called it quits after round six, refusing to get off his stool and continue the fight. It was an unheard-of way to lose a championship title. As Liston spat his mouthpiece out in defeat, Clay leaped from his corner, jumped high on the ropes, his patented mouth wide open in oval derision, a gloved hand raised in mockery and open defiance. Liston did not matter any more. Clay was beating up on the ringside press who had so gleefully predicted his slaughter. 'I am the king,' he proclaimed, 'King of the World. *Eat your words! Eat your words!*'[28]

Some did, and some did not. Soon a larger story was unfolding. Clay was no longer Clay. He was about to become Muhammad Ali, a convert to the Nation of Islam. Ali's relationship to the group, often known in the United States as the Black Muslims, had been developing for some time and preceded his title fight with Liston. But the connection had been kept somewhat in the background, in part by Clay and his handlers, for fear that it would scuttle the championship bout. There had been much talk of getting Malcolm X, who had befriended Clay and was something of a spiritual adviser to him as the Liston fight approached, out of Miami. Cassius Clay as the heavyweight champion of the world was bad enough; Muhammad Ali holding the title was, for most in the boxing world, unthinkable. Many saw Malcolm X leading an uprising of revolutionary African-American insurgents into the streets of America, the heavyweight titleholder among the throng.

Largely ignorant of what the Nation of Islam was, let alone how Malcolm X was moving decisively toward a more class *and* race program of social transformation, white America reacted to the birth of Muhammad Ali with barbed belligerence. It began at the morning-after press conference, with Clay quiet and subdued in responding to questions about the Liston fight, and who he would take on next. Then came the question: was Clay a 'card-carrying member of the Black Muslims?' Clay responded to the sting of the query, its wording reminiscent of a McCarthyism not all that distant in 1964, with a shocked but dignified pride. He refused the label 'Black Muslim,' explaining that it was coined by the press and was repugnant to all members of the Nation. 'I believe in Allah and I believe in peace. I don't try to move into white neighborhoods. I don't want to marry a white woman ... I know where I'm going and I know the truth, and I don't have to be what you want me to be. I'm free to be what I want.'[29]

It is almost unfathomable today that such words could unleash the rabid reaction they did in 1964. The Garden of Eden of integration, with its strange fruit born of centuries of racism, had been refused by an African American, and not only *any* black citizen of the United States, but the newly crowned heavyweight champion of the world. Freedom's road was the good Negro path of black accommodation, and Muhammad Ali was not following it. Fight journalist Jimmy Cannon was quick out of the gate, his prose an ugly caricature of Ali as a pawn of black racism:

> The fight racket since its rotten beginnings, has been the red-light district of sports. But this is the first time it has been turned into an instrument of hate. It has maimed the bodies of numerous men and ruined their minds but now, as one of Elijah Muhammad's missionaries, Clay is using it as a weapon of wickedness in an attack on the spirit. I pity Clay and abhor what he represents. In the years of hunger during the Depression, the Communists used famous people the way the Black Muslims are exploiting Clay. This is a sect that deforms the beautiful purpose of religion.

Clay and the Nation of Islam, Cannon concluded, were more pernicious in their symbolism of hate 'than Schmeling and Nazism.'[30] Malcolm had told Cassius that when he stepped in the ring with Sonny Liston, it was a modern Crusade, a truth that pitted the Crescent against the Cross. And now, in words that Malcolm had used in the aftermath of the assassination of John F. Kennedy on 22 November 1963, 'the chickens were indeed coming home to roost.'

In the months and years to follow, Ali's stand would feed into the spirit of the 1960s. He would become something of an outlaw. The World Boxing Association threatened to strip Ali of his title, ostensibly for 'conduct detrimental to the best interests of boxing,' a rather startling, if decidedly empty, expression of discipline given what it had condoned in the past.[31] Journalists steadfastly refused to refer to the champion as Muhammad Ali, insisting on calling him Cassius Clay. Howard Cosell, one of the very few in the media to break ranks with this pettiness, was branded a 'White Muslim.'[32] Floyd Patterson, who also declined to utilize Ali's chosen Nation of Islam name, likened the Black Muslims to the Ku Klux Klan; the former heavyweight champion saw it as his mission to regain the title, as a liberal, and personal, 'contribution to civil rights.' The bout was scheduled for 22 November 1965. Patterson, dubbed 'the Black White Hope' by Ali, did everything he could to politicize the contest. In a *Sports Illustrated* article he declared that the image of a Black Muslim holding the heavyweight title 'disgraces the sport and the nation.' He stated the necessity of removing the scourge of the Black Muslims from boxing, deploring the Nation of Islam's ostensible preaching of segregation, hatred, rebellion, and violence. 'No decent person can look up to a champion whose credo is "hate whites,"' Patterson fumed. Jack Johnson–like, Ali humiliated Patterson in the ring, physically and verbally, each punch followed with a taunt of 'Uncle Tom.' In defeat, white America shunned Patterson. Frank Sinatra, who had fêted Patterson as the man who would bury the brash Muhammad Ali, turned his back on him after the fight. Ironically, Ali buried the hatchet and treated the beaten Patterson with solicitous respect. Patterson acknowledged Ali's greatness in the ring and, in what was a final compliment, called him by his chosen Muslim name.[33]

Boxing was now firmly in the grip of the 1960s. When Ali took his stand against the Vietnam War, not only refusing induction into the army but insisting that no Viet Cong had ever called him 'Nigger,' the press hounded him mercilessly. Representative Frank Clark of Pennsylvania led a Congressional attack on Ali, denouncing the boxing champion as unpatriotic and calling for a boycott of his fights.[34] Ali responded in lines of characteristic verse: 'Keep asking me, no matter how long/On the war in Viet Nam, I sing this song/I ain't got no quarrel with the Viet Cong.'[35] The Veterans of Foreign Wars got into the act, threatening to picket any stadium where Ali fought or any theatre showing closed-circuit broadcasts of title bouts involving the now-notorious Nation of Islam member.[36] It was 'hardhat' America versus the loudmouth New Left, before that stereotypical opposition had actually emerged, but the situation was also obviously embedded in the explosiveness of race as well. It hit the powerful mob interest in boxing where it hurt the most, below the money belt. Ali was now turning all of his promotional and economic decision making over to an astute corps of Nation of Islam financiers, lawyers, and advisers.

Even this was not the big news. As Budd Schulberg noted in *Saturday Review*, Ali had come to personify the seething unrest of an era; he had become an anti-establishment figure in spite of himself.[37] Bertrand Russell sent Ali a telegram of congratulation, but the United States government revoked the heavyweight champion's passport and the FBI put him under strict surveillance. Compared in the sports columns of major newspapers with the 'unwashed punks who picket and demonstrate against the war,' Ali indeed joined forces with the anti-war students, speaking before college audiences and adopting an increasingly articulate and rebellious stand against the war. It made no sense to go halfway around the world to drop bombs on brown people in Viet Nam, he said, when 'so-called Negro people in Louisville are treated like dogs.' Threatened with incarceration, Ali quipped, 'We've been in jail for four hundred years.'[38]

Ironies of Identity: Canada, Chuvalo, and the Challenge of Ali

This was the embittered background against which the Ali-Chuvalo Maple Leaf Gardens fight unfolded. The bout had only come about, indeed, because no United States city would host an Ali title fight, and all manner of subterfuges and legal technicalities had been conjured up to thwart Ali and Ernie Terrell from squaring off against each other. Even Montreal had turned down the opportunity to host such a heavyweight championship. When Toronto was promoted as a possible venue for the Ali-Terrell face-off, the furor was instantaneous.

'Hopping on the local squawk wagon' were Liberal and NDP MPPs, who claimed the fight would lower Toronto's seemingly pristine image; they demanded inquiries into Terrell's mob connections and promised protests in the legislature.[39] *Toronto Daily Star* sportswriter Milt Dunnell deplored the phoniness of objections to the fight being staged in 'Hogtown.' He nonetheless betrayed views that were anything but progressive: targeting Ali as 'the showpiece of the racist' Black Muslims, Dunnell offered his defence of the champion's right to fight in ways that made it all too apparent that he had little regard for either the Nation of Islam or for the 'loud-mouthed egomaniac' he presented as 'the most unpopular champion of all time.'[40] Conn Smythe resigned as a director of Maple Leaf Gardens, disgusted that the enterprise had put 'cash ahead of class.' Ali's anti–Vietnam war statements were apparently grounds for locking him out of the iconic sporting complex. 'The Gardens was built for many things,' the legendary Smythe pontificated, 'but not garbage disposal. It is no place for those who want to evade conscription in their own country.'[41]

Terrell eventually nixed the fight, claiming there was not enough money in it for him. Rumours were flying that he had faced death threats from the mob. Apparently his underworld handlers sensed there was nothing to be gained by fighting the desperate Ali, now down for a serious sociopolitical count because of his anti-war stand. Better, they reasoned, to let Ali end up in jail and have Terrell take the title at some later date without too much fuss and muss.[42] So Chuvalo was parachuted into the Gardens matchup. It only added fuel to the fire.

From the United States and beyond came a flood of journalistic commentary that an Ali-Chuvalo contest was destined to be a dud.[43] Chuvalo was depicted as a has-been, loser of three of his last four fights, a luckless 'catcher' rather than a skilled boxer deserving of a chance at the title. Robert Lipsyte thought the build-up week before the fight was little more than a charade, one promoter confessing to him, 'This is strictly a salvage operation.'[44] Typical was the tirade of *New York Times* columnist Arthur Daley:

> The blindly stubborn promoters of the what-is-it involving Cassius Marcellus Clay and George Chuvalo at Maple Leaf Gardens tomorrow night have the consummate gall to charge $100 for ringside tickets. The fight isn't worth 30 cents. If the promoters were smart – which they obviously aren't – they would keep the ice making machines in operation at the erstwhile hockey arena. It would reduce the odor.

Daley continued the barrage with the usual anti-Ali rhetorical arsenal: Clay had attached himself to a 'hate organization,' lacking the decency of even 'a low-grade patriotism.' Perhaps most offensive, in a United States where the almighty coin did indeed rule, Ali had 'spoiled a multimillion dollar property.' Calling for a boycott, Daley asked that not a nickel be contributed to the coffers of Clay or the Black Muslims.[45] Others deplored the 'Tom Foolery in Toronto,' wrongly associated Chuvalo with unsavoury criminal elements, and railed against the Canadian city 'without sporting shame.'[46]

Not surprisingly, the race-political card was played prominently in the Canadian press.[47] Sports page articles asking 'What is a Black Muslim?' answered with the headline, 'Preach "white devils" are doomed to hell.'[48] Jimmy Breslin, tongue well in cheek, suggested that the title needed to be stolen from Ali for the good of the country, and as actual fight night approached U.S. journalists informed Canadian readers that Chuvalo was being cheered by millions of patriotic Americans, however unlikely it was that he would prove able to rise to the occasion.[49] In *The Vancouver Sun*, Jim Kearney mixed racial metaphor and a boxing aficionado's disdain for Chuvalo, 'a plodder whose best punch is a head butt.' Peppering his article with references to Ali as 'Allah's wordiest son' and the Black Muslims as 'the Negro counterpart of the Ku Klux Klan,' Kearney struck a rare materialist analytic note. He stressed that because Ali had remained beyond the grip of the mob, with the Nation of Islam controlling the closed-circuit television rights to his fights, the gangster element was more than a little miffed at the limited promotional possibilities available to it in the Ali-Chuvalo bout. This, and Ali's anti-war stand, had produced a strange set of boxing bedfellows. Cheering for Chuvalo, Kearney predicted, would be all Canadians, the super-patriotic American element, and the mob. 'Ain't society inconsistent,' Kearney closed. 'It says Muhammad Ali is unpatri-otic and cuts his financial windpipe. For saying much the same – and much more besides – Senators Kennedy, Morse and Fullbright are cru-sading liberals.'[50] If Ali recognized that Canadian columnists gave him a fairer shake than the nastiness he routinely encountered in the pages of the U.S. press, he was nevertheless hurt enough to remember a *Toronto Daily Star* headline, 'Clay Is Hated by Millions!' in his autobiog-raphy, *The Greatest*. The same paper's coverage of the bout referred to Ali as 'Mecca man.'[51]

The fight, of course, proved the pundits wrong, as is so often the case in boxing history. Ali, not surprisingly, won, but Chuvalo, in Dick Beddoes's words, gave people what they 'had hoped for and few expected – a fierce, primitive battle between a ponderous, rough-hewn slugger and a master hitter of polished skills.' The performance ele-vated boxing out of its doldrums. His column headed 'Chuvalo with Chauvinism,' Beddoes put the accent on the Canadian boxer's accom-plishment. On less than two weeks' notice, Chuvalo had given the world's best 'a stirring fight ... 15 bruising rounds ... blunt and punish-ing and exciting ... the liveliest in the heavyweight division since Rocky Marciano retired 10 years ago.' Chuvalo did this in 'absolute defiance of the experts.' To be sure, 'Chuvalo lost the fight' but, Beddoes insisted, 'he won the crowd.' If it sounded 'dramatic and maudlin' to see Chuvalo's defeat as something of a victory, Beddoes was willing to plead guilty. 'If a reporter doesn't care about a fighter who was born without any quit,' he concluded, 'he should hock his typewriter.' The coverage in the *Toronto Daily Star* was more restrained, but it played more directly into the mythic association of Canadians and their ongoing struggles to survive adversity. Chuvalo had put on a display of 'doggedness and gameness and durability that earned him admiration.'[52]

In Vancouver, Denny Boyd waxed enthusiastic about Chuvalo's showing: 'If you are a Canadian you can be a little prouder today because George Chuvalo is one, too. That he failed is not the point. That he is a Canadian and a proud man is something from which we can all draw.' Nothing irked Boyd more than hearing a fight fan declare, 'Chuvalo isn't bad, for a Canadian.' Even the doubter Jim Kearney proclaimed the fight 'a greater artistic' success than anyone had a right to expect, Chuvalo proving 'the most durable specimen of Canadiana since Maple Syrup and the Birch Bark Canoe.'[53] From the Canadian referee to the largely plebeian crowd that flocked to Maple Leaf Gardens at the last minute, the chorus of praise for Chuvalo was long, loud, and definitely tinged with nationalism.[54]

Jimmy Breslin was one of the few American commentators who echoed such sentiment. Chuvalo, he agreed, never had a chance, for he was little more than a 'plodding second-rate prize fighter.' That was not what mattered when he went into the ring with Ali and, above all, when he went out, standing up. 'He carried what he was born with for just as far as it would go and today he is a hero in Toronto, and he has a changed face.' Breslin, a liberal journalist unconcerned with the patriotic fear that responded with such venom to 'the nonsense' that came out of Ali's mouth, saw in Chuvalo a 'fighter at his trade,' a man's man, even in his loss, the anti-hero who turned a farce into 'a fight that you could watch.'[55]

For the most part, however, the American columnists and 'sweet science' cognoscenti took umbrage at Chuvalo's body punching, bemoaning what they considered a barrage of low blows. The referee, Jim Silvers, described in one *New York Times* article as 'a clothing salesman' who cultivated 'an almost mystical bond with Chuvalo,' came in for scathing critique, a homer who barely blinked at his countryman's fouls. Claiming that 'Chuvalo is not a dirty fighter by design, but by necessity,' Robert Lipsyte thought Silvers delivered 'an incredible exhibition of inaction,' a disgusting display of biased ineptness. The purple heart of anti-Chuvalo boxing prose went to the redoubtable Arthur Daley. Renowned for his animosity to Muhammad Ali, Daley put aside his usual rants against Black Muslims, race hatred, and Ali's disgraceful stand on the war to land a hard right on what seemed a Canadian conspiracy against fair fighting. His featured *New York Times* account of 'The Battle of Toronto' was weighted down with clichéd chauvinism:

> With the referee assuming the role of an innocent bystander, George Chuvalo pounded Cassius Clay from kneecap to skullcap at various times in Maple Leaf Gardens tonight ... Because rules were completely discarded, this became a rousing fight, contrary to all expectations. Ignoring at least a hundred low blows, Referee Jack Silvers behaved like a wooden Indian ... This was a weirdo all the way ... What brought the element of competition into it was the fact that Chuvalo was given free rein to use barroom tactics ... But when the decision was announced there was no need for anyone to summon the North West Mounted Police to investigate a bold-face robbery. Clay got what he deserved, a clear-cut victory over a most stubborn foe who neither knows nor cares where foul territory is located.

The Ali-Chuvalo contest was clearly regarded differently on either side of the forty-ninth parallel.[56]

The ironies of meaning, perhaps most significant in Canada, have largely escaped scrutiny and serious commentary. They turn on the particularities of race and class, filtered through an event that was hyper-gendered in its acute masculinization. The timing of all of this, the peculiarities of the 1960s, was also of critical importance, setting a particular stage on which the Ali-Chuvalo contest could take on so much and reach well beyond the ring.

Canadians seemed to enjoy, for instance, the seeming liberal tolerance with which they greeted Ali. They differentiated themselves from the ugly Americans, whose response to the Nation of Islam and any suggestion of a critique of the Vietnam war bristled the rednecks of most fight journalists and outraged Congressmen, moderate blacks such as Floyd Patterson, and state governors. Compared with Americans, it seemed, Canadians were an enlightened nationality. Yet this ignored an unmistakable history of racism in Canada.[57] In the coverage of the Ali-Chuvalo fight, in which the Canadian became 'the Great White Hope' for the hard racists of the American super-patriotic right, it was never pointed out that the original quest for 'the Great White Hope' had been initiated by Canada's own Tommy Burns. There was racism evident at ringside, with reports on taunts from the crowd: 'Kill that nigger, George. Hit him in the guts; the black boys can't take it there.'[58]

Chuvalo, to be sure, never racialized and politicized the fight in the way that U.S. boxing journalists and Floyd Patterson had constructed other Ali fights of the past. Was this a national trait or a class under-standing, growing out of the increasing recognition that with the 1960s the refrain of 'White Canada Forever' was growing obviously antiquated? Canadians may not have appreciated being judged, in the words of one Maple Leaf Gardens fight fan, as somehow 'second best,' a country that took on the heavyweight fight that the United States simply refused.[59] Many, undoubtedly, were wary about the rising climate of reaction in the United States and the dangers of its bellicose foreign policy. Looking for the nervous energy that accompanied most title fights, Robert Lipsyte found Toronto in late March 1966 quietly subdued and strangely out of synch with the atmosphere of aggression and retribution evident in the U.S. vilification of Clay/Ali: 'People feel a little sorry for Clay here, they feel he is a "dead man," with no future. If he loses he will be ridiculed; if he wins what good is a title with a pos-sible Army hitch or worse coming up? Many Canadians are frightened that American policy in Vietnam will drag them into a war, they think that those who speak against the war, as Clay did, are being perse-cuted.'[60] The telling point about Chuvalo, and Canada in the mid-1960s, was the extent to which white ethnics who had so long been racialized, structured very much outside the British traditions of the country, were now no longer marginalized and isolated.[61]

In some senses Chuvalo, too, was still constructed racially in 1966. Described as a boxer who fought 'with his face,' 'the best catcher since Bill Dickey of the Yankees,' Chuvalo was a 'rocky-faced Croat' with a 'thick hide,' and hitting him was like 'knocking on a hot water tank.'[62] In earlier times all of this would have been sufficient to designate him non-Canadian. But this was no longer possible. Unlike Tommy Burns, the son of German-Canadian immigrants who was born Noah Brusso, Chuvalo did not anglicize his name when he took to the fight hustings. Those who cheered for Chuvalo in Maple Leaf Gardens were the expression of a new Canada, struggling to be born, in which social place was no longer rigidly fixed for those who were not quite yet white, but were on the verge of being recognized as such. This broadening of whiteness had been brew-ing in the 1950s and 1960s. For many immigrant ethnic groups the advances registered as steps forward were simultaneously those of ethnic-ity *and* class, culture *and* materiality – the stuff of nationality remade.

As John M. Lee commented astutely in a *New York Times* article, the Ali-Chuvalo bout had a demonstrably proletarian and 'minority' air about it. Unlike the Archie Moore–James J. Parker championship fight held in Maple Leaf Gardens in 1956 and which set a Canadian boxing record of almost $150,000 in gate revenue, white jackets and evening gowns were not the attire at ringside in 1966. The fight fans at the Ali-Chuvalo match were dressed in 'narrow brim hats and fingertip coats.' Rompin' Ronnie Hawkins, Toronto's reigning rock star in the 1960s, was one of the few to wear a dinner jacket, and only three minks were in evidence among the ladies who braved the Gardens' crowd. In contrast to a Stanley Cup play-off game, where attendance was likened to 'going to church and being seen,' the 1966 fight was not a prestige event. 'In this predominantly Anglo-Saxon city of two million people,' Lee stressed, 'the Establishment couldn't be bothered with Clay or Chuvalo. The crowd reflected the minority groups one sees in the strip of taverns along Yonge Street – Italians, a smattering of French.' One ethnic Canadian welder in the packed $7 grey seats expressed the views of the new non-British Canadian: 'The attraction is Chuvalo. He at least gives you your money's worth. I don't want to see no Fancy Dan dancing around.'[63]

There was considerable irony in these multicultural beginnings. To begin with, they had not so much arrived with the fanfare of a government-proclaimed program, as is so often thought. Rather, they had been working their way into being over decades. Trudeau's Liberal multicultural policies and proclamations, in short, had been anticipated in popular culture. Sport had undoubtedly played an important role in this process. Indeed for the Ukrainians of the prairie west, the National Hockey League was a favoured route to Canadianization. Players like Turk Broda, Bill Juzda, Bill Barilko, and Bill Mosienko attained star status in the 1940s, followed by such 1950s and 1960s counterparts as Terry Sawchuck, Johnny Bucyk, Eddie Shack, and Eric Nesterenko. It may well have been that these kinds of sporting heroes set the cultural stage on which 'white ethnic' political breakthroughs of the 1950s and 1960s registered. In Manitoba, the country's first Ukrainian-Canadian mayor, Steve Juba, was elected in 1957, presiding over municipal politics for two decades. At the end of the 1960s that same province elected Edward Schreyer as the NDP premier. Schreyer, whose lineage was German-Austrian Catholic with links to the Ukraine, was the first social democratic leader in Manitoba who was not of Anglo-Saxon and Protestant background. His cabinet was dominated by Jews and Ukrainians.[64]

Chuvalo's boxing success in the 1950s and 1960s was thus part of a larger process that was unfolding across the country. Precisely because boxing illuminated the importance of race and its meanings in as stark a form as any other sporting endeavour, Chuvalo's brief moment of fame exposes a further, less benign, irony. Whiteness may well have broadened considerably in the 1960s, but it still had its limits. The most racialized of Canada's peoples, whose colour precluded their welcome into the fullness of citizenship, remained very much outsiders. African Canadians and Aboriginal people were still, as we will see throughout this book (as well as Asians, about whom I have far less to say), marginalized. They were denied what others, who had long been denigrated as not white, were now receiving. Muhammad Ali was still, even in liberal Canada, a black who needed to be put in his place by a Great White Hope (even if that historic force was now a white ethnic who, decades earlier, would not have been considered white).

In the years to come, few would espouse such sentiments. If we fast-forward to 1996, things looked very different than they did when Ali and Chuvalo faced off in Maple Leaf Gardens. Ali, hated and reviled as an enemy of the state and a defiler of things American in 1966, had been resurrected, even mythologized. Much had been forgiven. Largely forgotten was his refusal to make the communist Viet Cong into his enemy, his insistence that blacks should not kill in the name of freedom when they themselves were not free. Erased from memory was the equation of his Islamic religion and race hatred. Eclipsed was the ugly aftermath of Ali's Maple Leaf Garden battle with Chuvalo, which saw him refuse induction into the U.S. armed forces, sentenced to prison for his defiance, and stripped of his heavyweight title. Battling his conviction in the appeals courts, Ali fought his way back to boxing prominence in the 1970s. He entered the ring with Chuvalo again and, as Vietnam was increasingly recognized as an imperialist debacle, not only regained his dominance as the recognized heavyweight champion of the world, but also gradually came to be revered rather than reviled. By the 1980s and 1990s, Ali had become a worldwide symbol of black pride, recognized as arguably the greatest heavyweight fighter of all time. Now suffering from a debilitating case of Parkinson's disease, Ali was marketed by a resurgent, U.S.-centred global capitalism. At the 1996 Atlanta Olympics, Muhammad Ali (no one referred to him as Cassius Clay anymore) was the centrepiece of a spectacle selling NBC, Coca-Cola, and corporate capitalism to the entire world.[65]

In Canada, however, Chuvalo was largely forgotten. Championed in 1966 as Canada's Everyman, standing on his feet in the face of punishing odds, surviving when he should have been succumbing, Chuvalo had been dealt a series of cruel blows. He hung on too long in the fight game, losing credibility and financial security. His five children lived with Chuvalo's reputation as the quintessential tough guy, and some of them, especially the boys, fared poorly in the process. Masculinity came with a price tag for Chuvalo's sons, who bore the brunt of bullying youths out to prove they could beat up on the offspring of the man even heavyweight champions could not bring to his knees. Schoolyard fisticuffs gave way to more worrisome behaviour, and when some of the Chuvalo boys ran afoul of the law, they found out that the brutalizing police were little better than teenage tormentors. Three of Chuvalo's four sons turned to the hard drugs and criminal activity that often follow in the wake of substance abuse. They were all dead by their own hand or because of drug overdoses by the time Ali was lighting the 1996 Olympic torch in Atlanta. Chuvalo's wife committed suicide. George's life had descended from Canadian hero of the mid-1960s to the depths of a particular kind of hell. Boxers such as Ali and Joe Frazier did what they could for him, including sitting at the head table of a Rochester, New York, fundraiser for Chuvalo. Why could such an event not have been held in Toronto? But Chuvalo, like Canadian nationalism in an era of 'free trade,' was spiralling downward, and in 1993 there were reports that he had taken a sordid job 'encouraging' the tenants of a downtown Toronto apartment building to move out so that the owner could reap the financial rewards of turning the units into pricey condominiums. As had so often been the case in his past, Chuvalo was being badly used by others. He managed to climb out of this early 1990s pit, a project of personal rejuvenation that owed less to his status as a figure in the imagined community that is Canada than it did to the high price that he and his family had paid in the fighter's years of decline. Currently, in 2008, back on his feet, and dedicated to educating youth against drug abuse, Chuvalo had nevertheless not been promoted as part of the Canadian identity for a long time, until Stephen Brunt and the National Film Board put him back in the public eye in 2003.[66] This rejuvenated Chuvalo was no longer really a representation of Canada, as he had been in 1966. Indeed, how could he be, without exposing how fickle is the promise of the Canadian dream for the immigrants who changed the face of national identity in the mid-twentieth century?

The son of immigrants, a meatpacker and a chicken plucker, one in a long line of rugged European peasants in Old World coats, Chuvalo and those who supported him in 1966 were new Canadians whose place in the country of their choice and birth could no longer be denied. There was, however, a blindspot in the vision of Canada as a diverse and pluralistic homeland. Behind the making of Chuvalo as the symbolic Canadian of a particular era lay an underappreciated resurrection of the original Canadian quest for a Great White Hope. The anglophone establishment, no longer able to define being Canadian, was content to let others accent a new imaginary Canadian, embodied in the notion of Canada as something vastly different than an outpost of the British Empire, a vision that was forever buried by the time Chuvalo entered the ring with Ali. In the shadowed continuities of social inequality of the time, a waning whiteness needed a backdrop of differentiation against which new gestures toward 'the just society' could be showcased. Particularly because all of this involved something of a sideshow, in which the revolutionary challenge of the independently minded black American was the foil, the national identification with Chuvalo in 1966 borrowed from some rather long-standing chauvinisms. Moreover, the individualism of Chuvalo's stand obscured collective and historical experiences that needed to be more fully appreciated and assimilated if the attainment of change was to be anything other than stylized and mythic. The future of this identity was thus precarious in the extreme, precisely because it rested on a foundation always shifting in its oppositions and seldom all that secure in its attachments.

The 'Establishment' may indeed have been uninterested in Chuvalo and Ali in 1966, willing to let the changing Canadian identity be captured by a rugged representation of dogged, if defeated, separation from the United States. This nonchalant and transitory articulation of national identity would of course prove fleeting and easily displaced when a more suitable political imagery appeared on the scene, as it would in the Canada-Russia hockey series of 1972. There could be no lasting Great White Hope, however benign, that was not, in reality, truly white *and* green, the colour of moneyed power. Chuvalo's victory in defeat, as well as his later life, would make that abundantly clear. The irony of national identity, revealed in so many ways in the 1960s, and by the highly different but joined historical experiences of both Ali and Chuvalo, is that, in the lyrics of one 1960s poetic voice, if it 'is not busy being born' it 'is busy dying.'[67] Such experiences have as much long-term pain and disturbing anguish in them as they do the splendour and spectacle of the sporting stage. Translating recognition of that into the possibility of new identities in a twenty-first century distinguished not by the hopes of race superiority and attachments to national origin, but rather to the solidarities of humanity, is a fight indeed, and one destined to go far more than fifteen rounds.

Chapter Five

Celebrity and Audacity: Marshall McLuhan, Pierre Elliott Trudeau, and the Decade of the Philosopher King

In the mid-1970s, remembrances of the Sixties still fresh in their minds, thirty to forty people used to assemble each Monday evening in a nineteenth-century coach house at the University of Toronto. Formally a seminar offered by the Centre for Culture and Technology, the gathering actually brought together not only graduate students but university faculty and interested visitors as well. The drawing card was Marshall McLuhan, who had been christened by *Playboy* magazine 'the high priest of pop cult and metaphysician of media.' The 1960s saw huge advances in the mass marketing of celebrity, and McLuhan managed to become what was most unlikely: a Canadian academic whose 'star' stature resonated in increasingly wide circles. The cult of McLuhan was very much a product of Sixties thinking, the diffusion of ideas that seemed to fly in the face of convention. One social historian explained that 'the most extraordinary quality of McLuhan's mind is that it discerns significance where others see only data, or nothing; he tells us how to measure phenomena previously unmeasurable.' Jonathan Miller offered a rather shocking conclusion to his treatment of McLuhan in Frank Kermode's edited *Modern Masters* series: 'Perhaps McLuhan has accomplished the greatest paradox of all, creating the possibility of truth by shocking us all with a gigantic system of lies.' Whether such statements were true or not is certainly open to question, but there is no denying that for a time the University of Toronto professor, known as the 'Oracle of the Electronic Age,' had become, in the words of the *San Francisco Chronicle*, 'the

Marshall McLuhan and Pierre Elliott Trudeau (*Globe and Mail*).

hottest academic property around.' In France they coined a term, *mclu-hanisme*, as a synonym for thinking surrounding popular culture. That McLuhan achieved this recognition, largely as a result of his capacity to spin out commentary on the very media that created a new kind of celebrity, was of course ironic, and all the more so because McLuhan was hardly your run-of-the-mill famous person.[1]

McLuhan's fame, as fleeting as it would be, can hardly be separated from the politics of Canada in the 1960s. Indeed, a Conservative Party power broker, Dalton Camp, claimed to have been one of the first to appreciate the Toronto professor's insights, going so far as to take credit for 'launching' the 'guru of the global village.' As the Tories were cutting themselves to pieces in 1964, Camp, who was the deeply factionalized party's president, invited McLuhan to give the keynote address to a September conference in Fredericton. Camp hoped to use the New Brunswick think tank to shock Conservatives out of their doctrinaire obsolescence, to challenge them to see the mid-1960s for the period of change that it undoubtedly was. McLuhan was the man for the job. He spoke on what happened when people did not know the words to communicate, but his persuasive powers were apparently wasted on most of the delegates. They thought McLuhan provocative enough, to be sure, but found him difficult to understand. Some insisted he must be from the lunatic fringe. Camp, future New Brunswick premier Richard Hatfield, and Kingston's Flora MacDonald, however, were entranced by McLuhan, judging him a breath of fresh air, simultaneously hot and cool. As we shall see, however, if a select crew of Tories first found McLuhan enticing, it would be the decade's Liberal Party phenomenon, Pierre Elliott Trudeau, who would, in 1968, lean most decidedly in directions McLuhanesque. Strange bedfellows, indeed![2]

In the words of Tom Wolfe, who met the 53-year-old professor in 1965, his celebrity not yet quite secured, McLuhan was 'gray as a park pigeon.' A Catholic in an age of waning religious values, McLuhan was a teacher who had struggled through 'one of the most exquisitely squalid hells known to middle-class man,' the 'freshman English' lecture hall. He actually wore clip-on ties, the kind you might purchase off the Rexall revolving rack for 89 cents. They slipped under your collar, the telltale milky-white edge of plastic stripping exposing either your lack of knot-tying dexterity or your total nonchalance about appearing 'hip.' One interviewer summed up McLuhan as 'gray and gangly,' possessed of an 'eminently forgettable face,' sporting 'an ill-fitting brown tweed suit' and the distinctive 'clip-on necktie.' A biographer notes that he was likely to don mismatched socks or a fedora that was too small for his head, which, when his hair started to thin, might sport an ill-fitting toupée. Grey was clearly McLuhan's colour; the clip-on tie his signifier. Seemingly very uncool!

Yet, in contrast to countless others who aspired to nothing more than a place 'in the phlegmy grim dim world of EngLit academia,' McLuhan was not quite what he appeared to be. Throughout the 1960s he assailed intellectual sensibilities forged in the dungeons of past thought with ideas, observations, short quips, and lines of analytic outburst that related to the vast changes in everyday life and culture that had swept across the world. McLuhan, alone it seemed, had a handle on the cyclonic impact of media technologies and communication, most emphatically the single most important innovation that would mark the 1960s, television. Not prone to suffer fools gladly, McLuhan looked at his university teaching peers and delivered 'the most infuriating announcement of all: You are irrelevant.' This made him few friends among the scholastics and academically based literati. Many offered glib dismissals: 'the Dr. Spock of pop culture'; 'the guru of the boob tube'; 'the high priest of pop think'; 'conducts a Black Mass for dilettantes'; a 'Canadian Nkrumah who has joined the assault on reason'; 'swinging, switched on, with it and NOW. And wrong.' Such put-downs were of little consequence: McLuhan shot across the 1960s like a comet, commanding attention in the world's centres of metropolitan chic. He even enticed the quick-talking advertising men he simultaneously valorized and exposed into his corner. Soon they were preaching his power in the corridors of corporate capital. Before McLuhan quite understood what had happened to him he had become 'an international celebrity and the most famous man his country ever produced.'[3]

Small wonder that Pierre Elliott Trudeau, who also took Canada and, to some extent, the world, by storm in the same years, was a friend of McLuhan's and listened to the professor's judgments about how to market himself as a politician. Marshall primed Pierre on his television persona and its importance in enhancing Trudeau's message through effective use of the media. In the 1970s Trudeau would bounce into the Coach House Center for Culture and Technology seminar and exchange witticisms with the now-legendary McLuhan. Upon McLuhan's death in 1980, Trudeau wrote to his old friend's wife Corinne, and referred to the teacher's 'marvelous intellect' and 'global eminence.' Trudeau noted that the blithe commentator on technologies of communication, who seldom wrote on anything specific to his homeland, had increased his sense of pride in being a Canadian. This carried a special ironic charge inasmuch as McLuhan thought Canada 'the only country in the world that has never had a national identity.' In an age that McLuhan regarded as dominated by rapid technological change, the 'homogeneous nations' were destined to 'lose their identity images.' Canada, in the period when Trudeau would exercise his authority as the country's first minister, was thus situated alone among the advanced capitalist nations of the West in being able to 'keep its cool.' 'We have never been committed to a single course or goal,' McLuhan claimed. 'This is now our greatest assest.' Yet just around the corner lay the violent repudiation of McLuhan's observation/prediction, the October Crisis of 1970 and Trudeau's proclamation of the War Measures Act. In retrospect, it would seem that some in Canada, Trudeau included, did indeed embrace ideas of national identity and were in actuality committed to something that could be regarded as a 'single course.' Others, such as Trudeau's *indépendantiste* opponents in Quebec, certainly proclaimed their intentions with an unmistakable singularity.[4] A politics of the left would always be the blindspot in McLuhan's vision. Indeed, one 1970s critic would reduce McLuhan's oeuvre to a mildly contentious contest to realize its 'counterrevolutionary potential.'[5]

When the professor and the politician first commenced their friendship, sealed in an ongoing correspondence, Trudeau was minister of justice in the Lester B. Pearson Liberal government, having been appointed to the post in 1967. On 6 April 1968, however, Trudeau was elected leader of the Liberal Party following Pearson's retirement, and two weeks later he was sworn in as the prime minister. Trudeaumania galvanized the late 1960s electorate, infusing politics with a new and energetic sensibility of style, gesturing as well to the importance of modern ideas, and a combination of staunch stands and vague commitments. Riding a wave of media constructions, Trudeau marked a departure from the epoch of the Diefenbaker interregnum and the subsequent rule of Pearson. Globally, it may well have been the Age of Aquarius;[6] in Canada, the period had a more telescoped feel to it. The mid-1960s were thus in many ways the moment of McLuhan *and* Trudeau, days of celebrity in Canadian public life, an audacious staircase in the rise of the philosopher king.[7]

McLuhan I: Canada and Convention

Born on the prairie west, of Protestant parents displaced from Ontario, Herbert Marshall McLuhan grew up during the First World War, his childhood memories dominated by his comfortably middle-class view of Edmonton's North Saskatchewan River and a move to Winnipeg. Raised on an esoteric mix of metaphysics, phrenology, biblical reading, the *Oxford English Dictionary*, fundamentals of elocution, Shakespeare, Milton, and Browning, the young McLuhan was a precocious intellect, and one bred to believe in his maturing into greatness. His mother thought him university president material.

Educated at the University of Manitoba in the 1920s, McLuhan found his academic environment less than appealing. He felt he was not being sufficiently advanced in his learning, and according to him his professors in the English department were largely plodders and dullards. In his third and fourth years, attracted to some Oxford expatriots teaching in philosophy and history, McLuhan was prompted by new stimulations and the depressing lack of job prospects in the early 1930s to complete an MA, but his eyes, like so many Canadians oriented to the Empire, were set on Britain. In the mid-1930s he tested the waters at Cambridge, his Manitoba BA and MA counting for one year's credit toward the three-year 'superior' undergraduate degree of the elite British institution. He plugged into the New Criticism of notable literary scholar F.R. Leavis, who remembered McLuhan affectionately as the student 'from the wilds of Manitoba.' Mrs Leavis, no doubt the recipient of less fawning, and thus able to view McLuhan from a dispassionate social distance, judged him 'a rather loud, aggressive person, always running around arguing with everyone.'[8]

McLuhan was no Canadian nationalist, but his identity as a Canadian nagged at him, perhaps in ways that he could not quite figure out. An ascendant 1940s religious identity jostled with that of his national homeland and for a time displaced it. McLuhan felt his prairie roots gave him a unique vision, panoramic and liberated from the constraints of spatially confined goals. As a citizen of Empire's outpost, the aspiring academic understood himself advantaged in relation to the centres of civilization, his perspective fresh and uninhibited by varied constraints. How this related to his conversion to Catholicism is not known, but it did not ease his accommodation to the University of Wisconsin, where he secured his first teaching assistantship before completing his degree at Cambridge. McLuhan ended up furthering his apprenticeship as a professor at the Jesuit St Louis University, ostensibly the finest Catholic edifice of higher education in the United States. There, ironically, he began to break from the conventions of scholarship, building on non-conformist impulses first nurtured by Leavis, but reaching beyond poetry into the realm of popular culture.

The route he took was anything but radical and was built, at first, on firm antagonisms to both godless materialism (Marxism) and feminized emasculation (homosexuality), bêtes noires that had nagged at him throughout his Cambridge years. They would continue to irk McLuhan into the 1950s, when either they did not matter so much or he astutely kept his dislikes more and more to himself. As late as 1967 McLuhan would actually offer a rather silly prediction that gay men were going into decline.[9] McLuhan was manifesting growing impatience with the detailed excursions into the minutiae and trivia of historicized subjects and rejected prods to rein in his scholarship.

Instead he was tempted by the meanings of the mundane, most of which he saw as an assault on traditional institutions, like the family, that he championed. The comic strip *Blondie* was a launching pad for McLuhan's antifeminist homophobia.[10] Dale Carnegie's *How to Win Friends and Influence People* provided a provocation to explore critically the cynical manipulation of men and women driven by modernity's base acquisitive individualism. Having barely finished his Cambridge doctorate, McLuhan struck out for places perhaps more open to his emerging interest in cultural criticism, chairing the English department at Windsor's small Catholic institution, Assumption College. Many factors influenced McLuhan's decision to take what was commonly judged a 'step down' in moving from St Louis to Windsor. He was disillusioned with his St Louis colleagues and students, fearful of being drafted by the American government to fight in the Second World War. McLuhan was also attracted by personal connections to figures in Windsor and at Assumption, as well as the promise of a light teaching load, time to do his research and writing, and stimulations from 'congenial minds – Catholic minds.' The restless McLuhan no doubt thought that the grass on the Canadian side of the hill would be greener than it had been in St Louis. There was also a pull back to the land of McLuhan's birth, albeit one in which attraction and repulsion seemed to co-exist. McLuhan had long wanted to 'tear the hide off Canada and rub salt into it.' This would not really happen until the 1960s presented the increasingly idiosyncratic McLuhan with his opportunity.[11]

McLuhan did not take long to develop a condescending attitude to Assumption. He considered the college 'a little bay of silence – a little backwater.' It was not meant as a compliment, for however much McLuhan may have cherished moments of private silence, he longed to hear his own voice loudly in public discourse. Canada, at this point, he thought not much better, calling it a 'stagnant stream' and likening it to a 'mental vacuum.'[12]

In any case, McLuhan was not long for Windsor, making his way to the University of Toronto and St Michael's College in 1946. McLuhan judged his new job a final coming home, something of a passageway into permanence, and for the first time in his life he was faced with the need to do an 'uncompromising and unremitting job.' It was surely an irony that the prodigal prairie son, suspicious of traditional wisdom at the same time that he embraced the most orthodox of Christian religions, wary of metropolitan strongholds of conventional ideas but impatient with parochialism, would settle himself at the very centre of postwar Canadian cultural conformity, Toronto.[13]

Ambivalence was something of a McLuhan trait, and nowhere more so than in his understanding of Canadian identity. He often seemed, for instance, to regard Canada as barely worth 'taking seriously,' especially in the mid-1960s, with his fame spreading fast and furious outside of Canada's borders. To journalists, especially, he was likely to mouth comments on Canada that were little short of scathing indictment. The country was 'the most apathetic and unenthusiastic territory in all creation,' he huffed in the pages of *Mademoiselle* in 1967. 'The Canadian is mildewed with caution.' Yet he also found distance from the rest of the world a refreshing opening of space for intellectual possibility. 'The Canadian has freedom of comment,' he told one interviewer in 1971, 'a kind of playful awareness of issues, that is unknown in, say, Paris or London or New York.' Protected by 'layers of colonialism,' McLuhan suggested that Canadians were shielded from encountering themselves, and certainly insulated from undue seriousness. A part of McLuhan's message was to alert them to the dangers of the twentieth century, 'so they can duck out.'[14]

McLuhan II: The Suppression of Resistance and the Embrace of Communications

At the University of Toronto McLuhan may quickly have garnered genius status among a select few colleagues. Yet most faculty members saw him as odd at best, and a poseur at worst. McLuhan did attract graduate students who revered him, but his obvious shift away from mainstream literary studies and criticism meant he left many in his intellectual wake. He found a cohort of St Mike's philosophers deadly boring, and his relations with the man who would in many ways rival him, Northrop Frye, were never easy and grew increasingly strained as time went on.[15]

In 1951 McLuhan published his first book, *The Mechanical Bride*. Subtitled *A Folklore of Industrial Man*, it brought together images of newspapers, comic strips, pulp fiction covers, and, above all, advertisements, arranging them in fifty-nine sections that each contained a page or two of comments by McLuhan. Years in the making, the book had gone through what McLuhan considered a rough (and prejudicial) ride at New York's Vanguard Press. Editors were hard-pressed to select a reasonable number of representations from McLuhan's original submissions, which totalled in the hundreds. Paring down his prose in order to sharpen his analytic message, somewhat lost in the first submitted draft of 500 manuscript pages, was not easy. But the final product was a terse and evocative shredding of mass culture's technologies of selling itself. The ethical wasteland of industrial capitalism was laid bare in pointed, but effective, critique of the machine age and its defilements. McLuhan offered disdain aplenty for the philistine nature of contemporary culture, and was especially pointed in his digs at the moneyed elite. 'Why are the American rich such proletarians in mind and Spirit?' asked McLuhan, who a few pages later quipped: 'The top brass produces the low dream? Or is it the other way around?' Such an irreverent and glib attack on the class-divided house of the world's most affluent and powerful nation also hinted at a subtle process of accommodation that would ease McLuhan out of the role of social critic and into the place of the dispassionate observer. 'Got any light on why our intellectuals take such a dark view of pop kulch,' queried McLuhan casually towards the end of his text.[16]

Over the course of the next decade McLuhan shed his earnestness and stepped back from his criticism of the age in which he lived. He was learning, slowly, that critique did not pay. A few hundred copies of *The Mechanical Bride* were sold, and the book was soon remaindered. McLuhan himself bought a thousand copies at deep discount when the publisher faced the prospects of pulping it.[17] In the 1950s he cultivated his interest in electronic media, schooled in part by the last publications of his University of Toronto colleague, Harold Adams Innis, who would die in 1952. From Innis's prodigious researches on communications, and especially from his argument that print culture creates nationalism and displaces tribalism (a point that would be elaborated to considerable effect in the 1980s by Benedict Anderson), McLuhan undoubtedly learned much. But he drew on other wellsprings, too, even as he offered his mosaic of evidence/interpretation on the making of typographical man, *The Gutenberg Galaxy* (1962), as an homage to his colleague. For while McLuhan appreciated the specialized knowledge Innis commanded, he was also disappointed that the political economist seemed incapable of transcending specific intellectual boundaries.[18]

The two professors were in actuality quite different; whereas Innis wrote with a tortured, dense empiricism, McLuhan's prose was structured as a historicized poetics, influenced more by Dada and cubism than by positivism. Indeed, McLuhan's form in the immediate aftermath of Innis's death was increasingly unconventional. He offered an interpretive and historicized sequence of evidence and event, a packed canvas of cryptic probes that were defiantly anti-theoretical, chronologically disperse, and ordered by observation that was consciously satirical, even surreal.[19]

This was perhaps most evident in his 1954 *Counterblast*, provoked by what McLuhan viewed as the pompousness of the statement issued by a 1951 royal commission on the arts and sciences in Canada, the Massey Report. In a decidedly countercultural anticipation of the 1960s, McLuhan responded to the 'high culture' ponderousness of the report with 'blasts' of typed headlines. Almost Beat-like in its form, McLuhan's verse struck with force at the enduring myths of Canadian national identity:

BLAST england ancient GHOST of culture POACHING the EYES of
the Canadian HAMLETS
USA COLOSSUS of the South, horizontal HEAVYWEIGHT flattening
the canadian imagination
...
BLAST (for kindly reasons)
CANADA
The indefensible canadian border
The SCOTTISH FUR-TRADERS who haunt the trade routes and
folkways of the canadian psyche
BLAST all FURRY thoughts
The canadian BEAVER
Submarine symbol of the SLOW UNHAPPY subintelligentsias.
Oh BLAST
The MASSEY REPORT damp cultural igloo for canadian devotees of
TIME & LIFE
...
BLESS
The MASSEY REPORT, HUGE RED HERRING for
derailing Canadian kulcha while it is
absorbed by American ART & Technology.

Declaring this *samizdat* set of mimeographed sheets to be 'a view of the cradle, the bough, and the direction of the winds of the new media in these latitudes,' McLuhan was still, in the mid-1950s at least, enough of a voice of resistance to find himself the object of collegial apprehension. Peddling his cry against the Massey Commission for 25 cents at a local cigar store, McLuhan in 1954 was more likely to be mocked than mimicked. *Counterblast* was a typical McLuhan oddity, but it was more significant as a distilled and anguished last gasp of refusal. Soon McLuhan would put all of this aside to embrace the accommodations that were the building blocks of fame and fortune.[20]

McLuhan's celebrity required the suppression of critical, politicizing engagement, which much of the 1960s embraced, and in its stead the adoption of an admittedly participatory, but non-aligned, observation. McLuhan, in his later vernacular, needed to go from hot to cool.[21] For that to happen he had to brush off the singing embers of an entrenched Canadianism, what he abhorred in the hangover of the old imperialism, a dominion colonial containment that he referred to as 'the cringing, flunkey spirit of Canadian culture, its servant-quarter snobbishness resentments ignorance penury.'[22] As that dead weight was seemingly lifted from the nation's collective shoulders with the transition from the 1950s to the 1960s, McLuhan's oppositional temper quieted, his curiosity as an explorer peaked, and his stock as a celebrity rose. Ironically, the mainstreaming of McLuhan was premised on his simultaneous movement with and against his times. As Toronto broke loose of its provincialism and Canadian identity shifted gears into a new epoch of diversity and uncertainty, McLuhan found his niche. This was accompanied by a mellowing, and indeed eventual repudiation, of his earlier assault on a mechanical cultural conformity. This shift towards acceptance of the world as it was placed McLuhan increasingly distant from new voices of revolt. The vehicle of his incorporation was, in a further irony, a vibrant force for change: the media.[23] McLuhan's rise thus paralleled, somewhat, that of his counterpart in politics, Trudeau.

McLuhan III: The Cult of Celebrity

As McLuhan told *Playboy* in 1969, the making of McLuhanism had been premised on a major reconfiguration of his political sensibilities:

For many years ... I adopted an extremely moralistic approach to all environmental technology. I loathed machinery, I abominated cities, I equated the Industrial Revolution with original sin and mass media with the Fall. In short, I rejected almost every element of modern life in favor of a Rousseuvian utopianism. But gradually I perceived how sterile and useless this attitude was ... I ceased being a moralist and became a student.

Acknowledging that he was 'not a crusader,' McLuhan embraced his celebrity as a gift freely bestowed by a power that nevertheless expected detached acquiescence:

One must begin by becoming extraenvironmental, putting oneself beyond the battle in order to study and understand the configuration of forces. It's vital to adopt a posture of arrogant superiority ... I must move through this pain-wracked transitional era as a scientist would move through a world of disease; once a surgeon becomes personally involved and disturbed about the condition of his patient, he loses power to help that patient. Clinical detachment is not some kind of haughty pose I affect – nor does it reflect any lack of compassion on my part; it's simply a survival strategy. The world we are living in is not one I would have created on my own drawing board, but it's the one in which I must live, and in which the students I teach must live. If nothing else, I owe it to them to avoid the luxury of moral indignation or the troglodytic security of the ivory tower.

'I'm not *advocating* anything,' McLuhan insisted, his accommodation complete: 'why waste my time lamenting?' As he had declared in a 1966 essay, 'The Medium Is the Massage,' paraphrasing a nineteenth-century figure, 'I accept the universe.'[24] Cool was hot.

The book that launched McLuhan was *Understanding Media: The Extensions of Man* (1964). Its opening sentence concluded on the phrase that would stamp McLuhan's 1960s celebrity: 'In a culture like ours, long accustomed to splitting and dividing all things as a means of control, it is sometimes a bit of a shock to be reminded that, in operational and practical fact, the medium is the message.' McLuhan told his readers to stop grappling with something as fickle and as distinctly subordinate as content, and realize that humanity had become an extension of its technologies of communication. 'By consistently embracing all these technologies, we inevitably relate ourselves to them as servomechanisms,' McLuhan would later observe. *Understanding Media* assailed the 'banal and ritual remark of the conventionally literate, that TV presents an experience for passive viewers.' He insisted instead that 'TV is above all a medium that demands a creatively participant response.' McLuhan thus argued that TV would not work as a background: 'It engages you. You have to be *with it*,' a phrase that entered popular language with the rise of television. Or, in a classic McLuhanism: 'With TV, the viewer is the screen.'[25]

Ordered around oppositions, McLuhan's framework counterposed the machine to the electronic, the hot to the cool, meaning to effect. Television, as the archetypal electronic medium and the epitome of cool, was central to McLuhan's arguments, but not much more so than the telegraph, telephones, electric light bulbs, clocks, and automobiles. Often confused as hot because of its massive influence, McLuhan argued that television was cool precisely because, unlike other media – such as the press or radio – that galvanized opposing views and both demanded and enhanced sharply defined issues where difference was accentuated, TV projected 'the cool aura of disinterest and objectivity.' This was central to McLuhan's stress on television as participatory medium, since cool media 'leave much more for the listener or user to do than a hot medium.' But the irony was that in its cool character and structured need for audience participation, television as a *mass* medium could supposedly never galvanize hot issues and impassioned involvement. The extraordinary degree of involvement demanded of massive numbers of viewers invariably introduced 'a kind of *rigor mortis* into the body politic.' It also inevitably downgraded issues and raised higher 'the icon, the inclusive image.' Political platform, a hot statement, was ill-suited to representation on TV, which favoured in its stead 'political posture or stance.' Television, less a visual experience than it would obviously seem to be, was for McLuhan a cool intensification of inclusion, in which the viewer was drawn into his or her subjectivity.[26]

Understanding Media sold 100,000 copies, taking the world of ideas in the mid-1960s by storm.[27] Its author was soon discovered by California ad men, becoming the toast of New York literary society. Wined and dined by magazines such as *Esquire*, McLuhan was offered free office space by *Time* and *Life*, if only he would occasionally grace their building and drop a few *bon mots* their way. He managed to get himself immortalized in accounts of lunch at a San Francisco topless restaurant, Off-Broadway, where the straight-laced McLuhan seemed to take it all in and was anything but tongue-tied:

'Well!' he said. 'Very interesting!'
'What's interesting, Marshall?'
'They're wearing *us*.' He said it with a slight shrug, as if nothing could be

more obvious.

'I don't get it, Marshall.'

'We are their clothes,' he said. 'We become their environment. We become extensions of their skin. They're wearing us.'

McLuhan festivals were held in San Francisco and at Canadian universities. The communications commentator was now much in demand on the lecture circuit, commanding fees of $5,000 to $6,000, a not inconsiderable sum in the mid-1960s. Even these figures were dwarfed by the hyped fictions of magazine writers like Tom Wolfe, who circulated stories of $25,000 paid ($50,000 asked) for a McLuhan lecture. McLuhan hoped the state wouldn't be chasing him down in a financial audit.[28]

Articles and interviews proliferated, and McLuhan's venues were no longer staid, scholarly journals, but publications such as *TV Guide*, *McCall's*, *Look*, *Harper's Bazaar*, and *Vogue*. NBC's New York vice-president Paul Klein purchased twenty copies of *Understanding Media*, distributed them to fellow executives, and told them to read the book. Cartoons of McLuhan appeared in *The New Yorker* in 1966, and corporate groups regularly sought out his views, which sometimes disappointed them with their bluntness. It was in one of these executive conference talks that McLuhan announced, as much out of his penchant for bad puns as it was inspired by any analytic breakthrough, that he would no longer hold to the dictum that the medium was the message. It was now the *massage*.

A book of this title appeared in 1967, with the subtitle *An Inventory of Effects*, followed by a long-playing record in which McLuhan read portions of the text to the accompaniment of music. *The Medium Is the Massage* was not so much McLuhan writing his way into new thinking, but a composition of two McLuhanites, Jerome Agel and Quentin Fiore, who gathered together images and then paired them up with excerpts from McLuhan's past statements. They were arranged in a manner that juxtaposed arresting representations and jarring type presentations, which were laid upside down, slanted, shifted in size, varied in boldface. The author contributed the title and approved the text and layout. McLuhan had become a medium, his message conveyed in visuals and experimental forms, his authorship an almost collective undertaking.[29]

If all of this registered globally more than nationally, in Canada too there were signs of the McLuhan happening. To be sure, much Canadian comment placed the accent on the unfathomable nature of McLuhanism. A televised interview with Robert Fulford was introduced with the statement: 'His critics are almost as lively as his admirers. They call him a gadfly, a spellbinder, a word-merchant. But almost everyone agrees: no one can make sense out of more than ten percent of what the professor is saying, and that seems to include even the professor himself.' That 10 per cent apparently went a long way in the 1960s. At Montreal's Expo 67 McLuhan was all the rage: the theme pavillions of 'Man and His World' reflected McLuhan's writings, passages of which were transcribed to plaques that were then featured prominently as wall-hanging 'visual statements' inside the fair's buildings. In the last airing of the television program *This Hour Has Seven Days*, Patrick Watson reported that McLuhan had effected a shift in Canada's national image: 'After years of exporting wheat and aluminum and newsprint and Lorne Greene and Raymond Massey, we've finally come of age and now we're exporting ideas ... our own Herbert Marshall McLuhan has been labeled poet, philosopher, and prophet.'[30] A celebrity could also be a celebrated Canadian, even if he never ceased to provide a moving intellectual target.

McLuhan would eventually concede that the cool television medium produced effects quite striking in their destabilizations. In displacing the deeply institutionalized and culturally embedded values of an older print culture, television and its supporting cast in the 'new integral electronic culture create a crisis of identity, a vacuum of the self, which generates tremendous violence – violence that is simply an identity quest.' By the end of the 1960s, reflecting on the radicalism of the decade, McLuhan cavalierly reduced the rebelliousness of the era to the mindlessness of youth acting out 'its identity quest in the theatre of the streets, searching not for goals but for roles, striving for an identity that eludes them.' As the quieter multitudes yielded 'to the intensities of the new technology's electronic circus, it seem[ed] to the average citizen that the sky [was] falling in.'[31] And indeed it was. McLuhan's vast celebrity proved unable to shield even him from the fallout.

McLuhan IV: War and Peace in the Global Village

McLuhan found fame attractive, but it proved a cross for the aging Catholic intellectual to bear. He spent 1967–8 in New York City, the recipient of what was widely publicized as a $100,000 Albert Schweitzer Chair in the Humanities at Fordham University. He lived, fittingly, next door to Jack Paar, a TV personality of considerable stature. But the large salary ended up being contested by New York State, and McLuhan's research and teaching entourage ate up the bulk of this amount. At the University of Toronto, where English professors were earning a meagre $14,000 or less, however, McLuhan's celebrity was often seen as nothing more than a crass, commercial sell-out. McLuhan did little to deflect such criticism, and, indeed, he offered up more than enough transparently self-serving pandering to the celebrated dollar and those who dispensed it. Moreover, academic peers were not likely placated by their esteemed colleague's contemptuousness. They no doubt felt it on a day-to-day basis, but McLuhan's disdain might also leap off the pages of mass-circulation magazines and give them a rude slap in their complacent countenances. 'Some of my fellow academics are very hostile,' McLuhan told Peter Newman in 1971, 'but I sympathize with them. They've been asleep for 500 years and they don't like anybody who comes along and wakes them up.'[32]

McLuhan returned to Toronto in 1968 after an exhausting stint in New York, and one that had seen him operated on for a brain tumour. It was a year in which revolution was in the air. Asked if he liked McLuhan, one 1960s radical spokesman, Yippie leader Abbie Hoffman, replied: 'Let's say I think he is more relevant than Marx ... He experiments. For an old guy he does well.' McLuhan, according to Hoffman, 'understands how to communicate information. It's just that his living style – Catholic, university life, grants, the risks that he takes – is merely academic ... I respect him, but I don't love him.' The question had been triggered by Hoffman's easy assimilation of *mcluhanisme*: 'generational revolt has gone on throughout history ... But there are significant differences. The hydrogen bomb, TV, satellites, jet planes – everything is more immediate, more involving. We are the first internationalists ... We live in a global village.'[33] McLuhan was even linked to hallucinogenic drugs.[34] The University of Toronto professor was, however, anything but a New Leftist or a countercultural advocate. Oracles did not take sides, although they could pronounce haughtily with much disdain and arrogance. Asked to comment on the attraction of writers and scholars to the oppositional mobilizations of the post-1964 years, McLuhan managed to summon up a sentence of above-it-all dismissal: 'Moral bitterness is a basic technique for endowing the idiot with dignity.'[35]

As protests against the Vietnam war divided America, and ghetto rebellion rocked U.S. urban centres, McLuhan kept his distance from the politics of the moment, avoiding all moral stands save that of judgmental detachment. Yet he could not help but be affected by the apocalyptic mood, and he began to fear that his cool medium, television, was turning all too hot. In its coverage of napalmed villages, mass street protests, police beatings, and burning cities, TV threatened to stoke the flames of political Armageddon and in the process reverse its McLuhanesque meaning. Under such pressures, McLuhan's probes turned increasingly predictive, and extreme: the United States was destined to break asunder in a race war that would result in the balkanization of a series of regional and racial mini-states; African Americans faced extermination; political democracy was finished, and elections as they had been known were about to be rendered meaningless; urban transformation would obliterate the city–country dichotomy and reduce the automobile (which McLuhan personally hated) to an obsolete atavism. McLuhan even advocated that television take a sabbatical from covering certain inflammatory issues.

The prophet of doom was not without his up side. McLuhan had great faith in what he increasingly referred to as the 'human tribe.' In the new global village, a maximum of disagreement and an expansion of creative dialogue was inevitable, uniformity and tranquillity being displaced by conflict and discord. And yet out of this seeming chaos would come the 'customary life mode of any tribal people': love, harmony, and cross-fertilization. The retribalization of man promised an end to rampant individualism, alienation, and specialized privatization of points of view. If the transition to the global village was inevitably marked with 'profound pain and tragic identity quest,' the agony of the Sixties was nevertheless 'the labor pain of rebirth.' McLuhan expected 'to see the coming decades transform the planet into an art form,' and a new humanity would be 'linked in a cosmic harmony that transcends time and space,' its sensuality caressing, moulding, and patterning 'every facet of the terrestrial artifact.'[36]

This was the ground of McLuhan's second publication undertaking with the graphics designer Quentin Fiore and co-author Jerome Agel. The trio produced *War and Peace in the Global Village* in 1968. If global and American images predominated, McLuhan was nevertheless influenced by the slippage of Canadian national identity that was well underway by the late 1960s. He graced the middle of his book with a double-paged spread of a bloodied Maurice 'The Rocket' Richard, 1950s hockey star of the Montreal Canadiens, shaking hands with a battered Boston Bruin. The 1955 Richard–Clarence Campbell riot at the Montreal Forum had been a preface to Quebec's Quiet Revolution, indicating the limits to which insulting and chauvinistic behaviour would be tolerated in Quebec. In an abstract, textual generalization, under the heading 'War as Education,' McLuhan managed to avoid any direct reference to the imperialist carnage in Vietnam, declaring: 'When our identity is threatened we feel certain that we have a mandate for war.' The preordained clash 'of old and new environments is anarchic and nihilistic today,' wrote McLuhan, but 'violence, in its many forms, as an involuntary quest for identity, has in our time come to reveal the meaning of war in an entirely new guise.'[37]

As Donald Theall remarks, *War and Peace in the Global Village* is a utopian, mystical text, reliant upon an understanding of electronic technologies as catalysts of transformation in which aggression, pain, violence, and ultimately war are turned into the necessary evils that, through man's art, transcend themselves and consolidate a new birth of humanity. The problem with McLuhan's resolution of the apocalyptic height of the 1960s is that it managed to deal with the 'horrors of the modern world ... while seeming to never have encountered unpleasant subjects. Such a way of operating leads to accepting the way of war because it is a mode of education and to accepting aggressive fall-out from education because it is a way of war.'[38] For Larry Zolf the 'clash of ideas, classes, cultures dissolved into the one giant consensus of the Global Village.' This was nothing more than the 'end of ideology' thesis, imported from the United States 'and given the final stamp of absurd authority by Canada's own Marshall McLuhan.'[39]

By the beginning of the 1970s, McLuhan's celebrity was waning. A series of unsuccessful books undermined his reputation with scholars, while among the journalistic gonzos and glitterati he was no longer hot news. His stock had dropped considerably, not the least in the circles of commerce and consumption where his reputation had in part been secured. A man made by the media was unmade by them. *The New Yorker* cartoons that had solidified his avant-garde status only a few years before, took a dismissive turn in 1970, with the depiction of a young woman saying to a man as they departed a cocktail party, 'Ashley, are you sure it's not too soon to go around parties saying, "Whatever happened to Marshall McLuhan?"'[40] The naysayers were starting to get under his skin, McLuhan always having been prickly in the face of criticism: 'It's a nuisance having my books criticized,' he pronounced in 1971. 'It's like being caught with your fly open. It confuses my students.'[41] There were moments of respite, as in 1976, when Woody Allen called on him for a cameo appearance in the film *Annie Hall*, but even that retrieval of celebrity went poorly, and McLuhan's star did not shine brightly in Canada and the United States in the 1970s.[42] That decade, for better *and* for worse, belonged to Pierre Elliott Trudeau, the figure who donned the McLuhanesque mask of cool to such good effect in his 1960s rise to political celebrity.

Pierre (French) Elliott (English) Trudeau (Canadian): Born to Run (In Style)

With summer dawning in 1968, and after witnessing Pierre Elliott Trudeau's startling media-enriched surge into the leadership of the Liberal Party, Marshall McLuhan viewed a videotape of the debate between the neophyte (and never electorally tested) prime minister and his Conservative Party opponent, Robert Stanfield. He dropped a letter to the prime minister's office in the mail from his New York address. 'The witness box cum lectern cum pulpit spaces for the candidates,' opined McLuhan, 'was totally non-TV.' But Trudeau was nevertheless quite cool: 'Your own image is a corporate mask, inclusive, requiring no private nuance whatever. This is your "cool" TV power. Iconic, sculptural. A mask "puts on" an audience. At a masquerade we are not private persons.'[43] In the months following the 25 June 1968 election, which saw Trudeau and the Liberals capture 45.5 per cent of the popular vote, 155 seats, and a decisive majority government in a period of Canadian history and politics where minority rule had been the norm, McLuhan would advise Trudeau on how to work the electronic medium to best effect. Image triumphed over 'the production of packaged answers,' or what antiquated political animals might have called programs and policies. Problems needed to be addressed in other ways: they were best 'processed in dialogue,' traded in small group discussion that sought few answers and stayed away from a sterile 'stating mere points of view.' 'Instant and total participation' was McLuhan's sloganeering directive, his correspondence with the prime minister's office continuing past the Trudeaumania of February–July 1968: 'It is important to avoid all attempt at solutions ... always the mark of the 19th-century packaging mind. The real solution is in the problem itself, as in any detective story.' Such admonitions carried in their tail the pleasant sting of flattery: 'You are the only political image of our time able to use the T.V. medium without being forced to become a tribal buffoon or cartoon like De Gaulle. All other political figures of the Western world are merely faded photographs on the T.V. medium.' It all registered at the highest of levels, and McLuhan emphasized that the Trudeau government's commitment to 'participatory democracy' was ideally served by working out a televised interface with student-power leaders. The aim was not to plug the students into some 'existing bureaucracy,' but to situate them in a dialogue with Trudeau: 'Your own natural, easy, flexible way would relax them and alert them to many features of the world in which they live, in a totally new way.' Dispensing with all protocol, such a television encounter would place Trudeau 'in the Canadian living room as a "gap-bridger," the unifying image of our society that you became during the last election.' McLuhan likened this unprecedented politics of informal adventure to 'political mountain-climbing.'[44]

The man who climbed the mountain of creating a new style of politics in 1968, Pierre Elliott Trudeau, was the product of a uniquely Canadian union. His father was a gregarious, driven, and emotionally unpredictable French-Canadian lawyer turned businessman, Charles-Émile Trudeau. Pierre's mother, Grace Elliott, the Catholic-raised daughter of a Québécois, was also influenced by her practical-minded, tavern-owning, Protestant father, whose background was rooted in Scotland and New England–originating British loyalists. She would have a tremendous influence on Pierre, the first of her three sons who survived infancy. Pierre was born in 1919 just as the dynamic Charlie, who had been raised on a farm but graduated into the ranks of the francophone legal profession, was making the gutsy move of walking away from the practice of law to build an imaginative automobile association business that offered members discounts on gas, repairs, and towing. The Trudeau enterprise thrived, even as the Great Depression brought other firms to their knees, and the family, once characterized by its modest means, was well established in the centre of fashionable francophone Outrement. If home life, orchestrated by Grace, was unpretentious but comfortable, Charlie's public persona was brash and ostentatious, all the more so after he sold his automobile association to Imperial Oil for over $1 million. In his private, familial relations, as John English has shown, 'Papa' Trudeau was, however, capable of affection and genuine paternal warmth. Pierre grew to adolescence loving his formidable father. Charles Trudeau obviously had the Midas touch. Investments in mining, apartment buildings, an amusement park, and a piece of the Montreal Royals franchise funded his lavish lifestyle. Economic success allowed him access to the fraternity of boxers, ballplayers, and braying businessmen whose company he kept until, in 1935, he caught pneumonia on a Florida spring training visit to the camp of his baseball team and promptly died of a heart attack. The teenaged Trudeau was devastated.

With Charles Trudeau's death, Pierre was now entirely in the care of his mother, whose stature as the influential family matriarch grew year by year, and of his Jesuit teachers at the Collège Jean-de-Brébeuf. Rather frail as a child, the young Trudeau had been encouraged by his father to develop himself physically. Pierre soon turned from sports like hockey, baseball, and lacrosse, at which he had taken youthful turns, to the more individual pursuits of diving, canoeing, and skiing. He grew into a young man known for his wit, his intellect, and his incisive Jesuit-imparted Cartesian logic. Something of a 'snob,' Trudeau could on occasion be an obnoxious student, disruptive in the classroom. By the late 1930s and early 1940s he embraced decidedly corporatist views and endorsed a conservative variant of Quebec separatism that could harbour anti-Semitism. Not all that out of step with mainstream ideas in francophone Quebec, such views propped up attractions to an authoritarian, self-sufficient Catholic state, examples of which were Mussolini's Italy, Salazar's Portugal, and, after 1940, Vichy France. Trudeau's political ideas in these highly charged years, however, were anything but fixed. He could be strongly nationalist and was drawn to an underground movement of resistance, even battling police officers in the streets during the 1937–8 centennial celebrations of the Patriot rebellion. Yet he remained proud of his English heritage and, on occasion, became tired of pressures to always side with the French 'race.' Contradictory and conflicted, Trudeau was, like many young men, uncertain of his intellectual and political commitments, wavering in his early understandings of the Second World War and its meanings.[45]

There was no doubting his brilliance, however, and he went on to study law at the University of Montreal. He found the experience abysmal, but graduated nonetheless, spent enough time articling to know that the profession was not for him, and headed to Harvard for an MA. Maturing, and studying government and political economy, Trudeau increasingly saw the Second World War as exposing Hitler and Mussolini and revealing the ugly dead end of fascism. He moved away from his past politics and towards the more multicultural and civil-liberties perspectives that would feature forcefully in his 1960s rise to national prominence. He was interested in liberal theory and the sacrosanct rights of the individual. Reared in the conflicted traditions of a more collectivist, Catholic Quebec, Trudeau was galvanized by new insights and sought to further his intellectual aspirations at the elite École Libre des Sciences Politiques in Paris.

Parisian academic classrooms did not hold Trudeau's interest for long, animated as they were in the late 1940s by a Conservative–Marxist standoff. The young aspiring intellectual soon traversed the Channel to set up shop at the London School of Economics. There Trudeau gravitated loosely to Harold Laski's reform socialism and proposed to complete a thesis on 'Liberties in the Province of Quebec.' He was drawn to the question of what made people obey, a modern intellect pursuing the age-old questions of Niccolò Machiavelli's *The Prince*. The subject in fact bridged his seemingly youthful political schizophrenia, in which ideas and commitments of the left and the right contended. A doctorate was, ostensibly, the object of Trudeau's journey from Harvard to Paris to the LSE, but at thirty years of age he had still not written it. Instead, he travelled. His direction was east, and it took him on a backpacking excursion through eastern Europe, Turkey, the war-torn Middle East, India, and eventually China. He arrived back in Canada in 1949.[46]

It was an auspicious moment, defined by the fusion of class struggle and national aspiration in a strike at the mining town of Asbestos. Trudeau and his friend Gérard Pelletier, a reporter for *Le Devoir* who had been covering the labour battle for four months, drove out to the embattled picket lines in April 1949. What Trudeau encountered was a war for liberty, waged by the exploited and oppressed, against a powerful triumvirate: the authoritarian traditionalism of Quebec's government, presided over by *Le Chef*, Maurice Duplessis; foreign capitalists who symbolized the American takeover of Canadian natural resources; and the language of money, English. Trudeau, bearded and militant in his defence of freedom, delivered a powerfully radical tub-thumping address to the miners, urging them to accept no concessions in their quest for civil rights. He witnessed police brutality against striking workers and crossed paths with Jean Marchand, a union organizer who would later align with Trudeau and Pelletier in a quest to promote the cause of French Canadians within federalism. Writing in 1956, Trudeau would come to see the Asbestos conflict as 'a turning point in the entire religious, political, social, and economic history of the province of Quebec.'[47]

Upon his return to Montreal, Trudeau found that he was a marked man. In Duplessis's Quebec there was no room for the likes of a liberty-espousing Trudeau, and avenues of appointment to political and university posts were, routinely over the course of the 1950s, blocked. Trudeau at first headed to Ottawa and secured a position in the Privy Council Office, which was 'desperately poor in terms of Quebeckers.' As he wrestled with the tedium of his mundane tasks, Trudeau was also working to reconcile his Catholicism and his political-intellectual commitment to the rights of the individual. He found a forum in the circles surrounding the Montreal reform journal *Cité libre*, the first issue of which appeared in June 1950, Pelletier being its guiding hand. Trudeau brought to the fledgling publication not only his ideas, but his pocket-book and his intellectual connections to potential subscribers. Tired of the confinements and boring bureaucracy of Ottawa, Trudeau headed back to Montreal in 1951, convinced by Marchand that he had a role to play in Quebec's rising labour movement. For the next few years Trudeau juggled trips abroad – to Africa, Europe, the Soviet Union, and China – with labour education, giving classes in economics, accounting, and political science to union militants in the growingly secular Confé-dération des Travailleurs Catholiques du Canada (CTCC). Hopping on his motorcycle, Trudeau would breeze into labour action schools in Arvida, Rimouski, Shawinigan, or Chicoutimi, proselytizing among the local trade union activists. Soon he knew union leaders the length and breadth of the province. They, in turn, put him into the movement's harness, naming him as the union designate in labour arbitrations, tri-bunals where grievances were fought out by labour, capital, and the often state-appointed chairman judges. The young advocate prepared union briefs and even negotiated collective agreements. Trudeau was becoming widely known, and not only to Catholic labour leaders, but to figures in internationally affiliated unions, the legal community (judges and lawyers), and working-class activists in general.[48]

It was at *Cité libre*, however limited its influence, that Trudeau culti-vated his capacities as a polemicist and oppositionist. He railed at the containments of Duplessis's Quebec, willing to sustain faith in Catholi-cism only to the extent that the Church could be challenged to break with its complicity in 'the Great Darkness' and further the struggle for social reform. Trudeau combined the confidence and assurance of the rich with the intellectual incisiveness and passionate commitment of his immersion in the idea of liberty and the politics of civil rights. The record of the Duplessis government made it easy for Trudeau to point the finger of critique. Having suspended political rights in the 1930s Padlock Law (whereby communism and other forms of dissent were out-lawed), Duplessis was clearly no friend of liberal values. The late 1940s and 1950s were years that saw bitter eruptions of class conflict, reaching from 1949's Asbestos to the Murdochville strike of 1957. In the latter confrontation, in which CTCC and Canadian Labour Congress forces fought for steelworkers against police, hired thugs, and strikebreakers, one worker was killed and the combined unions almost bankrupted by legal costs. Trudeau's writings demanded democracy, rationalism, civil liberties. Stressing the critical importance of the sovereignty of the individual, Trudeau nevertheless recognized that the path to liberty lay in the recognition of collective reform. This project placed him, in the Quebec of the 1950s, in the vanguard of an individualist, egalitarian, anticlerical rebellion. *Cité libre* was its voice.[49]

Trudeau couldn't buy a professorship throughout the 1950s, but with Duplessis's death in 1959 he was offered two, and ended up in the law faculty at the University of Montreal. A year later, in 1960, the Quiet Revolution that Trudeau and others had been labouring for, unquietly enough since Asbestos, unfolded. It drove the remnants of the Duplessis machine, the Union Nationale, from office, catapulting the Liberal Party to power in Quebec. Trudeau's *Cité libre* articles of the 1950s had seldom been soft on the federal party of Louis St Laurent and Lester B. Pearson. French Quebeckers had little to thank federalists in Ottawa for, according to Trudeau, because outside of elections, when 'the tribe always evokes the aid of its witchdoctors,' there were few francophone Canadians other than St Laurent who figured forcefully in the politics of twentieth-century Canada. Suddenly, the darkness of Quebec's long night under Duplessis lifted. Liberalism was no longer radical and marginal. Rather, it was empowered, and *Cité libre* was increasingly drawn into support of the new state. Trudeau, less enthusiastic now that he was not in righteous opposition, reminded his colleagues not to get lost in the transitional moment. Against the ever-widening net of the technologies of governance, which advocated the institutionalization of identity cards in 1961, the civil libertarian raised his objections: 'Without doubt the logic of the thermonuclear age and the universe of the concentration camp will sooner or later put an end to our anachronistic freedoms,' he noted sarcastically. 'But please, let's give in only with regret, and at the latest possible date; and let's make sure the first concessions are not imposed on us by a handful of political amateurs struggling to prove their good intentions to us.'[50]

It was another identity card, however, that was about to be more forcefully played in the early 1960s. From quarters once congruent with Trudeau began to be voiced an aggressive nationalism, a contentious and authoritative articulation of the *separations* of Quebec. Trudeau and the old *Citélibreistes* were no longer cutting edge; they found themselves heckled as *vendus*. Ensconced in his law professorship, but itching to get back into the fight of politics, Trudeau honed his position on federalism and the French Canadians and distanced himself from the developing crescendo of radical nationalism. His longstanding audacity sharpened. Attacked, he struck back. He thought the closing of nationalist minds in the Quiet Revolution no better than the closures of intellect he had lived with under Duplessis. Separatists Trudeau considered guilty of 'criminal insouciance,' for they would inevitably hand back 'full sovereign powers to the very elites who were responsible for the abject condition' from which they were 'boldly offering to free us.' *Nationalism,* as opposed to a pluralist preservation of distinction and difference within a country and a widening world, Trudeau increasingly saw as a dead end. In the title of one of his more famous essays, it was nothing short of 'The New Treason of the Intellectuals.' Confronting 'Anglo-Canadian nationalism,' Trudeau feared, was pushing French Canadians into a kind of 'nationalistic shell,' which could only 'condemn them to the same stagnation.' The result would undermine Quebec and leave Canada's future precarious. Little would be left but a 'sterile soil for the minds of her people, a barren waste prey to every wandering host and conquering horde.' 'Open up the borders,' he shouted in metaphorical rebuttal to the rising nationalist chorus in Quebec. 'Our people are suffocating to death!'[51]

Trudeau marked time. But by 1965, enticed by Marc Lalonde and in consort with his long-standing allies Pelletier and Marchand, Trudeau made the trek to Ottawa. The 'three wise men' would eventually have the ear of the upper echelons of the governing federalist project, which had fallen into a political ineptitude in the mid-1960s that was surpassed only by a parallel but deeper descent on the part of the internally wracked Diefenbaker Tories.[52] The combination of labour union backgrounds, stinging journalism (Trudeau had been scathing in his 1963 indictment of Pearson's about-face on nuclear weapons, and Pelletier had recently likened the Liberal Party to a political garbage can), and electoral inexperience made 'the wise men' a tough sell in the backrooms of Liberal Ottawa. But the government's needs were large with respect to Quebec. What Lester B. Pearson wanted to hear was how to revive federalism in *la belle province* and stave off a nationalist revolt that had ironically been wooed in international circles. Charles de Gaulle's Paris had become something of a seedbed of radical thought for the connoisseurs of independence from below as well as a luxuriant banquet circuit for ministers of the Jean Lesage Liberal Quebec state. Pearson had tired of de Gaulle thinking that Quebec was a sovereign nation and separatists inside Quebec thinking that it was about time they had one. He had ceded too much ground to Lesage in terms of Quebec's special status within Confederation. What Trudeau gave Pearson was, at first, little more than a pragmatic commitment to work within a party that presented the most realistic and constructive option. But he soon warmed to the federalist task and the opportunities that cropped up to draft new policies and promote them. As Marchand recalled, the 'wise men' concurred that 'there is a vacuum [in Ottawa], and if we believe in this country and we want to do something ... we have to do it in Ottawa – and we have to do it in the party which has a chance to be in power.' After his 8 November 1965 election in the mixed anglophone-francophone Montreal riding of Mount Royal, where a former *Cité libre* comrade, Charles Taylor, ran against him on the New Democratic Party ticket, Trudeau was moving in ever-more-powerful Liberal Party circles. Enticed into Lester Pearson's office as parliamentary secretary, and then appointed minister of justice in 1967, Trudeau had accomplished much a mere sixteen months after coming onto the stage of federal politics. It was a meteoric rise. And it was about to get wilder and reach higher.[53]

Trudeaumania: McLuhan's Mask and The Public Kiss

Lester B. Pearson cashed in his political chips on 14 December 1967. The diplomat wanted out of politics. He had perhaps experienced one scandal too many. Diefenbaker had been dumped by the Conservatives three months before, replaced by former Nova Scotia premier Robert Stanfield.[54] McLuhan thought the Conservative leader's image some-what divided against itself. On the one hand, he was the 'Yankee horse-trader, as shrewd as sabbatical or hebdomadal.' On the other, he also appeared an '"Honest Abe" – the vote splitter.'[55] But he remained 'old school' politics nonetheless. This was his liability. Change was in the air; youth a commodity whose stock knew no bounds. Ironically, in an age associated with protest and the politics of socio-economic transforma-tion, style trumped substance. In this context, who would fill Pearson's shoes and, in the process, wear more fashionable footwear? Only one man in cabinet had been known to sport sandals, much to the chagrin of John Diefenbaker.[56]

It was not that Trudeau lacked substance. He had more of it, arguably, than any other prime minister of the twentieth century. As Ramsay Cook suggests in his intimate memoir of Trudeau, the preface to Trudeauma-nia was the novice Liberal politician's adroit handling of Criminal Code amendments and constitutional issues, especially relating to Quebec's status within Confederation and the long-contentious matter of lan-guage rights. This was where Trudeau shone brightest in the period leading up to the Liberal leadership convention of April 1968. At a February 1968 constitutional conference involving Ottawa and the provinces, Trudeau, encouraged by Pearson, had effectively taken hold of the reigns of federalism's renewal. He put forward views that had jelled earlier and that would run through many of the articles collected in *Federalism and the French Canadians* (1968). Laying the seeds of his future commitment to a Canadian Charter of Rights and Freedoms, Trudeau emphasized the need to determine the general values all Canadians might adhere to in terms of guarantees of personal freedom, political liberty, economic security, and cultural equality. Rejecting special status for Quebec, which he saw culminating only in the break-up of Canada, and which was being promoted in various quarters under the guise of a 'two nations' policy, Trudeau countered with arguments summarized in a government pamphlet entitled *Federalism for the Future.* His intention was to take 'the fuse out of explosive Quebec nationalism by making sure that Quebec is not a ghetto for French Canadians – that all of Canada is theirs.' Trudeau's televised confrontation with the Union Nationale premier of Quebec, Daniel Johnson, was, at this point, a rare instance of Ottawa facing down French Canada's demands. It was complemented by the minister of justice's refusal to back away from entrenching language rights, establishing bilingualism as a Canadian reality. This was of course resisted by parochial regionalists, be they in the west, Quebec, or elsewhere. John English writes of this in a language patently McLuhanesque: 'The intense television lights sharpened all the participants' features but were particularly favourable to Trudeau's chiselled face and striking eyes. Johnson, in contrast, appeared uncomfortable under the glare.' Trudeau's 'virile performance' made him a known political quantity across the country; he drew enthusiastic reviews from a range of federalist intellectuals. A broader public appeal no doubt congealed in living rooms throughout the land as television viewers saw a possible leader emerge on their screens. Jean Marchand later commented, 'At the beginning of February, Pierre Trudeau was really created.'[57]

Be this as it may, Trudeau's substance would soon be overshadowed by a new, youthful politics of style, promoted by the media to the point that it would catapult the minister of justice into the prime minister's office. Trudeau in 1968 seemed to possess the rare political gift of developing substance in politics at the same time as he allowed, encouraged, and facilitated the marketing of his person as something entirely new in the Canadian political experience. He was thus simultaneously a man of ideas *and* images. It was the latter, however, that would ultimately captivate Canadians and unleash Trudeaumania.

One measure of this phenomenon was how coyly Trudeau handled his run for the leadership of the Liberal Party. To be sure, there were substantive reasons why Trudeau could not declare himself a candidate early in the contest. As justice minister, he had work to do throughout January and February 1968, meeting with provincial premiers in preparation for the constitutional talks that could not develop properly if Trudeau was perceived to be campaigning rather than dealing with federal–provincial relations in a measured way. As Cook shows, a draft-Pierre movement had been gaining momentum in certain influential circles since Christmas 1967. Trudeau held his cards close to his chest, however, and even if this was a necessity dictated by pragmatic and principled concerns, it served Trudeau surprisingly well. An aura soon enveloped the young minister of justice, who seemed to be operating in the minefield of Canadian politics as a seasoned McLuhanite.[58]

Trudeau was later fond of telling reporters that they had 'invented him.'[59] But if they hadn't, they would necessarily have been looking for someone else who could fit the bill. No sooner had Pearson announced his decision to step down as prime minister, than *Maclean's* commissioned a handful of marketers and image connoisseurs to give the influential magazine the scoop on what it would take to make over the candidates. High on the list was youth, sex appeal, looks, clothes – indeed, almost everything *but* political ideas and a program. Dull was what was not wanted. And Trudeau was anything but dull: he dressed mod, drove flashy convertibles, cut a fine figure on the diving board of the pool at the Château Laurier, and, if he had hot, passionate ideas on federalism and French Canada, could convey them in the cool, dispassionate manner of reason and rational debate. Trudeau may well have garnered support in 1968 for his principles. He projected his vision of 'One Canada' forcefully from the podiums of debate in French Canada, as well as in his position as minister of justice, where he was increasingly recognized as Pearson's authoritative voice on the need for a renewed federalism. A part of his approach, however, was undeniably to strike a pose notable for its outrageous panache. When questioned about independence for Quebec, Trudeau brusquely dismissed the idea as a variant of 'African tribalism that even the Negro kings don't want for themselves.' Trudeau perhaps sensed that the glib quip could effectively promote a politics of substance to better effect than a learned discourse. After all, no statement reverberated more decisively throughout the country than Trudeau's earlier memorable one-liner, delivered in the context of a Divorce Reform Bill and, more directly, amendments to the Criminal Code around permissible abortion and homosexual acts between consenting adults: 'There's no place for the state in the bedrooms of the nation.' It was a sexy statement, delivered in a sultry, sexy voice, and Trudeau made it before television cameras, dressed in a very sexy, full-length leather coat, standing outside the House of Commons. As such it was an archetypal McLuhan 'probe,' testing the waters of Trudeau's appeal with a legislatively innocuous, but rhetorically powerful and eminently quotable, maxim. The medium offered a certain political massage. But was the medium television, or Trudeau himself?[60]

Trudeau's 'bedrooms' comment, which Stephen Clarkson and Christina McCall note was borrowed from a *Globe and Mail* editorial written by Martin O'Malley,[61] captured something of the justice minister's capacity to blur the lines between substance and style. Less an articulation of policy, it was a statement of a new politics of performance. If there were indeed significant legislative advances registered under Trudeau, he was hardly their sole architect, for they had been in the making for some time. Yet they would come to be associated with the new minister of justice. Moreover, their concrete particulars might well be underappreciated at the time,[62] but the quick-witted ways in which Trudeau was able to scaffold judicial reform on the cultural rungs of the moment was the talk of the Ottawa press corps. They managed to see to it that this image of Trudeau registered with Canadians. In his constitutional commitment to solidify Quebec within Confederation, Trudeau oscillated between public pronouncements that were diametrically different. On the one hand his statements could be understated in their rational, reasoned, and restrained nature, while, on the other hand, he could be angered into pugnacious assaults that struck out at his critics with a vengeance that at times bordered on a rare political vulgarity. In the paradoxical passions of Trudeau's federalism, the man somehow became as much the message as the content he conveyed. The magic of Trudeau thus worked on a number of levels. Trudeau appeared above it all, when he wanted to, yet he could also come across as fed up with the usual bureaucratic entanglements of politics, impatient with the 'same old same old,' struggling to effect much-needed change. It was a brilliant capturing of the mood of the moment.

One expression of his abstract sense of detachment that paid huge political dividends was Trudeau's non-commitment to the Liberal leadership race during much of the early candidate jostling for prominence.

Trudeau managed to attract press coverage by not declaring himself a candidate for the office of prime minister until mid-February 1968, following on the heels of Eric Kierans, Paul Hellyer, Allan MacEachen, John Turner, Mitchell Sharp, and J.J. Greene (only Robert Winters would declare after Trudeau, rounding out the field).[63] Prior to the busyness of his January-February 1968 constitutional travails, Trudeau took a Christmas vacation to Tahiti, returning to Canada tanned and rested midway through the second week of January 1968. He appeared, albeit deceivingly, as a man calm and easy in his assumption of responsibilities. Ironically enough, as Pearson later realized, 'his non-involvement in politics became his greatest asset, along with his personal appeal, his charisma.'[64]

'The swinger is the man to beat if he runs,' declared the *Toronto Daily Star*'s Val Sears on 29 January 1968, 'and the man to court if he doesn't.' George Bain commented two days later in the *Globe and Mail* on how Trudeau was reaping the benefits of non-candidacy at the end of January 1968, describing a scene that McLuhan could not have scripted better. Instead of being required to hold down a hospitality suite in the early days of the leadership campaign, the non-declared Trudeau merely hung out. Perched on a dresser in a hotel bedroom jammed to the ceiling with young students, the minister of justice talked about the law, especially as it related to marijuana, censorship, obscenity, and hate literature. 'It was all very free-and-easy,' noted Bain, 'a discussion more than a question-and-answer session.' For her part, Mrs Pearson, having observed Trudeau at the annual Liberal Christmas party, dancing with the youngest and most attractive women, charming in his bilingualism, at ease and self-effacing one moment, on stage playing the drums the next, concurred with her husband's appointments secretary Torrance Wylie that this freshly unique face might well head the party come the April leadership convention: 'Oh?' she replied to Wylie's enthusiasm. 'Do you really think he has a chance. See, Mike – I told you.' Trudeau-mania was about to make politics a romance.

On the eve of that April decision, pro-Trudeau editorials, such as the one that appeared in the *Edmonton Journal*, declared, 'All the other leadership candidates represent the greyness of orthodoxy.' In the pages of the *Montreal Star*, Ramsay Cook, well situated to know just how formidable a political mind Trudeau was, stressed his friend's commitment to civil liberties, his rejection of nationalist rhetoric, and his pragmatism. But even Cook was forced to acknowledge that the new leadership contender was a paradox, being clearly the most liberal candidate, but also the most imprecise. 'It is not in his nature to be imprecise,' explained the historian, 'yet he knows that if Canadians want a renewed and viable country, it would be misleading to offer them a complete blueprint evolved in a short seven weeks of furious campaigning.' Extolling Trudeau's 'taste for freedom,' Cook nevertheless understood that such abstractions were not the normal stuff of political campaigning, and in their vagueness could never carry a candidate to victory. In the end, Trudeau's appeal was, in part at least, his style: 'Personality has raised the Liberal leadership campaign from the level of dull mediocrity to one of excitement. M. Trudeau might just do the same for the country.' Cook was joined in his enthusiasm by other academics, among them the country's leading sociologist, John Porter. A part of the intelligentsia was the first to board the Trudeaumania bandwagon.[65]

Maurice Western of the *Winnipeg Free Press* declaimed in early April 1968 that Trudeau had been anointed by television, that his candidacy was rolling and nothing could stop it. The new liberalism, claimed Western, was unexplained, and it was likely to remain so, given that Trudeau, the trickster, was a puzzle. How could delegates vote into the prime minister's office a man who campaigned with the statement 'The only constant factor in my thinking over the years has been opposition to accepted opinions'? But they would, Western predicted. Moreover, Trudeau's capacity to defy understandings of what was required in a politician and still inspire support, was fundamental to the rising tide of Trudeaumania. Thus an Ottawa woman penned a letter to *Maclean's*, asking, as had Western: 'What could we sober, Canadian squares possibly be thinking of, wanting this strange little customer for prime minister? It's madness. The whole country needs a cold shower.' But the punch line was the alchemist's reversal: 'Yet I, like the rest, will vote for him anyway.' Nothing seemed to change this. Trudeau met charges of his competitors for the leadership that he had no experience with his patented shrug: 'Most of today's problems are not solved by experience,' he replied with a certain off-the-cuff thoughtfulness. 'The further we advance into the modern age, the less important experience will become. It's much more important to have the necessary adaptability with which to face and solve new problems.' It was pure McLuhan. As Gordon Donaldson, a television commentator and producer as well as an author of character portraits of Canadian prime ministers, noted in 1969, Trudeau understood that his medium would be his message: 'He had sidled his way into power with an air of cool detachment, discovering that there was more magic in that shrug than in all the pounding and roaring of his competitors.' The night after facing down reporters sceptical of his experience, Trudeau was mobbed while frugging away on a dance floor at the Château Laurier.

Conventional politics had been packaged in unconventional ways.[66] What was new was not the substance, but the style: TV images galvanized support and deflected worries about details. No politician captured television like Trudeau, who was the subject of a number of interviews and portraits from the time he became minister of justice through his eventual candidacy for the Liberal Party leadership. Trudeau was the toast of CTV and CBC shows such as *The Public Eye*, *The Way It Is*, and *W5*. Donaldson first met Trudeau in May 1967, working with Norman DePoe, who interviewed the fledgling justice minister for CBC's *Newsmagazine*. He captured something of the aura surrounding Trudeau when he confessed that somehow what the neophyte minister of justice actually said eluded him: 'I don't know what he said, because I was fascinated by the film possibilities of his face – the oriental serenity as he listened, fingertips together as in prayer; the graven elegance of the high cheekbones and the big nose; the sudden animation, the deprecating smile, and the depth of the huge eyes ... masterfully assembled for the lens.' Whatever TV needed, Trudeau had it. As McLuhan said, 'the medium [can't] take a real face. It has to have a mask.' Charisma, celebrity, audacity – television brought them together in the visage of Pierre Elliott Trudeau, beamed into hundreds of thousands of homes.

Some still didn't get it. A younger contender for the Liberal Party throne, John Turner, seemed bewildered as the April leadership convention revealed scene after scene of almost mob adulation for Trudeau, with delegates, gate-crashers, and swooning admirers crushing against one another to touch the new messiah. 'What's this guy got anyway?' he asked incredulously. Mike Pearson answered in his memoirs: 'He was the man to match the times, the new image for a new era.' 'There was about him a subtle, indefinable intensity, a suggestion of pent-up power and hidden dimensions that fascinated the nation's TV viewers,' concluded Peter C. Newman.[67]

That pent-up power exploded in the spring and summer of 1968. The fireworks were dubbed Trudeaumania. It was the pyrotechnics of a Canadian identity struggling to be born, shooting wildly out of the euphoria that had, for some, begun with the architectural imagination of Expo 67. This sociocultural happening promised a political realization with the coming to power of Pierre Elliott Trudeau. To be sure, the dialectic of this new national identity, so explosive in its capacities to out-dazzle the antiquated Diefenbaker-promoted, dominion-oriented, nineteenth-century notion of 'Canada First,' draped in its imperial attachments to Empire, was something of a minefield. The danger of implosion was always present. Trudeau rode the wave of this promise with his simultaneous 'hot' gunslinger persona, a franco-phone Quebecker doing battle with the separatists, *and* his 'cool' impenetrable mask, in which a youthful and casual indifference to the decorums and conventions of the past fit effortlessly on a celebrated countenance of audacious detachment. Trudeau thus mastered the dualism of McLuhan's past and present media technologies. He managed, almost, to be all things to all people in the summer of 1968. But the growing resentments in Quebec, spurred on by television coverage that threatened to go hot with Charles de Gaulle's July 1967 admonition, 'Vive le Québec libre,' were not to be easily quieted by Trudeau's magical mask. A former *Cité libre* editor, Pierre Vallières, had recently completed his powerful indictment of Québécois passivity and Anglo-American capitalist exploitation, *White Niggers of America*. It would be published the next year as Trudeaumania swept Canada. The tensions behind the mask were palpable; the contradictions at the core of national identity irresolvable.[68]

With Trudeau's victory in the April leadership convention all of this was swept under the rug of infinite hope. The delegates did not exactly stampede to make Trudeau prime minister. It took four ballots before the recognized front-runner finally bested the last two candidates, 1,203 votes to their combined 1,149. There was a good deal of antagonism towards Trudeau among old-guard Liberal Party figures, and much of it was translating into resentment at his rising star status and a stubborn refusal to give up the ghost of a Liberal Party of the past. Trudeau's speech was 'flat and uninspired,' according to Richard Gwyn. But none of this actually mattered. Trudeaumania had been unleashed and the candidate seemed embarrassed by the tumult that followed his lacklustre performance. Rival Paul Martin took his defeat the hardest, having proclaimed that 'democracy is not a system where truths are implemented by Philosopher Kings.' He obviously had not been talking to Marshall McLuhan.

Trudeau's image of cool was preserved to the end. He mugged for the camera, sliding down a banister at the Château Laurier, tossing grapes in the air and catching them in his mouth. As the third-ballot results were announced, Trudeau was reading a scrap of paper. 'Is it your acceptance speech?' asked a reporter almost breathless with excitement. 'No,' whispered the now obviously first wise man, 'It's a love letter.' When his victory was finally announced, Trudeau plucked a carnation from his lapel and tossed it from his box to admirers below, the men with tears in their eyes, the women fluttering with faintness. It had been a love-in of the sort never before seen in Canadian history, conducted under the banner 'New guys with new ideas.' There was talk of the 'Just Society,' a term Trudeau had used in the late 1950s and possibly refined in discussions with his social-democratic colleague at the University of Montreal, F.R. Scott. Ramsay Cook developed the concept further for Trudeau in his capacity as an astute speech writer, but it was largely drowned out in the stampede of crowds. The 'Just Society' clearly took second billing in the press to Trudeau's patented kisses. Reference to participatory democracy was there as well. Its meanings, however, not to mention the mechanisms by which it would be implemented, were commented on but weakly. It all blurred into the ballyhoo. But it was beautifully scripted and carefully orchestrated, down to the 50,000 Trudeau buttons and the hordes of bouncingly attractive young women who, hours after the chief threat, Robert Winters, had his organization issue green buttons declaring, 'It's Winterstime,' were sporting tags proclaiming, 'It's Spring!'[69]

Trudeaumania rode that love-in through the spring to a late June 1968 election. The Liberals with Trudeau as their deft leader trounced the Conservatives, more than doubling their seat count. Pierre kissed more beautiful women than any other politician alive ('If it puckers, he's there,' wrote the *Globe and Mail*'s George Bain), and flipped stingingly effective insults with gay abandon (when a heckler assailed his Criminal Code amendments as permissive, shouting, 'What about masturbation?' Trudeau's quick retort put him in his place: 'I suppose everyone has his problems.'). Supporters were enraptured, especially in urban centres. 'Vive le Canada; Merci Pierre,' said a hand-painted Regina banner. Pretty co-eds were invited to join him in the hotel pool. When one declined because she lacked a bathing suit, Trudeau garnered smiles from the reporters with his reminder that 'Marilyn Monroe did it.' Eighteen-year-olds asked the prime minister for a kiss, and he complied, often discreetly shielding faces with a briefcase. Even Robert Stanfield's daughter appeared out of a Halifax gathering, wanting a closer connection to Pierre Elliott Trudeau. The campaign was all about contact with Trudeau: crowds, often huge in number, wanted to see him; people needed to touch him.

It had some political journalists worried. Charles Lynch noted that Trudeaumania, 'minimizing the risks of failure, and maximizing the advantages of Mr. Trudeau's convention-born image,' was sacrificing content 'on the altar of the shopping centre.' Itineraries were set up, from the Yukon to Newfoundland, in order to get the prime minister 'in and out of as many crowds as possible on a given day. Speechmaking is minimal, promises are played down, and no effort is made to engage, much less challenge, the minds of those present.' For Lynch it was all 'a throwaway when you think of the man's intellectual capabilities, and the range of his mind as demonstrated before he committed himself to the role of the showbiz campaigner, showing himself to the hero-hungry people.' When he did offer statements, Trudeau made no commitments. Indeed, as a commentator in the left magazine *Canadian Dimension* noted, Trudeau's public policy statements were consistently conservative 'whenever he condescended to acknowledge the existence of most political and economic issues.' Like McLuhan before him, and as McLuhan would always advise, Trudeau was learning to cool down his politics, to take fewer and fewer stands, and to make his pitch with a decided lack of lamentation and a shrugging acceptance of the world as it actually existed. Other candidates might promise a bridge or a tunnel, but from the incumbent PM their push for patronage and public works was met with a lift of the shoulders, palms upturned but empty: 'Remember you have to pay for these things. The government has no money of its own – it's your money.' Anti-war protesters thinking the hip candidate would topple to their demands to stop selling arms to the imperialists were met with a rhetorical suggestion that the country might as well terminate nickel sales too. When western wheat farmers wondered in his presence how they could move more of their crop at increased prices, Trudeau let them know that he thought the commodity overvalued already. With answers like these, Trudeau's handlers soon decided they were better off pushing style, charisma, and cheering crowds.[70]

Not all screams were libidinal, however. It was in Quebec, not surprisingly, where Trudeau's unique courage and charismatic nonchalance played most effectively. There the politics of 'One Canada' could not be avoided. Even Trudeau's silent presence galvanized violent opposition. The prime minister had agreed to join Quebec premier Daniel Johnson and Montreal's mayor Jean Drapeau on the review podium for Montreal's Saint-Jean-Baptiste Day parade. Militant advocates of Quebec independence led by Pierre Bourgault's Rassemblement pour l'Indépendance Nationale (RIN) promised to make it hot for the coolest politician in Canada. A riot erupted and Trudeau alone sat implacable on the elevated stage, many other dignitaries scattering as debris rained down on them and glass bottles whizzed by their ears. Amid the favoured cry of street protest, 'Tru-deau au pot-eau' (Trudeau to the gallows), the federalist stood his ground. Police cars were overturned and torched, 123 persons suffered injury, including 43 policemen, and Bourgault and 291 other demonstrators were arrested. In the end, by just being there, and refusing intimidation, Trudeau emerged the victor. Police and journalists applauded him, most loudly when he angrily brushed back RCMP bodyguard attempts to shield him with a coat. René Lévesque, whose sovereignty movement had been engaged in merger discussions with the RIN, opted out of further talks with the more militant separatists: 'Too many people are playing with violence like sorcerer's apprentices,' he explained. The next day a nun expressed gratification that Trudeau had not been fatally injured. Never at a loss for words, Trudeau assured her he had nothing to fear. After all, he had been 'sitting beside the Archbishop.' Even God, it seemed, was a convert to Trudeaumania. When the exacting toll of the Saint-Jean-Baptiste riot was finally tallied it counted much suffering and a staggering surge in Trudeau's popularity. Dalton Camp thought a Liberal organizer's guess that the riot was worth 40,000 votes in Toronto alone likely an understatement.

Trudeau did not really need the bump in his popularity, which had already, in a 19 June 1968 rally of 50,000 at Toronto's Nathan Phillips Square, been established decisively. Nothing like the Trudeaumania crowd had ever graced Toronto the Good politics before. Young girls skipped school, hopping out of bed at 5 a.m. to secure an adequate view of the noon-hour proceedings; white-collar workers passed up lunch to flock downtown; secretaries swooned; journalists acknowledged that Trudeau's speech was dismal but that it could not cool the crowd's ardour. It was not even politics anymore, but rather, in Peter C. Newman's words, 'some kind of public rite, new and strange to the Canadian electoral process.' Keith Mitchell, a Vancouver lawyer and Trudeau campaigner, remembered the 1968 road show as 'a national celebration.' One journalist wrote, 'You can manufacture noise and screaming kids, but you cannot manufacture that excitement in the eyes, that glistening look of rapturous excitement which is on the faces Trudeau now sees when he makes his little speeches, saying nothing, in the hotel ballrooms where the delegates gather to see him. It is not madness, not in these excited matrons and lawyers, it is belief.' The irascible Peter Worthington called it '*machismo*, charisma, magnetism, plain old fashioned sex appeal,' adding that the prime minister 'turned on Toronto as it has never been turned on before.'[71]

Turned On, Turned Off: The Dance of the Dialectic

The 1968 election crowned Trudeau as a philosopher king. To be sure, as Lotta Dempsey wrote in the *Toronto Daily Star*, Canada had purchased the proverbial pig in a poke. 'But what a pig! and what a poke!'[72] Trudeau's appeal, the victory of style over a substance that was there but had been overtaken, now had to raise its political content and wrestle with a national identity forged, incompletely, implausibly, and in great haste, in the euphoria of youthful exuberance. Kenneth McNaught christened it all 'the new politics of "style,"' and as far away as Nigeria the *Lagos Daily Times* suggested that Canada's fascination with 'youth, charm, and intelligence' was likely to be repeated in other countries' electoral contests. A 'superbly managed swinging image' complemented by 'remarkable charm' and proven 'intelligence' was apparently an unbeatable political package. The *Peterborough Examiner* editorialized that in spite of Trudeau's avoidance of policy specifics and his tendency to lapse into vague abstractions, the politics of the 1968 campaign were 'refreshingly honest' in their refusal to reproduce the old platform manner: 'Not formulae or swift solutions; not promises of subsidy or sudden charity; but a man who recognized the problems for what they were and seemed to feel that *we* – not some government agency – were capable of solving them.' From coast to coast, all agreed, it had been Trudeau's victory: 'Fascination for the leader,' declared Montreal's *La Presse*, 'was the motor in this conquest of power.'[73] For his part, Trudeau was about to take off the mask: 'I certainly intend mounting some opposition to my former self and hope to be a Prime Minister which doesn't resemble in any way the Pierre Trudeau which existed until now.'[74]

Trudeau's promise was the illusion that the nation *was* as strong, and bright, and fresh, and new, and attractive as its prime minister. It was, as Larry Zolf discerned insightfully in a zany restrospective of the early Trudeau years, *The Dance of the Dialectic: How Pierre Elliott Trudeau Went from Philosopher-King to the Incorruptible Robespierre to Philosopher-Queen Marie Antoinette to Canada's Generalissimo Ky and then to Mackenzie King and Even Better* (1973), a historical (and McLuhanesque) irony that confrontational politics seemed to have been overtaken by the possibilities the new prime minister offered in 1968. Canadians found their appetites for a politics of endless standoff in a world of growing violence saturated. There was fear of the Americanized protests that seemed to grow daily, of the spread of ghetto rebellion from Watts to Newark to Detroit. Well aware that the rallying cry of 'Quebec libre' meant an end to Canada and a reproduction of scenes of barricades and burning cars that had graced the streets of Paris, many Canadians rallied to Trudeau's federalism and its espousal of protections for francophones and other minorities. The aged Canadian politics of Diefenbaker-Pearson standoffs, now more than a decade old in their failure to produce either change or resolution, had politically exhausted the country's citizens by 1968. They longed for the extension of the feel-good atmosphere of Expo 67 and the country's centennial celebration. Trudeau was the answer:

> The age of Mackenzie King was not only dead in Ottawa but all over the country. Canadians were no longer Uriah Heepish, but rather Great Forward Leapish. Our North American affluence, minus the Vietnam-race-riots-assassination-pollution syndrome of our neighbours to the South, had given birth to a new Canadian phenomenon: self-love. The Canadian Identity, hitherto lost in the lacunae of British Connection colonialism and Roosevelt Good Neighbour continentalism, had at long last been found in the New Canadian Nationalism.

As Zolf notes, Trudeaumania, while undoubtedly manufactured in part by the electronic and print media, was also a reflection of the broadcasting and reporting journalists' 'instinctive response to the new public mood.' This mood not only tolerated cockiness, arrogance, audacity, and celebrity: it embraced the whole package as the just deserts of the philosopher king. 'The Brightest and the Best' had earned a right to govern.[75]

Philospher kings and their courts, while they burn brightly with the fire of passionate promise for the future, often find the intense heat of their project difficult to sustain. As many have pointed out, the roaring flames of Canada's celebratory 1967 festivities and their political continuation in the Trudeaumania of February–June 1968 did not take all that long to die down, leaving an ashen disappointment in the mouths of so many. Judy LaMarsh noted that in the aftermath of Expo and Trudeaumania, 'no one has asked what it is to be Canadian.' Her faith in the possibility of articulating an answer is infinite, almost religious and mystical, tied to what she witnessed in that moment of the late 1960s: 'We cast off the bonds of our conformity and slipped out of our cloak of grey anonymity forever.' The change for LaMarsh had been profound. 'We will never look back,' she insisted, although she recognized that Canadians had failed to move to new plateaus of self-understanding in the wake of the events of 1967–8. Richard Gwyn offered a more direct acknowledgment of termination: 'The 1968 election was our last joyous collective experience together,' he argues, 'the last time we were wholly confident of ourselves as a country ... we'd fulfilled our dream, in Centennial and in Expo, and now in electing a prime minister whom almost everyone envied us for.'[76] Zolf went even further, suggesting that Canadians in 1968 revelled in besting the Americans at their own game: 'Trudeaumania and charisma – the twin Trudeau engines driving the 1968 election campaign – were purely presidential. In 1968 the only truly successful presidential candidate on the continent was Trudeau.' Canadians looked at whom they had chosen for *their* leader, and they compared him to 'the American presidential bores – Tricky Dicky Nixon and Hube the Boob Humphrey.' They shrugged and smiled knowingly, adopting the arrogance of their own anointed philosopher king. 'The 1968 election was the first in which Canadians felt that their leader was smarter, brighter, sexier than the American leader,' Zolf concluded.[77] Others agreed. In May 1968 the *Chicago Daily News* proclaimed that 'neither Canada nor any other nation in the world has had a leader like Pierre Elliott Trudeau.' A New Zealand travel agency tried to promote the possibilities: 'Fly to Canada and See Trudeaumania!'[78]

Decades later, Richard Gwyn, drawn to a phrase of Stephen Clarkson and Christina McCall, suggested that Trudeau 'haunts us still.'[79] His audacity and his celebrity were central to a new Canadian identity that emerged in the 1960s, the ironies of which would not be fully apparent for decades. It seemed a magical flame, carried by a philosopher king, and many do not want to think of it as extinguished, not only by events that unfolded after 1968, but by the swirling draughts that threatened to snuff it out at the very point that it burned brightest.

As Norman DePoe closed out CBC's coverage of Trudeau's stunning 1968 leadership convention victory, amid thoughts of participatory democracy and the coming 'Just Society,' the cult of celebrity and the politics of audacity went largely unquestioned. The newsman offered a salutation to the mercurial intellect that seemed unmistakably a part of the moment. 'Goodnight, Marshall McLuhan,' he nodded in acknowledgment, 'wherever you are.'[80] Was McLuhan's whereabouts really unknown to DePoe? Or would the irony of such a moment in the making of Canadian national identity being addressed to New York somehow depress the festive mood of the country? In any case, Canadians turned off their televisions on that night in April 1968 turned on to Trudeau and the possibilities of what now, seemingly, were his dance and his decade.

What looked like an ongoing party of youth and renewal, however, was about to be rudely crashed by radical challenges. Trudeaumania foundered on the shoals of late 1960s conflicts. By the time of the October Crisis of 1970, the love affair with Trudeau had long since faded into nostalgia as the liberal state and its leader reacted to threats against individual liberty with suspensions of that very same individual liberty. The origins of this implosion lay in the discontents of postwar Canada, and they would simmer in the early to mid-1960s before boiling over in a tumultuous series of post-1968 extra-parliamentary political upheavals. Canada, as a national identity constructed over the course of a century, would never be the same again.

PART III
Suggestions of Tumult

Chapter Six

Riotous Victorianism:
From Youth Hooliganism
to a Counterculture of Challenge

Canada's oldest public holiday, Victoria Day, predates Confederation. Established in 1845 to commemorate the birthday of Princess Alexandrina Victoria on 24 May 1819, the festive occasion was purposely constructed to tighten the ties that bound Britain's remaining North American colonies to the 'mother' country. By the late nineteenth century, a leading newspaper was able to declare that Victoria Day had 'cut a deep groove in Canadian history and Canadian life,' one angled in respectability and reverence for the monarchy and its meanings of order, stability, and good governance. Not until after the monarch's death in 1901 did the Canadian Parliament establish a legal holiday formally designating Victoria Day to be the Queen's Birthday, 24 May on each year, or 25 May if the actual date of celebration fell on a Sunday. There were soon grumblings, however, especially in French Canada: Victoria Day was failing to elicit the appropriate sense of national identity rooted in the relations of imperial connection it was created to sustain. The *Montreal Gazette* noted that 'little demonstration of a patriotic nature' was exhibited. Twenty years later some observers complained that the holiday had slipped into a sorry state of slumber, observed almost apologetically. The *Manitoba Free Press* stated: 'The deadliest seventh of the sins against nationality here is "showing off," and there is always a harassing fear of the Canadian mind that any demonstration may come under this head.' If two world wars revived a sense of the dominion connection to Empire, other developments worked in

Riverdale (Toronto) youth 'gang,' 1964 (York University, *Toronto Telegram* Fonds, FO433, 1974-002/088).

opposition to such trends. Commercialized forms of leisure and the erosion of the nineteenth-century imperialist ideology of 'Canada First'
undercut recollection of what Victoria Day was meant to symbolize.
There were no doubt locales where the festive remembrance of the
Queen's Birthday was more vibrant than in the rest of the country, the
aptly named Victoria, British Columbia, being perhaps the clearest
example. Yet the symbolism of Empire Day nonetheless seemed lost on
more and more Canadians. By the 1950s the 24 May long weekend was,
depending on where you stood in the class hierarchy, the official opening of the cottage, a night to watch the local fireworks extravaganza, or
the only day in the calendar year when the loud boom of children's firecrackers was not a shock.[1]

The *London Free Press* acknowledged editorially in 1968 that 'the patriotic quality' had long faded out of Victoria Day. While Canada stood
proudly 'alone among the nations of the Commonwealth' in celebrating
'the birthday of Good Queen Victoria,' it was perhaps time to recognize
that 'durable as Victoria was the holiday has outlived her by more than
60 years.' It was long overdue, the newspaper declared, to christen
Empire Day with a new name. The year before, the *Peterborough Examiner*
had taken Victoria Day as an opportunity to scrutinize how the 'ethos of
a nation' can change abruptly, resulting in the unfortunate and arbitrary discarding of historical experience. 'Attitudes towards Confederation, the monarchy, and the British connection,' it pointed out with
sadness, were not, in the year of Canada's centennial celebrations, what
they once were. Indeed, the foundation of Victoria Day 'had begun to
crumble.' Holiday headlines at the end of May in the mid- to late 1960s
focused more on the long weekend's traffic fatalities than on the forgotten meanings of the nineteenth-century celebration.[2]

As something was lost in the nature of the day commemorating
Queen Victoria, so, too, the ideology associated with her in decline. Victorianism, the appellation of an age that conveyed something of a sociocultural ethos, had been faltering since at least the First World War. Yet
it managed to hang on, atavistically, into the 1950s. Associated with
prudery and patriarchy, the powerful subordination of class inferiors to
their identifiable masters, Victorianism thrived, as Dorothy Thompson
has noted, as nothing less than an ironic, if not contradictory, politics of
complexity. Turbulence marked Victoria's reign, yet the accent of her
public persona stressed stability and continuity. She was the longest ruling of any British monarch. Inheriting a throne strapped for cash and
characterized by declining influence and respect, Victoria left her royal
family rich in revenues and the resources of hegemonic power. As a

woman in an age of aggressive imperialism and entrenched patriarchal assumptions, Victoria did much to confine women to the domestic sphere. Yet as a head of state in one of the world's pre-eminent powers, she also undermined age-old conceptions of 'the female station' and paved the way for considerable change in the twentieth-century world of gender relations. Victoria and Victorianism, then, were a contradiction in motion, poised to proclaim one set of values while their every working enterprise brought opposing developments closer and closer to fruition. As Perry Anderson notes, 'the "manifest" function of the monarchy was (by assertion) to unify the nation; its "latent" function was (by example) to stratify it.'[3]

At a distance, this Victorian social dynamic, transferred to Canada, was of course marking time in a slow demise. Within that seemingly gradualist decline lay the seeds of a violent implosion in which the embrace of authority was finally met with its repudiation; the reverence for institutions of stability was eventually confronted with the proclamation of disorder; age-old traditionalism, an invention of a previous epoch, found itself challenged by the birth pangs of the present's necessity to break out of confinement. The 1960s would unfold as a testing ground of such contentious impulses. It should come as no surprise that the springboard into this sociocultural cauldron of conflict would be a demographic cohort with little attachment to the past, a contingent of youth increasingly distanced from the moorings of the dominion's discernible ties to Empire. Small wonder that the divorce of the old and the new would unfold in what could be designated a riotous Victorianism. The origins of this lay in Canadian youth's mid-century alienations, a generalized movement disrupting the past certainties of integration into family and nation. By the 1960s, these ties of accommodation had been weakened considerably, if not frayed to the breakpoint.[4]

Youth, Identity, and Delinquency at Mid-Century

The problems specific to youth have long been the concern of Canadian and U.S. commentators. Definitions of delinquency were put forward in the nineteenth century and, with the rise of progressive thought in the immediate years after 1900, 'child savers' such as J.J. Kelso and the settlement house heroine Jane Addams offered their thoughts with respect to youth and social crisis in publications and on numerous podiums. A sociology of the 'city boy,' and his particular problems, often associated with a culture of poverty and the improvised street gang, emerged in the years before the First World War. Class deprivations overrode all other concerns in this literature, driven as it was by the obligation of improving conditions so that children would grow up to be good rather than bad. By the 1920s in Canada, with the first stirrings of mass culture and the recognized rise of modern youth, the 'teenager' was identified as a distinct social, economic, and demographic being.[5]

With the 1950 publication of Erik H. Erikson's *Childhood and Society*, identity emerged as a central analytic category of the social sciences. Concentrating on adolescence as the passageway leading from childhood to adulthood, Erikson understood youth as engaged in a search for identity, analogous in its liberal outcome in the sovereign individual to the realization of national identity in the process of nineteenth-century state formation. As such, given its intellectual formation in the context of the Second World War and the Cold War, the Eriksonian understanding of youth identity was that it was an anxiety-ridden stage in the struggle to realize political selfhood or subjectivity. It could only be appreciated in opposition to those totalitarianisms of Soviet communism and German fascism that defined the liberal American ideal of mid-century, and supposedly subordinated the individual to the collective, often in ways judged both socially and psychologically violent. 'Responsible Americans know the danger emanating from a "total war" machine and from its facsimile in peacetime,' Erikson asserted, his coded framework confident of its certainties. The problem of youth in this new age was thus posed in ways that broke from all past historical understandings. Precisely because youth was an identity subset, a conduit in the making of a larger national identity, children were now conceived as partners of adults. Adolescents were bodies in mid-passage, no longer merely dependents, but not quite fully autonomous agents.

As such, youth needed to nurture appreciations of what an identity of freedom entailed, in which rights and responsibilities were the reciprocities of entitlements and the largesse of consumerism. On a world historic scale, the bounty of U.S. capitalism was now a 'friendly coerciveness.' It threw 'gadgets and robots' into the world market and created 'revolutionized economic conditions' at home and abroad. If this was the ultimate weapon in the Cold War, its domestic fallout could be great. 'Our new and shiny goods,' wrote Erikson, 'so enticingly wrapped in promises of freedom,' had to be something more than merely 'sedatives' and 'opiates' lulling the masses into subservience to 'worn-out upper classes' and conditioning a 'new serfdom of hypnotized consumership.' Youth, in its perennial quest for identity, should not be granted freedom as a gift; instead, it needed to 'be given the opportunity to grasp it, as equals,' so that it could be savoured as earned. As Leerom

Medovoi has insightfully suggested, this Eriksonian understanding of adolescent identity, which proliferated as a popular and academic discourse in the 1950s, set the analytic stage on which youth identities clashed in a post–Second World War affluent parade, the underside of which was anomie, alienation, and angst.[6]

This gave rise to a newly intensified focus on the 'teenager.'[7] Nonconformist, rebellious youth emerged as a feature of modern capitalist society. This cohort figured forcefully in the 1950s writings of Robert K. Lindner, which built on his 1944 study *Rebel without a Cause: The Hypnoanalysis of a Criminal Psychopath.* With the immense appeal of Nicholas Ray's 1955 Hollywood film of the same name, James Dean was canonized as the symbolic representation of rebel youth.[8] As Edgar Z. Friedenberg would state, unequivocally, at the end of the 1950s, 'adolescence *is* conflict – protracted conflict – between the individual and society.'[9]

The 1950s discourse on a contentious youth identity stretched old continuities reaching back to the 1920s into newer, and more taut, sociocultural understandings. 'Expert' commentary and a widening popular culture of film, television, and printed text elevated the increasingly public significance of the 'teenager.' All of this was riddled in irony. Conceived as an *ideological* project in the making of national identity, youth as a separate stage in this realization was necessarily driven by ambivalences, expressions of a two-way traffic on capitalist North America's freedom road. Yet the adoption of rebel or conformist personas was never, for youth, predetermined, and the ultimate victory of conformity was itself dependent on the possibility of rebellion. This supposedly kept Canada and the United States distinct from other 'organized societies.' Conformity needed rebellion to rationalize its adaptations; rebellion confirmed the rightness of conformity.[10]

A prolonged baby boom massively expanded the demographics of consumption on the part of youth, an identity that was now a material mainstay of capitalist production. This coincided with the rising ideology and actuality of affluence, so central to the postwar years. In the 1950s and 1960s the commercialization of the teenager, and the growth of new sectors of mass consumption linked to youth markets of entertainment, leisure, fashion, and education, provided an unprecedented stimulus to economic growth and expansion. With children partnered to paying adults, they soon championed a sense of rights that expanded the marketplace significantly.[11] As U.S. pediatrician Dr Benjamin Spock advised: 'When children show a universal craving for something, whether the comics or candy or jazz, we've got to assume it has a positive, constructive value for them.' An advertisement in *Maclean's* took

this to entrepreneurial heart, asking its Canadian readers in 1953, 'How
are you tackling the serious business of play? For it is a serious business –
nothing could be more mistaken than the notion that there is anything
trivial in a child's preoccupation with its toys.'[12]

There were three difficulties with all of these developments. First, not
everyone welcomed them. Second, they opened a Pandora's box of
youth acts and aggressions that those dissatisfied with the developing
culture of adolescent entitlement feared and loathed. Third, with youth
not always able consciously to cultivate, even consistently to navigate,
their way on the road to identity's realization, adults, especially those in
positions of power, could well do it for them. This was most emphatically the case if that adult power was pitted against the direction of
youth activity, labelling and caricaturing behaviours that appeared, in
spite of an undeniable and lengthy historical presence, as new and
threatening.

Thus, as the teenager was constructed, so too was juvenile delinquency, ostensibly raging rampant, rediscovered and reconfigured as
the dangerous offshoot of youth's quest for identity.[13] Especially worrisome, in the words of one 1955 pop criminology tract, grandiosely titled
1,000,000 Delinquents, was the biological threat of the bad seed sprouting in good environments, a troubling process of cross-class fertilization:
'It can go on spreading and contaminate many good cells in our society
… Juvenile delinquency is already creeping from the wrong side of the
tracks to the right side.'[14]

Such fears would gain momentum as the Angry Young Men of the
Beat generation began, at the close of the 1950s, to flee middle-class
suburbs and settled, respectable working-class neighbourhoods, often
relocating to the metaphorical wrong side of the tracks. They inhabited
a world of Negroes, Hispanics, migrant labourers, and the casually
employed, crossing boundaries of respectability and criminality in their
drug use and disdain for convention. An embrace of marginality would
be evident in the frenzied mobility of their prose, boldly leaping off the
covers of books with titles such as *Go* and *On the Road*. Juvenile delinquency appeared to have grown into a movement of deviance and
detached dissidence, the birth of what Norman Mailer problematically
called 'The White Negro.' The Beats donned the dress of Lindner's
rebellion without a cause, sneering, as *Life* put it in 1959, 'at virtually
every aspect of current American society: Mom, Dad, Politics, Marriage,
the Savings Bank, Organized Religion,' and the entire edifice of suburban consumption and Cold War conformity.[15]

Many thus recoiled from 'the scourge known as Juvenile Delinquency,' even if crime statistics did not confirm a new threat to social
order.[16] Ostensibly promiscuous girls[17] and thieving, violent boys nevertheless proved a worrisome and potent mixture to fearful, respectable
adults, however exaggerated the narratives of transgression. Magazines
such as *Saturday Night*, *Maclean's*, and *Chatelaine* all contributed to a
growing Canadian chorus of concern with youth crime in the late 1940s
and 1950s. Cities such as Toronto convened conferences and commissioned reports on the perception that juvenile antisocial behaviour was
becoming a serious problem.[18] Conservative MP E. Davie Fulton railed
in the House of Commons about the pernicious influence of comics.
In concert with American anti-comics activist Dr Frederick Wertham,
Fulton led a crusade to ban such dangerous children's publications.
The Tory campaigner took his cause to a United States Subcommittee
to Investigate Juvenile Delinquency. Fulton's June 1954 testimony supported findings of Dr Frederic Wertham's recently published book,
Seduction of the Innocent, which stated that comic books were a cause of
juvenile delinquency.[19]

Reports of rising youth crime rates proliferated, but little attempt was
made to discern how crime was being defined and how it related to population change, more rigorous record keeping, increasing attention to
youth criminality on the part of police, the expanding number of jurisdictions reporting statistics relating to juvenile transgressions, and other
such questions.[20] At the time when Fulton and others first popularized a
late-1940s political panic around juvenile delinquency, youth conviction
ratios per 100,000 population were actually dropping and would continue to do so until 1954. Thereafter, the ratio rose until it reached and
then surpassed the comparable figure from 1946. Moreover, the raw
numbers of those between 7 and 16 years of age being convicted
seemed to be climbing over the last half of the 1950s. In a slightly older
group the statistics appeared even more alarming. Canadian Welfare
Council workers bemoaned 'the tragic trend' of youths in the 16–19-
year-old age group being convicted of major crimes and indictable
offences. Those found guilty in such cases between 1954 and 1959 had
supposedly jumped from 5,547 to 9,734.[21] The growing fear of juvenile
delinquency intensified in the late 1950s. By the end of the decade
Edgar Friedenberg's *The Vanishing Adolescent* would proclaim 'There is
obviously something in adolescence itself that both troubles and titil-
lates many adults. The "teen-ager" seems to have replaced the Communist as the appropriate target for public controversy and foreboding.'[22]

As Canada entered the 1960s, concern with juvenile delinquency showed no signs of abating, especially as reports from the British Isles highlighted a growing youth problem in the brawls of Mods and Rockers.[23] In 1961 Fulton, now the minister of justice, told a Winnipeg gathering of the Canadian Bar Association that the rise in juvenile crime was extremely troubling. Less than five months later, on 8 January 1962, he announced the striking of a special parliamentary committee to study delinquency and the 'mounting juvenile crimes of violence and moral offences.' It would finally report in 1965.[24] *Maclean's* estimated in July 1961 that if the trends of that year continued 'there will likely be between 14,000 and 18,000 juvenile convictions by 1966.' Delinquency rates in Vancouver were supposedly running at twice the national average, with drug addiction a serious problem. In Toronto, juvenile court judges reported a tripling of delinquents appearing before them in the 1958–61 period. 'We have the greatest workload in our history now before the courts,' claimed Judge Lorne Stewart, pointing to the annual total of 3,564 cases. Across the country, boy and girl convictions for various offences climbed from 15,215 to 18,352 over the course of the early 1960s, an increase of 20 per cent. Approximately 85 per cent of such youth crime was committed by males, with the bulk of the charges relating to theft and breaking and entering; serious crimes of violence, such as murder, manslaughter, and rape constituted only slightly more than 2 per cent of all young offender convictions.[25] Increasingly worrisome were 'the number of offences committed by adolescents from staid, respectable old neighborhoods and elaborately planned new suburbs,' the crimes perpetrated by the 'have' delinquents nurtured on the 'ultra-materialistic world' of their parents' consumer capitalism.[26]

A Communist Party of Canada publication, *Poison for the Young*, thought such figures 'ominous.' It pointed a left finger at a cast of usual suspects: sensationalist violence on television, smut pulp fiction, lurid newspaper headlines, pornography, and the much-maligned comic. Mark Frank, author of the treatment, lined up with Wertham and his *Seduction of the Innocent* screed. He cast his lot as well with James V. Bennett, director of the U.S. federal prison system, who insisted on the 'definite relationship' between teenage crime and television, studies having shown that 95 per cent of juvenile offenders watched TV three to four hours a day. The communist differed from the American conservatives in various ways. He insisted, for instance, that comics provided the kind of dulling of the senses towards violence that proved an 'ideal formula for those who argue about the inevitability of nuclear war.' Frank also proposed that the anti-communist narratives of Cold War pulp fictions were a particular variant of 'the deliberate inundation with horror for the sake of breeding a generation of youth that will with equanimity exterminate whole peoples by dropping nuclear bombs or splashing napalm on them.'

The communist pamphlet's strident anti-Americanism separated it out from the usual delinquency fear-mongering. Frank bemoaned the flooding of Canada by 'books for birchers,' in which the heroes and heroines were 'pimps, prostitutes, sadists, sex-maniacs, and opponents of state welfare, unions, socialism, and communism.' He deplored the cinematic excess of Hollywood: 'blood, decapitation, and barbarism' were supplemented by 'sex, crime, and atom-bombing.' But it was 'cold-war comics inciting race hatred and war' that garnered his particular ire. Such publications, 'U.S. poison pulps fed to children,' made their American corporate owners millions but left Canadian youth disturbed, neurotic, and prone to criminal activity. Calling for a massive clean-up of bookstalls, television programming, and radio broadcasting, *Poison for the Young* advocated the wide participation of churches, home and school organizations, trade unions, and farm bodies in meetings and conferences on juvenile delinquency. Probes into the effects of TV, radio, movies, comics, pulps, pornography, and pocketbooks on youth crime rates should be made. 'A citizen's machinery for controlling the spread of gutter-type publications' needed to be established. It could provide a mandate to 'cleanse the atmosphere' by developing 'restrictions at the border against the Made-In-U.S.A. ... tide of poison that is sweeping the land.' Likening the influx of such material to the selling of rotten meat or foodstuffs tainted with arsenic or strychnine, Frank denied that such restriction on 'mental poisons' constituted censorship. Instead, the adoption of such measures would make it 'entirely possible to muzzle the purveyors of violence, sadism, distorted sex values and the cold war, the unwholesome and massive character of which is doing so much incalculable harm to the younger generation.' To fail to act was to condemn Canada to a rising tide of violence, a prime example of which, in Frank's judgment, was the spring 1961 teenage riots at Toronto shopping plazas.[27]

In alluding to such youth riots, Frank inadvertently stumbled on a missing link. Between the socially constructed 1950s panic over juvenile delinquency and the rise of a 1960s politics of alternative and challenge lay the shadow of youth's conflicted rebel-conformist identity.[28] In Canada, this shadow first surfaced on the streets and sidewalks of Victoria

Day, as the children of the 1950s aged into the rowdies and hooligans of the early to mid-1960s. They, in turn, would give way to francophone youth chanting 'The Queen to the Gallows' in Montreal parks as the independence movement grew to prominence in 1963–4. This politics of challenge would later, in English Canada, be paralleled by the alternative message of the flower children of 1967–8 who congregated in Toronto's Yorkville.[29]

Riotous Victorianism

The 24th of May is the Queen's birthday
If we don't get a holiday we'll all run away.[30]

Victoria Day celebrations in the early to mid-1960s were varied and many. Across the country a diverse array of activities unfolded. The annual parade drew a huge throng of 75,000 in Victoria, British Columbia, in 1960. On the mainland, New Westminster kept alive a long-standing twenty-one-explosion salute, the crack of gunpowder placed between two anvils announcing the holiday festivities. At the Six Nations reserve near Brantford, 800 pounds of cheese and 700 loaves of bread donated in the Queen's name by the federal government were distributed to Aboriginal families on the annual 'Bread and Cheese Day,' a tradition dating back to the nineteenth century. Halifax marked its 1960 Empire Day with the fiftieth anniversary of the Royal Canadian Navy, the fleet coming home and 10,000 sailors swelling the eastern port's celebrations.[31]

There was also some running associated with the 24th of May holiday, as the popular children's ditty associated with Victoria Day suggested. The fleet-of-foot, however, didn't make haste quietly. Often they were pursued by police, and something other than patriotism and the British connection quickened their pace. The holiday weekend was associated with juvenile vandalism and pranks, directed at what was undoubtedly the primary institution of youth containment, the school. But the traditional spring feverish battering in of school doors, flooding of classrooms, setting of fires, smashing of inkwells against walls and blackboards, and ransacking of teachers' desks soon graduated to another level, one more threatening to public order.[32]

Victoria Day in the early 1960s was marred by riotous crowds of urban youths throwing firecrackers, lighting bonfires in city thoroughfares, torching sheds, and battling cops and firemen for control of the street.

As happened in countless south-central and western Ontario locales, Victoria Day in 1961 began with children tossing firecrackers into dilapidated and sometimes abandoned buildings, resulting in fire damages approaching $400,000. Such property loss, as well as injuries to persons and the mobilization of firemen and police, inevitably gave rise to calls that specific practices be curbed. A spate of local bylaws were passed restricting the sale and setting off of fireworks, but there was little that could apparently be done to harness the roving bands of youths that gathered annually for an evening of stylized riot.[33]

In Hamilton, the rioting was perhaps the most ritualized, concentrated at a specific set of intersections along James Street – Ferrie, Strachan, and Picton – and erupting for four years running from 1961 to 1964. 'Small gangs of disorderly children' roamed Hamilton on Victoria Day from early morning to early evening, tossing firecrackers with abandon, stuffing glass jars and bottles with explosives, lighting them, and running for cover. With dusk, however, the nature of the troublemaking changed. The first year of serious confrontation, 1961, saw 400 youngsters pelt the initial wave of law enforcement – six officers and a police dog named Sandy – with cannon-type firecrackers. As newspaper boxes were set ablaze, gasoline fires were lit in the streets, and tires put to the torch. The crowd soon overwhelmed the small police forces, refusing to disperse, and continued the bombardment of firecrackers, necessitating the calling out of reserves. Arrests were futile, it being impossible to establish who was throwing the incendiary missiles from the large and unruly mob. An ice cream vendor wheeled his truck into the melee and did a roaring business. It seemed the world had turned upside down, and youth were finally on top, slurping ice cream and tossing 'bangers' at uniformed authority. The *Hamilton Spectator* deplored 'the noisy climax to Victoria Day,' bemoaning the 'frightening defiance of the law.' In the end roughly twenty-five policemen were called in to cope with the crowd, the dog was forced into protective custody in a cop car, and it was not until midnight that the streets were cleared and safe.[34]

The next two years saw repeat performances. Local newspapers carried bold-print headlines: 'Hundreds Rampage, Attack Police, Set Fires' and 'Mob of 400 Throws Firecrackers.' Reporters concluded that 'violence and mob rampages have become a Victoria Day tradition in Hamilton.' Close to 1,000 'rampaging youths' burned a two-storey frame building to the ground in 1963. Police were assaulted; a cruiser immobilized when the crowd let the air out of its tires; those arrested struggled to free themselves; and the more audacious rioters made off with an officer's badge, nightstick, and hat, prized trophies in the field day of carnage. Those foolhardy enough to come to the aid of the embattled police found themselves trapped in their cars, which were surrounded and then rocked by hostile, menacing youth. Street fire flames roared fifteen feet high. It took twenty-four police and five arrests for 'creating a disturbance' and 'obstructing police' to quiet the scene, which produced only 'a stalemate' between the officers and the shouting youthful crowd, members of which carried gallon jugs of gasoline.[35]

In 1964 the police bumped their numbers up to 30 and the crowd dwindled to 300, resulting in subdued Victoria Day hooliganism. From the sidelines, 'teen age girls urged boyfriends to trample the flatfeet.' Braving insults and harassment, as well as countless 'canons' tossed at their feet, the cops made only three arrests and let the restless crowd of youths wear itself out. One veteran of Victoria Day riots past thought it all rather disappointing. 'The whole thing's a bust,' he complained, explaining that 'the older fellas – the ones who used to light cans of gasoline, slash tires, and fight with the police – are married with families. So they don't want any part of this, except to watch, and the younger crowd, well they just haven't got what it takes.'[36]

Despite threats that Hamilton's north end would riot again in 1965, police meandered among loitering youth, keeping 'the celebrants' in line and arresting three ringleaders of a 'disorderly gang.' After midnight a roving band of twenty youths took out their frustrations on a couple of Volkswagens, rocking them until they tipped over into the street.[37] A once-routinized Victoria Day clash of police and Hamilton hooligans failed to materialize. The bloom of youthful, riotous Victorianism had apparently faded in the Mountain City.

In nearby Toronto, riotous Victorianism was more subdued. An archetypal Victoria Day confrontation took place between 700 youths and onlookers and city police and firefighters in 1965. A 'gang of juveniles' set a fire in downtown Stanley Park, adjacent to the Canadian National Exhibition grounds, and then battled Toronto firefighters when they appeared on the scene to extinguish the conflagration. They wrestled firemen to the ground in a tug-of-war for the hoses, protecting and feeding the blazing pile of fencing, mattresses, and trash, throwing gasoline-filled bottles on the burning pyre as firefighters struggled to put it out. When twenty-five police appeared on the scene, the crowd jeered and booed.[38]

The year before, inflated fears of gang-related juvenile delinquency in the Regent Park public housing complex coincided with reports of rumbles and gang fights pitting the combined forces of the Regent Park Regents and the Spadina Spooks against teenagers from Clifton House, the Working Boys Home of Toronto. Bad blood had existed between the groups and associated gangs since a 1963 'Riverdale Rumble.' Police broke up two ostensible 1964 youth disturbances, one in the last week of May, another in the second week of June. A year later, on 10 June 1965, teenagers fought en masse on Toronto Island. A study conducted from November 1964 to January 1965 acknowledged that teens congregating at a Root N' Burger located in a Regent Park South shopping plaza had been targeted by police, who maintained a close surveillance of the juveniles, many of whom had minor brushes with the law and youth courts. Amid reports of seized weapons and charges of police racism directed against black youth, cruisers tailed young neighbourhood residents walking the streets and harassed them relentlessly. Frank Adams of the *Globe and Mail* thought the cops had a case of the 'youth gang rumble jitters.' He noted that police were breaking up baseball games in unauthorized areas, chasing teenagers out of schoolyards where they congregated at night, physically moving them off of street corners. In one case, sweeping down on a plaza parking lot in response to a reported battle of rival gangs, the police found an impromptu twist party on the go.[39]

Disorder also threatened the Yorkville district, as an emerging coffee-house culture drew alienated youth to late-night hangouts north of Bloor between Yonge and Spadina. Tensions mounted in 1964–5, especially in May and June, as long-haired youth thronged to the 'Village,' a cultural formation defined by liberated sexuality, availability of drugs, and the rising crescendo of rock 'n' roll which had overtaken an earlier folk scene.[40] Merchants complained of routine vandalism, of motorcycle toughs holding up traffic, and of 'near riots' in May 1964. With crowds of 13-, 14-, and 15-year olds wandering the streets at 2 a.m., fear of gang destructiveness gripped local businessmen. They were outraged that their establishments were being denied fire insurance, placed on what was commonly referred to in the racist terminology of insurance companies as 'Indian lists,' properties judged to be high-risk because of the 'danger of riots and fires.' 'There is an air of tension here,' reported one alderman, 'You feel like you are in a foreign … territory taken over by teenagers.'[41] As a moral panic swept the local newspapers, undercover and uniformed beat cops patrolled Yorkville's narrow byways and alleys in pairs, municipal authority declaring that it was on a crusade to clean up the streets. Toronto City Council toyed with legislative prohibitions to curb the 'rowdies,' 'toughs,' and 'punks,' but it was all to no avail: the young kept pouring into Yorkville. Three years later, in August 1967, 300 protesting flower children clashed with police as they sat in and lay down in the middle of Yorkville Avenue, demanding that the streets be liberated from the cars and turned over to the people.[42]

In the western Ontario resort town of Grand Bend, the mid-to-late 1960s were something of a war zone on Victoria Day holiday weekends. The annual riotous celebrations had their origins in earlier cottage-based teenage parties that routinely saw dozens arrested for underage drinking or consuming alcoholic beverages in a public place. Later in the decade, events took on a more public and confrontational character. Hundreds of teenagers roamed the streets, clashing with police, smashing beer bottles, lighting firecrackers, brazen in their defiance of the beefed-up Ontario Provincial Police (OPP) detachment of twenty-five that struggled, often unsuccessfully, to keep order. Suburban youth from regional urban centres such as London made a yearly trek to 'The Bend.' They camped out at nearby Ipperwash Provincial Park, hauling coolers and cases of beer into tents or stocking the fridges of parents' or friends' cottages. They were joined by border-crossing caravans of Michigan teenagers and young adults, as well as by local motorcycle gangs from as far away as Toronto and Windsor. By ten o'clock in the evening, the main street was lined with Harley-Davidsons, Nortons, BSAs, and other 'bikes,' many of them 'chopped' and customized with chrome extensions and luscious paint jobs. Cars loaded with kids made the promenade up and down the street, hooting, yelling, and whistling. As the clocks ticked toward midnight, ritualized clashes with police increased, culminating in gauntlets of youths lining the streets, insulting the cops, and showering them with lit firecrackers and beer bottles. Arrests followed.

Cold weather was the OPP's best friend, for it curbed the holiday influx into the resort village, kept the drinking down and the motorcycle gangs in check, and made it more likely that the crowds would thin as the night wore on and the temperatures dropped. In 1967, for instance, the arrest total was a meagre 23 and the crowd not much more than 700, the modest numbers attributed to the mercury falling well below freezing. For the first time in years it was reported that 'the first round in the annual confrontation with troublesome teenagers' had gone to the police. Still, it was a victory that shocked many of the law and order brigade, trucked into Grand Bend from other provincial police centres, trained in crowd control at a crash course in nearby Clinton. 'I've never experienced anything like this before,' reported one recent transferee, asking if reporters could provide him with a few pictures 'to send to the boys back at the detachment to see what we are doing here.'[43]

Not surprisingly, Montreal was also an early centre of riotous Victorianism. The city had a history of holiday hooliganism that predated the 1960s, and riots in 1959 were violent, culminating in fifty-eight arrests. Motorists who braved the fire-strewn streets of hard-hit districts were pelted with debris and lit firecrackers; burning barricades blocked main thoroughfares; and wooden staircases on the outside of the city's patented triplex row housing were often put to the match by 'rampaging youths.' Unlike Hamilton, there was no particular locale of preference, and fires and brawls were widely dispersed, although the main trouble spots were the southwest working-class districts of St Henri, Point St Charles, St Cunegonde, and Griffintown. With regular police forces supplemented by 20 extra squad cars, 22 unmarked vehicles, and 160 officers, as well as Montreal's entire firefighting personnel, the authorities had prepared for the worst in 1960. Precautionary measures included removal of all inflammable trash from the city's ubiquitous alleyways, but this did not seem to slow down the 'celebrants' from finding rubber tires, scrap wood, broken furniture, old clothes, and discarded sofas to pile into the streets and torch, the flames further fed by generous applications of coal oil. If the rowdy crowds were not using the match, they were flooding the streets by opening fire hydrants or baffling their police/firemen combatants with false alarms, estimated through the night at fifty per hour. Montreal's 1960 Victoria Day hooliganism led to twenty-four arrests, injuries to nine firemen, and a massive clean-up of charred street refuse.[44]

Next year municipal authorities were determined to put a stop, in Mayor Drapeau's words, to the 'disgraceful … criminal vandalism' of Victoria Day. Neighbourhoods were flooded with circulars denouncing past rowdyism; letters were sent to priests, ministers, and school trustees; visits were made to homes and classrooms. Municipal judges warned of stiff sentences for transgressors. A local member of the National Assembly staged a parade to appeal to all his constituents to be on their best behaviour. Walking beside him in the solemn procession were the widows and children of firemen who had died recently in the line of duty. The assistant police director assured all concerned that with almost 400 officers on duty and nearly 90 vehicles patrolling the streets, order would prevail. Montreal's fire director backed him up, promising the full force of his 200-man department. Predicting massive arrests if Victoria Day revellers broke the law, the police chief issued a stern rebuke: 'We are determined to put a stop to the nonsense that has been going on for years.' 'Get Tough' was the new slogan of Montreal's preparedness campaign in the war against riotous Victorianism.[45]

As the postmortem headlines of the holiday proclaimed, the campaign was not an immediate and unmitigated success: 'Hooligans Mostly Ignore "Get Tough" Warning.' The southwest districts were again ablaze, with bonfires, torched cars, false fire alarms proliferating up to 1 a.m. and gangs in the hundreds roaming the streets. They were observed by a trio of crowd, police, and fire control experts, brought in by the city to advise it on how best to contain the mob; one was a former chief of police from Hull, Quebec, another a past member of the Paris prefecture. The accent, however, was on a massive police and firefighting presence in the streets, with 600 patrolling, controlling crowds, and putting out burning refuse. They were complemented by rubbish trucks which prowled the districts scooping up anything that could be set afire, watering trucks able to flush fires into the gutter, and plainclothes detectives instructed to nab anyone stepping out of line. More arrests were made than in the previous year, thirty-five in total, but Montreal's variant of riotous Victorianism had been tamed. An assistant police chief declared the entire scene one of 'vast improvement' over previous years, noting that there was 'nothing to compare' to the 1961 events and the tumultuous hooliganism of 1959 and 1960. Damage was slight, and riotous Victorianism in Montreal appeared to be in decline.[46]

But as it happens, hooliganism would, like Marx's Old Mole, reappear, albeit in different circumstances and with a purpose now markedly changed. The riotous Victorianism of the early 1960s, a pre-political rowdyism that stood in stark defiance of all order, went into subterranean retreat in the face of a dual defeat, internal and external. On its own internal terms, traditional riotous Victorianism had undoubtedly illuminated the irrelevance of respect within the national identity for a British connection. This link to nineteenth-century Empire was, on the one hand, fading fast by the early 1960s. Yet, on the other, Victoria Day riots were by this late date an inadequate expression of popular disillusionments. It is not surprising that this process unfolded most violently and with an accelerated velocity in the poor francophone districts of Montreal, where the link to Empire was weakest in all of Canada. The forces of order within Quebec managed to drive riotous Victorianism underground, as indeed would be the case in other locales. It was ironic, of course, that riotous Victorianism would be seemingly defeated in the very place where it was apparently strongest. Yet the further irony was that this defeat was not permanent, and Montreal would witness the revival of a new and potent riotous Victorianism in the early 1960s, one which transformed youth hooliganism into a politics of challenge. The dialectic of development ensured that yesterday's rebels without a cause would, in future days, be replaced or altered, their rebellion more focused and direct. Victoria Day hooliganism, once a celebration of no order, was becoming a protest demanding a different order. 'Well grubbed, old mole!' Marx would proclaim, borrowing from Shakespeare's *Hamlet.*[47]

Separatist Celebrants of Victoria Day

Montreal's Victoria Day celebrations in May of 1963 were dreaded more than usual. For two and a half months the city had been traumatized by a new movement called the Front de Libération du Québec (FLQ/Felquistes). Inspired by Frantz Fanon's 1961 anti-colonialist manifesto *The Wretched of the Earth,*[48] repulsed by the centuries-long history of Québécois subordination and oppression at the hands of Anglo-American and English-Canadian capital, the Felquistes emerged in the early 1960s as the ultra-left, direct-action alternative to Jean Lesage's liberalizing Quiet Revolution.[49]

An underground, cell-ordered movement, the FLQ drew in its earliest days on three dissident constituencies. First were those gathered around the expatriate Belgian Georges Schoeters, whose formative experience lay in the anti-Nazi resistance of the the Second World War. Second was a growing corps of young and militant members of the Rassemblement pour l'Indépendance Nationale, or RIN. Their leading figure, Pierre Bourgault, had ostensibly tired of the seeming futility of building a mass separatist movement through legal propaganda, political organization, and public demonstration. Many in this quarter thought that the RIN should remain the legal arm of the *indépendantiste* movement, but it needed to be supplemented with a clandestine corps of activists. Third and finally was a left-separatist body, Action Socialiste.[50]

Composed of such activists, the FLQ burst on the scene with an 8 March 1963 Molotov cocktail assault on three Quebec armouries. The bombing of a railway track and an explosion at an army recruiting centre followed. In the case of the latter undertaking, an incendiary device supposedly abandoned in a garbage can by Felquistes scared off by police detonated tragically, inadvertently killing a night watchman, 65-year old Vincent Wilfrid O'Neill.[51] This loss of life created a huge backlash, one that gathered intensity as a mid-April Felquiste 'Message to the Nation' exploded on the public scene, where it was widely discussed, debated, and denounced.[52] Addressed to all 'Patriots,' the revolutionary statement was a ringing call 'to arms,' an unabashed refusal of colonial subordination and class exploitation. Proclaiming that 'The Hour of National Revolution Has Struck!' the subterranean FLQ, drawing for inspiration on Fidel Castro's late 1950s Cuban cry of 'Revolucion o Muerte,' demanded 'Independence or Death!'[53]

Victoria Day 1963 was overshadowed by these developments, which saw the initial phase of FLQ bombing come to a close in June, police arresting twenty-three people in what was the first stage of a massive crackdown that saw the entire Felquiste underground in jail or under police surveillance by the end of the year. Thirteen incendiary devices were discovered in Westmount mailboxes on Friday, 17 May 1963. One blew up as it was being dismantled by an army bomb-disposal expert, resulting in the loss of his arm. A dynamite explosion rocked a regimental building in a francophone district to rubble on the following Monday. Montreal's municipal authorities were in no mood to mollycoddle Victoria Day revellers.

Dedicated to the destruction and desecration of all institutions of colonial oppression and all monuments celebrating their history, the FLQ had authorities rightly convinced that a politicization of the traditional rowdiness associated with the monarch's birthday fête was in the making. City officials let it be known that fires and firecrackers were the last thing they wanted to see and hear on the holiday, let alone placards or cries proclaiming 'The Queen to the Gallows.' As the French-Canadian mainstream press denounced FLQ 'terrorism' as 'murderous madness,' military 'bomb-men' were flown into the city from Chilliwack, British Columbia. NATO envoys were put on full security alert for a three-day ministerial conference in Ottawa. Liberal Premier Jean Lesage placed a $50,000 price on the heads of any Felquistes arrested and convicted in the spring 1963 bombing wave, the city of Montreal kicking in a further $10,000. A relatively quiet 24 May 1963 weekend was assured, most of the old-time street revellers no doubt pressured to restrain themselves. But the FLQ did its best to make a bang: Operation Chenier, named after one of the heroes of the 1837–8 Rebellions, saw the Felquistes detonate their largest-ever bomb, composed of seventy-five sticks of dynamite, against the weapons room wall of the Sainte-Grégoire

Street Montreal barracks on the holiday evening of 20 May. To the east in Quebec City, after a respectable waiting period, Queen Victoria's statue was blown up in July. Fifteen months later Queen Elizabeth II and Prince Philip commemorated the centenary of the discussions leading to Confederation with a royal visit to Canada. She graced Quebec City with her presence on 10 October 1964. Independence forces gave her a warm, if unexpected, welcome. A hostile crowd lined the streets to jeer the Queen's entourage and turn their backs on the monarch as she drove by. Nightstick-swinging police charged the rude protest ranks, leaving six injured (including some innocent monarchist bystanders gathered to hail the royal couple) and arresting thirty-five. The event was quickly memorialized in an emerging radical reading of modern Quebec history, dubbed 'Truncheon Saturday.'[54]

Empire Day clearly was not a part of the annual calendar the emerging separatist movement, centred in Montreal, was content to continually let pass with a quiet beer on the porch. By 1964, FLQ supporters and other groups dedicated to the militant struggle for Quebec independence were ready for a confrontation, one that took on the trappings of riotous Victorianism but that infused it with the passions of a struggle for national liberation and socialist understandings of justice and equality. Ten hours of demonstrations and scuffles with police marked the Victoria Day protests, which saw a bomb discovered on a bridge spanning the St Lawrence River, wires cut along Canadian Pacific Railroad tracks, and massive traffic snarls. Students at a French-language high school showed up for classes in defiance of the official closing. To show their displeasure, they burned the Canadian Red Ensign flag, symbolic of the British connection, unfurling in its place a banner adorned with a red star. Asked what it was, a youth replied curtly: 'the call of the revolution.'

Separatists called on francophone Quebeckers to show their anti-Confederation sentiment and instead honour the heroes of the oppressed nation. The RIN organized a 7 p.m. demonstration below the Jacques Cartier Bridge on Notre Dame Street, site of the execution of twelve patriots in the aftermath of the 1837–8 Rebellions. Earlier in the day, Richard Bizier, a Felquiste recently released from prison after serving a six-month term on a bombing charge, laid a wreath at the Patriot Monument. Bizier called for remembrance of those who had recently suffered incarceration 'for wanting to defend the country they so dearly love – Quebec.' He was accompanied by relatives (including two mothers) and friends of jailed FLQ and Armée de Libération du Québec (ALQ) members.

Bands of protesters paraded the streets and parks of Montreal, chanting slogans, blocking streets with sit-ins, and raising placards. When met
by police, crowds jeered 'Gestapo,' booed, and threw rocks, bottles, and
firecrackers. Roaming gangs of 200–500 separatists and 'hoodlums'
carried 'broken bottles, bricks, and knives.' Broken up by mounted officers riding into their midst, the crowds dispersed, and then suddenly
reappeared, an unfathomable mixture of students, separatists, and
'goons.' As many as 300 Victoria Day celebrants/protesters were
detained by police, hustled into paddy wagons and removed from the
fray, but only 85 were officially arrested. In one subsequent arraign-
ment 'twenty-six men and a pert 18-year-old brunette' had to lay down
$50 deposits with the municipal court to secure release on charges of
disturbing the peace. The *Montreal Gazette* editorialized on 'unhappy
holidays,' bemoaning the 'disturbances' in the city and laying blame for
the 'start of the trouble' on 'separatist demonstrations.' But an older
appreciation of riotous Victorianism crept into its fear mongering: 'The
chief danger' in these protests, complained the newspaper, 'is the large
number of hoodlums' all too ready to join any street fracas 'for the
sheer love of destruction.'[55]

This troubling concoction of political protesters and 'vandals and
hoodlums' resurfaced in 1965 as 2,000 demonstrators and 'celebrants'
took to the streets.[56] With two underground FLQ commandos recently
sentenced to be executed for their part in the robbery of a gunsmith
shop on Bleury Street, which left two French Canadians dead, the atmosphere was strained from the outset. Matters worsened when police
blocked a march to Place Victoria. As nightsticks thudded on backs,
shoulders, and heads, Molotov cocktails sailed towards police lines. One
undercover officer, identified by separatists, was isolated and soundly
beaten. The arrest toll climbed to over 200 'after 24 hours of separatist-
inspired Victoria Day disorders left the city limp.' Public squares and
thoroughfares echoed with independence 'anthems and protests
against Commonwealth Day.' Some of those detained were subsequently
let go, but hundreds of charges were laid against the more than 130
eventually arraigned. Among them were several RIN activists; Pierre
Maheu, editor of the radical nationalist magazine of politics and culture, *Parti pris*; an ex-boxer, Reggie Chartrand, head of the separatist
Chevaliers de l'Indépendance, whose black-shirted group attempted to
form a protest ring around a statue of Queen Victoria; a smattering of
English-speaking youths from colleges and a private schools; and almost
a dozen women, including 'an attractive young brunette housewife'
caught daubing paint over a Royal Trust Company building. Attorney

General Claude Wagner decried the lack of respect for private property, the law, and the rights of individuals exhibited by the protesters. 'I think the moment has come to make them hear the only language they can truly understand,' he thundered, 'that of the rigor of the law.'

A four-stick dynamite bomb exploded outside a twelve-storey Dorchester Boulevard edifice housing the Prudential Assurance Company, the British Information Service, and the British Trade Commission, and a smaller incendiary device was discovered undetonated at the central post office. Molotov cocktails were seized from youths, as well as gasoline-soaked Red Ensigns. Police faced the usual injurious barrage of bricks, bottles, rocks, and firecrackers. Their vehicles were stoned or set on fire, and a police station was surrounded, under constant threat of attack, as youths demanded the release of those arrested. East-end francophone working-class districts were littered with debris as garbage was burned in neighbourhood streets, mailboxes overturned, and plate glass windows of commercial establishments smashed. Radical nationalist demonstrations and parades were called for a number of locales, the afternoon protests escalating 'into street brawls and vandalism as young hoodlums with time on their hands infiltrated [the] ranks.' With the coming of night 'reckless, leaderless hooliganism' supposedly reigned. Several thousand independence advocates amassed late in the evening in the east-end Lafontaine Park, columns of youths struggling to break through police lines and spill into Sherbrooke Street, hoisting signs proclaiming 'Québec Libre.' Cries of 'Lesage to the Gallows,' 'Gestapo,' and 'Revolution,' punctuated the proceedings. One English newspaper expressed disdain at the 'pointless destructiveness,' concluding that 'whatever the hard core may be, it has moved now toward a position of anarchy.' Montreal's chief of police, Adrien Robert, drew a finer line of political distinction through the disorder, commenting solemnly: 'We are no longer dealing with separatists, but with genuine revolutionaries.'[57]

In his 1972 retrospective account of the literary wing of revolutionary Quebec nationalism in the 1960s, Malcolm Reid confirmed this judgment, pointing out that those gathered around the journal *Parti pris* and the Mouvement de Libération Populaire (MLP) were enraged by Victoria Day. They took it upon themselves to mobilize slum streets and bohemian quarters against the apparatus of colonization:

Parti Pris regarded Victoria Day 1965 as a date in the revolution in Quebec. More so, perhaps, than even the FLQ arrests in 1963, or Nightstick Saturday in 1964 (when demonstrators went to the down-river capital of Quebec City to greet Queen Elizabeth), for in neither of these cases had there been so clear an appeal to the *colonisé*-in-the-street. On Victoria Day 1965, a number of policemen had been injured in late night brawls with leaderless demonstrators from the slums. It was new to the police, this action in the slum streets, and frightening.

Pierre Vallières, writing from his prison cell at the Manhattan House of Detention for Men in the winter of 1967, recalled the events two years previous to his arrest. They proved to be the inspiration of the mid-1960s FLQ strategy of underground acts of resistance. Part of a cataclysmic 1965 spring and summer, when strikes, anti-war demonstrations, unemployment protests, mass revulsion at the death of Gilles Legault, who hanged himself at Montreal's Bordeaux jail rather than face his trial for supplying *indépendantiste* activists with dynamite, and nascent party formations culminating in the birth of the MLP, the 1965 Victoria Day violence helped to move Vallières into the secret ranks of the FLQ.[58]

Outside of Montreal, the anti–Victoria Day action was less spectacular. But in Gatineau, Quebec, eight miles east of Ottawa, police were forced to fire warning shots to break up 'a near riot' that saw officers cut and bruised, their uniforms torn in street combat with juveniles and young adults. In Quebec City, radical nationalists defaced monuments commemorating General Wolfe's victory on the Plains of Abraham, Wilfrid Laurier's accomplishments as prime minister, and Canadians killed in South Africa during the Boer War.[59]

Next year saw the Montreal violence subside somewhat, but the 1966 'hooligan's march' and 'The Queen to the Gallows' protest, if they paled in comparison with the 1965 events, were nevertheless indicative of a growing radicalization among independence-oriented youth. Indeed, the federal holiday demonstration in Montreal appeared 'suddenly to be a tradition.' Leaflets announced the birth of an obscure 'Mouvement 23 Mai,' dedicated to a night of 'breaking out.' Consisting of joual-speaking young teens from Montreal's tough east-end neighbourhoods, the short-lived movement was regarded as a flood of 'three thousand Rolling Stones.' Combining orthodox separatist slogans and more class-inflected chants of '*Le! Qué! bec! aux! ouv! ri! ers!,*' the throng surged through the park on the eve of Victoria Day, flooded Sherbrooke Street East, and was soon embroiled in ritualized confrontation with the police and their roadblocks. Seemingly leaderless, the crowd was dispersed by the cops but managed to regroup in the back streets, popping out of alleyways en route to a westward march down the affluent artery of Sherbrooke Street. The more audacious elements shinnied up balcony posts to tear down Liberal and Union Nationale banners proclaiming the candidacies of mainstream party ward-heelers in the forthcoming 5 June 1966 provincial election. The Rassemblement pour l'Indépendance Nationale refused to countenance the protests and disassociated itself from the call of the Emergency Committee of the 23rd of May Movement: its placards were stoned by the more radical of the demonstrators, treated with no more respect than those of the traditional party bosses. Chartrand's Chevaliers were present, identifiable by their trademark black shirts, but the former pugilist-turned-separatist was noticeably absent, biding his time as an RIN candidate for the spoils of parliamentary office. Snaking their way down Sherbrooke towards McGill University, the protesters confronted a determined wall of police. As nightsticks flailed, and the more boisterous and confrontational of the youth were herded into police buses, the 23rd of May Movement was quieted, protesters retreating back into the east-end cul-de-sacs from which they had come. Arrests were down from the highs of previous Victoria Day rampages, and property damage was limited.

According to police, the rowdiness was confined to an 'older tougher element who led the crowd onto the streets.' This convenient analysis was disputed by others, such as Malcolm Reid, who saw the potent mix of juvenile rebelliousness and political challenge blur into each other on Victoria Day 1966. A month later, on Canada Day, a protest was called for late afternoon at Lafontaine Park. The gendarmes were so thick on the streets and sidewalks that only picknickers could make use of the public green space. No one else was able to clear a path through the corridors of cops to assemble in the now-notorious venue for rabble-rousing.[60]

Hippies, Peaceniks, and Diggers Redefine the Riotous 24th

Rumblings of a different kind animated the 24 May holiday weekend in English Canada. A 1964 Winnipeg holiday weekend confab brought together 170 left-thinking politicos in an idea exchange that had its origins in a desire to amalgamate elements of the Liberal Party and the New Democrats. Nothing much came of this Exchange for Political Ideas in Canada. Indeed, the youth sentiment of the times seemed to be running against conventional political organization, 'peace and love' being more in synch with the sentiments of the mid-to-late 1960s.[61]

In Vancouver, a 'Peace House' headed by a former University of British Columbia student, Peter Light, made the news on 22 May 1965. Light, a 22-year-old self-described anarchist, announced that he and others were waging a war for non-violence. A number of residents of the House had been arrested in sit-down demonstrations at the United

States consulate, their April protests of the Vietnam War drawing the police. They promised future actions against the war machine, in partic- ular a 4–5 June protest at the Vancouver Island Royal Canadian Air Force Comox base, where the target of the youthful dissidents would be nuclear arms. 'Peace House' hosted Wednesday night movies that revealed the horrors of the atomic bombing of Hiroshima and Naga- saki, promoted the reading of critical literature on social and political themes, and drew a contingent of bearded, booted, and blue-jeaned art- ists, students, and unemployed youth. Few among this new breed of activists placed much faith in the traditional political parties of either the mainstream (Liberals and Conservatives) or the left (the New Dem- ocrats and the Communist Party of Canada). Classes in civil disobedi- ence were taught and signs of protest painted, among them one that read 'Replace War with Love.'[62]

Over the course of the next three years, a New Left would galvanize the North American scene, and headlines in Canadian papers switched from riotous rampages of firecracker- and rock-throwing youths to inter- national protests. On 22 May 1968, for instance, the Students for a Democratic Society sit-in demonstrations at Columbia University were front-page news in Canada. Five days later, the media reported accounts of the Paris student and worker riots, whose burning barricades hear- kened back to the Commune of 1871.[63] Even more broadly influential was a countercultural wave of pulsating music, encompassing the British invasion (the Rolling Stones, Cream, and the Beatles), Jimi Hendrix, and psychedelic groups such as San Francisco's Grateful Dead and Jef- ferson Airplane. A U.S. folk revival headed by Bob Dylan and Joan Baez had its Canadian counterparts with Gordon Lightfoot, Ian and Sylvia, Buffy Sainte-Marie, and Joni Mitchell. If there seemed no time to read lengthy tomes, an alternative press – *Georgia Straight* in Vancouver was the archetypal example[64] – seemed always ready at hand. Drugs cranked the entire experience up a notch or two. When illicit substances took their users on a bad trip, communally run drop-in centres like Cool-Aid provided a safe space for them to come back down. 'There's something happening here,' sang Buffalo Springfield in 1967, 'what it is ain't exactly clear.' In this context, Victoria Day events associated with Cana- dian youth shifted gears dramatically, prefacing a wider process in which May 24th raucousness gave way to the Summer of Love.[65]

A contingent of so-called 'Diggers,' a group taking their name from seventeenth-century English radicals and inspired by the efforts in San Francisco to set up free clinics and meals for the homeless hippies of the Haight-Ashbury district,[66] mounted a 1968 holiday 'feed-in' at

Winnipeg's Memorial Park. The behind-the-scenes organizer of the event, according to one Winnipeger who attended, was actually a convert-seeking Anglican Church figure. Dining out on stories from the United States and Toronto of a new Digger phenomenon, the local press no doubt thought Winnipeg needed to juice up its countercultural content and made much ado about a local Digger nothing. But the actual happening was real enough. Peaceful and festive, the event was billed as an attempt to feed the city's growing population of underemployed long-hairs. It drew enough of the 'bearded, bedecked hippies,' to be sure, but it also attracted 'businessmen, housewives, and children,' not to mention a large number of unemployed and homeless youth happy to score a free meal. All gathered in a 'carnival atmosphere,' as youths in outrageous costumes blew soap bubbles in the spring air and clean-cut students handed out incense sticks. By evening the peaceful rally wound down, with participants ambling off to a folk concert at the nearby All Saints Church.[67]

If Winnipeg's Diggers were a social construction, in central Canada's metropolitan centre they made a fleeting appearance on the countercultural stage. Victoria Day 1967 was marked in Toronto by the city's first 'love-in.' Mocked in the press as 'a fresh air freak-out of flavored people,' the organized orchestration of spontaneous being was put on by youths who wanted 'straights' and 'hippies' to get to know one another. Its appeal, clearly, was to 'social drop-outs of all ages.' The press reported that 'weirdos came from miles around – as far as San Francisco.' A collection was taken up for the Diggers, 'Yorkniks who say they are going to establish a hostel for transient hippies.' Some 4,500 flocked to Queen's Park to see what the 1967 love-in was all about. A Roman Catholic priest asked if it was 'some sort of Victoria Day celebration.' If it was, the slogans were in marked contrast with those of previous years: 'Love Is Mudlicious'; 'Pot Is a Hobby, Not a Habit'; 'Trots Hate a System, Not People'; 'We Try Harder.' Amid 'the bomb-banners ... the New Left, the Trotskyites selling last year's propaganda ... the high school students, women walking their dogs, [and] hundreds of amateur photographers,' small groups broke into song, painted faces, and argued about Vietnam. *Globe and Mail* editors rained on the Digger parade. Victoria Day's flower children were considered little more than a wilted bouquet. One *Globe* columnist, Richard J. Needham, disagreed. He viewed the happening as a great success. Its 'color and movement and novelty' impressed him, as did the 'number of people' who came together in an 'atmosphere of peace and joy and goodwill.' Needham, aided by two teenage girls, Daring Denise and Perilous Pauline, distributed

150 roses throughout the crowd, which included celebrity authors and
singers Leonard Cohen and Buffy Sainte-Marie.[68]

June Callwood praised the hippies who nurtured the love-in and tried
to live its message in enclaves like Toronto's Yorkville, where they proclaimed themselves 'in the brotherhood business.' Consumed with
issues of 'inter-personal truth,' the flower children talked through
nights of 'acceptance, sharing, peace, love, freedom, *happiness*!' Discarding their pasts and their privileges (for many had come from affluent
families, some with famous fathers), they experimented with drugs and
sex, with clothes, and with ideas. Their encounter with new ways of living was a 'reckless adventure,' premised on refusals of much that conventional society valued, including acquisitive individualism. From
poverty, according to Callwood, 'they found they could learn.' Soon this
education would include clashes with police and rubbing shoulders with
older socialists and reform activists.

Digger House was set up in January 1968 as a hostel for transient hippie youth who needed a meal, a bed, a doctor, or a counselling session.
Originally established to deal with no more than a score of flower children, the House was almost immediately besieged, its unlocked door
offering sleeping space to as many as 115 youths on any given night.
Gradually things tightened up as Digger House evolved into a 'group living situation,' providing for twelve homeless young people at a time.
Staffed by Callwood and others, it was sustained by remnants of the hippie movement dubbing themselves Yorkville Digger Inc. The enterprise
was bankrolled by an array of charities, churches, and patrician women's
groups. But if Digger House came to rest on secure financial foundations
by the late 1960s, the movement it was founded to support was assailed
by forces of resentful fear and destruction. Tourists gawked and media
crews descended on the flower children. Their growing celebrity only
nourished the hatred of police, school authorities, city councillors, and
hostile parents, all of whom engaged in a war against the hippies.[69]

At Toronto City Hall, Allan Lamport, a municipal controller, seemed
bewildered by a contingent of Yorkville hippies whose unkempt appear-
ances, ostensibly unwashed bodies, and refusal to embrace the Protestant work ethic marked them as dangerously deviant. In a rowdy August
1967 debate, Lamport and the rebellious flower children clashed.
'We're fed up with a social system that puts the stress on production and
money and places individuals in pigeon-holes, when the most important
things are people's dignity and pride,' announced hippie spokesperson
Blues Chapman. Lamport was aghast, suggesting that if you did not
bathe you could not claim to be seeking dignity. Bare-footed, sporting

love signs, and decked out in the bright psychedelic colours of the moment, the young 'drop-outs' were clearly the physical antithesis of the greying city fathers. 'The greatest happiness in life is derived from working!' insisted Lamport as the hippies groaned and laughed. Lamport was eventually reduced to pleading with his apparently nihilistic opponents, asking them, 'Will you please tell us what we can do?' 'Practice leaving us alone!' was the sharp retort. City Hall demurred: 'Society doesn't work that way,' Lamport explained. In the end, the hippies and the politicians were reduced to statements of irreconcilable difference. When pressed as to *his* vision of what Yorkville should be, Lamport replied, 'I'd like Yorkville to grow up as a shopping centre.' The flower children hooted and guffawed. A few days later Lamport uttered what Pierre Berton characterized as 'a ludicrous statement about driving all the hippies out of Toronto.'[70]

Lamport did not follow through on his threat, but ultimately the hippies found themselves on the losing end of a protracted struggle for survival. Drug busts landed many in jail, and some of those who lived on the edge soon descended into psychological and physiological malaise. Ripe for the picking, hippies were targeted by thieves and toughs, 'greasers' who pilfered their meagre belongings, motorcycle gangs who pimped their young women, and drug dealers whose adulterated wares were laced with poisons. Nights of peace and love, by 1968–9, had given way to dawns of disillusionment. One part of this was the increasing threat of disease, particularly infectious hepatitis, which prompted the establishment of free clinics, such as the Women's College Hospital's hippie-serving Trailer program, or the health testing offered by a Yorkville 'head shop,' the Grab Bag.[71]

Digger House was soon displaced by Rochdale College, a larger, more institutionalized expression of the alternative experiment, but one that also travelled the quick road from innocence to destructive despair.[72] Established in September 1968, Rochdale loomed over Bloor Street like a grey, bleak Soviet high-rise, an architectural articulation of 'socialist realism' at its worst. Affiliated with Innis College and the University of Toronto, and named after the pioneering initiatives of Britain's mid-nineteenth-century cooperative movement, Rochdale was heralded as the largest free university in North America. It was ordered by a commitment to student-centred practices and was defiant of the structured curriculum, coercive learning, and repressive testing environment of conventional higher education. Idealism and innovation launched Rochdale, which was envisioned as a haven of democratic freedom in the heartless world of bland bureaucracy. But its cooperative spirit and proclaimed ideals, meant to pick up the increasingly jaundiced slack of Yorkville's fading Summer of Love, had no staying power against the growing external chorus of nay-sayers. They reached from the police to the pulpit, and their public assault was reinforced by the internal ravages of self-seeking opportunists and a chaos that seemed to overwhelm the supposed experimental community in its own contradictions. Barely a year after opening, a housing surplus at the University of Toronto prompted the inept and commercially minded administration to open Rochdale's doors to virtually any and all tenants. Street people and drug dealers thronged to the cheap accommodations and the opportunities for profit from easy pickings and lucrative sales. At the same time, most residents wanted an open-door policy that allowed those in need to 'crash' in Rochdale's halls. When the college's governing council locked the doors and issued keys to residents, a black market in keys soon emerged in Yorkville.

Rochdale's experiment in education soon degenerated into little more than a massive commerce in marijuana, hashish, LSD, and other illicit substances, the press labelling the building as nothing more than 'North American's largest drug distribution warehouse.' Outliving its promise of creative liberation and cooperative living and learning, Rochdale descended in a downward spiral. By 1970, it was a paranoid shell of its former 1960s self. A bad trip of accusation and fantasy, guilt and frustration, Rochdale was soon a captive of the conspiratorial view that building developers, health inspectors, university administrators, police, and the federal state's Central Mortgage and Housing Corporation had brought the institution and much else to a crashing halt. The creation of the new in the shell of the old had not happened at Rochdale. Its much-vaunted freedom had to be protected by a paid security force, composed in part of Vagabonds biker gang members. Police raids became routine and violence was commonplace. After a 1974 riot resulted in the trashing of the Rochdale rental office and the burning of bonfires in Bloor Street, political pressure to close the long-soured experiment in alternative living mounted. On 30 May 1975, Rochdale's last reluctant residents were physically carried from their homes by the cops, and the doors were welded shut.[73]

Riotous Victorianism and what Myrna Kostash has labelled 'the bugaboo of the Fifties,'[74] juvenile delinquency, had given way, then, to 1967–8 gatherings of flower children. Rituals of nihilistic combat with the police and authority were transformed into be-ins, love-ins, and sit-ins. The ease with which this movement unfolded was striking, as was its demise. No one predicted the transformation from 1957 to 1967, except perhaps a few of the more far-seeing of the Beat generation. And there was never any specifically identifiable *personal* transformation. The rock-throwing fourteen-year-old sauntering down James Street in Hamilton in 1963 did not become, inevitably, the eighteen-year-old Digger proselytizing among the hippies in Toronto's Queen's Park in 1967, although, of course, in some circumstances precisely that kind of shift did take place within an individual. Nor was the movement from juvenile delinquent to flower child animated by clearly discernible class mobilizations. The Victoria Day celebrants, from Grand Bend to Hamilton to Montreal, were undoubtedly drawn, especially in urban centres, from the proletarian and impoverished inner-city districts, but there were plenty of middle-class suburban youths pulled into the action as well, as there would be in the different context of 1967's hippie counterculture. What had happened was more abstract: youth had moved from the margins of social transformation, constructed as a 'problem' and criminalized, into the very core of a decade's understanding of sociopolitical meaning.[75]

In the process, an entire cohort of youth discarded age-old understandings of Canadian identity without knowing what new identity they wanted to embrace. Buried forever was the British imperial connection that had given birth to Victoria Day. A rampaging 'hooliganism' in the early to mid-1960s wrote *finis* to an antiquated Canadian identity without necessarily summoning another into being. One part of this was the meaning of alternative in the mid- to late 1960s, from the rise of Quebec's first militant independence movement to the countercultural catharsis of 1967–8.[76]

Margaret Wente captures some of the naive optimism of the moment, in which a political awakening of sorts was truncated in the giddiness of a passionate belief in love's endless possibilities: 'The Summer of Love was the best of times ... The world would never seem so fresh, so new, so full of cultural optimism again.'[77] Others saw 1967–8 more politically: 'Drop out. Start your own country,' animated one tendency, heralding a back-to-the land movement that decided to forgo the cosmopolitanism of urban life for the simpler subsistence of the earth's offerings.[78] What one struggled for, and, equally important, how this battle for a different world was undertaken, required resolution in a host of other sectors, including among trade unionists, in efforts to remake the politics of the left, especially with respect to the subordination of women, and in Quebec's ongoing challenge to Canada. 'Choose your weapons,' proclaimed the Diggers, 'guns or flowers.'[79] In the Summer of Love, perhaps, it was possible to conceive of a world born of the power that came from both. It would be the final, ironic dawn of an age of youthful innocence.

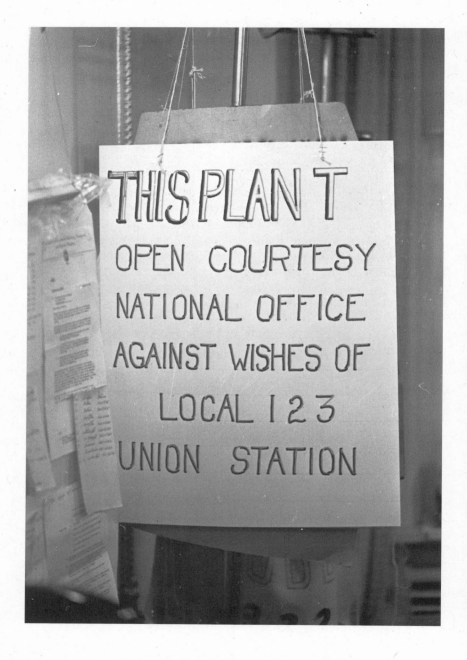

Chapter Seven

Wildcat Workers: The Unruly Face of Class Struggle

As part of the British Empire, Canada in the nineteenth century inherited much. One area where this legacy curbed the historical process of realizing identities forged in freedoms and feisty demands for entitlements in all kinds of realms related to how colonial society was stratified into contending classes. A market society that privileged those who owned property and productive apparatus over those who did not balked at workers' demands for more autonomy and greater compensation for their labours. This resistance often looked to the legal and social context of the 'mother country.' Yet economic differentiation within Canada and the expansion of the home market led to increasingly more extensive commercial economies of exchange in the staple-based resource sector. It also stimulated the rise of larger and more diversified manufacturing concerns; the expansion of urban, commodity-producing centres; and the consequent emergence of a language of 'labour reform' and the juxtaposition of 'the relations of labour and capital.' In this context, the struggle to secure working-class rights to form unions, bargain with employers collectively, and strike for just demands was always subject to the constraint of practices often regarded as either customary or illegal in the old country.[1]

Defining moments in Canadian class relations were not so much the outcome of the majesty and mercy of a far-seeing justice system. Rather, they were the product of labour–capital confrontations that ended up

Wildcat railroad strike placard, Spadina Yards, Toronto, 1966 (York University, *Toronto Telegram* Fonds, FO433, 1974-002/242).

clarifying the respective rights of workers and employers.[2] A less than
impartial umpire, the federal state, played an increasingly prominent
role in codifying these rights in the period 1880 to 1960. It constructed
an expanding infrastructure of legality, composed of legislative enactments, institutions, and the practices that grew out of them.[3]

Class Struggle's Ambiguous Resolution:
A Two-Sided Postwar Settlement

The second quarter of the twentieth century was a time of tumultuous
class conflict, marked by protest movements of the unemployed and
mass production organizing campaigns that aimed to establish working-
class citizenship. Central to this latter development were the industries
that marked Canadian manufacturing's movement from a nineteenth-
century Industrial Revolution to a different era of what has been called
Fordism. The assembly line, new technologies of production, higher
wages, and more far-reaching consumer purchasing power were the
hallmarks of an expansive capitalism and one of its offshoots, the modern labour movement. Economic sectors associated with the automobile
industry, steel making, electrical, chemical, and rubber products, as well
as a parallel expansion in resource extraction, paced by the growth of
mining and forestry were all the site of important organizing drives in
the late 1930s and 1940s. The Second World War, as a period of full
employment when capital and the state desperately needed to keep the
lid on potentially explosive class relations, opened the door to granting
labour's century-long struggle to secure the legal right to organize
in unions. A 1941–3 explosion of class struggle produced over
1,100 strikes involving unprecedented numbers of workers, roughly
425,000. A series of legislative enactments, such as Privy Council Order
1003, tried to tame this labour revolt by granting unions temporary
rights to represent workers. A combination of intensifying class struggle
– a massive 1946–7 strike wave swept the country, with hundreds of
thousands of workers on strike, and millions of worker-days lost in what
appeared to be a labour–capital Armageddon – and state intervention
produced what subsequent commentators have called a postwar settlement of industrial pluralism.[4]

This settlement has come to be understood as an unevenly applied
and reluctantly implemented accord. It drew trade unions, the state,
and employers into a mutually agreed-upon pact to keep the labour–
capital peace. Trade unions secured, in principle, the right to establish
unions under specific procedures of state certification, to bargain

collectively, and to sign binding contracts with employers that would, in the event of disagreement, be interpreted and enforced by provincial labour boards and a growing army of state-monitored lawyers, mediators, and arbitrators. Finally, while this would long be resisted by intransigent, often smaller, employers, union dues could now, in what was known as the union check-off, be collected by the employer. They would be deducted from workers' paycheques and deposited in trade union bank accounts. This would happen regardless of whether a worker wanted to belong to a union, as long as the labour organization had been certified as the legitimate bargaining unit of a specific workforce. The check-off was, in effect, a symbolic statement that unions were now a recognized reality on the industrial relations scene.

A critical architect of these late 1940s innovations in industrial relations was Justice Ivan Rand. His arbitration decision settling a tumultuous 1945 strike at the Windsor Ford plant advocated union check-off and various other entitlements so as to strengthen trade unions 'in order to carry on the functions for which they are intended.' These included the realization of an 'increasing harmony' among contending social forces, securing 'the interests of capital, labour and public in the production of goods and services which our philosophy accepts as part of the good life.' For Rand, workers' rights were necessary to achieve an 'industrial civilization' that was governed 'within a framework of labour–employer constitutional law based on a rational economic and social doctrine.' Private enterprise as the dynamic engine of socioeconomic development and a widening affluence was the privileged core of all concessions made to labour.[5]

What all of this meant was often puzzlingly unclear in the nitty gritty of workplace relations and class confrontations, which proceeded apace in spite of the changing circumstances geared to produce tranquillity on the industrial field. Yet a hurdle had been successfully vaulted in this late-1940s shift in the *ideology* and *apparatus* of class relations. Unions secured much, albeit always on the ground of capital's dominance. This, understandably, was *the* premise of any state-orchestrated program of incorporation. The brutal suppression of working-class initiative, characteristic of class relations for a century, was now somewhat mediated.[6]

What did the unions give up in this industrial pluralist legal bargain? First and foremost, the labour legislation that proliferated in the post-1945 years, and the techniques of governing class relations that evolved on the basis of such state pronouncement, named and proscribed a wide range of unfair labour practices. The most decisive and ultimately overwhelmingly significant of these newly designated 'illegal acts' was striking during the period of a collective agreement. Trade unions were now called on to police their members and keep them productive and profitable during the life of state-monitored contracts that bound workers, employers, and governing power together.

Second, the historic irony of the postwar settlement's promotion of the union check-off was that it enhanced *union* security at the same time that it eliminated one of the basic face-to-face connections of rank-and-file members and their organizational leaders. When unions had to collect dues, with labour movement activists circulating among the membership and gathering the monthly organizational tithe, they were linked, organically, to the masses of workers who sustained the union as an institution and its leaders as spokespeople of the labour cause. The check-off lessened the links between members and union officials.

Third, and further deepening this process of separation, precisely because so much attention had now to be paid to the *legalisms* of class relations, the expanding contractual arrangements of the workplace, and the state-orchestrated technologies of governance, trade unions became more bureaucratized and less openly democratic. It took an immense effort to wade through the dense and fattening sheaves of collective agreements, which grew over the period 1939–49 from five- or six-page documents to massive tomes that were hundreds, even thousands (in the case of some large employers) of pages in length. The culture of unionism changed gears, downshifting into a more grind-it-out daily routine in which a layer of union officialdom reacted more and more with non-working-class elements, including labour lawyers and state functionaries. As Ed Finn, a radical labour journalist and editor of the Canadian Brotherhood of Railway Trainmen's journal *Canadian Transport*, noted in 1965, the full-time labour leader was increasingly distant from the rank and file. Acknowledging that this was a necessity in the age of modern labour relations, Finn also concluded that it tended to produce business union leaders estranged 'to some extent from their membership.'[7]

Fourth, and finally, it was not purely accidental that Rand and other far-seeing proponents of a new industrial relations regime came to their positions as Cold War anti-communism was heating up in the aftermath of war's settlement and the targeting of Soviet Russia as the free world's major enemy. Responsible trade unionism could never be led by the nefarious reds, widely perceived to have been channelling much of the militancy of the 1930s and 1940s into the rise of an aggressive labour movement. The increasingly virulent postwar labour anti-communism saw Communist Party members and others of the revolutionary left driven from the unions in a kind of working-class McCarthyism. It was not, of course, directly linked to the late-1940s worker–employer accord, but it fed quite comfortably off the premises of Rand and others. If the trade union movement was to progress, and to avail itself of all the benefits an affluent North American capitalism of the last half of the twentieth century had to offer, it must serve the cause of freedom and respectability. Labour thus had to clean its house of all those elements discrediting it in the eyes of this undertaking. It would not take long for this labour anti-communism to drive many, if not most, potential opponents and radicals underground, even out of the trade union movement entirely. Such a development, moreover, furthered the trend toward bureaucratic conservatism that was being reinforced from so many other quarters.[8]

The legacy of such an ambiguous and two-sided resolution of the long history of Canadian class struggle was that by the 1950s workers and their unions appeared secure but were in effect caught in tightening ossification. Such a process would take decades to develop and would not really be discernible until the fiscal crisis of the Canadian state manifested itself blatantly in the mid-1970s. It was then that Pierre Elliott Trudeau's Liberals imposed wage and price controls and initiated the legislative assault on trade union freedoms that would be picked up with a vengeance by Conservative, even NDP, governments in the 1980s and 1990s. Masking the seething contradictions of the almost immediate cracks in the edifice of the postwar settlement were a host of 1960s developments. Among them were the expanding infrastructure of 'social safety net provisioning,' which encompassed tremendous growth and stabilization of health and education programs and facilities; state commitment to principles of universality in family allowances and unemployment insurance; and a range of initiatives that took aim at the reduction of poverty or targeted youth as specific beneficiaries of state largesse, training, and aid.[9]

Resentment and grievance in the arena of class struggle did nevertheless emerge in the 1960s.[10] In particular, it surfaced with a vengeance in 1964–6, at precisely the same point that radical nationalist agitation was developing in Quebec, English-Canadian youth were gravitating toward both countercultural alternative and the politics of challenge and dissent, and women were beginning to voice their discontents with a status quo that kept them confined to the constrained possibilities of a feminine sphere. Not surprisingly, as was the case elsewhere, the young led the way. Their vehicle of protest, driven by a rage and violence that was itself an expression of the frustrations of alienation and marginalization common to a wider generational revolt, was the single working-class

expression of rebellion that Justice Ivan Rand had been at pains to suppress. Wildcat strikes, protests in which workers walked off the job in
defiance of their contractual obligation not to disrupt the economics of
peaceful class coexistence during the life of collective agreements, were
the mid-1960s voice of an aggrieved, and youthful, layer of workers waging a most difficult war. For not only did this military-like campaign
array itself against the traditional enemy, capital, it also found itself confronting two other powerful structures: the seemingly benevolent state
and the embodiment of workers' mechanisms of defence, the trade
union and its increasingly hierarchical officialdom.

The Demography of Dissent[11]

The Canadian labour force, like Canadian society in general, grew
younger over the course of the 1960s. Whereas people between the ages
of 15 and 24 accounted for 15.3 per cent of the country's population in
1951, by the 1970s this figure was approaching 19 per cent. Within the
workforce, this demographic shift had a dramatic impact. In the decade
and a half between 1961 and 1975, the numbers of youth participating
in wage labour rose dramatically. The percentage of wage earners in the
14–19 and 20–24 age brackets increased from 36.2 and 68.9 per cent,
respectively, to 51.1 and 75.9 per cent. Throughout the 1960s the average annual participation rate increases of workers under 25 years of age
were between 4 and 5 per cent, outpacing the annual labour force
growth of 3 per cent. All of this lent an increasingly more youthful
appearance to the Canadian working class: there were more and more
young workers in paid employment, and they were, as each year passed,
a larger percentage of the entire workforce.

Moreover, factoring gender into the demographic equation in the
mid-1960s, when young males were more likely to enter the paid workforce than were young working-class women, skews these figures in a
decidedly masculinist direction. This explains much of the wildness of
the wildcats, which were most emphatically male undertakings, marked
by bravado and the macho posturing of youth in a pre-feminist working-
class cultural moment.[12]

In the pivotally important 1964–6 years with which this chapter and
its focus on wildcat strikes will be largely concerned, male youth were
overwhelmingly concentrated in waged employment. If these young
workers were the best-schooled generation of working-class youth in
Canadian history, they were nevertheless not yet the beneficiaries of a

mid- to late-1960s education boom that saw a tremendous expansion of college and university facilities and the first serious possibility of lower-income youth taking advantage of what higher education had to offer. Only 11 per cent of Canadians aged 18 to 24 were enrolled in university in 1965, with slightly less than 15 per cent of those 20 to 24 having any university experience at all. Of these, according to a survey undertaken by the Canadian Union of Students, roughly one-third of the undergraduate population could be considered to have come from working-class backgrounds.[13] Unlike young working-class women, moreover, males in this age bracket were less likely to be confined to family responsibilities, whether that involved care of the young or the old. The result was that in the mid-1960s, roughly 88 per cent of all 20–24-year-old males were in the civilian labour force, compared with approximately 54 per cent of women of the same age cohort. Understandably, as well, younger workers entered the workforce with less security than their older counterparts. Unemployment rates for the young in the mid-1960s indicated that their employment was far more precarious than those in the 25–44 and 45–65 age groups. Young workers from 14 to 24 years of age faced unemployment rates of from 16.4 to 9.7 and 11.8 to 5.3 per cent over the first half of the 1960s; comparable rates for older workers never reached much more than 7 per cent and sometimes bottomed out at just under 3 per cent.[14]

Working-class youth, of course, were drawn into the same countercultural cauldron as their non-proletarian peers.[15] Many young workers lived at home, and resentments of adult, often patriarchal, authority fused domestic and workplace resentments in a generational assault on 'the Establishment.' One 1968 study, addressing Canadian industrial relations, noted 'an undeniable tendency in this generation to question and challenge authority itself and those in a position to exercise it.'[16] As music, drugs, sex, fashion, and a youthful tendency to refuse all authority congealed in an increasingly public and often consumer-paced popular culture of age differentiation,[17] a 'them vs. us' discontent coalesced among Canadian youth. This echoed the lyrics of the 1965 British rock anthem 'My Generation.' Recorded by Pete Townshend and The Who, the song, presented with a patented stutter, was among the hardest-hitting statements of a newly combative rock 'n' roll:

People try to put us d-down, talking 'bout my generation
Just because we get around, talking 'bout my generation

Things they do look awful c-c-cold, talking 'bout my generation
Hope I die before I get old, talking 'bout my generation.[18]

Often perceived as a product of campus rebellion, this expanding youth culture of discontent was, in actuality, far more widespread, and it affected the trade unions as well as the university classroom. As Ed Finn commented in *Canadian Dimension* in 1965, the parallel revolts then unfolding on Canadian campuses and within the labour movement 'recruited from the same generation; both share the same discontent with the status quo, the same willingness to engage in civil disobedience to dramatize their feelings.'[19] As one old-timer in Winnipeg's Transcona and Symington railway yards later looked back on decades of class conflict, he was reminded of the rebelliousness of his younger co-workers in the postwar years. The impact of this youth militancy first surfaced in 1965–6, and this veteran of class struggle saw it as responsible for changing the terms of trade in the perpetual war between capital and labour. 'If it weren't for them we wouldn't be here now. They're different. They're fearless ... It's a new generation,' he proclaimed.[20]

The revolt of the young within unions thus had a profound impact on class relations in the mid-1960s. It not only upped the level and nature of conflict with employers; it also threatened the capacity of the state to contain struggles within respected boundaries of legalism and industrial pluralism. Finally, it rocked the boat of trade unionism itself. For youthful rebels had none of the political baggage of their older labour movement leaders: they had not experienced the anti-communist purges of the 1950s; cultivated no intense loyalties to a layer of social democratic trade union officials; and had not, for the most part, known the difficult, insecure, and often violently vindictive times of the Great Depression and before, to which their fathers and mothers had a more organic connection through family or direct experience.[21]

Younger workers thus took for granted much that their older predecessors and union leaders had struggled, often at great cost and considerable sacrifice, to achieve. And as the postwar settlement delivered tangible benefits to unions, older leaders had grown cautious in their protections of the valued stabilities that had resulted. As Finn noted:

Approximately 80 per cent of Canada's top labour leaders are between the ages of 50 and 70. Many of them have grown more conservative with the passing years, more wedded to the old ways and the old traditions. They fail to see the need for drastic changes in the structure and policies of the labour movement if it is to cope with automation, industrial and technological change, and other pressing challenges of the 1960s and 1970s. And while the leaders of most unions have aged, the turnover in their membership has brought in many thousands of young workers who are not tied to old union methods and traditions. Better educated, more aggressive, these younger workers have strong ideas about what they want and how to get it. They are taking over the leadership at the local level, and their radicalism often brings them into sharp conflict with the comparatively conservative leaders at the top.[22]

Writing in *Saturday Night*, Mungo James discussed the mid-1960s 'new ferment' in the trade unions, attributing it to 'the arrival, for the first time in any numbers, of the young, swinging, questing generation.' In Quebec, one local labour activist noted that 'it used to be that we waited for orders from the union representative, but that is not the way with the young people.' Murray Cottrell, a veteran unionist associated with the powerful United Steel Workers of America (USWA), told James that 'it's completely impossible to give these young people the old hogwash … You can't fool them by holding up the bogey of depression, the old you-ought-to-be-grateful-to have a job at all. These kids have no experience of the depression. All they know is that management needs their services now.' Concluding that the relatively recent postwar settlement was really rooted in assumptions that management was educated and far-seeing and the workers in need of discipline, Cottrell summed up the problem of class relations as it appeared in the mid-1960s: 'These kids won't take it. They expect to be treated like human beings.'[23]

The Meaning of Wildcatting

The wildcat strike might be regarded as the trade union equivalent of the students' sit-in.[24]

One aspect of Cottrell's conclusion that youthful workers were refusing to 'take it' was that this stand placed them not only in revolt against the employers and the state, but against the union as well. An illegal railway striker in Montreal said, simply, that dissidents were 'fed up with excuses from their union leaders.'[25] The 1968 Task Force on Canadian Industrial Relations, headed by McGill University's H.D. Woods, pointed out that worker dissatisfaction in the mid-1960s was sometimes running 'as deeply against the union and collective bargaining as against management,' producing a worrisome 'rebellion of union members against their leaders.'[26] Wildcat strikes were *the* most decisive articulation of this process, violating the legality of a contract and posing a threat to union security. Labour organizations found such rank-and-file rebellion threatening, for if they failed to uphold their legal responsibilities within the Canadian postwar settlement, trade unions could be subject to crippling financial penalties in the form of fines, often calculated as a daily sum per union member in defiance of the contract. Depending on the duration of the wildcat, such financial penalties might total hundreds of thousands, even millions, of dollars. As local and international treasuries were the material and symbolic measure of trade unionism's new-found security, this hit labour's developing bureaucracy where it truly hurt. Adding personal insult to the cash injury, these very same trade union tops who failed to stave off or muzzle wildcat strikes might well be jailed if they did not demonstrate sufficient zeal in getting their members back to work.

Wildcat strikes tend to be a combination of informal, but ongoing, organization and exuberant spontaneity, which marks them out from legal strikes. The latter are planned, coordinated, and announced by union officials well in advance. They have a timetable, which wildcats never do. Everyone involved in a legal strike knows that a collective agreement has run its course and management and labour have been unable to reach a consensus that a new contract will be signed. No one is quite certain where a wildcat will go. Wildcats are far less likely to be about wages, pensions, or what business unionists often see as the core issues of contract negotiations, than are legal strikes. They are thus more amorphous, but more likely to crystallize deep-seated working-class grievance, and suggest a wider reform agenda. If the legal strike is about securing a contract, the wildcat strike can either be about skirting the contract or, alternatively, present itself as a forceful statement from the shopfloor that workers are tired of waiting for one. No labour *movement* has ever been built without the enthusiasm and mobilizing potential of the illegal work stoppage, just as no *business* unionism, concerned overwhelmingly with narrow wage issues, has ever been comfortable with wildcats. As one observer told the *Canadian Forum*'s Louis Greenspan, 'The union leaders have fought the old fights and won the old battles; they no longer negotiate ideas, they only negotiate money.'[27] If this was an overly optimistic assessment of the success of conventional unions on the wage and job security front, it nevertheless articulated a sense of working-class frustration that existed as Canadian trade unionism appeared to be losing its protest movement character and lapsing into a merely economistic machine.

As John H. Crispo and Harry W. Arthurs reported in 1968, Canadian wildcats were an expression of 'rank-and-file restlessness' that was sometimes 'as much against the "union establishment" as against the "business establishment."' One investigator found that a diffuse sense of 'participatory democracy' animated the 1965–6 Canadian wildcat wave, with workers demanding an expansion of their role in decision making, especially on critically important issues such as technological innovation and automation. The intensity of commitment to a 'new version of Trade Unionism' surprised this commentator, who concluded that, 'just as the bureaucratized universities have created the militant student and faculty so have the bureaucratized plants created the new generation of union militants.' Talk of a 'new unionism' and 'the just society' spread in labour circles, prompting rebelliousness and commitment to widening the effort to eradicate poverty and create more equitable income distribution.[28]

The wildcat strike, then, was the perfect vehicle (in both form and content) for the expression of youthful labour rebellion in the mid-1960s. It was often a spontaneous eruption of anger, alienation, and anxiety, ordered by workers themselves rather than channelled through conservative union leaders and the procedural morass of the legally ordered trade union settlement. Like student protest meetings and demonstrations, wildcat strikes were happenings rather than highly structured and routinely scripted events. They took place outside of the boundaries of what had come to be conventional class relations, striking blows against the peaceful coexistence the postwar settlement was designed to secure for capital, labour, and the state.[29]

Class Struggle's Temperature Rising:
Wildcat Fever and Youthful Labour Revolt

The mid-1960s seemed wild enough, without the drama of illegal strikes being thrown into the mix. A 31 May 1966 *Globe and Mail* discussion of 'A Plague of Strikes' noted that for several months Canadians had 'been preoccupied with Mrs. Gerda Munsinger and the manner in which the CBC handled its employees,' a reference to a strike at the national television network. The country seemed in danger of 'losing the power to distinguish the picayune from the perilous.' Such work stoppages, according to a House of Commons statement by the minister of labour, John Nicholson, 'threaten[ed] the Canadian economy.' Nicholson was put off by 'a near epidemic of labour disputes and the hair trigger atmosphere that attends so many negotiations.' He feared a 'long summer of uncontrolled labour strife' that would 'exact its toll from every Canadian.' The *Globe and Mail* advocated a 'cold, dissecting eye of the researcher upon strikes.'[30]

A precise count of the strikes and lockouts of these years is difficult to establish. The major government publication upon which such a tally would necessarily be based, the Department of Labour's Economics and Research Branch *Strikes and Lockouts in Canada*, underreported levels of conflict. Nevertheless, two separate calculations, one conducted by Stuart Marshall Jamieson, a professor at the University of British Columbia's Institute of Industrial Relations in the 1960s, and another by Joy McBride, a PhD candidate at Queen's University in the late 1980s, confirm the unmistakable dimensions of an upturn in the class struggle. Jamieson, who ascertained the numbers of strikes and lockouts by surveying official statistics, records a total of 1,118 such conflicts in 1965–6, while McBride, studying the same period, but drawing on the aggregate data rather than reproducing the final published government statistics, suggests that 1,147 strikes occurred. Both scholars place the accent on the dramatic rise in class conflict, with the workers involved, worker-days lost to strikes and lockouts, and percentage of estimated working time sacrificed to such struggles soaring. The number of worker-days lost almost quadrupled over the period 1963–5, climbing to 7.5 million in the two years of intense mid-1960s conflict. Estimated working time that evaporated in the heat of class struggle tripled to .33 per cent, with almost 600,000 workers battling employers on picket lines in 1964–6.

Unemployment having been brought under control, contained at roughly 4 per cent, inflation was the primary scourge of the organized working class. Its rising wage demands, which in the case of some sectors appeared outrageously excessive, peaked with a 1966 Canadian Union of Postal Workers announcement that the union would seek a mammoth 50 per cent wage hike. When railway workers seemingly insisted on a 30 per cent raise in 1966, politicians from Liberal Prime Minister Lester B. Pearson on down to Ontario's minister responsible for provincial highways cried foul. Governments claimed they would be bankrupted. Contractors in Montreal were shocked when 10,000 building tradesmen and labourers associated with the Confederation of National Trade Unions (CNTU) brought $100 million worth of projects to a standstill. They rejected an agreement providing 'the largest and most rapid wage and fringe increases ever negotiated in Canada' for workers in the construction sector. Newspaper editorials and tavern talk turned on 'big unions' and their crippling inflationary wage demands. More sober calculations, however, indicated that while the salaries of Canadian executives had jumped 27 per cent from 1961 to 1965, workers' gains, while significant, had trailed such corporate cash-grabs by 10 per cent and more.[31]

More telling (and more open to dispute in terms of differences in the numbers) is the tally of wildcat strikes in 1965–6. Certainly their importance is obvious, but Jamieson's reliance on official statistics alone probably understates significantly the number of wildcats in these years. He puts the figure at 359, while McBride's survey of illegal strikes approaches 575. What is undeniable is that such wildcat statistics, encompassing by 1965–6 anywhere from 20 to 50 per cent of all strikes, highlight an earth-shattering departure from the practices of the past. Even official statistics, such as those gathered for Ontario, conceded that 27 per cent of the strikes in the province in 1966 were illegal, having been launched during the life of the collective agreement. And with this wave of wildcats, Canadian workers served notice that they were prepared to defy law and order, often resulting in violence. 'The peaceable kingdom,' with its attachment to orderly understandings of British constitutional practices, was being assailed from within by an increasingly unruly, wildcatting working class.[32]

Many of these wildcat battles were epic confrontations in which workers extracted much from capital. Often strikers – legal and illegal – were forced to defy court injunctions ordering them to cease and desist from specific picket-line activities and return to their work. So blatant was the hostility to injunctions in mid-1960s labour circles that it threatened to shatter the hegemonic hold of the law. It was difficult to mask the extent to which injunctions prohibiting picket lines were not obvious tools relied on by capital to crush working-class resistance, exposing the class prejudices of the state and its infrastructure of 'justice.' Central Ontario became a particularly hot site of contestation as strikes of typographers at the *Oshawa Times* and poorly paid female workers at the Tilco Plastics Company, both of which were slapped with restraining orders, culminated in a well-coordinated and province-wide Ontario Federation of Labour campaign against injunctions. Unionists declared that 'the war is on' and that they had 'no respect for the law.' Strikes of dozens of workers might be supported by thousands, leading to newspaper editorials deploring the explosive lawlessness of the times and chastising stubborn unionists for their nasty acts of intimidation. It did not stop the mass picket movement. When a sheriff in Oshawa tried to read an injunction to a huge crowd of union supporters he was pelted with snowballs and the offensive legal document was torn from his hands, shredded by its opponents. The New Democratic Party's Ontario leader, Donald C. MacDonald, told one group of defiant strikers 'that people who defy laws have in the past been at the center of historic events.'[33]

Labour spokesmen could barely stomach the crude way in which the proliferation of injunctions kneecapped striking workers. Paddy Neale, secretary of the Vancouver and District Labour Council, made no bones of his disdain for a judiciary that would grant employers injunctions without even glancing at sworn affidavits. 'The law is an ass,' he railed. Injunctions, by 1965, were a particularly dirty word in British Columbia's militant labour circles. 'We used them to decorate the office as wallpaper,' snorted one strike leader when asked what he thought of the proliferating court orders. Ambrose Casey, chairman of London's Local 311 of the Canadian Brotherhood of Railway, Transport, and General Workers (CBRT), issued a statement in the midst of a summer 1966 battle, declaring that if the government imposed 'a return to work ultimatum, civil disobedience will occur.' Young workers heard such statements and no doubt considered them a licence to flout the law in general, especially as the class war gave every sign of heating up in the 1965–6 years.[34]

Typical of the complex levels of developing antagonism were strikes of Hamilton and Sudbury steelworkers and miners and Montreal longshoremen in 1966. Contract negotiations at the northern Ontario International Nickel Company (Inco) plant were disrupted by a 16,000-member wildcat walkout that union officials subdued only after three weeks. In spite of the leadership's opposition to the job action, it helped win Sudbury's miners and metal processors an impressive pay hike. When the contract was eventually approved, however, only 57 per cent of the union membership thought it good enough and voted for ratification. To the south, in Hamilton, discontent erupted in a violent wildcat at the Steel Company of Canada, where workers fought police and union officials, destroyed property, and won themselves a reputation for militancy and the highest steelworking wage in the world. On the Montreal docks, the first illegal strike in years was fought by longshoremen resisting the stevedoring companies' demands that new cargo-handling machinery be used and gangs reduced in size accordingly. Workers refused to recommend a settlement that contained lucrative wage increases until a royal commission was established to inquire into the shipping firms' insistence that the size of work crews be pared down, cutting 600 jobs, thus guaranteeing that traditional longshoring gangs would be preserved for the duration of the contract, until 1968.

Similar developments on the railways forced Parliament to sanction 18 per cent wage increases before it ordered strikers back to work after an October 1964 protest in which 2,800 Canadian National Railway employees booked off sick in an en masse protest. Meanwhile, 12,000 postal workers were poised to lead one of the largest nationwide wildcats in the 1965–6 upheaval. They improved the depressed wage environment in which they had been incarcerated for some time. A *Globe and Mail* editorial worried over the spread of wildcat fever. It saw the postal conflict as a reflection 'of the loss of control by union leaders.' Meanwhile, the mail carriers' walkout 'spread like wildfire across the country despite efforts by the union leadership in Ottawa to douse it.'[35]

Many such strikes, commentators of the time were quick to point out, ended up headed by rebel leaderships and factions that 'refused to obey their national officers.' In the case of Ontario's 8,500 teamsters, a wildcat strike precipitated by Hamilton truckers was opposed vindictively by an employers' association that demanded damage suits, dismissals of workers, and other legally sanctioned penalties as the price of a new collective agreement. Rumours circulated that the illegal work stoppage was inspired by 'Reds, kooks, and nuts,' allegations that were disputed by a Teamster 'strongman,' D. Thibault, said to be spearheading 'the revolt' against both the companies and the union. He challenged in particular the communist characterization, suggesting that journalists 'check the records of the RCMP on any' of the dissidents. Union representatives were pushed to reject a conciliation board's award and manoeuvred themselves into a position to strike legally in January 1966, which they did upon receiving a 72 per cent strike vote. In the ensuing fourteen-week battle, fought largely to secure the forty-hour work week, a Hamilton foreman was shot at; scab trucks were showered with pop bottles and rocks from highway overpasses; pins connecting tractor trailers were surreptitiously removed and trucks were vandalized; and assaults erupted at a number of work sites. After twelve weeks a settlement seemed imminent. A militant, rebel faction mobilized to turn thumbs down on the deal. Union leaders were 'caught by surprise,' as strikers overwhelmingly rejected the terms negotiated by a Teamster bargaining committee. It took a further two weeks of haggling, considerable backtracking by the bosses, and state-orchestrated pressure to get the drivers back in their trucks. Sealing the settlement, eventually, was international union president James Hoffa's intervention, which began

with placing a key Toronto dissident local under trusteeship and suspending Thibault and another recalcitrant Teamster union official.[36]

The demographics of youth figured centrally in these class battles.
Time and time again, commentators underscored the origins of the wildcat movement in the impatience, intransigence, and volatility of workers
'new' to the game of stable industrial relations, uninitiated in the procedural practices of postwar settlement unionism, layered as they were in
bureaucratic legalism. The secretary treasurer of the CBRT noted in
1966 that three years earlier, during the most recent set of contract negotiations, fully half of his members had not been around at the time of the
last strike in the industry, in 1950. 'It is doubtful whether many of these
new members even know the names of the leaders, and they certainly
have no personal identification, as was the case in the past.'[37]

'Young workers,' according to one labour journalist, were 'pushing
their older leaders into more aggressive bargaining positions than
they've taken in the past. And by displaying the militant social consciousness now common to youth around the world, they've also set
their leaders to reappraising the labour movement's social role.'[38] The
Globe and Mail located the decisive, general causal element in the 1965–6
labour revolt in the influx into the unions of 'a new and largely undisci-
plined force of younger men with little or no trade union experience or
loyalties.'[39] Henri W. Joli, president of the Canadian Manufacturers'
Association, agreed. The employer spokesman attributed the worsening
mid-1960s climate of industrial relations to those young workers swelling the workforce, 'fresh from school who have no idea what the pre-
war world was like and who always have got what they wanted. Many of
them appear shocked when they find their demands are not going to be
met automatically.'[40]

Inco's wildcat rebellion was ostensibly sparked by a group of young
Newfoundlanders, all working at the Levack Mines and lodging
together at the company barracks. When two of their number opened
lunch boxes to munch on sandwiches before getting their daily work
instructions, they were ordered by a shift boss to return to the surface.
The pettiness of the arbitrary discipline, as well as accumulated grievances and the failure of contract negotiations to move forward, culminated in a massive shutdown of the entire international conglomerate's
Sudbury-region operations – mines, mills, and offices.[41] Across the
country, managerial personnel bemoaned the tendency of young workers to fly off the handle, precipitating illegal work stoppages, to inflame
the situation during legal strikes, to bog down negotiations, or to disrupt long-standing relations of stability with their inexperience and

inflexibility. For their part, the young might regard their elders, in the words of one young francophone Canadian National Railway wildcat striker, as 'vendus.'[42]

At Hamilton's Stelco plant, site of one of the more robust wildcats, it was young men in their twenties, according to various accounts, who precipitated the walkout. One older unionist told journalists that 'the hard core dissenters were young men who worked at the plant for only 6 to 9 months and were already up to their necks in trouble,' adding for good measure, 'you have that kind in any group, not just steelworkers.' As cranes congregated in the aftermath of a lunch break, their operatives gathering to foment dissent, it was noticed that they 'were all manned by young men.' Some of these youthful workers had entered the Stelco workforce, and the union, through family connections, their fathers having long histories in the steelworking community. With contract negotiations having dragged on from May into August, stalling in a deadlock that stretched past the expiration date of the contract, resentments mounted in the massive steelworks. With a foreman taunting an evening shift that, 'You guys haven't got the guts to walk out,' twenty young men marched to the plant gate and formed pickets. Two hundred others were quickly enlisted to circulate throughout the plant, calling workers out. Within a day the illegal walkout had spread throughout the sprawling Stelco works, idling 16,000 workers. Of 29 workers initially targeted as militants, arrested and charged with assault and various other picket line criminal acts, suspected as well of sabotage, the average age was 28.6 years, the oldest being 42, the youngest 20. Fully one-third of those arrested were 23 years old or less. When the reinstatement of these wildcatters became an issue of contention, management refusing to hire some of them back, one union leader responded to criticism with the comment, 'Look, Jesus Christ couldn't have got the jobs back of some of those guys. I know one. He was a good kid, too. His father was a personal friend of mine. He'd only been working at Stelco for six months, but he got caught inside the plant cutting electrical cables and that sort of thing … Now what are you gonna do about a case like that?'[43]

This Stelco veteran's words conveyed the dilemma that labour's established advocates found themselves in during the mid-1960s. On the one hand, there was recognition that young workers' resentments were justified. On the other, the actions of the rebellious youth within labour's ranks were often judged rash and irresponsible. This led union officials to struggle simultaneously to placate those who demanded that the class struggle take a more aggressive and expansive turn *and* contain instances where such rebelliousness crossed specific lines. At the head of the CLC, for instance, a youthful associate research director, Russell Irvine, moved with the times to embrace positions that labour organizations should not trap negotiations with employers in the cul-de-sac of a traditional quid pro quo in which capital's expectation was that any increase in labour's remuneration had to be met with rising productivity. Irvine refused such a profit–wage bargain, arguing that if workers accepted 'this line about being a responsible citizen and tying ... income to productivity, not only will [labour's] share not increase – it will get even smaller.' Tired of the assumption that unions had to act within the rules of a game that seemed to have been conceived and constructed by capital and the state, Irvine snorted, 'We're sick of being told to act responsibly. Let *them act* responsibly for a change.'[44] If this was the rhetoric of militancy emanating from the upper echelons of the trade union bureaucracy, as the wildcat wave peaked many a trade union top imploded in frustrated antagonism to young 'hotheads' who seemed to take labour spokesmen like Irvine at their word.

What, for instance, were trade union officials to make of the electricians at Ontario's Warkworth prison, who staged a four-day walkout in antagonism to a foreman's disputatious relations with workers? The irate unionists did not want lectures, and simply told the figureheads to butt out of the affair, that it would be handled by the men as they saw fit. When Thetford Mines municipal employees rankled under the ill treatment of a superintendent, they did not bother to launch a grievance. They simply barricaded him out of the repair shop where they worked. Electricians at the North Burnaby, BC, Lenkurt Company wildcatted in May 1966, outraged when 257 workers were fired in a dispute over overtime procedures. They defied their international union's orders to lay down picket signs and instead battled Royal Canadian Mounted Police. Arrests resulted, and, when a union business agent was suspended by his labour employer for his part in the fracas, the militant workers turned their anger on the union. They greeted the appointment of a local president from on high by changing the locks on the union hall, preventing their newly christened leader from gaining access to his building. Elsewhere, disgruntled workers blockaded a hotel where they knew their union president was engaged in contract negotiations, demanding that he face them; denounced negotiating committees; refused to ratify agreements; and called for votes of no confidence in their local officials.[45] As the Woods Report on Canadian Industrial Relations concluded in 1968, never before had the contention that union officials were essentially 'managers of discontent' been made with such conviction. It was proving difficult to 'reconcile employee rights and union responsibilities.'[46]

As railway workers employed by the express delivery wings of the Canadian National and Canada Pacific railways waged an illegal wildcat in the summer of 1966, a union official, prodded to get the workers back on the job, threw up his hands in despair: 'They said they weren't ready to go back, so what's the point of talking to them?' The strikers' words offered an elaboration on their antagonisms: 'This is a non-confidence vote (in the union executive), we are taking things into our own hands.' When Local 1005 president John Morgan and Steelworkers' area supervisor Stewart Cooke implored wildcat pickets at Stelco's gates to open the lines and return to work they were shocked by the vehemence with which they were denounced. 'We're fed up with you, we don't want you,' one picketer jeered in derision at his local union president. Morgan left in tears. One of his supporters reported: 'It was an ugly scene ... They were shouting at us like some of them had gone mad. We were lucky to get out of there alive.'[47]

The Wildness of the Wildcat

This report of fear and loathing on the illegal picket line conveys something of the unique wildness of the 1965–6 labour rebellion. If it did not manage to achieve the conscious radicalism or secure the decisive breakthroughs of previous strike waves in 1917–20, 1941–3, and 1946–7, it nevertheless marked a point of departure. Segments of labour were placing limits on how much they would be contained by the bureaucratic legalism of modern class relations. Writing a year after the wildcat wave, Ed Finn summarized the general importance of the new mood of labour militancy, drawing on his particular familiarity with railway workers:

> Impatient with the interminable delays, and with the seeming lack of assertiveness by their elected negotiators, they took measures into their own hands by staging several wildcat strikes. When they were ordered back to work by the strike-ending legislation, many thousands of them defied the government edict for several days before reluctantly submitting. Had they received the slightest encouragement from the leaders, Canada would have witnessed the spectacle of a mass defiance of Parliament by 120,000 citizens. These workers are now completely disillusioned with the whole railway labour-management system. Many are fed up with their own unions, or at least their present union leaders. The debacle that ended their strike last

summer put the finishing touch to their disenchantment. The only thing that prevented them from engaging in further mass demonstrations of their displeasure was the size of the final wage settlement ... more than double the 1964–65 wage increase.

Finn concluded that the bitterness engulfing Canadian labour ranks was liable to unleash a new round of 'illegal work stoppages,' and if it did not it 'certainly bodes ill for any peaceful settlement of the next round of negotiations.' More repression, he prophesied, would make working-class upheavals of 1966 seem 'like a tea party by comparison.'[48] It is critical to appreciate the wildness of the wildcat wave, for it proved a forceful, if transitory, reminder that the much-heralded postwar settlement was less than universally welcomed by the first generation of workers tasting the actual fruit, both bitter and sweet, of its offerings.

Not all of the wildness made front-page news or generated editorial attack in the nation's mainstream press. Some of it was so mundane that it often went unnoticed. It was no less wild for being unheralded. Workers routinely wildcatted in opposition to companies disciplining, suspending, or firing workers, as well as altering the speed of assembly lines or refusing to compensate employees adequately for transportation to and from work. A worker refusing to pay union dues, the suspension of a union committee man or shop steward, transfers of unionized workers to other sites, implementation of technological change or automation – all might precipitate workers into illegal strike action.[49] It was not particularly surprising that young autoworkers at Chrysler, Ford, and de Havilland plants routinely rebelled when the company imposed compulsory overtime. However, when they wildcatted and won the right to be let off work early to attend a hockey tournament in which their buddies were playing, it was a sign that the times were definitely changing.[50]

Stevedores seemed particularly susceptible to wildcat fever, usually of the kind that many would dismiss as rather frivolous. They walked off the Montreal docks, 3,500 strong, on a spring day in 1966 to voice their displeasure at police ticketing their cars parked adjacent to the waterfront. If any of their longshoring brethren were disciplined for transgressions involving drinking, job action was often immediate. The Toronto docks were shut down in June 1966 when harbour police manhandled a longshoreman accused of having an open bottle of beer in a public place. Hamilton's lakeside facilities were subjected to three wildcat walkouts over the course of ten days in November 1965.[51] All three apparently were in protest against suspensions that followed liquor violations,' the *Globe and Mail* reported soberly, noting that the job actions, unsupported by the union, were 'frustrating work at the docks at the peak of the busy end of the season.'[51]

Given what the postwar settlement was supposed to accomplish, and the order unions were expected to achieve in Canada's workplaces, this was all fairly wild. But the wildcats often got even wilder as pent-up frustrations exploded in violence. The largest wildcat in the 1965–6 upsurge, the illegal walkout of thousands of Inco workers, was a key case in point. Workers in the Sudbury region had a long history of militancy, having fought a lengthy 119-day strike against the company in 1958.[52] It ended badly, and to complicate matters union relations were embittered by a violent jurisdictional battle that pitted the communist-led International Mine, Mill, and Smelter Workers Union against the United Steelworkers of America (USWA). The latter was successful in wresting control of the huge Sudbury-area membership away from one of the few radical holdouts in postwar trade unionism. Some Inco workers' memories were nevertheless long in their recollection of the USWA's misdeeds. As contract negotiations faltered in the summer of 1966, the wildcat spread from one operation to another and eventually, outside of all official union control, it took on the trappings of a 'wartime military machine.' Illegal strikers used 'walkie-talkies' to communicate and threatened to disable a transport helicopter Inco was using to get supervisory personnel into company facilities. With provincial police appearing on the scene, the wildcatters armed themselves with lengths of pipe, baseball bats, steel bars, and ominous clubs. Roads were blockaded, hydro and telephone lines sabotaged, and a supply truck en route to the plant was stopped, overturned, and rolled down a hill. Shipments of nickel to the United States were stopped dead in their tracks. The *Toronto Telegram* reported that some pickets carried shot guns and were prepared 'to take on all comers.' One Steelworker official confessed his wonderment at the wildness: 'I saw the Molotov cocktails, the guns, and the dynamite. The union lost control of the situation. Eventually we took truckloads of arms of one kind or another away from the picket lines.' When a settlement was finally reached, and the dissident wildcatters tamed, worker discontent was barely assuaged by the company's wage concessions, which saw increases of almost 30 per cent for skilled tradesmen, a bonus of five-week vacations on top of regular holiday time for all workers with half a decade of service under their belts, and greatly enhanced indemnity benefits for those unable to work because of sickness or accident. Yet there were strikers who refused to report for the midnight shift as the Inco rebellion was declared over in mid-September 1966.[53]

Inco's wildcatters set something of a tone for their Stelco counterparts, who walked out in the first week of August 1966, their picket signs expressing irritation at the usual stalled collective bargaining talks. 'No Contract, No Work,' was a favoured maxim of wildcat workers in an explosive summer of illegal strikes. Resentments quickly boiled over, and wildcatters soon pitted themselves against not only the company, but their union officials, mainstream media photographers, foremen, and almost anyone who tried to rein in their rebellion. On the first full day of the wildcat, cars parked in the company lot, identified as belonging to supervisors and workers who refused to join the growing pickets, were vandalized. Journalists were jostled, their cameras seized, and a later company attempt to force a train carrying scrap metal through the line was physically rebuffed, the wildcat workers clashing with police in the process. When the company tried to sneak personnel into the plants by boat, wildcat 'vigilantes' organized to patrol the docks and prevent the surreptitious water brigades from making their way onto Stelco property. Union stewards dispatched to the wildcat picket lines to cajole the dissidents into stopping their illegal walkout were 'howled down and insulted.' The melee culminated in a physical charge against the union officers, who required a police escort to extricate them from the scene and secure their safety. When USWA leaders invited picket captains at the four struck Stelco gates to send a dozen representatives each to the union hall to meet with the negotiating committee, between 200 and 300 angry wildcatting workers rushed the building. Panicked by what they interpreted as a growing 'mob psychology,' union officials called the police, which merely made matters worse. 'Get the fuzz out of here. This is our hall. They have no right here!' screamed a militant striker. Labour officialdom cracked down. Union leaflets declared that there was no authorized strike at Stelco. They deplored 'leaderless, directionless, and futile' actions of 'irresponsible' elements, reminding the militants that there would be no strike relief or welfare for those engaging in the walkout. Anti-wildcat material was torn from stewards' hands, crumpled, piled in the street, and burned. Then, according to one obviously less-than-progressive union official, the militants danced and howled around the pyre, 'just like a load of ... indians.' The USWA placed newspaper advertisements urging the wildcatters to terminate their illegal actions, took to radio airwaves to suppress the strike, and asked police to close down taverns in the vicinity of Stelco, thereby depriving the discontented workers of both venues to meet and places to bolster their bodies with food and drink. Eventually idling 12,500 production workers and 3,500 non-union office staff, the Stelco strike, soon supported by wives of the wildcatters, erupted in a 6 August 1966 'fist-swinging, gouging' battle between police and company guards, on the one hand, and a 'surging mob of 2,000 steelworkers,' on the other. Arrests, assaults, and arson characterized the day, which also witnessed a mass sit-down of strikers that clogged a major Hamilton thoroughfare. Hanging over the USWA until 1 September 1966, the uprising at Stelco eventually cooled. Workers turned down one union-endorsed potential agreement before returning to work. Management promised it would at least review the cases of fifty-one workers fired or suspended for their role in the violent early August illegal job action and bumped its contract offer considerably.[54]

Labour violence in 1965–6 thus seemed endemic.[55] Quebec longshoremen blockaded the ports of Trois-Rivières, Montreal, and Quebec in early June 1966, their strike marked by two days of especially boisterous and rowdy proceedings. Automobiles were stolen, driven to the docks, torched and dynamited, pickets refusing to let firemen through their lines to extinguish the blaze.[56] At Chelmsford, Ontario, a strike of fourteen board of education caretakers required police to clear picket lines for students, one-third of whom refused to cross, and gave rise to mass demonstrations by the Sudbury and District Labour Council, denials by the attorney general that the cops were strikebreaking, and the blowing up of two school board members' cars with explosives.[57] Vehicles were also bombed by strikers at the Concrete Ready Mix plant in St Laurent, Quebec, and at the Scarborough Taggart Transport Company.[58] Striking Montreal longshoremen resorted to violence in a May 1966 battle, having rejected agreements engineered by the federal minister of labour and a judicial mediator. When the shipping federations tried to introduce non-union crews to the docks, the stevedores slashed tires, broke employers' windows, and reportedly used explosives on company property. It took 500 police dispatched to patrol the waterfront for order to be restored.[59]

The wildness of the 1965–6 class struggle prompted the Ontario government to haul the 82-year-old Justice Ivan Rand out of his judicial mothballs, setting him up to inquire into the increasingly tempestuous climate of industrial 'disputes.' Ostensibly instigated by the Peterborough Tilco strikers' violation of an injunction limiting them to twelve pickets, the Rand inquiry ranged broadly over a number of issues relating to strikes, lockouts, and the legal responsibilities of contending parties in the camps of labour and capital. Rand and his provincial royal commission entourage traversed the province (and undertook some international junkets as well), accumulating testimony that totalled 5,000 pages. So masculinist were the assumptions of the inquiry that, as Joan Sangster notes tellingly, not one woman testified before the whole commission. Ironically enough, as the Rand Commission convened in Toronto, 100 workers at Hiram Walker Limited wildcatted when their bosses refused three of their number an opportunity to attend the hearings.[60]

Rand was no longer the far-seeing progressive that he had been heralded as in 1946. Instead, his approach to the wildness of class battle as it had been enacted in 1965–6 was increasingly troubled. An advocate of progressive, responsible, freedom-loving unionism, Rand prided himself on his expertise in law and labour relations. He had no time for the new breed of unionist who refused to see the courts and the police as esteemed protectors of basic rights. Haranguing one labour figure who failed to bow in deference to the majesty of the law, instead arguing that it dripped with class unfairness and collusion, Rand railed: 'I am astonished you have the opinion of the police and the courts that you do when they protect you from thugs you talk as if they are utterly irresponsible. I know more about the courts than you do and I say there is nothing of the sort.' Rand recoiled from civil disobedience, mass picketing, and strike discipline that prevented scabs from entering workplaces – in short, the entire 1945 edifice of militant tactics that Windsor's Ford workers had used to good effect in prompting his arbitration decision that would stand for two decades as the cornerstone of the postwar settlement. Denying that strikers in the mid-1960s dealt with 'conditions of beggary or ruthless exploitation,' Rand now feared above all else a rampant lawlessness. 'What is essential to a democratic government under a regime of law,' the justice insisted, 'is that clashes of interests be settled by reason, not by muscle or guns.' The 1940s were long gone. Having helped to create the postwar settlement, Rand declared, in 1968, that it was no longer necessary.[61]

The learned justice was no fan of the wildness of wildcat workers. He claimed that history had not exactly absolved them. Small wonder, for Rand's survey of wildcat strikes showed that the law had been anything but a friend to the wild: in the approximately 110 Ontario strikes that Rand's data identified as having taken place during the life of collective agreements in the 1965–6 wildcat wave, almost 75 of these walkouts were slapped with some kind of disciplinary retribution. Fines were levied, arrests made, injunctions granted, employees dismissed, suspended, or reprimanded, and strikes declared illegal. Rand agreed with the notion that this kind of restraining rod should not be spared. Even granting that many union officials also took umbrage at the wildness of the wildcatters, few in the ranks of the workers' movement had much good to say about the final published Rand report. For the most part, it was regarded as 'a textbook for the promotion of conflict and turmoil in Ontario's industrial relations.'[62]

Politics and the Wildness of Working-Class Upheaval

Justice Ivan Rand saw little politics in the 1965–6 labour revolt, save for the bad manners of those who did not accept the boundaries of restraint required in civil society.[63] There was nevertheless no disguising the extent to which some of the wildness of the mid-1960s was related to the often intense politicization of the working class.

This was evident in Quebec, for instance, where some of the violence associated with working-class upheaval blurred into the class-ordered struggles of the rising independence movement. A shoe factory, for instance, was the site of ongoing picket line violence that pitted non-union workers against striking unionists. *Indépendantistes* associated with the Front de Libération du Québec (FLQ) stepped into the fray. Dragging on for the better part of a year, the 1965–6 battle culminated in a bomb explosion that killed a 64-year-old secretary and left eight others injured, closing the plant.[64] May 1965 saw a flurry of FLQ-associated bombings at various work sites and struck companies. In Drummondville, the Dominon Textile works were bombed as 5,000 CNTU-affiliated workers walked picket lines, their job action having commenced in March. Twenty-four hours before 4,000 Montreal postal workers commenced wildcat strike action a bomb was defused at the Peel Street post office. Job actions in a variety of economic sectors were marred by violence, dynamite and Molotov cocktails being the incendiary devices of choice. In an underground memo written in 1966, the FLQ's Pierre Vallières indicated that the organization's 'military action is limited to sabotage, bombings, and organizing strikers' self defence,' largely through detonating 'token explosions' during workers' walkouts.[65] Some Quebec strikes of these years were also joint efforts of unionists and members of the Rassemblement pour l'Indépendance Nationale. One such confrontation, involving the Dominion Ayers Company, a plywood concern in Lachute, began in the summer of 1966 and reached into early autumn. It culminated in a huge solidarity rally that was broken up by company guards on 'Tear Gas Sunday.' Security forces battled workers and their supporters with batons, tossing canisters into the crowd. Molotov cocktails sailed back in reply. The next day a bomb was left near the Ayers plant. Even the company president's domestic residence did not go unscathed, rampaging strikers and their allies stoning the house and setting its grounds on fire.[66]

New developments galvanized Quebec workers as the Confédération des Syndicats Nationaux (CSN/CNTU) shifted away from its Catholicism to chart new streams, especially for public sector workers, in the rising tide of sociopolitical class struggles. Paced by Montreal's Central Labour Council and its fiery president, Michel Chartrand, the CNTU unions moved aggressively to the left in the 1965–8 years, challenging imperialist war in Vietnam and issuing radical manifesto-like statements that widened the political parameters of trade unionism. Pressing for labour to struggle not only for the rights of organized workers, the CNTU embraced anti-imperialist resistance to war and colonization and took up the causes of the unorganized, the unemployed, tenants, and consumers. This, in turn, paved the way for the tremendous explosion of class militancy in Quebec's Common Front mobilizations of 1970–2. Industrial unionists and teachers, craft unions and radical supporters, marched arm in arm as French-Canadian workers launched massive work stoppages and general strikes in March–April 1972. The rebelliousness was tamed only with back-to-work legislation, crippling fines levied by the courts against the unions, and selective imprisonment of labour leaders.[67]

None of this class conflict was unrelated to the emergence of a radical nationalist movement that identified with the oppressed and exploited proletariat and found itself increasingly at odds with the centralized power of Canadian federalism. Montreal May Days in the 1960s became huge festivals of alternative thought and practice, the vessel of parade overflowing with working-class and radical nationalist content. The CNTU embraced the cause of incarcerated FLQ members, demanding their release, and separatists such as Vallières steeled themselves in class conflict defeats like the *La Presse* journalists' strike of 1964–5. Taxi drivers and students waged war at Montreal's airport, battling police in a 1968 show of force protesting the monopoly held by the Anglo-Canadian firm Murray-Hill over prime limousine and cab service pickup properties. An October 1969 demonstration of the Mouvement de Libération du Taxi turned violent as an encounter at the entryway to the

Murray-Hill Limousine Company ended with Molotov cocktails flying through the air and a security guard firing a twelve-gauge shotgun into the crowd. An undercover Quebec Provincial Police officer, rumoured to have been functioning as an agent provocateur among the militant protesters, was mysteriously killed. Cabbies were rivalled in their militance by Montreal mail-truck drivers. They formed their own cooperative company and eventually secured certification as a CNTU affiliate, managing, as well, to win the lucrative federal contract from Canada Post. This victory was soon undermined by the federal Liberal Party's decision, in February 1970, to divide the delivery of mail among four different companies. For two and a half years *les gars de Lapalme*, as the drivers dubbed themselves, battled Ottawa and eventually their own union. They employed sabotage, intimidated drivers who took their jobs, and were anything but reluctant in their use of violence. In the short span of six months, the striking mail drivers damaged 1,200 postal boxes, attacked 662 postal trucks, vandalized 104 postal stations, and inflicted and suffered 75 reported injuries. Seven dynamite explosions were attributed to them, their ranks thinned by 102 arrests. Still, *les gars de Lapalme* turned out in force to give Pierre Elliott Trudeau the proverbial jeering raspberry on Parliament Hill. They were not pleased at experiencing Trudeau's shift in gears from his days as a 1950s advocate of Quebec's working class to the federal government's minister of justice and, eventually, prime minister of the country. Faced with their taunts, Trudeau snapped back in kind: 'Mangez de la merde!'[68] The postwar settlement was impolitely imploding.

In English Canada, youthful, militant working-class nationalism often took the mid- to late-1960s form of antagonism to the old-guard, international unions headquartered in the United States.[69] Since the 1920s, a strictly Canadian labour movement had been espoused by some in the ranks of the trade union movement. By the 1950s, two key figures in the drive to organize workers into autonomous Canadian unions were Kent Rowley and Madeleine Parent. Driven from the United Textile Workers of America in a 1952 purge of a dozen Canadian staffers accused of 'disastrous and irresponsible leadership' and 'communist' leanings, Rowley and Parent countered by setting up the Canadian Textile Council. It languished until the populist and poorly conceived nationalism of the Diefenbaker years (1958–63) and Liberal Finance Minister Walter Gordon's anti-Americanism of the early 1960s helped to revive working-class concern with the national question. Rowley and Parent spearheaded a new national trade union movement named the

Council of Canadian Unions, later to be called the Confederation of
Canadian Unions (CCU). By the mid-1960s and into the latter half of
the decade a number of Canadian locals left U.S. unions to found small
Canadian bodies. Discontent with the United States and its imperialist
dominance often echoed on wildcat picket lines. One Inco wildcatter
insisted that Canada in 1966 was 'on the verge of a revolution ... when
we see what is being taken out of this country by the Americans we are
fed up. We want action.'[70]

International unions headquartered in the United States dominated
the Canadian labour movement in the mid-1960s. Fully 1,125,000 workers, or almost 72 per cent of the ranks of organized employees in
Canada, belonged to 110 such U.S.-affiliated unions, the largest of
which were the USWA, the UAW, and the Brotherhoods of Carpenters
and Joiners, Woodworkers, Electrical Workers, and Pulp and Paper Mill
Workers. Only the rising public sector unionists, concentrated in the
84,000-strong Canadian Union of Public Employees, as well as the
32,100 CBRT railway workers, cracked the top ten unions in Canada in
terms of their memberships. By the mid-1970s, public sector unionism
in Canada, necessarily organized in national unions and thus different
from the internationals of old, had expanded considerably and created
a dramatic shift in the relations within the upper echelons of the labour
movement. The percentage of organized workers belonging to international unions in 1975 had dropped to just over 51 per cent. CUPE and
the Public Service Alliance of Canada, with their combined memberships of 250,000 in 1970, now rivalled steelworkers and autoworkers in
terms of numerical significance. In the mid-1960s these developments
were in the making, rather than already accomplished. Canadian workers often represented small minorities within their international unions:
USWAers from Canada constituted just under 11 per cent of the international's dues payers, while the comparable percentages for machinists, labourers in the auto sector, and packinghouse workers ranged
from 4.5 to 6.7 to 21.9. Among Quebec workers, of course, nationally
organized unions were stronger, headed by the powerful CNTU, and
the francophone state was even known to launch assaults on the U.S.-
based internationals.[71] But in English Canada there was no mistaking
the weight of so-called international (really binational) unionism.[72]

As the rebellious atmosphere of the 1960s permeated the unions, the
U.S.-based internationals were often, rightly or wrongly, subject to critique by dissident Canadians, who regarded them as ossified junior partners in a project of imperialist colonization and class collaboration.[73] In

the USWA the critique of U.S. domination grew out of a highly politicized left–right factional split in the union that related to the long-standing feud between the ultimately victorious Steelworkers and their communist rivals, the Mine Mill and Smelter Workers Union. That battle was settled by the time of the wildcat wave of 1965–6, but advocates of Canadian unionism such as Rowley and Parent revived discontent with their calls for an autonomous labour movement. (Parent had, earlier in the decade, been caricatured by Sudbury's anti-communist USWA leadership as a red witch, riding into northern Ontario on her revolutionary broom.) In Hamilton, the Stelco wildcat of 1966 was led by an Autonomy Group, described by Bill Freeman as 'a loosely organized collection of young inexperienced activists,' who, in spite of their rather lackluster coherence, effectively parlayed a fusion of popular nationalism, militancy, and anti-establishment bravado into loud attacks on 'sell-out' contracts and the complicity of the local and international leadership with management. During the illegal walkout there was much talk that the U.S. leadership had cajoled Hamilton's USWA officials to force their dissident ranks back to work so that precious strike funds could be preserved in the event they were needed to support job actions in the United States.[74] If the Steelworkers were not necessarily guilty of bleeding Canadian unionists for dues (in the 1968–70 years Canadian USWA members contributed just over $4 million to the international's coffers, but drew out well over $12 million, in what amounted to a $55 subsidy for each Canadian member), other U.S.-based unions could not make the same claim. From 1962 to 1967 the internationals collected a massive $166,322,000 in Canada, but returned less than $99,000,000 to union locals north of the border. U.S.-based leaderships were not shy in using heavy-handed methods to coerce Canadians into compliance with their wishes. As the wildcat wave wound down, fully twenty-six Canadian union locals had been placed under trusteeship by their U.S. headquarters.[75]

In the late 1960s and early 1970s a series of breakaways and successions by Canadian union locals wracked the International Brotherhood of Pulp, Sulphite, and Paper Mill Workers, International Union of Operating Engineers, the International Molders and Allied Workers Union, and the Retail, Wholesale and Department Store Union, as well as other unions headquartered in the United States. This represented, in Finn's words, 'the first stirrings of the nationalist ferment now bubbling up within Canadian labour.' If stifled, Finn warned, the result would be that these 'incipient rumblings' would lead to a 'titanic – and ultimately successful – struggle for Canadian union emancipation.' The body of workers organized in truly independent English-speaking Canadian unions was small by the end of the 1960s, roughly 124 organizations with a membership of 60,000, but they were nevertheless a voice of discontent with the internationals and their often-staid union officials. Such breakaway unionists had served vocal notice that they would not allow themselves to be easily subordinated to U.S. leaders.

Particularly among metal trades and smelter workers in British Columbia and machinists whose shops were linked to Manitoba railway and aerospace industries there existed an ongoing challenge to the bureaucratized leaderships of the established internationals. This included a successful raid of the nationalist Canadian Association of Smelter and Allied Workers (CASAW) on the USWA local at the Alcan works in Kitimat as well as a contentious Winnipeg-based breakaway movement pitting the Canadian Association of Industrial, Mechanical and Allied Workers (CAIMAW) against the International Association of Machinists (IAM). In the latter case, CAIMAW parlayed rank-and-file discontents in the aftermath of a 1968 strike into a take-over of the bargaining unit at Bristol Aerospace. With the war for workers' affiliation unfolding, the Cleveland-based IAM leaders placed insurgent CAIMAW-inclined local Winnipeg trade union officers on trial. For their part, the targeted malcontents dismissed the distant Machinists' hierarchy as out of touch with their members: 'They're backward, conservative, old, wealthy people living in luxury who have less in common with the average guy in the plant than with the bosses.' This was a refrain that reverberated in rebellious working-class circles over the course of the mid- to late 1960s. As a former president of the Trail Steelworkers local proclaimed in 1969, 'The younger workers, because of the environment they've been brought up under and seeing the fallacies of their society, these have a stronger feeling of anti-Americanism. It's there, let's not kid ourselves, not only in Canada but all over the world.'[76]

Labour Walking a New Line

As young workers rampaged outside of plants closed by wildcats, as injunctions prohibiting picketing brought forth a deluge of denunciation in which the law was questioned if not repudiated, and as established unions and their conventional structures of collective bargaining, as well as their respectable leaderships, were chastised and jeered, labour seemed to be walking a newly unruly line in the mid-1960s. It threatened the postwar settlement. We are used to seeing this labour–capital accord undermined by capital and the state, a process that Leo Panitch and Donald Swartz have outlined rigorously in a detailed examination of post-1973 socio-economic trends and government 'back-to-work' and other kinds of restrictive, anti-labour, legislation.[77] The irony of the 1965–6 wildcat wave was that an initial blow at the system of so-called industrial pluralism was struck from within the House of Labour, albeit by workers who did not see themselves as owners of the respectable domicile. As this happened, long-established understandings of workers' place, in company and union, were challenged and, in particular instances, came under violent assault. A new identity, one more openly rebellious, was contending with past appreciations of the need for restraint, of conformity to duly constituted British understandings of authority and what it was owed.

Journalists referred to a 'new labour revolution, with all its threat of turmoil,' suggesting that it had 'only just begun.'[78] They spoke with more insight than they knew. For the true possibility of revolution lay in politicizing young and rebellious workers in the ideas and programmatic commitment to social transformation that grew out of workplace relations but that necessarily reached past the confining experiences of life on the assembly line or in the mine or mill. The task was to expand the political horizons of those trapped in the limitations of industrial legality and postwar trade unions, which were brokered at every point by their own containments. Around the corner of the wildcat wave of 1965–6 was a growing left challenge. Had it co-joined youth of the university and the unions, the result could well have reconfigured the nature of twentieth-century Canada. Class difference is a difficult hurdle to leap, however, and as campus youth, women, and Aboriginal advocates of 'Red Power' joined the unruly workers of the 1960s in an explosive embrace of dissidence and opposition, they did so, ultimately, divided from one another, in separate and unequal mobilizations.

PART IV

Radicalism, Revolution, and Red Power

Chapter Eight

New Left Liberations:
The Poetics, Praxis,
and Politics of Youth Radicalism

Canada's 'most forgettable generation' was the subject of a carping September 1969 *Saturday Night* article. It wrote *finis* to a phenomenon. A Montreal associate editor of the popular magazine, Peter Desbarats, had apparently come back from an evening stroll around McGill University, where, in a bowl-like depression at the north end of the campus, he had seen an apelike gathering of what he took to be the 'exhausted new wave of revolutionary youth.' Hair obscuring their faces, reminding Desbarats of nothing so much as 'the herd,' the students undoubtedly talked among themselves, but all the reporter could discern was 'a few guttural noises.' The journalist, obviously offended by the scene, took solace in the view that 'this is the end of it':

> The easy poetry and trite melodies have palled. Pot has settled into its humdrum place and even the strong drugs are hardly worth a television programme any longer. The only thing that seems to remain, for those who have been spoiled by the whole game is ... The hair. The sandals. The uniform. The liturgical slang and loose simian gestures.

Desbarats, like many others ensconced in a complacent repugnance, considered 1960s youth rebels little more than 'cases of arrested individual development.' He concluded that 'it will be a long time before the actual veterans of the movement, now moving into their twenties, will be able to evaluate their own mutilation.' Content to forget what the

Feminist protest, Abortion Caravan, 1970 (York University, *Toronto Telegram* Fonds, FO433, 1974-002/134).

1960s had symbolized, Desbarats closed the book on the 'silent, simian shapes squatting on the McGill campus,' and in thousands of other locales across the country, as 'a parody of the universe envisioned by McLuhan.' He wished this generational blight on individual creativity good riddance, if not good luck.[1]

There was no denying, by late 1969, that something of the taste of the 1960s had soured. Locales like Toronto's Yorkville, the site of demonstrations and street occupations in August 1967, were sorry shadows of their former selves.[2] The influence of the lost generation of the 1950s, captured in Jack Kerouac's frenzied mobility of *On the Road,* seemed now confirmed in the poetic despair of Allen Ginsberg's *Howl.* An archetypal 1956 statement of the Beats, its lines of freewheeling, hard-bop verse appeared, at the close of the 1960s, eerily prophetic:

> I saw the best minds of my generation destroyed by madness, starving
>   hysterical naked,
> dragging themselves through the negro streets at dawn looking for an angry
>   fix,
> angelheaded hipsters burning for the ancient connection to the starry
>   dynamo in the machinery of night,
> who poverty and tatters and hollow-eyed and high sat up smoking in the
>   supernatural darkness of cold-water flats floating across the tops of cities
>   contemplating jazz,
> ...
> who passed through universities with radiant cool eyes hallucinating Arkansas
>   and Blake-light tragedy among the scholars of war,
> who were expelled from the academies for crazy and publishing obscene odes
>   on the windows of the skull ...[3]

Too many radical youth had burned out.

Old Left ideas seem to creep back into the widening fissures of New Left thought. 'The revolutionary process cannot be set in motion merely by the ardor of our convictions,' lectured Irwin Silber in the pages of *Canadian Dimension.* 'It is still true that only a revolution based in the working class is capable of destroying capitalism and developing socialism.' There was a backing away from the nihilism of the new, as articulated by Jim Morrison of The Doors: 'We're interested in anything about revolt, disorder, chaos, and activity that appears to have no meaning.' Too often this seemed just a reproduction of old patterns of cultural and commercial ugliness: in 1969 the Rolling Stones hired

Hell's Angels to protect them from a crowd of love only to have that sea of emotion part in blood, with bikers swinging pool cues viciously, the almost scripted black male drawing his gun, the end a mournful, savage beating and deadly stabbing. Woodstock had taken a deep dive into a very bad Altamont trip. When the *Globe and Mail* featured a page-one image of a 14-year-old runaway girl, Mary Ann Vecchio, kneeling in anguish beside a dead Kent State, Ohio, student on 5 May 1970, the 1960s were, for many, spiralling downward. If the decade was not over that spring, it surely crashed sometime between September 1970 and July 1971, with Janis Joplin, Jimi Hendrix, and Morrison all dead of drug overdoses.[4]

Desbarats was not, then, so much wrong in his dating of a 1960s post-mortem as he was mean-spiritedly dismissive of its contribution when it had been in full flower. One of the New Left movement's most sensitive Canadian commentators and herself a Sixties veteran, Myrna Kostash does not consider herself scarred and deformed by the experience of the protest decade. Her book, *Long Way from Home: The Story of the Sixties Generation in Canada* (1980), confirms that by the end of the decade much was in disarray. By 1970 she wrote, after what seemed an eternity of police harassment, physical beatings at demonstrations, the state's endless parade of repression, and the disillusionment of so many campaigns turning into something other than their original expansive and visionary intentions, 'the hardest thing to bear was the nightmare that behind one's stumbling, fatigued and frightened stride came no one at all.' Kostash nevertheless refuses the victimhood Desbarats imposed upon her and so many others. 'While all about us insist that we failed and were absorbed into the consensus,'she wrote in recognition of the curtain of commentary that has descended on the 1960s and the New Left, it was nevertheless critical 'to remember that there was a moment, an hour, a day when we were successful, when the system could not ... proceed with impunity.' Indeed, Kostash remains grateful for having lived during a unique moment: 'What is special about growing up in the Sixties,' she writes, 'is how close our learning came to being revolutionary. You can't get much luckier than that.'[5]

Desbarats, then, seemed to have missed at least something of the march of the 1960s, including its purchase on many of its activists. Ellie Kirzner of Toronto's *Now* magazine, declared of her involvements in the decade that they constituted 'a delicious addiction.'[6] Milton Acorn, a Canadian 'people's poet,' put it slightly differently in his commemorative verse, 'Ho Chi Minh': 'We shall never have this sword again: / We will

always need it; / even when, instead of 'sword' / we may say "flower."'[7]
Canadian Dimension, founded in 1963 and arguably one of the strongest
and most sustained voices of the 1960s, declared with more confidence
in a 1988 commemoration of 'The Explosive 60s': 'We were brazen and
brave and we shook them badly despite our mistakes. We'll do it again.'[8]

The 1960s: A *New* Left

Few decades brand themselves with a political shift to the left. The
1960s did so. If the surge of oppositional thought and action was international,[9] Canada could hardly be exempt.[10]

Kostash presents the Canadian New Left as 'seemingly overwhelmed by
the American example yet fighting for its native life.' A New Left participant told her: 'We thought like Europeans and acted like Americans.'
Few could deny that in Canada's burgeoning and youthful New Left, the
1960s were a cauldron of British and French ideas and the proximate
practices of the United States, with echoes of black struggles (from 'We
Shall Overcome' to 'Burn, Baby, Burn') ringing in militant ears. Alder-
maston peace marches and the idea of unilateral nuclear disarmament;
Fabian socialism and the British Labour Party; the existentialism,
Marxism, and anti-colonialism of Albert Camus, Jean-Paul Sartre, and
Frantz Fanon – all jostled with the iconic personages, places, and pow-
derkegs of the U.S. movement: Selma and Newark, Tom Hayden and
Malcolm X, Students for a Democratic Society and the League of Revolu-
tionary Black Workers, Eldridge Cleaver and Stokely Carmichael.

New Left news outlets like the New York–based 'independent radical
newsweekly,' the *Guardian*, were especially influential. Originating in the
non-communist Old Left of the 1948 Henry Wallace campaign, and
founded as the *New York Guardian*, the paper shed much of its traditional
leftism in the mid- to late 1960s. After a 1968 clash between owner and
co-founder James Aronson and his increasingly New Left staff and columnists, the paper changed hands, shortening its name and broadening
its influence. Affiliated with no particular political organization, the
Guardian was nonetheless resolutely New Left, a guide to what was happening in the movement as well as a publication venue for a wide array
of writers staunch in their antagonism to imperialism, racism, and the
exploitation of the working class. For many young Canadian leftists,
searching for alternative reporting of the events of the 1960s and a radical perspective in which to situate them, the *Guardian* was their preferred source of information. It was supplemented by access to the

offerings of the Liberation News Service or the glossy monthly *Ramparts*. The latter publication, edited by Robert Scheer, rode the explosive growth of the New Left to massive subscription and newsstand sales approaching 250,000 each issue by the end of the 1960s. Compared with such venues of New Left thought, more mainstream left-of-centre publications like *The Nation* or *Canadian Forum* seemed oddly out of step with the 'movement' scene, far too staid and limp in their willingness to break moulds and rock boats.

Marxism did not initiate the decade's radicalism, but it did, eventually, come to influence it mightily, even if many would, in turn, reject it forcefully. It was not, however, the *old* Marx of political economy, long days of pouring over Blue Books in the British Museum, *Das Kapital*, and carbuncles. Rather, it was the *young* Marx of the yet-to-be-widely-published *Economic and Philosophic Manuscripts of 1844*, the rebel Hegelian, theorist of alienation, and beer-downing author of a sheaf of love poems. And, surprising in its influence, Mao Tse Tung's thought found its way from study groups through party formations and into street protests, no texts being more widely read in the late 1960s than the cream-coloured and embossed-covered pocket volumes of Peking's Foreign Language Press. The slogans of the time were a uniquely dualistic mix of Mao's materialism and the anarcho-surrealist graffiti of a metaphorical Parisian Left Bank. How could an era embrace simultaneously the maxims 'Political power grows out of the barrel of a gun,' 'Grasp revolution, promote production!' 'Workers of the world, have fun!' 'Boredom is counterrevolutionary,' 'Be realistic, demand the impossible!' and 'Those who take their desires for reality are those who believe in the reality of their desires'? Yet it was done.

When Parisian students scrawled 'Down with the Stalinist carcass. Run, comrade, the old world is behind you' on the walls of the Sorbonne, moreover, they were separating themselves from a past left. Its rigidities and ossifications were so entirely foreign to them that they had trouble grasping what the long march of revolutionary degeneration associated with the Soviet Union was really all about. They wanted not so much the program of revolution, as its adventure. The inspiration of the Cuban Revolution was seen in this way, elevating Che Guevara in the eyes of millions. This and much else forced the significance of decolonization movements and anti-racist struggles to the forefront of New Left appreciation. At few historical junctures was the trade in the theory and practice of revolution more exhilaratingly wild and seemingly pregnant with promise than in the 1960s.[11]

The promise dawned with a rejection of politics as it had been known. As Carl Oglesby wrote in the introduction to a collection of essays on the radicalism of the 1960s, 'The New Left is properly so called because in order to exist it had to overcome the memories, the certitudes, and the promises of the Old Left.'[12] C. Wright Mills, drawn to the newness of the first New Left in Britain, penned his transatlantic comrades a 1960 letter in response to their publication of a book of essays, *Out of Apathy*. Wright Mills situated himself in opposition to the twinned ideological pillars of Vulgar Marxism and Liberal Rhetoric. They were joined at the stiff hip by a bureaucratic denunciation of 'radical criticisms of their respective societies,' the socialist realist Soviet Union and the end-of-ideology United States. These power blocs in an oppositional global order governed by the arms race and complacency were what needed to be rejected. Their very connectedness conditioned outmoded, hierarchical thinking. Wright Mills wanted to shed the 'labour metaphysic,' that Old Left *faith* in the working class 'as *the* historic agency of social change,' as little more than the legacy of an unrealistic Victorian Marxism. He was equally insistent on the need to dump the disillusionment 'with any real commitment to socialism in any recognizable form' that was the foundational structure of the raging ideologies of non-ideology in Western capitalism. In their place, Wright Mills offered the relentless utopian drive of criticism, rigorous analysis of the agencies of historical change, and a moral commitment to act. When he looked at who, trapped in the ossified structures of both the East and the West, was waging war against 'all the old crap' (he was quoting Marx), Wright Mills saw only 'the young intelligentsia.' Content to let the old men ask sourly 'Out of apathy – into what?' Wright Mills revelled in the rise of the New Left. 'We are beginning to move again,' he concluded confidently.[13]

When the Port Huron Statement was drafted by Tom Hayden two years later as the manifesto of Students for a Democratic Society (SDS), it contained a number of C. Wright Mills–like formulations. Tragically, the rebellious New Left sociologist had died of a heart attack shortly before the first 20,000 mimeographed copies of the statement found their way across America as university classes commenced in 1962, hawked for 35 cents. Attacking communism as anathema to American democracy, Hayden's Statement also rejected the mirror image of anti-communism. These global power polarizations, configured as they were around colonizations of the world's resources and the menace of nuclear arms, threatened humanity. They made inevitable revolutionary movements of opposition. In the United States, SDS targeted racist discrimination as *the* decisive oppression disfiguring democracy. It was also inseparable from poverty, alienation, and the stalled historic New Deal drive of American workers to secure justice and just compensation. What was new in the Port Huron Statement was that in Wright Mills's call for identification of agents of change, it drew less on Old Left understandings of the laws of motion of capitalist accumulation than on a 'movement spirit.' The eclectic document did not so much promote a program as it set an agenda for a generation, seeing the university and its students as a decisive agency of social change, arguably the first time such a perspective had been put forward seriously and with passionate political conviction. In the end, the echoes of Wright Mills's brief for utopianism and his assault on apathy were perhaps the final loud endnote of a reverberating call to espouse values and struggle for change. 'A new left must start controversy across the land, if national policies and national apathy are to be reversed,' the Statement insisted, its refusals as well as its righteousness ringing in the last sentence of the sixty-three-page manifesto: 'If we appear to seek the unattainable, as it has been said, then let it be known that we do so to avoid the unimaginable.'[14]

One of the New Left's most esteemed theoreticians, Herbert Marcuse, framed the radical project in philosophical terms in his *Essay on Liberation* (1969):

> The new sensibility has become, by this very token, *praxis*: it emerges in the struggle against violence and exploitation where this struggle is waged for essentially new ways and forms of life: negation of the entire Establishment, its morality, culture; affirmation of the right to build a society in which the abolition of property and toil terminates in a universe where the sensuous, the playful, the calm, and the beautiful become forms of existence and thereby the form of the society itself.

This philosophy of praxis thus fused theory and practical activity, in an aesthetic and politics of the deed that promised a possibility of true social transformation and the ultimate realization of freedom, both individual and collective:

> If now, in the rebellion of the young intelligentsia, the right and the truth of the imagination become the demands of political action, if surrealist forms of protest and refusal spread throughout the movement, this apparently insignificant development may indicate a fundamental change in the

situation ... The political action which insists on a new morality and a new sensibility as preconditions and results of social change occurs at a point at which the repressive rationality that has brought about the achievements of industrial society becomes utterly regressive – rational only in its efficiency to 'contain' liberation.

Praxis, in the New Left sense, entailed the freedom to think about what the movement was going to do with new sensibilities, especially those cognizant of the extent to which 'revolutionary forces emerge in the process of change itself; the translation of the potential into the actual is the work of political practice.' In struggling to make history, New Leftists were engaged, in their view, in an unprecedented undertaking. The forms that such struggles took were as decisive in determining outcomes as any theoretical laws of social motion, specific predetermined agencies of transformation, or programmatic maxims.[15]

What was strikingly new was that 1960s radicals were in actuality well ahead of their times in locating an 'end to history' malaise that later writers – on the right and in the centre-left – would exploit with the collapse of the Soviet Union in 1989.[16] Understanding that both the Soviet Union and the United States, as bureaucratic societies curbing democratic initiative and the movement of progress, had stopped history in an end that silenced the soul and numbed the mind, prompted 1960s radicals to showcase the need to kickstart historical process anew. As Mario Savio, catalyst of the Berkeley Free Speech Movement, argued at a December 1964 sit-in of an administration building: 'Here is the real contradiction: the bureaucrats hold history as ended. As a result significant parts of the population on campus and off are dispossessed, and these dispossessed are not about to accept this a-historical point of view.' In Savio's conclusion he voiced the New Left insistence that history had not ended, and that its promise demanded struggle and sacrifice:

The most exciting things going on in America today are movements to change America. America is becoming ever more the utopia of sterilized, automated contentment. The 'futures' and 'careers' for which American students now prepare are for the most part intellectual and moral wastelands. This chrome-plated consumers' paradise would have us grow up to be well-behaved children. But an important minority of men and women coming to the front today have shown that they will die rather than be standardized, replaceable and irrelevant.[17]

Savio's interventions were not decisively severed from Old Left connection. His wife at the time was a member of the Communist Party, and Berkeley's Free Speech Movement had a part of its origins in defending the right of a Communist Party figure, the historian of African-American slavery, Herbert Aptheker, to speak on campus. Yet they were new in the nature of their argument. The accent was less on the class struggle than on the refusal to succumb to bureaucracy. Automation, alienation, and segregation were Savio's crucial problems, and, indeed, the Old Left had much to say about them as well. Savio, however, said what he had to say in New Left ways, using words, examples, inflections, and tones that were different from those employed by an older communist or social democratic left, let alone men and women from the Democratic Party.

In Canada, this newness of the New Left was evident from the beginnings of the movement. Born underneath the cloud of Hiroshima and Nagasaki, chilled by the deforming iciness of the Cold War, Canada's New Left distanced itself from 'centralized undemocratic decision-making,' which it claimed was 'inexorably related to the growth of the war-fare state.' Electoral politics was conceived as a dead-end: 'Despite all our glorification of democracy in Canada the real centres of power remain far out of reach of the electors and remain intact and totally undisturbed by elections no matter who is elected.' The New Left wanted a 'new and self-directing order.'[18]

As these tendencies crystallized over time, in actions, debates, and struggles over the political direction of diverse movements and groups, an increasingly fragmented New Left actually hardened in its distinctive separation from Old Left political formations. Many New Left figures had their origins in social-democratic youth movements, and, even as late as 1965, almost half of the 150 founding members of the Student Union for Peace Action were affiliates of the New Democratic Party. Nevertheless, over time a deep suspicion of the parliamentary reformism of the Co-operative Commonwealth Federation–New Democratic Party (CCF/NDP) tradition developed. The NDP was quite often seen as little more than centralized state planning of the kind that merited the derisive dismissal of 'liberals in a hurry.' Some New Left leaders, to be sure, chastised their movement for its isolation from important, established centres of social democratic politics, including the New Democratic Youth (NDY) movement. Most New Leftists, however, regarded the NDP as but one of many houses on which they would cast a plague of rather jaundiced disdain.[19]

Communist parties, whether of the staid Stalinist sort or of the ultra-left, usually fared no better, although, again, a number of Canadian New Leftists were red-diaper babies and certainly had connections to, if not direct membership in, the Communist Party of Canada.[20] Marcuse, widely read in Canadian New Left circles, nonetheless offered a broadly accepted critique of Soviet Marxism. Communist organization was often judged little more than an appendage to bureaucracy and oppression, 'a party of order.'[21] As Peter Gzowski noted in *Maclean's*, the New Left, unlike the Old, was not interested in 'isms,' which it regarded as a hang-over from the 1930s. 'The Communists, they're empty man,' a New Leftist was quoted as saying. 'They've got the same stale ideas, the same bureaucracy. When he gets mixed up with us, a Commie dies, and a per-son develops.' Not even sure they were right, Canadian New Leftists were capable of making a virtue of their necessary programmatic uncer-tainty. 'Lots of us have doubts,' one young radical told Gzowski in 1965. 'But maybe that's exactly why all the radical movements of the 1930s went wrong. When they found out they *couldn't* save the world they just felt defeated. Well none of us are sure we can save the world. I suppose we don't even *think* we can. But we know we have to try. And we're try-ing to find new ways to work for it.'[22]

Radical activities within university departments and classrooms, spreading to and growing out of communes, high schools, daycare cen-tres, and community organizations, were understood to be 'stepping stones towards a larger revolutionary movement, yet to be consti-tuted.'[23] A major figure in the western Canadian New Left and a presi-dent of the Saskatchewan NDY, James Harding, held to the pre-eminent importance of 'confrontation with the authoritarian bureaucracies.' Sounding very much like Mario Savio, Harding often put forward views remarkably similar to those in the Port Huron Statement, although he might also understate the connection, insisting that SDS's influence was regionally rooted in Ontario. By 1969 he widened the net the New Left would cast:

An extra-parliamentary opposition will have to struggle against liberal democratic bureaucracies at all levels in society: on campus, in trade unions, in all the institutions of the corporate society. This strategy must be explicit, to work; because the institutions of neo-capitalism are so all-encompassing, radical politics can not be abstracted from the people (as is, for example, the case with party politics or any form of bureaucratic poli-tics). Our struggle must be at the base of society, where the people are, not among the elites and those who yearn to become part of the elites. This means, ultimately, organizing in mental hospitals, prisons, offices and the military in addition to schools and factories.[24]

Within the segments of the New Left drawn to anarchism, the assault on 'bureaucratic manipulation,' the proclaimed virtues of civil disobedience, and embrace of the boldest concepts of a realizable utopia were perhaps most vehement. Such statements co-joined the attack on capitalist centralization, state authoritarianism, *and* the ideas and practices of the Old Left. Class discontent was valuable only inasmuch as it disgorged the young from the repressions of the work ethic, Puritanism, consumerism, and obedience to authority. Thus, a prominent Montreal New Leftist, Dimitrios I. Roussopoulos, borrowed the words of Murray Bookchin, arguing that 'the most promising development in the factories today is the emergence of young workers who smoke pot, fuck-off on their jobs, drift into and out of factories, grow long hair, demand more leisure time rather than more pay, steal, harass all authority figures, go on wildcats, and turn on their fellow workers.' Small wonder, given this rather indiscriminate list, that Roussopoulos also pilloried capitalist institutions and the entirety of Old Left experience in one stunning paragraph of repudiation:

At a time when hierarchy as such is being brought into question, we hear the hollow echoes of 'vanguards,' and 'trained cadres under our discipline.' At a time when centralization and the State have been brought to the most explosive point of historical negativity, we hear the hollow echoes of a 'centralised movement' and a 'proletarian dictatorship.' This search for security in the past, this attempt to find a haven in a fixed dogma and an organizational hierarchy – all as substitutes for creative thought and praxis – is bitter evidence of how many little 'revolutionaries' are capable of 'revolutionising themselves and things,' much less revolutionising society as a whole. And as to those conservatives who in the midst of a technological society wave the 'little red book' to rephrase Trotsky's juicy description of Stalinism, they are the syphilis of the radical youth movement today. And for syphilis there is only one treatment – an antibiotic not argument.[25]

That a statement such as this could appear in the first Canadian collection of articles on the New Left written by New Leftists themselves was an indication of the capacity of the new radicalism to define itself in opposition to older revolutionary claims, organizational forms, and histories. It was also an articulation of the implosion of the New Left by the end of the 1960s, as contending forces fed off the body of a movement struggling to keep its energy and momentum. In a sense this strident statement proved something of a eulogy for a New Left organizational intiative that had already passed into a long night of fractious encounter, its demise missed in the clash of perspective.[26] For its embittered and extreme tone was *not* characteristic of the radical decade's entirety of struggle, a contest carried on over years of challenging adversity, to be sure, but one that also rang with joy. In the myriad makings and mobilizations of Canada's 1960s New Left lay encounters in which glimpses of the origins of this ultimate angry sectarianism can certainly be seen. Yet a more insightful vision would reveal histories of comradeship and solidarity far more tender and affectionate in which Roussopoulos and countless others participated. Brief as it was, this New Left experience encompassed an eternity of meaning, and it helped to remake understandings of Canada in the years to come.

Peace or Cease:
The Unilateralist Origins of the Canadian New Left

> We are strangers in a strange land
> Of flesh and tissue and dead moving
> Under naked trees burnt in the holocaust
> Of passion that feeds on itself.
> Not from distances of land and water,
> We come from dwellings in the zenith of time
> Blind with gunpowder in the circle of the eye;
> This is the difference – no other.

Ruth Lisa Schechter[27]

Cold War stasis and the race to nuclear annihilation prodded the New Left into being. Canadians worried by the prospects of nuclear war – writers, scientists, liberals, unaligned radicals, socialists, and a smattering of students – formed the Committee for the Control of Radiation Hazards. This soon led to the founding of the Canadian Campaign for Nuclear Disarmament in 1959. A small but committed group of students and faculty pioneered the Montreal and Toronto chapters of the Combined Universities Campaign for Nuclear Disarmament (CUCND) in the same year. On Christmas day 1959, eighty of these opponents of nuclear weapons trekked through the cold, unwelcoming streets of Ottawa to lay a wreath at the base of the National War Memorial. It was said to be the first Canadian student political demonstration since the end of the Second World War.[28]

A coalition of radicals and liberals, 'red diaper babies,' and more moderate idealists, CUCND was a largely middle-class movement of often religiously inspired youth. The Student Christian Movement had been a formative experience for many. Echoes of the early twentieth-century social gospel might still be heard in CUCND chambers, just as a radical Catholicism, now associated with Dorothy Day's Catholic Worker Movement, could well be discerned. Early CUCNDers struggled to comprehend the contradictory character of Canadian public policy, animated by commitments to decency, equality, fairness, and peace. How could Canada claim to be a peacekeeper in the global community, wearing its benevolence proudly in international forums such as the United Nations, and even consider bringing atomic weapons onto Canadian soil to arm Bomarc missiles? Always aware of other social issues, CUCND presented a brief to Parliament in November 1960 that extolled 'the worth and dignity of the individual' and embraced 'equality and self-government as the rights and needs of all men.' CUCND youth were perplexed that Canadian society paid lip service to such values but failed to develop ways to live and act according to them. 'In the name of a decent standard of living,' CUCNDers pointed out, 'we destroy food surpluses while millions starve.'[29]

Soon CUCND students were attending workshops on non-violent disobedience run by Quakers on Grindstone Island, Ontario; sitting in meetings with Voice of Women journalists, professors, and authors like Lotta Dempsey and Ursula Franklin; even rubbing shoulders with hardened trade union radicals or soft-spoken communist-sympathizing clergymen in the Canadian Peace Congress. From people like these, experienced in organizing campaigns and raising a consciousness of opposition, CUCNDers learned much. They circulated petitions, held vigils, and picked up guitars as they sang for peace. Hanging out in Saskatoon's Humanity House, putting out an issue of the strikingly impressive Montreal theoretical journal, *Our Generation against Nuclear War,* mobilizing a pan-Canadian opposition to nuclear war, CUCND members were becoming a movement. The NDP was pressured to adopt variants of CUCND's 'positive neutralism' and unilateralist disarmament positions. These had developed out of discussions about Canada's role in the U.S.-dominated North Atlantic Treaty Organization (NATO) and the extent to which this contributed to the arms race and exacerbated the possibilities of nuclear war. Inroads were made in the labour movement.[30]

At a federal conference in Toronto in late February 1963, CUCND moved in tandem with its past and with the future of student radicalism, as outlined months before in the Port Huron Statement. It opposed the 'Cold War military and political policies of both nuclear blocs,' insisting that students had a special role to play in resisting the drive to war, suggesting that the university needed to take the lead 'in the mobilization of social forces internationally for the achievement of world peace.' And then Lester Pearson and the Liberals cut the ground out from underneath CUCND, signing a clandestine 1963 accord with the United States that committed Canada to accept U.S. nuclear warheads. With the euphemistically named 'special ammunition' secretly delivered to the La Macaza, Quebec, and North Bay, Ontario, missile silos in 1964, Canada became the fourth country in the world to embrace nuclear arms. Those who sported CUCND buttons on campuses across the land never recovered from this blow. For years they had faced ugly Cold War accusations that they were 'commie' sympathizers or worse, but they had the rightness of their cause behind them. Now they had lost.

The radicals among them, a minority of those CUCND forces still willing to continue the fight, led the way forward. They marshalled energies in a new organization founded in December 1964 in Regina, named the Student Union for Peace Action, or SUPA. No ideological conformity characterized this first New Left formation, but it had moved beyond the seeming fixation on a single cause that many associated, however wrongly, with CUCND. Many, to the extent that they were turned on by intellectual concepts, were captivated by the imaginative SDS formulation of 'the Triple Revolution.' Activism was seemingly ordered by the issues flowing out of revolutions designated as cybernetics (computerization, automation, and the transformation of human labour), nuclear weaponry (the ongoing struggle for peace in the atomic age), and civil/human rights (struggles of minorities such as African Americans, but also those linked to organized labour, the unemployed, and the poor).[31] A Canadian New Left had emerged, one animated by the possibility of participatory democracy.[32]

SUPA's Sixties, 1965–1967

SUPA, like the New Left as a whole, defied easy categorization. SUPA's raison d'être was in actuality a fusion of forms and contents in which

non-violence, participatory democracy, equality, non-hierarchical structures, and open-ended objectives that valued consensus became both
means and end. Talk tended to trump reading, writing, and seriously
reflective thought. To the extent that a national organization existed, it
was premised on a regionally ordered decentralization. There were
always acute differences separating SUPA's strong western Canadian
contingents, its cosmopolitan Montreal dissidents, and the 'centre,'
defined broadly as Ontario, but often casually and dismissively telescoped into 'Hogtown.' Meetings happened, and structures evolved,
with a growing recognition that decision making had to involve SUPA
members across the country, and not just in the seemingly privileged – if
often quite competitive and different – secretariats of Montreal and
Toronto. Tensions certainly existed. The theory of how SUPA was supposed to work often foundered on personalities and the ways in which
different leaderships emerged, counter to one another with respect to
place, imposing their will on others within a specific locale.[33] And yet, as
James Harding, one of western Canada's leading New Leftists in 1966
noted, SUPA managed quite early in its brief history to crystallize the
meaning of the movement in five interrelated features.[34]

First, SUPA acknowledged that it needed to undertake an analysis of
power in Canada in order to challenge the systematic inequality that was
foundational to the nation-state. This nation-state system was central to
the global crisis of a world order threatened with annihilation by competing communist and anti-communist blocs. It was also the primary
context in which alienating technologies of governance and repression
were unleashed on exploited workers, colonized peoples, students, the
unemployed, and minorities of all kinds. Second, SUPA, like CUCND
before it, was committed to non-alignment in a highly polarized world.[35]
This refusal to place itself on one side or another in the Cold War was
the only path to world peace. Third, SUPA took up the idea of student
syndicalism, in which it was understood, as it was in SDS, that students
had to foment controversy, organize campaigns, and take a lead in confronting social problems by bringing various possible agents of historic
change together in 'people's unions.' Fourth, it was absolutely necessary
that SUPA extend its theory and its practice to encompass the notion of
a totalizing order of oppression in which the linkages of war, peace, and
suffering on an everyday level were made visible and connected in ways
that they had not been in the past. Fifth, the political ends that SUPA
sought to achieve were to be consistent with the means it utilized to
secure them, which related to the organization's ideas and training in

non-violent direct action: 'Please don't believe / The use of force / Is how we change the social course / The use of force / You surely know / Is how we keep the status quo.'[36]

The notion of student syndicalism was particularly important because it launched SUPA on a series of initiatives, direct actions, and struggles to empower oppressed groups in Canada. Likening their educational experience to the routinized production of the assembly line, student syndicalists demanded something more than a business unionism content with wage increases and company paternalism. In its origins student syndicalism imagined a union of students battling university bosses to create a decentralized student control of their entire learning environment. SDS vice-president Carl Davidson promoted a student syndicalist movement that would 'sabotage the knowledge factory machinery' by promoting a countercurriculum guided by Paul Goodman and A.S. Neil; challenge professors by demanding student participation in shaping the structure, format, and content of courses; denounce, strike against, and picket excessively large classes; and hold mock trials of deans of men and women for their 'crimes against humanity.' Women students in particular, it was suggested, might take the lead in forming dormitory councils or soviets that could rewrite the 'rules' or eliminate them altogether. As Barbara Godard has recently suggested, in the earliest stages of student syndicalism at major universities in Toronto and Montreal over the course of 1963–4, the practical activities of university youth might be far less challenging of established norms. Indeed, student activists might well have embraced syndicalism less as Wobblies and more as liberal reformers, regarding their political mission as becoming 'intellectual workers' or serving an apprenticeship in citizenship. By the time SUPA was founded, however, radical student syndicalists were turning decisively toward the politics of community involvement. Most student syndicalist efforts in the crucial 1965–7 years were conceived as attempts to intersect with the poor and powerless in Canadian society so that students could both learn from direct experience with the dispossessed and, possibly, provide guidance as to how such people could overcome their subordination. Student syndicalism, in this undertaking, meshed with the movement's fundamental commitment to participatory democracy.[37]

The participatory democracy initiatives that SUPA undertook in the first year of its existence were almost all ad hoc undertakings growing out of local affinity groups of activists. There may well have been larger, national discussions, and funds were raised across the country, to be sure, but for the most part it was the fieldworkers themselves who came together and decided the direction their work would take. Among SUPA collectives different strategic understandings contended. Some wanted to 'enable' the poor and the dispossessed, others to offer a more traditional 'leadership.' If one SUPA member might stress the need to 'confront capitalism,' another would be as likely to locate their contribution in the group effort as 'equalizing opportunity,' or even merely 'helping' those who were disadvantaged by poverty or race or lack of education.[38] Yet at the base of community organizing projects, undertaken as summer initiatives, was perhaps a common, if unexamined, assumption that they would 'radicalize the student,' or at the very least broaden horizons and bring into view 'the basic contradictions within ... society.' Andre Cardinal, affiliated with the ongoing La Macaza research and non-violent civil disobedience project at Quebec's nuclear arms base,[39] was convinced that 'social action will develop in the student a social conscience, provided that the project has a revolutionary ideology and that the leadership of the project applies that ideology to the situations it has to face.'[40] Nothing of the sort, unfortunately, unfolded over the course of SUPA's first summer of fieldwork.

One of SUPA's early 1965 endeavours, illustrating well the ways in which the group worked, the influences it drew upon, and its limitations, was the Kingston Community Project (KCP). Community organizing had been embraced by SDS and its Economic Research and Action Project (ERAP) as a means of encouraging the dispossessed to voice their discontents; about 100 student radicals lived and worked in slums in the northern United States over the summer of 1964. Eight organizing projects, the best-known of which were the Newark Community Union Project and Chicago's Jobs or Income Now Community Union, identified housing, urban renewal, welfare, police brutality, and the limitations of state-sponsored 'wars on poverty' as fundamental issues animating black and white inner-city discontent. Led by national SDS spokesmen such as Tom Hayden and Todd Gitlin, with whom SUPA had direct connections, these projects conceived the poor to be 'the main thrust behind any broader movement for radical change – partly because their needs are more crude and insistent, and partly because they seem most insulated from some of the more deadening shibboleths of "the American dream."'[41]

Prodded by one of the last position papers of CUCND, co-authored by the organization's chairman, Art Pape, Kingston SUPA members struggled to link the movement against war to the social conditions of everyday life that nurtured violence. They cajoled student societies at Queen's University into giving them $3,000 to support the KCP; Liberal finance minister Walter Gordon and NDP leader Tommy Douglas wrote the young radicals modest cheques; a letter of commendation from John G. Diefenbaker came their way. The dozen or so Limestone City student activists then imported future United Automobile Worker and Canadian Labour Congress leader Dennis McDermott, at the time a young organizer with 'slum experience,' into the eastern Ontario city to direct their work. McDermott, two Queen's professors, and Tom Hathaway, Ontario regional head of SUPA, chose ten organizers, sent two of them off to a Toronto training session with Hayden and Pape, and then turned the neophyte organizers loose after they had written their final exams in May. It wasn't hard to find the poor in a city divided into town and gown. Segregated in the north end, Kingston's dispossessed lived on the wrong side of the city's main thoroughfare, Princess Street. It was relatively easy for SUPA organizers, all of whom eventually resided in two old ramshackle houses among those they wanted to interact with, to go out every day in groups of two or three, knock on doors, talk to people over cups of coffee and domestic chores, listen to accounts of hardship and resentment, and offer suggestive prods as to how things might be improved. Week by week the 'on the block' organizing proceeded. In the words of one KCP fieldworker, Bill Martin, this 'ordered procedure' carried with it the 'stench of unions or social workers.' Nonetheless, 'amid the piles of tedium, from around the edges of the clouds of everyday door to door conversations with housewives who are too busy to listen and husbands who are too busy listening to their spouses to give a guild edge damn, arises or glows the odd ray of light.'[42]

There was a sense of accomplishment in the KCP, then, but as it wound down for the summer in August 1965 the ironies of the activist season dawned on SUPA members. Journalists gave SUPA's confrontations with slumlords coverage, but at the expense of actually talking to the tenants, who were intimidated and who retreated into the background. Landlords seemed to be organizing faster than the poor renters, placing ads in the local newspaper suggesting the value of 'exchanging information about tenants.' One SUPA fieldworker reported caustically: 'Perhaps a landlord's cooperative is in the making.' One of the hardest blows to accept, however, was hearing a hated north-end housing magnate, his cash-clucking tongue well in cheek, praise 'the Queen's students' for stirring up his tenants to clean up their property and take pride in their living spaces. Joan Newman summed up the growing realization that SUPA's Kingston work seemed bogged down: 'We didn't know what made us different from ordinary social workers. We were supposed to be intellectuals activating the masses, but where do you begin?'[43]

In retrospect, many of the SUPA organizers of the summer 1965 initiative found themselves disillusioned and dispirited. Kingston was not Newark, and it did not have the explosive potential that a community dominated by racial poverty inevitably exhibited. Rent strikes were difficult to organize among tenants who did not inhabit ghetto high-rise apartments, and the rage that would explode in the 1967 Newark race riots was never simmering to quite the extent in Kingston that it obviously was in Hayden's New Jersey stomping grounds. The collective spirit of the enterprise left many wondering if the KCP's accent on trust, friendship, and community was enough. Women, the most adept at balancing the daily grind of domestic labour, part-time paid work, and connecting with poor working-class people (especially housewives), began to experience and then appreciate the gendered inequalities of SUPA's mission. Inherent assumptions about women's roles surfaced in a report from KCP 'leader,' Dennis McDermott. He reported in June 1965: 'The five boys will live in a combined office-house on the periphery of the project area, and commute for meals to the girls' apartment.' Students with romanticized misconceptions of poor people's innate radicalism instead found them often conservative and cautious. They could even be unwilling, as the intelligent dispossessed often are, to risk what little they had on a throw of the dice prompted by those who had many more tosses in their riskless pockets. Depression, self-deprecation, guilt, bewilderment, exhaustion, anger, resentment, and an unease with the emerging 'heavies' of the SUPA leadership, who were never centrally involved in the mundane 'block organizing,' set in.

All of this jostled uneasily with the exhilaration of having done something to develop change, of struggling to transform oneself as well as the social conditions of others, of learning from people quite different from themselves. The bottom line was not easily reduced to a single figure, for the balance sheet of SUPA's Kingston work was never merely a ledger-like set of plus/minus columns. Moreover, it laid the groundwork for further community organizing in 1966, paced by two SUPA women, Joan Newman and Myrna Wood. Their apartment became a place for local youth to gather, a coffee house was started, welfare recipients were given much-needed assistance, and Newman ended up elected to municipal office. Women such as Peggy Morton, Bronwen Wallace, and Sarah Spinks, who first cut their political teeth on the KCP, some little more than eighteen years of age, went on to contribute significantly to the New Left. Spinks was later involved in the Toronto Community Project at Trefann Court and was a mainstay, with George Martel, of the influential youth publication *This Magazine Is about Schools*. Edited by Bob Davis, the imaginative small-format collection of articles, poetry, and communications relating to education was a sounding board for alienations bred in the bone of the public school system. It made its way from its base in Toronto to the SDS stronghold of Ann Arbor, Michigan, where it was touted by Weatherman-to-be Bill Ayers. Soon radical educational theorists such as John Holt and Berkeley's Herbert Kohl were singing its praises. Pre-university youth, especially in south-central Ontario and metropolitan centres across Canada, turned its pages avidly. They found in them a rising crescendo of criticism of 'the school,' increasingly perceived as little more than a vehicle for indoctrinating students with the values of conformity and the ethos of the marketplace. Few Canadian voices of the New Left reached high school students with the same ease and vigour as *This Magazine*.[44]

There were other ventures in student syndicalism. Ten SUPA radicals spent the summer living with status Indian and Métis families in Saskatchewan. Having raised $3,000 (the going rate in 1965, it seemed, for a SUPA group of ten to twelve to make it through the summer), largely from the Student Council at the University of Toronto, a small group met in Saskatchewan. It then launched the Student Neestow Partnership Project, '*neestow*' being a Cree word for brother-in-law.[45] The Neestow initiative had its origins in a February 1965 Canadian Union of Students–sponsored conference on 'The Status of the Indian and Métis in Canada.' Held at the University of Saskatchewan, the gathering solidified ties that had developed between western SUPA figures such as Harding and socialist Métis organizer Malcolm Norris. Norris was the first person Harding encountered in Saskatchewan 'who could blend Marxism and libertarian politics ... [talking about] the importance of a racial analysis of class society ... about the colonization of the Indian and Métis.' Norris's dynamism, oratory, and analytic acumen galvanized the student conference, stimulating the young radicals to launch an American civil-rights-like summer of encounter with Aboriginal peoples. Guided by Indigenous and Métis activists such as Don Nielson, Jim Brady, and Norris, the students contacted Native bands, reserves, and Métis communities before fanning out across the province with their seemingly simple goal. They merely wanted to make contact, observe, live with Native peoples, and help them in the work of everyday life, achieving something of an education in the process. No doubt SUPA had a sense that social actions against the Indian agents of the federal government would take place.[46]

Instead they found that while they learned of the subtle ways in which colonial dependency was cultivated on the reserves, they had little political possibility of making inroads into communities which were sensibly suspicious of white students and kept their silence among 'visitors' they knew too little about. Struggling to break down images of whites as incapable of the kinds of everyday work that Native peoples do to survive, an American radical studying at the University of Toronto, Pat Uhl, washed clothes, baked bannock, weeded gardens, hayed, milked cows, chopped wood, beaded costumes, made butter, even laid a cement foundation for a house. As their skins browned in the sun, with hands blistered and necks ravaged by mosquitoes, backs stiff from sleeping on the bug-infested floor or in a tent on the ground, SUPA figures like Uhl felt they had proven their commitment. It was not quite enough to transcend the barriers separating them from those who would not be leaving the reserves in August to return to the Universities of Toronto or Saskatchewan. Naive fieldworkers, innocent in their enthusiasms to learn and to help and to politicize, were pained to find out that Native peoples were not what they had imagined them to be. Too often their Aboriginal friends seemed passive and submissive. It did not help to hear, via the rumour mill, that some on the reserve looked on radical students as undercover agents for the Department of Indian Affairs or spies for welfare agencies. Even more troubling was the complex problem of erotically charged competitions among young Native men, some of whom considered it a status boost to be hanging out with white women student radicals. Adding insult to injury, mainstream elements in the Canadian Union of Students denounced the SUPA leftists for ostensibly hijacking the project and making it 'political'; some of the sponsors, including Don Nielson, withdrew their support and denounced the students.[47]

As the project stumbled into a second summer, things did not improve. At the Métis settlement of Green Lake, where two SUPA Neestowers had wintered, protests developed around issues of land and logging payments. The Liberal provincial government was outraged that student radicals seemed to be fomenting discord, forcing the state to ante up with cash payments and property rights acknowledgments. 'Until the people of Green Lake ... kick out these communist interlopers ... we can do little for [the residents],' thundered one member of Parliament in the Legislature. The Green Lake Métis were threatened with material deprivations if they continued to harbour student radicals in their midst. SUPA's Neestowers were soon an unwanted element, and it was not long before they packed their bags, coming to the conclusion that 'native people must organize their own liberation.'[48]

Liora Proctor, who spent some time in the Métis community of Green Lake in the winter of 1965–6, wrote a critical assessment later in the autumn. She noted that Native people had no understanding of why white students had come into their midst, and, indeed, they had a right to feel resentful of the intrusion. Interviewed by Krista Maeots, Proctor later realized that SUPA's idealized 'picture of the Indian' as 'someone whose whole culture rejects what is hollow about Middle Class America' was a problematic foundation on which to build the Neestow initiative. Sadly, after three years, SUPA had come to be regarded in a number of Native communities as 'just white men who came and dabbled and went away again.' In a related commentary, Proctor's comrade and a summer Neestow fieldworker, Clayton Ruby, suggested that SUPA had undertaken its entry into the Saskatchewan reserves in order to help Native people assert power over their lives. Paraphrasing Stokely Carmichael of the Student Non-Violent Coordinating Committee [SNCC], Ruby concluded that power was 'white' and the 'whiteness' of SUPA fieldworkers was never really addressed. This meant that SUPA had to confront the extent to which its entire understanding of participatory democracy and struggling for power through such vehicles as education was a racialized dead end from its very beginnings: 'It may be that the road to education is power, but certainly not Indian power, because by the time you're successful all the Indians are white men – or as close as makes no difference.'[49]

It was one thing to conclude that race mattered on an Indian reserve, a 'discovery' difficult enough but also natural and inevitable. Among the Doukhobor communities of Castelgar, Krestova, and Ootoshenie, British Columbia, where another eight SUPA fieldworkers set up the Kootenays Project in the summer of 1965, neophyte activists faced a rude jolt to their assumptions about youth and radicalization. Doukhobor pacifism drew the New Leftists. They wanted to connect with the Union of Doukhobor Youth, and they expected that 'the older folk,' who spoke only Russian, would be less than receptive to their message. In understanding its project as persuading Doukhobors that they were agents of an unfolding social revolution, aligned with 'the poor, native peoples, radical students, the labour movement, and intellectuals,' SUPA discovered that not all youth were captivated by the prospects of social transformation, especially in the interior of British Columbia. Young Doukhobors, the Kootenays Project fieldworkers discovered, were actually less in tune with SUPA than the Old World elders. They had been educated in the Canadian public schools, worked in the region's pulp and paper mills, spent their money on car loans, and drank their evenings away in boisterous bars. The spiritual inner life of Doukhobor pacifism and the rejection of capitalist materialism that SUPA had seen from a distance was, up close among the assimilated youth, an illusive organizational straw to grasp in the modernizing winds of the immigrant milieu. Oddly enough, perhaps the most lasting lesson learned in the SUPA experiment in crossing cultural lines in British Columbia was that old was not necessarily inferior to young and new. As Lynne Butts wrote in a SUPA report for the Kootenays entitled, 'The Beauty That Is Age,' one of the Doukhobor women elders was a 'symbol of old age and what it could be, if we stopped fearing it.'[50]

SUPA's sole African-Canadian fieldworker, Rocky Jones, found his head so 'full of ideas' that he thought he could 'create a Utopia' within Halifax's black community. He ended up isolated, lonely, and desperate for help. Not a student, Jones, who grew up in Truro, Nova Scotia, had been motivated by Carmichael's SNCC work in the American south and Tom Hayden's Newark community organizing project. SUPA was the only connection he could establish in Canada, and he gave up a good government job in Toronto to return to the Maritimes and work with Halifax blacks, then suffering through the urban renewal dislocations of the assault on Africville. His dreams shattered, he concluded that 'Superman does not exist and I can't play the role he supposedly played.' SUPA reinforcements did arrive, sustaining the Nova Scotia project for two years. But by January 1967 it was on its last legs. A SUPA activist summoned up a recollection of the events years later: 'We sent [Rocky Jones] down without any money. I think he must have eventually given up on us.'[51] Other SUPA activists, such as Montreal-based Stan Gray, who toured the country to raise money for non-violent protest at the La Macaza missile base, and a contingent of civil disobedience practitioners in Comox and Courtney, British Columbia, kept the CUCND tradition of protesting Canada's nuclear arms and warfare state bases alive. Research on peace and the professions, for which many SUPA activists no doubt (and not wrongly) considered themselves destined, was undertaken. Yet regional discontents and differences chafed, even as commitment to non-alignment in the Cold War and the need to convert war industries to peaceful economic production deepened.[52]

The Toronto-based School for Social Theory revealed how things could fall apart rather quickly. Of all the 1965 SUPA projects, the school probably involved more activists than any other undertaking, with a dozen full-time participants, including a director, Matt Cohen, and upwards of fifty people drifting in and out of two on-going, part-time seminars. Discussions could turn on how to sabotage the Bell Telephone Company, later reported on under the title 'Hegel and the New Left.' An organizer from the Communist Party of India might drop in for an afternoon talk.[53]

It all seemed relatively straightforward in the beginning. SUPA activists were keen to learn about social change, hone their theoretical expertise, and discuss how it could be applied to specific areas. Among the subjects that seemed to suit SUPA's needs were Marxism, the New Left, and psychoanalysis. From the first day, however, Cohen indicated he would not lead. It was up to the participants to determine how the school would work, what would be taught within it, and how that pedagogical exercise would be structured. Faced with no structure, SUPA members immediately constructed a fairly rigid one, with daily written papers and oral presentations. But 'pressured by assignments, bugged by non-directed discussion, unsure of their own place in the school, and frustrated by lack of communication,' the students rebelled and decided instead to prepare what they thought useful to discuss the next day. This led nowhere: 'We really had no idea how to learn from each other. What seemed a disintegration of the school was blamed on the fact that we met too early in the morning, intellectual levels were different, other people weren't reading, there was no motivation.'

After a week at which an average of three people a day attended classes, Cohen stepped in, assuming more authority, lecturing, assigning papers. Expectations adjusted, people began to work on their own, and 'the school picked up again.' In the end, the lessons learned were negative ones, but no less significant for being so:

> The school was an experiment to provide an experience through which people can learn freely from each other, unhampered and unaided by limits and structures such as deadlines, exams, curriculum, systems of organization. I think we underestimated the frustration and confusion that occurs when accustomed structures are removed and people are forced to

confront themselves and each other. We failed to provide support for each other during this upheaval.

In its failures, SUPA's School for Social Theory was typical of all of the undertakings of the summer of 1965. It never became a 'nerve centre for the movement.' As with most of SUPA's intense summer work, the school confirmed among participants that two months was an insufficient time frame in which to accomplish what they had set out to do.[54]

Throughout all of this, SUPA was intimately connected to SDS in the United States. Few of those truly active in the Canadian New Left could, in 1965, discern that much separated Canadians and Americans in the student syndicalist movement. These were revolutionaries who knew no country, at least at this point in their youthful lives. As one of them told Cyril Levitt, 'the people that I knew didn't feel the profound sense that we were part of the same country that the powerful were part of.'[55] Asked to comment on how the movement differed in Canada and the United States, SUPA leader Peter Boothroyd replied bluntly: 'I don't think there is a difference.'[56] From ERAP literature sold on SUPA tables, to Tom Hayden coming to Toronto to chill out from the pressures of Newark and national SDS commitments, to the voter-registration drives in Mississippi, and SNCC support work, the Canadian and American New Lefts at mid-decade shared much that mattered.[57]

Indeed, prior to the summer 1965 projects, perhaps the single most important action that both galvanized SUPA and brought fresh forces of radicalizing youth into its midst was a March 1965 series of protests outside the United States Consulate on Toronto's University Avenue. Called in support of a civil rights march from Selma, Alabama, to the state capital in Montgomery which aimed at securing black voting rights in the violently segregated American south, the SUPA demos propagandized about the ways in which state troopers and racist vigilantes had unleashed a torrent of deadly abuse on the student activists, a handful of whom were Canadians. As the small daily sit-ins at the consulate gained press attention, publicizing racist atrocity and the growing opposition to it, the crowds gathering on the sidewalk outside of the U.S. consular grounds grew. Signatures on petitions mounted, and SUPA's numbers mushroomed. From this date on, SUPA retained close ties to SNCC through joint endeavours, a linked committee in which the key figures were Anne Cohen and Harvey L. Shepherd, and a May 1965 conference.[58]

It was of course the war in Vietnam that ultimately linked Canadians and Americans in the mid-1960s New Left. Indochina had been an outpost of European (particularly French) colonization for decades. Having defeated France in the 1950s, Viet Minh guerillas found themselves confronted with an oppressive, U.S.-backed Saigon regime headed by Ngo Dinh Diem. By 1960 a resistance movement was calling on the country to rise up and overthrow the Diem dictatorship; the National Liberation Front and its military wing, the Viet Cong, mounted a guerrilla war that threatened to take power. The United States moved to pacify the region. It quietly sent almost 20,000 military personnel, euphemistically designated 'advisers,' into Vietnam by 1963. It was not enough. Soon the United States was embroiled in an all-out war effort, one that necessitated drafting American youth to fight in a country halfway around the world, against an enemy few combatants understood. As of 1968, almost 500,000 American troops were stationed in Vietnam. The U.S. death toll had climbed to approximately 20,000. Roughly 150,000 Vietnamese were being slaughtered annually, many of them civilians with no actual involvement in armed resistance. With the United States detonating 700,000 tons of explosives a month and spending billions on an undeclared war against communism, American society fractured down the middle. An anti-war movement emerged and dominated politics of the mid- to late 1960s, eventually defeating President Lyndon B. Johnson. Millions of protesters marched on Washington and in every major metropolitan city of the country. Students for a Democratic Society, one of a number of anti-war organizations, exploded in growth to the point that it could claim 100,000 members in 1968. War, long the business of the nation, was now its decisive divide, and the New Left stood on one side of what was increasingly looking like a barricade-strewn society. Democracy took to the streets, youthful protests proclaiming at first, 'Bring the Boys Home,' and, as radicalism escalated, 'We Are All Viet Cong' and 'Ho, Ho, Ho Chi Minh, The NLF Is Going to Win.' An anti-war movement had become an anti-imperialist mobilization. Soon there would be those who would champion the need to 'Bring the War Home.'[59]

Vietnam registered with Canadian radicals, to be sure, but even as late as 1964 opposition to the war was posed rather mildly. *Canadian Dimension* offered an understated liberal editorial that opened with the weakly worded question, 'How much longer can the war in Vietnam go on?' as late as spring 1965. But from that point on the New Left grew increasingly concerned and prolific in its publications and criticisms of the Canadian state's complicity in imperialist atrocity. *Dimension*'s Cy Gonick offered a lengthy three-part article entitled 'What Every Canadian

Should Know about Vietnam' that ran from mid-1965 into the last published issue of the year, and many others also bent their pens in opposition to the U.S. military intervention in Indochina. By 1968 there were
few New Leftists in the country who had not read and researched the
imperialist imbroglio and its Canadian connections.[60]

SUPA's anti-war activities followed a similar course. A protest vigil at
the University of Toronto in the spring of 1965 formed a silent ring of
students and faculty, staring down the American liberal apologist for
Vietnam, Adlai Stevenson, as he bowed and scraped his way to an hon-
ourary degree. A passive media plug-in to a mid-May 1965 Washington
Teach-In on the Vietnam war was promoted by SUPA, but it proved disappointing. The audience of 400–500 was smaller than anticipated, and
the broadcast discussions rather staid. More robust protests, which
involved defiance of the university administration's ban on political
book tables, took place at the University of Alberta, forcing the censors
to back down.[61] SUPA participated in a Vietnam Conference organized
by the Canadian Friends Service Committee (Quakers) at Carleton University in mid-June 1965.[62] These and other demonstrative anti-war
undertakings, however, were soon overshadowed by the officially sanctioned International Teach-In on 'Revolution and Response,' organized
at the University of Toronto in October 1965, in which SUPA figures
Liora Proctor, Matt Cohen, and Henry Tarvainen had been early organizational contacts.[63]

The International Teach-In at Toronto quickly became top-heavy in
its institutionalization, and to radical students it appeared conformist
and ivory towerish. SUPA figures such as Art Pape, while drawn to some
of what could be accomplished in such settings, nevertheless rebelled at
the extent to which 'people were talked *to* about personal issues, not
talked *with*.' Governed by liberal premises – such as dropping from the
platform a Berkeley graduate student who had visited Hanoi when
another non-radical participant refused to share the front table with
him – the University of Toronto Teach-In was an *academic* and hierarchical undertaking, orchestrated by faculty and sanctioned by the university's president Claude Bissell. At a cost of $35,000, it hardly seemed a
model of mobilizing and participatory democracy. The liberal trajectory
of the Toronto International Teach-Ins was evident in the post-1965
drift away from the concern with war and revolution: future teach-ins
would address 'China: Co-Existence or Containment,' 'Religion and
International Affairs,' and 'Exploding Humanity: The Crisis of Numbers.' Yet the first International Teach-In, undoubtedly the most radical,

drew 4,000 students and 120 journalists, the proceedings transmitted by radio to an audience reported to top one million. It undoubtedly fired enthusiasm for more anti-war activity.[64] It was followed, for instance, by the chartering of SUPA buses to attend Washington anti-war rallies, open letters to Parliament, another teach-in at the University of Ottawa (featuring *Our Generation* editors and SUPA leaders Tony Hyde, Art Pape, and Dimitri Roussopoulos), and civil disobedience aimed at disrupting the business-as-usual attitude of the Canadian state. In the latter March 1966 event sixty-one SUPA activists were arrested, many of whom were found guilty on charges of obstruction.[65]

By 1966, SUPA was playing an increasingly important role in aiding American draft resisters who wanted to come to Canada in order to avoid being forced into the armed forces and sent to Vietnam. Clayton Ruby and others set up an office next to a SUPA house; established a telephone roster and a counselling service; found temporary housing for draft dodgers, putting them up with sympathetic families; and even helped smuggle young war resisters into the country. Over the course of the last half of the 1960s thousands of such legal and illegal draft evaders came to Canada, materially aided by SUPA and well informed about the nature of the country and their prospects by reading a text that the Toronto radicals had inspired. A SUPA associate, Martin Satin, edited *A Manual for Draft-Age Immigrants to Canada*, building on an earlier New Left pamphlet that had been produced to ease the war resister's entry into a new country. The tremendously successful *Manual* sold 65,000 copies in the latter half of the 1960s. Draft dodgers were a mixed lot. Many simply wanted to avoid military service and settle into comfortable lives. Others, however, were committed leftists who would have an important, immediate impact on the small Canadian New Left, as well as in decades to come.[66]

There were nevertheless signs of trouble on SUPA's anti–Vietnam war horizon. The Ottawa Vietnam Week had been characterized by a growing divisiveness, with some claiming decisions were being made in bureaucratic ways by an elitist cohort of Toronto leaders. Resentments grew over 'power plays' and 'oligarchies.' George Grant, who was supposed to address the teach-in withdrew because of conflicts with SUPA leaders. Attendance never really reached much past 100.[67]

Subsequent anti-war activities in Canada from 1966 to 1968 revealed how an increasingly sluggish SUPA was being left behind by a growing anti-war mobilization. The University of British Columbia's Vietnam Day Committee led the way and was quickly followed by the formation of some twenty-two pan-Canadian campus Committees to End the War in Vietnam. In Montreal anti-war mobilizations culminated in a large mid-November 1967 protest at the U.S. consulate. Organized by the Quebec Union of Students, the demonstrators were militant and vocal in their condemnations, shouting 'Johnson, napalm, murderer.' They linked the wars of resistance abroad with those at home: 'Vietnam for the Vietnamese/Québec for the Québécois.' Thousands strong, the Montreal marchers arrived at the American embassy and showered it with missiles, precipitating a police attack that left twenty people injured and forty-six arrested. SUPA, while involved in such actions, was now clearly a waning force. Students, pacifists, and a rising anti-imperialist movement, a part of which was composed of Marxist organizations with Trotskyist or Maoist programs, was supplemented by the Old Left ranks of the Communist Party, which retained a presence of importance in locales such as Vancouver and Winnipeg. Committees of such united fronts mobilized Vietnam protests across the country, militant expressions of a rising crescendo of opposition, much of it youth oriented. But SUPA was less and less visible, its role increasingly marginal.[68]

In 1965, after a 'Fall Institute' gathering of eighty fieldworkers and SUPA leaders in St Calixte, Quebec, Peter Gzowski had seen the roughly 1,000 students and youth radicals comprising the Union as the best and the brightest of a new generation of thinking, doing, dissident youth, 'the heart of the new left.'[69] Yet as Kostash records, 'it was downhill from St. Calixte.' SUPA conferences in Saskatoon (December 1965), Waterloo (December 1966), and, finally, Goderich (September 1967), were wracked by increasingly pessimistic reflections on the summer projects. The numbers of committed cadre took a nosedive: from 200 to 40. As a vehicle of revolutionary advance, SUPA was stuck in reverse. More and more activists were asking themselves just what it was that was guiding them in their fieldwork. They didn't have answers. And as they questioned, the distinctiveness of the New Left, with its accent on community organizing, faith in the dispossessed, and deeply engrained opposition to all structures and hierarchies, seemed to drift into spaces occupied by the Old Left.

Where do you do revolutionary work and why? If power oppresses, how can power be mobilized to counter this? Who, or what, has the power to challenge the state? Can the trade unions, the Communist Party, the NDP all be written off as irrelevant? Was not Marxism something more than merely a relic of antiquated Victorianism? Paul Goodman, invited by SUPA to facilitate a session at its Waterloo conference, found his audience impatient with his subjective orientation, with its understanding of alternative as a project of self-education. The old libertarian departed the conference muttering that in Canada, of all places, there seemed to be a lot of Marxism. Certainly more than Goodman was used to in the United States, and a tad in excess of what he perhaps would have liked.

How *could* SUPA transcend a materialist analysis when it ran questions like this in its newsletter: 'Your father wants you to go back to University in September and to graduate next May, but you want to stay out a year to work for SUPA. So your father says, "OK, but if you go back this year, I'll not only pay your fees, but I'll give SUPA a post-dated cheque for one thousand dollars ($1000.00) which they may cash in May of next year provided you graduate."' SUPA polled individual members as to what they would do if they found themselves in this 'true to life actual problem.' 'Just say No' was not, apparently, in the vocabulary of SUPA's 1960s.[70]

SUPA Slip Slidin' Away

As facetious as it may sound, the individual dilemma of a father bribing his son or daughter to stay in school while he bankrolled the New Left captured the reality of a larger threat to SUPA. The biggest of daddies, with the blankest of cheques, was the state. At the same point that SUPA began to charter the political territory of community organizing the prime minister's office of Lester B. Pearson was promoting citizen participation through a series of well-funded government programs. One of these was the Company of Young Canadians (CYC). In April 1965 Parliament was asked to approve a project 'through which the energies and talents of youth can be elicited in projects for economic and social development both in Canada and abroad.' Enticing one of SUPA's leading figures, Toronto's Art Pape, onto the CYC governing council proved an early state coup, and one that fostered divisions and animosities within the nascent New Left. CYC funded SUPA's 'Fall Institute' at St Calixte to the tune of $4,000. It sent observers to cultivate the notion that CYC and SUPA shared an approach to community organizing that should bring the bodies together. Key CYC figure and former Canadian Union of Students activist Stewart Goodings promoted close relations between the Company and SUPA, visiting with KCP fieldworkers, addressing members through contributions to the newsletter, and developing connections with a number of New Left figures.[71]

There were many in SUPA, understandably, who wanted nothing to do with state bureaucracy. They cautioned that there was much to be lost if the hand-outs of state grants and incorporation into elite structures came to define the New Left. *Our Generation*'s editor, Dimitrios Roussopoulos, was quick to denounce anyone who snuggled up to the state.[72] Pape seemed, to some, to have succumbed to the lure of office and its largesse as he argued: 'Man, there's four hundred million dollars on the table. If we don't pick it up somebody else is going to.'[73] It didn't help that in January 1967 a SUPA anti–Vietnam war rally in which two CYC volunteers – David DePoe and Lynn Curtis – were organizers brought the wrath of the prime minister's office down on the head of the Company.[74] There were, it was now clear, limits to what the paymasters in Ottawa were willing to put up with.

Furthermore, rumours abounded that the CYC was a nest of corruption. There had supposedly been an automobile buying spree, netting eight Volvos for the use of Quebec volunteers. Pape's trips to left-wing think tanks in Santa Barbara or civil-rights training camps in New Orleans were bankrolled, replete with $25 helicopter trips from the California airport. It mattered little that this may well have been an economical means of transport. When it was bandied about in Parliament at the end of 1968 that Pape had drawn $17,000 as a CYCer over the course of a year, the damage in some New Left quarters was irreversible. An *Our Generation* editorial closed the CYC book bitterly, drawing on Marcusian notions of repressive tolerance to condemn the 'seasoned radicals' and 'intellectual eunuchs' who 'turned a tender day-dream into a nightmare' and, in the process, aborted 'a movement of youth that was *feeling* its way towards an effective opposition.' The moral of this sad tale of state intervention and attractive accommodation was that 'more activists should take horror films seriously.'[75]

Kostash concludes that after the disappointingly small and politically acrimonious September 1967 Goderich conference, SUPA simply disintegrated. There were, of course, many lesser SUPA lights than Art Pape. Over the course of 1966–7, they quietly took the CYC bait rather than struggle in uncertainty and confusion. There seemed so little difference between being a SUPA fieldworker or a CYC volunteer except the level of poverty one was expected to endure. As SUPA's ranks thinned dramatically in 1967, the CYC recruitment of youth volunteers picked up. By the end of 1967, the CYC 'had absorbed most of SUPA's Toronto-based leadership in staff or consultant jobs, had hired half of its project workers into its own volunteer groups, and had linked up with most of

SUPA's extant projects.' The eulogy was definitively blunt: 'SUPA was dead and the chance to mature politically was forfeited.'

SUPA stalwarts charged those who went over to the CYC with career-ism, compromise, and complicity, the three C's of co-optation's cash-induced 'sell-out.' 'I can remember when CYC came out to Saskatche-wan to court us,' recalled one New Leftist disdainfully. 'They picked us up in their big, beautiful van, took us to the hotel, fed us filet mignon and wine and asked us, would you like to work for us, we pay well, blah, blah. We said no, this is an attempt to co-opt us, its crap, it's bullshit.' But the bullshit travelled far, wide, and with considerable effect. At its highwater mark in 1967–8, the Company of Young Canadians had 228 volunteers working in dozens of projects, many of them in the polit-ically volatile environment of Quebec. New Leftists Art Pape and a non-SUPA former University of Buffalo SDS high-flyer, Rick Salter, were now centrally involved in the CYC, trying to push it in a 'harder left' direc-tion and gaining some ground. But their plans would soon be scuttled, resisted by the bureaucracy in Ottawa as well as by critics who remained wedded to New Left principles, what Salter would later refer to as 'all the old, clichéd radical reasons.' As 1968 closed, Pape and Salter had made their exit from CYC, and its last years, before being incorporated directly into the state bureaucracy in 1970, were a winding down of any New Left impulses that remained within the government-affiliated orga-nization. With the passing of the 1960s, the Company of Young Canadi-ans was both 'idealistically and for all practical purposes, dead.' Its volunteers in May 1970 numbered barely one-third of those who criss-crossed the country in 1968, and, while it lived on until 1977, the CYC was but a pale and inconsequential reflection of the radical purpose and commitment that it had fed off of from its founding in 1965–6.[76]

The irony was an old one. SUPA's destination, the building of a revolu-tionary youth opposition that could truly live up to the promise of a New Left, seemed so close in 1967–8. The loose affinity groups of the organi-zation and their commitment to a radical praxis that co-joined critical thought and socially transformative action had nonetheless slipped away. There is no denying the role of the CYC, as a state agency, in not only co-opting SUPA's leaders and ranks but, more importantly, in culturally dis-rupting the solidarity and collective experience of the nascent New Left formation. This happened, in part, because SUPA lacked a clarity of per-spective and anything approximating a programmatic orientation to the illusive revolutionary change it embraced with such fervour. But as the CYC held out the carrot of officialdom's call – access to state power,

Bomb shelter graffiti, University Avenue/College Street, Toronto, with Department of Public Works employees painting over slogan, 1960 (York University, *Toronto Telegram* Fonds, FO433, 1974-001/168 [1147]).

CUCND anti-nuclear arms demonstration, Toronto, 1961 (York University, *Toronto Telegram* Fonds, FO433, 1974-001/168 [1147]).

Police controlling 'Ban the Bomb' demonstration, 1962 (Library and Archives Canada/PA 152325, *Montreal Gazette*).

Voice of Women peace vigil, Toronto, 1963 (York University, *Toronto Telegram* Fonds, FO433, 1974-002/285).

(MTL 3) MONTREAL, MARCH 11--MODEL POSE--Gerda Munsinger,
who lived in three different Montreal apartment buildings,
is shown in another pose as an aspiring model.
(CP Wirephoto) 1966 dxb645p

Gerda Munsinger (Library and Archives Canada/PA 152499, *Montreal Gazette*).

George Chuvalo Training, 1958 (York University, *Toronto Telegram* Fonds, FO433, 1974-002/388).

Marshall McLuhan, 1966 (York University, *Toronto Telegram* Fonds, FO433, 1974-002/390).

Pierre Elliott Trudeau and Lester B. Pearson, Federal-Provincial Conference, Ottawa, 1968 (Library and Archives Canada/ Duncan Cameron/PA117463).

Pierre Elliott Trudeau, Liberal leadership convention, 1968 (Library and Archives Canada/Duncan Cameron/PA111212).

Teenagers, Root & Burger Restaurant, Regent Park, Toronto, 1964 (York University, *Toronto Telegram* Fonds, FO433, 1974-002/165).

United Steel Workers of America strikers burn contract, INCO, Thompson, Manitoba, 1964 (Library and Archives Canada/Murray McKenzie/*Winnipeg Free Press*/PA 120633).

Postal Workers' strike, Burlington, 1968, with Frances Donovan, the only female letter carrier in Ontario at the time (York University, *Toronto Telegram* Fonds, FO433, 1974-011 [3166]).

Student protest, United States Embassy, Montreal, 1965 (Library and Archives Canada/PA139979, *Montreal Gazette*).

SUPA Anti-Draft Programme Office, Toronto, 1967 (York University, *Toronto Telegram* Fonds, FO433, 1974-002/243).

Vietnam War protest, Montreal, 1967 (Library and Archives Canada/PA 139985, *Montreal Gazette*).

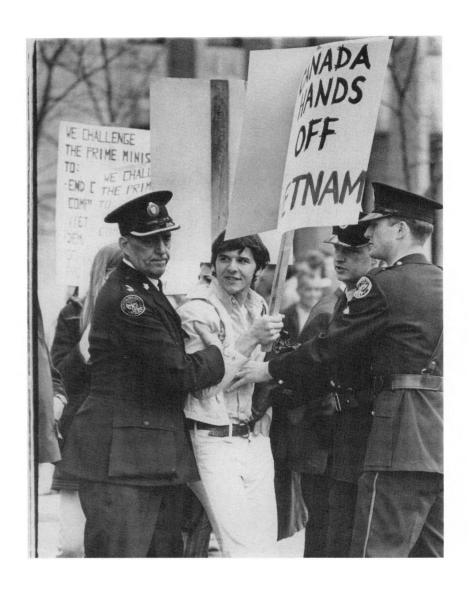

Anti–Vietnam war protest, United States Consulate, Toronto, May 1968 (York University, *Toronto Telegram*, Fonds FO433, 1974-001/167 [1146]).

Anti–Vietnam war protest, United States Consulate, Toronto, October 1968
(York University, *Toronto Telegram* Fonds, FO433, 1974-002/284).

Free Vallières-Gagnon rally, Montreal, 1968 (Library and Archives Canada/PA 117474, *Montreal Gazette*).

CEGEP student protest, Montreal, 1968 (Library and Archives Canada/PA 139982, *Montreal Gazette*).

Debris on the street after Sir George Williams University protest occupation, 1968 (Library and Archives Canada/PA 139988, *Montreal Gazette*).

McGill Français demonstration, 1969 (Library and Archives Canada/PA 110517, *Montreal Gazette*).

Rochdale College Student Room, 1969 (York University, *Toronto Telegram* Fonds FO433, 1974-002/167).

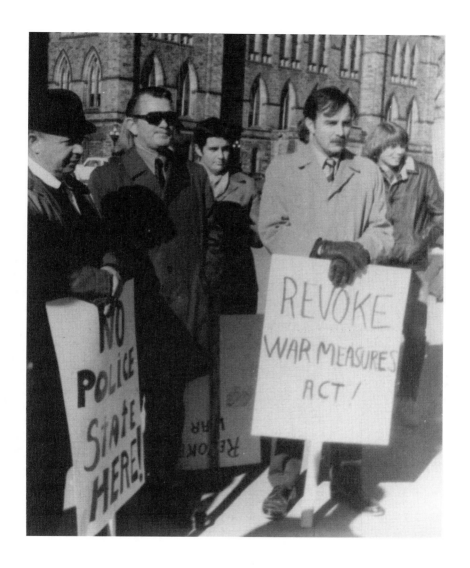

Opposition to the War Measures Act, Ottawa, 1970, Communist Party of Canada (Library and Archives Canada/PA 126354).

Protest against arrests made under the War Measures Act, Toronto, 1971 (York University, *Toronto Telegram* Fonds, FO433, 1974-002/086).

funds to pay for meals, books, and good works, and, seemingly, a structure that could carry on beyond the summer – there were those wielding the stick of what was increasingly called 'ideology.'

As early as the end of 1966, *Canadian Dimension*'s Cy Gonick had penned an incisive and widely read critique of SUPA. A radical born and bred in Winnipeg, a city rich in the multicultural diversity of the Old Left, Gonick had gravitated to the rather wilder Berkeley-based California New Left. There, as a graduate student, he connected with many figures prominent in 1960s mobilizations. Somewhat harsh in his characterization of SUPA as made up of 'part-time radicals' and 'coffee-house revolutionaries,' Gonick claimed that notwithstanding 'a few outstanding exceptions' northern student syndicalists couldn't hold a militantly activist candle to SDS, SNCC, and the Berkeley Viet Nam Day Committee. He thought the Canadian New Left 'more of a myth than a reality.'

Aside from this jaundiced outlook, however, Gonick's more serious qualms about SUPA were that it had failed to move beyond a nebulous, if evocatively promoted, assault on bureaucratism. This led inevitably to a concentration on the means by which power elites ruled rather than the substance and content of that dominance. In the New Left reification of participatory democracy, Gonick claimed, lay the seeds of political indifference to the actual content of power. There was, he discerned, a problematic willingness to concentrate the struggle for social transformation on forms that were undemocratic and hierarchical. Thus, Gonick suggested that the logic of SUPA's New Leftism was that, if 'an inhumane, illiberal programme was arrived at at the "grass roots" level and represented a "consensus," and provided it were implemented by the "grass roots," then it would be acceptable to the New Left.' Rejecting all 'traditional agencies of protest,' from the NDP to the trade unions, the New Left, according to Gonick, embraced the alienated and the powerless and, in the process, elevated understandings of 'counter communities' to a place of prominence in revolutionary social change that such marginalized people could never fulfill. Questioning the notion that the poorest and most dispossessed in any society have no stake in the status quo, the *Dimension* editor suggested that their utter helplessness and dependency on the state made them dubious material to lead the revolutionary struggle for overthrowing contemporary capitalist society. Isolated in ghettoized communities of their own mind, as well as those of capitalist inequality's making, SUPA New Leftists, Gonick suggested, had been irresponsible in placing all of their revolutionary eggs in the one basket of 'a national network of community organizing.' The need of the hour, in Gonick's view, was not avoidance of established venues of already-established organization, but the absolute necessity of penetrating 'the major institutions where people are – trade unions, churches, teachers' societies, student organizations, the NDP, to create within them constituencies which can be harnessed to a political movement aimed at national independence and socialism, to guard against elitism, and to insist, in all of these activities, on member participation in decision-making.' To do this, the New Left needed what, according to Gonick, it lacked: 'a political programme.'[77]

Gonick spoke out of two sides of the radical mouth, which was not necessarily a bad thing. As a New Leftist attentive to the message and meaning of Old Leftism, he was looking for bridges to build between the young and those who were, in their oppositional commitments, young at heart. In Canada, Gonick argued, this resonated with historical practice. The formation of dissident third-party movements, the possibilities of realizable socialism, and the viability of Marxism as a theoretical and analytic guide were less awkwardly posed in Canada than they were in the United States. There, the hegemony of anti-communism and the inviolate sanctities of individualism and private property were weighty ideological anchors that sank the appropriation of Marxist sensibilities deeper in conservative waters than was the case in Canada. Indeed, as SUPA faltered and then fell by the wayside in 1967–8, a new New Left emerged, one that could never quite, ironically, manage to be as centred as was the admittedly decentred SUPA, but one that rode out what remained of the revolutionary wave of the 1960s. In this discontinuous continuity, the New Left shifted gears, accelerating its growth but doing so in ways that moved people into different political and interpretive lanes. No easy pigeon-holing of these emerging post-1967 tendencies could ever capture either the diversity or the commonality of the New Left's brief, but powerfully creative, last Canadian gasp. Yet within the pattern of a broad, common political development, three complicatedly related, albeit often eventually divided, radical trajectories emerged: Marxism, left nationalism, and feminism.

Political Reproduction: New Left Expropriations of Marxism and Campus Revolts

As SUPA quietly imploded at the end of 1967's summer,[78] its failures and its successes led its more reflective members to seek out a more rigorous analytic praxis. The limitations and frustrations of community organizing, as well as the problem of why America was in Vietnam, all pushed activists in the direction of theory. In January 1967 one SUPA activist had declared:

> Things are pretty grim at the moment. Can anything be done about this? The Left on campus has been failing for one fundamental reason – it has always reacted to specific crises ... rather than educating the campus, and in this way, establishing a base of support upon which to draw ... By educating the campus, I mean the setting up of a broadly-based organization of the Left which would conduct seminars, invite speakers, hold conferences, and possibly even publish a periodical of some kind. This is necessary to combat the widely-accepted 'non-political' quasi-ideology which asserts the irrelevance of the student in society.

It was difficult to avoid the obvious analytic authority of a body of writing that placed the accent on the structured class inequalities and imperatives of accumulation evident in capitalism or the ways in which that same economic order, blocked by its inner contradictions, turned to colonialism, making imperialism its highest stage. Student radicals could see that the weak links of the global chain of oppression and exploitation were exposed in revolutionary struggles that might actually *defeat* capitalism in Third World movements of guerilla warfare or colonial liberation. The New Left began the process of congealing different strands of revolutionary thought, from Marx and Lenin, on the one hand, through Che Guevara, Regis Debray, Frantz Fanon, and Kwame Nkrumah on the other, into a mix in which Mao often percolated to the surface. His ideas were championed by groups like The Internationalists, led by former University of British Columbia student radical leader Hardial Bains. This had the ironic impact of moving the praxis of the New Left away from fieldwork projects and more and more into what was increasingly called 'ideological communication.' For a brief moment in 1967 this effort was concentrated in a New Left Committee of a dozen ex-SUPA figures who put out a *Bulletin* that aimed to draw student radicals across the country together: 'O we can't organize, it's a pity / In country or campus or city. / We need an analysis / To stop our paralysis / So we'll set up another committee.'79

The New Left Committee wrote and thought and spoke in an idiom different than had SUPA. When it looked back on the brief history of the Canadian New Left, it was clear to some where predecessors had faltered:

Key to SUPA's failure was its inability to develop a coherent strategy of the structure of modern capitalism and of its specific characteristics in Canada. Instead SUPA remained ideologically confused, uncritically eclectic. It drew on various elements of the pacifist-direct action approach and ill-defined SDS notions of 'participatory democracy.' But the war in Vietnam, the powerlessness of the poor, the authoritarian governing of the universities were never traced to their structural roots in the political economy of modern capitalism, and the constituencies essential to revolutionary change were vaguely defined and analysed.

In this short paragraph of judgment lay the approach that would define the New Left's engagement with what remained of the 1960s.[80] The road of simultaneously interpreting *and* changing the world, however, would not be an easy one.

To the extent that SUPA had failed, it was apparent in 1967 that there were those prepared to resist the growing tide of Marxist theory that seemed to be crashing the New Left shorelines of praxis. Some continued to base an understanding of the revolutionary possibilities of the youth movement on the counterculture. 'Politics in the widest sense,' insisted one student activist, 'must be made as interesting as pot.' For another, protest needed to be inspired, as it was throughout the world, by avant-gardes and those who refused all incorporation in the establishment's machineries of governance. Among the exalted were the Provos of Amsterdam, Timothy Leary, Bob Dylan, Dadaists, Surrealists, and civil rights marchers; tactics championed included 'chalk drawing on the sidewalk, Black Masses, public 15-minute semi-spontaneous orgies, a poet on every corner, the right of spontaneous spectacle – enthusiasm, participation, IMAGINATION AND BEAUTY: spontaneous solidarity and creativity.' Some thought the vanguard was destined to be those who refused all complicity in capitalism's drudgery and addictive consumerism – the hoboes, tramps, and permanently unemployed.[81]

This anarchistic intransigence to the fundamental program of Marxism certainly characterized a segment of Canada's New Left. It was, however, countered in the growth of new organizations that championed the energy and activism of 1960s youth radicalism at the same time that they engaged with a range of issues posed in the decidedly Old Left accent on party structure, political program, and proletarian orientation. The history of the proliferation of revolutionary organizations in the period 1967–77 has yet to be written.[82] This breathtaking explosion of Trotskyist, Maoist, and revolutionary direct action groups lay in the late-1960s encounter of the New Left and Marxism. Out of this would emerge the New Left Caucus, Red Morning, Rising Up Angry! Canadian Party of Labour, Progressive Worker, Communist Party of Canada/ Marxist-Leninist (formerly The Internationalists), League for Socialist Action (an older body, but we can enter it on the list), Socialist League/ Forward Group, Spartacist League (later Trotskyist League of Canada), Revolutionary Marxist Group, Revolutionary Workers League, En Lutte/In Struggle, and Workers Communist Party.[83] To have lived in the intense crossfire of this late-1960s/1970s cauldron of revolutionary thought, activity, and organizational commitment was an experience of endless and sharpening debate, argument, and exchange over the tactics and strategy of a new kind of left practice. Some would recognize the contribution that this made to deepening and developing the project of dissent, opposition, and socialism in Canada. Thus, Mel Watkins was generous in his understanding of how the left push in the New Democratic Party was accelerated by what he termed 'the sectarian groups in Canada,' naming the Trotskyists in particular as playing an important role in building the 'anti-war movement in Canada.'[84] Yet there were also those who saw in all of this an ongoing fragmentation and acrimony deserving of censure. 'There were a whole lot of splits then,' one SUPA leader told Myrna Kostash. 'The Trots were getting heavy and there were the Hegelian phenomenologists and the hard-line Marxists. I remember one night at the NDY house when people were screaming, roaring, practically having fist fights over the issues of where we were politically. This was supposed to be a party.'[85]

A party, or *the* Party? The word had different connotations, according to accents and capitalization. Increasingly this was the issue posed, and with it came, inevitably, questions of affiliation. Marxist or not-Marxist further divided along axes of distinguishable Marxisms, in the plural. Veteran Canadian New Left liberationist Jim Harding penned a decisive 1970 rebuke of an intellectual and political opponent, labelling him 'a reductionist, mechanist, vulgar maoist Marxist, and anything else I can say with tongue in cheek. He wants to stay outside humanity and its struggles for freedom with his grand, deterministic theory of revolution.' Harding's mindset spoke to 'the poles on the left in Canada' that were widening in these 1967–70 years.[86]

One pole within SUPA's political contestation was represented by Stan Gray, who in the spring of 1967 was working on a dissertation in England. His view was that a turn to Marxist understandings of class struggle was precisely the direction demanded. Gray, who had grown up

in a communist family, was for the first half of the 1960s a quintessential
New Leftist. Later in the decade he began to reflect on where youth radicals had been going and whether they were not missing something. 'If
there is one thing that the new left, at least in Canada, has consistently
sought to avoid,' thought Gray after his years in CUCND and SUPA, 'it is
the radicalizing experiences and organizational importance of the productive process, and thereby of the working class as a class.' Gray wrote
to Don McKelvey, a member of SDS who had left the United States to
work with SUPA and who advocated the writing of a Canadian equivalent of the Port Huron Statement, in the summer of 1967. He expressed
opposition to the drift into what he judged the excessive subjectivity of
middle-class students. In contrast, Gray championed 'Marxist emphasis
on class and workers control.'[87] A year later, Gray was adamant that
'Marxism is coming more and more to be the common denominator of
all student movements in North America and Western Europe.'[88]

The New Left, born of the campus but separated somewhat from it in
the mid-1960s engagement with 'community,' would ironically make its
prodigal return via a commitment to working-class analysis and Marxism. A first phase of the Canadian New Left gave way to a second, in
which former SUPA activists figured prominently but were supplemented by a younger wave of disaffected youth. Marxism was to be a
necessary component of their radical, growingly anti-capitalist, arsenal.
To be sure, *some* veterans of the New Left were now well placed to lead
the emerging student movement, and of those males who survived the
demise of SUPA, many embraced Marxism and class analysis in one way
or another. But few joined the Trotskyist and Maoist organizations that,
by 1968–9, were a force to reckon with on the left in general, and within
student radical politics in particular. 'Student syndicalism,' undertaken
in particular ways in the mid-1960s, came increasingly to mean a
worker–student alliance orchestrated by a party formation which understood its ultimate aim as the creation of a revolutionary vanguard organization.[89] Even if such bodies did not lead, they were ubiquitously
present. Moreover, the ethos of the New Left in this period meant that
'participatory democracy' and 'community organization,' evident in
1969–70 in the anti-poverty agitations of Toronto's Just Society Movement and its links to a contingent of radical social workers, academics,
and urban rebels who took the eminently New Left name Praxis,[90] were
overtaken by more boisterous protests. Increasingly, these aimed to disrupt the university and its pretence of civility or to organize picket line
militance in support of striking workers.[91]

This, then, was an intellectual movement of radicalization that affected many university youth, often those affiliated with the Canadian Union of Students (CUS). It was an oddly uneven development, characterized by what one participant/commentator, Andrew Wernick, dubbed 'a quasi-Marxism' in which 'much talk of movement-building' was sobered by 'an acute suspicion of leadership and organization.' As much as all seemed to agree that 'theory lagged far behind practice,' the importance of acting on one's radical beliefs was nevertheless paramount. The New Left lived on in the accent on spontaneity and the significance of 'the grassroots.' Centralization was to be avoided, used only when formal structures were necessary for fulfilling the objectives of local activism. The enthusiasm of a loosely Marxist, theoretically inclined student left in 1968 was summed up in Wernick's account of a CUS gathering in Winnipeg: 'The history of those ten days seemed to suggest that mainstream middle-class Canadian students placed in the intense hothouse of a "free" community and prodded a little by radical ideas and experiences, are but ten days from revolutionary consciousness.'[92] Sometimes, of course, this 'revolutionary consciousness' required nurturing, and this often came in the form of specific local developments. -

A case in point was the Toronto Student Movement (TSM), organized in the summer of 1968. TSM largely leapfrogged over its immediate student radical predecessors, CUCND, SNCC, SUPA, and the anti–Vietnam war coalitions that, by 1966–7 were being pieced together by Trotskyist organizations such as the League for Socialist Action.[93] Its eyes at first set on radicalizing university life, TSM soon found itself supporting striking newspaper guild members in Peterborough, pursuing Marxist analyses of power that connected the obscure dots of corporate profit and research, the state and higher education, and capitalist culture and the ideological pacification of the oppressed and exploited. Along with the Canadian Union of Students, TSM adapted to the militancy of the moment, evident in student revolts in France, Italy, Germany, the United States, and elsewhere. Marxist classics and anti-colonialist writers were now supplemented by attention to the speeches and positions of European student leaders such as Red Rudi Dutschke, Karl Dietrich Wolff, and Daniel Cohn-Bendit. The latter's 1969 *Obsolete Communism: The Left-Wing Alternative* soon became a New Left bestseller. Campus revolt was now front-page news. Tom Hayden, his New Jersey community organizing terminated by the 1967 Newark riots, saw SDS's revitalization in linking campus upheaval to the anti-war drive. When students occupied Columbia University in April 1968, Hayden called for 'Two, Three,

Many Columbias.' The SDS leader's formulation suggested that in the heart of the imperialist empire student radicals could draw state repression and its material resources to them, thereby directly aiding the Vietnamese and other Third World revolutionaries.

University of Toronto never quite managed to rise to the 1968 occasion. But there were plenty of rallies and disruptive actions. TSM gave way to the New Left Caucus (NLC), broadly Marxist in its approach, but uninterested in direct alliance with any party formation. Toronto student radicals prevented University of California president and industrial relations authority Clark Kerr from speaking at the Royal Ontario Museum, 150 of them piling onto the stage, pantomiming Kerr's suppression of Mario Savio's freedom of speech. They protested the university's connection with Dow Chemical, a corporation whose products and profits were widely, if rather loosely, seen as fuelling the imperialist war drive. Classrooms became challenging stand-offs between dissident students and professors as the NLC refined its tactic of 'spectacular radicalism.' The ideology of higher education was assailed by a 'theatre of revolt,' exposing its sham hypocrisy and empty platitudes. Commencement ceremonies were heckled and unaligned students treated to an extemporaneous NLC lecture on youth's sexual oppression. As the meaning of the female orgasm became a hot topic of political discussion, button-wearing radicals popped up at the multiversity's various colleges sporting a slogan that immediately generated a playful mass appeal: 'Bring U of T to a Climax.'[94]

At the University of Toronto, the New Left Caucus broke the back of a draconian disciplinary code. In Montreal, Sir George Williams University had a rougher student radical ride. There, protesters almost cracked the university's bank, trashing and torching the room where computers, tapes, and punch cards were kept. The damages were reported to have reached from $2 to $5 million. Race ignited the explosive protest, a special committee convening at the end of January 1969 to hear student testimony on allegations of a biology professor's racism and incompetence. Rawl R. Frederick's poem, 'Man Trap,' articulated black students' rage:

> They designate institutions
> we disintegrate in infernoes.
> They consumate animals
> that abort us.
> Nursing grounds for dysgenic beasts.

Developing ghettoes/employing social workers
to create negroes.
Man-trap, I know your name, your face.

Montreal in the mid-1960s had been a magnet attracting black student activists and radicals, many of whom had origins and interests in the Caribbean. Robert and Anthony Hill, Ann Cools, Roosevelt (Rosie) Douglas, Alfie Roberts, and others formed a Conference Committee on West Indian Affairs. They drew deeply on the presence of C.L.R. James, who was sojourning in Canada over the course of late 1966 and into 1967. With James as a stimulus, this group of Montreal blacks organized a number of conferences, workshops, and talks. These culminated in a 1968 Sir George Williams symposium that addressed black grievances in Canada, as well as a major black writers conference held at McGill University in mid-October 1968, at approximately the same time that West Indian student resentments were rising at Sir George Williams University. Speakers at the influential McGill forum included the charismatic James; Black Power advocate Stokely Carmichael, then at the height of his legendary status as the movement's most powerful orator; Guyana's Marxist historian Walter Rodney; Olympic athlete and protester Harry Edwards; and Halifax's Rocky Jones.[95]

The atmosphere approaching the Sir George Williams hearing was tense and untrusting. Administrators and most faculty had done little to convince black students that their complaints of professorial racism, classroom inadequacies, and dissatisfaction with how students were treated by instructors were going to be addressed sensitively. Grievances had been launched as early as April 1968, but they were largely swept under the university's bureaucratic rugs. There they gathered resentments over the summer and fall. A number of the Caribbean students were older and more experienced than their Canadian counterparts; many had considerable education under their belts and were training to work in the medical profession. They were not about to be put off. As the fall of 1968 gave way to the winter of 1969, the January hearing to finally address the matter was shaping up to be an explosive event. The black students were rightfully incensed with the university's prevarications, and the consciousness of Black Power that had been raised and emboldened by the almost life-transforming oratory of dazzling speakers like James and Carmichael was not to be denied.

With the meeting about to begin, demonstrators overtook the stage, disrupted the proceedings, shut the hearing down, and 200 students occupied a number of rooms and gathering places, including the faculty club and the computer centre in the multi-storied Hall Building. The sit-in dragged on for two weeks. On 11 February 1969, however, there was every indication of an agreement that would have seen the occupation end. But the faculty vetoed it being signed, and a first entry of municipal police inspected the computer room and withdrew. Things took an ugly and destructive turn as those occupying university space heard on radio that the riot police were about to descend on them. Uncertain of their role and purpose, apparently, this second wave of police entered the rooms taken over by the students, departed, and then barricaded the building, their behaviour menacing in its threatened violence. When they returned and broke in a glass door, the protesters ransacked a cafeteria and the computer room was torched.

As the smoke cleared, 87 Sir George Williams students were arrested: 38 of them were black, the majority from the Caribbean. Many of those taken into police custody were badly beaten, racist taunts ringing in their ears as they were roughly escorted from the building. Douglas, a future prime minister of Dominica, and Cools, later appointed by Trudeau to the Senate, were among those who landed in jail. The university ostensibly spent hundreds of thousands of dollars to lay a total of 1,044 criminal charges, of which, one year after the event, only 50 had been heard, a mere 9 upheld, with 22 dropped. Singled out as the leader, Kennedy Frederick, a West Indian from Grenada, endured a twenty-five-day hearing, during which time he was held without bail (later granted) and was on occasion brought to court in a cagelike vehicle, his hands shackled behind his back. Frederick faced twelve charges, six involving conspiracy and six relating to arson and damage to and prevention of lawful use of property. Most such charges, blanketing the scores arrested, were later dropped for 'lack of proof.' Across Canada, the media denounced the 'gang of hooligans,' 'rampaging criminals,' 'anarchists,' and 'thugs' responsible for the destruction of property. In Ottawa federal politicians pointed the finger of blame at Caribbean students and the lax immigration laws that allowed them access to Canadian higher education. They were soon demanding that more restrictive practices govern the entry of foreigners to universities.[96]

There were those quick to claim that there was little that was overtly Marxist that could be discerned as the rubble was cleaned up and the bruises healed in the Sir George Williams University affair. There had undoubtedly been more left rumblings of dissidence in the complicated making of the upheaval than many were willing to acknowledge. One western conservative did claim that the occupation had featured much chanting of slogans and direct quotation from 'copies of Mao Tse Tung's Little Red Book.' This did little to impress some older Marxist critics, who saw nothing more than 'obscurantism, egocentric pseudo-existentialism, and abstract moralizing' as the computer cards fluttered from atop the Sir George Williams building onto McKay Street below. Some grew increasingly hostile in their refusal to countenance 'the romantic incendiarism and apocalyptic messianism of many segments of the new left.' One professor at Sir George Williams, an associate editor of *Canadian Dimension*, condemned the nihilism that was 'always at war with the idea of civilization – socialist civilization as well as bourgeois civilization.' Charles Taylor, whose experience in the British New Left commenced in the *Universities and Left Review* of the late 1950s and reached into Canada and Quebec in the 1960s, translated the growing unease with the practice of youth radicalism into a theoretical interrogation of one of the movement's analytic pillars, Herbert Marcuse. Taylor questioned the New Left theorist's 'blithe unconcern with what rebellion is *for*, as long as it's stridently enough against.' He also deplored Marcuse's ruling out 'the possibility that a paroxysm of rebellion could destroy the discipline and character-form of one civilization without building those of another, higher one.' The result could only be 'disillusionment and despair: a binge of agitation followed by a prolonged hang-over.'[97]

Down the road from Sir George Williams, McGill University had been a centre of agitation since November 1967. With Stan Gray as its president of the local Students for a Democratic University (SDU) chapter, calls went out for a campus-wide general strike. The galvanizing event proved to be the disciplining of some *McGill Daily* staff. They had published a satirical extract from Paul Krassner's *The Realist* that higher education officials considered 'obscene libel.' In retaliation, students occupied all six floors of the administration building. It took a brigade of policemen and liberal use of nightsticks to clear the occupiers off McGill property; Stan Gray was knocked unconscious and arrested, and many students suffered injuries. A year and a half later, Gray, anything but subdued, headed a 15,000-strong 28 March 1969 demonstration outside of the gates of the anglophone university, chanting, 'McGill français! McGill aux Québécois! McGill aux Travailleurs!' Police barricaded the university, helicopters hovered overhead, while some diehard Tory teenagers circled the wagons of retrenchment, standing strong for nineteenth-century values. Proud to protect McGill from the radical hoards, they planted themselves firmly on university property and sang 'God Save the Queen.' Victorianism *sans* riot! A coalition of trade unionists, students, socialists, and independence advocates, the McGill Français movement cost Gray his teaching job at the prestigious bastion of English-speaking Montreal, catapulting him into prominence in the increasingly militant milieu of the Quebec revolutionary left. He soon headed an agitational mass movement of extra-parliamentary opposition, the Front de Libération Populaire, playing a prominent role in the establishment of a Quebec Committee for Solidarity with the Black Panthers. As the repressive atmosphere worsened, the provincial legislature passed anti-demonstration laws. FLQ kidnappings of British High Commission staffer James Richard Cross and Quebec minister of labour and immigration Pierre Laporte provoked the 1970 declaration of the War Measures Act and the October Crisis. Gray was eventually swept up in the post–War Measures Act repression, the culmination of which was the Black Friday arrest and detention of 500 leftists. McGill's SDU, for its part, had denounced the university in 1969 as responsible for 'more than two hundred years of economic exploitation and national oppression.'[98]

From east to west, SDU chapters at Canadian universities agitated in 1968–9, their demands paralysing campuses. Libraries were locked down, buildings occupied, faculty clubs invaded by squealing pigs and gas-masked students screaming, 'Thought police! Thought police!' Teach-ins, boycotts of classes, marches on department chairs, challenges to traditional behaviours and curriculum, and students petitioning for and rallying around a small but significant number of victimized Marxist professors were commonplace.[99]

The conflict peaked at Simon Fraser University (SFU), where a long-standing battle involved not only radical students and teaching assistants, but New Left Marxist faculty and some committed liberal colleagues. It confronted the class power of the university, demanding open admissions for working-class students. Student researchers uncovered the not terribly well-hidden story of corporate capital's dominance of Simon Fraser, how its senate was ruled by presidents and directors of major enterprises. Labour unions and Native, welfare, tenant, and teacher organizations, however, had nary a voice in the corridors of power. Former SUPA activists Jim Harding and Sharon Yandle were among the shit disturbers. When hundreds of students occupied the administration buildings in November 1968, rifling through files as they lunched on peanut butter sandwiches, they discovered that RCMP dossiers had been compiled on 600 students, including a number of

American war resisters. At 2:15 a.m. on the fourth day of the occupation, the Mounties broke in on the sit-in, arresting 114 students as a
public address system blared, 'The Party's Over.' Cries of 'police state'
echoed on Burnaby Mountain.

During the course of the next summer, the experimental red centre
of SFU radicalism, its political science, sociology, and anthropology
department, was attacked by the administration. The program's
elected committees of students and faculty were disbanded, its Chairman removed, a trusteeship was imposed, and a number of faculty,
including senior professors, were refused tenure or renewal of existing
contracts. A strike was declared on 24 September 1969. After six weeks
the academic walkout, which had the support of thousands of students,
and gave rise to arrests and injunctions, was broken. The largely New
Left–Marxist faculty was locked out and subsequently purged. SFU
president Kenneth Strand could not countenance the bold and utopian exercise in critical thinking and radical democracy that his political science, sociology, and anthropology professors, students, and staff
pioneered. He told them: 'The society and economy is capitalist and
the university serves that system.' At SFU Strand brought the 1960s to
an abrupt halt.[100]

Canada: The Wealthiest Colony[101]

And what's good for GENERAL MOTORS
obviously benefits the kingdom of
heaven not to mention certain suburbs and
the dominion of
Canada
tho some
(communists!)
might disagree.

A.W. Purdy[102]

The New Left was born talking about liberation, independence, even
socialism. This was the discourse of its being. It did not, before the mid-
1960s, voice much concern about how all of this related to Canadian
identity. Indeed, in the general political context of the early 1960s,
national identity was hardly a raging concern north of the forty-ninth
parallel. Where there were rumblings, they came from the left.[103] As
Philip Resnick has suggested, in the period 1955–65 nationalism in

Canada was largely a dead letter. In the latter half of the 1960s, however, nationalisms of many kinds floated in and out of a variety of politics. They structured much of the economic agenda of the Liberal Party, influenced cultural policy and priorities, and permeated the organizations and arguments of the Canadian left, old as well as new.

Central to the emergence of an effervescent nationalism was a rising anti-Americanism, evident in a poem, '1966,' published in *Canadian Dimension*:

America America
the burnt seed lies by the side
of your turnpikes
auto graveyards
motel cities
military camps
the heaped-up contempt of every dream of paradise on earth
stinking your greens
the burnt seed
shines darkly
blasting out
the sun[104]

The politico-intellectual trend that words such as these articulated, lapsing into essentialist condemnation, could not but shake New Left thought to its foundations, aligned as it was with developments in the United States.[105]

There were many reasons for the late-1960s birth of left nationalism in Canada. The most serious conservative thinker who sustained a critical and supportive engagement with the SUPA-style New Leftists, George Grant, did so unashamedly as a nationalist. He ended what was, in effect, a 1966 Open Letter to the New Left, with the conviction that 'our greatest obligation as Canadians is to work for a country which is not simply a satellite of any empire.' This resonated with the Canadian New Left in the mid-1960s, searching as it was for a direction unambiguously differentiated from imperialist aggression and the brutal practice of power. Gad Horowitz, for instance, was voicing the need for 'Canada to be something other than a collection of disintegrated particularisms of the American Mind.' He and Grant would carry on something of a dialogue as the 1960s gave way to the 1970s. With Grant willing to voice his challenging opposition to the war in Vietnam in a language of imperialism, many New Leftists seemed equally amenable to opposing warmongering with words championing a distinct Canadian nationhood. Horowitz summed up the emerging argument for a popular front of all Canadian socialists and nationalists to turn back the tide of Americanization in ways that appealed directly to Grant: 'The Canadian tory might want to stay out of a society in which the masses are given to excesses of violence and intolerance, noblesse oblige nowhere to be found, tradition is a dirty word and individual greed rides roughshod over all feelings of community.' Only socialism, Horowitz suggested, could in the long run preserve Canadian independence, because it would require the class forces of a mobilized revolution to decisively defeat the coordinated, massive power of continental capitalism in Canada. But 'this dream may never be realized,' and in the interval much could be done to ensure that Canadians would not 'be stuck with Americanism.'[106]

By the early 1970s, confronting just how overwhelming a left nationalist anti-Americanism could become, even Horowitz acknowledged that the socialist/nationalist dilemma was not quite as easily bridged as he had suggested a few years before.[107] But as the New Left emerged out of its 'community organizing' phase to embrace a more Marxist analytic accent on the political economy of Canada, the exploration of foreign ownership of the country's resources and industries and understanding of its role in supplying the U.S. war machine with much-needed materials pushed many to embrace left nationalism and espouse an independent socialist Canada.[108] In nascent party formations, especially those with a Maoist tinge, such as the Progressive Worker movement in British Columbia, independence and socialism were twinned. More and more classroom discussion turned on the political economy of dependency and the struggle for an autonomous Canada.[109]

As the left went, so went the nation. (Would that it were so!) In a *Toronto Daily Star* poll published in *Canadian Dimension* (something of a rarity), the magazine's left-wing readership was treated to a progressive variant of 'meet the Ugly American.' The survey indicated a woeful ignorance on the part of a U.S. citizenry that clearly wanted no controls placed on its imperialist reach into Canada. In contrast, Canadians polled seemed worried about their country's independence. With the Liberal newspaper declaring that 'most Canadians believe that in our relationship with the US we are trading our soul for the American way of life,' *Canadian Dimension* applauded the bourgeois publication as 'one of the leading nationalist forces in Canada today, strengthening the will to resist further Americanization.' Its next cover was adorned with a red maple leaf, over which was superimposed a red and black, bold-printed 'Open Letter to Canadian Nationalists.' Segments of the New Left were clearly going new nationalist.[110]

As this happened the debate that might have taken place over the political economy of *formal* dependency within a U.S.-dominated continental capitalism versus the *substantive content* of domestic capitalist exploitation and the autonomous role of the Canadian bourgeoisie in its own imperialist penetration of the developing world was largely postponed until the 1970s.[111] Instead, the Pandora's box of nationalism, however much it was draped in socialist intent, once opened proved a difficult politics to keep within Marxist bounds. Left nationalists soon embraced a plethora of essentialist positions.

With the denouement of SUPA, James Laxer utilized a newly found nationalism to tar the entire New Left with the brush of American domination. He explained the failure of youth dissent to light the spark of mass resistance as a result of relying on the inappropriate guide of U.S. New Left radicalism. Laxer thought Canada's 1960s ideas of dissent had been 'conceived out of the conditions of the heart of the empire rather than the conditions of a dependent country.' If Laxer's critique contained insight – like Gray he was dubious of New Left disdain for organized labour and working-class struggle and raised important questions about the ways in which SUPA and others isolated themselves from Canadian traditions of resistance – it nevertheless retreated too easily into a hectoring insistence that the national question, in and of itself, was 'the most powerful force for combating the American empire that exists in Canada.'[112] Ironically, this New Left assault on empire often proved a substitute for more sustained inquiry, drifting in the direction of moral condemnation.

John W. Warnock, for instance, entitled one assault on American liberal individualism, 'Why I Am Anti-American,' opposing the United States as a 'Sick Society.' America's justification of inequality, worship of property and profit, and cultivation and dependence on violence relegated it to ethical condemnation. Warnock managed to avoid discussion of just how different Canada actually was in being similarly diseased.[113] Robin Mathews and James Steele launched a broad-ranging crusade to revive Canadian culture in the throes of its incessant Americanization, the most effective component of which was their pressuring of universities to hire Canadians. Few subjects proved more divisive to a New Left that leaned intellectually on contributions from the United States. The problem was exacerbated by the significant contribution genuinely radical and often Marxist expatriots had made to the growing sophistication of critical, oppositional thought in Canadian universities, especially with respect to anti-imperialism. The pages of both mainstream and left publications bristled with debate as the relentless Mathews pursued his course of opposition to Americanization, drawing other left nationalists such as Mel Watkins into his cause.[114] Mathews could, however, push the envelope too far. In an article on 'Draft Dodging and U.S. Imperialism in Canada,' he argued that war resisters, while worthy of Canadian compassion, carried Americanization with them as they fled induction into the U.S. army and refused the patriot's cry to wage war on the communist Vietnamese. For Mathews, these exiles were little more than agents of the colonial empire, and he found himself 'past the sentimental outpourings about Morality and the tender souls of U.S. draft dodgers.' It seemed that Mathews would have preferred that the American war resisters return home. Barring that, he thought they might write a letter of thanks to the federal minister of manpower and immigration, an Ottawa 'representative closest to the fact that they' had been able to secure sanctuary in Canada. Such a request, posed in a magazine of the Canadian left, was a long way from the spirit of SUPA's pioneering projects of smuggling draft evaders across the border at Niagara Falls.[115]

Mathews thought that draft dodgers might also want to write an appreciative cheque to the Waffle Manifesto Group. The ardent nationalist claimed that this body was the only serious force fighting U.S. imperialism in Canada. Originating as a youthful dissident caucus within the New Democratic Party, the Waffle was part of a 1968–9 ferment over left nationalism that spilled out of the fragmentation of the initial SUPA New Left and the turn to Marxist-inspired political-economic analysis of Canada. It was built by a 1960s radical who had close connections with both the Old and New Lefts, Jim Laxer, and former liberal economist, Mel Watkins, who was moving to the left over the course of a decade that saw him increasingly committed to taking up 'the dismal science' cudgels against foreign ownership of Canadian industry.[116] Laxer and Watkins quickly rallied to their cause figures such as *Canadian Dimension* editor and Manitoba NDP MLA Cy Gonick; Nova Scotia NDP leader Jeremy Akerman; and a half-dozen prominent British Columbia NDPers. Their support grew among a younger, New Left–inspired cohort of activists. An NDP–Waffle Labour Committee was formed. Although it never attracted mainstream union support,

being anathema to the leading layer of officialdom within the hegemonic international unions, it did promote militant struggles for workers' control, rank-and-file administration of trade unions, women's
rights in the labour movement, and the organization and support of
immigrant, unemployed, and non-unionized workers. It also raised the
obligatory demand to increase Canadian autonomy and authority
within the institutions of the working class.[117]

With its main strength in Ontario, the Waffle also garnered support on the prairies and in British Columbia.[118] It promoted its left-
nationalist message within the NDP through publication of a 1969 Manifesto, which carried its barbed politics of challenge in a combined New
Left rhetoric and a strong assault on the Americanization of Canada. Six
of the twelve authors of the document for an independent socialist
Canada were graduate students in the Queen's University history
department and their spouses: Laxer and Krista Maeots; Pat and John
Smart; and the Saskatchewan radicals Caroline and Lorne Brown.[119]
The Manifesto first surfaced with a bang at a Winnipeg convention, and
before long NDP votes on policy matters were being posed as a left–
right party division, with Wafflers leaning decidedly left. Carrying as its
banner of preference the linked demands of national independence
and socialism, Wafflers threw the more cautious and bureaucratized
reform-minded NDP leadership – ensconced in the Lewis family and
buttressed by the trade union tops – into quite a tizzy in the 1969–72
years. Then, able to take it no longer, Stephen and David Lewis, the
lapsed New Leftist Dennis McDermott, now a heavy in the United Automobile Workers, and a triumvirate of United Steelworkers of America
officialdom – William Mahoney, Lynn Williams, and Bob Mackenzie –
forced the Waffle out of the party at an Orillia, Ontario, gathering of
the NDP provincial council. This was not before the Waffle had challenged the hegemony of the international unions' leaders in the trade
union movement, questioning their commitment to labour militancy;
spread the radical left-nationalist position throughout social democratic
circles, claiming the support of 3,000 of the country's 50,000 NDPers;
and managed to run Laxer against David Lewis for the federal leadership of the party, it taking four ballots for the elder Lewis to defeat his
Waffle opponent, 1,046 to 612, at the party's sixth convention in
Winnipeg in 1971. In pressing what many felt was a strident anti-
Americanism, the Waffle did nonetheless expose the vulnerabilities to
the left of Canada's mainstream social democratic tradition. It pro-

moted a vigorous anti-imperialist Canadian nationalism that differentiated itself from both staid social democrats and the rising, narrowly
economistic bourgeois nationalism of the Liberal Party's Walter Gordon.[120] As New Leftists struggling to make common cause with Old Leftists found themselves finally referred to in the 1970s as 'social misfits,'
as 'a cancer' that needed to be cut out of the New Democrats, or warned
that they were about to receive 'a lesson in gutsmanship today,' they
knew, deep in their heart of liberation theory, that something of the Sixties had definitely passed.[121]

When the Waffle was wound down by its NDP opponents, Cy Gonick
editorialized in *Canadian Dimension*. His New Left lament for a socialist
nationalism lost was cynically downbeat in its repudiation of a moderate
electoralism: 'The Liberals have coopted the nationalist issue because it
has been shorn of its socialist content. David Lewis sounds like an angry
Trudeau or a petulant Stanfield. Maybe his driving fist and his outraged
indignation will be enough to win a few more seats for the N.D.P. in the
upcoming federal election. Somehow it doesn't seem to matter.'[122] The
wealthiest colony, understandably enough given a materialist analysis,
could not quite sustain an anti-imperialist mobilization within a core
constituency of the Old, albeit moderate, Left. The ironies of the situation could only go so far politically. When the Saskatchewan Waffle
finally exited the NDP after a 6–8 October 1973 Moose Jaw conference
decided that it was time to break from social democracy and 'establish a
socialist party,' the movement for an independent socialist Canada
seemed to some to be growing. In actuality it would fragment and prove
stillborn.[123]

Further complicating the situation was an irrepressible demand,
developing within the Waffle, but also generalized throughout New Left
circles, that women now be heard. Largely male-led, the Waffle har-
boured a contingent of vocal and authoritative feminists who widened
the discussion of what an independent socialist Canada would look like.
Among them, Krista Maeots, Kelly Crichton, and Varda [Burstyn] Kidd
were powerful advocates of creating a new politics in which women's
place would not be one of subordination and silence. As Burstyn
recalled in 1990, early women's liberation registered strongly in the
Waffle and, through it, exercised a considerable impact on the NDP:

Prior to the onslaught on the Party's program led by Waffle women at constituency associations, provincial conferences and national conventions,

NDP policy on women's issues was bland and unobjectionable, shaped by a
mild (not to say gutless) fifties-style social democratic rhetoric of equality
which had little substance or meaning. Waffle women, with Waffle men supporting them often enough to register their presence as different from
many mainstream NDP men, tackled the big issues: childcare (universal, for
the first time); abortion rights (fireworks that still explode on a predictable
basis); equal pay; quotas for women on party bodies; the right to caucus.

NDP loyalist Douglas Fisher noted that the Waffle had 'used brilliantly
... the women's liberation movement. The women cry outrage over
under-representation on councils, committees, etc. of the party. This
unsettles, diverts, and gives the Wafflers a popular support which swells
over into other areas.'

Wafflers and New Democrats clashed repeatedly in the period 1969–
72 over issues associated with Quebec self-determination, the influence
and seeming conservatism of a powerful layer of trade union officialdom, nationalization of key resource industries, and promotion of the
NDP as a *socialist* party. Yet it was resolutions on the women's question
that provoked an initial, and embittered, rupture at the party's 1971
Winnipeg convention. The social-democratic establishment defeated
two constitutional amendments designed to increase women's representation. On the last day of the gathering, those in control adopted a tepid
policy statement on women that infuriated Waffle feminists and many
other women in the NDP as well. With delegate hostility rising, the convention chair, Eamon Park, a United Steelworkers of America official
and well-connected NDP insider, ran the proceedings with a dictatorial
proceduralism that outraged left-leaning feminists. Park ruled out of
order a referral motion calling on the NDP to convene a women's conference within a year to redraft party policies relating to women. Stung
by this contemptuous silencing, women implored the NDP to make
amends, only to find their pleas drowned out as union-affiliated delegates broke into a deafening chorus of 'Solidarity Forever.' Cries of
'Sieg Heil' were directed venomously at the podium. Gender politics
such as these have tended to be lost sight of in the titanic clash of male
leaders (Laxer vs. Lewis) and the seemingly gender-neutral politics of a
period dominated by discussions of Americanization, Quebec independence, and nationalization, but they were nonetheless quite important
at the time. In the end much kept Burstyn and other Waffle feminists
separate from conventional social democratic men and women in the

NDP, as well as from those hardened left nationalists who would, upon being forced out of the NDP, go on to form the Movement for an Independent Socialist Canada in 1972. Burstyn nevertheless remembers the positive impact that women's liberation exercised in radical political circles at the end of the 1960s.[124]

Something of this would characterize the New Left as a whole, but like the Waffle it was not destined to survive the post-1960s political traumas of the early 1970s, at least not on the gendered terms it had set for itself from 1967 to 1970. A feminist challenge both extended and enriched the New Left experience and, ultimately, fragmented and divided it. This was all the more evident as the relatively coherent first phase of late-1960s women's liberation itself soon fractured into various 1970s camps.

'Typers of Letters and Distributors of Leaflets No Longer'

As Simon Fraser University's political science, anthropology, and sociology department erupted in September 1969, the venerable New York–based independent socialist magazine *Monthly Review* published a fourteen-page article entitled 'The Political Economy of Women's Liberation.' Its author was an unlikely pioneer of a Marxist analysis of women's oppression, a feminist critique of orthodox historical materialism's blindness to the fundamental importance of unpaid household work as 'socially necessary production.' Few would have expected such an article to be written by a member of a university chemistry department, unschooled, by all accounts, in the workings of Old or New Left throughout her period of formative intellectual development in the 1950s and 1960s. Of working-class background, and trained in the United States as a scientist, Margaret Benston had no deep connection to left or Marxist praxis until 1966, when she came to Simon Fraser and was immediately caught up in the intellectual turmoil of a campus enlivened by revolutionary thought. Benston was transformed by the atmosphere of the later 1960s, her identical twin sister, Marian Lowe, later describing what amounted to a political conversion experience:

> She used to credit the dancing of the 60s and its freedom of movement with allowing her to hear what the radicals were saying. Freedom of the body helped to free the mind. Marxism as a framework made sense, something that for the first time offered the possibility that social forces could

be understood and then changed. It was a revelation, and her life and work began to be informed by political ideas.

Drawing on largely male Marxist theoretical writing, including unpublished papers that had been delivered at SFU by the Trotskyist economist Ernest Mandel, as well as the influential 1966 Juliet Mitchell *New Left Review* essay, 'Women: The Longest Revolution,' Benston insisted on the necessity of revolutionary social transformation, one that would in fact 'end women's oppression.'

'The Political Economy of Women's Liberation' fused Marxism and feminism and, in a few pages, crystallized understandings that had been circulating in a nascent New Left women's movement in Canada and the United States and had been reverberating around the world. Travelling across Canada in mimeographed, *samizdat*-like versions, the essay's before-publication impact registered in the women's consciousness-raising groups that were springing up in the post-1967 implosion of the first New Left. Soon Benston's short article was grinding its analysis into male-dominated theoretical discussions in bodies like the New Left Caucus, where feminism now registered as a potent challenge to a rekindled interest in Marxist theory. It left a lasting impression on a peculiarly and insightfully rich Canadian theoretical debate about housework and its meanings within the capitalist mode of production, resonating internationally in the writings of Mariarosa Della Costa and Selma James. Translated into Spanish, French, Italian, German, Swedish, and Japanese, 'The Political Economy of Women's Liberation' affected the developing global women's movement as an interpretive statement unlike almost any other. In Italy segments of the women's movement.called themselves Benstonistas. German feminists considered Benston's article 'one of the first to analyze women's housework from a new left perspective.' Soon copies of Benston's article were coming out of every radical movement pamphlet-producing plant: the United Front; the Radical Education Project (Detroit or Ann Arbor); the Eugene, Oregon, SDS chapter; Boston's New England Free Press; the San Francisco Bay Area Radical Education Project. It would later be anthologized in countless collections of the pivotal writings of so-called 'second wave' feminism. Benston's argument anchored a particular materialist feminist approach rooted in the briefly happy marriage of Marxism, women's liberation, and the New Left in the last years of the 1960s. Many young women, among them Adrienne Rich, considered Benston's article 'one of the milestones of passage into women's liberation.'

Benston had many sides to her wonderfully engaged and influential life: a chemist who jumped ship from her discipline to find a home in computer science, she also helped create SFU's women's studies program. Benston was as well a founding member of the Euphoniously Feminist Non-Performing Quintet. In her commitment to community organizing, her love of people, and her important feminist labours, she made possible a part of the rising of the women that grew out of the New Left and transformed it in the 1967–70 years. The Vancouver Women's Caucus and its publication, *The Pedestal*, would have been unimaginable without women like Maggie Benston, as would like bodies and forums throughout the country.[125]

'The Political Economy of Women's Liberation' began as a 1967 draft and found its way into print two years later. This chronology marks the birth of New Left feminism in Canada, a major statement appearing in the fall of 1967.[126] Judy Bernstein, Peggy Morton, Linda Seese, and Myrna Wood, four SUPA women, wrote a position paper for the ill-fated Goderich conference. Entitled 'Sisters, Brothers, Lovers ... Listen,' it quickly became the founding document of the Toronto Women's Liberation Movement. SUPA women had read Betty Friedan's *The Feminine Mystique* (1963) early on their road to activism, but it was the movement itself that registered with them the experience of being female in a male-dominated world. When women began to talk in SUPA about their discontents – in and of itself perhaps a sign that the first phase of student radicalism was about to implode – their male comrades responded with jokes and gendered put-downs. 'We talked about how it was men who did the writing and women the Gestetnering, about how our political influence in the group was directly related to how "heavy" the guy was that we were coupled with,' one budding feminist told Myrna Kostash years later. Word spread of women's caucuses sprouting up throughout North American radical student circles. Even the Canadian government was recognizing that the 'status of women' was a legitimate topic of inquiry and struck a royal commission to investigate and 'ensure for women equal opportunities with men in all aspects of Canadian society.'

Unlike Benston's analysis, the SUPA women's document was more quintessentially New Left in its accent on liberation and love, alienation and anger, conformism and creativity. They drew as well on early feminist anthropology and their direct experience in African-American struggles for freedom, where the gendered differentiation of race in the deep south led them to acknowledge how black men and women lived through systemic racism and came out of it formed in contradictory ways. Mourning 'the loss of manhood of Negro men,' these early New Left feminists regretted that so few cared about the 'loss of humanity of the exploited half of the human species – the women.'

Anything but radical separatists, the SUPA women recognized that it was necessary to 'attempt the most humane interaction,' insisting that men and women in the New Left must 'act as though the revolution had occurred by our relationships with one another.' They drew attention, for the first time, to the reality of those relationships, and the extent to which the New Left suffered 'the same hang-ups, frustrations, and neuroses as the rest of society.' SUPA had, for many women, been a quest to transcend their Marcusian one-dimensionality by developing ego identity through attachment to the New Left itself. But this project of substitutionism had failed: 'We created father figures or allowed them to be created ... we never gained the principles of participatory democracy. A few people were allowed to lead. Many people were excluded from leadership. The largest excluded group was women. SUPA, in respect to women, totally accepted the mores of the dominant society.' In what was undoubtedly a series of barbs that brought painfully home to male leftists the seriousness of feminist discontent, 'Sisters, Brothers, Lovers ... Listen' pointed to Black Power advocate Stokely Carmichael's claim that 'the only position for a woman in SNCC is prone.' Such a statement had never been publicly proclaimed by SUPA men, they noted. It was bad enough, however, that they might well have been thinking it. Old Leftists often seemed astounded with the level of male chauvinism in the New Left, these SUPA feminists reported with regret. They went so far as to suggest that SUPA women sometimes felt that they were in a 'civil rights organization with a leadership of southern racists.' Confronting 'masculine intellectualism' and 'feminine emotionalism,' the SUPA position paper addressed issues that would ring loudly in feminist writing for decades. Seeing first hand that to be accepted by men as theoretical and political equals was often to sacrifice their emotional lives as lovers and partners, Bernstein, Morton, Seese, and Wood refused the either/or dichotomization. Instead they realized that in their struggle for equality lay 'a feeling of beauty and power.' They closed their manifesto-like document with the simple assertion, 'We are going to be the typers of letter and distributors of leaflets ... *no longer*.'[127] A phase of the New Left had definitely ended.

Women ended this phase when they spoke out against their own oppression. Their voices unleashed, the meaning of their words expanded. Soon a perspective, drawing women, pushing them to act to develop it, and stimulating deep attraction to basic rights of equality, provided a sense of social movement. Women's liberation as a loose structure of discussion groups, as a mobilizing possibility, and as a demand for new theoretical clarity on a range of orthodox Marxist questions became, in 1967–70, an increasingly vocal presence in the renewed but fragmenting New Left. Feminist consciousness-raising groups emerged in Regina and Saskatoon, Winnipeg and Halifax, Sudbury and Thunder Bay, Kingston, Ottawa, Galt, Guelph, and Edmonton, as well as, of course, in Vancouver, Toronto, and Montreal. As Nancy Lubka noted in an early assessment of this development, women were claiming 'their share of the freedom which this decade has wrested from history.' They did so, not as some new social formation on the left, however, but as part of 1960s radicalism. As such, early Canadian women's liberation was a challenge to the decade's New Left as well as something that grew organically out of it. One part of its making was the oppressive, confining, and maddeningly traditional repression of women's capacities, initiatives, and needs, in the wider society as well as in circles of the radical left. Another component was 'the thought-expanding perspectives offered by the new left.' It was no accident that when Women's Liberation surfaced in Montreal it grew out of the repression of the Québécois struggle for national liberation as well as the mobilizations at McGill and Sir George Williams.[128]

New Left women's liberation advocates, like their male counterparts, read Marx, and read him through standard 1960s sources such as Marcuse.[129] Increasingly they also read Betty Friedan, Simone de Beauvoir, and Juliet Mitchell.[130] As Naiomi Black remarks, they brought with them from the student movement 'a significant commitment to a Marxist or at least an economic, class-oriented analysis of women's situation; they were to identify themselves as Marxists or socialist feminists.'[131] This was where Benston's 'The Political Economy of Women's Liberation' had come from. At McGill University, a young Marxist sociologist, Marlene Dixon, who had just published an important article entitled 'Why Women's Liberation?' in the American radical magazine *Ramparts*, gathered around her a group that would later be described as 'certainly one of the first self-consciously feminist women's groups in Montreal.' Soon connections were being made among various left socialist organizations and young women's liberationists. Debates unfolded as to how women were not all of the same class and race, and their oppression, while universal to some degree, also needed to be viewed in light of other aspects of their identity. When Black Panthers promoted insulting views of women's role in radical movements, referring in public meetings to women using their 'pussy power' to support revolutionary men, bodies such as the Maoist Canadian Party of Labour might walk out in protest, chanting opposition to such blatant male chauvinism.[132] Many left women struggled to maintain their Marxist perspective alongside of their realization that male domination of the left and of society was deforming them as women and as human beings.[133]

In this, the women's liberationists of the late 1960s differentiated themselves from the liberal state's project of promoting gender equality through agencies such as the Royal Commission on the Status of Women.[134] Their consciousness-raising, however, also often attacked frontally the seemingly *private* dimensions of women's oppression, thus marking women's concerns as different from an older New Left's focus on *public* issues, such as poverty and dispossession. Hidden from history, the meanings of women's sexual objectification or the particular experience of grappling with pregnancy and childbirth in an age when abortion was illegal and inaccessible, were brought to the forefront of women's liberation thought and practice.

Women's liberationists thus translated their growing refusal to accept subordination into performative attacks on beauty contests that included staging denunciations of the proceedings from the podium.[135] Judy Darcy, a member of Toronto Women's Liberation Movement (TWLM), entered the 1969 Miss Canada University Pageant, having talked the student government into letting her be Miss York University. 'Okay, but don't tell us what you are going to do,' the lefty student politicos said with a wink and nod. Then, with Darcy one of the seven semi-finalists, she awaited an attack on the event, being televised live. One of her TWLM comrades burst into the room, approached the podium chanting, and began a public argument with the master of ceremonies. Darcy marched off the stage into the audience, proclaiming, 'It's a meat market, and they do exploit women,' singing 'Solidarity Forever' as she exited the pageant.[136]

Advocates of women's liberation also played roles in the widespread dissemination of birth control information, which at the time was technically illegal. The McGill Student Society's 1968 *Birth Control Handbook*, arguably the most widely circulated pamphlet in Canada in the late 1960s and early 1970s, was distributed in massive quantities at the time. Fifty thousand made their way throughout the country in the first eight months of its publication. Within a few years three million of the newsprint booklets had been distributed. Often, university women's caucuses spearheaded mobilizations for daycare, as they did at Simon Fraser in the spring of 1968. Supported by the New Left Caucus, Toronto women's liberationists occupied a vacant house on the outskirts of the University of Toronto, converting the dilapidated domicile to a cooperative nursery. Blocked by bureaucracies, the daycare struggle moved directly into the university senate chamber, 200 New Leftists sitting in. They extracted concessions from the administration, which agreed to renovate the seized building so that it would meet standards. Across the country the gaining of daycare facilities was proclaimed a victory of the women's liberation movement.

Above all, the early women's liberation movement, in 1969, began the impetus that would sustain a national campaign against the liberalized, but still inadequate, federal abortion law of that year. Within Trotskyist organizations such as the League for Socialist Action and its youth wing, the Young Socialists, ideas of women's liberation were debated and discussed, gaining ground and adherents, and forcing shifts in understanding that translated into active commitments. Such bodies participated with women's groups across the country in the Vancouver Women's Caucus April 1970 call for an Abortion Caravan to make its way from the west coast to Ottawa demanding 'Free Abortion on Demand' and 'Every Child a Wanted Child.' As the women's automobile convoy picked up people, cars, and vans en route, it gathered petitions signed by thousands upon thousands of women, demanding the repeal of all abortion legislation, and the right to truly choose the freedom to give birth. Eventually hundreds of women and their supporters descended on Parliament Hill, 24 Sussex Drive, and even into the House of Commons. They chained themselves in the gallery, closing down the seat of Canadian government for the first time in history. Behind them they left a coffin, symbolic of the women who had died seeking unsafe and illegal abortions. It overflowed with women's petitions and the tools of the trade of back-room abortionists: knives, coat hangers, cans of Lysol.[137]

As women New Leftists in 1967–70 battled their oppression inside the left and in the mainstream society, they also built links with women who worked for wages and were part of the trade union movement. A slogan of the Abortion Caravan had been 'Just Society Just for the Rich.' Women's liberationists were well aware of the class inequalities that affected women's, children's, and men's lives. Much of this would bear fruit in campaigns of the 1970s, when Canadian feminists inside and outside of trade unions would be actively involved in making the International Women's Day marches major local and national events. In Vancouver, bodies such as Working Women's Association grew out of the New Left. Feminist activists often saw as their goal developing liberationist ideas among trade union women and convincing all radicals, male and female, that organizing women in the workplace was an essential activity, one that would enhance fundamental collective strengths. As the women's movement in Quebec emerged out of the national liberation struggle, it grappled with the ways in which women had been sidelined in both the left and in the labour movement. By the early 1970s, such feminists were, like their SUPA counterparts of 1967, defiant in their refusal to countenance any longer their relegation to a place of inferiority in the movement: 'We have typed their papers, painted their placards, listened to their speeches, marched in their demonstrations, marked the measure of their slogans, "Power to the Workers!"'[138]

There were, of course, also developing divergences *within* the women's liberation camp, evident in the TWLM, which experienced a number of splits and breakaways in 1969–70. One of these, the New Feminists, saw the course of radical politics determined by exclusion of women from power. 'Trudeau and Trotsky are just another pair of men,' they declared. They were not prepared to grant 'impartial credence to the gospel according to Mark, to Marx or Marcuse, to Mohammed or to Malcolm X.' For such women the New Left project, and with it a good part of the 1960s, had ended with their realization that 'the total society is based on the discrimination of sex roles, and the total society must be changed.' They would align with anyone – 'whether these friends are found on the left, the right or the center' – who supported their goals; they would consider as enemies those who threatened 'the realization of their radical feminist goals.'[139] This kind of movement, along with other fissures in the New Left, spelled the end of an era, just as the rise of contingents of liberal and socialist feminists after the Royal Commission on the Status of Women marked a departure from the youth radicalism of the 1960s.[140]

The 'Sixties Generation' and Canadian Identity

As the decade of the 1960s closed chronologically, then, the ethos of the Sixties was fracturing in some quarters, fading in others. The contagious exuberance of a seemingly generational revolt could no longer be maintained as the first wave of radical youth aged and found itself arguing over the direction the revolutionary movement should take: into the unions, against Americanization, for Marxism (and which Marxism!), against the state (or utilizing the state in some form), back to the NDP, or, alternatively, into a widening range of new party formations, Maoist and Trotskyist, in which the woman's question would invariably be discussed, leading to new organizational possibilities. The university campus, which had for so many radical youth been a nursery of oppositional thought and organization, seemed, moreover, no longer *the* place to be: with the lock-down of radicalism at McGill, Sir George Williams, and Simon Fraser, the classrooms of higher education in the 1970s were less promising venues of dissent than they had seemed to be in 1968. Experimental forms of living, be they communes in rural regions or urban endeavours such as the University of Toronto's Rochdale College, had apparently run their course. The Canadian Union of Students, after a brief but intense effort to become 'a national liberation front for Canada,' explicitly anti-imperialist, socialist, and militantly activist, was buried in an avalanche of local resistance. Its ostensibly strident agenda apparently failed to address the mundane, material needs of its student constituency. In October 1969, in what was a decisive blow, students at the large and centrally powerful University of Toronto voted in a referendum to withdraw from CUS, as other student bodies across the country had done before and would do in the immediate future. Its financial support evaporating, a national centre of the Canadian student left folded up its once revolutionary tent, disbanding in the spring of 1970.[141]

The disruptions and destabilizations of these years were of course pressured by varied repressive onslaughts, including infiltrations and extensive surveillance orchestrated by the Royal Canadian Mounted Police and its security state forces.[142] Nevertheless, as Howard Adelman noted in a *Canadian Forum* 'coroner's report,' the death of these institutions and movements of the Sixties also resulted from a fundamental paradox, one that the New Left never proved able to address.[143] Its poetics, praxis, and politics of liberation were, deep into the radical root of New Left thought, unable to grasp that structure and agency, institution and movement, direction and freedom, were not, in actuality, ever counterposed as merely and simply bureaucracy vs. participatory democracy. Rather, such organized structures of resistance, from parties, programs, and perspectives, were (as they have always been and remain today) simultaneously threats to freedom and social transformation as well as the only vehicle capable of its realization. They need to be built and guarded in particular ways, rather than rejected out of hand. The New Left, inspired and insightful as it was, had one-half of the praxis that could have secured a political shift to the left. Strong on poetics, it was weaker on the politics of program; born with the aspirations of agency already formed on its young lips, it needed to learn the language of structure. It struggled to do this, in part via a revived, late-1960s encounter with Marxism as analysis and as political program. Tragically, its demise strengthened a poetics of anti-program, evident, for instance, in the renewal of antagonism to Marxism that began to appear in certain circles by 1970. If, in the early 1960s, the New Left knew little of Marxism and had much to gain by an encounter with the theory and history of revolutionary communism, it had at least grasped that the crude ideology of anti-Marxism was a part of the Cold War conventionality that all radicals were required to shed. By 1970, a changed context and a revived hostility to Marx that would gain momentum throughout the remaining years of the century meant the New Left's point of departure had a freshness to it that had to be resuscitated.

Irving Layton's poem, 'Marxist,' appearing in the social-democratic *Canadian Forum*, articulated this sad development:

out of certitude
or terror a Marxist
will knock out your teeth

break your jaw
with a crowbar

hang you from
your feet your head
in scalding water

crush
your balls before
your wife and children

and make you
spit
on friends and convictions

he will flay you
while still alive rip-
pling the skin
in neat strips of
three: thesis, etcetera ...

when you are nothing
he'll wipe you out with
machine-gun executions:
negation of the negation

he will my sons
do this and more
if you let him

look for no pity
in this highest product
of evolution: dialectical
of course[144]

This poetics would have been unlikely in much of the New Left, even as it was spawned in some of its select enclaves. The irony of 1960s radicalism was that as it so fruitfully challenged the dream of capitalist affluence and equality that had done so much to stamp its particular being, it also nurtured a part of that deep sleep of traditional prejudice that inhibited conscious human agents of liberation from realizing their ends. But seeing those ends, in and of itself, was an advance of monumental significance. The Sixties had, in part, been very much about this vision.

To speak of Canada and the generation of the 1960s is, of course, to overgeneralize. For every radical SUPA fieldworker, for every militant anti–Vietnam War protester, for every women's liberationist, there were countless Canadian youth who followed no rebel road. Minorities nevertheless sometimes make history, and they are certainly capable of putting a strong stamp on it, as elites have always understood. In the 1960s, the impact of youth revolt was unmistakably evident on the pages of the decade, and it remains there to this day. For those who lived the radicalism of the decade, and even for people who merely walked softly and often silently in its shadows, the Canada of their times had been changed. Future generations would be unable to think complacently and quietly of the settled British imperial connection after experiencing a sit-in, a protest march, or a reading of Marx, Marcuse, or Mitchell. From the ashes of Sir George Williams's computer centre, to the pages of the *Birth Control Handbook*, to protests against the imperialist war – the times they were indeed 'a changing, and there was no going back. Women's liberation, if it did not transform gender relations in its 1960s praxis, nevertheless laid the foundation for unanticipated advances for women, a movement that changed forever the *politics* of sexual being and our appreciation of essential *human* rights. As ideas of justice, equality, entitlements, and freedoms – to choose this path and designate that necessity – permeated the consciousness of an era, nothing would, in the future, look quite the same. Gays and lesbians, for instance, were neither very visible in the New Left of the 1960s, nor were they accorded much sensitive treatment in the movement, either theoretically or practically. Even the New Feminists that emerged out of the TWLM, and that contained lesbian members, did not handle the issue adequately in their public presentation of the group's concerns and purposes. Yet in spite of this less-than-admirable history, new doors would open in the aftermath of the 1960s because of what had taken place within that decade of altercation and change. When, eventually, a gay and lesbian liberation movement did emerge in Canada it would surface, in part, in circles originating in the late 1960s. Its relationship to Marxism was fractious, but undeniable.[145]

Nowhere was this general process more evident than in Quebec, where the New Left actually threatened to achieve a serious destabilization of the social order. In the process, it unleashed, as it did in English Canada, but with a much more wide-ranging and powerful force, the hounds that would rip apart forever the old, entrenched, and ossified body of Canada as it had been conceived for generations. In the New Left struggle for liberation in Quebec, the intensity of the drive for emancipation had many of the same impulses, innovations, and intentions, but it was placed on an entirely different level by the realization, for the first time historically (at least in a revolutionary sense), that the national question was not just the Canada question, but it was also the Quebec question. In its insistence that Quebec could only be understood as an ongoing *history* of exploitation, oppression, misery, *and* consequent nationalist aspiration, the 1960s broke the back of a complacent Canadianism. And as Canada, in turn, crushed Quebec's New Left liberationists, turning to a ruthless repression, it ironically secured

its continuity at the cost of its long-standing, socially constructed identity. A good deal of the 1960s ended, for all Canadians, in the October
Crisis of 1970. So too did a significant part of the mythology of 'the
peaceable Kingdom.'

Chapter Nine

Quebec: Revolution Now!

October 1970. It was the worst of times for many Canadians. Two separate Front de Libération du Québec (FLQ) cells, in acts spread over five days, had kidnapped British Trade Commissioner James Cross and taken a major figure in the provincial government, Pierre Laporte, hostage. The purpose of these acts was to call attention to the desperate struggle for national liberation, now almost eight years old, and which involved, in the beliefs of its advocates, an end to both the exploitation of the workers and the colonial oppression of the Québécois people.

Pierre Elliott Trudeau assumed the pose of the nation's law-and-order conscience, decrying the 'bleeding hearts' and 'weak-kneed people' who counselled consideration of Canadian civil rights in the face of terrorist acts. Ontario's premier, John Robarts, declared loudly, 'It's war ... total war.' Police were quick to raid the homes of Quebec's easily identifiable revolutionary nationalists. Even before Laporte's kidnapping some forty-four arrests had been made. Armed troops patrolled the streets of Quebec City, Montreal, and Ottawa. In the dead of night, at 4 a.m. on 16 October 1970, the federal government invoked the War Measures Act, which gave it unimpeded powers to set aside conventional legal niceties as it pulled out all the stops to thwart an ostensible 'apprehended insurrection.' Within hours there were 238 new arrests, and scores more would follow over the course of the next month. Almost immediately an anonymous phone caller revealed the location where Laporte's body

St Jean Baptiste Day Riot, Montreal, 1968 (Library and Archives Canada/PA 152447, *Montreal Gazette*).

could be found, stuffed in the trunk of a car parked near an air base. With confirmation of the murder of the Quebec minister, the mood in Canada and Quebec became even uglier in its cries for vengeance.[1]

Laurier Lapierre, a social democrat being pushed to the left, was 'angry, mad, disturbed, sad, and frightened.' Trudeau he saw 'behaving as if he were a modern Mussolini,' and it pained Lapierre greatly that the prime minister's right-hand man, Jean Marchand, known in Quebec labour circles as a staunch foe of 'repression, distortion and political manipulation,' now appeared as 'an incarnation of Maurice Duplessis.' Lapierre asked rhetorically if 'the sceptre of separatism, of the breakup of Canada that we see ... everywhere,' could possibly prove 'a foundation for the maintenance of a country?' Is Canada to be preserved, he wondered, 'by means of blackmail, intimidation, war measures act, and political terrorism' of the official, sanctioned kind? No friend of the FLQ, Lapierre recounted that since 1963 Quebeckers had lived through 200 bombings and six resulting deaths, as well as countless bank robberies and other intimidations. Still, this terrorism had been knowable, an evil that might be coped with. Why, Lapierre then worried aloud, had the entire country succumbed so easily to the violence of Trudeau, so much more threatening in its ultimate implications than the acts of the FLQ?

The October Crisis had politicized the already quite political Lapierre. 'I am more determined than ever that the Revolution is needed,' he wrote. Acknowledging so much that was wrong and unacceptable, Lapierre could not quite chart a way forward:

> What is going to happen to that Revolution and us within it? We just can't live anymore this way – isolated, frightened, our freedom limited in the name of national unity and security: our poor becoming poorer; the rich, richer; more of our land, our resources, our souls, our children being sold for a song of affluence to the American: our streets clogged with traffic and garbage; our cities polluted; our lives shattered by noise and lies; our political system manipulated, used, and abused; our communities forever prisoners of majorities that do not care and just look after themselves.

Refusing both 'REVOLUTION À LA FLQ' and 'DEMOCRACY À LA DRAPEAU, BOURASSA, TRUDEAU, AND SPIRO AGNEW,' Lapierre wanted 'REVOLUTION IN OUR FREE, NON-VIOLENT, DEMOCRATIC WAY,' without the co-optations of the system or the pressured evils of terrorist violence.[2]

The cry of 'Revolution Now!' rang out in many quarters in the 1960s, but perhaps nowhere was it voiced more loudly and with more feeling than in Quebec.[3] There were many ironies at work in this undeniable development, however. Few would have predicted, in the first part of the twentieth century, that Quebec would be on the cutting edge of a new radicalism in the post-1950s period of broad demands for social transformation.[4] Quebec's particular oppression meant that it was in the forefront of both socialist and countercultural challenges to the mainstream of the Canadian nation in the 1960s. It did so out of a fusion of class and national aspiration premised on the expectation, indeed the demand, that the nature of Canadian identity be interrogated, if not overthrown. In arguing for the realization of *their* freedom, Québécois nationalists necessarily called into question the freedom of Canada to continue a project that many on the revolutionary left were quick to characterize as colonialist. Liberation's unfolding 1960s project in Quebec could never be separable from the prospects of independence, a cause championed not only by francophones, but by many English-Canadian socialists: Canadian Union of Students position papers had, by 1968, endorsed Quebec's right to self-determination, a position pushed consistently by left NDPers and eventually taken up by the Waffle, a number of Marxist groups, and *Dimension* writers such as Gad Horowitz.[5]

The consequences for Canadian identity, always forged in the face of the awkwardness of the Quebec–Canada duality, were both decisively disruptive and long-lasting. Poet laureate of the Canadian left, Al Purdy, captured something of this momentous and ironic change. In the immediate aftermath of Trudeau invoking the War Measures Act, his 'The Peaceable Kingdom' mythologized the past, feared for the present, and anguished over the future:

> In Quebec the Fifth Combat Group
> from Valcartier occupies Montreal
> paratroopers fly in from Montreal
> infantry from the Maritimes
> ...
> as a man's life turns right or left
>   from the norm
> No change in the news
> N.D.P. and P.C. members condemn
>   the government

Creditiste Real Caouette does not
Diefenbaker thunders at the P.M.
a prophet grown old
Police raids continue in Montreal
...
the little eddy that is my life
and all our lives quickens
and bubbles break as we join
the mainstream of history
with detention camps and the smell
    of blood
and valid reasons for writing great novels
in the future the past closing around
and leaving us where I never wanted
    to be
in a different country from the one
where I grew up
where love seemed nearly an affectation
but not quite
beyond the Peaceable Kingdom

In looking at Canada's 'unguarded existence,' Purdy could only conclude that for too long it had been ransomed 'day by day of our short lives.' His verse captured the final destabilizing comprehension that lay at the heart of much of the turmoil of the 1960s.[6]

Embittered Background: Class Struggle and the Quebec Nation

Prior to the 1960s, for almost three decades, Quebec balanced a kind of political schizophrenia in which the economic largesse of a hegemonic federal Liberal Party was counterposed by a provincial political *partitocratie*, headed by Maurice Duplessis and institutionalized in the Union Nationale.[7] Duplessis skillfully and cynically constructed and maintained his hold on the reins of regional governance through an effective orchestration of a coalition of interests. Local elites, farmers and the landed poor, and urban workers were all to varying degrees placated and cajoled into the Duplessis camp through an adept exploitation of patronage, the rhetoric of populism, and selective use of an enervated nationalism. The material base of Duplessis's authority was a willingness to cede economic control of sectors of the economy to American and

Anglo-Canadian capital, in return for a variant of colonialism that touched lightly if at all on the hegemonic institutions of everyday life: education, the church, and the local state. Quebec was granted certain terrain. The federal Liberals, in turn, were given a free hand to develop their political economy of continentalism, in which the integration of Canadian manufacturing and resource extraction into the rising colossus of U.S. imperialism proceeded apace.[8]

If Quebec's urban working class, decimated during the Great Depression, turned to Duplessis and the Union Nationale for protections in the 1930s,[9] it did so within a more limited set of possibilities than were present in the rest of Canada. Workers provided early votes for Duplessis, whose 1936 electoral victory ushered in the infamous 1937 Padlock Law, which gave the government wide latitude in suppressing those who would propagate ideas that were regarded as Bolshevist.[10] By the 1940s and 1950s, however, Duplessis and the Union Nationale found that they could count less on industrial working-class protest votes than on bases of traditionalism in the Quebec countryside. Evident in the Union Nationale's harsh record of anti-labour legislation (both tabled and passed) from 1944 to 1954, the Duplessis regime's hostility to trade unionism tended to bring workers together in the province of Quebec over the course of the late 1940s and 1950s. While this growing solidarity was by no means without its divisions and difficulties, it would prove vitally important in stimulating opposition to what came to be referred to as 'the great darkness' of the Duplessis-dominated pre-1960 years.[11] Central to this process was the rise of a progressive francophone intelligentsia whose ideas and social engagements intersected with the uprisings of Quebec workers.[12]

Entering the 1940s, Quebec labour was fractured into three competing centralized bodies: the Confédération des Travailleurs Catholiques du Canada (CTCC), headed by the aging and conservative Alfred Charpentier;[13] their long-time craft union rivals in the Fédération Provinciale du Travail (FPT), affiliated with the American Federation of Labor (AFL) and its Canadian counterpart, the Trades and Labor Congress of Canada (TLC); and the emerging industrial unionist wing of the bi-national U.S.–Canada labour movement, the Congrès Canadien du Travail (CCT), associated with the Congress of Industrial Organization (CIO) unions linked to the Canadian Congress of Labour (CCL).[14] The rivalries and clashes of these often hostile labour centrals were an essential backdrop against which class conflict with employers and the state unfolded. Old animosities died hard, especially when they

seemed confirmed by the actions of employers. Companies often reinforced a conception of the Catholic unions as inherently compromised,
enticing the CTCC with wage agreements that were relatively high for
Quebec, but lower than the standard rates in either English Canada or
the United States. To be sure, there were other large enterprises, often
branch plants of American corporations, preferring to deal with a more
familiar class enemy. They opened their doors to AFL unions. This cod-
dling up to one or another of rival union bodies, or resisting any union-
ization efforts with a commitment to the open shop, understandably
kept many workers and their leaders, as well as contending voices of support within the intelligentsia, perpetually off balance.[15]

In such circumstances, moreover, the voice of godly authority might
speak into both sides of working-class ears, admonishing the self-
interested as well as the easily swayed to stick with those organizations of
the working class that were truly able to address their ultimate well-
being. Priests quietly advised wives that husbands might be refused the
sacrament if they were disloyal enough to join in sacrilege with AFL
international unionists. Playing a trump card in the Duplessis deck, an
auxiliary bishop spoke out decisively, advising all in the province to have
nothing to do with 'neutral unions, albeit they may have made gains in
the great cities. Communism glides in their shadow like a snake. It
attempts to fish in troubled waters and tries to turn the workers against
the employers ... against religion, and against the clergy.'[16]

Nevertheless, the CTCC and its secular rivals were not so much separated in the 1940s as they were persistently drawn together by their
opposition to Duplessis's anti-union drive and by the relentless logic of
an escalating class struggle, which forced even the most compromised
of local unions into combat with employers. In addition, Catholicism
itself underwent a mild radicalization, prodded to endorse workers'
rights to share in corporate profit by Pope Pius XI's encyclical 'Quadrag-
esimo Anno.'

The consequences of these changes registered in an upturn in aggressive
working-class militancy and mobilization. A record-breaking 154 strikes
were fought out in Quebec in 1942–3, involving 48,000 workers. CTCC
membership almost doubled in 1943–8, with over 93,000 Quebec workers
enrolled in 428 *syndicats*. Non-Québécois and non-Catholic workers diluted
the traditional cultural homogeneity of the Catholic unions, weakening
the hold of religion and strengthening more secular working-class concerns. The inclusion of women in significant numbers altered the nature of
the *syndicats* as well. Older ideas of corporatism, compromised by their

associations with fascism and its defeat in the Second World War, gave way to newer commitments to industrial democracy. Between 1945 and 1950 this potent combination of diverse forces meant that the CTCC was shedding its accommodationist skin. With the rise of Gérard Picard to the presidency of the CTCC an older, more conservative generation of leaders linked to the Church was replaced by lay activists. A group of dynamic young organizers, among them Jean Marchand, was recruited from Laval University. The long-standing tie between church and state unravelled as Catholic unionism's incorporation broke at the weak link where the counterposed interests of Duplessis, big business, and labour shattered.[17]

It was in one of the strikes of this period, a 1949 confrontation at the asbestos mines and mills of Quebec's Eastern Townships, that the trends of the decade came together. A militant solidarity combined with a festive sense of community to oppose the state and the employers. Strikebreakers were imported, workers were evicted from company houses, and mass demonstrations and silent processions brought intellectuals and working-class families together in exhilarating protests. Union rivalries retreated in the face of a common front against the state, its laws and police, and a group of obstinate employers, whose otherness was all too evident in both the language they spoke and the imperial tone in which they delivered the message of U.S. dominance. By early May, the Eastern Townships were polarized. Tensions rose as striker pickets turned into barricades by which workers secured control of the town of Asbestos. Not until the Riot Act was read was 'order' restored. The resumption of legal authority was secured only through hundreds of arrests, police beatings of strikers, and a violent routing of the unionists that engendered much resentment and long-lasting bitterness. After five months of pitched battle, class war in the Eastern Townships left an indelible mark on the modern history of Quebec. In the words of Gérard Pelletier, editor of the CTCC's Le Travail: 'By its breadth, its duration, its style and the particular character of its objectives, this conflict forced everyone ... to take part. For the first time, the attitude of polite indifference became impossible ... For the first time they were involved with a social problem, no longer in theory, detached, but concretely and with terrible immediacy.'[18]

Asbestos would thus remain forever embedded in the consciousness of Quebec workers, indeed, in the self-understanding of the Québécois nation. To be sure, the 1949 strike would come to be conceived differently in various oppositional quarters, its symbolic importance standing as something of an invented tradition by which counterposed camps lined up their evidence of what a future Quebec was and what it needed in terms of political strategy. In its refusal to bow to authoritative American capital and to prostrate itself before an all-powerful and deeply compromised political oligarchy, Asbestos became a cornerstone of the imagined and increasingly disgruntled community of Quebec nationhood.[19] Asbestos, according to Fraser Isbester, was 'the key that unlocked the door to the quiet revolution,' the latter term a reference to the post-1960 liberalization of Quebec society.[20]

For a militant minority, however, far more than 'quiet revolution' was demanded in the 1960s. Among some radicals, it was the defeat of the Asbestos strikers that stood as a forceful reminder of the many interests that would be marshalled to turn back the loud voices of revolutionary demand within Quebec. Pierre Vallières's *White Niggers of America* declared bluntly: 'The fervor aroused by the heroic strike of the miners in Asbestos died down and went out in discouragement.' As Léandre Bergeron would state unequivocally in his much-reprinted and highly influential *Petit Manuel d'histoire du Québec*, Asbestos was a crushing defeat, one in which U.S. imperialism was the victor. Crucial to this display of power were those elements of the Québécois nation that aligned themselves against liberation and with the imperialist exploiter, the compliant caretakers and 'Negro-King' oppressors like Maurice Duplessis and much of the Church hierarchy. For Bergeron, as for many revolutionary nationalists in Quebec in the 1960s, Asbestos clarified 'the composition of post-war Quebec society.' If the war for Quebec's liberation was to be waged against capitalist imperialism, it would also inevitably strike blows against those cautious Québécois who refused to swim with the revolutionary tide.[21]

The 1949 strike thus registered decisively in reorienting understandings of postwar Quebec. There was now no love lost between Duplessis and his forces of darkness, and the CTCC, which would soon launch a 1952 anti–Union Nationale Political Action Committee. Across the province a corps of labour-sympathetic intellectuals championed the cause of workers, and from their ranks would come the 1950s voice of reform, *Cité libre*.[22] In 1952, the CTCC led a strike at the bastion of French-Canadian retail, the Dupuis Frères department store. Elderly, disabled, and female sales personnel waged a successful struggle for increased wages, the forty-hour work week, paid holidays, and union security. Denounced as communists, the strikers were defended by a rising CTCC spokesperson, Michel Chartrand, who insisted that labour in

Quebec would have no truck with those 'who defended the French language while starving those who used it.'[23] CTCC and Quebec's Canadian Labour Congress unions united in a 1956 merger of TLC and CCL locals, then came together in the 1957 United Steelworkers of America–led Murdochville strike of copper miners. Defeated by police, hired company goons, strikebreakers, and bankrupting court costs, the unions nonetheless gained insight into the extent to which capital and the state were willing to go to suppress their mobilizations. One worker was killed on the 'Murderville' picket lines.

On the eve of the 1960s, the Quebec labour movement had transformed French Canada through its willingness to confront one of the most viciously anti-labour provincial regimes in Canada. CTCC unionists, in 1960, were poised, at 102,000 in number, to become the cutting edge of a radical syndicalism that would be celebrated by elements of the revolutionary left throughout Canada and the United States.

They had their work cut out for them. As late as 1960–1, the markers of a distinct, and continuing, Québécois oppression were both acutely real and undeniably visible: francophones controlled less than 20 per cent of Quebec's economy; with 27 per cent of Canada's population, the dominantly French province nevertheless had 40 per cent of the nation's unemployed; French Quebeckers' average income was 35 per cent lower than that of English-speaking Canadians; and, across the country, francophone Canadians, overwhelmingly concentrated in Quebec, ranked twelfth of fourteen ethnic groups identified according to income, with only Italians and Native peoples poorer.[24] Rural Québécois no doubt suffered the worst poverty and most debilitating unemployment rates, which in some isolated northlands could climb to 75 per cent, but urban Montreal, poised to give birth to 'red belts' in working-class districts such as St Henri, was anything but affluent. In the commercial metropolis, for instance, French-speakers comprised 65 per cent of the labour force, but held a mere 17 per cent of the administrative jobs. A 1962 report of the Economic Research Corporation of Montreal claimed that 36 per cent of the families in St Henri lived in uninhabitable dwellings, the figures for other poor working-class neighbourhoods ranging from 11 to 34 per cent. Childhood in these mean streets and humble abodes, well into the 1960s, was stalked by malnutrition and disease, too often accompanied by abuses in familial and institutional settings.[25] Out of such combustibles the spark of 'Revolution Now!' would ignite a political conflagration.

The Lull before the Revolutionary Storm: 'Quiet Revolution'?

With Quebec stuck in the long freeze of the Duplessis regime, the 1950s nevertheless nurtured a creative effervescence of rationalist, democratic thought among a growing layer of dissident intellectuals. Gathered around the *petit journal* of civil libertarian, anti-clerical, and reform-oriented principles, established in 1950 under the banner *Cité libre*, figures such as Trudeau, Pelletier, Charles Lussier, Pierre Juneau, Jacques Hébert, and others promoted an eclectic radicalism that crossed over into other circles of opposition. Poets of revolution such as Gaston Miron; stormy petrels in the now more combative labour movement, like the always fiery Michel Chartrand;[26] and alienated youth from the rough alleyways of Montreal's working-class districts or the barren proletarian suburban outskirts of the metropolitan centre – such were the varied constituencies that found something on offer in *Cité libre*'s pages.

As long as Duplessis reigned, this highly differentiated collection of critical thinkers was in many ways forced together in their radicalism, exclusion from the seats of power dictating a certain solidarity and sociability. But the social, cultural, economic, and political climate was over-ripe for change and many radical Quebeckers of the 1950s were poised to become new voices of authority in the 1960s. When Duplessis died in September 1959, ushering in the 1960 provincial Liberal Party victory of Jean Lesage, floodgates opened as a pent-up demand for Quebec's modernization transformed, finally and irrevocably, a society long considered traditional and rural. The primary agent of this *rattapage* (catching up) was the French-Canadian state. A massive infrastructure of education, health, and welfare mushroomed. Sustaining this was an economic drive to both extract much-needed funds from Ottawa *and* sustain provincial programs that could ensure workplace retraining and labour mobility, as well as megaprojects of growth and expansion in specific sectors, such as the nationalization of Hydro-Québec in 1963.[27]

The mindset of Quebec had changed. In the words of Marcel Rioux:

> The Quiet Revolution saw whole classes of people 'take the floor,' people who had never before spoken for themselves, but had let the clergy and the professions be their spokesmen. From 1960 on, the 'quiet ownership of Truth,' which Lesage himself called a French-Canadian characteristic, was violently questioned by the new elites. The Quiet Revolution was more a mental liberation, a development of critical attitudes towards men and affairs than it was a revolutionary action per se. It was, above all, a reevalua-

tion of ourselves, a reappearance of a spirit of independence and of inquiry which had been smothered in the snows of a hundred-year winter. Quebeckers grew confident that they could change many things if they really wanted to. They began to shrug off the fatalism of a conquered minority who had come to think that they were born to lose.

As Léon Dion, chairman of the Laval University political science department, argued forcefully at the time, this expansive politicizing climate was spreading throughout Québécois society. A part of its strength came from 'impoverished city neighbourhoods ... depressed areas ... the grim misery of the poor.' Protests from this quarter, the academic predicted, 'may well prove more intractable than that of the more affluent radicals.'[28]

La Revolution Tranquille clearly changed Quebec dramatically in its realignment of sociopolitical forces and shifting material priorities. This was evident in the streets as well as in the corridors of power, especially as they related to Quebec's constitutional battles with Ottawa. One measure of this was the crisis of federalism necessitating the establishment of a Royal Commission on Bilingualism and Biculturalism.[29] It also created an ideological climate as different from the Duplessis years as it would be possible to imagine. Religion, arguably a central touchstone of French Canada's historic sense of *survivance*, was eased out of its place in public life and increasingly confined to the private sphere, where its influence no doubt remained great, but perhaps not as pervasive as it had once been.[30] A Québécois nation, with the provincial state charting its redefined connection to Confederation, thus demanded a widening of authorities and fiscal claims, as well as linguistic, economic, and symbolic equality with Canada. In the new Quebec of the early 1960s, much was promised and not a little delivered. For some it would nevertheless prove too little too late.[31]

In a context of rising expectations, with the radical nationalist genie now very much out of the Duplessis bottle, the demanding politico-intellectual culture of democratic challenge split apart. Trudeau, Pelletier, Marchand and others soon came to embrace the federalist alternative to a rising nationalist cry for Quebec's ultimate independence and separation from Canada.[32] The 1956 Trudeau-inspired effort to bring democracy to Quebec, Le Rassemblement, had foundered on the shoals of political disagreement over whether the struggle for liberal democracy was to be a sufficient foundation on which to resurrect the possibilities of humanity in Quebec. By 1962, these debates returned with a vengeance as the Lesage Liberals promised to move Quebec into a democratic age, only to have many on its militant margins cry that this was not enough. Trudeau found the revival of nationalism, however radical its guise, a retreat back into the unreason and irrationality of the past, in which the advances achieved were to be sacrificed on the old altars of *race* and *nation*. He opted for a functional politics that would be his springboard into the upper echelons of the federal Liberal Party. The result was a mercurial late-1960s ascent that left Trudeau in command of the heights of Canada's culture, politics, and economic life. In the process Quebec's radical intelligentsia was increasingly forced onto narrower and narrower ledges, where only the most sure-footed could maintain their balance.[33]

Pierre Vallières captures well the confusingly creative moment of 1960–2. *Cité libre* seemed almost simultaneously to stimulate the radical nationalism of a growing separatist chorus within Quebec at the same time that it choked off *indépendantiste* aspiration and activity. According to Vallières, *Cité libre* 'was in power, and the freedom of expression manifested in the press, on the radio, and on television, as well as in private conversations, was in sharp contrast to the timid thinking of the Duplessis era … Now revolt was coming up out of the catacombs, publishing reviews, building a "lay movement," and beginning to formulate a body of doctrine, still more or less confused, which was to give birth to separatism, the "quiet revolution," and the questioning of all traditional institutions and values.'[34] As a perception arose that the 'Negro King' Duplessis had been buried, only to see other, more sophisticated, 'Negro Kings' rise on his grave, it was apparent that the Quiet Revolution was truly a lull before the more violent storm brewing in the contradictions of Quebec society in the early 1960s. 'Could a *Quiet* Revolution signify anything but continuity?' was a question many on the left were prodded to ask. Vallières, banished from *Cité libre* with a Trudeauesque shrug, would soon come to see the Lesage period of reform as 'nothing else but an entry for Quebec into the capitalist world.'[35]

'The Hanged Sheep' in the Pastures of Anti-Colonialism

The Quiet Revolution unleashed the words of revolt that had too often been suppressed and silenced in the coercive limitations of the Duplessis years. Gaston Miron, poet of the sorrowed alienation of the Québécois, later to be heralded as the spiritual founder of the FLQ, had struggled to find his voice in the late 1950s. A socialist before he was a nationalist, he ran for office in Outrement under the banner of the Co-operative Commonwealth Federation in 1958–9. A futile exercise in electoral sacrifice that tallied a nonetheless respectable 1,900 votes, Miron's campaigns convinced him that English-Canadian socialists had no comprehension of the particularities of oppression in Quebec. In the early 1960s he would rail against the totality of containments that pressured and deformed his yearnings. Miron embraced the view that 'Quebec must break out of this national repression to move toward socialism on its own path':

> now I am in the city of plenty
> great St. Catherine street clops and gallops
> through a Thousand and One Nights of neon
> while I cringe, walled up inside my cranium
> with my language and kinship depoetized
> decentered and disoriented in my convergences.
> memory and flesh I ransack and dig
> down to rooted roots and a rotted being I dig
> to unearth some trace of myself torn & swept away
> to find my voice in the crowded dark of reality
>
> now I go down toward the seedy districts
> squatting and breathing in their mould
> rambling back streets I drift along
> here is my true life – built like a shed –
> History's dump – and I reclaim it
> I'll not accept a deserter's personal salvation
> my life starts from the humiliated man's condition
> I swear it upon our shared and unseen breath
> I want all men to know that we know

These 'Monologues on Raving Alienation,' under the growing weight of revolutionary nationalist aspiration, gave way to 'A Lesson in Commitment': 'Brothers, if in the course of my youth / I once inhabited the sacred shrine of my poems, now / I am with my people in the public square / and my poems have taken the dark bit of our struggles.'[36]

Miron's commitment came to privilege what he designated 'fundamental alienation' over 'Marxist alienation.' The latter, gruesome enough on its own terms, involved the classic exploitation of labour by capital, but Miron insisted it was compounded by the ravages of colonialism:

deculturation, depersonalization, dehumanization. Québécois workers chaffed under Marxist alienation, to be sure, but Miron eventually saw their ultimate tragedy as subjection 'to another very fundamental sort of alienation' in which they risked 'becoming someone else': 'colonization superimposes a new blueprint over your own which becomes antiquated due to an outsider who is in you and among you, this "other" whom you have interiorized and now regard as part of yourself. He is inside you and you are living life according to *his* conditions.'[37]

Such ideas rebounded throughout the emerging militant minority of Quebec's revolutionary nationalists who, by the opening years of the 1960s, were beginning to piece together a movement culture of opposition. Its tortured creation lay in the formation of overlapping organizations, propaganda organs, and literary journals,[38] knitted together by networks of individuals committed to the cause of Quebec independence. Differences shaded into commonalities, just as hard-headed sectarianism bred isolations. The Rassemblement pour l'Indépendance Nationale (RIN) formed three months after Lesage and the Liberals assumed provincial power in 1960. Composed of writers, artists, Ottawa civil servants, and Montreal lawyers, RIN was always too resolutely petty bourgeois[39] to draw into its ranks the likes of Raoul Roy, founding editor of *La Revue socialiste* (1959–65), and the animating spirit behind Action socialiste pour l'indépendence du Québec. But Roy and many others read RIN spokesperson Marchel Chaput's *Pourquoi Je Suis séparatiste* (1961), nodding in agreement with at least a part of its message. They were drawn as well to the Rassemblement's willingness to put forward a militant style, which might include demonstrations, pickets, support for strikes, and the fiery oratory of Pierre Bourgault, a one-time military officer turned journalist. Students in the Association Générale des Étudiants de l'Université de Montréal, under the leadership of Bernard Landry and Pierre Marois, grew increasingly restive in the autumn of 1962, emboldened by the Lesage Liberals' slogan 'Maîtres chez nous/Masters in our own House.' When Donald Gordon, president of the Canadian National Railways (CNR), responded to pointed questions as to why there were no French Canadians among the seventeen vice-presidents of the powerful Crown corporation with the curt rejoinder, 'Promotions are made on the basis of merit!' all hell broke loose. The Queen Elizabeth Hotel, head office of the CNR, was besieged by demonstrators. A pig's-headed effigy likeness of the corporate mogul was soon torched. At one protest rally, thousands of students stripped flag poles of the Red Ensign and the Union Jack and, putting the symbols of empire to the match, smashed windows and battled charging police.

Among the slogans chanted at such violent rallies were anti-colonialist calls for a 'Free Quebec.' The 1960s was an epoch of rising anti-imperialist sentiment and protest, and independence movements in Africa, Asia, and Latin America galvanized much support in French Canada. Frantz Fanon's *Les Damnés de la terre* (1961), Albert Memmi's *Le Portrait du colonisé* (1957), Herbert Marcuse's *Soviet Marxism: A Critical Analysis* (1961), Albert Camus's *L'Étranger* (1942), and the example of China's Mao and Cuban revolutionaries such as Fidel Castro and Che Guevara loomed large in the emerging left nationalist milieu. Walls began to be spray-painted with independence graffiti. Roy's *La Revue socialiste* argued that the peace-loving traditions of the *Francs-Canadiens*, a term the former translator for the Communist-led Canadian Seamen's Union preferred to the RIN's terminology of 'Québécois,' should be preserved. The radical journal also acknowledged, however, that it was perhaps time to recognize that 'shaking up the structure of colonial occupation in Quebec and putting it out of action' might have to proceed 'through violence.' Even the RIN seemed to endorse this in its symbolism, a fighting ram's head, emblazoned in red and black, the traditional colours of revolution. Such imagery consciously reconfigured one of the representations of francophone submission, the sheep that walked with unresisting docility beside the patron saint of French Canadians in the national holiday of Saint-Jean-Baptiste Day. One day before the bleating lamb was to make its 1962 annual 24 June trek, a clandestine body taking as its name the Mouvement de Libération Nationale announced that it had 'kidnapped' the hapless mascot. The underground wanted to strike a blow against this acquiescent parading of the people's alienation. Raoul Roy no doubt thought stunts like this of limited validity, but they were at least 'training for a tougher battle.'

For his part, the seasoned socialist converted the back room of a small shop in Montreal's working-class east end into a café, hoping to draw militants to nightly forums addressing issues posed in the struggle for revolution. Christening this gathering place for youthful socialist separatists Le Mouton Pendu ('The Hanged Sheep'), Roy offered evening meals of Lenin and the increasingly influential Fanon. The *indépendantiste* menu provided mimeographed copies of out-of-print writings or digressions on the significance of language in the flexible 'socialism of decolonization.' A few years later Pierre Vallières would address his 1968 revolutionary rallying cry to the cheapened labour of Quebec –

the 'white niggers' of the textile mills, shoe factories, canneries, department stores, pencil-pushing offices, mines, railroad companies, ports, lunch counters, marginal farms, and clothing sweat shops – with the hard acknowledgement, 'We are not cowards, but we are still a little too much like sheep.' Hanging the Québécois sheep was Roy's graphic reminder that in the making of a nation it was necessary to end a part of what had kept it from coming into being. This message resonated in the minds of militants with the experiences of Algeria, Cuba, Vietnam, Ireland, and the Spanish Basque country.[40]

The Felquiste Underground

Out of quarters such as these congealed, over the course of late 1962 and early 1963, a secret underground composed of various committees of national liberation and resistance networks. Refugees from the RIN and Action Socialiste, the initial Montreal recruits to clandestine activism were soon joined by commando groups in Quebec City and the Ottawa-Hull region. University students and white-collar workers, most of whom were in their twenties, dominated the ranks. An additional corps of shock troops came from the more marginal corners of the Québécois dispossessed. Some had been disciplined for their Marxist ideas in the RIN, and they eagerly gravitated to the 'training schools' of the new movement, where they read Fanon, studied the history of anti-colonialism, and boned up on their understanding of the 1837–8 Patriote rebels of Lower Canada. But they yearned to act. In nights of exhilarating raids on the symbolic edifices of Quebec's subjugation, they desecrated monuments of empire. They also spray-painted mail boxes and buildings, penned treatises, even burned property and vehicles of the hated pinnacle of Anglo-Canadian capital, the CNR, or tossed Molotov cocktails through the window of the English establishment's favoured radio station.

Such informal networks and their public proclamations of '*Le Québec aux Québécois*' constituted less than a movement. They nevertheless provided sufficient evidence that there were those impatient with the quietude of not only the Lesage Revolution Tranquille, but also of the above-ground voices of dissent. Drawing out the RIN elements who shared a sense of urgency with respect to Quebec's national liberation, such clandestine undertakings served as a magnet pulling recruits to a new cause. More likely to be working-class than the precocious original recruits to the underground, this next contingent of militants founded the FLQ in February 1963. Leading the way was a trio composed of 19-year-old Raymond Villeneuve, a working baker fresh out of high school but rich in experience with the RIN, Action Socialiste, and the NDP; a secretary of the Association du Comité Ouvrier de Sainte-Marie, Gabriel Hudon, who at 21 had been working in an aircraft parts factory for four years, hanging around the RIN national secretariat; and, the odd man out, an older Belgian, Georges Schoeters, who brought to the making of the FLQ a Marxist-humanist anti-colonialism and experience as a teenager in the anti-Nazi resistance of his European youth. The three men shared the view that the RIN would serve as the above-ground independence movement, while the new subterranean body, named the FLQ by Villeneuve, would make contact with radicals already working in secretive cells for Quebec's liberation and socialism. Hopefully this might lay the basis for a clandestine revolutionary network that could carry out direct actions paralleling the 'legal' work of the RIN. With the Rassemblement breaking from its electoral abstentionism in March 1963, crowning its entrée into the parliamentary arena with declarations that 'Independence by itself means nothing. Independence must be accompanied by social revolution,' and 'Revolution is an act of love and creation,' FLQ bombs exploded at three targeted military barracks. A communiqué declared: 'The independence of Quebec cannot be achieved without social revolution.' The RIN immediately distanced itself from the FLQ's 'criminal acts,' claiming that while the Felquiste demands for independence were admirable, the 'extreme means' adopted to promote this end were regrettable.[41]

With a federal election in the offing, early April 1963 saw escalating FLQ activity, which continued throughout the month and into May, setting the stage, as we have seen, for fears of a tumultuous Victoria Day, 1963. The underground was now clearly cut loose from any moorings with its legal, RIN, counterpart. Federal tax buildings, the CNR, the Canadian Broadcasting Corporation, the Royal Canadian Mounted Police headquarters, the Sherbrooke Street Canadian Army recruiting centre, the central post office, the offices of the Solbec Copper Company, then being struck by the United Steel Workers of America, a Royal Canadian Air Force Ville Mont-Royal technical service unit, and mailboxes in suburban anglophone Westmount, labelled a 'colonial stronghold' by the FLQ, were all either bombed or had unprimed incendiary devices planted in their midst. A series of manifestos were issued by 'the suicide commandos of the FLQ' in March–April 1963. The first, addressing 'the French nation of Quebec,' was authored by Schoeters. It

drew on his Belgian resistance experience to claim for the FLQ the status of partisans engaged in legitimate war with an occupying army of
conquering oppression and its varied collaborators:

> The National Liberation Front (FLQ) is a revolutionary movement consist-
> ing of volunteers ready to die for the independence of Quebec ... aiming
> principally at the complete destruction, by sabotage, of the colonial institu-
> tions, of all means of communication in the colonial language, of the
> enterprises and commercial firms practicing discrimination against the
> Quebeckers. The FLQ will proceed to eliminate all persons collaborating
> with the occupant. All the volunteers of the FLQ will carry, during their
> acts of sabotage, identification papers of the Republic of Quebec. We
> demand that our wounded and our prisoners be treated according to the
> Geneva Convention concerning the laws of warfare. The dignity of the peo-
> ple of Quebec requires independence. Students, workers, farmers – form
> your clandestine groups against Anglo-American colonialism.

With the accidental death of Vincent Wilfrid O'Neill, night watchman at
the military recruiting centre, as a consequence of one explosion, and
the mid-May assault on Westmount resulting in one serious injury,
antagonisms and denunciations proliferated. Anglo-Quebeckers burned
the Quebec flag, and the English-Canadian Montreal radio station,
CJMS, suggested that all separatist parties be outlawed. Among the radicals and reformers of the 1950s, such as *citélibriste* Gérard Pelletier, the
response was more reasoned at the same time as it was unambiguous in
its refusal to countenance the methods of the FLQ: 'When democratic
processes are available and yet terrorism is chosen instead, this choice
can only lead to a harvest of shame, of blame, and of contempt.' Léon
Dion pleaded in the aftermath of the coroner's inquest into O'Neill's
death that Quebec's independence movement not slip into a moment
of 'collective unconsciousness,' creating 'a psychological climate which
will turn the young accused into heroes or martyrs. We would then see,
with the gradual suppression of the moral conscience's resistance
against violence, arising around our freedoms the infernal circle of
terrorist activities and police repression.' State power exercised no such
restraint. The Felquistes were marked as terrorists with prices on their
heads, the bounty proclaimed with lurid fanfare by the Lesage provincial government and the municipality of Montreal. An informant inside
the thirty-five-member FLQ collected $60,000, turned his comrades
over to the police, and walked away as twenty-three arrests were quickly

made. Aside from Schoeters, 33, and his 25-year old wife, a Montreal General X-ray technician, Jeanne Pépin, those arrested were all between the ages of 18 and 23, most of them students. Against some there was little or no evidence of criminal activity, necessitating release, acquittal, or suspended sentences. But eleven defendants received jail time, totalling sixty-eight years. The underground, seemingly, had been grounded.[42]

Weapons of the Weak

This original Felquiste initiative had been cobbled together quickly, drawing on the passionate resentments and commitment to active opposition of the young, the bulk of whom were as inexperienced as they were indignant. The two suicide commandos responsible for placing the bomb that inadvertently killed O'Neill illuminate the problematic political maturity of the forces that sustained the early FLQ. Jacques Giroux and Yves Labonté had never themselves met before they ventured forth to plant an explosive device at the base of the John A. Macdonald monument in Dominion Square on the evening of 20 April 1963. Finding the public square packed with people, the duo decided, apparently under some pressure associated with the traffic of vehicles, night walkers, and police, to instead deposit the ultimately fatal bomb in a deserted alleyway behind the Sherbrooke Street recruiting centre of the Canadian Armed Forces. Giroux, a 19-year-old aspiring photographer and son of a barber shop owner, had completed high school with some difficulty and then moved relatively quickly into the Felquiste underground. He had graduated, in less than a year, from painting the Dominion Square statue of Canada's pre-eminent 'Father of Confederation' with the ironic words, 'Je suis séparatiste,' to the more serious endeavour of blowing the monument up. His compatriot, Yves Labonté, was a primary school drop-out with an irregular history of employment and, in all likelihood, an incomplete grasp of the politics of anti-colonialism. Whatever the abilities of those in leadership positions in the FLQ cells, then, there is little doubt that the clandestine body lacked anything approximating the sense of security that could have shielded it from the repression of the state: its escalating adventurist program was amateurish in its lack of discipline and direction.[43]

Yet there is no denying that the majority of first-wave Felquistes were animated by a sense of national identity and grievance that took to extremes positions widely dispersed throughout Québécois society. If the ranks of consciously committed revolutionary advocates seemed as weak as the historical demand for forthright independence among French Quebeckers, it was nevertheless the case that more and more of the francophone population of the province identified with a sense of class exploitation and national oppression. *Citélibristes* such as Pelletier understood as much when they cautioned against harbouring 'a glimmer of deep-down sympathy for the terrorists.' Such feelings, however contradictory, were widespread because so many francophones were tired of being weak in the face of bosses and bigots. If they were not open advocates of violence, they had some empathy for those who were willing to take up weapons in the interests of creating a climate of long overdue change. There was, moreover, an intuitive understanding, in Léon Dion's words, that 'the weapons of the weak can only be shattering ones.'[44]

The initial FLQ thus achieved an almost mythical stature in early 1960s Quebec. Notwithstanding their fated failures and almost total routing by the state, radicals in the independence cause achieved a propaganda victory of sorts. This ensured that, with largely different personnel, the underground was destined to be born again. In the pages of *Le Devoir*, 'Isocrate' warned that the terror of the FLQ deed would indeed, inevitably, be back:

> Beside those FLQ members who were before the court, there are other victims, to various degrees, of patriotic illuminism, who are already engaged – and who are making military preparations – to stage the Battle of the Plains of Abraham again with the opposite results ... In their revolutionary mysticism, they know that there will be victims. They expect this. Not to combat by force an army of three united police forces, but to 'stimulate' the separatist chiefs, to 'strain' the situation, to intimidate responsible politicians and manipulate public opinion. There will be other explosions, other attacks, other threats: at least to accelerate the march to independence.[45]

Indeed, underground and above-ground advocates of independence, some of them with brothers sitting in jail, soon revived the spirit, as well as the organizational body, of the FLQ. One measure of this was a subterranean current of violence, spontaneously generated by young sympathizers (17–21 years old) of the Felquiste cause, who continued to use graffiti, dynamite, and arson against the symbols of Québécois oppression and exploitation.[46] This activity was soon complemented by three separate, but more organized, developments.

First, the most resolutely underground contingent formed the Armée de Libération du Québec (ALQ). This consciously militaristic guerrilla force would see itself as a clandestine corps committed to campaigns of harassment that would arouse sympathy for the *indépendantiste* movement. It saw itself as a partisan army of liberation engaged in the primitive accumulation of the arms, ammunition, vehicles, training camps, communication equipment, and funds necessary to materially sustain a later stage of more overt armed struggle.

Second, an FLQ propaganda network emerged separately, establishing an official publication, *La Cognée* (*The Axe*), its first number appearing in October 1963. The journal's name was not without its ironies. It was taken from a highly controversial and best-selling Québécois criticism of popular French, or *joual*.[47] The deficiencies of this language of the street were laid bare in Jean-Paul Desbiens's *Les Insolences du Frère Untel* (1960), a book that in part attributed the debasement of the French language in Quebec to the Catholic Church. Anything but pro-separatist, Desbiens's has a character proclaim: 'I do my work with an axe. This is no time for being subtle in Quebec.' This obviously resonated with the views of Felquistes, who christened their first propaganda organ *The Axe*. They also took as their banner the red, white, and green flag of the Patriote rebels of 1837–8. These new Felquistes managed to put out *La Cognée* for two and a half years, the editors campaigning under pseudonyms and evading police arrest and suppression. A twice-monthly mimeographed sheet of eight pages, the paper stressed that Quebec's independence was the necessary first step to the realization of the 'overall social revolution.' It appealed to workers and their allies in other classes to break decisively from 'the colonial rulers in Ottawa and their whores in Quebec.' If it sidestepped discussions of socialism, the pages of the FLQ organ were dedicated to the memory of past class battles, such as Asbestos and Murdochville. Committed to 'follow the trail blazed in 1837,' drawing from the well of resistance movements in Algeria and Cuba, *La Cognée* nevertheless insisted that Quebec's national liberation struggle and its demand for revolution were embedded in modern, North American society.

The social basis for both the *La Cognée* groupings and the ALQ was an overlapping network of students from bourgeois Outrement and young workers from east-end Montreal. They connected through clandestine liaisons, and rubbed shoulders in other *indépendantiste* circles, which formed a third milieu in which the idea of the FLQ experienced reinvigorated support. This included the RIN, but more decisively important was the young *Parti pris* group, the leading figure of which was Pierre Maheu. *Parti pris* published a left-wing monthly (1963–8) dedicated to

independence, socialism, and secularism. 'We are in unanimous agreement about one basic step,' declared Maheu, 'revolution.' In 1963, *Parti
pris* was unambiguously fresh and defiantly dissident. Malcolm Reid
remembered picking up the first number at a Parti Socialiste du Québec
(PSQ) gathering, shortly after the organization declared its break from
the parent pan-Canadian New Democratic Party. Reid was surprised as
he leafed through the pages: 'When it tackled religion it was from the
point of view of atheism: not from agnosticism or from a dismay at the
abuses of the clergy, but from the idea that religion was, yes, the opium
of the people. This was new. The socialism was Marxist; the separatism
struck the tone of the FLQ's manifesto; and it was anti-colonialist. *And
somehow it was all one thing, not three.*' One year later, another publication,
more of a blend of *indépendantiste* generations, drawing on young separatists as well as an experienced cadre of social democratic, communist,
and Trotskyist political formations, appeared under the masthead, *Révolution québécois.* Behind its creation, and writing in its first number (as
well as for *Parti pris*) would be a young militant and alienated refugee
from the *Cité libre* camp, recently returned from a disappointing self-
imposed exile in France and employed at *La Presse*, Pierre Vallières. By
1965 *Parti pris* and *Révolution québécoise* had forged a political unity based
on the promotion of a Mouvement de Libération Populaire (MLP),
which quickly disappeared into the social-democratic PSQ. May Day
1965 dawned with the creation of the Comité de Coordination des Mou-
vements de Gauche (CCMG), orchestrated by the PSQ but drawing into
its fold six established groups and three socialist journals. Dormant for
two decades, May Day revived in this mid-1960s context as 250 leftists
gathered to hear speeches by Léandre Bergeron of Club Parti Pris and
Trotskyist trade unionist Jean-Marie Bédard of the International Woodworkers of America. For his part, Vallières, convinced that the PSQ was
firmly in the hands of 'senile graybeards,' secretly joined the FLQ with
Charles Gagnon and some other comrades. By October 1965 he was
writing for *La Cognée*.[48]

The weak were growing stronger. A series of armed holdups, burglaries,
and theft of arms undertaken by the ALQ from the end of September
1963 into April 1964 culminated in the arrest and conviction of the second-
wave of underground Felquistes. In August 1964, a reconstituted Armée
Révolutionnaire du Québec (ARQ), hungry for arms to outfit a modest
lakeside training camp near St Boniface, Quebec, and no doubt emboldened after nights of drinking discussion at an FLQ watering hole, Le
Cochon Borgne (The One-Eyed Pig), assailed a Bleury Street gunshop.

The exercise ended badly. A vice-president of International Firearms was shot fatally in the stomach by one of the commandos, and, in a later standoff with the cops, a store employee was killed by police fire. A number of Felquistes were quickly captured. Their leader, François Schirm, was wounded and later arrested, as were all of those subsequently rounded up at the FLQ training camp. *La Cognée* had struck a note of defiance in the May 1964 aftermath of police arrests: 'Every time one of our people is put in jail,' it declared, 'ten others step forward to take his place.' It actually seemed to be happening, as pro-FLQ organizations mushroomed: Front Républicain pour l'Indépendance (FRI), Partisans de l'Indépendance du Québec (PIQ), Groupe d'Action Populaire (GAP), Chevaliers de l'Indépendance. But with the Schirm group's break-up and accumulating evidence that its head man had been a dictatorial leader, given to impatience and adventurism, many in the intellectual wing of the FLQ thought it was time to regroup and tighten precautionary measures. Upon his conviction, Schirm was at first given the death penalty, later to be commuted to life imprisonment. He served fourteen years, the longest of anyone imprisoned during the entire 1960s and 1970s history of the FLQ, while the 20-year-old who shot the International Firearms executive remained behind bars for eleven. From his jail cell, one FLQ activist, Pierre Schneider, no doubt sensing the demoralization accompanying these defeats, urged the forces of independence to hold firm: 'Independence,' he wrote, 'is a class struggle, the struggle of the Quebec working class against exploitation, wherever it originates and whatever form it takes.'[49]

Not long before Schneider's appeal, the distinguished Québécois writer Hubert Aquin had signed out of the RIN, declaring himself the revolutionary commander of an underground 'Special Organization.' Aquin, who had been a figure of importance in the Rassemblement, was one of Quebec's most distinguished and anguished literary figures of the 1960s and 1970s. He would prove an intensely passionate advocate of Quebec's independence until 1977, when he tragically took his own life. Of humble background, educated at the University of Montreal and the Institute of Political Studies in Paris, Aquin worked in radio and television in 1959–60 before throwing himself directly into the growing nationalist ferment in Quebec. He edited an important review, *Liberté*, but resigned in protest when the publication stood silent in the aftermath of the October Crisis of 1970. The author of a number of prize-winning novels, written between 1968 and 1975, Aquin refused the Governor General's Award in 1969 as a statement of his long-standing political discontents. Little came of Aquin's erratic 1964 promise to wage 'total war on all the enemies of complete independence for Quebec.' He was soon arrested and, after a lengthy trial, acquitted, largely on grounds of a disordered mental state. Confined for a time to a psychiatric institute, Aquin produced his first novel, a widely acclaimed account of political commitment and the failure of the struggle for liberation, *Prochain Épisode* (1965). It was further evidence, were any needed, that the fervour of revolution was anything but dead in mid-1960s Quebec. Animated by a grasp of the linked destinies of international revolution and the troubled psyche of the individual revolutionist, *Prochain Épisode* opens with the memorable line: 'Cuba sinks flaming in Lake Geneva while I sink to the depth of things.' It closes with a declaration of the coming redemptive violence that would figure so prominently in Vallières's *White Niggers of America*: 'The time will have come to kill and to organize destruction by the ancient doctrines of strife and the anonymous guns of the guerilla! It will be time to replace parliamentary battles with real ones. After two centuries of agony, we will burst out in disordered violence, in an uninterrupted series of attacks, and shocks, the black fulfillment of a project of total love.' For Aquin, the struggle for liberation was destined to be ongoing: 'When the battles are over, the revolution will continue.'[50]

The Vallières-Gagnon Group

At this point, in 1965, the FLQ's success registered in the extent to which it had managed to realize itself as an *ideal*. Felquistes, to be sure, were flesh-and-blood human beings, and they met, put out propaganda, owed their discipline to a group, and carried out activities. Yet they were few in number, and their deeds were directed at destruction rather than construction, although underground *indépendantistes* would have refused such an oppositional distinction. In the end, the FLQ was as much myth as movement; its power lay in its capacity to galvanize the left wing of a growing aspiration for national liberation.

Anti-colonialist movements, once confined to struggling segments of the Third World, were, by 1962, registering victories, the most notable of which was in Algeria. The Palestine Liberation Organization (PLO) was founded in 1964, and Yasser Arafat's Al-Fatah (Victory), the beneficiary of Algerian aid, was about to confront Israeli power directly. In Latin America, Uruguay's Tupamaros bombed the U.S. Embassy in September 1964, signalling the beginning of a violent armed struggle that would redefine guerrilla warfare as an urban as well as rural undertaking. Not all national liberation struggles pitted themselves against *foreign* imperialist power. Resistance to internal colonization by the militant wing of the African-American civil rights movement struck its blows against domestic racism and the super-exploitation of the black working class by white capital and its compliant states, be they located in Washington or Alabama. This dynamic and multi-faceted Black Power movement would influence greatly developments and personalities within the FLQ. The speeches of Malcolm X; the example of an anti–Ku Klux Klan armed self-defence movement in Monroe, North Carolina; and various mobilizations that marched under a plethora of names: Student Non-Violent Coordinating Committee, Congress of Racial Equality, Black Liberation Front, Black Panther Party, League of Revolutionary Black Workers – all of this came, by 1965–9, to represent perhaps the most critical line of solidarity/defence uniting black nationalists in the United States and revolutionary nationalists in Quebec.[51]

This potent concoction was given further punch by Students for a Democratic Society–led anti–Vietnam war protests and a mid-1960s upsurge in class struggle, which, as we have already seen, witnessed an eruption of violent, wildcat strikes across Canada. In Quebec, this working-class upheaval had been prefaced, in 1964, by a militant mobilization of trade unionists against the Lesage government's increasingly anti-labour legislation and a bitter seven-month strike at *La Presse*, as well as growing awareness among militants that particular trade union tops were outright barriers in the road to freedom.[52]

It was in this context that Pierre Vallières and his friend and associate Charles Gagnon joined the FLQ. They were pushed by the state, as well as pulled towards the FLQ by their own political evolution, the offices of *Révolution québécoise* having been raided in June 1965, its subscription lists and library resources confiscated, and Vallières taken into custody. He was promptly fired from his job at *La Presse*. Soon after, writing under the *nom de guerre* of Mathieu Hébert in *La Cognée*, Vallières described the underground independence movement as 'a vague collection of tiny, more or less active groups, whose members are all known to the police and to each other.' A February 1965 series of arrests grew out of a Federal Bureau of Investigation (FBI) 'sting' in which a black agent, Raymond Wood, posed as a leading member of the New York Black Liberation Front in order to entice Felquistes into transporting dynamite across the border. The Statue of Liberty, referred to as 'that damned old witch,' was supposedly targeted for demolition by a group of Felquiste and Black Power advocates. Undercover agents in Canada and the United States claimed that they had unearthed growing international connections of the FLQ with Algeria, Cuba, and militant African Americans. Sadly for the FLQ, the whole episode confirmed how vulnerable the *indépendantiste* underground was to infiltration and the slippery, seemingly radical, tongues of agents provocateurs. Charged and convicted in the engineered act of terrorism were Michele Duclos, a 28-year-old television announcer closely connected to the RIN's Pierre Bourgault; Michele Saulnier, a Normal School teacher of educational psychology affiliated with *Parti pris*; and three male workers, one of whom, Gilles Legault, hanged himself in the Bordeaux jail awaiting his trial for supplying dynamite to Duclos, two legitimate members of the Black Liberation Front, and the undercover FBI agent Wood. The latter had travelled to Montreal to entice Duclos and others into the criminal plot, coordinating his every move with the RCMP and the head of the recently created Montreal Anti-Terrorist Section, Detective-Sergeant Claude Desautels. In the aftermath of this successful entrapment, the Pentagon included Quebec in its ongoing monitoring program aimed at destabilizing revolutionary movements in foreign countries, code naming its surveillance of French Canada 'Operation Revolt.' Small wonder that over the course of the spring and summer of 1965, bombs signed FLQ were deposited near the U.S. consulate and at the RCMP headquarters in Quebec City. The Macaza Commando Unit, composed of remnants of the ARQ network of François Schirm, ostensibly planned an assault on the nuclear-armed Bomarc missile base nestled in the Laurentian forests near Mont-Laurier.[53]

This ongoing skirmishing indicated to Vallières and Gagnon the absence of a coordinated strategic direction. Disappointed with the lack of grassroots activists as well as revolutionary thinkers, Vallières called on the FLQ to become a disciplined party. He stressed the need for a theoretical understanding of Quebec's place in North America and the world, aiming not only to make noise, but to overthrow the state and its capitalist order, substituting in their place 'a government of and for the people of Quebec.' What emerged out the Vallières-Gagnon underground Felquiste cell was a more consciously socialist rallying cry for Quebec independence, a more explicit attempt to address working-class struggles, and a concerted effort to cultivate relations with U.S. leftists. Notable among these were the New York–based publishers of the independent socialist magazine *Monthly Review* as well as various Black Power bodies and their white youth supporters, like Students for a Democratic

Society and Youth Against War and Fascism.[54] If other elements of the FLQ, including a founding editor of *La Cognée*, were growing increasingly dispirited, abandoning the underground *indépendantiste* ship in order to climb back aboard the RIN and regroup on its 'legal' and electoral decks, Vallières and Gagnon expanded their clandestine commando corps and championed the prospects of revolutionary change. For the time being, Vallières conceded, FLQ military action was limited to sabotage and bombings, but the long-range view was to create 'a genuine revolutionary army, supported by a popular militia,' the aim of which was to liberate Quebec so that the 'people can exercise power.' According to Vallières, Quebec was the 'only place in North America where conditions are ripe for revolution to break out and succeed. The way is open for the FLQ and for revolution, on the Americans' doorstep, to make Quebec the first socialist country in North America.'[55]

An orientation toward the trade unions was cultivated. Admittedly, it owed more to nineteenth-century anarchist advocates of exemplary deeds like Johann Most than it did to the united-front proposals of V.I. Lenin, who, in any case, left Vallières, at least, rather cold. He was drawn instead to Mao and Che, whose revolutionary contribution was not so much to accent the centrality of the working class in the insurrectionary toppling of capitalism as to highlight the importance of guerilla warfare and the possibility of exporting revolution. Not surprisingly, given this programmatic guidance, the Vallières-Gagnon wing of the FLQ, in the words of Marc Laurendeau, may have 'reasoned as orthodox Marxists,' but it 'acted like anarchists.'[56]

Dynamite blasts did $25,000 damage to an Expo 67 construction site embroiled in a labour dispute; strikes of dock workers, truckers, and garbage men, as well as workers at a factory producing envelopes were 'supported' by FLQ bombs and Molotov cocktails. A year later, on 5 May 1966, the struck Lagrenade shoe factory, which was refusing to countenance the organization of its plant by the CNTU, was bombed. A 64-year-old secretary, Thérèse Morin, died in the process. Two and a half weeks later, another strike-bound establishment, the large Dominion Textile plant at Drummondville, was also rocked by an FLQ explosion. Later in the summer, in mid-July, a teenaged courier for the FLQ, Jean Corbo, was killed while trying to plant a bomb. This tragic accident demoralized many Felquistes, and, the underground in a state of confusion and disarray, the police were quick to follow up on tips that led to a number of arrests and the decimation of the Vallières-Gagnon cell. The two leaders were charged with criminal responsibility for the Morin and Corbo deaths but managed at first to evade the police dragnet. They soon surfaced in New York City, where, rather than retreat into hiding, Vallières and Gagnon protested the arrest of their comrades, announced a hunger strike, and picketed the United Nations to call attention to 'political repression in Quebec.' Interviewed by the CBC, they were promptly arrested by New York police and transported to the Manhattan House of Detention for Men.[57]

White Niggers of America

It was there, in the 'cunningly organized dehumanization' of the American prison system, among the mentally ill, the murderers and rapists, the drug addicts, the jaundiced and often sadistic guards, and the brutalizing rigidities of the jail colloquially known as 'The Tombs,' that arguably Canada's most quintessential New Left text was written. With a title that would still shock and provoke forty years later, Pierre Vallières offered up an inflammatory Molotov cocktail of a book, one that was part autobiography, part manifesto, part lament, part history, part philosophy. Published in French and English, in Quebec, the United States, and Canada, as well as in West Germany, Italy, and Mexico, *Nègres blancs d'Amérique: Autobiographie précoce d'un 'terroriste' québécois* (1968) had a greater circulation throughout the world than any other book published in Canada addressing revolutionary possibility, save perhaps for a few titles officially sanctioned by the Soviets, translated in their Moscow Foreign Languages Publishing House offices, and dumped on the captive markets of 'actually existing socialism.' The book spoke to a working-class Québécois audience in languages of sentimentality and rage. Its discourse was one of philosophical digression as well as uncompromising denunciation. A telescoped reading of Marxism and an embrace of the black nationalism of Stokely Carmichael existed alongside the lesser-known revolutionary positions of Robert F. Williams on armed self-defence of black communities and James Lee Boggs on the centrality of African Americans in the unfolding U.S. revolution. Vallières's *White Niggers of America* was an articulation, simultaneously, of despair *and* hope. As such, it captured precisely the raison d'être of the Felquiste underground, foregrounding as well the raw nerve of empathy for the guerilla warriors of the *indépendantiste* cause broadly exposed in the French-Canadian body politic. Vallières's arguments and analysis came to rest repeatedly on the dualisms of his book's development: white/nigger; bourgeois/proletarian; religion/rationality; Quebec/

Canada; alienation/freedom; work/life; man/woman. *White Niggers of America* made the case for independence, not by arguing that Québécois society was *different*, but by suggesting that it was impaled on the same capitalist contradictions that produced exploitation and oppression throughout the modern world.[58]

This universalism, within which the particular struggle of the colonized Québécois could be inexorably linked to the explosive international movements that radicals everywhere in the 1960s looked to, explains the Vallières title. It mattered not that the French in Canada, however subjugated, were not marked with a visible blackness. As francophone Quebeckers understood intuitively, they had been racialized historically from at the very least the time of Lord Durham in the 1830s. They bore the material scars of this subjugation in their depressed housing conditions, their lowly place on the national wage scale, and their coerced subservience to Anglo-American authorities, be they empowered by their money and control of workplaces or dominance within the federal state. To be sure, as Vallières would later acknowledge, the outrageous phrasing of his title, 'white niggers,' was in some ways a conscious device that allowed him to break through walls of a particular *American* construction. It forced consideration of the plight of the Québécois within a United States left that grasped the significance of race but had difficulty appreciating the oppression experienced by francophones inside North America. Vallières was letting his U.S. comrades know that in Quebec, white was not simply and only white. There is thus a dialectic at work in Vallières's title, obvious in the juxtaposition 'white/nigger,' but also apparent in his purpose and direction, the end result being a widening solidarity. In playing on what in North America were the most basic of separations, those of the racialized difference of white and black, with the negative consequences of this all too apparent, Vallières was recognizing the commonplace divisions of a socio-economic and political order the better to further the creation of a revolutionary movement and what it could positively accomplish. 'We desire, we say, the total liberation of man, and we risk our lives for it every day,' Vallières declared, adding that this struggle took place 'in Guatemala, in Vietnam, in the Congo, in Angola, in the United States itself, and in Quebec' (270). This *we* was thus an embrace of *négritude* as a universal struggle of all of those oppressed and exploited, all of those who could join the ranks of anti-colonialist, anti-capitalist insurgents to create a society in which the oppositional clash of *white* and *nigger* would be transcended.[59]

In his message of 'revolution now,' by whatever means necessary, Vallières was imploring the alienated to act, to end slavery, to choose liberation and fraternity rather than incarceration and isolation. He was, like the period in which he wrote, not terribly concerned with nuances and subtleties. Placed alongside texts like Malcolm X's *Autobiography* (1965) and Eldridge Cleaver's *Soul on Ice* (1968), Vallières's *White Niggers* appears to suffer the same limiting deficiencies, most notably its robust masculinist attraction to what Ian McKay has rightly identified as redemptive violence. It is difficult not to see the book as an extended diary struggling for the realization of a mass Québécois manhood. In scaffolding his appeal to collectivity, solidarity, and commitment to revolutionary change on a highly individualized accounting of alienation and anguish – Charles Gagnon would later dismiss *White Niggers of America* as 'an act of extreme narcissism,' dangerous in its cultivation of ego, celebrity, and craving the making of mythology – Vallières certainly grasped that 'the personal was political.'

Yet his book betrayed barely a hint that women existed as anything other than carping, controlling, and conservative mothers and elusive sexual objects. Indeed, from the vantage point of the 1990s and beyond, the text might be read as misogynist. As early as 1971 Vallières was acknowledging that when he wrote *White Niggers of America* he had been a 'male chauvinist,' the book betraying 'a deeply ingrained male bias.' In this failing he was not alone. Aquin's *Prochain Épisode* and Jacques Godbout's *La Couteau sur la table*, both published in 1965, exhibited some of the same conventional gendered shortcomings. There was no denying the intensity with which Vallières and other Québécois writers in the mid-1960s masculinized the revolutionary subject, a process not unrelated to their understanding of the cathartic capacities of violence.

As a strategy for socialism, the book was far more resolutely direct than its counterparts in the radical black nationalist circles of the mid- to late 1960s. It was, nonetheless, perhaps all the more disappointing because its declarative call to revolutionary, anti-capitalist, anti-imperialist class and national struggle tended to reduce the organization of this enterprise of liberation to the mobilization of violence, side-stepping so many important questions. Ironically, after so many words, many of rambling reference to philosophical thought (Sartre is a significant influence, but there is much reference as well to Husserl and Heidegger), *White Niggers of America* delivered little of programmatic, theoretical value. This was because Vallières believed very much in the imperatives of the moment. A crisis had been reached in capitalism, and, 'in time of crisis, theory is a very small weapon' (225).[60]

It is therefore rather easy, reading *White Niggers of America* decades after its publication, to dismiss its message. The crisis in capitalism may well have been unfolding in the 1960s, but we can perhaps better now appreciate the staying power of this major architect of exploitation, oppression, and accumulation. The view, so common in the 1960s, that revolution was indeed around the corner, is hardly sustainable today. In contrast to the period in which Vallières wrote, our time is one of theory, and we valorize this over action in countless ways, often extracting unfortunate political costs in our reification of concepts and endlessly arcane analytic refinements. And so today we tend to look on *White Niggers of America* with complacent, if not mocking, condescension, deserving of nothing but a well-earned obscurity. To leave it at this would be to miss the fundamental meaning of *White Niggers of America*. The book can be interpreted in a number of ways.

First and foremost it is an outline of the long night of oppression's many darknessess, reaching through a childhood whose pillars of identification were a 'mother's disenchantment' and a 'father's timid but tenacious hope' (80) to an adolescence housed in the drab *papier brique* proletarian suburb of Ville Jacques-Cartier and a half-built Franciscan *collège*. As a sociology of the Québécois working-class districts, and the stultifying and pervasive limitedness imposed upon French-speaking youth in the years reaching from the Great Depression into the 1950s, *White Niggers of America* chronicles the relentless containment of life. Education, for example, was overseen by 'old maids.' Vallières presented schooling as little more than a jail term: 'Ah! cursed school that constipated us and paralyzed us! Prison where, day after day, *they* bored us to death with their disgusting, maternal stupidity. School of childish despair, which gradually turns into a monstrosity ... [maintained by] all the tactics of dictatorship and the degradation of minds through humiliation.' Resentful in his recollections, Vallières declares emphatically, '*The only thing I remember having learned in school was to be ashamed of my – of our – condition*' (102–3). Not unlike Gabrielle Roy's *The Tin Flute* (1945), the author of *White Niggers of America* conveys the misery of the disadvantaged, but it is a portrait more devastating and unforgiving than any literary text. The power of Vallières's representation of the prices paid by working-class men, women, and children resides in his refusal to ever let capitalism and its servant, the clerical state, off the hook.

It is, of course, bad enough that male labourers are exploited at the point of production, and Vallières is not unmindful of the ways in which his father, who 'never missed a day of work' at the Canadian Pacific Railway Angus shops, was, in the end, discarded at the age of 53, a broken machine no longer capable of generating surplus (88). He would, in short order, succumb to exhaustion, dying of the cancer that generalized itself throughout his body. Vallières no doubt thought his father's disease was related to the environments of work and home that his father alternated within, alive as they were with toxins physical and psychological. The workplace, for all of its grinding subordinations, at least had the potential to generate fraternity and solidarity. But the elder Vallières, after a generation in the trenches of class struggle, was overcome by a weariness of political mind as well as of labouring body. Aligned for a time with the communists, who ran 'the union of the Angus employees,' Vallières's father soon learned that the work of the shop militants would eventually be sabotaged by 'the Stalinist bureaucracy.' It proved all too willing to hand the reins of working-class power over to 'capitalists and the gangsters of the big-business-style unionism' (96). Faced with the sorry history of a trade union compromising with the employer and the state, the Angus workers retreated into being compliant, non-combative toilers. As the fight went out of them, so too did hope for the future. Vallières saw his father slip into this tired resignation.

It was in the working-class Québécois family, however, that this sad denouement registered most profoundly. For it was there, within a union blessed of church and state, in which the gender relations of want and deprivation were deepened, that man's debasement and woman's isolation fed off each other. The result was whatever love had once existed was finally relinquished. This state of affairs affected adversely all who lived within its vise-like grip:

> If love was there in the beginning, a host of factors very soon forced it out of this world monopolized by the million little worries that poverty engenders ... Only priests imagine that love can adapt itself to misery, to a stupefying daily routine, to crass ignorance of the laws and beauties of sexuality, to Jansenism and the dictatorship of capitalism ... And when children grow up in an atmosphere of constant frustration, how can joy reach them? Sometimes it seemed to me that my father was ashamed of himself, and that my mother was afraid of her own desperate eagerness to preserve present security and ensure it in the future ... The terrible thing about the working-class family is the function, imposed on it by the present system,

of renewing and perpetuating the supply of slaves, of niggers, of cheap labor to be exploited, alienated, oppressed. And the inhuman thing about a working-class childhood is the child's powerlessness to resist the conditioning not only of the system itself but of all the frustration of the life around him, frustrations that are generated by the capitalist organization of society and that contaminate him even before he becomes aware of their existence. (84–5)

The physical surroundings held a mirror to the face of this caricature of human domesticity: 'On days when it rained hard, everything turned black. The houses, flattened and ashamed, took on a sinister, tormented look. The people picked their way through streets transformed into rivers of mud. The few puny trees, which each family had tried to preserve on its lot, bent their branches toward the wet earth. It was as if they wept at being powerless and ridiculous witnesses to the empty misery that was obstinately trying to persuade itself the future would be better' (110). Such a landscape permitted little genuinely human interaction: 'People came and went too fast; they did not have time to get to know each other. Hopes were built up hurriedly, at random, and crumbled a little later amid general indifference' (119).

As a totalizing anti-aesthetic of the suburban proletarian 'slum,' then, *White Niggers of America* is an evocative and unrivalled dissection of the destructive capitalist structures of everyday life. In this it was anything but an objective, academic survey, dispassionate and learned. Rather, it was an enraged recollection, filtered through 1960s sensibilities and engagements, a statement part remembrance and part propaganda in which objective reporting, subjective feeling, and the resurrection of resentments were processed, two decades later, through the filter of new-found radical commitments. Vallières's representation brought interpretation of Duplessis's darkness out of the politics of metaphor and into the politicized construction of memory. It fused past and present in the demand for revolution now. Vallières was convinced that the contradictions of generations of oppression were finally, in the 1960s, giving rise to a consciousness of the need for social transformation. Out of the 'wretched ground' that was the 'garbage dump' of the conditions of life for working-class Québécois had come 'something stronger than humiliation ... a hard and enduring fraternity' (119) that *White Niggers of America* struggled to harness.

Very much a text of its times, it did this in specific ways. Its interpretive direction was a particular kind of appreciation of Marxism, one that owed far less to the laws of capitalist accumulation as outlined in *Capital*, and much more to the philosophical notebooks of the 1840s, with their concern with subjectivity, ideology, and alienation. Indeed, it was this triumvirate of ideas that stamped *White Niggers of America* with its peculiarly powerful language of refusal. This was a New Left Marcusian accent that demanded an end to tyranny; a repudiation of all accommo-dations that denied the validity and possibility of ultimate, utopian socialist transformation; and the removal of all forces silencing the per-petual human cry for the realization of dreams and possibilities. 'Not to be engaged is always to collaborate with the enemy. Neutrality does not exist anywhere' (270). The ideal of an uncompromised freedom achieved in a revolutionary upsurge of collective humanity explodes throughout the pages of *White Niggers of America*. Sometimes the book is an almost unconscious revelation. In his 1960s antagonism to women, for instance, Vallières ended up addressing, in spite of himself and in ways that were unique and unanticipated, the isolating deformation of Québécois femininity. *White Niggers of America* looked deep into the soul of the working-class family and saw relations of conformist containment that were troubling in their implications. Bravely challenging the qui-etude of the Québécois, Vallières called for people to be different so that they could embrace life rather than suffer it as little more than death. *Survivance* could never again be championed in its traditional ways after Vallières demolished the facade that had masked much of the malignant dysfunctionality associated with it.

White Niggers of America was thus a classic New Left statement. It assailed the privileged (Canadian and American capital), but it demanded a new accounting from the French-Canadian poor themselves. It looked to no established venues of protest and was 'based neither on the opportunis-tic pragmatism of the capitalist parties, nor on the obsession with "revo-lutionary inevitabilities" [*sic!*] of the ... Communists' (220). Voluntarist in its foundational assumptions, Vallières's book was passionate in its insistence that socialist transformation would only come with a proletar-ian revolution that emerged out of the limits that workers would eventu-ally come to place on the exploitation that they were subjected to from other human beings. If that revolution was inevitable, it required organi-zation to bring it to the fore and free men from the shackles capitalism had placed on their minds and bodies. 'The overthrow of the established Order, and the collective dealienation of the working class that must accompany it, is a problem of conscious and collective organization of the people' (222). The question was, 'What kind of organization?'

Vallières's answer was most emphatically not an orthodox one: no party, no union, no technology, and no program could free the workers of the world.

For Vallières, revolutionary violence, orchestrated by conscious opponents of the regime of capital, was itself the *party* of liberation:

> The important thing, for the revolutionaries of the whole world as for those of Quebec, is not to expect the revolution to come from the *natural* and so-called *autonomous* development of the productive forces, but to organize immediately the spontaneous violence which in various ways (from workers' strikes to student demonstrations to juvenile delinquency) springs from the profound and cruel frustrations generated by the present organization of society ... violence that has been systematically practiced for centuries by the minority ruling classes ... This popular, organized, and conscious violence is based on the needs, aspirations, and *rights* of the majority of men. It is demanded every day by the age-old negation of those needs, aspirations, and rights by a minority of thieves, exploiters and murderers whose economic, political, military, and legal strength (Capital, the State, the Army, Justice) has been built, over the centuries, on the pitiless oppression of billions of men ... I have repeatedly emphasized the savage hatred that inhabits humiliated men, a hatred without definite object ... Revolutionaries ... organize the people's violence into a conscious and *independent* force. (223–4)

In organizing and orchestrating a popular and focused revolutionary violence, in Vallières's view, men remake themselves and make history. Only then would ordinary men 'no longer be the niggers of millionaires, the warmongers, and the preachers of passivity, but will be free at last to subject the world to their "whims": love, scientific curiosity, creation ... in solidarity and equality, in modesty and pride' (254).

As a politics and as a literary endeavour *White Niggers of America* almost immediately attained a grudging recognition for its 'savage readability.' An expression of brutal truthfulness, it drove a stake of fear deep into the national bosom. Malcolm Reid suggests, not without condescension, that Vallières's book had a certain pathetic appeal, likening it to the rant of a man who 'across the tavern table sobs out the story of his life ... a politics of chickenflesh.' Precisely because such an attack on the fusion of two nations in one country was posed in an unambiguous language of anti-capitalism, it also successfully grafted appreciation of class exploitation onto the more digestible understandings of national oppression.

After *White Niggers of America*, whose title, after all, proclaimed the plight of the Québécois in words no one could misconstrue, the Quebec–Canada relation could never quite be promoted as the great accomplishment of nation-building that many desperately needed it to be. This was a considerable, and in many ways unrivalled, accomplishment for any left-wing contingent, let alone one as new and inexperienced as the FLQ. Moreover, the fact that it was written in the midst of a repressive state assault, in the aftermath of a hunger strike, its pages growing through a period of enforced and debasing confinement, merely highlights what is unique about Vallières's book. Few are the texts in the entirety of Canadian history that have been written out of the experiences of class exploitation, national oppression, and the hope for socialism, at the same time as they have spoken so passionately of liberation across boundaries of different kinds. This is what Vallières managed to bring with him out of the Tombs. When looked at in this way, it is possible to forgive *White Niggers of America* much, at the same time as it is necessary to recognize that its postures demand redress in any subsequent political accounting.[61]

1967: 100 Years of Injustice

Canada entered its centennial year with FLQ bombs exploding in the financial district of Montreal. The RIN promoted a Quebec licence plate holder that proclaimed, '1867–1967: 100 Years of Injustice.' *La Cognée*, when it was not deploring the increasingly repressive development of a Quebec police state, found time to denounce the century of exploitation of the Québécois people that 1967 was commemorating. Vallières and Gagnon, after nearly four months in the Manhattan Detention Centre for Men, during which time they successfully turned back the Canadian state's demand that they be extradited to Montreal to face legal charges, were released. They were immediately illegally kidnapped by U.S. Immigration officials. Put on a plane to Montreal, the independence activists were delivered into the hands of the RCMP, who promptly slapped them in handcuffs. On 15 January 1967, Quebec's two 'most wanted' Felquistes appeared in court facing charges of murder, bombing attacks, and hold-ups. The infamous duo would not actually come to trial for a full year, and they would spend over forty months in jail before their eventual acquittals. But these legal victories would come only after a series of convictions and appeals, dragging on for months, kept the two advocates of revolution in their jail cells. A Comité

d'Aide au Groupe Vallières-Gagnon, formed in November 1966, demonstrated, raised money, attracted a number of prominent francophones
to its banner, and splashed the cause of independence and defence of
the FLQ across the pages of mainstream newspapers. In the corridors of
state power, with Trudeau about to be appointed minister of justice in
Lester B. Pearson's Liberal government, Quebec separatism now outdistanced communism as a threat to Canadian national security. Aiming 'to
destroy Confederation by subversive and seditious machinations,' the
indépendantiste cause was very much in the federal government's sights as
Canada's one hundredth anniversary unfolded.[62]

With Vallières and Gagnon awaiting trial and the RCMP moving more
aggressively to infiltrate FLQ cells, *La Cognée* finally collapsed. Its last
issue, no. 66, appeared two weeks before Expo 67 was scheduled to
admit people to its extensive grounds. Individuals such as Jacques
Desormeaux, arguably the longest-serving soldier in the ranks of the
Felquiste army of national liberation, were placed under surveillance by
the combined RCMP, Quebec provincial police, and Montreal anti-
terrorist unit for eighteen months. Special agents infiltrated the underground, enticing Felquistes by supplying them with dynamite sticks that
had been siphoned of their nitroglycerine, reducing them to harmless
props. Such agents provocateurs suggested terrorist acts, supplied the
'explosives' that could be used, and then testified in the trials of those
arrested for possessing incendiary materials. Almost anyone connected
to the underground was hauled in for 'interviews.' If no charges could
be laid, as was often the case, the security forces nevertheless congratu-
lated themselves on 'neutralizing' individuals who were made all too
aware that their political attraction to the independence cause had now
caught up with them. Quebec's university campuses were, by late 1967,
judged to be nurseries of radicalism and dangerous ideas. They were
infiltrated by police spies. Student-led anti-war protests produced
pitched battles with the cops outside the U.S. consulate, the most violent of which was a mid-November 1967 demonstration against the U.S.
bombing of Hanoi. The countersubversion forces of the Mounties were
directed to pursue 'terrorist sympathizers ... active in the universities
and other institutions of higher learning in Quebec.'[63]

At this point the FLQ was probably at its lowest ebb. It had martyrs
aplenty, but its capacity to engage in the actions it valued had been
severely curtailed. Yet the Felquistes had, along with their above-ground
counterparts, sown the seeds of a new consciousness of revolutionary
possibility and national liberation. When Charles de Gaulle capped his

July 1967 visit to Canada with the declaration, 'Vive le Québec libre,' he was applauded and cheered wildly. An increasingly vocal left wing inside the RIN linked Quebec's working class and its struggles against American capital with the project of national liberation. RIN head Pierre Bourgault spoke in Paris, insisting that independence was now attainable only with a program of the left, that it was a matter of 'life and death' not unrelated to the long-standing 'revolutionary mood' that had been evident in Québécois society for some time. Malcolm Reid ends his *The Shouting Signpainters* (1972) in this post-Expo environment with the words, 'The young people I am speaking of will not stop shouting until the walls come down.'[64]

The Spark of May 1968: Revolution! Revolution!

Some thought the walls were indeed collapsing. In Paris, Prague, London, Mexico City, Rome, Tokoyo, and New York the period reaching from April through November 1968 was marked by protests, general strikes, demonstrations, and an atmosphere of rebellious upheaval. It was during May 1968 in Paris that the archetypal 'feverish *journées*' of riot and revelry exploded spectacularly. With protest rallies now surging forth 200,000 strong, a leading French Gaullist intellectual, Raymond Aron, acknowledged that 'such a fund of violence and indignation in the masses' was a surprising and staggering statement of resentment and hostility, a bitter pill for the regime to swallow. As nine million workers put down their tools in support of the students, closing mines, railways, shipyards, offices, schools, and factories, the red flag flew over many barricaded workplaces. After a month of this assault on the bastions of sociopolitical and economic order, the revolt cooled, but May 1968 would live in popular memory as perhaps the defining moment of late capitalism's revolutionary challenge.[65]

In Canada, nothing so momentous unfolded. If we were to look for a locale of May '68 upheaval, however, it would most certainly be Montreal. Gagnon and Vallières had issued ringing calls to arms from their jail cells, their words carrying the charge of martyrdom. 'The people of Quebec are angry,' thundered Gagnon. 'All they need is the spark to start the fire. And that is precisely our role as the revolutionary vanguard – to set off that spark. We must start fires everywhere ... speak fiery words, do fiery deeds, and repeat them over and over.' Vallières concurred, and in a prison essay entitled *Indépendance et révolution* he counselled 'bombings, sabotage, kidnappings, and propaganda ... [as well as] a network of hideouts, warehouses, and print shops.' This was the infrastructure necessary for a people's uprising.[66]

These calls to push forward revolutionary nationalism were issued in a climate when the political temperature of the *indépendantiste* cause was rising. René Lévesque was assuming the voice of a respectable push for Quebec sovereignty, his independence sensibilities soon stifled in the provincial Liberal Party, where he ran headlong into the opposition of Eric Kierans, Robert Bourassa, and others. With Trudeau taking on the uncompromising captainship of the federalist forces in Ottawa, a showdown was inevitable, and Lévesque's *Option Québec* (1968) stated the case for a negotiated separation of Canada and Quebec. A Lévesque-inspired Mouvement Souveraineté-Association (MSA) gathered momentum and soon entered into talks with the RIN to merge the divided forces advocating Quebec's independence. This precipitated an acrimonious round of splits and the founding of new, more left-wing, political formations as Lévesque shepherded the more liberal separatist elements in the direction of the Parti Québécois (PQ), founded in mid-October 1968 with the merger of the MSA and a smaller moderate body, Ralliement National. What remained of the RIN immediately threw its *indépendantiste* towel into the Lévesque ring, almost doubling the size of the PQ and allowing it to assume the mantle of a 'National Front' for Quebec's liberation. If the PQ managed to draw some on the left to its ranks, stealing NDP thunder with its fundamentally social democratic program, radical and revolutionary opponents, committed not only to independence but also to socialism, formed the Front de Libération Populaire (FLP), the Comité Indépendance-Socialisme (CIS), and the Mouvement pour l'Intégration Scolaire (MIS). The FLP's newspaper, *La Masse*, appeared under the banner 'For a Québécois revolution.' The CIS, in turn, drew on a constituency of former *Parti pris* figures (the group had split over whether or not to support Lévesque, and the publication ceased), Marxist intellectuals, and young socialist militants connected to the FLQ underground. Workers' committees were formed in proletarian districts such as St Henri, their declarations sounding the death knell of a social order that no longer commanded the respect and trust of its lower echelons. At the annual convention of the Confédération des Syndicats Nationaux (CSN/CNTU), Marcel Pépin delivered his report on radical labour's embrace of a Second Front, in which trade unionists were urged to expand their activism and militancy beyond the workplace and collective bargaining, into the general struggle for social justice. If

Pépin avoided a direct endorsement of the *indépendantiste* movement and a commitment to fight with it for national liberation, his message was nonetheless clear enough and intersected the widening cries for direct action: 'In the past two years the economic grip has been tightened on the population. This additional twist has provoked more suffering, increased the social malaise, but it has stimulated the desire to fight on.'[67]

In this context the FLQ was reborn, as small concentric circles of underground militants formed to revive the direct-action wing of the *indépendantiste* movement. Class struggle formed the immediate backdrop against which these clandestine cells regenerated, an especially violent demonstration at the end of February 1968 pitting almost the entire francophone workers' and nationalist movements' advocates against the state. Called in support of striking Seven-Up workers, who had been picketing for more than eight months, the protest turned ugly at the gates of a Ville Mont-Royal bottling plant: marchers, some carrying red flags, clashed with a substantial police detachment, Molotov cocktails were the heady drink of the day, and many arrests and injuries resulted. Weeks later a bomb was placed at the Seven-Up plant. In the months to follow some thirty bombing incidents, many of them in support of striking workers, were attributed to an underground FLQ cell. Some explosions coincided with protests of the Vallières-Gagnon support committee, which sponsored a gala 27 May 1968 benefit for Quebec's political prisoners, in which poets, rock musicians, actors, writers, and other celebrities donated their time and talents to the *indépendantiste* movement and its martyrs. Less than a month later the violent Saint-Jean-Baptiste Day 'Trudeau au Poteau' riot revealed dramatically how inflamed the political situation in Quebec was becoming. Two of the 250 injured and 292 arrested on Police-Club Monday, 24 June 1968, were Jacques Lanctôt, a 22-year-old taxi driver, and Paul Rose, a teacher two years his senior. They first met in a paddy wagon en route to a police station, bloodied and battered after doing battle in front of the podium on which Trudeau sat unmoved as he was pelted with projectiles. In the twenty-seven months after their June 1968 arrest, Lanctôt and Rose would piece together a working-class Felquiste commando unit that largely replicated the orientation of Vallières and Gagnon. Their final act would be the kidnapping of Pierre Laporte.[68]

If May 1968 had been the spark of an incendiary call for Québécois revolt, the year ended with a number of brush fires. Felquiste cells stepped up their campaign of bombing, among the targets the Chamber of Commerce building in Quebec City, police cars in a large garage, Montreal's Ministry of Labour offices, Union Nationale and Liberal Party clubs, and the Eaton's department store, long a symbol of anglophone economic domination. Especially prominent in the late-1968 flurry of direct action attacks were firms embroiled in acrimonious strikes: the Quebec Liquor Commission; the Molson Street headquarters of the paper company Domtar; steelworks in Montreal; the Voyageur bus terminal; the Chambly Transport Company; and a factory near Shawinigan. The Murray-Hill Company, which had a monopoly on transporting passengers to the Montreal airport, drew the ire of the radical Mouvement de Libération du Taxi (MLT), founded in September 1968 by an old *gauchiste*, Germain Archambault, and militantly endorsed by Jacques Lanctôt. A day before Halloween, an MLT-led protest that attracted over 1,000 taxi drivers, radical students, and militants from the FLP and CIS, surrounded Dorval Airport with 250 cabs, brought traffic to a snarling standstill, and torched buses in the Murray-Hill fleet. Five days later a bus in the Murray-Hill garage was destroyed.[69]

With Quebec's labour–capital relations rocked by such events, the province's students took to the streets in a series of protest mobilizations that championed a countercultural affinity for libertarianism, autonomy, and self-expression. The expanding CEGEP system, which had grown to seventeen general and professional educational institutions meant to replace the age-old classically oriented *collèges*, was envisioned as a means of preparing Quebec's students for university and for the job market. Instead, its expanding classrooms became catalysts of revolt. Tens of thousands of students closed the schools, occupied the premises, and marched in angry demonstrations.[70] An SDS-like body, the Mouvement Syndical Politique (MSP), crystallized out of the ferment, elements within it gravitating to a now-widening circle of agitation that brought students, anti-war activists, trade unionists, and Black Power spokesmen together. As we have seen, radical students and militant West Indian blacks at Sir George Williams University and McGill were central to this mobilization. A Montreal African-Canadian newspaper emerged out of the upheaval under the banner UHURU ('freedom' in Swahili), espousing increasingly radical views. Black and white students, their arms linked with community activists, marched on the American consulate, demanding the release of Black Panther Eldridge Cleaver, recently arrested in California. At the end of November the Hemispheric Conference to End the War in Vietnam attracted 2,000 militant anti-imperialists to Montreal. With the presence of delegates from the

Vietnamese National Liberation Front, the Latin American Solidarity
Organization, headed by Chile's Salvador Allende, the Black Panther
Party (which sent Bobby Seale and a group of bodyguards only after the
staid conference organizers were pressured by the ranks to cough up
$1,200 in airfare), the government of Cuba, and the Palestinian Resis-
tance, Québécois revolutionaries rubbed shoulders with compatriots
from around the world. They also decided to make some noise. Four
bombs were planted outside the homes of executives of Canadair and
United Aircraft, targeted because their firms produced war materials for
the U.S. army.[71]

Towards October 1970

Nothing much changed in 1969. Escalating FLQ violence in January
and February of that year saw repeated bombings, threats of impending
explosions, and intimidating placement of dynamite. Police were receiving 500 calls a month, many of them clearly bogus, of incendiary
charges planted and ready to go off. After a dramatic bombing of the
Montreal Stock Exchange on 13 February 1969, injuring between
twenty and thirty people and causing nearly a million dollars in property
damage, the police arrested Pierre-Paul Geoffroy, charging him with
129 criminal counts relating to 31 separate bombings. His apartment
had yielded 200 sticks of dynamite, 100 detonator camps, and two
recently constructed bombs ready to be activated, as well as a library of
communist literature and posters of Marx, Lenin, and Che. Refusing to
implicate others, Geoffroy pled guilty and was sentenced to an extraor-
dinarily punitive 124 life sentences. In St-Jérôme, northwest of
Montreal, Geoffroy's brother Jacques worked for the Company of Young
Canadians, helping to distribute a radical journal, *Pouvoir ouvrier*
(*Worker's Power*). Rumours circulated that he was implicated in the theft
of dynamite from a padlocked warehouse. As the bourgeois press
howled for blood, Michel Chartrand, headquartered at the stronghold
of proletarian radicalism, Montreal's Central Council of National Trade
Unions (CNTU/CSN), shot back: 'Terrorists didn't create violence.
It created them.' Decrying 'the violence of the capitalist system,'
Chartrand advocated revolution: 'We must destroy the capitalist system
and reorganize the economy to meet the needs of people. The CSN in
Montreal will come to the assistance of all demonstrators, protestors,
and revolutionaries whose aims are the same as ours.'[72]

Words such as these echoed in the ongoing student radicalism, which exploded in Montreal universities in February 1969 and escalated throughout the winter, spring, and summer. At McGill, militants assailed a symbolic core of anglo Montreal's cultural and intellectual elitism, an institution reinforcing the material differentiation of French and English. Aiming to make McGill a French-language institution within three years, to secure the abolition of the University's French Canada studies program, and to democratize life in Quebec's quintessential ivory tower by loosening admission standards considerably, lowering tuition fees, and opening the McLennan Library to the public, 'McGill Français' put the fear of a revolutionary Québécois god in English-Canadian administrative circles of higher education. Four days before a 28 March 1969 protest rallied 15,000 rowdy demonstrators outside of the McGill gates, a vice-president (administrative) warned the Montreal Bar Association that it needed to reflect thoughtfully about the 150-year-old university. 'It is under attack,' he wailed, and it could well be 'destroyed overnight.' The threat 'to one of the world's great universities' was tangible and easily identifiable. It came, he said,

From Stanley Gray and his revolutionaries
From Lemieux and the Ligue pour l'Integration Scolaire
From Chartrand and his violent separatists
From the taxpayers who foot the bills
From restless youth who demand change in society – your society.

McGill would indeed weather the 1969 storm. But radical students and professors formed a new theoretical magazine, *Mobilization*. Close working relations with the Comité Vallières-Gagnon were forged, along with ties to Chartrand's CNTU, militant cabbies in the MLT, and a number of other radical nationalist, socialist, and working-class organizations, some of them now consciously Maoist in their programmatic affiliations.[73]

Things went from bad to worse as Montreal faced an illegal strike of police and firemen in October, prompting disgruntled taxi drivers to launch an unimpeded assault on the hated Murray-Hill limousine service. Buses were driven into walls, Molotov cocktails were thrown, and lethal gunshots exchanged. Bill 63, proposed by the recently elected Union Nationale government, inflamed the language issue by giving free rein to parents in choosing the language of instruction in their children's schools. This opened the door to the assimilation of the sons and daughters of non-francophone immigrants by the English minority and the encouragement of the deculturation of the Québécois. Chartrand, punctuating his outburst with declarations that in Quebec the bosses spoke English while the workers talked in French, threatened the dynamiting of English-language universities if the hated legislation was made into law, earning him a few days in jail on charges of sedition (bombs did indeed explode at McGill and Loyola in November 1969). Indeed, the charge of sedition, which had been rare in the history of Quebec, was now seemingly commonplace: in less than two months six people were allegedly guilty of this offense, among them leaders of the MIS opposition to English in Quebec's schools and the former pugilist and head of Les Chevaliers de l'Indépendance, Reggie Chartrand. Tens of thousands of protesters amassed on the lawns of the provincial legislature in Quebec City on Halloween eve 1969, their dress one of defiant opposition to the bill. It took tear gas, liberal use of police clubs, seventy injuries, and forty arrests before the crowd was dispersed. The bill eventually passed, further dividing Quebec. After a throng of 3,000 supporters of Vallières and Gagnon demanded the release of the Felquistes from prison at a 7 November 1969 rally, the demonstrators, some of them cradling Molotov cocktails, torched a barricade, fought with the cops, and dispersed throughout the city's business district, where they lobbed incendiary devices at police headquarters, City Hall, the *Montreal Star* building, and any accessible bank or insurance corporation. Mayor Jean Drapeau had had enough. He secured a vote in city council banning demonstrations and public meetings in Montreal. In one of the first visible, articulate promotions of women's liberation within the ongoing national/socialist struggle, 200 women decked themselves in chains and paraded the streets. Their slogan: 'No liberation for Quebec without women's liberation; No women's liberation without Quebec's liberation.' The women's protest resulted in their immediate arrests. Not to be silenced, the organizers went on to form the Front de Libération des Femmes (FLF), espousing socialist, feminist, and *indépendantiste* positions.[74]

The End of the Sixties

By the end of 1969 more and more *indépendantistes* had experienced first-hand the repression of the state at various levels. It was well known that above-ground organizations of dissent were infiltrated by undercover RCMP and provincial/municipal police forces. Stanley Gray's FLP gradually withdrew into workers' committees in 'red' districts such as St Henri. From there, entrenched in surroundings they felt could be kept under their control and direction, they developed ways and means of evading agents of the state. FLQ cells mushroomed in the subterranean circles of revolutionary nationalists. If no lines of distinction could be drawn between legal bodies promoting independence and underground groups committed to the violent propaganda of exemplary deeds, even the mildly social democratic PQ being suspect in the eyes of the expanding counter-subversion security apparatus, some in radical circles clearly wondered why they should put their collective heads in the gendarmes' widening noose.

As secret collectives sprang up spontaneously, there was at first little in the way of coordination among them. Jacques Lanctôt and Paul Rose formed the leadership core of one cell, while another contingent involving former ALQ veteran Robert Hudon and long-time Felquiste Jacques Desormeaux coalesced at the same time, bankrolling its activities by 'fundraising' robberies. At the Université du Québec à Montréal (UQAM), a 25-year-old academic historian, Robert Comeau, gathered around him an FLQ communication nucleus. It issued a communiqué defending the use of terror against 'the violence of the existing system,' calling on a common front of workers to establish a combat party guided by its commitment to socialism and Quebec's national liberation.

Lévesque and the Parti Québécois mounted their first serious electoral challenge in April 1970. They found that underhanded scare tactics limited their success at the polls to a mere seven seats, six of them in the proletarian ridings of east-end Montreal. Even moderate sovereignty-association advocates could understand why some thought a tame approach to independence had come up short. Lévesque himself was defeated in his bid for a provincial seat. The PQ had to become more radical. 'It isn't hard to understand why the youth of Quebec go around setting off bombs,' snorted Lévesque.

Some of those bombs, which began exploding with more regularity in the spring and summer of 1970, supported workers under attack. Among the most infamous would be the 450 *gars de Lapalme*, truck drivers whose mail pick-up contract with the federal government had been terminated. Conventional symbols of English economic power, such as Montreal's Board of Trade building, were targeted. A non-incendiary bomb landed in the lap of the judiciary as Vallières and Gagnon were finally released from prison in 1970, their message one of international revolutionary struggle. Proclaiming his belief in violence as the necessary first step in the creation of an effective national liberation front, Vallières insisted that the FLQ was in the forefront of such endeavours, not only in Quebec but abroad. Urging organization on a North American and international basis, Vallières and Gagnon, in concert with Stan Gray and the FLP, representatives from the Comité Ouvrier de Saint-Henri, the CSN, and the UQAM magazine *Socialisme*, and supported by the French writer Jean Genet, set up a committee for solidarity with the Black Panthers. Panther leader Fred Hampton, fresh from speaking engagements in Alberta and Saskatchewan, was murdered in his Chicago bed, succumbing to a barrage of police bullets; Eldridge Cleaver escaped victimization by going into exile; H. Rap Brown was underground, finding his way to Quebec, where he declared it 'a cornerstone of the North American revolution'; and Huey P. Newton and Bobby Seale were in jail. The FLQ–Panther connection was, to many in the connected paranoid security state circles of Canada and the United States, but a visible tip of an international conspiracy. It reached from Cuba, Algeria, Vietnam, Ireland, Latin America, and Europe into North America through the clandestine U.S.-based Weather Underground (a subterranean terrorist network that had emerged out of Students for a Democratic Society, hastening the demise of that prototypical 1960s body) and the FLQ.[75]

As early as the summer of 1968, Vallières had written to a comrade suggesting that if he and Gagnon were ever to be released from prison someone had to be prepared to 'organize a spectacular operation.' He thought a political kidnapping, in which influential members of the Quebec or Trudeau governments, or perhaps two judges, would be taken hostage, to be released only when the freedom of the jailed Felquistes was secured, was what was required. It was a desperate and indiscreet proposal, one that would later result in Vallières pleading guilty to a charge of incitement to create a criminal offence. By 1969–70 the Paul Rose–Jacques Lanctôt network was perhaps the most developed and radical component of the FLQ. It was committed to an immediate release of political prisoners and socialist independence for Quebec. Among its clandestine ranks discussions turned to the increasing prominence of political kidnappings in Europe and Latin America. Some advocated going after Harrison W. Burgess, United States consul in Montreal. With Vallières and Gagnon now out of jail, a wider-ranging movement to release all political prisoners in Quebec and to raise bail and legal fees for those arrested while engaged in oppositional activity, emerged. The Mouvement pour la Défense des Prisonniers Politiques

(MDPPQ) was joined by the 1970 formation of the Front d'Action Politique (FRAP) and, as the summer wound down, the Gagnon-inspired Partisans du Québec Libre (PQL). Violent construction worker strikes involving tens of thousands of CNTU unionists, the ongoing and increasingly violent *gars de Lapalme* controversy, and a three-month strike at an auto assembly plant sparked by the use of French as the working language all highlighted how the *indépendantiste* cause was now centrally important in a broad and increasingly militant workers' movement.[76]

It was in this context of escalating struggle and pressured discussion and debate in the FLQ underground that the Rose and Lanctôt forces divided over whether a major operation should be launched. The latter pressed for immediate action, and Opération Libération, which would ultimately result in the kidnapping of James Cross on 5 October 1970, was put into motion. The Libération cell alerted radio stations that written demands had been deposited in an envelope at a university building in Parc Lafontaine and that Cross would be released when they were met. Among the demands were the publication of an eight-page FLQ manifesto, the release of twenty-three named political prisoners, the rehiring of the *gars de Lapalme*, an airplane to take the kidnappers to Cuba or Algeria, and $500,000 as a 'voluntary tax' in aid of the struggle for Quebec's national liberation. In the days that followed the state unleashed a series of police raids aimed at the intimidation and incarceration of known Felquistes. This repression, in conjunction with the broadcasting of the Libération cell's manifesto, which was a mixture of *indépendantiste* advocacy and a highly charged workerist rhetoric that appealed to broad populist and socialist sentiments, crystallized sympathy for the FLQ. This, in turn, hardened the state in its refusals.

The FLQ manifesto opened with the claim that the organization's intention was to achieve 'the total independence of the people of Quebec, to have them united in a free society, without the clique of ravenous sharks, the "big bosses" of business and politics, and their lackeys, who have turned Quebec into their private preserve of cheap labour and unscrupulous exploitation.' Alluding to the historic struggle of the Québécois, the kidnappers closed by likening themselves to the Patriotes of 1837–8. With ample reference to labour struggles, reaching back to the late 1950s and Murdochville, the manifesto carried with its nationalist appeal the unambiguous class demand that the 'workers of Quebec' need to 'start today to take back what belongs to you.' The declarative spontaneity of the manifesto rang out in the assertion, 'Only you know your factories, your machines, your hotels, your universities, your trade unions; don't wait for some miracle of organization. MAKE YOUR REVOLUTION YOURSELVES.'[77]

The Libération group's bold seizure of Cross galvanized their Rose-led counterparts, known as the Chernier cell, to act. Paul Rose, his brother Jacques, a mechanic at the CNR shops, and their long-time ally, Francis Simard, had been in the United States when the kidnapping was announced, en route back to Quebec after having travelled as far south as Texas in search of funds to support their underground activities. With Trudeau maintaining an absolute refusal to concede anything to the Cross kidnappers except safe passage to another country, the Chernier commando unit targeted Pierre Laporte, the acting premier of Quebec and minister of labour in the provincial cabinet, as the FLQ's next victim. On 10 October 1970, they took Laporte hostage outside his home a little after six o'clock in the evening. Promising to execute Laporte in short order if the Libération cell's prior demands were not met in their entirety, a handful of FLQers had managed to convince the country that its underground organization was a sophisticated and capable military operation, one able to carry off a coordinated campaign of terror. In reality, the Libération cell was as shocked as anyone to hear that it had been bolstered by the Chernier group's kidnapping. If few Québécois endorsed the acts of the underground, 'the FLQ's highwayman élan and the government's inept responses' left many 'inwardly pleased.' On 25 October 1970, a Montreal sociologist would write, ' For the time being, the government has won, but the real victor is the FLQ ... the FLQ has gained more than is generally believed.'[78]

Laporte's kidnapping scotched any possibility that the October Crisis would be resolved in negotiation. Those in Quebec who promoted this option, such as Le Devoir's Claude Ryan, PQ head René Lévesque, the leaders of most trade unions, and many public intellectuals, found their voices drowned in the hawkish rhetoric of state retribution. In Ottawa, Trudeau's Principal Secretary and his increasingly hard-line conduit to a wavering Quebec Premier Robert Bourassa, Marc Lalonde, gave every sign of gearing up for an all-out war against the FLQ and anyone who breathed a syllable of support for the underground indépendantiste movement. Montreal's police and anti-terrorist forces adopted a similarly unyielding stand. Talk of imposing the War Measures Act floated in such circles for days, and drafts of like-minded municipal legislation were in various stages of revision. Arrest lists were compiled indiscriminately and cavalierly. The tense atmosphere and escalating repression brought those sympathetic to the FLQ's ends, if not its means, out of the shadows and into the open air of public debate. University classes ground to a halt. Three thousand gathered at Paul Sauvé Arena in mid-October to hear Vallières, Gagnon, Chartrand, and FLQ lawyer-negotiator Robert Lemieux defend socialist independence and denounce the state of siege instigated by various levels of governing authority. Vallières declared to his supporters: 'The FLQ is each of you. It is every Québécois who stands up.' The crowd chanted in unison, 'FLQ, FLQ, FLQ.'

Two nights later, the War Measures Act proclaimed, the arrests mounting, the tanks and military personnel filling the streets of Montreal and elsewhere, it was more and more difficult to keep one's *indépendantiste* and socialist posture erect.[79] It was not just the hundreds of arrests of comrades and friends, held without legal rights. An avalanche of intrusion, registered in over 31,000 searches of individuals and homes and other buildings, almost 5,000 of which resulted in seizure of property of some kind, struck terror into the hearts and minds of dissidents from all walks of life: trade unionists, political leftists, nationalists, students, community and citizens' group activists, intellectuals and professors. Laporte's death on 17 October 1970 cast a pall over an already-divided and rancorous Quebec. As Louis Fournier, whose detailed outline of the FLQ's history is unrivalled in its careful reconstruction of the underground movement, notes, 'the murder aroused general condemnation and helped swing public opinion over to the side of law and order. The sympathy the kidnappers had enjoyed disappeared. The FLQ had lost the second round – and the war.'[80]

The full weight of the liberal state's coercive apparatus was brought to bear on the revolutionary initiative, with ongoing arrests, trials, and a widening net of coercive containment. Protests were registered across the country, but the outcome was a foregone conclusion. Legal advocates of revolutionary transformation, such as the FRAP, were tarred with the now-bloody brush of terrorism, their candidates for electoral office arrested. Leading public figures associated with the FLQ or known to defend its ideas rotted in jail, held under the provisions of the War Measures Act without any charges being laid. Among them were a group that would come to be designated 'The Five': Vallières, Gagnon, Chartrand, Lemieux, and a journalist associated with the mid-1960s anti–nuclear arms movement, Jacques Larue-Langlois.

Slowly but surely the Felquiste fox was hunted down, its lairs of isolated rural farmhouses, non-descript apartments in francophone working-class districts, and networks of professors, students, and workers

penetrated by spies and turned inside out by police raids. Eventually the
authorities were able to zero in on the house where Cross was being
held, captured two of the Libération cell members, and, after five days
of surveillance, cut the hydro to the building. In the negotiations that
followed, Jacques Lanctôt and his comrades were guaranteed safe passage to Cuba and James Cross was released on 3 December 1970, after
fifty-nine days in FLQ captivity. Paul and Jacques Rose, Francis Simard,
and some others were not so fortunate: while they managed to evade
police capture for many weeks, they were eventually rounded up. Paul
Rose surrendered to police at the end of December 1970, stoic in his
resignation: 'We wanted to speed up history and perhaps we belong to a
lost generation. We have no regrets, even though in principle we are
opposed to violence. We accept responsibility for the violence that
occurred and we will pay for it.' Pay he did: Rose was one of roughly
a score of convicted Felquistes sentenced to terms ranging from
six months to life imprisonment.[81]

The armed forces withdrew from the streets of Quebec on 4 January
1971, but the state of emergency, in which the War Measures Act was
replaced by a December passage of the Public Order Act, remained
until the end of April 1971. Oddly enough, the police did not entirely
crush out the FLQ. At least one cell, the Information Viger group
responsible for communications, but also thoroughly compromised by
informants, was allowed to continue to exist, apparently in order to
'protect' those supplying the police with 'intelligence.' Other subterranean commando units came into being after the October 1970 events,
including some that were actually created and guided by agents provaca-
teurs. The writing was now on the FLQ wall. Upon his release from jail
in the winter of 1971, Michel Chartrand, the rabble-rousing voice of
militant Quebec labour, was uncharacteristically subdued. Still an advocate of total revolution, Chartrand insisted that nothing would be won
by killing individuals, advocating instead that the trade unions and their
allies 'become more politically conscious' and pursue the democratic
road to social transformation.[82]

The cruellest blow was undoubtedly delivered by Pierre Vallières, who
had, in the aftermath of October 1970, suffered through yet another
arrest, secured his release, faced new charges and, in the midst of differences with Gagnon and others over the question of revolutionary violence, gone underground. Then, in mid-December 1971, Vallières
shifted strategic gears, withdrawing his support for what had been the
practice of the FLQ, terrorism. He now cast his lot as an *indépendantiste*

with the Parti Québécois. In a lengthy essay published in Claude Ryan's *Le Devoir*, and later expanded into his 1972 *Parti pris*–published book, *L'Urgence de choisir*, Vallières declared unequivocally: 'If until October 1970, the FLQ was the radical expression of the spontaneous and anarchic character that every national liberation movement experiences at its outset, it has today become the unconscious but objective ally of the strategy of those in power.' This repudiation, on the eve of mass struggles of the Québécois working class, was all the more galling precisely because the author of *White Niggers of America* castigated trade union leaders precisely at the point when they were adopting radical and far-reaching critiques of capitalism and putting themselves in the forefront of militant mobilizations and resistance. Rejecting the primacy of class as an engine of social transformation, Vallières challenged the viability of a workers' party and refused the notion that orthodox left thinking and understandings of revolutionary organization had much to contribute to overcoming what the former Felquiste now increasingly referred to as 'national alienation.' The PQ was presented as the only socially transformative game in town. Vallières embraced its statism unequivocally, arguing, 'The only collective instrument the Quebec society can use is the state,' which he rather mystically defined as 'the whole of the Quebec collectivity.'

Staunch revolutionaries, underground or not, found this change of position difficult to accept. With Vallières soon securing a job studying the effects of unemployment on a rural forestry-dominated enclave north of Montreal, a posting funded by the federal government's manpower minister Bryce Mackasey, recantations coming from the FLQ's leading public figure proved a bitter pill for those to whom it now seemed force fed. Charles Gagnon, for one, gagged on the politically medicinal message. Convinced that the road to Quebec's liberation and the realization of socialism lay in the creation of a Marxist-Leninist revolutionary party, Gagnon was also now disaffected with the FLQ. His choice, however, was not that of Vallières. Gagnon worked as a political adviser for the Montreal Central Council of National Trade Unions and put out a Maoist bulletin, *Vaincre*, that would point toward the later founding of a Gagnon-led group, In Struggle/En Lutte. Although he was branded an opportunist and a traitor by many of his former comrades, Vallières's embrace of the PQ nevertheless proved one of a number of political paths rooted in the 1960s but leading out of it.[83]

Not surprisingly, for all the repression that rolled over Quebec, it remained a centre of radical working-class mobilization in North America.

October 1971 would be hailed as Quebec's 'Blue Collar' crisis. A momentous strike at *La Presse* culminated in a 15,000-strong rally that was viciously attacked by Drapeau's 'Gestapo' police. Hundreds were injured, and a young female student, Michèle Gauthier, was killed. As Quebec labour rallied to overcome its historic divisions, bringing together the Quebec Federation of Labour (QFL), the CNTU, and the increasingly important Quebec Teachers Corporation (QTC), a Common Front jelled throughout the winter months of 1972. As rural protests assailed the monopolistic corporations in the forestry sector and mining towns revolted against the shutdown of the sole industrial employer in their midst, Montreal's red districts seemed rivalled by a rebellious hinterland. Townsfolk in Cabano blew up bridges and blockaded roadways utilized by K.C. Irving, the company having failed to deliver a promised plant and its much-sought-after jobs. They threatened to torch the enterprise's buildings, even the valued wooded terrain itself. 'The people feel the forest, the natural resources, belong to the people,' explained the local priest to bewildered reporters. Demonstrations by the unemployed rocked Shawinigan and numerous other locales in the Gaspé and the Eastern Townships.

A social crisis was in the making. By spring 1972 some 210,000 public sector workers had walked off their jobs in a general strike that was met with injunctions, fines, and other forms of discipline. Bourassa's liberal state passed legislation that would eventually break the back of the escalating work stoppages. Three key union officials – Pépin, QFL head Louis Laberge, and Yvon Charbonneau of the QTC – were jailed. As riotous assemblies of workers voted to 'overthrow the regime,' thousands of disgruntled union residents of Sept-Îles, an iron port, rebelled when the government passed back-to-work legislation aimed at subduing two construction unions embroiled in a jurisdictional dispute. They sealed off the roads, closed stores except those they deemed acceptable to keep open, and seized the radio stations, playing revolutionary music and broadcasting radical and union manifestos. Two thousand steelworkers and 1,500 machinists walked out of their American-owned operations, while 72 per cent of the region's teachers and civil servants opted to defy the law and refuse to report to work. Malcolm Reid, instructed by one machinist to keep his reporting leftist, opened his story on the 'Sept-Iles Revolts' for the *Last Post* by acknowledging, 'They don't read much Trotsky in Sept-Iles. But the workers of this iron port way out east on the St. Lawrence put themselves at the head of the May revolt in Quebec with something that looked like what Trotsky called "dual power."' 'It doesn't shock me,' declared Labor Minister Jean Cournoyer. 'This could have been predicted five years ago. The nationalist movement was due to become class conscious.'[84]

This class upsurge would succumb to the generalized assault on labour as the shifting terms of trade in an international class struggle hoisted militant workers on the petard of a post-1973 fiscal crisis of Western capitalist states. As Ralph Surette noted insightfully in 1972, Lévesque's suggestion that the PQ would move to the left after its 1970 electoral defeat did not materialize. The October Crisis nipped such a possibility in the bud, perhaps adding a repressive push to the PQ's instinctually moderate inclinations. A year later, as the *La Presse* strike provided a glimpse of the class battles in the making, Lévesque denounced the ostensibly fanatical labour leaders of the emerging Common Front and earned himself the gratitude of even the anglophone Montreal bourgeoisie. By 1972, a year of increasingly militant, even revolutionary, labour manifestos, the PQ and the left labour movement were on a collision course. This drove the 'statist' technocrats who served as Lévesque's brains trust increasingly into a cul-de-sac where sovereignty-association was twinned with the Quiet Revolution's half-state/half-private enterprise 'mixed' economy characterized by Hydro-Québec and its counterparts in the forestry and minerals sectors.[85] Socialism, syndicalist aspirations for workers' control and self-management, and anti-imperialism were wrenched apart from the struggle for national liberation. Independence was all too routinely boiled down, on the one hand, to the practical realization of a constitutional accord or, on the other hand, to a conceptualization of nationalism as *étapisme*, a strategic commitment to the one-step-at-a-time gradualism of political horse-trading.

As the tides of reaction rose, the islands of revolutionary politics receded from view. New Right governments came to power in Britain and the United States; the political climate changed. Within twenty years the implosion of the Soviet Union would condition theses on 'the end of history.' The ringing declaration of 'Revolution Now!' which bellowed throughout the mid- to late 1960s in Quebec was barely audible amid the din of common-sense counter-revolutionary platitudes that were the stock in trade of a 1980s and 1990s ideological about-face. The Sixties had become memory.[86]

So too had conventional conceptions of Canada. If anything laid to rest the understanding of the country as a northern outpost of the British Empire, it was the making of a loud, rather than quiet, revolution that had figured so prominently in Quebec in the years reaching from the early 1960s into the October Crisis of 1970. No longer could Quebec be contained as a racialized appendage, the 'second' of two nations in the *one* country that *was* Canada. The demand for revolution that was first whispered beneath the sign of the Hanged Sheep and then shouted in FLQ bombings and manifestos, and nurtured in a generalized radicalization of workers, students, peoples of colour, and their mobilizations, turned out to be less tied to an organization and a program of social transformation than floating in an atmosphere of challenge and critical thought. This allowed the individualism of resistance to follow paths of extreme expression, deepening the representational significance of the 'FLQ,' which came to be far more of a rallying cry than it was a coherent political formation. This is precisely why, from 1963 to 1969, each wave of repression, snuffing out actually existing underground FLQ bodies, was always followed by the rebirth of the clandestine 'movement.'

These waves of revival were, however, driven deeper and deeper underground. This both removed Felquistes more and more from mass mobilizations on the *indépendantiste* surface of Quebec's politics and upped the ante of what kind of exemplary acts were conceived as useful to the cause of socialism and national liberation. The FLQ was pushed inexorably towards its tragic end point. Overreaching itself in October 1970, the FLQ as icon then toppled. Its advocates were no longer willing to be captivated by its magnetism; the state was now able to turn the Felquiste myth against itself.[87]

Canada's 1960s lost momentum with the October Crisis. Certainly the book did not close on Quebec radicalism as the 1970s opened with repression, but a new chapter would be written with the changing times. More than anywhere else in Canada the spirit of the 1960s lived with the development of small, but politically spirited, revolutionary organizations and the continuity of more amorphous rebellious impulses. Nonetheless, the tone of political and cultural life changed as the mythology of the FLQ succumbed by the mid- to late 1970s to the struggle for parliamentary power exemplified by the rise of Lévesque and the PQ.

Along the way, however, the call for revolutionary change galvanized not merely the few hundred FLQers who worked in successive 'generations' for independence, but tens, even hundreds, of thousands of Québécois. A vision of a different Canada, one more egalitarian and one not divided against itself, either 'racially' or materially, flourished as a possibility, expanding daily in ways that were quite rare. This called into question both the capitalist foundations of the Canadian economy and its servile federal and provincial states. In the struggle for national liberation inside Canada's most obvious ongoing exercise in colonization, moreover, awareness of other instances of special oppressions slowly percolated to the surface of radical politics. As the FLQ, born of recognitions that 'the wretched of the earth' shared a common struggle to realize their dreams of liberation, moved towards October 1970, one of its communiqués spoke in the commonplace 1960s idiom of internationalism, connecting the struggles of francophone Quebec to those of 'all the peoples who are victims of American imperialism.' It added a concluding note that was entirely new: 'We also support the struggle of the first exploited people of the continent: the American Indians.'[88] If the 1960s cry for 'Revolution Now' grew far more subdued with the death of Laporte, one of the decade's belated discoveries was the plight and power of Canada's Native people.

Chapter Ten

The 'Discovery' of the 'Indian'

To write about Native peoples and Canadian identity is fraught with difficulty. The various Indigenous groups that inhabit the land mass now known as Canada never asked nor agreed to be 'Canadians,' and their complex and often quite different identities, while sharing much, can hardly be congealed into a commonality. This has often been what has happened in the course of white colonization, and it remains a pitfall when interpretation, however sensitive, strives to generalize rather than confine itself to a particular case study.

The experience of the Aboriginal population of the northern half of North America, and its relations with white colonizers and their increasingly powerful and interventionist Canadian state, transcends the ironic motif that has animated this study of the 1960s and national identity. Yet it is also difficult not to appreciate just how ironic the historical intermingling of the country's First Nations with the 1960s preoccupation of being Canadian had become. For perhaps at no point in Canada's history was it so apparent that in 'creating' Canada something decidedly ugly had not only been countenanced, but had existed at the core of the national being from its inception. When Native peoples across Canada began to align with their counterparts in the United States in a Red Power movement of challenge and opposition, demanding redress of centuries of grievance, national identity found itself tested in ways that both threatened and struggled to confirm what was unique about being Canadian.[1]

Mohawk activist Kahn-Tineta Horn, 1964 (*Look*, 28 January 1964; Photographer: Bob Henriques).

The brief but important emergence of Red Power in the 1960s is, at this point, a little-studied phenomenon. It was no doubt as multifaceted and as wildly oscillating as the New Left or the advocates of national independence in Quebec, forces and movements with which Red Power was loosely connected, as it was to the Black Power mobilizations in the United States and the anti-imperialist agitations of the decade. So continuous had been Aboriginal oppositions to colonization, through struggles for title to land and water or defence of traditional rights, be they related to treaties, fishing and hunting, or cultural practices,[2] that there will be those who question whether the emergence of a new militancy in the 1960s marks any kind of break with a Native past in which Indigenous resistance was never far from the surface of Aboriginal–white relations. All of this is further complicated by the undeniable extent to which youthful Native militants came to appreciate and seek sustenance through developing connections with elders, a phenomenon that existed only weakly in the history of white New Leftists. This meant that what was new in the Red Power movement was always dialectically related, indeed inseparable from, what was old in Native experience. This process was highlighted in the ways that young Aboriginal militants, relatively innocent of Indigenous spirituality, often came to situate their challenges to the colonizing white state within a return to traditional customs, such as dance, that were religious confirmations of Native identity and its superiority to that of the rapacious market-driven fetishes of late capitalism.[3]

Yet for all of this there is no denying that something changed as the Sixties placed its stamp on Indigenous peoples. They, in turn, left their mark indelibly on that decade. An entrée into the emergence of Red Power in the 1960s is the Aboriginal fiction and life stories that developed in its aftermath. It is no accident that Native writers such as Jeanette C. Armstrong, Lee Maracle, and Eden Robinson have worked their prose around young Aboriginal militants of the 1960s, born in British Columbia, who found inspiration and new direction for their lives in the United States–based American Indian Movement (AIM) and Vancouver's Native Alliance of Red Power (NARP).[4]

Arguably the most compelling of these accounts presents a history of the emergence of Native radicalism in the 1960s in the guise of a fictional account of the journey of an Okanagan youth from the reserve into an urban malaise of anomie and self-destructive behaviour that culminates in an all-too-common denouement of incarceration. Jeanette C. Armstrong's Tommy 'Slash' Kelasket discovers in Red Power a critique of colonialism and a path back to pride in being Native. *Slash* (1985) offers a richly human encounter with the experience of dispossession *and* the historicized particulars of the ways in which Aboriginal militancy grew out of this experience in the specific context of the 1960s. In Slash's movements across borders – national and sociocultural as well as those separating the reserve and the city – he discovers a politics of resistance that takes him into political meetings of Red Power advocates in Vancouver; AIM encampments along the 'Trail of Tears'; protest caravans descending on the U.S. federal government and its Bureau of Indian Affairs in Washington, DC; an arrest at Wounded Knee; Youth Conferences in Akwesasne; BC chiefs' meetings in Port Alberni; and land claims protests and blockades. Running away from the reserve, Slash returns to it; at first rejecting the ways of the elders, he later finds in them solace and answers, for himself as an individual, and for Native politics and protest. *Slash* outlines a 1960s-originating Red Power agitation that seemed poised, by the early 1970s, to transform the everyday relations of Native peoples, white colonizers, and the state:

> So many things were going on all at once even the newspapers and television couldn't seem to keep up. Roadblocks were being thrown up sporadically everywhere in the province over the cut-off land issue. Occupations of the D.I.A. district offices in different parts of the province were in progress. Sit-ins and demonstrations in government offices and on Parliament Hill were continuous. Rallies at almost every Band in the province went on to keep the people informed on all the stuff that was happening ... People were urged to harvest all Indian foods and exercise their aboriginal rights in their traditional territories and begin trade patterns with other Bands and tribes to spread the food around to insure nobody went hungry. Everywhere, on every reserve, there was a feeling of high activity and energy. If people weren't occupying or attending rallies they were busy hunting, fishing, berry-picking and planting gardens. Wherever there was a gathering people brought out the drums and sang the protest songs and the friendship songs ... A strong feeling of unity persisted among the people. Nobody questioned which Band or which Tribe a person belonged to; everybody was Indian and that was good enough. It seemed for a while that we were going to make it. It must have seemed that way for a while to the government as well. We heard some reports that a statement had been issued to the R.C.M.P. which said that Indian people were the biggest threat to national security since the F.L.Q. thing in Quebec.[5]

Lee Maracle offers a similar, if ultimately less optimistic, trajectory in the life story of a Métis woman, Bobbi Lee. Lee's radical odyssey begins as a Yorkville hippie, encounters anti-war demonstrations and Trotskyist organizers in Toronto, encompasses readings of Malcolm X, Frantz Fanon, Marx, and Mao, and finds its culmination in West Coast fish-ins and the Skid Row proselytizing of NARP in Vancouver. At first resistant to the rhetoric of 'Revolution, socialism, communism, and "offing the pig" and so on,' Lee felt like she was being bombarded with 'all the talk,' worrying that she was being 'sucked into this great wave of whatever it was' that these leftists were doing. But gradually she was transformed by this 'new world' that she had entered; a love of Red Power was rooted in a love of learning, reading, political engagement, and struggling to 'Think Native,' the title of a project NARP worked on with Aboriginal students at the Vancouver Community College. By the end of the 1960s, 'all at once every major city turned out Native youth who were talking about the same kinds of things,' Lee recalled. 'We had minds; we could think.' Anything but mundane, this discovery was a breakthrough, in which past barriers were transcended, and new possibilities embraced passionately: 'Youth everywhere were holding conferences, chiefs were meeting, everyone was talking about our rights; rights we didn't dare to believe existed in the 1950s.'[6]

To understand why the 1960s proved something of a watershed in the development of Native militancy, and to appreciate what this meant in the ironic formation/deformation of Canadian identity, it is necessary to situate, however incompletely, Aboriginal–white relations historically.

Colonization's *Longue* (and Lethal) *Durée*

Precisely because Canadian identity prior to the 1960s was so decisively understood to be dominantly British, Aboriginal–white settler relations in the imperial dominion seemed easily incorporated into appreciations of progress, civilization, and socio-economic advance. Colonization by Europeans was often regarded as an act of benign improvement. Its end product was to elevate the 'Indian,' to educate the 'savage,' and to benefit an 'inferior race.' The path to such betterment lay along the resolute road of racial subordination that was always measured by the yardstick of money, which purchased both property and propriety.

This path, however, was never simply one of Native peoples succumbing to white power. Indeed, in the formative 'fur trade' period reaching from the eighteenth century into the 1850s in eastern and central

Canada, decades of colonizing wars and 'development,' waves of competitive and imperialistic Europeans needed to exercise tact and diplomacy in their dealings with Indigenous bands in order to consolidate trade and military alliances. They desperately needed connections with and enduring ties to what was in effect an Aboriginal lifeline extended to segments of empire's reach into the New World. There were times, then, when a relatively peaceful coexistence seemed to characterize the early period of Native–white contact.[7]

As years of overt military colonization and mercantile trading company dominance gave way, in the 1860s, to nation-building and efforts to consolidate an industrial-capitalist order, white reliance on Native peoples was replaced by a more explicit attempt to forcibly assimilate the Indigenous population. The continued existence of Aboriginal groups thus came to be posed as an 'Indian' problem, a crack in the edifice of nation-building. For much of the post-Confederation century reaching from 1867 to 1967, Native peoples were routinely constrained, the purpose being to make them appendages to white power. Lands that for centuries had been regarded and utilized in specific ways became defined differently, owned as property by acquisitive individuals and authoritative 'companies.'[8] Customary cultures faced invasive and debilitating challenges. Political economies were reconfigured. The material substance of Aboriginal life sagged under the weight of devastating change: pious religious certainties spelled out in letters of destructive conversion an unmistakable cultural genocide; infectious and devastating diseases left a trail of death across lands that had faced much but that had never before encountered such a relentless and catastrophic assault; the mind-altering and wildly intoxicating introduction of alcohol further weakened the Native capacity to resist; and the proliferation of trade items as seemingly innocuous as the copper pot or as brutally lethal as firearms all did their work in undermining Indigenous traditions and practices. After centuries of 'contact' with whites, the landscape of Native–white relations was irrevocably altered.[9]

The violence of this process of colonizing primitive accumulation, in which the dispossession of Native peoples was a prerequisite to the capitalist development of British North America, has long been recognized.[10] It registered, after all, in a reverse Malthusianism. The toll, in hemispheric terms, was staggering. An Aboriginal population that could have reached as high as 125 million was decimated over the course of centuries, reduced by an almost unbelievable 90 per cent. At the time that Europe's colonizing imperative commenced in the 1490s, the Aboriginal population of what is now Canada and the United States – what Native peoples refer to as Turtle Island – likely totalled somewhere between 7 and 18 million. Such population estimates have long been a matter of controversy, in which understating the numbers of Indigenous people has been a cornerstone anchoring white denial of the genocidal nature of a 'contact experience' that many have wanted to portray benignly. For some time the 1492 Native population of North America was conservatively estimated to hover around one million, but this clearly understated the diverse populations of Indigenous peoples who inhabited territories now known as Canada and the United States. Estimates by Russell Thornton, Lenore A. Stiffarm, and Paul Lane, Jr, as well as the political challenge of writings by David E. Stannard and Ward Churchill, have buried forever the seemingly scientific data on Native underpopulation prior to the arrival of white colonizers in North America. And the result is appreciation of the extent of the genocidal obliteration of the Indigenous peoples of what is now Canada and the United States: from possibly as many as 18 million in 1492, Native population plummeted to a few hundred thousand in the nineteenth century. Between 96 and 99 percent of Turtle Island's original population had been exterminated.[11]

Demographic demise was paralleled and culturally extended by Aboriginal marginalization and subordination, processes central to the tangled histories of European colonization's two critical institutions, church and state. These encompassed educational initiatives such as the residential school[12] and processes of dispossession that co-joined coercive campaigns of physical displacement from land and its habitats, broken treaties, and the abuses of the reserve system. Canadian Native peoples – whether they be northern Inuit,[13] the demographically blended Métis populations whose origins lay in the decisively important fur trade, status Indians recognized as retaining their Aboriginal heritage through residence on or historical connection to lands ceded to particular bands, or non-status Indigenous people living in cities or rural regions where they were a decided minority – were at once impoverished and socially marked as 'outcast others.'[14] As capitalism sank its roots, moreover, Aboriginal lives of isolation were deepened by a 'primitivist' reduction of their social being to that of the 'noble savage.' In this caricature Native political economies were typecast as bounded by the harvests of forest and stream. Aboriginal peoples found themselves by the mid-twentieth century curbed in the relentless march of market society and its vehicles of accumulation and exploitation, private property and wage labour, which were also *the* toe-holds that ordinary Canadians relied on for economic security.[15]

To be sure, labouring in the marketplace or securing property as a liveli-hood were anything but 'foreign' to Native peoples, who had deep histories of early involvement with the transatlantic economy of eighteenth-century merchant capital.[16] With the coming of industrial capital and the consoli-dation of its servile state, however, Aboriginal peoples struggled through-out the late nineteenth and early twentieth centuries to secure a place at colonialism's economic table.[17] They did this, of course, on terms that accorded with their culture and the strengths they drew from language, heritage, and a sense of spiritual difference from the white world around them. Yet we should not be overly insistent that Native peoples consciously *chose* traditional economic pursuits and shunned the opportunities of wage labour and the new options offered by the capitalist marketplace. As Robin Jarvis Brownlee has suggested in a perceptive discussion of Mohawk and Anishinabe women's labour in southern Ontario during the interwar years, it is of course true that Aboriginal people objected to the expropriation of their lands and rights, but this did not mean that they refused to enter into market relations and paid employment.[18]

Whether this ordered Native options more than racist exclusion, how-ever, is questionable. As an Anishinabe trapper wrote to officials in Indian Affairs in 1930, 'In a great many places of employment they will not employ an Indian to do their work.'[19] Many Indigenous peoples thus combined particular kinds of paid labour that were seasonal or migratory, and that were for a variety of reasons open to them, with resi-dence on reserves and continued connection to Aboriginal ways of liv-ing. These work options, however, were increasingly defined by the white state through a variety of restrictive laws. Waged employment, then, was possible as long as the economics of casualism could be sus-tained, be it on the docks of west coast shipping, in the migratory har-vests of particular regional crops, or in sectors of urban building trades. The waged work such Native labour contributed was evident from coast to coast and reached far into the developing north as well as penetrating established enclaves of specific expertise at the pinnacle of metropoli-tan capitalism's urban high-rise development. Nevertheless, against the *particular* instances of Aboriginal integration into the advanced capital-ist economy and its waged relations, the *general* process of dispossession and marginalization was markedly evident.

The constricting job possibilities of the 1930s, relieved only briefly by the labour shortages of the Second World War epoch, were deepened by technological innovations that struck repeated blows at all forms of casual labour. Especially pronounced were developments in agriculture that lessened reliance on migratory hands by the 1960s and 1970s. Native peoples experienced declining job opportunities in such sectors as the southern Alberta sugar beet harvest and cross-border migration from Nova Scotia to Maine to pick potatoes and blueberries. Institution-alized racism and the growth of urban and welfare social services in the same period widened the nets of dependency evident among status Indians residing on reserves as well as within an expanding contingent of displaced Aboriginal youth, for whom the lure of the city proved quite pronounced.[20]

This was, however, something less than a 'choice' freely made given the options for Indigenous peoples. Its consequences, with the chang-ing nature of employment possibility by the 1960s, were economically devastating. Native peoples made less money than whites, worked more irregularly, and were confined to the worst-remunerated and least-appreciated employments. Far more reliant on public sector jobs than their dominantly private-sector-employed white counterparts, Aborigi-nal workers found themselves increasingly relegated to the outposts of Canadian occupational history in a racialized constriction of opportu-nity. Less integrated into wage labour, less likely to be found in better-paying and/or unionized jobs, and more commonly unskilled, Indige-nous peoples were the last in the long line looking for work and the first to be laid off, fired, or reduced to welfare dependency. This tightening history of containment is undoubtedly complex and complicated. Many Native acts of agency run counter to its broad outline. Its general con-tours, over the course of decades leading into the 1960s, are neverthe-less undeniable.[21]

Canadian Native peoples were structured into this material cul-de-sac, in part, by a state ideology quickly ensconced in law, one that sustained a pernicious paternalism and cultivated Aboriginal dependency. Evi-dent from the history of treaties commencing in the late seventeenth century, but accelerating with nineteenth-century efforts to pacify Indig-enous populations, was a paternal articulation of 'Crown concern.' Native people were made out to be 'children' or 'wards' of the govern-ment. This proved a legal shield behind which lay generations of racist assumptions and premises. A proliferation of legislation crafted a series of Indian Acts and their revision, reaching from 1850 to 1951, as well as formally creating the Department of Indian Affairs in 1880. This arse-nal of enactment and governmentality limited Aboriginal initiative and freedom of movement under the guise of a state responsibility that was itself the cause of circumscribed Native possibility.

This process unfolded with the creation of barriers to Aboriginal integration into the advanced capitalist economy, blockades that were indeed the building blocks of the historical foundations of the Indian Act. Native bands were forcibly removed from regions where mining or agricultural were being consciously developed by white colonizers and corporate interests. Aboriginal people were prohibited from involving themselves in commercial fisheries, even as these thrived in their own recognized jurisdictions. Limitations were placed on Native people's movements. Doors were closed to Indigenous involvement in the growing infrastructure of competitive, market-based capitalism, as institutions like marketing boards, licensing bodies, and regulatory agencies proved unwelcoming or worse to those perceived as Indian. Native organizers who necessarily travelled off reserves to rally resistance had their status revoked by vindictive Department of Indian Affairs agents through forcible enfranchisement. Legislation often prohibited Native peoples from financing legal claims against land theft and other acts of expropriation without the explicit permission of Indian Affairs officials.[22]

Such restraints to a materially realizable assimilation were reinforced by outlawing aboriginality itself. Rituals and cultural touchstones such as Indian dance or the potlatch were criminalized on the grounds that they contributed to dissipations unworthy of an entrepreneurially acquisitive citizenry. Indigenous healing practices were attacked at the same time that traditional diets and subsistence economies were assailed by state practices and policies. All of this produced something of an undeclared war on the aboriginal body. 'Protected,' even 'defined,' by a colonizing state, the 'Indian' was one of many managed inconveniences in the march of capitalist progress.[23]

Sixties Sensibilities

When reviewed dispassionately, the tortured history of Aboriginal–white relations over the course of the last three centuries reveals abundant indications of colonizing coercion and violent subjugation, as well as much evidence of Native people's agency and creative adaptation. Ironically, contemporary liberal historiography, emerging in the 1970s, and blurring with postcolonial studies in the 1990s, has tended to dull the sharp edge of an early radical recognition of the brutalizing suppression at the core of the colonizing experience, one in which whites ended up decidedly dominant. Three separate but related interpretive accents have contributed to this outcome.

First, accounts of Native-European trade in the first phases of colonial expansion into North America began to rewrite the contact experience as one of shrewd Aboriginal exchange and hard bargaining. Contact had not been, it turns out, a necessarily one-way street of tawdry whites taking easy advantage of innocent and unsuspecting Indigenous hunting and gathering bands.[24] Second, the particularities of Native achievement and accomplishment in the post–fur trade 'age of irrelevance' began to be given interpretive priority. A stress came to be placed on Aboriginal adaptability and survival, rather than on the generalized historical record of subordination, marginalization, and deepening oppression.[25] In response to this analytic trajectory two historians suggested in 1994 that scholarly writing was exhibiting 'an insidious tendency to turn Native agency into colonialist alibi.'[26] Third, re-evaluation of Aboriginal political culture, especially late nineteenth and early to mid-twentieth-century efforts to establish influence with colonial governing authority, has recently paid homage to the reciprocities of Native–white agendas for organization and reform.[27]

All of these interpretive directions contain insight and suggestive reconsiderations of scholarship of varying kinds. They advance knowledge and widen our perspective. Yet it must also be recognized that they are resolutely post-1960s in their attentions and analytic accents. They extol particularities and eschew a larger, generalized experience that a decade of militant and vibrant Red Power activism took aim at with its demand for rights and entitlements and the at times harsh condemnation of a society and its structures of governance claimed to be responsible for Native oppression.[28] Moreover, in the 1960s Aboriginal dissidents saw themselves as part of a large, historic struggle against colonialism, one that linked them to upheavals of peoples of colour around the world.

Native political organizing of course pre-dated the 1960s. Aboriginal scholars have indeed demonstrated the breadth and diversity of Indigenous political traditions, exploring the continuous histories of what Taiaike Alfred has described as 'a consistent struggle to revitalize various Indigenous cultural and political institutions in the hope of restoring the integrity of national communities.' Alfred, born a Mohawk of Kahnawake, begins his book *Heeding the Voices of Our Ancestors* (1995) with the statement, 'It has been said that being born Indian is being born into politics,' an apt aphorism coming from a scholar whose 'nested Mohawk

identity' is rooted in the broad Iroquois political culture of the Longhouse. The Iroquois confederacy, rooted in oral political traditions
reaching back to the fourteenth century, evolved a Great Law of Peace,
the *Kaienerekowa*, that many regard as the foundation of 'a truly democratic system of political organization and the first genuine North American federal system.' Colonization, as Alfred points out, has complicated
immensely the pan-Native identities and politics that were reconfigured
as the Canadian nation-state was born on the backs of Aboriginal dispossession.[29] But throughout centuries of Native–white contact and conflict,
Indigenous peoples engaged in a wide variety of political struggles to
defend themselves and all that sustained them. Often, as in the case of
the negotiations of treaties by the Plains Cree and other western bands in
the 1870s, these undertakings revealed different Aboriginal perspectives,
strategies, concerns, and approaches to living with the colonizer.[30]

This Native political history blossomed in the conflicted histories of
the Ontario Grand General Indian Council; British Columbia's Confed-
eration of the Tribes of the Mainland and its provincial rival, the Native
Brotherhood; endeavours to organize prairie Native peoples from the
1870s through the 1940s; and even a short-lived effort to sustain a
North American Indian Brotherhood in the Second World War period.
Native leaders such as Fred Loft, Andrew Paull, John Tootoosis, and
Jules Sioui built organizations and established traditions of resistance
that played out across Canada throughout the twentieth century.[31]
Métis organizers Malcolm Norris and Jim Brady present an insightful
example of decades of political commitment and engagement, traversing a twentieth-century rebirth of Métis nationalism in Alberta in the
1930s; the formation of various movements and organizations, among
them L'Association des Métis d'Alberta et des Territoires du Nord Ouest
and the Indian Association of Alberta; links to white-dominated parties
of dissidence, such as the Communist Party and the Co-operative Commonwealth Federation, the latter being particularly significant given its
governing authority in Saskatchewan in the late 1940s, when a provincial Métis Society in which Norris and Brady involved themselves experienced a brief rejuvenation; and complicated efforts to recharge the
politics of Aboriginal people in the 1960s.[32]

In this ongoing political struggle, reaching from the eighteenth century into the mid-twentieth century and beyond, differences of region
and identity proliferate. For Norris and Brady the 1950s were, according to their biographer Murray Dobbin, a decade of 'political stagnation.' Yet for the Kahnawake, as Alfred details, a break with 'the Indian

Act mentality' and its reliance on colonial institutions heightened in this period as Mohawk resistance to the expropriation of Aboriginal lands associated with the development of the St Lawrence Seaway produced a tangible shift in consciousness. As band council legal challenges and petitions protesting Seaway expropriations proliferated in 1956–7, the long arm of the federal government's intransigence reached into Kahnawake. Its mailed fist was the enforcement power of the Royal Canadian Mounted Police. 'No surrender' became the watchword of a rising Native nationalism as the Seaway development project 'drove Kahnawake away from a position of trust in the Canadian government.' The stage was set for a new politics of Native organization and challenge in the 1960s, as ideas and answers began to surface that would have been 'inconceivable to Mohawk leaders in the 1950s.'[33]

What I suggest, then, in the pages that follow is that the 1960s were a period of self-discovery as Aboriginal people themselves charted new paths of opposition, demand, and protest. For the colonizing state, and for whites in general, this process had its ironic twist, in which a further belated 'discovery' of Native peoples unfolded. Thus what I call the 'discovery' of the 'Indian' in the 1960s was an unmistakable dialectic of reinvigorated political sensibility. It was conditioned, on the one hand, by the response of a new generation of Aboriginal leaders and youth, whose assertions of their rights, on the other hand, conditioned a liberal state's blundering attempts to resolve Canada's 'Indian problem.' Native peoples, wrongly and lately 'discovered' by their paternalist superiors, 'discovered,' with the help of national and international currents of dissent, a new and vibrant sense of themselves as something more, something other, than what they had been constructed as by the state and white colonial authority.[34]

As Georges Erasmus told *Canadian Dimension*'s Fred Gudmundson in 1984, 'It really wasn't until the very late 1960s that things started to change. Younger leaders started coming forth, finally being able to clearly analyze the position of Native people in the Canadian context, and they began speaking out loudly and publicly expressing our discontent. What we started to see happening was that the squeaky wheel gets the grease, and the grease, in this case, was government programs that were supposed to remedy the situation.'[35] Many Native peoples began to conceive of themselves as part of a Fourth World of anti-colonial resistance. Buoyed by the vitality of Quebec's 1960s revolutionary nationalism, and schooled in the manifestos and radical rhetoric of the U.S. Black Power movement and the escalating demands for independence emanating from African and Asian liberation struggles, militant 'Indians' began challenging Canada and its meaning under the banner of Red Power in the late 1960s.[36] Many more major Native political voluntary associations were formed in the years 1960–73 (86), for instance, than in the entire period from the late eighteenth century to 1959 (61).[37]

One legacy of the 1960s that has refused to be easily put to rest is thus the layered complexity of issues associated with the Aboriginal–Canadian relation, and Native people's justified impatience with an impasse that has existed for generations. The origins of this contested conjuncture, which continues to this day, lay, as Native studies scholar Peter Kulchyski suggests, in the 1960s: 'In Indian Country, the sixties was a time when sea changes led to crises and conflict, and ultimately a new paradigm in Indian-government relations ... For just over 100 years policies were developed at the whim of officials; after 1970 Aboriginal people became major players in policy development.' A fitting final chapter in the ironic narratives of identity in Canada's 1960s, then, centres on the 'discovery' of the 'Indian.'[38]

Material Legacies of Dispossession

As late as 1932 Canada's eminent anthropologist Diamond Jenness would write of the inevitable disappearance of Native peoples.[39] Indeed, it appeared on the eve of the First World War and over the course of the 1920s that conditions on reserves and in the residential schools had taken such a toll that the obliteration of the 'Indian' was a distinct physiological, as well as cultural, possibility. Disease and neglect, as well as systemic and overt racism, all contributed to a slow and seemingly irreversible demographic decline. During the 1930s and 1940s the demographic tide turned. Native populations stabilized and then began to grow, perhaps as a consequence of improved health and welfare, growing immunity to white disease, and increased government spending. For the first time since Confederation, the numbers of registered status Indians living on reserves in Canada topped 110,000, a figure that grew incrementally over the next two decades and began a new, mid-twentieth-century surge. By the end of the 1950s Native peoples had disproportionately high numbers of children under the age of 16, and one government-commissioned report referred to an 'extremely rapid rate of population growth since World War II.'[40]

By the 1960s Canada's Aboriginal population had not disappeared, then, but had grown in numbers. There were about 850,000 Native peoples in Canada at this time. Just under 250,000 of them lived on 2,000 reserves in 1968 and were thus within the jurisdiction and control of the federal government, placed under the provisions of the Indian Act. A further quarter of a million Indigenous peoples lived in urban or rural areas as part of the broader Canadian society. Many assimilated so thoroughly, through intermarriage with whites and other means of adaptation, that they would lose touch with their Aboriginal heritage, or preserve it in quite particular and limited ways. In addition, some 350,000 state-classified Métis, whose ancestors were white and Native, lived in clearly defined western communities as well as being scattered throughout the general Canadian population.

What was striking about Native people in the 1960s, a decade that would pride itself on reform and the expansion of welfare services that was often heralded as a War on Poverty and the creation of the Just Society, was the dire circumstances they lived within. Yet they had managed to survive, their families and collective dignity largely intact, their resiliency and sense of Aboriginal identity preserved. Surveys of the time tend to record the experience of Native peoples who were part of more established, secure, and well-off Aboriginal bands and groups. Nevertheless, the evidence was undeniable. The vast majority of Native peoples living on reserves were trapped in an unrelenting cycle of underemployment, economic destitution, constricting material possibilities, ill-health, and inadequate living conditions. The experience of Canada's Indigenous population was too often one of brutal, debilitating poverty.

In a 1964 sample survey of over 35,000 status Indians living on (73 per cent) and off (27 per cent) thirty-six reserves, it was reported that per capita annual income was just over $300. This compared with an overall Canadian average of $1,400. The average annual duration of employment was a mere 4.8 months. Of 6,327 employable males, only 28.5 per cent worked more than nine months, with 61 per cent employed less than half a year and fully 23.6 per cent able to secure barely two months' work in a given twelve-month period. Average yearly incomes for Aboriginal workers were an inadequate $1,361, when the comparable Canadian figure was $4,000. Only slightly more than 10 per cent of Native *households* boasted combined earnings totalling that much, while more than half of all such domestic units brought in less than $2,000 annually and more than a quarter claimed yearly incomes of $1,000 or less. Heavily dependent on welfare, such Aboriginal families eked out livings of underemployment and low earnings by securing almost 10 per cent of their total cash intake from government cheques. One-third of all families surveyed depended on subsidies from the Indian Affairs Branch. By the end of the 1960s, this government department was spending about $175 million a year on welfare, education, housing, economic development, and the ever-present costs of administration, as well as a further $100 million on health expenditures.[41]

Such state funding was, when registered against acute need, a drop in the proverbial bucket. Reserve living conditions were abysmal. Nine out of ten homes lacked indoor toilets; barely half had electricity; 60 per cent of the reserve population lived in houses of three rooms or less. To be sure, some relatively affluent reserves, close to centres of white population, were much better off. In many remote Aboriginal communities of the north or in isolated prairie locales, however, living conditions were clearly unacceptable. In Alberta, for example, the Slavey Indian reserve of Hay Lake, situated at the northwestern corner of the province near the border of the Northwest Territories, was dotted with log houses with mud floors and leaking roofs. Furniture consisted of sagging beds covered with coats and dirty blankets, metal tubs for melting snow into drinking water, and wood stoves. One-room domiciles, these dwellings lacked space and amenities most Canadians took for granted: the rafters hung with smoked moose meat, dried fish, and wet clothes; and they might shelter ten to fifteen people. At the Manitoba reserve of Norway House-Rossville in the late 1960s one water tap serviced 109 Aboriginal homes, a ratio not out of step with Frederick Engels's Manchester slums of the 1840s or contemporary Third World shanty-towns. With potable water almost non-existent, reserves were incubators of disease, and health problems were exacerbated by malnutrition and alcoholism. Infant mortality rates doubled that of the general Canadian population, while life expectancy on the reserves was almost half that of non-Aboriginal Canada. If anything, the Native situation worsened as mortality rates increased by 8 per cent between 1965 and 1968.[42]

And yet Native peoples persevered. The sums spent on their education, welfare, and health paled in comparison to government expenditure on urban and rural Canadians, who saw their standards of living soar as per capita outlays on schools, universities, hospitals, and other infrastructure improvements peaked in the affluent and expansive 1960s. Native poverty, which in and of itself had not yet severed Aboriginal peoples from their heritage and sense of themselves, was of course not unrelated to the material violence of colonial dispossession, which had, by this point, abrogated treaty rights, restricted commercial and

economic opportunities, appropriated valuable lands, and swindled
Native peoples out of millions of dollars of legal assets.[43]

Even more debilitating, however, was the way in which the state and
its burgeoning social welfare apparatus used Aboriginal poverty as a justification for a decisive assault on Native culture. The residential school
had long been premised on colonialism's need to decisively corrode
Aboriginal identity. It forcibly assimilated the 'Indian' by taking young
children away from their parents, training them in work discipline, and
separating them from the languages and cultural practices of their
ancestors. By the 1960s this was no longer as easily justified as it had
once been, but the residential schools, which many advocated closing
down or phasing out of existence, were given a new lease on life. They
became institutions saving Indigenous children from the supposed
abuses of impoverished First Nations families. Beginning in the 1950s
and escalating into the 1960s, in tandem with the expansion of welfare
services, more and more Native children were forcibly removed from
their families by state agencies claiming that they were 'neglected' or
that 'home conditions [had] been judged inadequate.' As early as 1961,
fully half of the children enrolled in British Columbia's residential
schools were ostensibly there because of parental neglect. At one residential school, half of the children in 1960 were said to have come from
'broken homes' where 'immoral conditions' prevailed; by 1974, this figure had risen to 83 per cent. Nova Scotia's Subenacadie School was no
different, an official reporting in 1967 that 'practically all of the children now in residence have been placed there mainly for reasons other
than to facilitate school attendance.' Subenacadie had become, in the
words of one religious commentator, 'a welfare institution.' Of the
10,000 Aboriginal children attending Canadian residential schools in
1966, fully 75 per cent had been 'placed' because their parents were
judged by white social service workers and other officials as somehow
inadequate.[44]

Known as the 'sixties scoop,' this was the unkindest appropriative cut
of all. It unleashed a decisive and destructive process of familial disloca-
tion, deepening fundamental alienations for both parents and children,
and extending them into worsening social pathologies. Skyrocketing
rates of Aboriginal incarceration, alcoholism, sexual abuse, suicide, and
the flight of Native youth from the reserves and residential schools to
skid row were but the visible tip of the iceberg of dysfunctionality that
colonialism conditioned. For the residential schools lacked both the
resources and the trained personnel needed if the acute problems that

flowed in the wake of this welfare scoop were actually to be addressed meaningfully, which, of course, was never a serious consideration. A 1966 Indian Affairs–commissioned study by George Caldwell, a child-care specialist working for the Canadian Welfare Council, made this abundantly clear. The most telling testimony of the ways in which the 'sixties scoop' ravaged Native communities, however, appears in Aboriginal fiction and life stories, such as Beatrice Culleton's *In Search of April Raintree* (1983) and Maria Campbell's *Halfbreed* (1973).[45] It was also decisive background to later Aboriginal Healing Foundation initiatives and to the findings of the 1996 Royal Commission on Aboriginal Peoples, co-chaired by René Dussault and Georges Erasmus.[46]

An extreme case of the decimation of Aboriginal lives and traditional ways in these years was the tragic destruction of the Ojibwa Grassy Narrows reserve, nestled in the English River–Wabigoon River–Ball Lake region north of Kenora, Ontario. The reserve was relocated in 1963, concentrating Native peoples who had hunted, trapped, and gathered wild rice across a wide expanse of territory into a narrow and claustrophobic cluster of residences. Clan alignments were disturbed, separating people from lands and waters that were integral to their way of life. The Ojibwa of Grassy Narrows were, as a consequence, quickly broken in their spirits. Many became dependent on a state that was taking a more regulatory approach to their traditional avenues of sustenance: hunting, trapping, and fishing. Grassy Narrows degenerated into, in the words of one elder, 'a diseased place to live,' one of desperate rage and unfathomable frustration. A joyless anomie of family breakdown and violence against persons left Native residents painfully reduced to a state of self-destruction. Men, women, and children could not believe that they mattered, that their lives had a future.

Adding lethal insult to this historic process of injury was the decision of Reed Paper, a subsidiary of Dryden Chemicals Limited, a pulp and paper mill located 80 miles upstream from Grassy Narrows, to dump 20,000 pounds of mercury effluent from its chlor-alkali plant into the English-Wabigoon river system. When the Ontario Ministry of Energy and Resource Management finally put a stop to the dumping of mercury pollutants in 1970, after almost a decade of irreversible damage, 300 miles of the Ojibwa's 'River of Life' had been transformed into a 'River of Poison.' Native peoples who had experienced the trauma of being wrenched from the moorings of their traditional way of life on their old reserve now found it difficult to grasp how they could be subjected to this new assault. Not only was taking fish for food now seemingly dangerous, but relatively lucrative commercial fishing and income from guiding were abruptly terminated. As blood tests on Grassy Narrows men, women, and children revealed increasing possibilities of toxic levels of mercury poisoning between 1971 and 1975, Reed corporate executives denied responsibility. The state tried to buy off growing discontent among Aboriginal commercial fishers who had lost their livelihoods with modest forgivable loans that totalled a meagre $6,000. Later in the 1970s, as the crisis of Native poverty, ill-health, and self-destructive behaviour deepened, Grassy Narrows became newsworthy, but residents grew increasingly agitated as their reserve pathology became the stuff of sensationalist journalism. An Ojibwa Warrior Society aligned with the radical American Indian Movement; an Anti-Mercury Ojibwa Group incorporated and lobbied for state aid; and hundreds of thousands of dollars eventually made their way into reserve development from Ottawa and Queen's Park.

Native peoples found themselves trapped in a no-win situation. To shut down the Grassy Narrows region's sport fishery, with its lodges and guiding jobs, would, on the one hand, cripple Native prospects for employment. Succumbing to state pressure to keep the sport fishery open because it was the lynchpin in a lucrative tourist industry, on the other hand, did little more than tell Aboriginal people that their lives were expendable. In the end, the Grassy Narrows Ojibwa opted for jobs. 'We recognize,' they concluded in a seventeen-page 1975 brief to various cabinet ministers of the Ontario government, 'that through employment lies the key to the revitalization of a solid social fabric for our reserve and its people.'[47]

Grassy Narrows may have presented an extreme picture of Aboriginal demise. Yet it was undeniably illustrative of broad trends.[48] Between the 1940s and the mid-1970s thousands of Native peoples were forcibly relocated by the state, their removals from traditional lands and waterways justified by the needs of capitalist development and paternalist argument that improved living standards and sustainable economies lay somewhere else. Nova Scotia's Mi'kmaq, the Labrador Mushuau Innu and Inuit of Hebron and Davis Inlet, respectively, Chemawawin Cree and Sayisi Dene in Manitoba, groups of the Yukon territory's First Nations, and the coastal British Columbia Gwa'Sala-Nakwaxda'xw all experienced the dislocations of state-orchestrated relocation, a process of dispersal, disruption, and quite often unambiguous decline.[49]

In this context, paid work was little more than an impossible dream. Meaningful education became an illusory attainment. In Saskatchewan,

3 per cent of Native people completed high school and 15.5 per cent of the Indigenous population reported that they had no formal education whatever. Bodies were ravaged by the unknown, often unidentifiable scourges of pollutants, bacteria and infection. It is hardly surprising that many isolated reserves fed various beasts of social dysfunction.

Crime ran rampant through 'Indian country.' By 1970 it was estimated that 30 per cent of the inmates in Canada's jails, penitentiaries, and juvenile 'training schools' were Aboriginal, although Native people constituted no more than 3 per cent of the population. In provinces such as Saskatchewan, where Indigenous populations and reserves registered even more of an impact than in more populous and industrially developed regions, Aboriginal incarceration rates reached the astounding figure of 60 per cent. Native peoples constituted no more than one in ten residents in the prairie province. The number of Indigenous men and women in federal penitentiaries soared in the decades 1950–70, increasing fivefold to more than 2,500. Ratios of 'Indian'/Métis to non-Aboriginal incarceration varied in the late 1960s and 1970s from 88 to 1 to 19 to 1, depending on gender and status. Confirming the 'sixties scoop,' Native children were almost eight times more likely than non-Aboriginal infants and adolescents to be placed in childcare programs by various government social services. Between 1955 and 1964, for instance, the population of Native children in relation to the total number of infants and youths under the care of British Columbia child welfare services climbed from less than 1 per cent to more than one-third.[50]

Those whom crime did not claim, death often took. Reserves, especially those physically remote ones, were beset by a rash of suicides and accidental deaths in which out-of-the-way train tracks and highways were the final escape from a soul-destroying immiseration. In a 1965 Saskatchewan Region Indian Health Services report, a doctor noted that 'accidental death' was greatest in the 15–24-year-old group, and included 20 vehicular deaths, 12 drownings, 10 murders, 10 cases of alcoholism and acute exposure, 5 suicides, and 4 deaths by burning. 'They choose methods which are quite final in their result,' he concluded. This same tragic finality and the same methods ostensibly 'chosen' reappeared across the country in 1965 with British Columbia's coast and the Indian Affairs Central Region of Manitoba, northwestern Ontario and Keewatin recording an alarming spate of fatalities. Rarely acknowledged as suicides, the majority of these deaths were young Native men. Their drownings, manglings on railway tracks, hunting mishaps, deaths due to exposure, suffocations, and loss of life behind the wheel were telling testimony to the self-destructive road that many Aboriginal youth took as the only exit they could find from the intolerable nature of their lives.[51]

Most, fortunately, departed the reserve in a more traditional way. They simply left. Between 1959 and 1972, with population growth proceeding, the percentage of status Indians in Canada who lived in urban centres rose from 17 to 28. Ten thousand Manitoba Native people migrated to Winnipeg in the 1960s, swelling the urban Aboriginal population to over 50,000. Drawn to seemingly improved prospects of employment and education, Indian and Métis migrants to the city found themselves mired in similar conditions of unemployment, substandard housing, and higher rates of criminal charges (53 per cent of those arrested in Winnipeg in 1969 were Native). They had escaped what they came to refer to as the 'concentration camp' reserve system only to be incarcerated in the destitution of 'skid row.'[52]

Yet as bad as conditions on reserves were, they were often understandably regarded by Native peoples as not only a last refuge, but as *home*, 'the Indian's only material asset ... without [which] he would be as poor as his poorest cousin, the Metis.'[53] The reserve was a place of many comforts, something of a haven in the heartless world of capital's dictates and the hardened racialized powers of a hierarchical social order. Peter Gzowski wrote in *Maclean's* in 1963 that 'the reserve is the Indian's one guarantee against anonymity, the one reminder of his heritage and his one bulwark against the discrimination he will feel in the city. While no one will get rich on a reserve, no one will starve either.'[54] Wilfred Pelletier, for instance, remembered 'childhood in an Indian village' as a different place, one in which power was not institutionalized, and where authority rested on ability and recognition of how it could be used to further the collective good. Children learned from stories and experience, not from arbitrary dictates. Organization happened when it was needed, but was not preserved as a rigid reminder of power. 'Everyone did something in that community,' Pelletier insisted, but if you tried to find out who managed this process, 'you couldn't.'[55] When Jeannette C. Armstrong's fictional Slash returns to the reserve, as so many Red Power activists did in the aftermath of the 1960s, moreover, he rediscovers the familiar attractions his peripatetic radicalism and urban activism have all but obliterated. 'Like a warm blanket,' they 'wrapped around' his being, melting 'the hard things' inside of him and warmed his soul.[56]

The push off the reserve was thus never only about deplorable conditions. The elusive promise of improvement through assimilation could only be effective if it was sustained by funds from the Department of Indian Affairs. In the mid-1960s, committed to a policy of acculturation through enticement, Ottawa offered Aboriginal families $5,000 to relocate to the city, sweetening the urban inducement with a $10,000 home-purchase grant in 1967. Further cash allotments were available to fund the acquisition of furniture and appliances. More punitive measures were also being imposed on those who chose to stay on the reserve. At Fox Lake, Alberta, where Native people were almost entirely dependent on welfare payments and relief provisions from Indian Affairs, the ration allotment was cut from $7,000 in October 1965 to $1,800 in February 1966. If the carrot would not entice Aboriginal migration to urban centres, the well-applied stick might beat a path in that direction. In the two decades reaching from 1966 to 1986, the number of off-reserve Native peoples climbed by 254 per cent, from 47,496 to 158,944, while reserve populations grew by a relatively modest 27 per cent.[57]

Conditions of deprivation and dependency – on and off the reserve – of course bred resentments and resistance. Native people were practitioners par excellence of James C. Scott's 'weapons of the weak,' as countless Indian agents could testify and the wry humour so evident among Native peoples often confirms.[58] Pelletier, for instance, insists that

Indians are expert at making all programs that the Indian Affairs Branch has ever come up with, a failure by withdrawing. The Indians embrace everything that comes into a community. If you want to build a church, that's fine. We'll help you build that church, etc. Then once they see that they can't relate to that church in any way, they withdraw and the thing falls apart. If you want to build a road, they'll help you build one, with the result that some reserves have roads running all over the place, but nobody uses them.[59]

Protests on and off reserves were hardly rare in the early to mid-1960s.[60] But the everyday sense of grievance that developed on reserves governed by Indian agents and subject to Indian Act dictate was as evident in mundane happenings as it was in organized political challenges to established authority.

A case in point is an anecdote from the Nelson House reserve in northern Manitoba in the winter of 1962. Amid reports of starvation on the reserve, where the entire Native population was reduced to living almost entirely on welfare, the Salvation Army airlifted hundreds of pounds of potatoes into the isolated community, dumping the load on

the frozen expanse of an adjacent lake. The produce lay there, hardening in the frigid air and snow. 'Well, aren't you going to carry your potatoes up to your homes?' demanded the Indian agent. 'Pay us for our
labour,' said the residents of the reserve. The agent retired in dismay,
and the frozen spuds rotted in the spring thaw, eventually washing away
in the melt. Here and there the dialectics of discovery, in which Native
peoples repeatedly confirmed their identities in acts of refusal that
might grow into resistance, bobbed to the surface.[61]

The Dialectics of Discovery, I: The Hawthorn Report, 1964–1966

Anthropologists, as Aboriginal people well know, have some large debts
outstanding to Canada's Indigenous populations. The beginnings of
cultural anthropology, for instance, were infused with late eighteenth-
and nineteenth-century 'scientific' racism, an ideological component of
European imperialism that justified conquest of societies inevitably
judged inferior to those of advancing empire. Ethnocentrism dominated the conceptual universe of early cultural anthropologists. It
gained a further foothold with the caricature of Charles Darwin's evolutionary science that unfolded in the crude perversions of late nineteenth-
century Social Darwinism. Theories of natural selection, competition,
and survival of the fittest were implausibly grafted from the world of
flora and fauna onto the inappropriate physiology of human beings.
The result was an 'evolutionary scale' that placed Caucasians of Europe
and North America above all others. Even if early to mid-twentieth-
century anthropologists could get past their deeply ingrained biases,
which left them captive to a range of assumptions about Native peoples
– most decisively that they were a doomed race, long down the sorry
road to extinction – they found it difficult not to see the Aboriginal
world as one that needed saving by enlightened and superior civil-
izations. And so progressed a history of anthropologically ordered
condescension that began with 'study' and too often ended with misun-
derstanding and worse, including the looting of Native artifacts and the
material undermining of traditional cultures. As Vine Deloria, Jr, commented in 1969: 'Indians have been cursed above all other people in history. Indians have anthropologists.'[62]

It has taken radical, progressive, and humanitarian anthropologists
decades of diligent intellectual and practical labours to begin to overcome this troubled legacy.[63] A small, if indecisive, step forward would be
taken in the mid-1960s by an unlikely candidate, Harry B. Hawthorn, a

traditionally trained anthropologist. Hawthorn commenced his academic career with a study of Maori acculturation in New Zealand, an undertaking supervised by Bronislaw Malinowski and eventually published in the 1944 proceedings of the American Anthropological Association. This accent on acculturation rocked few boats in the 1940s and 1950s, either in scholarly circles or in the corridors of Canadian policymaking in the St Laurent and Diefenbaker governments. In both sectors assimilation was the preferred solution to Canada's 'Indian problem.' A. Grenfell Price, an Australian scholar of comparative Aboriginal policies, reinforced views dominant in government circles and long attributed to Canada's leading anthropologist, Diamond Jenness. Price reported on the advancing assimilationist tide in the late 1940s, assuring the ruling Liberals that 'the ultimate fate of the Canadian Indian must be absorption.'[64]

A mid-1950s study of social adjustment among contemporary British Columbia Indians by Hawthorn, C.S. Belshaw, and Stuart Marshall Jamieson reported widespread evidence of such acculturation. It viewed Native reserves as likely to remain a part of the Canadian landscape because of 'the material and psychological security' they understandably provided a beleaguered population. Yet the 1958-released Hawthorn, Belshaw, and Jamieson publication predicted that 'the acculturative change of the Indian is irreversible and is going to continue, no matter what is done or desired by anyone.' If Aboriginal communities were indeed separate and different from the non-Native Canadian population in many ways, it was also the case that they had not survived unscathed by centuries of white contact. 'No customary actions, elements of belief or attitude, knowledge or techniques,' declared the University of British Columbia academic trio authoritatively, 'have been transmitted from earlier generations to the present without major alteration.' On the eve of the 1960s, Hawthorn, like his anthropological discipline in general, was confident that ongoing change in Canadian Native–white relations was irreversible and destined to result in a 'final point of nearly complete cultural assimilation and racial amalgamation.'[65]

Hawthorn's use of the word *nearly* perhaps signalled some doubts in his certainties of Aboriginal acculturation. In early 1963 Hawthorn was asked by the federal government to canvass Native people's conditions of life and offer suggestions for policy initiatives. The very subtitles of the 1950s vs. 1960s Hawthorn studies – the first stressing social adjustment, the second outlining needs and policies – hinted at the changing sensibilities of the two decades, with the rising concern over problems and addressing them taking pre-eminence by 1963.[66] Hawthorn assembled a research team of fifty-two social scientists, and their two-volume compendium, *A Survey of the Contemporary Indians of Canada: A Report on Economic, Political, and Educational Needs and Policies,* was published by Ottawa's Indian Affairs Branch in 1966–7. It proved a landmark in the 'discovery' of the 'Indian.' This was not so much because of its recommendations, which remained very much framed within an ideology of liberal acculturation, but because of its reasonably objective presentation of Aboriginal malaise. As a copious and stark compilation of evidence confirming Native poverty, substandard housing, marginalization in the wage-labour economy, ill-health, and a poorly functioning residential schools educational system, the Hawthorn report opened eyes long sleepily shut. The high price Aboriginal peoples had paid for the systemic racist barriers blocking full entry into Canadian society was exposed. Hawthorn's report gave scholarly credibility and seeming state endorsement to a series of more informal journalistic accounts of policy failures and abuses. With respect to the residential school system, for instance, Hawthorn and his colleagues pointed out that Native peoples sustained a drop-out rate of 94 per cent before high school graduation. They urged the teaching of Native peoples in their own languages, and found counterproductive the practice of using school texts that routinely depicted Amerindians in inaccurate if not viciously insulting ways. Moreover, given the sorry record chronicled in the 1966–7 publications, Hawthorn and his team could not entirely skirt the irksome issue of Native self-government. They outlined a political culture of dependency on Ottawa and its Indian Affairs Bureau that stifled initiative on reserves and structured Aboriginal bands into reliance on welfare rather than development of local autonomy. Such a state of governance worked decisively against any meaningful acculturation and could not help but highlight the pitfalls of paternalism.

Out of all of this, which was little more than a gesture toward scholarly objectivity and an attempt to grapple honestly with the contradictions of the assimiliationist and paternalistic practices of decades of federal governance, came, however, the Hawthorn Report's most startling 'discovery.' Despite their material location at the bottom of Canada's socioeconomic ladder, and unable to any longer promote assimilation through political dependency and subordination, Hawthorn and his research associates declared Indigenous peoples 'citizens plus.' 'In addition to the rights and duties of citizenship,' they wrote, 'Indians possess certain additional rights as charter members of the Canadian community.' The Indian Affairs Branch thus had a 'special responsibility' to respect Aboriginal difference. Indeed, acknowledging aboriginality and providing funds and programs to enhance it and better offer opportunities of advancement to all Native peoples in various walks of economic, political, and sociocultural life was a cornerstone of the state's responsibilities and crucial to IAB's functioning. Non-Native Canadians, moreover, should be educated in the particularities and 'plus' privileges of Canada's first peoples, a point that many First Nations leaders had impressed upon Hawthorn. While integration or assimilation would undoubtedly be the chosen route of many Indigenous people, these were not 'objectives which anyone else could properly hold for the Indian,' including the federal state. The ninety-one specific policy recommendations put forward by Hawthorn and his extensive network of scholars were developed to further the general 'discovery' of the 'Indian.' In subtle ways, they tried to establish aboriginality as a central component of Canadian identity, one less circumscribed and materially starved than had been the case for many generations.[67]

In the years immediately following the Hawthorn Report, similar views would emerge across a spectrum of increasingly radical Canadian thought. Inquiries into poverty, for instance, generated understandings that Aboriginal problems demanded new and creative programs, solutions lying well beyond conventional sights.[68] Prodded by this post–Hawthorn Report sensibility, Lester B. Pearson's Liberal government used its last months in office to consult with the expanding number of late-1960s Native organizations, seeking advice as to how the Indian Act might be revised and government policy be improved.[69] But the writing on the wall of Aboriginal–white relations was taking a contentious turn, as the battle over the words that accompanied the murals and exhibitions at Expo 67's Indians of Canada Pavilion revealed. Arthur Laing, minister of the Department of Indian Affairs, pleaded with Native leaders 'to turn away from brooding on the past' and to work with him to present a story of national accomplishment. When he previewed the mildly critical Aboriginal pavilion storyline, which contained restrained rebuke of white churches and their attempts to obliterate Native culture, Laing was taken aback. It was reference to his own department as historically treating 'the welfare of the Indians ... as proper work for retired soldiers' who regarded Indigenous peoples as 'amiable backward children' that, in the words of one DIA official, caused Laing to 'just about shit.' The minister threatened to close down the pavilion. He demurred only when it was impressed on him that the resulting political scandal would prove far more embarrassing than the brief passages he regarded as 'the anguished cry of the frustrated.'[70]

The Expo pavilion's message was nothing compared with the realizations slowly germinating in other quarters, where the dialectics of discovery took turns that Laing could barely have imagined. As the 1960s unfolded there would be those – Native and white – who would embrace a revolutionary acknowledgment that at the core of Canadian nationhood and identity festered an ugly reality that was not going away. The dialectics of white 'discovery' of the 'Indian' thus moved over the course of the late 1960s. They shifted away from Hawthorn's liberal gift of 'citizens plus'[71] to the brutal pessimism of one radical journalist who had spent much of the late 1960s experiencing the reality of the reserve:

> The Indians, rats in psychologists' wire cages, have been our subjects for between 100 and 350 years. They have been on the receiving end of almost every bureaucratic program, religious crusade, and psychological gimmick conceived by the Canadian mind. They have been poked, prodded, berated, praised, analyzed, frightened, studied and theorized about. They have been treated like guinea pigs and supermen, like children and saints. They have been ignored, brainwashed, flattered and ridiculed. Each new wave of crusaders which has surged over the reservations, only to stagnate in sloughs and ditches, has been convinced that it was going to succeed, that it was going to turn these savages, these barbarians into civilized human beings, into citizens who would be an integrated and productive part of Canada. Something has always gone wrong. The wells have been poisoned; the wave has turned into slimy backwaters breeding infection. Every day more disinfectant is needed, the walls have to be built higher, the lid is harder to keep on.[72]

The Dialectics of Discovery, II: The White Paper, 1969

To bury this national shame, the newly elected Liberal government of Pierre Elliott Trudeau moved to revive the assimilationist goals of previous administrations. It completely rejected the recommendations of the Hawthorn Report. On 25 June 1969 – exactly one year following Trudeau's electoral victory – Jean Chrétien, minister of Indian Affairs, delivered the White Paper on Indian Policy to the House of Commons. It was so named because of its preliminary status as a position document developed prior to any potential legislative enactment approved by cabinet. Commencing with an acknowledgment of difference as well as recognition of disadvantage, the White Paper nevertheless struck out in a new direction. It laid responsibility for the 'Indian problem' at the feet of governing authority, to be sure, but it did so in an odd way, singling out the 'special treatment' Native peoples had received from Canadian society and its state. 'Special treatment has made of the Indians a community disadvantaged and apart.' In order for the country's Indigenous population to lead 'full, free, and non-discriminatory' lives 'a break with the past was required.' That entailed jettisoning 'the separate legal status of Indians and the policies which have flowed from it,' keeping 'Indian people apart from and behind other Canadians.' The Trudeau government proposed to end forever any semblance of a 'plus' tagged to Aboriginal citizenship.

To do this the state would offer enhanced and positive recognition of 'the unique contribution of Indian culture to Canadian life.' It would develop services for Natives through the same channels and from the same agencies as other Canadians drew upon, help those who needed aid the most, recognize lawful obligations, and begin the process of transferring lands into the hands of Native people. But there was a catch. In the process the Indian Act would be repealed. Responsibility for Aboriginal people would be shifted from the federal government to the provinces. Most importantly, the Department of Indian Affairs and Northern Development would be wound down, and Ottawa would appoint a commissioner to consult with Native people in order to establish procedures for the adjudication of land and other claims. Many Native leaders during the 1950s and 1960s had requested just such reform. More ominously, treaty claims and obligations, while acknowledged, were declared 'limited.' They were judged both inequitable in terms of their capacity to address all Indigenous peoples as well as inadequate as a means of coming to grips with Aboriginal economic, welfare, health, and educational needs.

Complications of implementation aside, and with due consideration given to consultation and a viable transition period, the Canadian state was advocating an end to the frustration of being colonized by doing away with all vestiges of aboriginality enshrined in legal status and the practices, policies, and institutions of the state. In sounding the death knell of 'different status,' Trudeau's Liberals offered Indigenous peoples 'full social, economic, and political participation in Canadian life.' The road that the White Paper outlined had no name, but it was undoubtedly a one-way street to assimilation. Once taken, there was no looking back.[73]

The premise of the White Paper's break with the past was not racist, at least not overtly so. Trudeau's purpose was undoubtedly to strike a blow against racist structures of 'being Indian' in the 1960s. But in its ahistorical and abstracted commitment to individual rights and freedoms it stubbornly refused to grasp that deep structures of oppression cannot be undone by rational declaration. Not unlike his attitude toward Quebec, where Trudeau was adamant that long-standing grievance not be redressed by appeals to special status, the new prime minister's 'Indian policy' was governed by the axiom that no sector of society could sign treaties with another. The rights and good of all depended on each and every Canadian being absolutely equal. It was a heady and powerfully seductive ideology, eminently bourgeois in its liberal, individualist, rationalism, and entirely divorced from the material realities within which Native peoples lived.

Chrétien's and Trudeau's White Paper had not fallen from the sky, although to some in the Aboriginal community it appeared to have landed with a surprising, indeed shocking, thud. Rather, Trudeau's rhetorical commitment to participatory democracy and a new politics of consultation had led to a series of 1968–9 meetings that many in both the Aboriginal leadership and the Indian Affairs bureaucracy undoubtedly felt were the right step in formulating new and needed policy changes. A National Indian Council, first established in 1961, was but one of many Native organizations that, throughout the 1960s, garnered more state funding and became better organized and more effective, albeit in a moderate way, in lobbying for the interests of Aboriginal people. Over the course of the summer of 1968, and into the spring of 1969, such bodies, although troubled by the snail's pace of progress in their talks with Indian Affairs functionaries, nevertheless commended Chrétien on what they thought was a new era in Native–white relations. Some of the more mainstream Aboriginal leaders sensed a partnership in the making, rather than a continuing subordination in which Indigenous people were always subject to official directives.[74] New Native leaders, however, were suspicious of the state and its agenda, troubled by Chrétien's arbitrariness in reorganizing the Department of Indian Affairs in September 1968 without so much as a nod in the direction of Indigenous input. It was this militant section that would help lead the offensive against the White Paper's perceived coercive acculturation, opening a decisive, final door in the dialectics of discovery.

The Dialectics of Discovery, III: The Birth of Red Power

With the notable, if partial and incomplete, challenge of the Hawthorn Report a liberalization of Aboriginal–white relations reached from 1950 to 1970. Directed from above, mandated by the federal state, the revisionist drift as an unambiguous drive to forced assimilation culminated in the proposed 1969 White Paper dismantling of Native people's unique legal status. What shocked Aboriginal leaders in 1969, however, was that alongside a seemingly fresh and welcomed rhetoric of participatory democracy, consultation, and negotiation lay the same governmental arrogance and arbitrary top-down politics of rule by directive as well as the seeming continuity of state efforts to deny Indigenous identity.[75]

Reforms of the Indian Act in 1951 eased or eliminated many restrictions that had been introduced in the 1880–1930 years. The small print of these changes, however, tended to suppress Aboriginal culture and force status Indians to give up their identity as Native if they pursued involvement in Canadian society. Along with the granting of federal voting rights to Native people in 1960, these were bricks in the assimilationist causeway. They were able to be laid in less coercive ways precisely because the past restrictions on Aboriginal freedoms had so egregiously circumscribed Indigenous cultures. The notorious apartheid-like pass system, which required prairie Native peoples to secure the permission of the Indian agent to leave designated areas in search of work, to visit distant relatives, or to purchase items in nearby towns, seemed altogether antiquated in its obvious denial of freedom of movement. The outlawing of customary rituals, such as the Sun Dance or the potlatch, no longer seemed necessary. A liberal loosening of state containment was thus a useful hegemonic initiative. For Native peoples to vote, drink in public establishments, or go to non-residential schools with other Canadians, to become lawyers, doctors, or priests, they had to relinquish their state-constructed 'status' as Indians. Generations lived with this arbitrary 'choice,' and the consequences for Native peoples were sufficiently debilitating that some in Aboriginal circles embraced the White Paper's agenda.[76] Had this history of the state elaboration of Indian policy, which took on new vigour and wider significance in the 1960s, been the entirety of the narrative of Aboriginal identity formation, then the process of 'discovery' would have been one-sided and undialectical.

Things were not to prove so simple. For arguably the critical inducement to the post-1950 climate of change was the rise of Aboriginal activism, with its widening circle of demand that soon reached into the very heart of colonization's historic project, culminating in demands for self-determination and self-government. In the process the assertion of Aboriginal identity complicated immeasurably the understanding of Canadian identity. A particular 1960s chapter in this long book of protest and challenge would be the text of Red Power, an Aboriginal statement written in the vernacular of a particular moment.

Native political organization prior to the 1950s has undoubtedly been inadequately researched and perhaps unfairly caricatured as insufficiently militant. Kiera L. Ladner's blunt conclusion that successful Canadian Aboriginal organizations were little more than 'puppet regimes which were to aid in the goal of "civilizing" the Indian' may well be unduly dismissive. Yet her general stress on the Canadian state's sorry record of dealing with Native peoples is hardly open to challenge. Few such pre-1950 Aboriginal movements and political bodies embraced tactics and strategies of militant opposition. Even F.O. Loft's trade union–influenced League of the Indians of Canada, founded at the end of the First World War from a base on the Six Nations Reserve near Brantford, Ontario, and spreading across the country in the 1920s, premised itself on cultivating government sympathy and assistance. It proved too much of a thorn in the side of Duncan Campbell Scott's Indian Administration: amid state fears of alien-endorsed revolution in the epoch of the Winnipeg General Strike, Indian agents accused Loft and his co-workers of 'Bolshevism.' Police vigilance and the 'unrelenting opposition of Indian Affairs' played their part in helping to bring the League of the Indians of Canada to a state of 'near collapse by the early 1930s.' It is thus impossible to understand the limitations of pre-1950s Aboriginal activism, as the struggles of the Métis organizers Malcolm Norris and Jim Brady make abundantly clear, without appreciating the colonial state's capacity to constrain it in a variety of ways.[77]

By the late 1950s and 1960s a new day of Native political organizing was dawning. Veteran Native organizer Andrew Paull is a case in point. Paull's activism began in the first third of the twentieth century. He founded British Columbia's Allied Tribes movement in 1916 and helped establish the Native Brotherhood of British Columbia in 1931. In the 1940s Paull was involved in the formation of the North American Indian Brotherhood (NAIB), which championed land claims and Native rights and headed a drive to forge a cross-country mobilization of Indigenous peoples. Tutoring a rising activist in BC's interior, George Manuel, in the 1950s, Paull also challenged the newly ensconced head of

Indian Affairs, Jack Pickersgill. When the long-time Liberal Party func-
tionary first enunciated the reinvigorated liberal drive to abolish the
Indian Act and dismantle all special legislation concerning Native rights
in 1956, Paull was outraged. With half a century of social activism under
his belt, he told a *Vancouver Sun* newsman in 1958 that Indigenous peoples were not interested in Pickersgill's coercive program of assimilation. Such whites, Paull spat out, were 'the lowest form of animals.'[78]

Under Paull's guidance, Manuel emerged as a powerful regional
voice in the NAIB. From there, the rising BC activist struggled to bring
Native organizations together in the west coast province. He believed
that a unified Indigenous movement would be more effective in prying
concessions and change from Ottawa. Such efforts resulted in an
Aboriginal Rights Committee, which presented submissions to the federal government in 1960 and, eventually, a broader-based NAIB under
Manuel's leadership. These BC-based mobilizations were paralleled by
developments in Manitoba leading to the formation of the National
Indian Council (NIC), its founding taking place in Regina in August
1961. Led by future White Paper advocate and promoter of the privatization of Indian reserves, Saskatchewan's William Wuttunee, the NIC
made room for the more militant Manuel on its six-person executive.[79]

Meanwhile, in central Canada and in upstate New York, Iroquois activists were spurred to protest by the land expropriations, relocations, and
disruptions associated with the late-1950s development of the St Lawrence Seaway. While legal battles launched by the Kahnawake Mohawks
failed to secure what they referred to as 'Sovereign Territory,' by 1957
an Aboriginal language of resistance came to be premised on understandings of armed invasions of their land. Condemning their reduction
to the status of 'Displaced Persons,' 'the Band of Caughnawaga Indians'
railed against the pretences of 'Conquest' and 'Expropriation,' declaring, 'We Indians are the primordial inhabitants placed here by the Great
Spirit and universally recognized as the only true Citizens of North
America. Humanity blushes at the events of this period of Colonial History and Dictatorship, and Usurpation.' Among the Awkwesane, strad-
dling the United States–Canada border at Cornwall, similar frustrations
and angers seethed in the 1950s. At the central Ontario Six Nations
reserve in Grand River country, the largest Aboriginal reserve within the
borders of Canada, a rebellious contingent dedicated to the traditions of
the Longhouse seized the reserve Council House in March 1959. They
declared themselves the sole ruling body on the reserve, independent of
both the provincial Ontario state and its federal counterpart in Ottawa.

The RCMP raided the occupied Council House and restored the authority of the Department of Indian Affairs–recognized system of an elected band council. Such developments marked the late 1950s, in Laurence M. Hauptman's words, as a breeding ground for the Red Power strategies of the 1960s. They were destined to be the springboard into new developments in both Canada and the United States, where Iroquois militants would figure prominently in the rise of the American Indian Movement and in the revival of Native nationalism.[80]

Regional difference (coastal vs. interior organizing in BC as well as regional/provincial/national separations across the country), compounded by divergent strategic orientations that now separated increasingly militant and more mainstream leaderships, hampered Aboriginal organization in the late 1950s and early 1960s. The movement never quite managed to follow the road of unification that many such as BC's George Manuel advocated. But there was no mistaking the growth in what was now a discernible 'Indian movement.' The Indian-Eskimo Association of Canada was formed in Toronto in the first years of the 1960s. It aimed to bring Indigenous people's complaints to public attention and to broaden understanding between Natives and white Canadians. Although it contained Native people among its leading officials, it was staffed primarily by whites committed to Aboriginal rights and was thus something of an anomaly in a decade characterized by the struggle for Native people's self-determination.[81] From Newfoundland to the Yukon Aboriginal activists forged new organizations over the course of the 1960s, with BC in the forefront, eight Native associations being established on the west coast during the decade. Ontario was not far behind, its long-established and relatively affluent reserves sustaining six new 1960s-founded Aboriginal bodies.[82] By 1967–8 and the publication of the Hawthorn Report, the National Indian Brotherhood had appeared to represent status Indians, and the Métis Council of Canada was founded as the voice of non-status Aboriginal peoples.[83]

This vibrant organizational and agitational context was further complicated by the growing belief that Canada's 'Indian problem' was the equivalent of the U.S. crisis of race relations, out of which came an escalating civil rights struggle. Peter Gzowski, writing in *Maclean's*, found 'Our Alabama' in Saskatchewan, where 'Indian lover' was an epithet hurled with the same abusive vitriol as the Dixiecrat's snarled 'nigger lover.' Gzowski detailed the racism of the prairie province, where an 11 May 1963 killing of Allan Thomas, a Saulteaux man, near North Battleford, one hundred miles northwest of Saskatoon, brought national attention to the impoverishment of the region's 7,500 status Indians and Métis. Exposed in the process was a long and deep history of racism embraced by the area's white population of 12,000. The nine white males arrested the day following Thomas's murder had descended on an Aboriginal encampment, pulling down tents, and fighting with the unsuspecting Thomas and his friends. They were, like many in the vicinity, farmers and small businessmen. 'There *is* race prejudice in North Battleford,' concluded Gzowski, 'and it is ugly and in some ways frightening to behold.' Gzowski could nevertheless not refrain from qualifying this racism as peculiarly 'Canadian,' differentiating it, seemingly, from other (possibly 'American') racisms: 'It is, if this is possible, the race prejudice of a gentle, friendly people.'[84]

When Malcolm Norris wrote in support of an Aboriginal march of 400 on Kenora's city hall late in November of 1965, an early protest demanding the preservation of Native rights and resources ostensibly secured by treaty, he espoused the need for militant action. Kenora's march, he argued, had done more to 'dramatize ... the Indians' plight than all the conferences held ... in the past three years. ... Not a major paper in the country ignored the incident.' Red Power, Norris clearly thought, was long overdue. Norris also took aim at the Gzowski-like view that Canadian racism was somehow more benign than the seemingly overt direct discrimination against African Americans in the U.S. south. He acknowledged that 'the white Canadians' attitude to the Indian is different,' but asked rhetorically, 'is it more defensible?' Norris thought that drawing fine lines of distinction between types of discrimination was less than useful, and he decried the viciousness of Canada's capacity to ignore its First Nations and to marginalize them with a dismissive 'we don't give a damn.' The Kenora protest, he suggested, showed that racism could be fought against in Canada, and he hoped 'the Indians learn this lesson.' Norris's relatively understated remarks made him a marked man in government circles and among moderate Aboriginal leaders and organizations.[85]

By 1969, however, few could close their eyes to the new reality of Native protests and the backlash against them. Northern Saskatchewan, site of killings and unexplained deaths of Métis families and Aboriginal activists, was being reported on by the Canadian Broadcasting Corporation as the 'Mississippi of Canada.'[86] A white social worker who supported Native people's struggles was brutalized by police, and communities like North Battleford looked to some little different than Selma, Alabama. Saskatchewan premier, Ross Thatcher, an ardent assimilationist chilled by talk of 'Indian' culture, treaty rights, and self-government, warned that Aboriginal grievance in Saskatchewan was a ticking time bomb. Progressive Conservative MP, Don Mazankowski, stood in the House of Commons to report on a supposed plot to train Canadian Indians in 'riot techniques.' In the anti-terrorist wing of the RCMP, documents were produced warning of a dangerous, AIM-inspired Aboriginal movement, part of an international conspiracy that, in its demands for social and economic equality for Native peoples, as well as insistence that their land claims be recognized, 'had become the principal threat to Canadian stability.' Red Power was giving the RCMP a bad case of the security state jitters.[87]

'Indian country' appeared to be, by the late 1960s, in a state of race conflagration. The dialectics of discovery gave rise to Aboriginal rebellion. It voiced its discontents and opposition to white violence with a militancy that was foreign to an older Aboriginal leadership's quiet, often stoic, gentility. Indeed, the Black Power movement in the United States, its banners emblazoned with Malcolm X's phrase 'By any means necessary,' was increasingly influential in young Native activist circles. This emerging layer of radical leadership took to heart African-American critiques of internal colonialism, such as those of Stokely Carmichael, which alluded to the subordination of Aboriginal nations. All of this prompted Native militants to take increasingly aggressive stands of opposition to white power that were theoretically informed by the growing anti-imperialism of the epoch. Anti-colonialist, pan-African movements led by figures such as Kwame Nkrumah and theorized by Frantz Fanon and others permeated the thought of young Canadian Aboriginal militants. Black Panther spokesmen received a warm welcome among Native activists in the Canadian west, where they were embraced as fellow revolutionaries.[88]

A dissident Aboriginal leadership emerged out of the ferment of the 1960s, and it soon expressed its impatience with the old ways. Silent vigils and protest marches, such as a 1965 Slavey demonstration that carried placards into the Alberta legislature crying out for 'Help' and declaring, 'We Want Work,' or 'We're People First, Not Just Indians,' gave way to angrier, more robust rallies and occupations. Even as staid a publication as the mainstream *Time* magazine appreciated that radical change was in the air, declaring in May 1967: 'For the first time, Canada's Indians have begun to think of themselves as a single ethnic group ... an Indian civil rights movement is in the making.' In November 1969, Aboriginals on both sides of the Canada–U.S. border seized

Alcatraz Island in the San Francisco Bay and defiantly declared the former prison site Indian territory. 'We are a proud people. We are Indians! Our Mother Earth awaits our voices. We are Indians of All Tribes. *We hold the rock!*' One of the leading Aboriginal Alcatraz activists was Richard Oakes, an Akwesasne Mohawk who had grown up at St Regis, near the Canadian border, on a 'big reservation, six miles square, with three thousand people and three thousand problems.' A young iron worker who dedicated his life to Red Power in the late 1960s, Oakes was shot and killed in 1972 by an outraged YMCA caretaker. The security-minded camp official exploded in murderous anger as Oakes argued with him about Native boys who had ostensibly been taking the camp's horses without permission. Only months before the Alcatraz occupation, a Mohawk woman, Kahn-Tineta Horn, addressed a Canadian student audience, her rage at Trudeau's White Paper program exploding as she cried: 'Why don't you all go back where you came from. We were doing fine before you came. We own the land; we're your landlords. And the rent is due.'[89]

A 1970 collection of essays by Aboriginal writers and activists in Canada gathered together thirteen distinct statements addressing aspects of Red Power. Typical in his views was Andrew Nichols, a Malecite and executive director of the Union of New Brunswick Indians:

> There is a definite element of determination in the Malecite and Micmac of New Brunswick to seek changes, to be active in bringing about changes and to play a meaningful responsible role in process of changes. I've seen Indian people gritting their teeth for a fight; that's what it is, you know, change a way of life for a hundred years. That's the proverbial way of attracting a mule's attention – hit the son of a bitch right between the eyes. If that's what Indian people have to do to bring about changes – they're going to wield the biggest goddam two-by-four on a stubborn 'power structure' which has been screwing them for generation after generation. The destiny of Indian people will not be determined by the fickle finger of Fate; it's going to be determined by Indian people – and let no one forget it![90]

Harold Cardinal, author of the highly influential *The Unjust Society* (1969), and a mere 24 years old at the time of the book's publication, warned of the consequences of continued federal government suppression of Native organizations. If the state insisted on following the path of coercive assimilation, 'then the future holds very little hope for the Indian unless he attempts to solve his problems by taking the dangerous and explosive path traveled by black militants of the United States.'[91] By 1968, spokesmen like the Okanagan Tony Antoine of the Vancouver-based Native Alliance for Red Power, the Manitoba Métis George Munroe, and the Saugeen-Métis Duke Redbird all articulated and represented a new explosiveness that characterized Aboriginal militancy.[92] 'I am the Redman / I look at you White Brother / And I ask you / Save not me from sin and evil / Save yourself,' declared Duke Redbird.[93] Saskatchewan Métis author Howard Adams penned *Prison of Grass: Canada from the Native Point of View* (1975), a powerful Aboriginal New Left assault on white colonialism and the imperialist subjugation of Native peoples. He later confirmed: 'In the 1960s there was a parallel between Red Power in Canada and Black Power in the U.S.' Indeed, when Malcolm X was assassinated in 1968, Toronto's Native activists co-sponsored a memorial for the martyred black leader with their African-Canadian counterparts.[94]

The White Paper's arrogant and arbitrary expression of the starkness of the state's resurgent program of repressive acculturation no doubt galvanized further the growing militant Red Power movement of the later 1960s.[95] But it was centuries of subordination and generations of abuse, 'discovered' in the changed climate of radicalism that was 1967–8, which really ushered Red Power into being. As a *Star Weekly* journalist reported in May 1968, 'The strong talk of the militants [was] far more common than the whispers of the conservatives.' The state's rhetoric of participatory democracy conditioned rising expectations. They were soon squashed, however, in a coercive denial that Canadian Aboriginal peoples would be granted something of the 'plus' of their historical claims on citizenship rights. In the new revolutionary tone of the 1960s lay an inevitable clash that Trudeau's complacent liberal reification of individual rights and the marketplace of meritorious economic advance merely hastened. 'I don't think we should encourage the Indians to feel that their treaties should last forever so that they are able to receive their twine or their gun powder,' Trudeau declared contemptuously in a Vancouver speech in August 1969. 'They should become Canadians as all other Canadians and if they are prosperous and wealthy they will be treated like the prosperous and wealthy and they will be paying taxes for the other Canadians who are not so prosperous and not so wealthy whether they be Indians or English Canadians or French or Maritimers and this is the only basis on which I see our society can develop as equals.'[96]

This was no longer acceptable. As Cardinal's *The Unjust Society* made abundantly clear, Red Power militants had no love for the Indian Act that Trudeau proposed discarding. The 'legal' construction of Aboriginal identity was about as far from the growing consciousness of Indianness among Native peoples as it is possible to imagine. To those Indigenous youth and their elders who had 'discovered' a sense of Red Power in the 1960s, obliterating this aboriginality 'from above' was no solution to centuries of dispossession, exclusion, and bigotry that whites had visited upon Native people. Cardinal coined the term 'buckskin curtain' to convey a sense of the racist indifference that had been lowered over Canadian society with respect to the accumulated wrongs done to the country's Indigenous population. Carefully chosen to mock Western 'democracies,' which prided themselves on their superiority over communist societies that needed 'iron curtains' to contain their populations, Cardinal's 'buckskin curtain' was an ironic reminder of the arrogance of countries like Canada. Playing on well-known metaphors of Canadian identity, contrasting seeming Canadian pluralism with the less-tolerant United States, Cardinal demanded the right to remain 'a red tile in the Canadian mosaic.' He insisted that the buckskin curtain had to go up. Native people wanted no part of 'a white paper for white people created by the white elephant.' They would no longer listen to words spoken with 'the forked tongue' of the white state. If all the Just Society could offer Canada's status Indians and Métis was 'cultural geonocide,' Cardinal insisted that Trudeau and Chrétien had merely amended the American adage, 'The only good Indian is a dead Indian.' The revised Canadian axiom may have been more palatable, but it was no less lethal: 'The only good Indian is a non-Indian.'[97] Canadian identity had been trumped with metaphorical cards drawn from its own self-proclaimed deck.

Cardinal's book articulated as text what Native peoples across Canada were undertaking in practical protests and everyday undertakings that proclaimed a rebirth of Aboriginal identity. Akwesasne militants blockaded the International Bridge at Cornwall on 18 December 1968, protesting duties levied on articles valued in excess of five dollars. Hundreds of Natives, mostly women and youth, battled the RCMP, who arrested forty-one of the Mohawk dissidents, including Kahn-Tineta Horn from the Kahnawake community immediately south of Montreal. After months of negotiations, the Native militants wrung important concessions from the state, securing Aboriginal rights to freely traverse the international border that bisected their 'nation.' Out of this struggle came the *Akwesasne Notes*, a militant Aboriginal newspaper that would prove of considerable importance in spreading the message of Native rights and Red Power throughout Canada and the United States. Mohawks rooted in the St Regis reserve led a spiritual revival that utilized a cross-continent caravan to rebuild Aboriginal appreciations of traditional religious values and spirituality. By 1969 they had reached California, where they met with students of the newly established San Francisco State College's Indian Studies program. They lectured on the Longhouse tradition, conducted Iroquois dances, and discussed the International Bridge protest. All of this linked loosely with the development of the American Indian Movement, whose pivotal leader, Russell Means, had been involved in a 1964 symbolic claiming of Alcatraz Island for all Aboriginal peoples.

AIM, established in Minneapolis in 1968, had at first little connection to Canadian reserves or American reservations, and was in 1968–9 a nascent, but growing, pan-Indian movement. An urban-based organization, it welcomed *all* Indigenous peoples into its ranks and aspired to be a national voice of Red Power. The mobilizing Mohawks of Akwesasne would eventually include Richard Oakes, who led the November 1969 seizure and nineteen-month jurisdictional control of Alcatraz in the name of 'Indians of All Tribes.' The same year saw revived protest on the Six Nations reserve as an Iroquois Declaration of Independence was drafted in opposition to the Canadian Liberal government's White Paper. One month after the U.S. publication of Vine Deloria Jr's powerful indictment of internal colonialism and embrace of Amerindian spiritual revival, *Custer Died for Your Sins: An Indian Manifesto*, a November 1969 Winnipeg meeting of religious elders decided to hold an Indian Ecumenical Conference. Aboriginal militants were, by this time, routinely crossing the Canada–U.S. border, often in defiance of immigration officials, on their way to various political meetings and strategy sessions. On 29 August 1969, for instance, a large intertribal motorcade crossed the Cornwall International Bridge en route to the Algonquin Maniwaki reserve, refusing to pay the bridge toll. The Maniwaki Labour Day weekend gathering, with hundreds in attendance representing seventy-five distinct Native nations, heard angry testimony of Aboriginal discontents: police brutality, residential school abuses, unemployment, and alcoholism topped the list. But it was the direction of the emerging Native rights movement that animated many, who were tired of going slow and fed up with soft talk of the need to avoid violence. Rose Ojek, an Ojibway from Upper Slave Lake, Alberta, was adamant: 'The violence is here already! There are young Indians in Alberta who are going to burn the schools and the churches ... I can't stand it when I hear of talking peace!'[98]

The birth of Red Power in Canada thus unleashed a flood of demand
that encompassed a range of change, from advocating national self-
determination to championing government-assisted development of
Indian business, or 'red' capitalism. Given the rich resources of some
reserves, which in 1970 included gas and oil potential on Aboriginal
lands estimated to total $2 billion in value, it was indeed possible that
specific bands could promote and profit from development projects.
This had long been curtailed by the Indian Affairs Branch's support for
what one official in 1967 characterized as 'marginal, low profit enterprises' that did not threaten large capitalist domination of the Canadian
economy. 'How is it that rich people are so poor?' asked the anonymous
Ottawa bureaucrat. 'Why can't Crown corporations and commercial corporations be set up, primarily under Indian control but with expert help,
to exploit the resources? Why can't the Indians hire their own management talent?' These were questions also asked by Harold Cardinal. His
assault on the unjust society was in part motivated by a belief that the late
1960s represented a final moment of reform possibility, one that needed
desperately an infusion of state funds into programs of assistance, training, and development on Canada's reserves.[99]

Most Red Power advocates were to the left of Cardinal. Even before
the White Paper they represented a revolutionary refusal of incorporation into the Canadian capitalist state and marketplace. One expression
of this was the non-reserve–based Native Alliance of Red Power (NARP),
a decidedly youth-oriented New Left Vancouver body with connections
to west coast Maoist and Trotskyist political organizations. Founded in
1967, NARP was led by a small but committed cadre. It nevertheless
managed to produce and distribute 5,000 copies of its international
newsletter; to staff a 'Beothuck Patrol' that provided protection to the
most vulnerable of urban Aboriginal street people, whose intoxication,
poverty, or work in the lowest sectors of the sex trade subjected them to
the abuse of police and others; to hold educational forums and a variety
of socials; and to propagandize in the interests of various Aboriginal
actions, including the Akwesasne International Bridge protest and the
occupation of Alcatraz. NARP intersected directly with various local
Aboriginal initiatives in the late 1960s, including the Nisqually fish-in
near Olympia, Washington. This action was supported by the Seattle
Liberation Front, actress Jane Fonda, the Cree activist and celebrated
folksinger Buffy Sainte-Marie, and the Black Panther Party, arguably the
model for NARP's understanding of Red Power. NARP also supported
the Fort Lawton, British Columbia, efforts to repatriate Native land

expropriated for military use by the Canadian state. At a Vancouver conference of residential school officials, NARP targeted those attending
with a leaflet of condemnation, then followed with a protest rally. As a
founding member of NARP, Henry Jack, noted, this Vancouver voice of
Red Power was composed primarily of 'ex-convicts, young Indian run-
aways from the schools, young drop-outs from school, some academics
(those who suck-holed their way through school) and unemployed as
well as young workers who lived in the city.' Committed to end the racism they experienced in their everyday lives, NARP activists were drawn
into the wider struggle for self-determination and the realization of
their destinies as human beings. Like other Red Power advocates across
the country, they were firm in their belief that 'all the Indian peoples of
North America are cousins, members of the same country, INDIAN;
that we are not of Canada or the United States,' and that it was necessary for the 'scattered Indian groups' to consolidate and collectively
oppose 'a fat, degenerate, ignorant enemy.'[100]

The program of the Native Alliance of Red Power appeared in the
organization's newsletter of January–February 1969. Its eight points
refused the taxation of 'a racist government that has robbed, cheated,
and brutalized us'; demanded an education that exposed 'the true history of this decadent Canadian society'; called for an immediate end to
the arrest and imprisonment of Indian and Métis peoples, freedom for
all Indigenous 'brothers and sisters now being unjustly held in the prisons of the country'; and trials for Native peoples to be conducted before
juries, judges, and officials of their Aboriginal peers. In addition, NARP
insisted that all treaties were to be honoured but that this alone was
insufficient atonement for the loss of Native land, which required nothing less than full and fair compensation for Canada's Indigenous peoples in their entirety. Deploring the divisions fostered among status and
non-status Native people, Amerindian and Canadian, Métis and Indian,
the Red Power statement singled out the large capitalist corporations
that had 'raped the natural resources of the country' as especially culpa-
ble for Native exploitation. Insisting that Aboriginal people should be
paid foreign aid to allow them to develop territories justly constituting
the Indian Nation, NARP declared defiantly, 'We want to develop our
remaining resources in the interests of the red man, not in the interests
of the white corporate elite.' Red Power was about 'Resistance, Love for
Our People, Coming Together to Fight for Our Liberation,' and it was,
in 1968–9, very NOW![101]

Ironically, this ringing manifesto had commenced with a commitment to self-determination that NARP insisted could never be furthered as long as the Indian Act and the colonialist Indian Affairs Branch continued to exist and exercise power over Native peoples. It called for the abolition of such statutes and institutions. With the June 1969 White Paper embracing exactly this course of action, the ramifications of such a legal and institutional dismantling of Aboriginal–state connections became anathema to most Native leaders and their constituencies on and off reserves. The White Paper managed to do, in the charged climate of the late 1960s, what centuries of past oppression could not: it brought Canada's Indigenous peoples together in a broad consensual opposition to the white state. But this shift also tended to drown the young and militant voices of Red Power in the deeper waters of Aboriginal negotiation with various levels of government. As Bobbi Lee concludes, the Red Power momentum of 1967–9 sank in the post–White Paper Aboriginal activism, which moved increasingly back into a state-funded series of chiefs' conferences and other more moderate developments. By 1972, she concludes, 'the tactics of the movement were usurped by the growing presence of government-funded organizations. Fewer people came out to the demonstrations organized by Red Power militants. They began to look like fringe fanatics.'[102]

From his base in Alberta, Harold Cardinal helped to orchestrate what would subsequently be heralded as the response of Canada's Métis and Indian population to the Trudeau-Chrétien mythology that such white heads of state could 'lead Indians to the promised land.' Under the authorship of the Assembly of Indian Chiefs of Alberta, what came to be known as the Red Paper offered a point-by-point refutation of the federal government's proposed revision of Indian policy. The document demanded a serious negotiation of the 'Indian problem' through dialogue, reform, and state commitment to materially improve the chances of Native people to emerge from the deplorable conditions of reserve destitution and urban squalor. Adopted by the National Indian Brotherhood, and presented to Trudeau by 200 Indian leaders gathered in Ottawa to meet with state officials on 2–3 June 1970, the Red Paper stopped the implementation of the White Paper's policy shift. It proved an embarrassment for Indian Affairs head Jean Chrétien. Increasingly radical Native mobilization nevertheless did not lead to recognition of the Red Paper's essential demand, which hearkened back to Hawthorn's view that 'Indians should be regarded as citizens plus.'[103] In the brief but momentous period of Aboriginal–white relations from 1966 to 1970, the 'dialectics of discovery' had come full circle. Nowhere was this more apparent than in the title of Harold Cardinal's 1977 book *The Rebirth of Canada's Indians.*[104]

The Legacy of Red Power

In the nearly forty years since the clash between the White and Red Papers, Canada's 'Indian problem' remains as contentious as ever. Aboriginal peoples, however, have mounted a consistent and often quite successful set of campaigns to secure title to their lands, preserve their culture, and redress lives of poverty, ill-health, educational abuse, and neglect. At times they have even managed to win reparations of a sort, as in the admittedly inadequate material compensation finally secured for the suffering many generations of Native children endured in the residential school system. Slowly and always in the face of much resistance, Native people have pushed past Trudeau's 1969 speech on Aboriginal and treaty rights, in which he proclaimed that compensation for past injustices was an impossibility in a bourgeois democratic order. 'We will be just in our time,' he said. 'That is all we can do.'[105] Every victory, however, has been overshadowed by the continued oppression of Native peoples.

During the 1970s the struggle for Native self-determination took on a new character.[106] Much of this was related to the brutal suppression of Red Power in the United States. The cross-border transnational nature of the Native rights movement was evident in the reception accorded Dee Brown's *Bury My Heart at Wounded Knee* (1970) in both Canada and the United States. As AIM mythologized Wounded Knee further with its 1973 occupation and armed standoff against the Federal Bureau of Investigation at the Pine Ridge Indian Reservation, Red Power activists in the United States such as Dennis Banks and Russell Means became well known in Canada. In the aftermath of a series of 1972–5 trials and aggressive repression that signalled an undeclared war on the part of the U.S. government against the most militant section of the Aboriginal movement, it was apparent that to the south no quarter was being allowed AIM radicals. They were now the targets of a virtual extermination order by the state. An AIM warrior, Leonard Peltier, a Sioux-Ojibwa brought up on the border of Canada and the United States, escaped north, seeking refuge in familiar territory. Indicative of the meaninglessness of the border to Native peoples, Peltier moved among relatives and friends in British Columbia, Manitoba, and Alberta. He was eventually arrested at a remote Cree encampment, 160 miles west of Edmonton and imprisoned at Oakalla, outside of Vancouver, awaiting extradition hearings that would see him returned to the United States and railroaded into prison. While incarcerated at Oakalla, Peltier was adopted by the Kwikwasutainwook people of the Kwakewlth in a Vancouver Island potlatch ceremony, given a plot of land and the name 'He Leads the People.' In Vancouver, the Indian Centre coordinated a Peltier defence campaign that utilized protest marches as well as traditional Aboriginal ceremonies involving sacred pipes, sweat lodges, and medicine bags, drawing support from Native peoples in both Canada and the United States. Unfortunately, such efforts could not roll back the repressive tide. Peltier's victimization and the more general assault on AIM was a transnational declaration that Red Power would be obliterated by the state, which was willing to use any means necessary to rid itself of an irksome foe.[107]

Given the brutal and relentless suppression of AIM in the 1970s, it is not surprising that Aboriginal activism in Canada combined protest and more moderate methods of opposition. New organizations such as the Native Women's Association of Canada and the Inuit Tapirisat of Canada complemented the institutional developments and political organizing of the 1960s. Major land claims and sex-discrimination (involving the 'out marriage' provisions of Aboriginal women losing their status entitlements through marriage to non-Natives) cases were fought through the Supreme Court of Canada in 1973. Native blockades at Kenora contested ownership of Anicinabe Park. The Quebec government's proposed hydro-electric development of James Bay culminated in a successful opposition movement of Cree and Inuit peoples, who wrestled the state to negotiate the first modern treaty involving hundreds of millions of dollars of compensation for Aboriginal cooperation. In the Northwest Territories the Dene blocked the construction of the Mackenzie Valley gas pipeline, resulting in a state inquiry headed by BC Supreme Court Justice Thomas Berger. By the 1980s Aboriginal civil disobedience was commonplace as the Lubicon Lake Cree fought militantly for recognition of land claims in Alberta, the Innu in northern Quebec and Labrador battled to stop NATO flights over their homeland, and the Temme-Augaina Anishnabii in the Temagami region of northern Ontario struggled to restrict lumbering in a 40,000 hectare area of six townships. Major land claim victories were secured in the courts of British Columbia. The 1990s saw an eruption of militancy at Oka/Kanesatake in Quebec and at Stoney Point in

Ontario. In both cases, Natives occupied lands and clashed with provincial police. An officer was killed and the army called in to face off against armed Natives in the former case. In the latter an unarmed militant, Dudley George, was shot dead by the Ontario Provincial Police (OPP). Nothing much had changed as the 1990s gave way to the opening decade of the twenty-first century.[108]

Of course not all Aboriginal peoples were militant opponents of capitalism and the state. As Métis radical Howard Adams, who led a cross-Canada caravan of Native protest that descended on Parliament Hill in 1974, only to be violently rebuked by the RCMP, has suggested, the success of post-1960s Aboriginal demands forced material concessions from the state that further divided Indigenous peoples. As the crumbs from the governing table of Indian appeasement grew, opportunities for red capitalism proliferated and with expanding possibilities for Native business came an increased class differentiation in the Aboriginal community. Conservatives and radicals clashed, as indeed they always had within Indigenous circles, but the standoffs grew more and more embittered as the stakes rose and the opportunities for corruption and chances to garner cash proliferated. The result, according to Adams, was a leadership layer of conservative, pro-capitalist, and corrupt Native 'politicians' whose elitism separates them from the masses of Aboriginal people and whose lock on Indigenous organizations provide 'havens for multinational investment' and conduits for state aid. Adams went so far as to declare much of the Métis/Indian leadership of our times as little more than 'mafia gangs' whose purpose it has been to eradicate the radical political potential of 1960s Native organizing.[109]

Yet it remains undeniable that the legacy of the militant 1960s survives in Canada's growing Aboriginal movements, more so perhaps than in any other section of society.[110] This was symbolized dramatically in 1990 when attempts to implement federal constitutional reforms resting on recognition of Quebec as a distinct society, orchestrated by Conservative Prime Minister Brian Mulroney and agreed to by the provincial premiers in the Meech Lake Accord, were scuttled in the Manitoba legislature by the sole Aboriginal MPP, Elijah Harper, an Oji-Cree from Red Sucker Lake. Procedures required that there be unanimous consent in the legislature before constitutional amendments could be debated. Harper held an eagle feather for spiritual strength. Quietly refusing to follow his fellow politicians, the Aboriginal parliamentarian held his ground of refusal, knowing well that Native peoples resented deeply a constitutional recognition of Quebeckers as a distinct society without similar acknowledgment of the cultural and historic differences marking out Native peoples from all other Canadians. Harper delayed his assent and the Meech Lake Accord died.

Elijah Harper's national prominence in 1990 signalled the irony of the dialectics of the 'discovery' of the 'Indian.' That process, so much of which took complicated and complex turns in the 1960s, left Canadian identity irrevocably tied, for better or for worse, to the conditions of Native peoples. It is surely not accidental that from the mid-1960s to the mid-1990s there have been some 900 royal commissions and other government inquiries/reports on Aboriginal matters, roughly 35 such studies and hearings a year.[111] If the colonial white state preferred a coerced assimilation that rocked few boats of conventional, capitalist authority, Native peoples rediscovered and revived in their Red Power the possibility of resistance and refusal. They would countenance no more the brazen denial of their past and subordination of their being.[112] This was a discovery of Aboriginal power that had a long history, one chapter of which surfaced meaningfully and with considerable political creativity in the 1960s and that has proven impossible, in the years of change that followed, to stifle and suppress.[113]

PART V
Conclusion

Chapter Eleven

Ironic Canadianism:
National Identity and the 1960s

In 1967, Canada's centennial year, Blair Fraser published a book entitled *The Search for Identity: Canada – Postwar to Present.* It was a thoughtful reflection by one of the country's leading mainstream journalists. Fraser, a force at *Maclean's* from the mid-1940s until his death in a canoeing accident in 1968, was known for his connections to politicians in power and officials in the Ottawa bureaucracy. He also had an acute sense of the post-1945 remaking of Canada. Fraser understood well the destabilizing cauldron of the early 1960s in which an old Canada melted down. Chapters in his book touch on much of the material outlined in this account: Diefenbaker's populism; the Cuban missile crisis and nuclear weaponry; the scandals of politics, reaching their high point in the Munsinger affair; and the changing mood in Quebec.

At its roots, Fraser's argument was a simple one that culminated in complexity. Canada, prior to the 1960s, was understandable. For all that Quebec mattered, English Canadians mattered more. 'O Canada,' for instance, while eventually proclaimed the country's national anthem in 1980, was but one of a number of such songs that competed with one another for this official recognition in the century after Confederation. Its main rivals were undoubtedly *God Save the King* and *The Maple Leaf Forever,* but *Rule Britannia* retained pride of place among many Canadians:

> In days of yore, from Britain's shore,
> Wolfe the dauntless hero came

Expo 67 (York University, *Toronto Telegram* Fonds, FO433, 1974-002/069).

And planted firm Britannia's flag
On Canada's fair domain ...

Children of the 1940s, grown to adulthood in the 1950s and early
1960s, remembered chanting in their grade school classrooms: 'Over all
these children, in all the far-flung lands of the British Empire, the
Union Jack will be unfurled in the breeze. The sun never sets upon our
flag. It flies on every continent, in every ocean – a symbol of freedom,
justice, fair-play, and honest dealing for every man who dwells beneath
its folds.' Canadian identity, prior to the 1960s, was a subset of British
identity, and it was, whatever its uniqueness, unmistakable in its attachment to empire and to understandings of colonizing superiorities. By
the mid-1960s, however, 'this Canada had, if not quite vanished, at least
faded into quaintness and old age.' A new Canada was being born,
Fraser concluded, but that is where the simplicity ended and the complications, seemingly endless, began. For, as had long been evident, 'tensions in Canada are never merely two-way. Nothing so simple as north
against south, English against Irish, French against German. In the patterns of hostility are a kaleidoscope of regional and religious, personal
and political, social and economic, cultural and linguistic prejudices in
which no combination is reliably predictable.' This had been known,
intuitively, for decades. But the mid-1960s would mark a moment when
'the nation's normal malaise' suddenly became 'acute.'[1]

In understanding that the old Canada was now forever gone, Fraser
was grappling with what others, from George Grant to Hugh MacLennan,
also appreciated. This original, largely conservative, sensibility wrestled
with the ways in which Canadian demography and economics twisted in
the winds of change after the Second World War. Left views, by the mid-
to late 1960s, also began to wrestle with the meaning of a changing
Canada. Immigration altered the sociocultural and political terms of
trade, not only between French and English, but among all Canadians.
Few could ignore the ways in which a rising American empire, riding a
tide of expansive consumerism, had managed, by the 1960s, to thoroughly displace older attachments to the British Empire of the mid- to
late nineteenth century. Like George Grant and Gad Horowitz, Fraser
asked, 'Home-owned or not, can a small nation resist absorption into the
culture, the folkways, the patterns of life in a neighbor ten times as big,
twenty times as rich, a hundred times as strong?'[2] 'Development' seemed
to deny it.

Fraser clung tenaciously to long-standing associations of Canadian identity with the land and a northern environment. This was perhaps an exercise of wishful thinking. Like many ardent Canadian nationalists, Fraser insisted that the true north was too different in its barren bleakness to ever truly be colonized, thereby ensuring that 'Canada will not die.' As television sets, washing machines, and the explosion of the suburbs left their indelible imprint on the landscape north of the forty-ninth parallel, however, these convictions waned. 'Superhighways devour uncounted acres of fertile land, and the second highest incidence of automobiles achieves, in the metropolitan areas, a second highest air pollution,' moaned Fraser. 'Ugly little towns prosper,' he continued, 'all calling themselves cities and all looking like faithful copies of Omaha, Nebraska.' His response to this value-added alteration of the physical and cultural environment was blunt: 'This is not a Canada to call forth any man's love.'[3]

For his part, one of Canada's premier authors of the period, a friend of Fraser's and five-time winner of the Governor General's literary award, whose novels included *Barometer Rising* (1941), *Two Solitudes* (1945), *Each Man's Son* (1951), and *The Watch That Ends the Night* (1959), concurred. Hugh MacLennan's 1961 *Seven Rivers of Canada* had celebrated a sense of Canada as geographically determined by the efforts of white colonizers to utilize its rivers to control the northern half of the continent. Intellectually indebted to Laurentian historians such as Donald G. Creighton, whose *The Commercial Empire of the St. Lawrence, 1760–1850* (1937) posited the centrality of the St Lawrence river system to the mercantile success, settlement, and ultimate birth of Canada, MacLennan, over the course of the 1960s, came to think differently. As Neil S. Forkey has recently suggested, MacLennan's reissuing of *Rivers of Canada* (1974) backed away from constructing Canadian identity as a heroic utilization of its river environments. Instead, the author chastised Canadians for squandering their resources and hoped for a day when it would indeed be 'possible to regard the rivers of any land as precious in themselves, as more than raw materials for human convenience.' Rivers, once conceived as conduits of national identity, were, with the 1960s, now deserving of appreciation on their own terms. Like so much else, they too, had a discrete identity, and one that need not be subordinated to the nation.[4]

In the introduction to his 1974 book, entitled 'Thinking Like a River,' MacLennan confessed that his first book on rivers, which he began writing in 1958, was a product of his contentedness in the settled understanding of Canada. The rivers that he wrote about then rescued him from his subjective immersion in his last novel, *The Watch That Ends the Night*, an exploration of the youthful idealism so evident in the Spanish Civil War. That liberation transported him back into his Canadian being, which he saw, at the time, as 'an enormous landscape' that was 'eternal.' Soon, however, MacLennan, who lived in Montreal and taught at McGill University, experienced 'the crack in the human psyche – universal, terrible, possibly wonderful, affecting everyone on our planet – which produced the watershed of the 1960s and caused the rivers of human thought, emotion, and morality to flow in new and strange directions.' National identity, for MacLennan, fractured, splintered, and could hardly have been pieced back together so that it looked the same. Its eternal being was little more than a social construction of a specific historical moment: 'A Canadian of 1945 could barely recognize the Canada of now.' In a comment that relates directly to the opening chapter of this book and the dollar crisis of the early 1960s, MacLennan wrote: 'We lost more than our old sense of the value of money – a very dangerous thing to lose for the reasons that money, as Somerset Maugham so shrewdly noted, is a sixth sense which conditions the functions of the other five. The poor did not lose their sense of the value of money; they never do. But this time the rich did. And worst of all, the governments lost it.'[5] Like George Grant, MacLennan was lamenting what the powerful and the governing elite had sold for a song, and no repetitive chorus could reclaim the Canada that had been turned into a financial transaction.

Recognition of this was not unrelated to the populist polemics of one of Canada's most iconoclastic journalists of the 1960s, Pierre Berton. His *The Comfortable Pew: A Critical Look at the Church in the New Age* (1965) and the subsequent *The Smug Minority* (1968) assailed the complacency of an old order, drawing on the more substantial researches of John Porter's classic sociology of stratification, *The Vertical Mosaic: An Analysis of Social Class and Power in Canada* (1965) to suggest that the Canadian Establishment, while undeniably self-perpetuating, was dangerously close to facing is own particular Waterloo. Transformative tendencies seemed very much in the air.[6]

This was evident in the youth revolt of the decade, one that Hugh MacLennan and Pierre Berton, unlike so many of their generation, were not simple-mindedly repulsed by. MacLennan wrote of the young of the 1960s that they often went crazy in their rage and contempt for an older generation which had ruined the cities and produced a system that looked like a cross-hatch of the assembly line and the boxes within boxes of the modern high-rise. In those years I literally swam in the broth of students in the most harassed university in the land and I could not have dodged their anger if I had tried. Which I didn't. I learned that they were rejecting, either with fury or with despair, nearly all of the values and many of the methods which had produced the stupendous power of humanity in the mid-twentieth century.

Berton, too, saw this momentum of refusal mounting in the decade: 'The hippies in their rejection of the timetable and the clock represent everything the establishment has been preaching against. Their real blasphemy is that they do not believe in the virtue of work for work's sake.' So much of Canadian national identity in the era of empire's colonial expansion had been related to work and its ethics that this quintessentially 1960s development, which departed dramatically from the conventions prevalent up to mid-century, altered significantly the touchstone of being Canadian. For many of a specific generation this had became an unknown: 'The end of an epoch, the dawn of something else and nobody knew what.' MacLennan, unlike Berton, appreciated that the shake-ups of the 1960s rocked Canadian national identity to its roots. In this sense MacLennan grasped what Berton could never, given his diehard commitment to Canadian nationalism, acknowledge. The symbolic celebrations of 1967 notwithstanding, MacLennan observed: 'In Canada the bright promise of the Centennial Year and Expo 67 did not last as long as the Centennial Year itself. During the kidnapping crisis of 1970 we asked ourselves how it was possible for such things to occur in what we had been accustomed to believe was the most orderly country on earth.' Even if Marx and Engels were not being quoted, their words echoed in many an ear: 'All that is solid melts into air, all that is holy is profaned.' MacLennan, struggling to 'think like a river,' rightly took the 1960s as having written *finis* to an outmoded understanding of Canada: 'Ours is not the only nation which has out-travelled its own soul and now is forced to search frantically for a new identity. No wonder, for so many, the past Canadian experience has become not so much a forgotten thing as an unknown thing.'[7]

This is not exactly the conventional wisdom. J.L. Granatstein's concluding volume to the Ramsay Cook–edited 'Canadian Centenary Series,' for instance, certainly acknowledged that there was much divisiveness in the Canada of the middle 1960s. It nevertheless concluded

that the tone of national identity was upbeat in these years, especially as
the country celebrated its one hundredth birthday. By 1967, Granatstein suggested in the last lines of his book, 'the doubts and hesitations
that had dominated the nation since 1957 seemed to have been swept
away in a splendid surge of optimism. In their place was a new decisive-
ness and leadership. Or so many Canadians believed.'[8] Berton was even
more effusive in his suggestion of the great triumph of national identity
in this period, on which he waxed eloquently and enthusiastically in
his own nationalistic literary monument, *1967: The Last Good Year.*
Published in 1997, Berton's thirty-year retrospective account of the
decade's symbolic centre concluded of Canadians' accomplishments:
'The greatest revolution was the revelation that we had created a world-
class, forward-looking nation.' The great triumph of 1967 was 'an awakening of spirit that seduced us all ... we shared an invisible bond as we
pondered our past and present and resolved to build a brighter future.'
Berton's hindsight highlighted *The Smug Minority*'s contemporary
paean to 'Progress' while conveniently sidestepping the extent to which
he had previously scaffolded this sense of history's march on a 1960s
irreverence, stressing the social fissures of the era and their erosion of
conventional certainties. Quoting one of his favoured Liberal politicians, Judy LaMarsh, Berton looked back in pride on how, by the late
1960s, Canadians had grown 'up to be one hundred together, and we
all shared that experience. We learned to have our own style.' Whereas
Canada in 1967 had, for Berton, been a land of them vs. us, a great
mythical subtreasury 'open to challenge' and indicative of the power of
vested material interests, a site where freedom was too often lacking
and needed to be struggled for, in 1997 the aging maverick seemed to
reverse political judgment. Growing older, he had come to highlight
not difference and change, but consolidation and consensus. Canada,
as an imagined community, seemed, in Berton's nostalgic reassessment
of 1967, born of the 1960s.[9]

A sober consideration of the actualities of the era suggests otherwise.
No sooner had this national identity emerged from its tortured past
than it imploded as new challenges and new discontents littered the
landscape and clouded the horizons of being Canadian. The 'things' of
national identity were, by 1968, clearly falling apart. The mythologies
and symbolic representations of Canadian national identity that consolidated, for instance, in the mid-1960s, seemed assailed from many quarters in the immediate post-1967 years. Understandings of the peaceable
kingdom were rocked by the escalating violence of the *indépendantiste*

movement in Quebec, just as they were rejected with authority by Aboriginal militants. It was difficult to see Canada in a peaceful, consensual light after the publication of Pierre Vallières's *White Niggers of America* (1968) or Harold Cardinal's *The Unjust Society* (1969). The violence of wildcat strikes in 1965–6 was followed by bomb explosions in Montreal and Native fish-ins, occupations, and protest blockades. Trudeaumania's euphorias, the enthusiasms of the mainstream, gave way to the unruly demonstrations of New Left radicals as the margins moved menacingly toward the centre, the politics of 'Revolution Now' a threat that could not be ignored. Universities, so long priding themselves on staid civilities and the deference of the young, became raucous playgrounds of a youthful generation of often wild, imaginative, even apocalyptic dissidents.

Women who had, not so long ago, seemed content to live out their days and nights encased within Betty Friedan's *feminine mystique*, comfortable in the suburban roles of housekeeping and childrearing, now demanded much more.[10] As they insisted on their liberation and the rights that it bestowed on them as persons, the world changed: sex and fashion, politics and everyday life, workplaces and communities, would never be the same again. With Canadian women refusing to succumb to biological determinism, proclaiming their right to choose when they would give birth and when they would not, advocating free abortion on demand, the most basic of social relations were reconfigured. Just as the Cold War thawed in the early to mid-1960s, lifting for a time the nuclear threat that had shadowed the seemingly complacent 1950s, so too did the feminist assault on the rigidities of gender relations raise the curtain on the behind-the-scenes confinements that women had lived within for generations. No longer would it be possible, on any number of fronts, for a Gerda Munsinger to be typecast in the ways that made her a household name in 1966.

The roughly 1.6 million non-British newcomers who immigrated to Canada from 1947 to 1966 were also unlikely to embrace seamlessly the kind of British-Canadian identity that had figured prominently in representations of nationality prior to the 1960s. More of these displaced persons, refugees, and migrants from other lands came to Canada in any given year after 1948 than had been admitted to the country in the entire decade of the 1930s. As José Igartua has recently suggested, the stretching of the boundaries of citizenship that occurred in various postwar debates over immigration policy taxed national identity to the point that many questioned the precipitous jettisoning of 'the British connection.' In the late 1940s, those who promoted the official changing of the name of Dominion Day to Canada Day drew the ire of newspaper editors who asked, 'Surely it is possible to love Canada, to give her our first affection and loyalty, without going about with a chip on our shoulders in narrow nationalism, and seemingly in dislike and suspicion of other countries of our own British Commonwealth?' Answering its own query, the *Ottawa Journal* noted in 1946 that this 'sort of thing' wasn't 'Canadianism.' Rather, it was 'an inferiority complex.' These words appeared under the title 'Young Men in a Hurry.' Fifteen years later, Victoria Day celebrations had given way to rowdy street confrontations between urban working-class youth and police. Young men were in a hurry to do different things. The rhetoric of a national identity certain of its British-Canadian essence had given way, in a decade and a half, to the language of riotous nihilism. The signs in the street pointed in the direction of national identity's troubled 1960s future.[11]

One reflection of this was, ironically, supposedly a defining moment in Canadian national identity's consolidation: the 1964 parliamentary debate over replacing the Red Ensign with a new and distinctive Canadian flag. From Confederation in 1867 into the 1950s, one measure of the hybrid nature of Canadian national identity, unmistakably entwined with British dominion status, was the country's flag. At Canada's birth in the 1860s, the official national standard was the Union Jack, commonly perceived 'to the immigrant and to the Canadian-born ... as being the patriot signal of his national defence.'

It's only a small bit of bunting,
    It's only an old coloured rag,
Yet thousands have died for its honour
    And shed their best blood for the flag.

It's charged with the cross of St. Andrew,
    Which, of old, Scotland's heroes has led;
It carries the cross of St. Patrick,
    For which Ireland's bravest have bled.

Joined with these is our old English ensign,
    St. George's red cross on white field,
Round which, from King Richard to Wolseley,
    Britons conquer or die, but ne'er yield.

Over the course of the twentieth century, however, the Red Ensign, which situated a Union Jack in the upper hoist, defaced in the fly with the Canadian coat of arms, both of these symbols appearing on a red background, gradually became the de facto Canadian flag. A 1945 order-in-council stipulated that this Red Ensign should fly over all federal buildings in Canada and abroad until such time as Parliament adopted a national flag.[12]

When, in 1964, Prime Minister Lester B. Pearson proposed that Canada indeed adopt a new flag, he drew attention to the waning of Canada's British dominion national identity. Pearson's public statements that neither the Union Jack nor the Red Ensign could possibly appeal to the majority of Canadian citizens, who were not British descendants, drew the ire of an old guard centred in bodies like the Royal Canadian Legion. Dispensing with the Union Jack, either flying on its own or integrated into the Red Ensign, invoked shrill cries that the new flag was an irreverent slap in the face of 'God, the Bible, and all those attributes usually understood by the general term "Christianity."' Moreover, cutting the Union Jack adrift slighted 'the number of brave men who have given their lives in defence of that Flag.' In the words of Mabel Harbour, writing for the British-Israel-World Federation, the Union Jack/Red Ensign were proper expressions of Canada's place in the 'Family of Nations which now compose the BRITISH COMMON-WEALTH OF NATIONS.' This was a unique constellation of countries that 'gradually grew up from small beginnings and their National Heraldry kept pace, until it developed into something of great significance in the world, each Nation having its own distinctive insignia, yet all using the UNION JACK showing their participation in the Common-wealth, and their allegiance to one King.'[13] Divides of language, region, and ethnicity articulated the contentiousness of the issue. Almost three-quarters of French Canadians supported designing a new Canadian flag, but less than one-third of anglophones agreed. Among English-speaking Canadians 35 per cent preferred the Union Jack, 23 per cent opted for the Red Ensign, 31 percent thought a new flag a good idea, and 11 per cent had no discernible opinion.[14]

Commencing in June 1964, and heating up in November-December, the parliamentary flag debate, the corresponding newspaper editorials across the country, and the all-party committee struck to adopt a flag design were the last hurrah of an entrenched nineteenth-century British-Canadian imperialist attachment to empire, its institutions, and its

values. As representations of a new flag featuring various configurations
of the maple leaf contended with the symbolism of the Union Jack and
combinations of colours, most Canadians came to accept the inevitability of change. Diehards nonetheless expressed their discontent in
extreme statements of admonishment. An Ottawa correspondent complained in a letter to the editor, 'The Karl Marx plan for world conquest
decreed that national corruption and spiritual decay must be the first
fruits of ultimate victory ... We now understand the Liberal Party's
desire to strike the Canadian Red Ensign.' A like-minded Toronto opponent of jettisoning the British-inspired colours declared a new flag little
more than 'a rag of appeasement, thrust upon us by a dictator who has
split the country.'[15]

Reaction of this nature notwithstanding, including John Diefenbaker's
last-ditch effort to derail Pearson's initiative, a new Canadian flag was a
fait accompli by mid-December 1964. Mike Pearson's preferred design of
three red maple leaves bordered by blue bars (the 'Pearson Pennant')
was rejected by the all-party parliamentary committee. Ottawa's irrepressible ex-mayor, Charlotte Whitton, voiced a harsh, all-too-common aesthetic judgment with her comment that Pearson's proposed flag looked
as if the country had suffered a nose-bleed. Dropping this obviously
unpopular design like the proverbial hot potato, the committee
endorsed a single red maple leaf on a white background centred between
two red stripes. Only the Tories on the panel dissented. There was talk of
the Conservatives demanding a plebiscite over the flag controversy, but
the political will to oppose the new flag was now exhausted. The old
national identity having slipped in stature to a relic of the past, its old
flags no longer had sufficient sociocultural political authority to keep
them prominent as symbols of Canada, unfurled and flying high.[16]

Canada's new official flag was first flown on 15 February 1965, a
mid-decade pronouncement that the old national identity of a British
dominion had passed into history. Thousands gathered on Parliament
Hill. Some mourned the passing of the Red Ensign, but many of the
tears shed were prideful, exuding what the *Toronto Daily Star* called 'a
pledge to our future.' Declaring, 'we are a nation and ... we can define
our nationality without recourse to the symbols of older nations,' the
newspaper was hopeful for the future. As the new flag rose, the bang of
a new national identity did not in fact make a very loud noise. 'The
whole fuss seemed to be forgotten within weeks,' noted Blair Fraser.
Some commentators, such as historian Jack Granatstein, concluded:
'The maple leaf flag quickly became *the* Canadian symbol, and the

divisiveness of the debate that gave it birth was largely forgotten.' Others came to think differently, suggesting retrospectively that 'the new flag did not symbolize a nation secure in its identity, but a nation that had just shed one identity and was searching for a new one.'[17]

The promise of the flag, as a representation of Canada's imagined community, was, in the words of Mike Pearson, great indeed:

> As the symbol of a new chapter in our national story, our Maple Leaf Flag will become a symbol of that unity in our country without which one cannot grow in strength and purpose; the unity that encourages the equal partnership of two peoples on which this Confederation was founded; the unity also that recognizes the contribution of many other races ... May the land over which this new Flag flies remain united in freedom and justice; a land of decent God-fearing people; fair and generous in all its dealings; sensitive, tolerant and compassionate towards all men; industrious, energetic, resolute; wise and just in the giving of securing and opportunity equally to all its cultures; and strong in its adherence to those moral principles which are the only sure guide to greatness. Under this Flag may our youth find new inspiration for loyalty to Canada; for a patriotism based not on any mean or narrow nationalism, but on the deep and equal pride that all Canadians will feel for every part of this good land.[18]

Pearson's words, like most nationalist pronouncements, were 'more of an aspiration than a fact.' A flag could not a nation make. And a piece of bunting, as much as it was devised to develop national identity, would, in the years after 1967, fly as much in the face of those it purported to inspire as it would cultivate a consensus of Canadian commonality. The developments of 1968–70 would reveal that Canada's flag did not necessarily rally all youth, all francophones, all First Nations, or all Canadians to its standard. A deluge of dissent that flowed forth from 1968 on often left Canada's new flag in tatters; notions of national identity balanced precariously in such circumstances.

Before this was made glaringly obvious, there was one more socially constructed 1960s effort to cultivate Canadian national identity. The Universal and International Exposition, or Expo 67, was a centennial megaproject of previously unimagined proportions. It planted the new flag of Canadian national identity atop the high modernist enterprise of a world's fair that, in its grand mix of outlandish structures (both futuristic and traditional) and shapes, brilliant colours, and jarringly imaginative maze of concrete, steel, glass, and other substances, many of them unimaginable to ordinary Canadians, surpassed any previous exhibition's imaginative chutzpah.

Expo 67 was conceived in the late 1950s, the offspring of Montreal mayor Jean Drapeau's insatiable need to put his city on the global map and to make the capital of Quebec's cosmopolitanism the centrepiece of the nation's centennial celebrations. Drapeau was a high roller unafraid to fly now and pay later, his proclivity for grandiose developments saddling Montreal, the province of Quebec, and their federal allies with an interest-bearing debt that, like the Energizer Bunny, just kept on going – decades past 1967. As early as 1963 official fears were that Expo 67's costs were skyrocketing out of sight. Some officials worried publicly that the world's fair was simply not going to be ready on time, proving a colossal embarrassment to the federal, provincial, and municipal governments bankrolling its building. The city of Montreal's share of the construction costs – a mere 12.5 per cent of the total – had soared from an original estimate of $12 million in the late 1950s to a 1963 figure of $35 million. With hundreds of millions of dollars at stake in each of a series of multiple expenditure packages, and the Bank of Montreal estimating that the spin-off economic stimulus of the exposition was going to exceed that generated by the binational development of the St Lawrence Seaway in the 1950s, the naysayers were rudely rebuked. They should keep their gloom and doom predictions to themselves.

To make Expo 67 happen the middle of the St Lawrence River was reconstructed. Twenty-five million truckloads of landfill transformed a barren peninsula and some mud flats into what one commentator named a 'utopia.' Islands emerged; the planned environment of the world's fair and its national pavilions were crisscrossed with pedestrian-friendly byways, beautifully crafted canals, an elevated monorail, and a sculpted landscape of arresting visual extravagance. The global race for technological sophistication and dominance, as well as avant-garde expressions in the arts and popular culture, were everywhere in evidence. If the USSR pavilion, impressive in its architectural reliance on glass, stuck to presentations of scientific, industrial, agricultural, and economic advance behind the Iron Curtain, Soviet Czechoslovakia was a crowd pleaser with its film presentations that allowed the audience to determine the plot line. A 250-foot-diameter geodesic dome designed by Buckminster Fuller housed the United States pavilion, its magic lighting dominating Expo 67's night skyline. It featured NASA space exploration equipment as well as iconic artifacts of American popular culture, such as an Elvis Presley guitar, Raggedy Ann dolls, and an Andy Warhol painting. Canada's pavilion, in which no expense was spared (at $21 million its cost exceeded the expenditures of the Americans and the Soviets), encompassed white tentlike buildings through which crowds could wander and ponder various exhibits, and a huge upside-down pyramid, composed of blue-green glass, weighing an astonishing 1,000 tons, known as Katimavik, Inuit for 'meeting place.' Playful provincial pavilions were complemented by National Film Board constructions such as Labyrinth, where multiple screens mounted on ceilings, floors, and walls presented a kaleidoscope of cinema in which presentation was as much spatial as it was visual. On the north shore of the Expo 67 site, architect Moshe Safdie's Habitat housed 158 families in 354 preformed modular units. This complex, dedicated to Man and His Environment, offered an aesthetic of a terraced Mediterranean village, blended into the bustling commercial byways of the St Lawrence Seaway. It symbolized the energetic commitment to transnational urban modernism that reverberated throughout Expo 67 and that was quintessentially Sixties and eminently McLuhanesque.[19]

Not surprisingly, comment on Expo 67 accents its contribution to Canadian national identity. Pierre Berton considered it 'one of the shining moments in our history,' and Peter Newman agreed. He wrote of being overwhelmed with the accomplishment: 'If this is possible, ... if this sub-Arctic, self-obsessed country of 20 million can put on this kind of a show, then it can do almost anything.' International comment, especially from Americans to the south, was equally laudatory. It was as if Canada was the Little Nation that Couldn't but that finally Did. *Time* magazine declared that Expo 67 was 'a symbol of the vigor and the enthusiasm of the Canadians who conceived an impossible idea and made it come true.'[20]

This was what the fair's political architects in various levels of the state had been working to accomplish. As Gary R. Meidema has recently concluded, the imagined Canada that was put on display at Expo 67 was an exercise in conscious reconstruction, a revision of history that understated the conflicts and tensions that had, over centuries, been central to the making of Canada. Out of the constraints of wilderness, Canadians had carved a political and economic culture of compromise and consensus, their material conquest of the environment advanced by technology, their success as a nation rooted in the ongoing commitment to unity. A work in progress, however, Canadian national identity – if hearkening back to a 'love of liberty' that it was now judged imprudent to associate with a British imperial order no longer fashionable to actually name politically – was a possibility that resided in all of the nation's citizens. Yet it still awaited realization. Expo 67, in its concrete and dazzling display of unity in diversity, was the first province in a new Confederation.[21]

Certainly that must have been how the record numbers attending Expo 67 between 27 April and 29 October 1967 saw things. Montreal's gala was arguably the most successful world's fair in the twentieth century: 50 million people passed through its turnstiles, and on the first Sunday that it was open the exposition shattered the single-day attendance record, with 569,500 surging on to the man-made St Lawrence islands.[22] One of Expo 67's visitors was Pierre Elliott Trudeau, a rising star in the Liberal government making his mark as minister of justice. He bewildered the staid guards at the Romanian pavilion; they could not quite grasp that the RCMP-accompanied man wearing sandals, dressed so casually, and wandering about like 'a hippie,' was actually a state official. Trudeau rode the wave of Expo 67 and then, surfing his own Trudeaumania momentum, made his fleeting stab at further consolidating national identity.[23]

The seeming 1967 centre of this bandwagon soon collapsed inward. When U.S. President Lyndon Johnson came to the Montreal World's Fair on 25 May 1967 he received an unenthusiastic welcome. The state dignitary whom many in Quebec considered responsible for atrocities in Vietnam was clearly worried, as were his counterparts in the upper echelons of Canada's governing authority and its security apparatus. Fear was that demonstrations and protests would mar the presidential visit. Secrecy shrouded the proceedings, but there was enough word on the street of LBJ's coming to town that Montreal newspapers carried half-page protest petitions signed by hundreds of university professors demanding an end to the bombing in southeast Asia, recognition of the Vietnamese National Liberation Front by the United States, and the termination of Canada's trade in arms with its military partner to the south. Activist/writer Barry Lord shouted 'Murderer' and 'Bloody Butcher' when he caught sight of Johnson touring the Expo site. He was immediately pounced on by police, who manhandled him, escorted him off the Expo grounds, and charged him with disturbing the peace. Eventually convicted and fined $100, Lord was the metaphorical fly in the ointment of Expo's celebration of Canadian national identity. 'Man and His World,' the theme of Expo 67, registered with Lord differently than our conventional wisdoms would have it. He thought the enterprise 'a carnival, an irrelevant distraction.' His mind was not on what the state architects of flags and pavilions wanted to be uppermost in Canadians' consciousness in 1967. Instead, Lord was thinking of 'black people's struggles for liberation in the United States, victories of the Vietnamese, and the determination of the Arabs to recover Palestine for its refugees.' For Lord, 'Gaza, Da Nang, Newark – these names, rather than Expo, are on the signposts of the future.' Within a matter of months, Quebec itself would be added to this list.[24]

From 1968 to 1970 the vehicle of Canadian national identity imploded. The 1960s proved a car bomb in the making and the ultimate unmaking of this identity. Guided by a directive hand that was at first difficult to discern, it drove the streets of the imagined community of Canada in the years up to 1965. The signs in these thoroughfares pointed only towards the unmistakable reality of change, always one-way in their flow away from an older, entrenched understanding of Canada as a British imperial dominion. Then, with travel that came to rest on that antiquated passage no longer possible, the vehicular decade seemed content to park and rest on the laurels of a new Canada. The symbolic alleyways of 1965–7 provided a lull in which the ticking bomb of the 1960s was obscured and muted as it was draped in the flag and seemingly outdistanced by the fast pace of Expo 67. In the end, however, the youthful revolt of the later 1960s provided a legion of suicide bombers, all of whom, be they advocates of the New Left, Quebec independence, or Red Power, would drive the last miles of the 1960s, ready and willing to crash their motherlode into the uncertainties and conflicted contradictions that had always plagued Canadian national identity and that would continue to do so.

The great irony of the Sixties was thus that while it decisively declared the end of one Canada, it defeated, for a generation or more, the possibility of realizing a new national identity that so much of the decade seemed to both demand and promote. We live, to this day, in the infinitely creative and politically destabilizing wreckage of a period in Canada's past that brought down with decisive finality what needed dismantling, but that could not, having accomplished this, build the kind of alternative that was required. The 1960s, as a consequence, remain with us still, even if the decade and its meanings seem so long ago, buried in the rubble of a past that laid claim to the promise of the future.

A final ironic question, like the sensibilities and political passions of the 1960s, has yet to be put to rest. To be sure, in our times, it recedes from view. Canada's current crisis of national identity seems to deepen daily, and just what Canada is remains a vexing, seemingly unanswerable, project of interrogation. In the process all Canadians are pressured, from various quarters and directions, to think that what they have seemingly lost, even if it never existed, is somehow to be cherished, whatever its history of undeniable costs, impossible contradictions, and ongoing uncertainties. Is Canadianism, for so long a seemingly known quality that suddenly became unknown in the 1960s, not related to this decade of tumultuousness in a myriad of ironic ways? Is its achievement, like the promise of the Sixties, not something we search for still? Could its realization, if that is possible, ever actually fulfill the varied ways in which that decade of discovery charted new paths for humanity and asked so many questions of it? And so the decade of the 1960s, and what it was all about, lives into the twenty-first century, haunting us with its simple but critical demand that we question ourselves, asking 'Is national identity really what we need?'

Notes

Prologue: Canada in the 1960s: Looking Backward

1 See two of many journalistic accounts: 'Caledonia Tensions Reach Boiling Point,' *Globe and Mail*, 23 May 2006; 'Fury, Confrontation at Caledonia,' *Toronto Star*, 23 May 2006. The *Globe and Mail* also carried a small photograph of an anti-monarchy protest at Toronto's Yonge and Dundas Streets, sponsored by Citizens for a Canadian Republic.

2 Roy MacGregor, 'Fontaine Walks the Line between Abuses Past and Protests Present,' and Bill Curry, 'Parliament Hill to Serve as Campground for Natives,' *Globe and Mail*, 28 June 2007; 'National Protests Disrupt Travel,' *Toronto Star*, 29 June 2007; 'Trains Halted Ahead of Blockades,' *Globe and Mail*, 29 June 2007.

3 A book published as I was completing this study explores the demise of older understandings of British Canada among anglophones in the post-1945 years. It provides detailed background to this study. See José E. Igartua, *The Other Quiet Revolution: National Identities in English Canada, 1945–1971* (Vancouver: UBC Press, 2006). I do not bemoan the passing of the old Canada and its supposed promise, as does Michael Bliss in 'Has Canada Failed? National Dreams That Have Not Come True,' *Literary Review of Canada* 14 (March 2006): 3–5. What is curious about Bliss's dismay is his failure to address what it was about the 1960s that made the continuity of Canada as it was in the immediate post–Second World War period an impossibility.

4 See, for instance, Philip Resnick, *The European Roots of Canadian Identity* (Peterborough, ON: Broadview, 2005). One measure of Canadian identity's shifting nature in the post–Second World War period is related to 'race' and ethnicity and the challenges posed to older notions of 'One Canada.' See, for instance, Contance Backhouse, *Colour-Coded: A Legal History of Racism in*

Canada, 1900–1950 (Toronto: University of Toronto Press, 1999); Himani Bannerji, *The Dark Side of the Nation: Essays on Multiculturalism, Nationalism, and Gender* (Toronto: Canadian Scholars' Press, 2000); Ross Lambertson, *Repression and Resistance: Canadian Human Rights Activists, 1930–1960* (Toronto: University of Toronto Press, 2005); Franca Iacovetta, *Gatekeepers: Reshaping Immigrant Lives in Cold War Canada* (Toronto: Between the Lines, 2006). This theme also surfaces, albeit with subtlety, in Norman Levine, *Canada Made Me* (London: Putnam, 1958), which begins with the epigram 'It is well known that one's native land is always recognized at the moment of losing it. – Albert Camus.'

5 As an introduction to the 1960s internationally see Arthur Marwick, *The Sixties: Cultural Revolution in Britain, France, Italy, and the United States, 1958–1974* (Oxford and New York: Oxford University Press, 1998); Ronald Fraser, ed., *1968 – A Student Generation in Revolt: An International Oral History* (New York: Pantheon, 1988); Paul Berman, *A Tale of Two Utopias: The Political Journey of the Generation of 1968* (New York and London: Norton, 1996); David Widgery, ed., *The Left in Britain, 1956–1968* (Harmondsworth, England: Penguin, 1976); Lin Chun, *The British New Left* (Edinburgh: Edinburgh University Press, 1993). For different approaches to Canada's 1960s see Dimitrios J. Roussopoulos, ed., *The New Left in Canada* (Montreal: Black Rose, 1970); Cyril Levitt, *Children of Privilege: Student Revolt in the Sixties* (Toronto: University of Toronto Press, 1984); Doug Owram, *Born at the Right Time: A History of the Baby Boom Generation* (Toronto: University of Toronto Press, 1996); and the selective synopsis in Ian McKay, *Rebels, Reds, Radicals: Rethinking Canada's Left History* (Toronto: Between the Lines, 2005), 183–92.

6 Benedict Anderson, *Imagined Communities: Reflections on the Origin and Spread of Nationalism* (London and New York: Verso, 1991), 205.

7 On the nineteenth-century birth of the nation see E.J. Hobsbawm, *Nations and Nationalism since 1780: Programme, Myth, Reality* (New York and Cambridge: Cambridge University Press, 1992).

8 For general statements, see Anthony D. Smith, *The Nation in History: Historiographical Debates about Ethnicity and Nationalism* (Cambridge: Polity, 2000); Smith, *Nationalism: Theory, Ideology, and History* (Cambridge: Polity, 2001).

9 Note the reasoned discussion in Amartya Sen, *Identity and Violence: The Illusion of Destiny* (New York: Norton, 2006), and also Ray Taras, *Liberal and Illiberal Nationalisms* (New York: Palgrave Macmillan, 2002).

10 Note the discussions in Ernest Gellner, *Nations and Nationalism* (Ithaca and London: Cornell University Press, 1983), 1–7, 53–62, with quotes from 48–9, 56; Gellner, *Encounters with Nationalism* (Oxford and Cambridge: Blackwell, 1994); Hobsbawm, *Nations and Nationalism*, 1–13. These treatments

challenge Smith's view that nations precede nationalism, but I find Smith's historical argument unconvincing and indeed logically inconsistent. For instance, how can it be that 'nations are a much older phenomenon than nationalism,' as Igartua claims in endorsing Smith if, in the latter's words, nationalism is 'an ideological movement for attaining and maintaining autonomy, unity and identity for a population which some of its members deem to constitute an actual or potential "nation"'? Too much in this formulation *requires* that nationalism precede nation. See, Smith, *Nationalism*, 9; Igartua, *Other Quiet Revolution*, 3; and for further discussion of the salience of ethnicity and 'race': Anthony D. Smith, *The Ethnic Origins of Nations* (Oxford: Basil Blackwell, 1986).

11 Hobsbawm, *Nations and Nationalism*, 11.

12 For a critique of the soft constructionism of identity as it is currently being used in scholarly discourse see Roger Brubaker and Frederick Cooper, 'Beyond "Identity,"' *Theory and Society* 29 (2000): 1–47.

13 Brubaker and Cooper, 'Beyond "Identity,"' lay out five ways in which identity has been used in contemporary scholarly writing (6–8), and further discussion can be found in Philip Gleason, 'Identifying Identity: A Semantic History,' *Journal of American History* 69 (March 1983): 910–31; Charles Tilly, ed., *Citizenship, Identity and Social History* (Cambridge: Cambridge University Press, 1996); Igartua, *The Other Quiet Revolution*, 5–9.

14 See, for instance, Alan Wilde, *Horizons of Assent: Modernism, Postmodernism, and the Ironic Imagination* (Baltimore: Johns Hopkins University Press, 1981).

15 Wayne Booth, *A Rhetoric of Irony* (Chicago and London: University of Chicago Press, 1974); Stanley Fish, *Doing What Comes Naturally: Change, Rhetoric, and the Practice of Theory in Literary and Legal Studies* (Durham and London: Duke University Press, 1989), 180–96.

16 In Canada this destabilizing, oppositional, and postmodern view of irony has been put forward by Linda Hutcheon in a number of works, including *Splitting Images: Contemporary Canadian Ironies* (Toronto: Oxford University Press, 1991); *Irony's Edge: The Theory and Politics of Irony* (London and New York: Routledge, 1994); and an edited collection, *Double-Talking: Essays on Verbal and Visual Ironies in Canadian Contemporary Art and Literature* (Toronto: ECW Press, 1992).

17 It is pertinent that Hutcheon emblazons her interpretive banner with what she designates the 'irony-marker' 'Not!' See Hutcheon, *Irony's Edge*, 8.

18 See, among many possible texts and statements, Georg Lukacs, *The Theory of the Novel: A Historico-Philosophical Essay on the Forms of Great Epic Literature* (Cambridge, MA: MIT Press, 1970), esp. 92–3; Terry Eagleton, *After Theory* (New York: Basic, 2003), 179–80.

434 Notes to pages 9–10

19 See especially Hutcheon, *Irony's Edge*, but for Hutcheon's answer note the comment in Hutcheon, 'The Power of Postmodern Irony,' in Barry Rutland, ed., *Genre, Trope, Gender: Critical Essays* (Ottawa: Carleton University Press, 1996), 33–49. I find it unfortunate that Hutcheon too often misstates Marxism's relation to the ironic in a problematic reductionism, authors such as Fredric Jameson and Terry Eagleton being caricatured as disapproving of 'irony as both a humorous and critical mode' (reproducing Hegel's dismissiveness of it as lacking in seriousness), or, even, as 'trivial and trivializing.' See Hutcheon, 'Power of Postmodern Irony,' 35; Hutcheon, 'Introduction,' *Double-Talking*, 12, citing Jameson, 'Postmodernism, or the Cultural Logic of Late Capitalism,' *New Left Review* 146 (1984): 53–92, and Terry Eagleton, 'Capitalism, Modernism, and Postmodernism,' *New Left Review* 152 (1985): 60–73.

20 See, for instance, Eagleton, *After Theory*, 59, 180.

21 Hutcheon, *Irony's Edge*, 4.

22 As evidenced in a recent discussion of the ironies of law and rhetoric in Canadian civil culture. See Michael Dorland and Maurice Charland, *Law, Rhetoric, and Irony in the Formation of Canadian Civil Culture* (Toronto: University of Toronto Press, 2002).

23 Terry Eagleton, *The Illusions of Postmodernism* (Oxford: Blackwell, 1996), 61–2.

24 Stanley Ryerson, *Unequal Union: Roots of Crisis in the Canadas, 1815–1873* (Toronto: Progress Books, 1973).

25 John Marlyn, *Under the Ribs of Death* (Toronto: McClelland and Stewart, 1993), 17–18.

26 On the Group of Seven see Robert Wright, *Virtual Sovereignty: Nationalism, Culture and the Canadian Question* (Toronto: Canadian Scholars' Press, 2004), 23–56; F.B. Housser, *A Canadian Art Movement: The Story of the Group of Seven* (Toronto: Macmillan, 1926); Jonathan Bordo, '*Jack Pine*: Wilderness Sublime or the Erasure of the Aboriginal Presence from the Landscape,' *Journal of Canadian Studies* 27 (Winter 1992–3): 98–128. On the Mounties note R.G. MacBeth, *Policing the Plains: Being the Real-Life Record of the Famous Royal North-West Mounted Police* (London: Hodder and Stoughton, 1921); Keith Walden, *Visons of Order* (Toronto: Butterworth's, 1982); Michael Dawson, *The Mountie from Dime Novel to Disney* (Toronto: Between the Lines, 1998). For a broad discussion of Canadian myth symbols see Daniel Francis, *National Dreams: Myth, Memory, and Canadian History* (Vancouver: Arsenal Pulp Press, 1997). A different perspective, in which continentalism figures prominently, is articulated in Allan Smith, *Canada – An American Nation? Essays on Continentalism, Identity, and the Canadian Frame of Mind* (Montreal and Kingston: McGill-Queen's University Press, 1994).

27 Until the 1960s, recognition of the abuse of Aboriginal peoples was under-stated at best. Note that the hegemonic suppression of Native cultures and political economies proceeded from first contact through eighteenth- and nineteenth-century dispossession (treaties and trade relations) to twentieth-century projects of 'freeing' Indian and Inuit peoples through forced relo-cations and the educational-religious violence of the residential school and legal systems. Among many texts see E. Brian Titley, *A Narrow Vision: Duncan Campbell Scott and the Administration of Indian Affairs in Canada* (Vancouver: UBC Press, 1986); Frank James Tester and Peter Kulchyski, *Tammarniit (Mistakes): Inuit Relocation in the Eastern Arctic, 1939–1963* (Vancouver: UBC Press, 1994); J.R. Miller, *Shingwauk's Vision: A History of Native Residential Schools* (Toronto: University of Toronto Press, 1996); John S. Milloy, *A National Crime: The Canadian Government and the Residential School System, 1879–1986* (Winnipeg: University of Manitoba Press, 1999); Shelagh D. Grant, *Arctic Justice: On Trial for Murder, Pond Inlet, 1923* (Montreal and Kingston: McGill-Queen's University Press, 2002).

28 Donald H. Clairmont and Dennis William Magill, *Africville: The Life and Death of a Canadian Community* (Toronto: Canadian Scholars' Press, 1997).

29 Hilda Glynn-Ward, *The Writing on the Wall* (Toronto: University of Toronto Press, 1974); Patricia Roy, *A White Man's Province: British Columbia Politicians and Chinese and Japanese Immigrants, 1858–1914* (Vancouver: UBC Press, 1989); W. Peter Ward, *White Canada Forever: Popular Attitudes and Public Policy toward Orientals in British Columbia* (Montreal and Kingston: McGill-Queen's University Press, 1978); Kay J. Anderson, *Vancouver's Chinatown: Racial Dis-course in Canada, 1875–1980* (Montreal and Kingston: McGill-Queen's University Press, 1995).

30 Consider for instance Donald Avery, *'Dangerous Foreigners': European Immi-grant Workers and Labour Radicalism in Canada, 1896–1932* (Toronto: McClelland and Stewart, 1979); Patricia Roy, J.L. Granatstein, Masako Lino, and Hiroko Takamura, *Mutual Hostages: Canadians and Japanese during the Second World War* (Toronto: University of Toronto Press, 1990).

31 Backhouse, *Colour-Coded*, 176. See also Terrence Craig, *Racial Attitudes in English-Canadian Fiction, 1905–1980* (Waterloo: Wilfrid Laurier University Press, 1987).

32 For 'racialization' and French Canada note the train of thought that links Lord Durham, André Siegfried, and others. The 1960s, I would suggest, was the last gasp of this 'racialization' of French Canada, as would be evident both academically and politically in John Porter's classic statement of Cana-dian sociology and in the outcry of Pierre Vallières. See, for instance, Gerald M. Craig, ed., *Lord Durham's Report* (Toronto and Montreal: McClelland and

Stewart, 1971), 22–3; Siegfried, *The Race Question in Canada* (London:
Eveleigh Nash, 1907); Ferdinand Roy, *The Call to Arms and the French-
Canadian Reply: A Study of the Conflict of Races* (Quebec: J.P. Garneau, 1918);
John Porter, *The Vertical Mosaic: An Analysis of Social Class and Power in Canada*
(Toronto: University of Toronto Press, 1965), 60–103; Vallières, *Nègres blancs
d'Amérique: Autobiographie d'un 'terroriste' québécois* (Montreal: Éditions Parti
Pris, 1968), a book that appeared in translation in New York and Toronto
under the title *White Niggers of America.*

33 See, among other works that could be cited, Carl Berger, *The Sense of Power:
Studies in the Ideas of Canadian Imperialism, 1867–1914* (Toronto: University
of Toronto Press, 1970); Paul Romney, *Getting It Wrong: How Canadians Forgot
Their Past and Imperilled Confederation* (Toronto: University of Toronto Press,
1999), 181–99; S.E.D. Shortt, *The Search for an Ideal: Six Canadian Intellectuals
and Their Convictions in an Age of Transition, 1880–1930* (Toronto: University
of Toronto Press, 1976).

34 Harold A. Innis, *The Fur Trade in Canada: An Introduction to Canadian Economic
History* (Toronto: University of Toronto Press, 1984; original 1930), 385.

35 Quoted in both Donald Creighton, *Dominion of the North* (Toronto:
Macmillan, 1962), 291, and R.T. Naylor, 'The Rise and Fall of the Commercial Empire of the St. Lawrence,' in Gary Teeple, ed., *Capitalism and the
National Question in Canada* (Toronto: University of Toronto Press, 1972),
36, albeit to different effect, a point that is not irrelevant to appreciation of
the ironies of Canadian identity as they shifted in the 1960s.

36 Quoted in W. Stewart Wallace, *The Growth of Canadian National Feeling*
(Toronto: Macmillan, 1927), 1.

37 Note the beginning words of Kenneth McNaught, *The Pelican History of
Canada* (Harmondsworth, England: Penguin, 1986), 7: 'From the time of
the earliest records Canada has been part of a frontier, just as in her own
growth she has fostered frontiers. The struggle of men and of metropolitan
centres to extend and control those frontiers, as well as to improve life
behind them, lies at the heart of Canadian history.'

38 Note especially W.L. Morton, *The Canadian Identity* (Toronto: University of
Toronto Press, 1972; original 1961), esp. 88–9, 93, 109; John Wadland,
'Wilderness and Culture,' in Bruce Hodgins and Margaret Hobbs, eds.,
Nastawagan: The Canadian North by Shoe and Snowshoe (Toronto: Betelgeuse,
1985), esp. 223–6; Carl Berger, 'The True North Strong and Free,' and Cole
Harris, 'The Myth of the Land in Canadian Nationalism,' in Peter Russell,
ed., *Nationalism in Canada: By the University League for Social Reform* (Toronto:
McGraw-Hill, 1966), 3–42. For antecedents see George Heriot, *Travels
through the Canadas, Containing a Description of the Picturesque Scenery on Some of*

the Rivers and Lakes; With an Account of the Productions, Commerce, and Inhabitants of the Those Provinces, To Which is Subjoined a Comparative View of the Manners and Customs of Several of the Indian Nations of North and South America (London: Richard Phillips, 1807); John J. Bigsby, *The Shoe and Canoe; Or, Pictures of Travel in the Canadas, Illustrative of the Scenery and of Colonial Life: With Facts and Opinions on Emigration, State Policy, and Other Points of Public Interest,* 2 vols (London: Chapman and Hall, 1850); Susanna Moodie, *Roughing It in the Bush: Or, Life in Canada* (London: Richard Bentley, 1852).

39 Northrop Frye, *The Bush Garden: Essays on the Canadian Imagination* (Toronto: Anansi, 1971), esp. vi; Frye, 'Conclusion,' in Carl F. Klinck, ed., *Literary History of Canada: Canadian Literature in English* (Toronto: University of Toronto Press, 1965), esp. 830; Morton, *Canadian Identity,* 112; Margaret Atwood, *Survival: A Thematic Guide to Canadian Literature* (Toronto: Anansi, 1972).

40 Frank H. Underhill, *The Image of Confederation: The Massey Lectures of 1963* (Toronto: Canadian Broadcasting Corporation, 1965), 58–9. The point had been emphasized one year earlier by Eugene Forsey, 'Canada: Two Nations or One?' *Canadian Journal of Economics and Political Science* 28 (November 1962): 485–501.

41 Morton, *Canadian Identity,* 88–9.

42 Leonard Cohen, *Beautiful Losers* (New York: Viking, 1966), 118, 121.

43 See Laurier LaPierre, 'Canada's Eldridge Cleaver and Malcolm X,' *New York Times Book Review,* 11 April 1971; Ian McKay, 'For a New Kind of History: A Reconnaissance of 100 Years of Canadian Socialism,' *Labour/Le Travail* 46 (Fall 2000): 115–19.

44 See, for instance, Léon Dion, *Quebec: The Unfinished Revolution* (Montreal and London: McGill-Queen's University Press, 1976), 187; Morton, *Canadian Identity,* 58–87, 114; Underhill, *Image of Confederation,* 69–70.

45 George Grant, *Lament for a Nation: The Defeat of Canadian Nationalism* (Ottawa: Carleton Library, 1970), esp. x, 8. In a 1970 introduction to the republication of his original 1965 text, Grant stated that he had come to emphasize 'this failure in irony because many simple people (particularly journalists and professors) took it to be a lament for the passing of a British dream of Canada. It was rather a lament for the romanticism of the original dream' (xi). But romanticizations, of course, are the very stuff of 'imagined communities.'

46 Karl Marx and Friedrich Engels, 'Manifesto of the Communist Party,' in *Selected Works* (Moscow: Progress Publishers, 1968), 38. See also Marshall Berman, *All That Is Solid Melts into Air: The Experience of Modernity* (New York: Simon and Schuster, 1982).

47 Among relevant studies: Carol Lee Bacchi, *Liberation Deferred? The Ideas of the English-Canadian Suffragists, 1877–1918* (Toronto: University of Toronto Press, 1983); many of the essays in Franca Iacovetta and Mariana Valverde, eds., *Gender Conflicts: New Essays in Women's History* (Toronto: University of Toronto Press, 1992); the evocative contemporary novel by Francis Marion Beynon, *Aleta Day: A Novel* (London: C.W. Daniel, 1919); Craig Heron, ed., *The Workers' Revolt in Canada, 1917–1925* (Toronto: University of Toronto Press, 1998); Ward, *White Canada Forever*; Hugh J.M. Johnston, *The Voyage of the Komata Maru: The Sikh Challenge to Canada's Colour Bar* (Delhi: Oxford University Press, 1979). For an articulation of Canadian nationality informed by such developments, appearing in the pressured context of post–First World War reconstruction and increasingly tense labour–capital relations, see C.W. Peterson, *Wake Up, Canada! Reflections on Vital National Issues* (Toronto: Macmillan, 1919).

48 Thus Donald Creighton could proclaim in an article originally published in 1942 that 'the forces of industrialism and nationality, internal and external to British North America, had finished their work. And the Dominion of Canada completed its programme of national unification with the National Policy of Protection.' See Creighton, 'Economic Nationalism and Confederation,' in Ramsay Cook, ed., *Confederation* (Toronto: University of Toronto Press, 1967), 8. See as well Craig Brown, 'The Nationalism of the National Policy,' in Peter Russell, ed., *Nationalism in Canada by the University League for Social Reform* (Toronto: McGraw-Hill, 1966), 155–63.

49 *Canada First: A Memorial of the Late William A.Foster, Q.C.* (Toronto: Hunter, Rose, 1890), 39–40. See as well Goldwin Smith, *Canada and the Canadian Question* (London and New York: Macmillan and Company, 1891), 253–66.

50 Consider, for instance, Isaac Buchanan, *The Relations of the Industry of Canada with the Mother Country and the United States* (Montreal: John Lovell, 1864), and the discussion of the 'producer ideology' in Bryan D. Palmer, *A Culture in Conflict: Skilled Workers and Industrial Capitalism in Hamilton, Ontario, 1860–1914* (Montreal and Kingston: McGill-Queen's University Press, 1979), 97–122.

51 W. Frank Hatheway, *Canadian Nationality: The Cry of Labor* (Toronto: William Briggs, 1906), esp. 13–28.

52 Berger, *Sense of Power*, esp. 53, 128–33. See as well *Canada First: A Memorial of the Late William A. Foster*; Wallace, *Growth of Canadian National Feeling*.

53 Norman Penlington, *Canada and Imperialism, 1896–1899* (Toronto: University of Toronto Press, 1965); T.G. Marquis, *Canada's Sons of Kopje and Veldt: An Historical Account of the Canadian Contingents* (Toronto: Canada's Sons, 1900).

54 Almost anything J.L. Granatstein has written on war and Canada is pertinent to this point, but his argument about the centrality of war in the making of modern Canadian identity is presented succinctly, if rancorously, in Granatstein, *Who Killed Canadian History?* (Toronto: Harper Perennial, 1999), 109–36. For an interwar statement see W. Eric Harris, *Stand to Your Work: A Summons to Canadians Everywhere* (Toronto: Musson, 1927), esp. 1–17.

55 See the stimulating discussions in Donica Belisle, 'Rise of Mass Retail: Canadians and Department Stores, 1890–1940,' PhD dissertation, Trent University, 2006; Cynthia Wright, 'Rewriting the Modern: Reflections on Race, Nation, and the Death of a Department Store,' *Histoire Sociale/Social History* 33 (May 2000): 153–67.

56 Arthur Irwin, 'What It Means to Be a Canadian,' *Maclean's*, 1 February 1950. Note as well *Canada in the Fifties: Canada's Golden Decade – From the Archives of Maclean's* (Toronto: Viking, 1999); Wallace, *Growth of Canadian National Feeling*, 70–7; and the more contemporary postcolonial literary analysis of texts such as Sara Jeanette Duncan's archetypal *The Imperialist* in Glenn Willmott, *Unreal Country: Modernity in the Canadian Novel in English* (Montreal and Kingston: McGill-Queen's University Press, 2002), esp. 19–29. Frank Watt offered a wonderfully prescient comment on the role of Canadian poets in 'inventing Canada' as early as 1966: Watt, 'Nationalism in Canadian Literature,' in Russell, ed., *Nationalism in Canada*, 242–6. Note as well Francis, *National Dreams*. For a general statement, see the essays in Eric Hobsbawm and Terence Ranger, eds., *The Invention of Tradition* (New York: Cambridge University Press, 1983).

57 Studies of Americanization of the Canadian economy would figure forcefully in radical nationalist research of the 1960s, but the evidence had long been available. For an influential early examination, see Herbert Marshall, Frank A. Southard, Jr, and Kenneth W. Taylor, *Canadian-American Industry: A Study in International Investment* (New Haven: Yale University Press, 1936). Arguably the most significant of the books on this subject to come out of the 1960s would be Kari Levitt, *Silent Surrender: The Multinational Corporation in Canada* (Toronto: Macmillan, 1970).

58 On Lower's understanding of liberal democracy see *This Most Famous Stream: The Liberal Democratic Way of Life* (Toronto: Ryerson, 1954).

59 I draw on A.R.M. Lower, *Canadians in the Making: A Social History of Canada* (Toronto: Longmans, 1958), esp. 410–46. See as well, especially for Lower's understandings of liberal order, nationalism, and opposition to particular kinds of immigration, Weif H. Heick, ed., *Arthur Lower and the Making of Canadian Nationalism* (Vancouver: UBC Press, 1975). Note also the discussions in Levine, *Canada Made Me*, esp. 44, 60, 235, 277.

60 Berger, *Sense of Power,* 265. See also Hanly, 'Psychoanalysis of Nationalist
Sentiment,' in Russell, ed., *Nationalism in Canada,* 314, a book whose editor
concluded that 'many who have written about Canada in recent years have
noticed how much the nationalism of the loyalists and the British colonists
has receded from the centre of the Canadian ethos. What is remarkable
here is that the members of this group take this so much for granted' (367).
This kind of argument also animates Allan Smith, 'Metaphor and Nationality in North America,' *Canadian Historical Review* 51 (September 1970):
247–75, where this exaggerated statement appears: 'Canada does not possess this basic impulse toward conformity because there has been nothing in
Canada to which conformity could be urged. There is no overarching Canadian Way of Life, nor can there be an ideological Canadianism' (272). Contrast this with the presentation in Francis, *National Dreams.*

61 The 1940s were of course marked by a dual integration. On the one hand,
Canada as an *economy* moved out of the sphere of influence of Britain and decisively on to the path of continentalist integration, unambiguously dependent
on U.S. capital. On the other, class relations witnessed a corporatist harnessing,
as a more liberal regime of conciliation and containment drew labour and capital together, their relations monitored by an increasingly attentive state. These
economic processes also laid the groundwork for immigrant Canadians to
assume the rights of citizenship as the mass production and resource extractive
economies grew and offered ethnic Canadians the protections of trade unionism and the rights of industrial citizenship for the first time. But the full impact
of these developments would not really be felt for another two decades. On this
see, among many possible sources, Philip Resnick, *The Land of Cain: Class and
Nationalism in English Canada, 1945–1975* (Vancouver: New Star, 1977), esp.
72–100; Peter McInnis, *Harnessing Labour Confrontation: Shaping the Postwar
Settlement in Canada, 1943–1950* (Toronto: University of Toronto Press, 2002).
On the ironic mix of the 1920s, see, for instance, Roger Graham, *Arthur
Meighan: A Biography – And Fortune Fled,* vol. 2 (Toronto: Clarke, Irwin, 1963),
esp. 414–77; Graham, ed., *The King-Byng Affair, 1926: A Question of Responsible
Government* (Toronto: Copp Clark, 1967); W.L. Morton, *The Progressive Party in
Canada* (Toronto: University of Toronto Press, 1967); Ernest R. Forbes, *The
Maritime Rights Movement, 1919–1927: A Study in Canadian Regionalism*
(Montreal and Kingston: McGill-Queen's University Press, 1979).

62 Allan Smith offers useful comment on the depth of old Ontario's capacity to
construct itself as the nation and on the imperial nature of provincial life in
the country's westernmost coastal province. See Smith, 'Old Ontario and
the Emergence of a National Frame of Mind' and 'Defining British
Columbia,' in Smith, *Canada – An American Nation?* 253–314.

63 For background to the Canadian National Exhibition see Keith Walden, *Becoming Modern in Toronto: The Industrial Exhibition and the Shaping of a Late Victorian Culture* (Toronto: University of Toronto Press, 1997).

64 Vincent Massey, *On Being Canadian* (Toronto: Dent, 1948); Massey, *Canadians and Their Commonwealth* (Oxford: Clarendon Press, 1961); and, for an earlier statement, Massey, *The Making of a Nation* (Boston: Houghton Mifflin, 1928). Note for the early twentieth-century progressive qualms about pluralism: J.S. Woodsworth, *Strangers within Our Gates, or Coming Canadians* (Toronto: Missionary Society, 1909); Woodsworth, *My Neighbor: A Study of City Conditions, a Plea for Social Service* (Toronto: Missionary Society, 1911).

65 Sara Jeannette Duncan, *The Imperialist* (Westminster: Archibald Constable, 1904).

66 Malcolm Ross, ed., *Our Sense of Identity: A Book of Canadian Essays* (Toronto: Ryerson Press, 1954).

67 Ross, 'Introduction,' *Our Sense of Identity*, x–xi.

68 Ibid., xi.

69 Lower, 'Bonnie Chairlie's Gone Awa',' in Ross, ed., *Our Sense of Identity*, 162–3. Lower would have taken particular glee in the 2005 fall of Conrad Black. Black (a Canadian commoner nevertheless born with the silver spoon of immense wealth in his mouth), having utilized his Canadian riches to amass a global fortune and rise to prominence as a newspaper mogul in the English-speaking world, renounced his Canadian citizenship to secure entry to the British House of Lords. His empire crumbled, however, and amid allegations of fraud, Lord Black was accused of depriving shareholders of millions of dollars. Facing criminal charges in Chicago, Lord Black found that his lightly lost Canadian citizenship offered him protections he now found attractive.

70 Ross, 'Introduction,' *Our Sense of Identity*, ix–x.

71 For a somewhat wild romp through the literature of contemporary 'Canada's identity crisis' see Ian McKay, 'After Canada: On Amnesia and Apocalypse in the Contemporary Crisis,' *Acadiensis* 28 (Autumn 1998): 76–97. Among the many relevant texts of this crisis, see Leslie Armour, *The Idea of Canada and the Crisis of Community* (Ottawa: Steel Rail, 1981); Tony Wilden, *The Imaginary Canadian* (Vancouver: Pulp Press, 1980); and the conclusion to Francis, *National Dreams*, 172–6.

72 There is much to ponder with respect to such issues of periodization and politics in the essays collected in Sohnya Sayres et al., eds., *The 60s without Apology* (Minneapolis: University of Minnesota Press, 1984). See as well Max Elbaum, *Revolution in the Air: Sixties Radicals Turn to Lenin, Mao, and Che* (London: Verso, 2002).

73 Barbara L. Tischler, ed., *Sights on the Sixties* (New Brunswick, NJ: Rutgers University Press, 1992), 5–6, lists seven possible chronological groupings of years that could constitute different 1960s.

74 Fredric Jameson, 'Periodizing the 6os,' in Jameson, *The Ideologies of Theory: Essays, 1971–1986,* vol. 2, *Syntax of History* (Minneapolis: University of Minnesota Press, 1988), 178–208.

1: When the Buck Was *Bad*: The Dollar and Canadian Identity Entering the 1960s

1 For an older survey see W. Stanley Jevons, *Money and the Mechanism of Exchange* (New York: D. Appleton and Co., 1896).

2 For specific accounts see the pioneering overview in Robert Brenner, *The Economics of Global Turbulence: The Advanced Capitalist Economies from Long Boom to Long Downturn, 1945–2005* (London: Verso, 2006), and an older Canadian treatment, Cy Gonick, *Inflation or Depression: An Analysis of the Continuing Crisis of the Canadian Economy* (Toronto: Lorimer, 1975). Note as well, Philip Resnick, *The Land of Cain: Class and Nationalism in English Canada, 1945–1975* (Vancouver: New Star Books, 1977), 149; Eric Helleiner, *States and the Reemergence of Global Finance: From Bretton Woods to the 1990s* (Ithaca and London: Cornell University Press, 1994); Helleiner, *The Making of National Money: Territorial Currencies in Historical Perspective* (Ithaca and London: Cornell University Press, 2003); Ernest Mandel, *Decline of the Dollar: A Marxist View of the Monetary Crisis* (New York: Monad, 1972); Susan Strange, 'From Bretton Woods to the Casino Economy,' in Stuart Corbridge, Ron Martin, and Nigel Thrift, eds., *Money, Power, and Space* (Oxford: Blackwell, 1994), 49–62; William Wiseley, *A Tool of Power: The Political History of Money* (New York: John Wiley and Sons, 1977), esp. 143–76.

3 Georg Simmel, *The Philosophy of Money,* translated by Tom Bottomore and David Frisby (London: Routledge and Kegan Paul, 1978); Gianfranco Poggi, *Money and the Modern Mind: Georg Simmel's 'Philosophy of Money'* (Berkeley: University of California Press, 1993); Max Weber, *Economy and Society: An Outline of Interpretive Sociology* (Berkeley: University of California Press, 1978), vol. 1, esp. 166–78; Bernard F. Dukore, *Money and Politics in Ibsen, Shaw, and Brecht* (Columbia and London: University of Missouri Press, 1980); Ernest Bornemann, ed., *The Psychoananalysis of Money* (New York: Urizen Books, 1976).

4 Marx's most pertinent comment on money, from which I draw above, appears in his 'Economic and Philosophic Manuscripts of 1844.' I quote from the translation that appears in Karl Marx and Frederick Engels,

Collected Works, vol. 3, *1843–1844* (London: Lawrence and Wishart, 1975), esp. 322–6, containing the discussion, 'The Power of Money.' Note as well S.S.Prawer, *Karl Marx and World Literature* (Oxford: Clarendon Press, 1976), 56–85; Michael Neary and Graham Taylor, *Money and the Human Condition* (New York: St Martin's Press, 1998); Robert Paul Wolff, *Moneybags Must Be So Lucky: On the Literary Structure of Capital* (Amherst: University of Massachusetts Press, 1988).

5 G. Poggi, *The Development of the Modern State* (Stanford: Stanford University Press, 1978), 93; Anthony Giddens, *The Nation-state and Violence* (Cambridge: Polity, 1985); Eric J. Hobsbawm, *Nations and Nationalism since 1780* (Cambridge: Cambridge University Press, 1992), 28.

6 See Eric Helleiner, 'National Currencies and National Identities,' *American Behavioral Scientist* 41 (1998): 1409–36; Emily Gilbert and Eric Helleiner, 'Introduction – Nation-states and Money: Historical Contexts, Interdisciplinary Perspectives,' in Emily Gilbert and Eric Helleiner, eds., *Nation-states and Money: The Past, Present, and Future of National Currencies* (New York and London: Routledge, 1999), 1–21.

7 For fuller elaboration of these issues and for the quotes provided, see Bryan D. Palmer, *A Culture in Conflict: Skilled Workers and Industrial Capitalism in Hamilton, Ontario, 1860–1914* (Montreal and Kingston: McGill-Queen's University Press, 1979), 102–15.

8 Gilbert, 'Forging a National Currency,' in Gilbert and Helleiner, eds., *Nation-states and Money*, 38–42; Helleiner, *The Making of National Money*, 153; A.F.W. Plumptre, *Central Banking in the British Dominions* (Toronto: University of Toronto Press, 1940), 162.

9 Paul Wonnacott, *The Canadian Dollar, 1948–1962* (Toronto: University of Toronto Press, 1965), 4–6, 64; Kari Levitt, *Silent Surrender: The Multinational Corporation in Canada* (Toronto: Macmillan, 1970), 122; Wallace Clement, *Continental Corporate Power: Economic Elite Linkages between Canada and the United States* (Toronto: McClelland and Stewart, 1977), 107–8; A.E. Safarian, *Foreign Ownership of Canadian Industry* (Toronto: McGraw-Hill, 1966); Libbie and Frank Park, *Anatomy of Big Business* (Toronto: James Lewis and Samuel, 1973).

10 For accounts of this complex currency history see Wonnacott, *Canadian Dollar*, 48–81; Robert Bothwell, Ian Drummond, and John English, *Canada since 1945: Power, Politics, and Provincialism* (Toronto: University of Toronto Press, 1989), 172–3; Donald M. Fleming, *So Very Near: The Political Memoirs of the Honourable Donald M. Fleming*, vol. 2, *The Summit Years* (Toronto: McClelland and Stewart, 1985), 487–90. The most recent discussion is Eric Helleiner, *Towards North American Monetary Union? The Politics and History of Canada's*

Exchange Rate Regime (Montreal and Kingston: McGill-Queen's University Press, 2006), esp. 19–104.

11 Wonnacott, *Canadian Dollar,* 112–25; Michael Babad and Catherine Mulroney, *Where the Buck Stops: The Dollar, Democracy, and the Bank of Canada* (Toronto: Stoddart, 1995), 93–136; Peter C. Newman, *Renegade in Power: The Diefenbaker Years* (Toronto: McClelland and Stewart, 1963), 49–78, presents an accessible account of the 1957–8 elections. Also, Peter Stursberg, *Diefenbaker: Leadership Gained, 1956–1962* (Toronto: University of Toronto Press, 1975).

12 Fleming, *So Very Near,* 2: 490; Bothwell, Drummond, and English, *Canada since 1945,* 72.

13 As an indication of the unprecedented public clash of the minister of finance and the governor of the Bank of Canada see, for instance, 'M. Fleming opposé à M. James Coyne un dementi categorique,' *La Presse* (Montreal), 15 March 1958. It was common for economists to note that more criticisms had been levelled at the Bank of Canada and its policies in the post-1954 years than had been raised in the entire history of the institution since it was established in 1935. For a sampling of economists' concerns in a year of considerable controversy, 1958, see H.S. Gordon and L.M. Read, 'The Political Economics of the Bank of Canada,' *Canadian Journal of Economics and Political Science* 24 (November 1958): 465–82; E.P. Neufeld, 'The Bank of Canada's Approach to Central Banking,' *Canadian Journal of Economics and Political Science* 24 (August 1958): 332–44.

14 The figure on deficit spending comes from Newman, *Renegade in Power,* 121.

15 Wonnacott, *Canadian Dollar,* 238.

16 For a full account see J.L. Granatstein, *Canada, 1957–1967: The Years of Uncertainty and Innovation* (Toronto: McClelland and Stewart, 1986), 62–100.

17 The above paragraphs draw on Babad and Mulroney, *Where the Buck Stops,* 109–43; Fleming, *So Very Near,* 2: 302–49, 490–4; Wonnacott, *Canadian Dollar,* 203–253; David Smith, *Rogue Tory: The Life and Legend of John G. Diefenbaker* (Toronto: Macfarlane, Walter, and Ross, 1995), 390–450. On Coyne's battles with the Diefenbaker government and its final public outcome, which ended with Coyne speaking before the Senate and then resigning, see also J.W. Pickersgill, *Seeing Canada Whole: A Memoir* (Markham, ON: Fitzhenry and Whiteside, 1994), 545–75; Peter Stursberg, *Diefenbaker: Leadership Gained, 1956–1962* (Toronto: University of Toronto Press, 1975), 229–50; Patrick Nicholson, *Vision and Indecision* (Toronto: Longmans, 1968), 310–13. For comment on the dollar prior to its devaluation see, for instance, the following *Financial Post* articles: Allen T. Lambert, 'He Says Peg It,' 16 December 1961; W. Earle McLaughlin, 'Let It Float Free,' 20 January

1962; Leslie Wilson, 'How Canada Kept Dollar Down,' 20 January 1962;
C. Knowlton Nash, 'Latest Background Facts on Dollar Exchange Rate,'
24 February 1962; 'Please Fix Dollar Rate IMF Again Asks Canada,' 10 March
1962. Fleming and the Conservatives railed against the speculators who
brought the dollar down but would not name them. See Forbes Rhude,
'Speculation against Dollar Is Major Cause of Pegging,' *Halifax Chronicle
Herald*, 4 May 1962; 'Will Not Name Dollar Traders, Fleming Says,' *Globe and
Mail*, 8 May 1962; 'Europe Talks of Capital Removal from Canada,' *Halifax
Chronicle Herald*, 21 June 1962; 'Fleming Says Speculators Caused Dollar
Instability,' *Globe and Mail*, 4 May 1962; Stursberg, *Diefenbaker: Leadership
Gained*, quotes cabinet minister Alvin Hamilton: 'Diefenbaker knew the
names of every person who raided the dollar. Every single one was Canadian, every single one was in Toronto. He would not divulge their names
because he didn't think prime ministers and cabinet ministers should
divulge this type of information, even though that was a deliberate political
ploy in the middle of the election to destroy him' (258).

18 See, for instance, George Grant, *Lament for a Nation: The Defeat of Canadian
Nationalism* (Ottawa: Carleton Library, 1970; original 1965), 17.

19 Blunt repudiations of Coyne appear in Wonnacott, *Canadian Dollar*, 215–39;
Lawrence H. Officer and Lawrence B. Smith, eds., *Canadian Economic Problems and Policies* (Toronto: McGraw-Hill, 1970), 33–4.

20 The above paragraphs draw on material in Newman, *Renegade in Power*, 51,
295–305, although they present a different interpretation. Coyne is quoted
on 303–4.

21 For standard accounts in the business and popular press see 'Pegging the
Canadian Dollar,' *Wall Street Journal*, 4 May 1962; Tim Creery, 'U.S. Sees Cut
as "Emergency,"' *Calgary Herald*, 3 May 1962; Lynceus, 'The Dollar,' *Calgary
Herald*, 22 May 1962; Alan Donnelly, 'Canadian Dollar Pegged at 92.5,' *The
Vancouver Sun*, 3 May 1962; 'Dollar Move Gets Mixed Reaction,' *Winnipeg
Free Press*, 3 May 1962; 'Dollar Devaluation,' *Saturday Night*, 26 May 1962;
Patrick Nicholson, 'Ottawa Newsletter,' *Business Quarterly* 27 (Summer
1962): 7, 81; Neville Nankivell, '92.5c Dollar Still Only a Big Experiment,'
Dalton Robertson, 'Where New Pegged Canadian$ Will Give Business Push,'
'What Foreign Press Says about Dollar Devaluation,' and 'Pegging the Dollar
Is Only a Start,' *Financial Post*, 12 May 1962; 'Canadian Dollar Is Fixed at
92.5c,' *New York Times*, 3 May 1962; Tania Long, 'The Canadian Dollar,' *New
York Times*, 4 May 1962; 'Canadian Dollar Is Pegged at 92.5 Cents in U.S.
Funds,' *Globe and Mail*, 3 May 1962; 'Fleming Says Speculators Caused Dol-
lar Instability,' *Globe and Mail*, 4 May 1962; Robert Duffy, 'London Thought
Currency Overvalued, Welcomes Pegging of Rate,' *Globe and Mail*, 4 May

1962; 'Mixed Reception Greets Cut in Value of Dollar,' *Halifax Chronicle Herald*, 4 May 1962.

22 Nicholson, *Vision and Indecision*, 316.

23 Newman, *Renegade in Power*, 322.

24 New immigrants would find Diefenbaker's attachment to an understanding of Canada's British dominion status unappealing and somewhat distanced from their own preoccupations. For one account of an admittedly atypical immigrant that addresses ambivalences of identity in this period see Michiel Horn, *Becoming Canadian: Memoirs of an Invisible Immigrant* (Toronto: University of Toronto Press, 1997), esp. 165–214.

25 Newspaper coverage of various heckling and riotous clashes includes: 'Devalued Dollar Still Hot Topic,' *St John's Evening Telegram*, 11 June 1962; *Vancouver Sun*: Bill Galt, 'Diefenbaker Hecklers Find Shouting Just Doesn't Pay,' 24 May 1962; 'Tories Battle Demonstrators at Riotous Diefenbaker Rally,' Jack Wasserman, 'PMs Big Show Like Nazi Bedlam,' Frank Walden, 'Diefenbaker Shouts Over Crowd's Ceaseless Roar,' 31 May 1962; Bob Porter and Bryce Williams, 'NDP Supporters Admit Plot to Disrupt Diefenbaker Rally,' Bob Porter and Bryce Williams, 'Campaign Well Planned,' 1 June 1962. Note as well the recollections of violence on the campaign in Stursberg, *Diefenbaker: Leadership Gained*, 268–71, and in John G. Diefenbaker, *One Canada: The Memoirs of the Right Honourable John G. Diefenbaker*, vol. 3, *The Tumultuous Years, 1962–1967* (Toronto: Macmillan, 1977), 129–30. On Doukhobor protest and other accounts of violence see 'Doukhobors Riot, Burn Fifty Homes,' *Halifax Chronicle Herald*, 9 June 1962; 'Douks Burn 3 More,' *Calgary Herald*, 15 June 1962; Newman, *Renegade in Power*, 304, 322–32; Smith, *Rogue Tory*, 439–40, 655.

26 Alan Donnelly, 'Devaluation, Unemployment Key Election Issues,' *Winnipeg Free Press*, 4 June 1963; 'Dollar, Unemployment Causes of Downfall, Metro PCs Declare,' *Globe and Mail*, 20 June 1962.

27 'Diefenbaker Hecklers,' *Vancouver Sun*, 24 May 1962; Editorial, 'The Dollar Election,' *Winnipeg Free Press*, 16 June 1962.

28 'Dollar Kindles Election Fires,' *Calgary Herald*, 15 June 1962.

29 Stursberg, *Diefenbaker: Leadership Gained*, 251–71.

30 On Smallwood's intervention see *St John's Evening Telegram*, 'Fleming A-heming but Not a Word,' 8 June 1962; 'Rotary Club Issue Score Even at 3–3,' Editorial, 'Rotary Convention,' 11 June 1962; and letters to the editor, including from Smallwood, 12, 13, 14 June 1962; 'Joey Said Don't, Fleming Didn't,' *Winnipeg Free Press*, 8 June 1962; 'Say Fleming Chose Topic,' *Winnipeg Free Press*, 9 June 1962; *Globe and Mail*, Editorial: 'Mr Smallwood Devalued,' 9 June 1962; 'Smallwood Ban an Issue: Fleming,' 13 June 1962; Diefenbaker, *One Canada*, 3: 130–1.

31 The press commentary on rising prices was voluminous. I draw on thirty-three articles in the *Calgary Herald*, the *Vancouver Sun*, the *Winnipeg Free Press*, the *Globe and Mail*, the *Halifax Chronicle Herald*, the *London Free Press*, and the *Financial Post* published in May–June 1962.

32 Charles Lynch, 'Sagging Dollar Dropped,' *Calgary Herald*, 3 May 1962. Lynch's point was echoed by New Democratic Party East Vancouver candidate Harold Winch, who claimed that devaluation was a gift to the Tory backers from their servile state. Big business, claimed Winch, was the only Canadian sector benefiting from the slumping Canadian dollar. 'Who finances the Tories,' he asked rhetorically. 'Big business – that's who.' Mike Valpy, 'Devalued Dollar Pays Off Tory Business Backers,' *Vancouver Sun*, 8 June 1962.

33 Letters to the Editor, 'Critical': 'Canadians Ashamed,' *Vancouver Sun*, 18 May 1962; Letter to the Editor, 'Realist': 'Prosperity or Austerity,' *Halifax Chronicle Herald*, 26 June 1962. Note also Letter to the Editor, 'Canadian': 'Jumpy Currency,' *Winnipeg Free Press*, 16 June 1962.

34 Editorial, 'Discipline and the Dollar,' *Globe and Mail*, 4 May 1962, and the jocular Lex Schrag, 'Mortgage Manor: Dollar a Dollar for a' That: Wife,' *Globe and Mail*, 11 June 1962.

35 'Dollar Pegging Dictated,' *Vancouver Sun*, 24 May 1962; 'Kennedy Move Forced Dollar Dip,' *Globe and Mail*, 24 May 1962. A more sustained Communist discussion is in Brian Elliott, 'Canada's Dollar Crisis,' *Marxist Quarterly* 3 (Autumn 1962): 3–25. Buck's views were later paralleled in the somewhat paranoid response of Diefenbaker himself, whose eventual assessment of the dollar crisis was bluntly conspiratorial: 'The only explanation of the 1962 financial crisis that makes any sense is that it was orchestrated for political reasons. Its object was to get rid of my government … The crisis began with a "spooking" of the New York money market. I believe that it is more than possible, indeed highly probable, that the administration of President Kennedy used its influence to bring this about … There is now public evidence proving the Kennedy administration's culpability in the most outrageous acts of direct interference in the domestic political affairs of other countries, and the extent to which the Kennedy administration is now known to have aided the Liberal Party in the 1962 election.' For Diefenbaker's views on the dollar devaluation and its political meaning, see *One Canada*, 3: 108–36, quote at 124. Note, as well, Nicholson, *Vision and Indecision*, 314–17.

36 Arnie Myers, 'Liberal Leader Says Party Will Save Canadian Dollar,' *The Vancouver Sun*, 31 May 1962; Frank Rutter, 'Pearson Promises to Save Dollar,' *Winnipeg Free Press*, 31 May 1962. For Pearson's subsequent views of the

dollar devaluation and the exchange-rate crisis, see Lester B. Pearson, *Mike: The Memoirs of the Right Honourable Lester B. Pearson*, vol. 3, *1957–1968* (Toronto: University of Toronto Press, 1975), 59–63.

37 Leonard A. Kitz, Letter to the Editor, 'Our Shattered Dollar,' *Halifax Chronicle Herald*, 9 June 1962.

38 *Globe and Mail*: Editorial, 'Steady Dollar Rate Pledged by Fleming,' 11 June 1962; 'Value of the Dollar,' 12 June 1962; *Winnipeg Free Press*: 'Backs 90 Cent Dollar,' 9 June 1962; Editorial, 'Confidence Lacking,' 13 June 1962; 'Hamilton's Confession "Proved Panic,"' 11 June 1962; *Vancouver Sun*: 'Tory Favors 90 c Dollar,' 8 June 1962; 'More Devaluation Forecast by Regier,' 6 June 1962; Fleming, *So Very Near*, 2: 510–11; Stursberg, *Diefenbaker: Leadership Gained*, 257–64; Pickersgill, *Seeing Canada Whole*, 576.

39 *Calgary Herald*: 'Dollar Value Dips Near Critical Point,' 16 May 1962; Editorial, 'The Position of Our Dollar,' 18 May 1962; 'Financial Crisis Seen from Slumping Dollar,' 23 May 1962; '"Political Storm Cloud" Builds Up Over Dollar,' 4 June 1962; 'Fleming Stresses Dollar to Remain at Pegged Rate,' 11 June 1962; Michael Barkway, 'Restoration of Confidence in Dollar May Necessitate Drastic Measures,' 20 June 1962; *Globe and Mail*: 'Canadian Dollar at Twelve-Year Low in New York,' 26 May 1962; Bruce Macdonald, 'How Will Cabinet Plug the Leak on the Dollar?' 20 June 1962.

40 Frank Walden, 'Fulton Warns Bread Firms Price Boosts to Be Probed,' *Vancouver Sun*, 9 June 1962; Victor Mackie, 'Dief Pledges War on Price Raisers,' *Winnipeg Free Press*, 8 June 1962; Editorial, 'The Spiral Begins,' *Winnipeg Free Press*, 8 June 1962; Editorial, 'The Dollar Election,' *Winnipeg Free Press*, 16 June 1962. The New Democratic Party and Tommy Douglas also promised to deal with 'price-fixing conspiracies.' See 'Consumer Protection Promised by Douglas,' *London Free Press*, 9 May 1962.

41 'Thompson Raps Diefs Funny Money,' *Winnipeg Free Press*, 28 May 1962; Pat Clayton, 'Bennett Says Diefendollars Too High; Wants 90 Cents,' *Winnipeg Free Press*, 2 June 1962; 'Manning Fires Broadside at Tory Debts, Devaluation,' *Winnipeg Free Press*, 7 June 1962.

42 For political cartoonists the dollar devaluation was a boon to creativity. A quite early representation appeared in the *Halifax Chronicle-Herald*, 5 May 1962, with a butterfly-winged Canadian dollar bill driven by a nail labelled Fixed Exchange Rate, a headstone beneath numbered 92.5 c. The *St John's Evening Telegram*, 10 May 1962, offered an unusually benign representation in which the Canadian dollar bill was represented by a tourist influx from the United States, with Fleming offering his welcome. From there matters worsened. See *Winnipeg Free Press*, 7 June 1962, depicting Diefenbaker as a

Man in the Moon scowling at the Cost of Living Cow, draped in a 92.5-cent dollar, jumping over him; Diefenbaker and Fleming were depicted on a silver dollar, trying to shoot the rapids in an imperilled canoe, in *Halifax Chronicle Herald*, 23 June 1962. In Vancouver Diefendollars turned up at the riotous rally of 30 May 1962, Fleming on their face, and the right portion of the bill with a 7.5-cent section declared 'non-negotiable, please detach' (*Vancouver Sun*, 31 May 1962). The Pas bills, used as Liberal Party election props, borrowed from a Peter Kuch Diefendollar cartoon that appeared in the *Winnipeg Free Press*, 12 June 1962, and, before that, on 4 May 1962. For a full account of Kuch cartoons and Diefenbaker see Peter Kuch, *Dief the Incredible 'Chief'* (Winnipeg: Christian Press, no date, but after 1978). See, on the Diefenbuck, *Globe and Mail*: 'Diefenbucks Minted by Manitoba Publisher,' 31 May 1962; 'Diefendollar Label Threatening,' 5 May 1962; *Halifax Chronicle Herald*: '"Diefenbucks" Worth 92.5 Cents Sell for 1 Cent,' 31 May 1962; and a Liberal Party ad headlined 'The Diefenbaker Dollar Wallops Your Pocketbook!' 13 June 1962; *Winnipeg Free Press*: 'The Diefendollar Becomes an Issue,' 14 May 1962.

43 Consider Diefenbaker's key statement of his political program, 'One Canada, One Nation,' in John G. Diefenbaker, *Those Things We Treasure* (Toronto: Macmillan, 1972), 139–55. This speech (and others in that text) reads, in the aftermath of his 1962 humiliation and the passage of the 1960s, as an articulate atavism. Note, as well, Diefenbaker, *One Canada*, 2: 248–266; and for a discussion of how such ideas left Diefenbaker stranded, even among Conservatives, by 1966, see Robert C. Coates, *The Night of the Long Knives* (Fredericton: Brunswick Press, 1969), 107–29.

44 Michael Barkway, 'Dollar Near Bottom Limit,' *Calgary Herald*, 30 May 1962.

45 See Marshall McLuhan, *Understanding Media: The Extensions of Man* (Toronto: Signet, 1968), 123–34.

46 Note the Liberal Party campaign advertisement, Jack Nicholson, 'Tory Bungling Brings 14c Drop in Dollar,' from 'The Liberal Challenge,' an insert in *Vancouver Sun*, 8 June 1962; Bruce Macdonald, 'How Will Cabinet Plug the Leak on the Dollar?' *Globe and Mail*, 20 June 1962; 'Story of the Dollar: A Fall from Grace,' *Globe and Mail*, 22 June 1962.

47 Indicative of ambivalences around the dollar's devaluation in the aftermath of the 1962 campaign were the contradictory positions expressed in *Canadian Forum*, an organ of liberal social democratic thought. See Harry C. Eastman, 'On Pegging Us to a Cross of Gold,' *Canadian Forum*, June 1962, 50–1, vs. Trevor Lloyd, 'Correspondence,' *Canadian Forum*, July 1962, 84–5.

2: Shelter from the Storm: The Cold War and the Making of Early 1960s Canada

1 See http://www.kicanada.com/nuke/news/bomb_shelter2.htm (accessed 6 January 2006).

2 This position, in which the Cold War is extended back in time, as well as perhaps forward into the future, seems to me congruent with positions adopted by William Appelman Williams. See, for example, his pioneering statement in *The Tragedy of American Diplomacy* (New York: Delta, 1962); Paul M. Buhle and Edward Rice-Maximin, *William Appelman Williams: The Tragedy of Empire* (New York and London: Routledge, 1995). On McCarthy, see Thomas C. Reeves, *The Life and Times of Joe McCarthy: A Biography* (New York: Stein and Day, 1982); David M. Oshinsky, *A Conspiracy So Immense: The World of Joe McCarthy* (New York: Free Press, 1983); Richard M. Fried, *Nightmare in Red: The McCarthy Era in Perspective* (New York: Oxford University Press, 1990). For an American-translated and -published propaganda statement that exaggerated the extent of the Soviet nuclear threat, see V.D. Sokolovskii, *Soviet Military Strategy: Fully Analyzed and Annotated* (Englewood Cliffs, NJ: Prentice-Hall, 1963).

3 The best recent overview addressing the impact of the Cold War on Canada is Reg Whitaker and Gary Marcuse, *Cold War Canada: The Making of a National Insecurity State, 1945–1957* (Toronto: University of Toronto Press, 1994).

4 On anti-communism in the labour movement, for instance, see Irving A. Abella, *Nationalism, Communism and Canadian Labour: The CIO, the Communist Party, and the Canadian Congress of Labour, 1935–1956* (Toronto: University of Toronto Press, 1973).

5 See Len Scher, *The Un-Canadians: True Stories of the Blacklist Era* (Toronto: Lester 1992).

6 For Gouzenko see Robert Bothwell and J.L. Granatstein, eds., *The Gouzenko Transcripts: The Evidence Presented to the Kellock-Taschereau Royal Commission of 1946* (Ottawa: Deneau, 1982); John Sawatsky, *Gouzenko: The Untold Story* (Toronto: Macmillan, 1984). Discussion of E.H. Norman is extensive, but see Lester B. Pearson, *Mike: The Memoirs of the Right Honourable Lester B. Pearson*, vol. 3, *1957–1968* (Toronto: University of Toronto Press, 1975), 166–73; James Barros, *No Sense of Evil: Espionage and the Case of Herbert Norman* (Toronto: Deneau, 1986); Roger W. Bowen, *Innocence Is Not Enough: The Life and Death of Herbert Norman* (Vancouver: Douglas and Macintyre, 1986).

7 Richard Cavell, ed., *Love, Hate, and Fear in Canada's Cold War* (Toronto: University of Toronto Press, 2004); Mark Kristmanson, *Plateaus of Freedom: Nationality, Culture, and State Security in Canada, 1940–1960* (Toronto: Oxford University Press, 2003).

 8 Anthony P. Michel, 'To Represent the Country in Egypt: Aboriginality,
   Britishness, Anglophone Canadian Identities, and the Nile Voyageur Contin-
   gent, 1884–1885,' *Histoire Sociale/Social History* 39 (May 2006): 45–78; Roy
   McLaren, *Canadians on the Nile, 1882–1898* (Vancouver: UBC Press, 1978);
   Norman Penlington, *Canada and Imperialism, 1896–1899* (Toronto: Univer-
   sity of Toronto Press, 1965); T.G. Marquis, *Canada's Sons of Kopje and Veldt:
   An Historical Account of the Canadian Contingents* (Toronto: Canada's Sons,
   1900); Carman Miller, *Painting the Map Red: Canada and the South African
   War, 1899–1902* (Montreal: McGill-Queen's University Press, 1998); Desmond
   Morton and J.L. Granatstein, *Marching to Armageddon: Canadians and the
   Great War, 1914–1918* (Toronto: Lester and Orpen Dennys, 1989); J.L.
   Granatstein and Desmond Morton, *A Nation Forged in Fire: Canadians and the
   Second World War, 1939–1945* (Toronto: Lester and Orpen Dennys, 1989).
 9 See, for instance, Robert D. Cuff and J.L. Granatstein, *Ties That Bind: Canadian–
   American Relations in Wartime from the Great War to the Cold War* (Toronto:
   Samuel Stevens Hakkert, 1977).
10 Sherene H. Razack, *Dark Threats and White Knights: The Somalia Affair, Peacekeep-
   ing, and the New Imperialism* (Toronto: University of Toronto Press, 2004), 34.
11 Ibid., 35–6; Razack, '"Simple Logic": Race, the Identity Documents Rule,
   and the Story of a Nation Beseiged and Betrayed,' *Journal of Law and Social
   Policy* 15 (2000): 181–209; James Eayrs, *Northern Approaches: Canada and the
   Search for Peace* (Toronto: University of Toronto Press, 1961).
12 Among many sources see Geoffrey Hayes, 'Canada as a Middle Power: The
   Case of Peacekeeping,' in Andrew Cooper, ed., *Niche Diplomacy: Middle
   Powers after the Cold War* (New York: St Martin's Press, 1997), 73–89; Donald
   Gordon, 'Canada as Peace-keeper,' in J. King Gordon, ed., *Canada's Role as a
   Middle Power: Papers Given at the Third Annual Banff Conference on World Devel-
   opment* (Toronto: Canadian Institute of International Affairs, 1965), 51–66;
   J.L. Granatstein and David J. Bercuson, *War and Peacekeeping: From South
   Africa to the Gulf – Canada's Little Wars* (Toronto: Key Porter Books, 1991);
   Gregory Wirick, 'Canada, Peacekeeping, and the United Nations,' in Fen
   Osler Hampson and Christopher Maule, eds., *Canada Among Nations, 1992–
   1993: A New World Order* (Ottawa: Carleton University Press, 1992), 94–114;
   Razack, *Dark Threats and White Knights*, esp. 32–6; George Ignatieff, *The Making of a Peacemonger: The Memoirs of George Ignatieff* (Toronto: University of
   Toronto Press, 1985).
13 Philip Resnick, *Land of Cain: Class and Nationalism in English Cnaada, 1945–
   1975* (Vancouver: New Star Books, 1977), 82.
14 See, for an excellent brief discussion of 'A Middle Political Power,' as prelude to Vietnam, Victor Levant, *Quiet Complicity: Canadian Involvement in the*

Vietnam War (Toronto: Between the Lines, 1986), 12–19. Middle-power politics are also surveyed in Alvin Finkel, *Our Lives: Canada after 1945* (Toronto: Lorimer, 1997), 102–23.

15 See as a starting point of analysis, Fred J. Cook, *The Warfare State* (New York: Macmillan, 1962); Seymour Melman, *The Permanent War Economy* (New York: Simon and Schuster, 1974).

16 Michael Bliss, *Northern Enterprise: Five Centuries of Canadian Business* (Toronto: McClelland and Stewart, 1987), 475; John G. Diefenbaker, *One Canada: Memoirs of the Right Honourable John G. Diefenbaker*, vol. 3, *The Tumultuous Years, 1962–1967* (Toronto: Macmillan, 1977), 38.

17 On Howe and his importance in this period see Robert Bothwell and William Kilbourn, *C.D. Howe: A Biography* (Toronto: McClelland and Stewart, 1979).

18 Bliss, *Northern Enterprise*, 474–7; James Dow, *The Arrow* (Toronto: James Lorimer, 1979); Ronald A. Keith, 'I Flew in the Avro, Our New Jet Fighter,' *Maclean's*, 1 November 1950.

19 Denis Smith, *Rogue Tory: The Life and Legend of John G. Diefenbaker* (Toronto: McFarlane, Walter and Ross, 1995), 308–11, which contains the Howe quote; John G. Diefenbaker, *One Canada*, 3: 33.

20 Patrick Nicholson, *Vision and Indecision* (Don Mills, ON: Longmans, 1968), 200–1; Dow, *The Arrow*, 113.

21 *Globe and Mail*, 13 January 1959.

22 Dow, *The Arrow*, Smith, *Rogue Tory*, 308–25; Peter C. Newman, *Renegade in Power: The Diefenbaker Years* (Toronto: McClelland and Stewart, 1963), 347–50; Jon B. McLin, *Canada's Changing Defense Policy, 1957–1963: The Problems of a Middle Power in Alliance* (Baltimore: John's Hopkins, 1967), 60–7; E.K. Shaw, *There Never Was an Arrow* (Toronto: Steel Rail, 1979); Bliss, *Northern Enterprise*, 474–7; Robert Bothwell, Ian Drummond, and John English, *Canada since 1945: Power, Politics, and Provincialism* (Toronto: University of Toronto Press, 1989), 228–30; Diefenbaker, *One Canada*, 3: 31–43; Nicholson, *Vision and Indecison*, 204, explains the commitment to the Arrow as follows: 'National pride was deeply involved ... the largest single factor urging the overlong continuation of the Arrow project.' The widespread unemployment the termination of the project induced was also a critical factor. See Thomas Van Dusen, *The Chief* (Toronto: McGraw-Hill, 1968), 33–7. The quote on museums and technology is from Pearson, *Mike*, 3: 47–8. In October 2006 Toronto's Downsview Park Aerospace Museum unveiled a full-scale model replica of the Avro Arrow. It took 140 volunteers sustained by corporate sponsors and donations eight years to assemble the aircraft, guided in their project mostly by second-hand documents, but aided as well by draftsmans' plans smuggled out of A.V. Roe as production of the Arrow was

halted. More than 2,000 people, many self-confessed semi-obsessive fans who have adopted the appellation 'Arrowhead,' flocked to the official launching of the mock jet. Some embraced the view that the denouement of the doomed plane was the result of 'behind the scenes work of the Americans,' who could countenance no competition from a superior Canadian aircraft. See Jeff Gray, '47 Years Later, It's Still Arrow Dynamic,' *Globe and Mail*, 9 October 2006.

23 This oscillating response, moving from exuberant optimism to fearful retrenchment, was something of a theme of the postwar nuclear age. See Elaine Tyler May, *Homeward Bound: American Families in the Cold War Era* (New York: Basic Books, 1988); Allan Winkler, *Life under a Cloud: American Anxiety about the Atom* (New York: Oxford, 1993); Paul Boyer, *By the Bomb's Early Light: American Thought and Culture at the Dawn of the Nuclear Age* (New York: Pantheon, 1985); Boyer, *Fallout: A Historian Reflects on America's Half-Century Encounter with Nuclear Weapons* (Columbus: Ohio State University Press, 1988); Margot A. Henriksen, *Dr. Strangelove's America: Society and Culture in the Atomic Age* (Berkeley: University of California Press, 1997); Lisle A. Rose, *The Cold War Comes to Main Street* (Lawrence: University of Kansas Press, 1999); Valerie J. Korinek, '"It's a Tough Time to Be in Love": The Darker Side of *Chatelaine* during the Cold War,' in Cavell, ed., *Love, Hate, and Fear in Canada's Cold War,* 166–8.

24 The U.S. nuclear arsenal expanded from 50 bombs in 1948 to 840 in 1952 to 2,000 in 1955 to an amazing 28,000 in 1962. The Soviet stockpile grew from 5 in 1950 to 1,700 by the end of the decade. See Tony Judt, *Postwar: A History of Europe since 1945* (New York: Penguin, 2005), 247–8.

25 The above paragraphs draw on Smith, *Rogue Tory,* 310–53; Bothwell, Drummond, and English, *Canada Since 1945,* 229–32; H. Basil Robinson, *Diefenbaker's World: A Populist in Foreign Affairs* (Toronto: University of Toronto Press, 1989), 85, 115, 132–4, 144; Thomas Van Dusen, *The Chief* (Toronto: McGraw-Hill, 1968), 45; Nicholson, *Vision and Indecision,* 165–221; *Toronto Daily Star,* 2 February 1960.

26 For brief reference to Canadian opposition to the nuclear arms race see Dimitrios J. Rouossopoulos, ed., *The New Left in Canada* (Montreal: Our Generation Press, 1970), 8–9; Myrna Kostash, *Long Way from Home: The Story of the Sixties Generation in Canada* (Toronto: James Lorimer, 1980), esp. xxii–xxiv; Cyril Levitt, *Children of Privilege: Student Revolt in the Sixties – A Study of Student Movements in Canada, the United States, and West Germany* (Toronto: University of Toronto Press, 1984), 39–43; Doug Owram, *Born at the Right Time: A History of the Baby-Boom Generation* (Toronto: University of Toronto Press, 1996), 165, 218–19; Bothwell, Drummond, and English, *Canada since*

1945, 241; Robinson, *Diefenbaker's World*, 203. For the views of Diefenbaker's defence and external affairs ministers, which accent the anti-nuclear campaign's influence on the Tory leader and its essential wrong-headedness, see Peter Stursberg, *Diefenbaker: Leadership Lost, 1962–1967* (Toronto: University of Toronto Press, 1976), 25–6. Note, as well, Ignatieff, *The Making of a Peacemonger,* 183–98.

27 There are countless accounts of the Cuban revolution and the U.S. response. The above paragraphs draw selectively on Richard E. Welch, Jr, *Response to Revolution: The United States and the Cuban Revolution, 1959–1961* (Chapel Hill and London: University of North Carolina Press, 1985); Morris H. Morley, *Imperial State and Revolution: The United States and Cuba, 1952–1986* (Cambridge: Cambridge University Press, 1987); William Appleman Williams, *The United States, Cuba, and Castro* (New York: Monthly Review, 1962); Robert Tabor, *M-26: Biography of a Revolution* (New York: Lyle Stuart, 1961); James O'Connor, *The Origins of Socialism in Cuba* (Ithaca: Cornell University Press, 1970); Hugh Thomas, *Cuba or the Pursuit of Freedom* (London: Eyre and Spootiswoode, 1971). For the New Left and Cuba's importance see Van Gosse, *Where the Boys Are: Cuba, Cold War America and the Making of a New Left* (London: Verso, 1993).

28 I rely for much of the above on an engaging journalistic account, Max Frankel, *High Noon in the Cold War: Kennedy, Khrushchev, and the Cuban Missile Crisis* (New York: Ballantine Books, 2004), esp. 1–22. Other accounts include Herbert S. Dinerstein, *The Making of a Missile Crisis: October 1962* (Baltimore and London: Johns Hopkins University Press, 1976); Roger Hilsman, *The Cuban Missile Crisis: The Struggle over Policy* (London: Praeger, 1996). The Canadian press reported in early September that a Cuban arms buildup was underway and that a Khrushchev–Kennedy standoff could culminate in atomic war. See 'Reds Threaten West with Monster Bombs,' *Oshawa Times*, 8 September 1962; 'Any Assault on Cuba Means Atomic War: K – Appeals to U.S. "Common Sense,"' *Oshawa Times*, 11 September 1962. On Berlin's importance see Judt, *Postwar,* 254.

29 Robert A. Divine, ed., *The Cuban Missile Crisis* (New York: Markus Wiener, 1988), 9–11.

30 Frankel, *High Noon in the Cold War,* 36–42; Dino A. Brugioni, *Eyeball to Eyeball: The Inside Story of the Cuban Missile Crisis* (New York: Random House, 1991).

31 Frankel, *High Noon in the Cold War,* 101–23; Divine, *Cuban Missile Crisis,* 3–4; Hilsman, *Cuban Missile Crisis,* 67–78

32 Kennedy's speech is quoted at length in Frankel, *High Noon in the Cold War,* 118–19. The full text, as well as extensive commentary, appears in 'JFK Orders Cuba Blockade,' and 'Text of Kennedy's Statement On Crisis Over Cuba,'

Toronto Daily Star, 23 October 1962. While Canadians undoubtedly backed Kennedy, the immediate reaction in the press was indicative of specific concerns, namely that the American president was engaged in a horrific gamble of potentially devastatingly destructive consequence, and that there was indeed another side to the question of why the Soviets were positioned to establish nuclear weapon bases in Cuba: they, after all, faced the threat of similar American warheads stationed in Italy, Turkey, and so on. For the range of comment see *Toronto Daily Star.* 'UK Press Raps Kennedy,' Editorial, 'Kennedy Plays with Fire,' 'How Canadians Reacted to Kennedy Ultimatum,' all 23 October 1962; Mark Gayn, 'Mood of Futility Pervades UN on Cuba Crisis,' John Bird, 'Ottawa Fear: That U.S. Decisions on Cuba May Now Pass from the White House to the Pentagon,' George Bryant, 'K. Too Knows What It's Like to Be under Nuclear Gun,' Ron Haggart, 'Americans Are Sometimes a Frightening People,' William R. Frye, 'Scrap Your Own Bases, Soviet Tells U.S.,' Editorial, 'The Double Standard,' 'Most Canadian U.S. Papers Back JFK Blockade of Cuba,' all 24 October 1962. Carl Mollins, 'United Church Policy on A-Weapons Sought,' *Oshawa Times,* 19 September 1962, provided an early indication of the diversity of views that would crystallize five weeks later.

33 Smith, *Rogue Tory,* 454–7; Diefenbaker, *One Canada,* 3: 77–90; Nicholson, *Vision and Indecision,* 145–77; Robinson, *Diefenbaker's World,* 285–95. A blockade was, by definition, an act of war, but quarantine was supposedly something different. See the response of the Canadian press in Carman Cumming, 'Question of Definition: "Quarantine" – Act of War or Piracy?' *Ottawa Citizen,* 27 October 1962; Jack Best, 'Uncertainty in Canada – Resolve in Russia,' *Ottawa Citizen,* 24 October 1962.

34 Robinson, *Diefenbaker's World,* 290–1; Smith, *Rogue Tory,* 457–60; Bothwell, Drummond, and English, *Canada since 1945,* 234–5; Frankel, *High Noon in the Cold War,* 121, 145–7; John Bird, '"No A-bombs for Canada" Policy Strengthened by Debate on Cuba,' 'Truman Raps Canada for Cuban "Attitude,"' and 'U.S. Boards First Red Ship but Finds No "Offensive Weapons" Now Americans Talk of "Further Action,"' *Toronto Daily Star,* 26 October 1962. Diefenbaker was no doubt embarrassed by an ultra-defender, Tory backbencher Terry Nugent, who was outspoken in his criticism of the Cuban blockade and of the Kennedy administration's treatment of Canada. Applauded by the NDP, Nugent insisted that Canada tell the U.S. that 'we cannot, as a nation with a national conscience, permit ourselves to be associated in an action which constitutes unprovoked aggression.' See John Walker, 'Tory MP Strongly Criticizes Blockade of Cuba,' *Ottawa Citizen,* 24 October 1962; 'Cuba Move Illegal Tory MP Tells House,' *Toronto Daily Star,* 24 October 1962.

35 Arthur M. Schlesinger, Jr, *A Thousand Days: John F. Kennedy in the White House* (Boston: Houghton Mifflin, 1965), 840–1. For more critical assessments of Kennedy and the Cuban missile crisis see I.F. Stone, 'The Brink,' *New York Review of Books*, 14 April 1966, 12–16; Leslie Dewart, 'The Cuban Missile Crisis Revisited,' *Studies on the Left* 5 (Spring 1965): 24–40; Barton J. Bernstein, 'The Cuban Missile Crisis: Trading the Jupiters in Turkey,' *Political Science Quarterly* 95 (Spring 1980): 97–125. An excellent collection of essays posing the debate around the question is Divine, ed., *Cuban Missile Crisis*. Typical Canadian press comment appeared in 'U.S. Boards First Red Ship but Finds No "Offensive Arms" Now Americans Talk of Further Action,' *Toronto Daily Star*, 26 October 1962; 'Kennedy, Mr. K End Cuba Crisis,' *Toronto Daily Star*, 29 October 1962.

36 Newman, *Renegade in Power*, 354.

37 For accounts, see Smith, *Rogue Tory*, 462–510; Peter Stursberg, *Diefenbaker: Leadership Lost, 1962–1967* (Toronto: University of Toronto Press, 1976), 3–100; Robinson, *Diefenbaker's World*, 296–311; Newman, *Renegade in Power*, 355–400, with quote on defence on 366; Donald M. Fleming, *So Very Near: The Political Memoirs of The Honourable Donald M. Fleming*, vol. 2, *The Summit Years* (Toronto: McClelland and Stewart, 1985), 577–621; Thomas Van Dusen, *The Chief* (Toronto: McGraw-Hill, 1968), 44–6; Lester B. Pearson, *Mike*, 3: 69–76.

38 The above paragraphs draw on Newman, *Renegade in Power*, 387–8, 395, quoting *Toronto Daily Star*; Pierre Berton, *Maclean's*, 6 April 1963, 62; Diefenbaker, *One Canada*, 3: 3–4; Bothwell, Drummond, and English, *Canada since 1945*, 235; Judy LaMarsh, *Memoirs of a Bird in a Gilded Cage* (Toronto: McClelland and Stewart, 1968), 36–44; Knowlton Nash, *Kennedy and Diefenbaker: Fear and Loathing across the Undefended Border* (Toronto: McClelland and Stewart, 1990), 278–93; Peyton V. Lyon, *Canada in World Affairs, 1961–1963*, vol. 12 (Toronto: Oxford University Press, 1968), 202–7; Smith, *Rogue Tory*, 500–4.

39 Note the brief comment on Diefenbaker in George Woodcock, *Canada and the Canadians* (Toronto: Macmillan, 1970), 210.

40 For accounts of other even more awe- and fear-inspiring hangovers of the high noon of the Cold War, see the brilliantly evocative and iconoclastic presentations in Mike Davis, *Dead Cities and Other Tales* (New York: New Press, 2003); Tom Vanderbilt, *Survival City: Adventures among the Ruins of Atomic America* (Princeton, NJ: Princeton Architectural Press, 2002), as well as Tom Vanderbilt, 'Fallout Shelters,' *Metropolis*, April 2001, at http://www.metropolismag.com (accessed 10 January 2006), which details how John F. Kennedy's private Peanut Island (near Palm Beach) family fallout shelter,

which had fallen into near ruin by 1995, and was taken over by homeless people, has been leased and refurbished by the Palm Beach Maritime Museum. The Diefenbunker paled in comparison to the slightly larger luxurious Greenbrier Resort in White Sulphur Springs, West Virginia, its 112,000-square-foot American counterpart. Meant to house the entire U.S. Congress, the facility boasted decontamination showers, dormitory and meeting space, a medical clinic, a television studio, food for 1,000 people for two months, and, to beat all, a crematorium. See Stephen I. Schwartz, 'Bunker Down,' *Bulletin of the Atomic Scientists* 59 (May/June 2003): 67–70.

41 John G. Diefenbaker, *One Canada: Memoirs of the Right Honourable John G. Diefenbaker*, vol. 2, *The Years of Achievement, 1956–1962* (Toronto: Macmillan, 1976), 246; http://www.diefenbunker.ca/english/default.asp (accessed 5 January 2006); CBC Archives, 'Clip: From Einstein to the A-Bomb: Early Milestones,' broadcast date: 8 August 1961, television, http://archives. cbc.ca/400i.asp (accessed 6 January 2006); *Duck and Cover*, Archer Productions, 1951. The government bunker was identified and located in Carp in 'Ottawans Remain Calm in Face of Cuba Crisis,' *Ottawa Citizen*, 26 October 1962. For United States commentary see Guy Oakes, *The Imaginary War: Civil Defense and American Cold War Culture* (New York: Oxford University Press, 1994); Laura McEnaney, *Civil Defense Begins at Home: Militarization Meets Everyday Life in the Fifties* (Princeton, NJ: Princeton University Press, 2000).

42 Henriksen, *Strangelove's America*, 200; Kenneth D. Rose, *One Nation Underground: The Fallout Shelter in American Culture* (New York: New York University Press, 2001), reviewed by Stephen I. Schwartz, 'Bunker Down,' *Bulletin of the Atomic Scientists* 59 (May/June 2003): 67–70.

43 Rose, *One Nation Underground*; Schwartz, 'Bunker Down,' 67–70. *Your Basement Fallout Shelter: Blueprint for Survival No. 1* (Ottawa: Alger Press/Queen's Printer, 1961). Subsequent booklets in the *Blueprint for Survival* series were issued by the Department of National Defence and addressed such topics as *11 Steps to Survival* (Ottawa: Queen's Printer, 1969; original circa 1961), which again extolled the virtues of fallout shelters and emergency cleanliness, but also provided instruction in first aid and other matters. See also CBC Archives, 'Clip: How to Survive; Life in a Fallout Shelter,' broadcast date: 17 September 1961, Radio, http://archives.cbc.ca/400i.asp (accessed 12 January 2008).

44 CBC Archives, 'Clip: Bomb Shelters for Sale,' broadcast date: 6 November 1958, Radio, http://archives.cbc.ca/400i.asp (accessed 12 January 2008).

45 For accounts of early civilian defence programs in the United States, which included grappling with the thorny problem of segregating bomb shelters in the American south, see Andrew D. Grossman, *Neither Dead nor Red: Civilian*

Defense and American Political Development during the Early Cold War (New York and London: Routledge, 2001); McEnaney, *Civil Defense Begins at Home*, 121–51.

46 Hyman Solomon, '$50 Million Spent to Meet an A-attack but Canadians Are Still Sitting Ducks,' *Toronto Daily Star,* 27 October 1962; 'Ottawans Remain Calm in Face of Cuba Crisis,' *Ottawa Citizen,* 26 February 1962; Editorial, 'The World Breathes Easier No Thanks to Canada's Gov't,' *Lindsay Daily Post,* 29 October 1962; 'JK Jitters: Sirens Alarm Oakville,' *Toronto Daily Star,* 25 October 1962.

47 'To Step Up Shelter Plan,' *Oshawa Daily Times,* 27 October 1962; 'Ottawans Remain Calm in Face of Cuba Crisis,' *Ottawa Citizen,* 26 October 1962; 'No EMO Meeting on Cuba – Mayor,' *Ottawa Journal,* 25 October 1962; 'Order Emergency School Radios,' *Ottawa Citizen,* 26 October 1962.

48 Schwartz, 'Bunker Down,' 67–70.

49 Vanderbilt, 'Fallout Shelters'; Rose, *One Nation Underground,* 191–213; Schwartz, 'Bunker Down,' 67–70; Paul Boyer, 'Review of *One Nation Underground,*' *Journal of Social History* 36 (2002): 249–51. On suburbs and shelters see especially Grossman, *Neither Dead nor Red,* 72–85; McEnaney, *Civil Defense Begins at Home,* 47–67.

50 Korinek, 'The Darker Side of *Chatelaine,*' 169–70, quoting Christina McCall, 'Can You Protect Your Family from the Bomb,' *Chatelaine,* April 1962. On the mixed results of raising women's bomb consciousness in the United States see McEnaney, *Civil Defense Begins at Home,* 88–122.

51 'Ottawans Remain Calm in Face of Cuba Crisis,' *Ottawa Citizen,* 26 October 1962; Hyman Solomon, '$50 Million Spent to Meet an A-attack but Canadians are Still Sitting Ducks,' *Toronto Daily Star,* 27 October 1972.

52 Solomon, '$50 Million Spent to Meet an A-attack but Canadians are Still Sitting Ducks.'

53 'Claims Ottawa Does "Next to Nothing" Urges Shelter Plan,' *Toronto Daily Star,* 25 October 1962; Solomon, '$50 Million Spent to Meet an A-attack but Canadians are Still Sitting Ducks.' James G. Eayrs would later author *In Defence of Canada* (Toronto: University of Toronto Press, 1965) and was arguably one of Canada's leading foreign policy political scientists.

54 For a later statement on the ludicrousness of the shelter defence argument see Marshall Windmiller, 'Shelters and Anti-Ballistic Missiles,' *Canadian Dimension* 4 (May–June 1967): 4–6, 9.

55 George Grant, *Lament for a Nation: The Defeat of Canadian Nationalism* (Ottawa: Carleton Library, 1970; original 1965), 5, 68, 86–7.

56 Smith, *Rogue Tory,* 502.

57 A measure of this would emerge in the insights of Gad Horowitz, *Canadian Labour in Politics* (Toronto: University of Toronto Press, 1968), 10, 23.

Horowitz and Grant represented the coming together of a certain kind of
socialist and a particular type of conservative in the mid-1960s, with Grant
making a quite specific (and limited) united bond with New Leftists as they
emerged in the later 1960s, an alliance forged on radio shows and in the
left-wing nationalist pages of *Canadian Dimension*, where Grant was a fre-
quently published contributing editor. See, for instance, Andrew Potter,
'Introduction to the Fortieth Anniversary Edition,' *Lament for a Nation: The
Defeat of Canadian Nationalism* by George Grant (Montreal and Kingston:
McGill-Queen's University Press, 2005), xxx–xxvii; William Christian, *George
Grant: A Biography* (Toronto: University of Toronto Press, 1993), 10; George
A. Rawlyk, 'Lament for Canadian-American Relations?' *Journal of Canadian
Studies* 26 (Summer 1991): 169–72; George Grant, 'Tories, Socialists, and
the Demise of Canada,' *Canadian Dimension* (May-June 1965): 12–15; Grant,
'Canadian Fate and Imperialism,' *Canadian Dimension* (March-April 1967):
21–5; 'Horowitz and Grant Talk,' *Canadian Dimension* (December-January
1969–70), 18–20.

58 Grant, *Lament for a Nation* (1970), 71.
59 Potter, 'Introduction,' *Lament for a Nation* (2005), xxix–xxx. For details of
   Grant's biography see also Christian, *George Grant.*

3: Scandalous Sex: A Cold (War) Case

1 Larry Zolf, *Just Watch Me: Remembering Pierre Trudeau* (Toronto: James
   Lorimer, 1984), 17–28; Gordon Donaldson, 'The Prime Minister's
   Bedroom,' *Fiteen Men: Canada's Prime Ministers from Macdonald to Trudeau*
   (Toronto: Doubleday, 1969), 259–60.
2 Zolf, *Just Watch Me*, 24–5, 28. Further comment on Trudeau and sex can be
   found in Linda Griffiths, 'The Lover: Dancing with Trudeau,' and Rick
   Salutin, 'Trudeau and the Left: Violence, Sex, Culture,' both in Andrew
   Cohen and J.L. Granatstein, eds., *Trudeau's Shadow: The Life and Legacy of
   Pierre Elliott Trudeau* (Toronto: Random House, 1998), 35–46, 177–94. On
   the marriage of Margaret and Pierre and its public implosion see Stephen
   Clarkson and Christina McCall, *Trudeau and Our Times*, vol. 2, *The Magnificent Obsession* (Toronto: McClelland and Stewart, 1991), 126–42, where
   McLuhan is quoted; Margaret Trudeau, *Beyond Reason* (New York: Padding-
   ton Press, 1979); Margaret Trudeau, *Consequences* (Toronto: Seal Books,
   1982); Celeste Fremon, 'Margaret Trudeau,' *Playgirl*, September 1979;
   Stevie Cameron, 'Maggie: Happy at Last,' *Chatelaine*, June 1985.
3 There is much written on the sexual revolution, and it will figure in later discussions in this book of feminism and the New Left. For introductions only,

see Robert Bothwell, Ian Drummond, and John English, *Canada since 1945: Power, Politics, and Provincialism* (Toronto: University of Toronto Press, 1989), 310–11; Doug Owram, *Born at the Right Time: A History of the Baby Boom Generation* (Toronto: University of Toronto Press, 1996), 248–72; and the fearful Simma Holt, *Sex and the Teenage Revolution* (Toronto: McClelland and Stewart, 1967). W.E. Mann's edited *The Underside of Toronto* (Toronto: McClelland and Stewart, 1970) contains a number of essays that address what might be considered aspects of the sexual revolution.

4 See Barbara Roberts, '"They Drove Him to Drink": Donald Creighton's Macdonald and His Wives,' *Canada: An Historical Magazine* 3 (December 1975): 51–64; Gail Cuthbert Brandt, 'National Unity and the Politics of Political History,' *Journal of the Canadian Historical Association* (1992): 3–11; Donald Swainson, 'Schuyler Shibley and the Underside of Victorian Ontario,' *Ontario History* 65 (1973): 51–60.

5 As is evident in Canadian literature. See John Moss, *Sex and Violence in the Canadian Novel: The Ancestral Present* (Toronto: McClelland and Stewart, 1977).

6 Among many sources that could be consulted see the essays in Gary Kinsman, Dieter K. Buse, and Mercedes Steedman, eds., *Whose National Security: Canadian State Surveillance and the Creation of Enemies* (Toronto: Between the Lines, 2000); Richard Cavell, ed., *Love, Hate and Fear in Canada's Cold War* (Toronto: University of Toronto Press, 2004); Mary Louise Adams, *The Trouble with Normal: Postwar Youth and the Making of Heterosexuality* (Toronto: University of Toronto Press, 1997); Gary Kinsman, '"Character Weakness" and "Fruit Machines": Towards an Analysis of the Anti-Homosexual Security Campaign in the Canadian Civil Service,' *Labour/Le Travail* 35 (Spring 1995): 133–62; David Kimmel and Daniel Robinson, 'The Queer Career of Homosexual Security Vetting in Cold-War Canada,' *Canadian Historical Review* 75 (1994): 319–45; John Sawatsky, *Men in the Shadows: The RCMP Security Service* (Toronto: Doubleday, 1980).

7 Blair Fraser, *The Search for Identity: Canada – Postwar to Present* (Toronto: Doubleday, 1967), 117.

8 Unfortunately, where such recognition appeared it did so filtered through the security state's problematic characterizations. Thus, there is both insight and insensitivity in the Royal Canadian Mounted Police's 1952 view of Gerda Heseler as part of a postwar cohort of young women of which it would say, 'the sense of values developed by many of these girls demanded a "protector," preferably a prominent person of means with whom they could associate themselves.' See The Honourable Mr Justice Wishart Flett Spence, Commissioner, *Report of the Commission of Inquiry into Matters Relating to One Gerda Munsinger* (Ottawa: Queen's Printer, September 1966), 4. This report, a synopsis of the

wider hearings, is hereafter cited as Spence, *Munsinger Report*. Background
on European women coming to Canada, and their relationship with Cold
War security, can be gleaned from Franca Iacovetta, 'Freedom Lovers, Sex
Deviates, and Damaged Women: Iron Curtain Refugee Discourses in Cold
War Canada,' in Cavell, ed., *Love, Hate, and Fear in Canada's Cold War*, 77–107;
Iacovetta, 'Making Model Citizens: Gender, Corrupted Democracy, and Immi-
grant and Refugee Reception Work in Cold War Canada,' in Kinsman et al.,
eds., *Whose National Security*, 154–67; Iacovetta, *Gatekeepers: Reshaping Immigrant
Lives in Cold War Canada* (Toronto: Between the Lines, 2006). For a sensitive
journalistic assessment see Gordon Donaldson, 'Washington Calling: Sex and
Spying May Go Together, but Not Always,' *Galt Reporter*, 21 March 1966. This
article, sometimes attributed to Patrick Nicholson, appeared in a number of
Canadian newspapers under various titles.

9 The literature on this is extensive, and one Victorian case, that of Arthur
Munby, has been detailed in a number of texts. See, for instance, Derek
Hudson, *Munby, Man of Two Worlds: The Life and Diaries of Arthur J. Munby,
1812–1890* (Cambridge: Gambit, 1974); Liz Stanley, *The Diaries of Hannah
Cullwick: Victorian Maidservant* (New Brunswick, NJ: Rutgers University Press,
1984); Carol Mavor, *Pleasures Taken: Performances of Sexuality and Loss in Victo-
rian Photographs* (Durham, NC: Duke University Press, 1995), 71–116; Anne
McClintock, *Imperial Leather: Race, Gender, and Sexuality in the Colonial Contest*
(New York: Routledge, 1995), 132–80; Bryan D. Palmer, *Cultures of Darkness:
Night Travels in the Histories of Transgression* (New York: Monthly Review,
2000), 143–6. Note, as well, Seth Koven, *Slumming: Sexual and Social Politics
in Victorian London* (Princeton: Princeton University Press, 2004).

10 On Gerda Munsinger's name see, for instance, The Honourable Justice W.F.
Spence, 'Commission of Inquiry into Matters relating to One Gerda
Munsinger,' 9 May 1966, National Archives of Canada, RG 33, Series 96,
Testimony of Jacqueline Delorme, 476 (hereafter Commission of Inquiry);
Patrick Nicholson, 'Liberals Welcomed Gerda; Paid Fare and Cleared Her?'
Sudbury Star, 24 March 1966; 'L'affaire Munsinger,' *Le Nouveau Samedi*,
19 March 1966; Alan Harvey, 'Newsmen Frustrated by Gerda's Cash Deal,'
Globe and Mail, 14 March 1966. In citing newspaper articles on Munsinger I
rely on original research in the Canadian press as well as on newspaper and
magazine article files compiled in Commission of Inquiry, RG 33, series 96,
labeled volumes, 2, 3, 4, 5, which contain files of articles by date, i.e., 20
March 1966 – 31 March 1966. In what follows I cite only the newspaper or
magazine article, avoiding unnecessarily cumbersome referencing.

11 The facts of Munsinger's personal history in this period are further problematized in that many of them were conveyed by Munsinger in 1966 as she

became an international news story. German tabloids (*Neue Illustrierte* and *Nachtausgabe Am Sonntag*), drawn to the Munsinger affair by the flood of Canadian journalists and the increasingly cloak-and-dagger nature of tracking Gerda down and securing her story, paid handsomely for interviews and sensationalized first-person accounts. This no doubt 'colours' the veracity of much of Munsinger's representation of her history, which was embellished for commercial reasons. Finally, the serialized Munsinger articles in *Neue Illustrierte* contain a number of contradictory statements and are overall a confusing mélange of what is obviously fact and fiction. Chronology is often blurred and presented in overlapping layers of narrative that could not possibly have happened sequentially. In my view these articles are suggestive of Munsinger's self-perception, but they are something of a non-fiction novel. They clearly contain exaggerated claims, as well as distortions and mistruths. When I quote them below, I do so as indications of Munsinger's representations of herself and other people, useful for what they are, but not a straightforward presentation of what happened. For accounts of the Munsinger commerce see Alan Harvey, 'Newsmen Frustrated by Gerda's Cash Deal,' *Globe and Mail*, 14 March 1966; Harvey, 'Gerda (or Was It?) Makes a Break, Throws the Press Corps Off the Scent,' *Globe and Mail*, 15 March 1966; Bruce MacDonald, 'At Last! Canada Gets Some Space in the U.S. Papers,' *Globe and Mail*, 16 March 1966; 'She Loved Sévigny,' *Cape Breton Post*, 24 March 1966; 'Arrêtée pour espionage par les Américains mais relâchée immédiatement,' *Le Journal de Montréal*, 21 March 1966; 'Gerda Show Starts Feud in CBC News,' *Globe and Mail*, 16 March 1966; 'Shapely Gerda Still in Hiding,' *Swift Current Sun*, 16 March 1966; Charles Lynch, 'The Nation,' *Winnipeg Tribune*, 23 March 1966; 'Gerda Gets Columnist Off the Hook,' *Sarnia Observer*, 29 March 1966; Ken Pritchard, 'To Probe Allegations; Achieve Space Docking,' *Victoria Daily Times*, 19 March 1966; 'Latest Gadget for Gerda Girl to Be Satirical Moving Film,' *Sarnia Observer*, 29 March 1966.

12 Don Delaplante, 'U.S. Denied Gerda Entry: Ex-Husband,' *Globe and Mail*, 14 March 1966; 'Son mari a joué au baseball à Ottawa,' *Le Petit Journal*, 13 March 1966; 'George Shuba fut le "grand amour" de Gerda,' *Nouvelles Illustrées*, 26 March 1966.

13 'Made No Trips aboard Canadian Official Aircraft, Gerda Says in Interview,' *Globe and Mail*, 16 March 1966; Patrick Nicholson, 'Liberals Welcomed Gerda; Paid Fare and Cleared Her?' *Sudbury Star*, 24 March 1966; *Neue Illustrierte* 15 (10 April 1966). In this tabloid citation and future reference to its Munsinger series, which ran from no. 13 (27 March 1966) to no. 17 (24 April 1966), I rely on an English translation by P.A. at RCMP Headquarters, in Commission of Inquiry, RG 33, vol. 3, *Neue Magazine*, file 5. The RCMP identification of

Munsinger's father as a communist is suspect because it suggests that he was
a teacher in a KPD (German Communist Party) school prior to 1939. Yet
such communist schools could not have been functioning for some time well
before the outbreak of the Second World War. See Spence, *Munsinger
Report*, 6.

14 *Neue Illustrierte* 15 (10 April 1966), 5–6; Don Delaplante, 'U.S. Denied
Gerda Entry: Ex-Husband,' *Globe and Mail*, 14 March 1966; Anthony Westell
and Geoffrey Stevens, 'The Munsinger Report: What It Must Answer and
Why,' *Globe Magazine*, 2 July 1966, 7–8; 'Arrêtée pour espionage par les
Américains mais relâchée immédiatement,' *Le Journal de Montréal*, 21 March
1966; Thomas Van Dusen, *The Chief* (Toronto: McGraw Hill, 1968), 187.
Munsinger's criminal acts in the 1947–9 period included taking some
clothes from the wife of a British army captain while working in his house
as a maid in 1947 and rifling the pockets of a U.S. army private in 1949,
stealing 1,000 German marks. An espionage link was asserted but never
elaborated on. See Spence, *Munsinger Report*, 4.

15 Westell and Stevens, 'The Munsinger Report,' 8; Van Dusen, *The Chief*, 189;
Bruce MacDonald, 'U.S. Told Canada of Gerda Ban,' *Globe and Mail*, 15 March
1966; '"Moral Terpitude" [*sic*], "Security Risk" Still Keeping Gerda out of
U.S.,' *Free Press Weekly Farmer's Advocate* (Winnipeg), 23 March 1966; Delaplante, 'U.S. Denied Gerda Entry,' *Globe and Mail*, 14 March 1966; 'Made
No Trips aboard Canadian Official Aircraft, Gerda Says in Interview,' *Globe
and Mail*, 16 March 1966. Munsinger was incorrectly linked in the French-
Canadian press with a woman deported from Canada for communist espionage in 1954, Ursula Schmidt. See Roger Nadeau, 'Oui Gerda était une
espionne! Pearson sauterait et Paul Martin le remplacerait,' *Le Petit Journal*,
17 March 1966; 'Le nom d'Ursula Schmidt rebondit,' *Dimanche-Matin*,
13 March 1966.

16 'Newspaper Says She Worked at NATO,' *Free Press Farmer's Weekly Advocate*,
23 March 1966; *Neue Illustrierte* 13 (27 March 1966), 7; 14 (3 April 1966),
12; 15 (10 April 1966), 7–9.

17 *Neue Illustrierte* 14 (3 April 1966), 6–9; Department of Citizenship and
Immigration, Government of Canada, Emigration Warrant #84938, Gerda
Munsinger, 18 July 1955, Minutes of a Meeting of the Committee of the
Privy Council, 14 March 1966, RG 14, series D-2, file SP 240-240B, National
Archives of Canada.

18 Spence, *Munsinger Report*, 65–7, would claim that Munsinger did indeed try
to mislead Canadian authorities in entering the country in 1955, especially
by avoiding use of her maiden name Heseler and providing false information relating to her mother and a woman designated both her mother and a

landlady. Such apparent subterfuges could, however, relate to the difficulty of locating Mrs Heseler and are not necessarily only interpreted as the actions of a guilty party.

19 *Neue Illustrierte* 14 (3 April 1966), 8–9.

20 The above paragraphs draw on and quote from *Neue Illustrierte* 14 (3 April 1966), 9; 15 (10 April 1966), 2; 'Des agents de la RCMP dans le même immeuble,' *Dimanche-Matin*, 13 March 1966; Robert Rice, 'Montreal Recalls Gerda,' *Globe and Mail*, 14 March 1966; Robert Reguly, 'Gerda veut revenir au Canada,' Robert McKenzie et John Brehl, 'La vie mouvementée de Gerda à Montreal,' *Dernière Heure*, 13 March 1966; 'Des agents de la RCMP dans le même immeuble,' *Dimanche-Matin*, 13 March 1966; Robert Reguly, 'Gerda the Vanishing Playgirl,' *Star Weekly*, 2 April 1966, 4; 'L'affaire Munsinger,' *Le Nouveau Samedi*, 19 March 1966; 'George Shuba fut le "grand amour" de Gerda,' *Nouvelles Illustrées*, 26 March 1966; '"Is It about Sévigny?" Said the Shapely Frau in the Comfy Flat,' *Globe and Mail*, 12 March 1966; *Toronto Telegram*, 11 March 1966, quoted in Deborah Van Seters, 'The Munsinger Affair: Images of Espionage and Security in 1960s Canada,' *Intelligence and National Security* 13 (Summer 1998): 79; Spence, *Munsinger Report*, 6; Commission of Inquiry, Delorme Testimony, 482.

21 The above paragraphs draw on *Neue Illustrierte* 14 (3 April 1966), 9–10; 16 (17 April 1966), 5–10; 'George Shuba fut le "grand amour" de Gerda,' *Nouvelles Illustrées*, 26 March 1966; Spence, *Munsinger Report*, 5. It is possible that Munsinger first met Sévigny at this Montreal golf club in 1958, as stated in Peter C. Newman, *The Distemper of Our Times* (Winnipeg: Greywood, 1968), 367, which contains a chapter on the Munsinger affair (354–68). It reappears in Peter C. Newman, *A Nation Divided: Canada and the Coming of Pierre Trudeau* (New York: Knopf, 1969). Spence, *Munsinger Report*, 5, would later claim that Munsinger did not fully pay back the Canadian state and its Department of Citizenship and Immigration until she was tracked down in November 1960 and forced to cough up the balance owed in one lump payment.

22 Sévigny dated his contact with Munsinger to August 1959 in Robert Rice, 'Ex-Minister Cries Slander; Knew Munsinger Woman "Socially,"' *Globe and Mail*, 12 March 1966. On Sévigny's connection to Doyle, troubling to Diefenbaker, see John G. Diefenbaker, *One Canada: Memoirs of the Right Honourable John G. Diefenbaker*, vol. 3, *The Tumultuous Years, 1962–1967* (Toronto: Macmillan, 1977), 192. Sévigny would later claim that Doyle played a prominent role in initiating the mudslinging around Munsinger, operating behind the scenes to bring the affair to light in order to embarrass the Conservatives and deflect attention away from matters the Liberal Party wanted to avoid having scrutinized. See Peter Stursberg, *Diefenbaker:*

Leadership Lost, 1962–1967 (Toronto: University of Toronto Press, 1976), 153, 157. See also Commission of Inquiry, Delorme Testimony, 491–2; and Van Dusen, *The Chief,* 213.

23 Commission of Inquiry, Delorme Testimony, 471–2, 491.

24 Munsinger would later claim that her relations with Sévigny started earlier in 1958 and involved travelling to Boston with him in a private jet owned by a friend of the Quebec businessman-politician, but she contradicts her statement in the same source that a first meeting with Sévigny occurred in 1959 at a Montreal cocktail lounge. See *Neue Illustrierte* 15 (10 April 1966), 2–3; 16 (17 April 1966), 4; Robert Reguly, 'Comment j'ai retrouvé Gerda Munsinger à Munich,' *Dernière Heure,* 13 March 1966. When asked about the Boston flight, however, Sévigny acknowledged that it could have happened. See 'Sévigny Tells of Shock Call from Gerda – "A Very Beautiful Girl,"' *Globe and Mail,* 14 March 1966.

25 There was later unconfirmed speculation that Munsinger visited Sévigny at his Beacon Arms hotel in Ottawa. See Benoit C. Hebert, 'Niant avoir été une espionne, Gerda Munsinger veut venir au Canada pour "éclaircir les choses,"' *Dimanche-Matin,* 13 March 1966; '"Is It about Sévigny?" Said the Shapely Frau in the Comfy Flat,' *Globe and Mail,* 12 March 1966.

26 The above paragraphs draw on Patrick Nicholson, 'Liberals Welcomed Gerda; Paid Fare and Cleared Her,' *Sudbury Star,* 24 March 1966; 'L'Affaire Munsinger,' *Le Nouveau Samedi,* 19 March 1966; Commission of Inquiry, 'Testimony of Jacqueline Delorme,' 'Testimony of Joseph Pierre Albert Sévigny,' 470–526; *Neue Illustrierte* 14 (3 April 1966), 3–5, 10–11. Sévigny's candid statements of his attraction to beautiful women were paraded throughout the tabloids and mainstream press. See 'J'aime les femmes c'est vrai!' *Le Nouveau Samedi,* 19 March 1966; Langevin Cote and Robert Rice, 'Gerda a Spy? Never, Says Sévigny,' *Globe and Mail,* 14 March 1966. For comment on Hees as something of a playboy see Judy LaMarsh, *Memoirs of a Bird in a Gilded Cage* (Toronto: McClelland and Stewart, 1969), 162.

27 *Neue Illustrierte* 14 (3 April 1966), 3–5, 10–11. For the contrasting representations of Munsinger's view of Hees see *Neue Illustrierte* 14 (3 April 1966), 4; 16 (17 April 1966), 6.

28 *Neue Illustrierte* 16 (17 April 1966), 3, 7; Commission of Inquiry, Delorme Testimony, Sévigny Testimony, 470–526; 'Pierre Sévigny: "This Is What Really Happened,"' *MacLean's,* 6 August 1966, 16.

29 Mark Kristmanson, *Plateaus of Freedom: Nationality, Culture, and State Security in Canada, 1940–1960* (Toronto: Oxford University Press, 2003), 173.

30 Commission of Inquiry, Delorme Testimony, 477–8; Sévigny Testimony, 509–10; 'This Is What Really Happened,' *Maclean's,* 6 August 1966, 17.

Further confirmation of Munsinger as a 'name-dropper' appeared independently in the recollection of another nightlife acquaintance. See *Toronto Telegram*, 11 March 1966, cited in Deborah Van Seters, 'The Munsinger Affair:
Images of Espionage and Security in 1960s Canada,' *Intelligence and National
Security* 13 (Summer 1998): 79. Spence, *Munsinger Report*, 39–47, 50, presents evidence relating to Sévigny's parliamentary assistant Gaston Levesque,
which it suggests establishes that the Sévigny-Munsinger relationship in this
period was more intimate. Yet all it really proves is that Munsinger tried to
see Sévigny, and that on one or two occasions more than Sévigny recounted
the cabinet minister did meet with Munsinger.

31 On the 'dirty tricks' campaigns of the RCMP see Ross Dowson, ed., *Ross Dowson
v. RCMP* (Toronto: Forward Publications, 1980); Bryan D. Palmer, 'They Ride
Horses Don't They? Historical Musings on the Canadian State and Its Agents,'
Our Generation 14 (1981): 28–41; Sawatsky, *Men in the Shadows*.

32 See Commission of Inquiry, Delorme Testimony, 479–82; Spence, *Munsinger
Report*, 5; 'This Is What Really Happened,' *Maclean's*, 6 August 1966, 17. The
problem with Munsinger's accounts in *Neue Illustrierte* is that they jumble
chronology and congeal events from different periods, but see 16 (17 April
1966), 1–10.

33 Commission of Inquiry, Delorme Testimony, 483, notes that the Munsinger
citizenship application was 'sometime late in the summer,' but recent scholarship dates it to June 1960. See Van Seters, 'The Munsinger Affair,' 72. This
is confirmed in Spence, *Munsinger Report*, 3, which dates the citizenship
application 28 June 1960. This report also makes much of the efforts of
Sévigny and his aide, Levesque, to facilitate Munsinger's problems with
documents (43–5).

34 'William 'Willie Obie' Obront,' http://www.geocities.com/wiseguywally/
WilliamObront.html?20062 (accessed 2 February 2006); Diefenbaker, *One
Canada*, 3: 176; Commission of Inquiry, Delorme Testimony, 500; Fulton
Testimony, 420; *Neue Illustrierte* 13 (27 March 1966), 6; 'Gerda Munsinger:
Zwei Gangster und ein letztes Wort,' 17 (24 April 1966), untranslated; 'She
Loved Sévigny,' *Cape Breton Post*, 24 March 1966; Van Dusen, *The Chief*, 189;
Denis Smith, *Rogue Tory: The Life and Legend of John G. Diefenbaker* (Toronto:
Macfarlane, Walter, and Ross, 1995), 351; 'This Is What Really Happened,'
Maclean's, 6 August 1966, 17; 'Gerda connaissait bien les locaux de la Sûreté
Municipale de Montréal,' *Le Journal de Montréal*, 21 March 1966; Van Seters,
'The Munsinger Affair,' 72, 76, 84; Westell and Stevens, 'The Munsinger
Report,' 11–12; Erik Nielsen, *The House Is Not a Home* (Toronto: Macmillan,
1989), 151; Robert Reguly, 'Gerda the Vanishing Playgirl,' *Star Weekly*, 2
April 1966, 4; 'Olga Case May Be Worse Than Profumo's: Cardin,' *Globe and*

Mail, 10 March 1966; '"Is It about Sévigny?" Said the Shapely Frau in the Comfy Flat,' *Globe and Mail,* 12 March 1966; 'L'Affaire Munsinger,' *Le Nouveau Samedi,* 19 March 1966; 'Sévigny Got 2 Warnings,' *Edmonton Journal,* 21 March 1966.

35 Quoted in Van Seters, 'Munsinger Affair,' 76–7 and in Spence, *Munsinger Report,* 72. See also Westell and Stevens, 'The Munsinger Report,' 10; Commission of Inquiry, Fulton Testimony, 388. On Munsinger as femme fatale see Roger Nadeau, 'Oui, Gerda était une espionne! Pearson sauterait et Paul Martin le remplacerait,' *Le Petit Journal,* 27 March 1966. On the mythologizing of Mata Hari and women spies see Julie Wheelwright, *The Fatal Lover: Mata Hari and the Myth of Women in Espionage* (London: Collins and Brown, 1992). Note the extensive discussion of evidence against Munsinger spying alongside the RCMP insistence that she was an ideal candidate to be engaged in espionage in Van Dusen, *The Chief,* 187–90.

36 The RCMP, according to Van Seters, went to 'considerable lengths to establish Munsinger's prostitution and her possible links with the Montreal underworld.' In the 1966 Commission of Inquiry, RCMP evidence would be drawn on by commission counsels as well as by counsel for cabinet minister Lucien Cardin, but it is critical to appreciate that this evidence is, as Van Seters has noted, largely unavailable for first-hand analysis. It is either not present in the commission files or is classified. See Van Seters, 'The Munsinger Affair,' 75–7; 'This Is What Really Happened,' *Maclean's,* 6 August 1966, 41; Commission of Inquiry, Fulton Testimony, 402–3, 411, 425–7; Westell and Stevens, 'The Munsinger Report,' 6–7; Patrick Nicholson, '6 Points to Watch When Probe Opens,' *Daily Journal Record* (Oakville), 29 March 1966; Spence, *Munsinger Report,* 6.

37 'L'affaire Munsinger,' *Le Nouveau Samedi,* 19 March 1966; *Neue Illustrierte* 13 (27 March 1966), 6; 'Gerda connaissait bien les locaux de la Sûreté Municipale de Montréal,' *Le Journal de Montréal,* 21 March 1966; 'Gerda a un dossier!' *Le Petit Journal,* 13 March 1966; Commission of Inquiry, Fulton Testimony, 398; Smith, *Rogue Tory,* 351, 642n81; Diefenbaker, *One Canada,* 3: 176; Westell and Stevens, 'The Munsinger Report,' 11. Note that Van Dusen, *The Chief,* 189, cites a Montreal RCMP report indicating that Munsinger had no criminal record as of mid-October 1960. Robert Rice, 'Montreal Recalls Gerda,' *Globe and Mail,* 14 March 1966, notes that Montreal police did indeed have a file on Munsinger relating to the department store bad cheque incident, but that it had been taken out of central records and locked in the office of Chief Inspector Leslie Hobbs, who refused to comment on the case.

38 Munsinger suggested that 'Obie' would have been a likely candidate to have started the rumour of her death, but others, such as Jacqueline 'The

Duchess' Delorme and Sévigny himself soon came to believe, for their own, sometimes convenient, reasons that Munsinger was dead. See 'Gerda the Vanishing Playgirl,' *Star Weekly*, 2 April 1966, 4; Commission of Inquiry, Delorme Testimony, 488–91; 'This Is What Really Happened,' *Maclean's*, 39.

39 Details from Commission of Inquiry, Fulton Testimony, 385–99, esp. 387; Sévigny Testimony, 521–6; Smith, *Rogue Tory*, 350–1; Stursberg, *Diefenbaker: Leadership Lost*, 155, 158. Van Dusen, *The Chief*, 189–90, cites three separate local RCMP Montreal reports that Munsinger was not engaged in spying.

40 Commission of Inquiry, Delorme Testimony, 486–92; 'This Is What Really Happened,' *Maclean's*, 6 August 1966, 39.

41 Tommy Douglas would later indicate that New Democratic Party MPs 'had heard vague rumors of a case involving Cabinet ministers for some time and the name Munsinger was used.' See Don Delaplante, 'Munsinger File Smuggled away during Tory Rule, Douglas says,' *Globe and Mail*, 16 March 1966.

42 Newman, *Distemper of Our Times*, 356; LaMarsh, *Bird in a Gilded Cage*, 162. Sévigny's memoirs are not terribly forthcoming or illuminating on anything associated with Munsinger. See Pierre Sévigny, *This Game of Politics* (Toronto: McClelland and Stewart, 1965).

43 Larry Zolf, *The Dance of the Dialectic* (Toronto: James Lewis and Samuel, 1973), 11.

44 For brief comment on the 1965 election see Smith, *Rogue Tory*, 531–6; J.L. Granatstein, *Canada, 1957–1967: The Years of Uncertainty and Innovation* (Toronto: McClelland and Stewart, 1986), 285–6.

45 For accounts see Newman, *The Distemper of Our Times*; Judy LaMarsh, *Bird in a Gilded Cage*, 129–60; Nielsen, *The House Is Not a Home*, esp. 133–54; Fraser, *Search for Identity*, 280–300; Gordon Donaldson, *Fifteen Men: Canada's Prime Ministers from Macdonald to Trudeau* (Toronto: Doubleday, 1969), 225–32.

46 Granatstein, *Canada: Years of Uncertainty and Innovation*, 286–8; Stursberg, *Diefenbaker: Leadership Lost*, 144–51; Nielsen, *The House Is Not a Home*, 150–1; LaMarsh, *Bird in a Gilded Cage*, 159; Lester B. Pearson, *Mike: The Memoirs of the Right Honourable Lester B. Pearson*, vol. 3, *1957–1968* (Toronto: University of Toronto Press, 1975), 173–80.

47 Pearson, *Mike*, 3: 180; Smith, *Rogue Tory*, 521–2; James Johnston, *The Party's Over* (Don Mills: Longman, 1971), 87–8; Diefenbaker, *One Canada*, 3: 269; LaMarsh, *Bird in a Gilded Cage*, 164; Stursberg, *Diefenbaker: Leadership Lost*, 147; Newman, *Distemper of Our Times*, 357; Bain is quoted in Granatstein, *Canada: Years of Uncertainty and Innovation*, which also makes reference to Pickersgill, 287, 289. See also 'Gerda the Vanishing Playgirl,' *Star Weekly*, 2 April 1966, 4; Patrick Nicholson, '6 Points to Watch When Probe Opens,' *Daily Journal Record* (Oakville), 29 March 1966; 'This Is What Really

Happened,' *Maclean's*, 6 August 1966, 15; 'Fulton Accuses Favreau as 2 Men
Clash over Gerda,' *Globe and Mail*, 15 March 1966; George Brimmel,
'Munsinger Inquiry Underway,' *Ottawa Citizen*, 18 March 1966; George
Bain, 'How Friendly Mr. Favreau Told Fearless Mr. Fulton to Beware,' *Globe
and Mail*, 12 March 1966. See also Nielsen, *The House Is Not a Home*, 152–5,
for the claim that the Conservatives knew the Liberals were going to raise
the Munsinger affair in the House.

48 Stursberg, *Diefenbaker: Leadership Lost*, 124–5, 152–4, 156–7; Commission of
Inquiry, Delorme Testimony, 491. Spence, *Munsinger Report*, 62, dismisses
out of hand any role of Ducharme in spreading information about
Munsinger. On the Profumo-Keeler scandal much has subsequently
appeared, but see two early reports: Lord Denning, *Lord Denning's Report:
The Circumstances Leading to the Resignation of the Former Secretary of State for
War, Mr. J.D. Profumo* (London: HMSO, 1963); Clive Irving, Ron Hall, and
Jeremy Wallington, *Anatomy of a Scandal: A Study of the Profumo Affair* (New
York: William Morrow, 1963). On the Cardin statement see John English,
The Life of Lester B. Pearson: The Worldly Years, vol. 2, *1949–1972* (Toronto:
Knopf, 1992), 355; Newman, *Distemper of Our Times*, 362–3. Note as well
Rene Hould, '"L'Affaire Monsignor" le "cas Profumo" du Canada?' *Ottawa
Le Droit*, 5 March 1966; 'Est-ce une affaire "Profumo" bien à nous? Pour
comprendre les aspects politiques de l'affaire Munsinger,' *Dimanche-Matin*,
13 March 1966. For background on Sévigny, who quit the Diefenbaker
cabinet in protest over the government's nuclear arms policy and was
defeated in the 1963 election, see 'Sévigny Was Quebec Lieutenant,' *Globe
and Mail*, 12 March 1966.

49 For an account see Thomas Van Dusen, *The Chief* (Toronto: McGraw–Hill,
1968), 168–71.

50 Van Dusen, *The Chief*, 170–6; Stursberg, *Diefenbaker: Leadership Lost*, 148; *Globe
and Mail*, 9–10 March 1966; Westell and Stevens, 'The Munsinger Report,'
10. Tommy Douglas muddied the waters with the suggestion that a copy of
the RCMP file on Munsinger had been 'smuggled out of the House of Commons' during the Diefenbaker years. See Don Delaplante, 'Munsinger File
Smuggled away during Tory Rule, Douglas Says,' *Globe and Mail*, 16 March
1966. The press was blanketed with coverage of the Munsinger affair in the
week following Cardin's House of Commons statement. For only a sample of
some of the journalistic immersion in the debates and ongoing mudslinging
see Anthony Westell, 'Chaos in Commons: PM Offers Munsinger Inquiry,'
Westell, 'Tories Split Over PM's Offer of Inquiry into Munsinger Affair,'
Geoffrey Stevens, 'Cardin Claims More Than One Tory Minister Involved In
Olga Case,' *Globe and Mail*, 11 March 1966; 'Another Day of Chaos in the

Commons,' *Globe and Mail*, 12 March 1966; Geoffrey Stevens, 'Cardin Summarizes Gerda-Case Charges in Letter to Pearson,' *Globe and Mail*, 12 March 1966; 'Sévigny Named by Caouette as Conservative Minister Involved in Munsinger,' *Globe and Mail*, 12 March 1966; Anthony Westell, 'One Word from Cardin, Monseignor, Lit the Fuse that Leads to Political Dynamite,' *Globe and Mail*, 14 March 1966; 'PC Leader Wants Names before Munsinger Probe,' and Langevin Cote and Robert Rice, 'Gerda a Spy? Never, Says Sévigny,' *Globe and Mail*, 14 March 1966; Anthony Westell and Norman Webster, 'PM Refuses to Alter Terms: PCs Balked, Gerda Probe On,' *Globe and Mail*, 15 March 1966; 'Munsinger Case File Won't Support Charges, Fulton Says,' *Globe and Mail*, 15 March 1966.

51 'Gerda the Vanishing Playgirl,' *Star Weekly*, 2 April 1966, 2, 4.

52 William Kaplan, *Everything That Floats: Pat Sullivan, Hal Banks, and the Seamen's Unions of Canada* (Toronto: University of Toronto Press, 1987), 155–6.

53 'Gerda the Vanishing Playgirl,' *Star Weekly*, 2 April 1966, 2–6; Newman, *Distemper of Our Times*, 363; '"Is It about Sévigny?" Said the Shapely Frau in the Comfy Flat,' *Globe and Mail*, 12 March 1966; Benoit C-Hebert, 'Niant avoir été une espionne, Gerda Munsinger veut venir au Canada pour "éclaircir les choses,"' *Dimanche-Matin*, 13 March 1966; Robert Reguly, 'Gerda veut revenir au Canada,' and 'Comment j'ai retrouvé Gerda Munsinger à Munich,' *Dernière Heure/Le Petit Journal*, 13 March 1966.

54 I will not cite the extensive March 1966 newspaper reporting of the Munsinger events. Profuse clippings exist in the Commission of Inquiry volumes. For specific coverage cited in this paragraph see 'Gerda the Vanishing Playgirl,' *Star Weekly*, 2 April 1966; *Le Nouveau Samedi*, 19 March 1966, in which various articles and photographs appear under the heading 'L'affaire Munsinger,' an eight-page spread; and 'Pierre Sévigny: "This Is What Really Happened,"' *Maclean's*, 6 August 1966. The *Maclean's* limerick appears in Newman, *Distemper of Our Times*, 366. Sévigny is further quoted on a man meeting a woman in Stursberg, *Diefenbaker: Leadership Lost*, 157, and for more on the code of parliamentary silence on private behaviour see LaMarsh, *Bird in a Gilded Cage*, 161. When Cardin first introduced the matter of the Munsinger affair and thus implicated Sévigny, the latter had referred to him as 'a despicable, rotten little rat' and as a 'cheap, despicable little man.' See 'Sévigny Tells of Shock Call from Gerda – "A Very Beautiful Girl,"' *Globe and Mail*, 14 March 1966; Robert Rice, 'Ex-Minister Cries Slander; Knew Munsinger Woman "Socially,"' *Globe and Mail*, 12 March 1966. For more on Sévigny's sense of outrage that parliamentary honour had been breached see the interview with Norman DePoe, 'Munsinger Speaks,' CBC Television News, CBC Archives, broadcast date, 12 March 1966. Journalists

who violated Sévigny's sense of honour might also feel his wrath. Larry Zolf tried to interview Sévigny in the early days of the Munsinger affair, sent by the public affairs television program *This Hour Has Seven Days* with a film crew to the politician's home. In a haze of chaos and confusion Sévigny and Zolf scuffled, the former cabinet minister tried to strike Zolf with his cane, Sévigny's wooden leg was kicked out from underneath him, and Zolf beat a hasty retreat, having the entire episode on film. See Larry Zolf, 'Citizen Cane,' CBC News Viewpoint, 9 April 2004, http://www.cbc.ca/news/viewpoint/vp_zolf (accessed 25 January 2006). Note, as well, Dalton K. Camp, 'Liberal Party: Group Terror in Disguise,' *Cape Breton Post*, 22 March 1966, which likens Cardin's use of the Munsinger affair to McCarthyism.

55 Newman, *Distemper of Our Times*, 368.

56 'Gerda Sells Her Story to the World,' *Globe and Mail*, 14 March 1966; Alan Harvey, 'Gerda (or Was It?) Makes a Break, Throws the Press Corps off the Scent,' *Globe and Mail*, 15 March 1966; 'Made No Trips aboard Canadian Official Aircraft, Gerda Says,' *Globe and Mail*, 16 March 1966.

57 See *Neue Illustrierte* 13 (27 March 1966) to 17 (24 April 1966).

58 An exception was Charles Lynch, who wrote of Gerda Munsinger behaving graciously in letting him bow out of an agreement he had made with respect to securing her story. His description of Munsinger is anything but that of an opportunistic shark. Lynch wrote that 'the lady's conduct was exemplary throughout ... Gerda turned out to be all heart.' See Lynch, 'The Nation,' *Winnipeg Tribune*, 23 March 1966; 'Gerda Gets Columnist off Hook,' *Sarnia Observer*, 24 March 1966.

59 Norman DePoe, 'Munsinger Speaks,' CBC Television News, CBC Archives, 12 March 1966.

60 Granatstein, *Canada: Years of Uncertainty and Innovation*, 289; J.L. Granatstein and David Stafford, *Spy Wars: Espionage and Canada from Gouzenko to Glasnost* (Toronto: Key Porter, 1990), 125–9; John English, *The Life of Lester B. Pearson: The Worldly Years, 1949–1972*, vol. 2 (Toronto: Knopf, 1992), 355. Pierre Berton wrote glibly of Munsinger as 'the German-born call girl ... found to have been inappropriately intimate with more than a dozen figures including at least one Russian official and Pierre Sévigny, who held the sensitive position of associate defence minister.' Berton, *1967: The Last Good Year* (Toronto: Doubleday, 1997), 98. The latest account of Munsinger is more sympathetic but glosses over much of the episode's political meaning. See Iacovetta, *Gatekeepers*, 281–287, which draws heavily on Van Seters, 'Munsinger Affair.'

61 'Gerda Sells Her Story to the World,' *Globe and Mail*, 14 March 1966; Harvey, 'Gerda (or Was It?),' *Globe and Mail*, 15 March 1966; 'Made No Trips aboard

Canadian Official Aircraft,' *Globe and Mail*, 16 March 1966; '"Is It about Sévigny?" Said the Shapely Frau in the Comfy Flat,' *Globe and Mail*, 12 March 1966; *Neue Illustrierte* 13 (27 March 1966), 3; 15 (10 April 1966), 4; 'Gerda Delays Wedding,' *Toronto Telegram*, 26 August 1966. One of the few commentators on the Munsinger events to draw attention to her respectable status in 1966, referring to her 1968 marriage, is Van Dusen, *The Chief*, 212–13.

62　For relevant accounts see Anthony Westell, 'Chaos in the Commons: PM Offers Munsinger Inquiry,' *Globe and Mail*, 11 March 1966; Geoffrey Stevens, 'Cardin Summarizes Gerda-Case Charges in Letter to Pearson,' *Globe and Mail*, 12 March 1966; Anthony Westell and Norman Webster, 'PM Refuses to Alter Terms: PCs Balked, Gerda Probe On,' *Globe and Mail*, 15 March 1966.

63　On Spence and the Commission and views of the time see Norman Webster, 'Judge Is Empowered to Probe Statements on Munsinger Case by Cardin,' *Globe and Mail*, 15 March 1966; 'Spence: A Tough-minded Jurist,' *Globe and Mail*, 15 March 1966; Anthony Westell, 'Will Gerda Be Kiss of Death for PC Chief?' *Globe and Mail*, 4 June 1966; George Brummel, 'Munsinger Inquiry Underway,' *Ottawa Citizen*, 18 March 1966.

64　For a critical, albeit partisan, account of the Spence Commission see Van Dusen, *The Chief*, 178–230. The best accessible synopsis, which reveals the commission's conclusions clearly, is Spence, *Munsinger Report*, with 60–1 comparing the Profumo and Munsinger cases. See, as well, LaMarsh, *Bird in a Gilded Cage*, 163–4; Nielsen, *The House Is Not a Home*, 156–8; Newman, *Distemper of Our Times*, 367–8; Pearson, *Mike*, 3: 183–4; Smith, *Rogue Tory*, 540–1, quoting *Globe and Mail*.

65　Commission of Inquiry, Delorme Testimony, 473; Sévigny Testimony, 508–9, 532–3; Van Seters, 'The Munsinger Affair,' 75; 'This Is What Really Happened,' *Maclean's*, 6 August 1966, 17; Langevin Cote and Robert Rice, 'Gerda a Spy? Never, Says Sévigny,' *Globe and Mail*, 14 March 1966.

66　Robert Rice, 'Montreal Recalls Gerda,' *Globe and Mail*, 14 March 1966.

67　Van Seters, 'The Munsinger Affair,' 77; Fraser, *Search for Identity*, 295–300; Newman, *Distemper of Our Times*, 354.

68　Bruce Macdonald, 'At Last! Canada Gets Some Space in the U.S. Papers – Thanks to Gerda,' *Globe and Mail*, 16 March 1966; Art Buchwald, 'Sex and the Single Government,' *Telegraph-Journal* (St John, NB), 23 March 1966; Newman, *Distemper of Our Times*, 366, quoting Braithwaite.

69　See Mariana Valverde, 'Building Anti-Delinquent Communities: Morality, Gender, and Generation in the City,' in Joy Parr, ed., *A Diversity of Women: Ontario, 1945–1980* (Toronto: University of Toronto Press, 1995), 23.

70　'This Is What Really Happened,' *Maclean's*, 6 August 1966, 41.

71 See 'Why All French Names Says CBC's Lapierre,' *Globe and Mail*, 14 March 1966; Van Seters, 'The Munsinger Affair,' 79.

72 For a survey of Canadian newspaper views indicating a growing scepticism among Canadians that Munsinger was a spy, see Van Seters, 'The Munsinger Affair,' 79–81. This disbelief was also driven by a chorus of opinion from those who knew Munsinger, in Canada and Europe, all of whom found the idea of her engaged in espionage risible. See, for instance, Alan Harvey, 'Gerda (or Was It?) Makes a Break, Throws the Press Corps off the Scent,' *Globe and Mail*, 15 March 1966, quoting an Austrian woman with whom Munsinger lived as saying, 'She's not the girl to keep a secret,' laughing at the thought of Gerda as a spy. Munsinger herself was blunt, telling her friend Jackie Delorme: 'You know very well I am too dumb to be a spy.' Commission of Inquiry, Delorme Testimony, 493. In contrast see Spence, *Munsinger Report*, 4–5, 68–73.

73 McClellan's views are outlined in Van Dusen, *The Chief*, 212.

74 Zolf, *Dance of the Dialectic*, 11.

75 LaMarsh, *Bird in a Gilded Cage*, 162–3; Pearson, *Mike*, 3: 185; English, *Life of Pearson: Worldly Years*, 2: 356–7; Nielsen, *The House Is Not a Home*, 157–9.

76 James Johnston, *The Party's Over* (Toronto: Longman, 1971), 89.

4: Canada's Great White Hope: George Chuvalo vs. Muhammad Ali

1 C.L.R. James, *Beyond a Boundary* (New York: Pantheon, 1983), xix.

2 See John Sugeden, *Boxing and Society: An International Analysis* (New York: Manchester University Press, 1996); Mike Marqusee, *Redemption Song: Muhammad Ali and the Spirit of the Sixties* (New York and London: Verso, 1999); Jeffrey T. Sammons, *Beyond the Ring: The Role of Boxing in American Society* (Urbana and Chicago: University of Illinois Press, 1988).

3 S.F. Wise, 'Sport and Class Values in Old Ontario and Quebec,' in W.H. Heick and Roger Graham, eds., *His Own Man: Essays in Honour of A.R.M. Lower* (Montreal and Kingston: McGill-Queen's University Press, 1974), 93–118; Michael S. Cross, ed., *The Workingman in the Nineteenth Century* (Toronto: Oxford University Press, 1974); Charles Anthony Joyce, 'From Left Field: Sport and Class in Toronto, 1845–1886,' PhD dissertation, Queen's University, 1997; David Di Felice, 'The 'Richard Riot': A Socio-Historical Examination of Sport, Culture, and the Construction of Symbolic Identities,' MA thesis, Queen's University, 1997; Roch Carrier, *The Hockey Sweater* (Montreal: Tundra, 1984); Scott Young, *The Boys of Saturday Night: Hockey Night in Canada* (Toronto: Macmillan, 1990); Richard Gruneau and David Whitson, *Hockey Night in Canada: Sports, Identities and Cultural Politics* (Toronto: Garamond, 1994).

4 For background see Harry Sinden, *Hocky Showdown: The Canada-Russia Hockey Series* (Toronto: Doubleday, 1972); Jack Ludwig, *Hockey Night in Moscow: Behind the Scenes in the USSR–Canada Series* (Toronto: McClelland and Stewart, 1972).

5 Obviously race is a social construction. Biologically there is one human race, and all artificially designated groupings within it based on skin colour and other physiological traits obscure more than they clarify. Within any such 'racial grouping' there will be significant numbers of individuals who share more characteristics with other so-called races than they do with their ostensible group. Nevertheless, the racialization of specific population groups has been an undeniable historical phenomenon, one of particular significance in the United States, where African Americans have long existed in the shadow of chattel slavery. I thus use the term race in this book, without the cumbersome inverted quotation marks, as a shorthand for how processes of racialization construct specific population groups as 'other.'

6 Trudeau's elephant–mouse metaphor was part of a speech he delivered in 1969 to the Washington National Press Club. See Matt Mossman, 'Canada's Camelot Remembered as Trudeau Dies,' *The Independent*, 29 September 2000.

7 Stephen Brunt, *Facing Ali: The Opposition Weighs In* (Canada: Knopf, 2002), 48, 57.

8 Alvin Finkel, Margaret Conrad, and Veronica Strong-Boag, *History of the Canadian Peoples: 1867 to the Present* (Toronto: Copp, Clark, Pitman, 1993), 415.

9 W.E. Mann, 'The Lower Ward,' in Mann, ed., *The Underside of Toronto* (Toronto and Montreal: McClelland and Stewart, 1970), 37. See also Franca Iacovetta, *Such Hardworking People: Italian Immigrants in Postwar Toronto* (Montreal and Kingston: McGill-Queen's University Press, 1992).

10 Edmund Bradwin, *The Bunkhouse Man: Life and Labour in the Northern Work Camps* (Toronto: University of Toronto Press, 1972), 112; Bryan D. Palmer, *Working-Class Experience: The Rise and Reconstitution of Canadian Labour, 1800–1980* (Toronto: Butterworth, 1983), 182; J.S. Woodsworth, *Strangers within Our Gates: The Problem of the Immigrant, 1909* (Toronto: University of Toronto Press, 1972).

11 See, for instance, Cecil Foster, *Where Race Does Not Matter: The New Spirit of Modernity* (Toronto: Penguin, 2005).

12 Murray Greig, *Goin' the Distance: Canada's Boxing Heritage* (Toronto: Macmillan, 1996), 111.

13 Brunt, *Facing Ali*, 52–3; Greig, *Goin' the Distance*, 111.

14 On Burns and the death of the Great White Hope see Greig, *Goin' the Distance*, 9–55; Jim Christy, *Flesh and Blood: A Journey into the Heart of Boxing* (Vancouver and Toronto: Douglas and McIntyre, 1990), 75–6.

15 Lawrence Levine, *Black Culture and Black Consciousness: Afro-American Thought from Slavery to Freedom* (New York: Oxford University Press, 1977), 432.

16 The above paragraphs draw on and quote from Randy Roberts, *Papa Jack: Jack Johnson and the Era of White Hopes* (New York: Free Press, 1983); Al-Tony Gilmore, *Bad Nigger! The National Impact of Jack Johnson* (Port Washington, NY: Kennikat Press, 1975); Sammons, *Beyond the Ring*, 30–47; William J. Baker, *Sports in the Western World* (Totowa, NJ: Rowan and Littlefield, 1982), 205; Gail Bederman, *Manliness and Civilization: A Cultural History of Gender and Race in the United States, 1880–1917* (Chicago: University of Chicago Press, 1995), esp. 1–20; Varda Burstyn, *The Rites of Men: Manhood, Politics and the Culture of Sport* (Toronto: University of Toronto Press, 1999), 89–90.

17 Characterization of Schmeling as a Nazi and a racist was unfair and inappropriate. Hitler praised Schmeling and the heavyweight served as a German paratrooper during the Second World War, but the boxer never joined the Nazi party, disliked Hitler, had a Jewish manager, saved Jewish lives during the Nazi attacks on Jewish homes, businesses, and synagogues known as Kristallnacht, 9 November 1938, and befriended Joe Louis, being one of the black fighter's pallbearers in 1981. For the significance of the Louis–Schmeling contest see David Margolick, *Beyond Glory: Joe Louis vs. Max Schmeling and a World on the Brink* (New York: Knopf, 2005). Note as well Bob Bensch and John Pickering, 'Schmeling Was Joe Louis's Friend and Foe,' *National Post*, 5 February 2005.

18 Much has been written on Louis and I draw on summaries in David Remnick, *King of the World: Muhammad Ali and the Rise of an American Hero* (New York: Vintage, 1999), esp. 151, 226–7. See, as well, Sammons, *Beyond the Ring*, 96–129.

19 For a general statement see Sammons, *Beyond the Ring*, 130–83. Remnick, *King of the World*, contains much on the typecasting of Patterson and Liston.

20 *New York Times*, 23 July 1963, quoted in Sammons, *Beyond the Ring*, 192. Black America's views of boxing would shift dramatically with the rise of Ali. See, for instance, Eldridge Cleaver, *Soul on Ice* (New York: Dell, 1968), 85–95.

21 Quoted in Marqusee, *Redemption Song*, 6.

22 Karl Marx, 'The Eighteenth Brumaire of Louis Bonaparte,' in Marx and Engels, *Selected Works* (Moscow: Progress, 1968), 97.

23 Charles Lemert, *Muhammad Ali: Trickster in the Culture of Irony* (Cambridge: Polity Press, 2003), esp. 1–50.

24 Cannon quoted in Remnick, *King of the World*, 158–9.
25 I address the gendered nature of boxing, the hypermasculinity and overt violence associated with it, only in passing because of the obviousness of these features of 'ring culture.' See Burstyn, *Rites of Men*, 166–7.
26 Marqusee, *Redemption Song*, 53.
27 Quotes from Remnick, *King of the World*, xi–xii, 180.
28 Remnick, *King of the World*, 200. For a different view of the Clay-Liston fight, and of Liston's significance, see the hard-boiled Nick Tosche, *The Devil and Sonny Liston* (New York: Little Brown, 2001).
29 Remnick, *King of the World*, 207.
30 Ibid., 209–10.
31 Sammons, *Beyond the Ring*, 195.
32 Howard Cosell, *Cosell* (Chicago: Playboy Press, 1973), 177.
33 Remnick, *King of the World*, 267–83.
34 Sammons, *Beyond the Ring*, 200–2.
35 Lemert, *Ali: Trickster*, 51–119; Muhammad Ali, *The Greatest: My Own Story* (London: Hart-Davis, MacGibbon, 1976), 120–51.
36 Paul Rimstead, 'U.S. War Veterans' Picket Lines Could Bankrupt Clay Fight TV,' *Globe and Mail*, 9 March 1966; Jim Kernaghan, 'Fight Finds a Home but Faces Problems,' *Toronto Daily Star*, 9 March 1966.
37 Budd Schulberg, 'Chinese Boxes of Muhammad Ali,' *Saturday Review*, 26 February 1972, 23–5.
38 Remnick, *King of the World*, 287–91.
39 Frank Orr, 'Fight Bid Stirs Teacup Tempest,' *Toronto Daily Star*, 7 March 1966; 'Clay Fight? Rowntree Feints, Ducks, and Dodges,' *Toronto Daily Star*, 8 March 1966.
40 Milt Dunnell, 'The Sound and the Fury,' *Toronto Daily Star*, 8 March 1966.
41 'Conn Smythe Quits Gardens in Clay Row,' *Toronto Daily Star*, 9 March 1966; John M. Lee, 'The Establishment Stays Away in Belief Fight Lacks Status,' *New York Times*, 30 March 1966.
42 Robert Lipsyte, 'Showdown in Boxing: Underworld Death Threats Are Seen as Outgrowth of Struggle for Power,' *New York Times*, 28 March 1966; 'Crime Syndicate, Ring Figures Summoned for Grand Jury,' *Globe and Mail*, 28 March 1966; 'Gangsters Tried to Muscle in on Clay-Terrell Tilt,' *Halifax Chronicle-Herald*, 28 March 1966.
43 Jack R. Griffin, 'Clay: Once Funny, Now Despised,' *Toronto Daily Star*, 19 March 1966; Milt Dunnell, 'Toronto's Big Fight, Big Yawn in Florida,' *Toronto Daily Star*, 19 March 1966; Ken McKee, 'Vegas Bookies Hide From Chuvalo Bets,' *Toronto Daily Star*, 26 March 1966; McKee, 'World Press Knocks Bout – But Still Covers It,' *Toronto Daily Star*, 29 March 1966.

44 Robert Lipsyte, 'Title Fight Buildup Is Just a Charade,' *New York Times*,
    27 March 1966.

45 Arthur Daley, 'Is This Trip Necessary,' *New York Times*, 29 March 1966; also
    in *Globe and Mail*, 29 March 1966.

46 'What Others Are Writing from around the World,' *Globe and Mail*, 29 March
    1966; 'Ali's Toronto Bout,' *Toronto Daily Star*, 30 March 1966.

47 Jack R. Griffin, 'Clay: Once Funny, Now Despised,' *Toronto Daily Star*, 19
    March 1966; Milt Dunnell, 'The Bust Is a Boom,' *Toronto Daily Star*, 25 March
    1966.

48 *Toronto Daily Star*, 19 March 1966.

49 Jimmy Breslin, 'Way to Beat Clay – Steal His Title,' *Toronto Daily Star*, 2 March
    1966; 'What Others Are Writing from around the World,' *Globe and Mail*,
    29 March 1966.

50 'Jim Kearney,' *Vancouver Sun*, 29 March 1966.

51 Ali, *The Greatest*, 141; Jim Kernaghan, 'Cassius Clay: Hated by Millions – But
    He Can Fight,' *Toronto Daily Star*, 26 March 1966; 'Ali's Toronto Bout,'
    Toronto Daily Star, 30 March 1966.

52 Dick Beddoes, 'Chuvalo with Chauvinism,' *Globe and Mail*, 31 March 1966;
    'Ali's Toronto Bout,' *Toronto Daily Star*, 30 March 1966.

53 'Denny Boyd,' *Vancouver Sun*, 30 March 1966; Jim Kearney, 'Clever Clay
    Keeps Title,' *Vancouver Sun*, 30 March 1966.

54 Paul Rimstead, 'Referee Says Chuvalo Deserves All Credit; Took Clay's
    Arsenal,' *Globe and Mail*, 30 March 1966; '"No Prestige," Establishment
    Ignores Fight,' *Globe and Mail*, 30 March 1966.

55 Jimmy Breslin, 'Fighter at His Trade: Chuvalo Turns Farce into Cheers for
    The Bull,' *Toronto Daily Star*, 30 March 1966.

56 Robert Lipsyte, 'Champion Jabs Baffle His Rival,' Gerald Eskenazi, 'Cham-
    pion Hails His Rugged Rival,' and Arthur Daley, 'The Battle of Toronto,' all
    in *New York Times*, 30 March 1966; Daley, 'A Foul Business,' *New York Times*,
    31 March 1966.

57 See Constance Backhouse, *Colour-Coded: A Legal History of Racism in Canada*
    (Toronto: University of Toronto Press, 1999). In the immediate context of
    the mid-1960s, indications of racism in Toronto are evident in Martin
    O'Malley, 'Blacks in Toronto,' in W.E. Mann, ed., *The Underside of Toronto*
    (Toronto: McLelland and Stewart, 1970), 131–40; Austin Clarke, 'A Black
    Man Talks about Race Prejudice in White Canada,' *Maclean's*, 18, 55–8; and
    in the troubled history of one black neighbourhood in Halifax: David Lewis
    Stein, 'The Counterattack on Diehard Racism,' *Maclean's*, 20 October 1962;
    Sylvia Fraser, 'The Slow and Welcome Death of Africville,' *Star Weekly*, 1 Janu-
    ary 1966; Raymond Daniell, 'Nova Scotia Hides a Racial Problem,' *New York*

Times, 14 June 1964; Susan Dexter, 'The Black Ghetto That Fears Integration,' *Maclean's,* 24 July 1965; Donald H. Clairmont and Dennis William Magill, *Africville: The Life and Death of a Canadian Black Community* (Toronto: McClelland and Stewart, 1974).

58 'Denny Boyd,' *Vancouver Sun,* 30 March 1966.

59 Gerald Eskenazi, 'Tickets for Bout Moving Slowly,' *New York Times,* 29 March 1966.

60 Robert Lipsyte, 'Title Fight Buildup Just a Big Charade,' *New York Times,* 27 March 1966.

61 'Clay Predicts Quick End if Chuvalo Becomes Dirty,' *Globe and Mail,* 28 March 1966.

62 'Denny Boyd,' *Vancouver Sun,* 30 March 1966; Daley, 'Battle of Toronto,' *New York Times,* 30 March 1966; 'Ali's Toronto Bout,' *Toronto Daily Star,* 30 March 1966.

63 John M. Lee, 'The Establishment Stays Away in Belief Fight Lacks Status,' *New York Times,* 30 March 1966.

64 I am indebted to Cy Gonick for pushing me to address this issue.

65 Marqusee, *Redemption Song,* 3.

66 Brunt, *Facing Ali,* 56–66; *The Last Round,* produced by Joseph Blasioli, directed by Silva Basmajian, written by Stephen Brunt, National Film Board of Canada, 2003.

67 Bob Dylan, 'It's All Right Ma (I'm Only Bleeding),' Columbia Recording, 1965.

5: Celebrity and Audacity: Marshall McLuhan, Pierre Elliott Trudeau, and the Decade of the Philosopher King

1 The above paragraph draws on and quotes from Eric Roher, 'The PM and the Media Meister,' *Globe and Mail,* 29 December 2005; Jonathan Miller, *McLuhan* (London: Fontana/Collins, 1971), 132; Richard Kostelanetz, 'Marshall McLuhan: High Priest of the Electronic Village,' in Kostelanetz, *Master Minds* (New York: Macmillan, 1969), 82–114; Fred Thompson, 'Monday Night Sessions,' in George Sanderson and Frank Macdonald, eds., *Marshall McLuhan: The Man and His Message* (Golden, CO: Fulcrum, 1989), 131–7; W. Terrence Gordon, *Marshall McLuhan: Escape into Understanding* (Toronto: Stoddart, 1997), 270; Philip Marchand, *Marshall McLuhan: The Medium and the Messenger – A Biography* (Toronto: Vintage Canada, 1989), 264–5; Barrington Nevitt with Maurice McLuhan, *Who Was Marshall McLuhan?: Exploring a Mosaic of Impressions* (Toronto: Comprehensive Publications, 1994), 41–68.

2 Geoffrey Stevens, *The Player: The Life and Times of Dalton Camp* (Toronto: Key Porter Books, 2003), 142–3. I thank Ramsay Cook for drawing this source to my attention.

3 Tom Wolfe, 'What If He Is Right?' in *The Pump House Gang* (New York: Bantam, 1968), 105–33; for a critique of this representation, Donald F. Theall, *The Virtual Marshall McLuhan* (Montreal and Kingston: McGill-Queen's University Press, 2001), 81–94. For a Wolfe update on McLuhan see Tom Wolfe, 'Foreword,' in Marshall McLuhan, *Understanding Me: Lectures and Interviews*, edited by Stephanie McLuhan and David Staines (Toronto: McLelland and Stewart, 2003), ix–xxii. On dress and appearance see Marchand, *McLuhan*, 188. McLuhan seemed to appreciate that Wolfe had bumped his celebrity stock considerably. See Matie Molinaro, Corinne McLuhan, and William Toye, eds., *Letters of Marshall McLuhan* (Toronto: Oxford University Press, 1987), 330. See as well 'Playboy Interview: A Candid Conversation with the High Priest of Popcult and Metaphysician of Media,' in Eric McLuhan and Frank Zingrone, eds., *Essential McLuhan* (Concord, ON: House of Anansi, 1995), 233–69; Roher, 'The PM and the Media Meister.' In 1968 students in McLuhan's overflowing classes were prone to note that 'he was a celebrity at that time, perhaps the biggest celebrity most of us would ever see so close at hand.' Marchand, *McLuhan*, 1.

4 For McLuhan–Trudeau correspondence see Molinaro, McLuhan, and Toye, eds., *Letters of Marshall McLuhan*, esp. 351–2, 359, 547. McLuhan reviewed Trudeau's *Federalism and the French Canadians* in the *New York Times Book Review*, 17 November 1968.

5 John Fekete, *The Critical Twilight: Explorations in the Ideology of Anglo-American Literary Theory from Eliot to McLuhan* (London: Routledge and Kegan Paul, 1977), 146. As McLuhan burst on the scene in the mid-1960s, he was responded to almost immediately with orthodox Marxist critique. See Sidney Finkelstein, *Sense and Nonsense in McLuhan* (New York: International, 1968). There was also, however, a left empathy for some of McLuhan's views, especially as they related to technology and alienation. See G. David Sheps, 'Utopianism, Alienation, and Marshall McLuhan,' *Canadian Dimension* 3 (September–October 1966): 23–6.

6 William Kuhns wrote of McLuhan in an essay entitled 'The Sage of Aquarius,' in Kuhns, *The Post-Industrial Prophet: Interpretations of Technology* (New York: Weybright and Taeley, 1971), 169–201.

7 Robert Fulford would indeed refer to 'The Age of McLuhan' in Fulford, *The Best Seat in the House* (Toronto: W. Collins and Sons, 1988), 162–84.

8 See, for instance, Marchand, *McLuhan*, 5–40; Gordon, *McLuhan*, 3–79.

9 Marshall McLuhan and George B. Leonard, 'The Future of Sex,' *Look*, 25 July 1967. McLuhan would later claim that he had not authored the article,

which is entirely possible given that in this period of high celebrity much writing was done in his name that he allowed to be promoted as his product.

10 For a later interview relating to McLuhan's views on women see Linda Sandler, 'An Interview with Marshall McLuhan: His Outrageous Views about Women,' *Miss Chatelaine*, 3 September 1974. On homosexuality, see Marchand, *McLuhan*, 45, 74, 118, 129.

11 Marchand, *McLuhan*, 48–87; Gordon, *McLuhan*, 69–135; *Letters of Marshall McLuhan*, 86.

12 *Letters of Marshall McLuhan*, 165.

13 Ibid., 186.

14 Gordon, *McLuhan*, 159; 'Understanding Canada and Sundry Other Matters: Marshall McLuhan,' *Mademoiselle*, January 1967, 114–15, 126–9, quoted in Marchand, *McLuhan*, 221–2; Marshall McLuhan, 'Canada: The Borderline Case,' in David Staines, ed., *The Canadian Imagination* (Cambridge, MA: Harvard University Press, 1977), 226–48, also in Marshall McLuhan, *Understanding Me*, 105–23; Peter Newman, 'The Table Talk of Marshall McLuhan,' *Maclean's*, June 1971, reprinted in Nevitt and McLuhan, *Who Was Marshall McLuhan?* 108–12. McLuhan's ambivalence about Canada and its national identity is noticed in Pierre Berton, *1967: The Last Good Year* (Toronto: Doubleday, 1997), 206–20, which presents a less-than-laudatory assessment of 'the guru of the boob tube.'

15 For attempts to address the Frye–McLuhan relation which, despite their antagonism, contain some parallel themes, see Richard Cavell, *McLuhan in Space: A Cultural Geography* (Toronto: University of Toronto Press, 2002), 207–22; Fekete, *Critical Twilight*. Frye, in what was undoubtedly a later attempt to be generous, commented that McLuhan was 'celebrated for the wrong reasons in the sixties, and then neglected for the wrong reasons later.' He further added, somewhat cryptically, that McLuhan's greatest contribution was to understand 'the role of discontinuity in communication.' See Nevitt and McLuhan, *Who Was Marshall McLuhan?* 126.

16 Marshall McLuhan, *The Mechanical Bride: Folklore of Industrial Man* (New York: Vanguard, 1951), quotes from 55, 102, 159. For a more critical assessment of this period of McLuhan's development, and for a general periodization of McLuhan that is far more attentive to lines of demarcation in the years after 1951, see Fekete, *Critical Twilight*, 146–62.

17 Marchand, *McLuhan*, 119.

18 Harold Adams Innis, *Empire and Communications* (Oxford: Oxford University Press, 1950); Innis, *The Bias of Communication* (Toronto: University of Toronto Press, 1951); Marshall McLuhan, *The Gutenberg Galaxy* (Toronto: University of Toronto Press, 1962), esp. 50; Paul Heyer, *Harold Innis* (London: Rowman

and Littlefield, 2003); Miller, *McLuhan*, 88–91; James W. Carey, 'Harold
Adams Innis and Marshall McLuhan,' in Raymond Rosenthall, ed., *McLuhan:
Pro and Con* (Baltimore: Penguin, 1969), 281–2; Marchand, *McLuhan*, 120–
45; Gordon, *McLuhan*, 147–51, points to McLuhan's critiques of Innis; and
Theall, *Virtual McLuhan*, 48–9, also has comment on Innis, as does William
Kuhns, *The Post-Industrial Prophets: Interpretations of Technology* (New York:
Harper and Row, 1973), 169–70. More generous is Glenn Willmott, *McLuhan,
or Modernism in Reverse* (Toronto: University of Toronto Press, 1996), 104–9.
Note as well Graeme Patterson, *History and Communications: Harold Innis,
Marshall McLuhan, and the Interpretation of History* (Toronto: University of
Toronto Press, 1990); John Watson, *Marginal Man: The Dark Vision of Harold
Adams Innis* (Toronto: University of Toronto Press, 2006), esp. 404–13. See,
finally, Benedict Anderson, *Imagined Communities: Reflections on the Origins and
Spread of Nationalism* (London: Verso, 1983).

19 *Letters of Marshall McLuhan*, 448; Theall, *Virtual McLuhan*, 29, 70, and on
McLuhan as satirist, 187–210. Note as well the discussion of McLuhan and
satire in Nevitt and McLuhan, *Who Was Marshall McLuhan?* 187–202. In
many ways, McLuhan was very much a man always ahead of his political
time. He foresaw much, both in the future of cultural practice as well as the
fashion of intellectual trends. But he also saw a great deal that never happened and gravitated in directions as problematic as they were probing. His
spirit both anticipated developments in critical theory and postmodernism
that unfolded in the last three decades of the twentieth century and stood
distanced from their substance. There is food for thought along these lines,
albeit not always aligned in agreement, in Willmott, *McLuhan, or Modernism
in Reverse*; and especially in Theall, *Virtual McLuhan*, esp. 125–37, which
addresses pre-postmodernism and French theory.

20 H.M. McLuhan, *Counterblast* (No place: no publisher, 1954). On this self-
publication see Marchand, *McLuhan*, 117–18. The Massey Commission is
detailed in Paul Litt, *The Muses, the Masses, and the Massey Commission*
(Toronto: University of Toronto Press, 1992).

21 For a succinct introduction to these terms, which will be discussed below, see
Dennis Duffy, *Marshall McLuhan* (Toronto: McClelland and Stewart, 1969),
38–42.

22 The quote comes from a recollection of McLuhan by his colleague Edmund
Carpenter. See Carpenter, 'That Not-So Silent Sea,' Appendix B in Theall,
Virtual McLuhan, 250–1.

23 This shift is discussed, albeit in ways different than I briefly suggest here, in
Donald F. Theall, *The Medium Is the Rear View Mirror: Understanding McLuhan*
(Montreal and Kingston: McGill-Queen's University Press, 1971). Paul

Heyer, *Harold Innis*, 85–6, notes that Innis and McLuhan shared a 'full-blown critique of commercial culture, circa 1950,' but that a decade later the latter 'jettisoned the critical stance.'

24 'Playboy Interview,' *Essential McLuhan*, 264–9; McLuhan, 'The Medium Is the Massage,' in *Understanding Me*, 107.

25 Marshall McLuhan, *Understanding Media: The Extensions of Man* (Toronto: Signet, 1968; original 1964), 23, 268–94; 'Playboy Interview,' *Essential McLuhan*, 264. Television in Canada developed later and more cautiously than in the United States, which meant that its full impact was just being felt as McLuhan made the new medium the focus of commentary. See Paul Rutherford, *When Television Was Young: Primetime Canada, 1952–1967* (Toronto: University of Toronto Press, 1990); Doug Owram, *Born at the Right Time: A History of the Baby-Boom Generation* (Toronto: University of Toronto Press, 1996), 88–90. McLuhan first introduced the medium/message phrasing in 1959, albeit rather cautiously. See McLuhan, 'Myth and Mass Media,' *Daedalus* 88 (Spring 1959), 346, and the discussion in Fekete, *Critical Twilight*, 160.

26 McLuhan, *Understanding Media*, 268–94; 'Playboy Interview,' *Essential McLuhan*, 233–69.

27 On the critical acclaim and response see Harry H. Crosby and George R. Bond, *The McLuhan Explosion: A Casebook on Marshall McLuhan and 'Understanding Media'* (New York: American Book Company, 1968).

28 The above paragraph on celebrity, and the ongoing account of this mid-1960s phenomenon below, draws on a range of sources. See, among much writing: Marchand, *McLuhan*, 168–22; Gordon, *McLuhan*, 173–298; Wolfe, *Pump House Gang*, 105–33; Herb Caen, 'Rainy Day Session,' *San Francisco Chronicle*, 12 August 1965; Gerald M. Feigen, 'The McLuhan Festival: On the Road to San Francisco,' in Sanderson and Macdonald, eds., *McLuhan*, 65–9; *Letters of Marshall McLuhan*, 330.

29 Wolfe, *Pump House Gang*, 105–33; Marshall McLuhan with Quentin Fiore and Jerome Agel, *The Medium Is the Massage: An Inventory of Effects* (New York: Bantam, 1967); Malcolm Muggeridge, 'The Medium Is McLuhan,' *New Statesman*, 1 September 1967. For a relevant postmodern reading of McLuhan's involvement in the construction of his celebrity see Willmott, *McLuhan, or Modernism in Reverse*, 135–55.

30 Nevitt and McLuhan, *Who Was Marshall McLuhan?* 99, 135; Robert Fulford, *This Was Expo* (Toronto: McClelland and Stewart, 1968), 116; Theall, *Virtual McLuhan*, 126; Berton, *1967: The Last Good Year*, 206–24; Robert Fulford, 'On Marshall McLuhan: What One Communications Expert Discerns – But Has Trouble Getting Across,' *Maclean's*, 20 June 1964.

31 'Playboy Interview,' *Essential McLuhan*, 249.

32 Marchand, *McLuhan*, 192–3, 204–5; Peter Newman, 'The Table Talk of Marshall McLuhan,' *Maclean's* (June 1971), reprinted in Nevitt with McLuhan, *Who Was Marshall McLuhan?* 108–12, quote 111.

33 Abbie Hoffman, *Revolution for the Hell of It* (New York: Dial Press, 1968), 58. McLuhan clearly had an early purchase on the New Left in Canada, in spite of his jaundiced view of youth radicalism. See for instance the publication of McLuhan in the first issue of the New Left publication *This Magazine Is about Schools*: Marshall McLuhan, 'Electronics and the Pyschic Drop-Out,' in Satu Repo, ed., *This Book Is about Schools* (New York: Pantheon, 1970), 383–9.

34 Marchand, *McLuhan*, 218; 'Playboy Interview,' *Essential McLuhan*, 254.

35 McLuhan quoted in Tom Wolfe, 'Foreward,' *Understanding Me*, xxi.

36 The above paragraphs draw on 'Playboy Interview,' 258–69.

37 Marshall McLuhan, Quentin Fiore, and Jerome Agel, *War and Peace in the Global Village* (Toronto: Penguin, 2003; original 1968), 113–15, 97, 149, 82, 123.

38 Donald F. Theall, *The Medium Is the Rear View Mirror*, 164–5; Marshall McLuhan, *Counterblast* (New York: Harcourt Brace and World, 1968), 58. Almost a decade later, in 1977, McLuhan was prone to acknowledge the problematic refusal of events to lead in the direction he had clearly wanted them to. See McLuhan, 'Violence as a Quest for Identity,' *Understanding Me*, 264–76, but his tone was somewhat cavalier. See, as well, Marshall McLuhan and Bruce R. Powers, *The Global Village: Transformations in World Life and Media in the 21st Century* (New York: Oxford University Press, 1989). For a recent retrospective appreciation of McLuhan that contains discussion of what he had right and what he posed wrongly in his understanding of the global village see John Moss and Linda M. Morra, eds., *At the Speed of Light There Is Only Illumination: A Reappraisal of Marshall McLuhan* (Ottawa: University of Ottawa Press, 2004).

39 Larry Zolf, *Dance of the Dialectic: How Pierre Elliott Trudeau Went from Philosopher-King to the Incorruptible Robespierre to Philosopher-Queen Marie Antoinette to Canada's Generalissimo Ky and then to Mackenzie King and Even Better* (Toronto: James Lewis and Samuel, 1973), 11.

40 Marchand, *McLuhan*, 232.

41 Quoted in Nevitt and McLuhan, *Who Was Marshall McLuhan?* 111. For a subsequent critique of McLuhan's views on television see Rutherford, *When Television Was Young*, 26–38.

42 Gordon, *McLuhan*, 278; Judith Fitzgerald, *Marshall McLuhan: Wise Guy* (Montreal: XYZ, 2001), 158–9. Willmott, *McLuhan, or Modernism in Reverse*, 136, notes that McLuhan retained readers in the Latin world, with his

largest following in Mexico and South America, a point McLuhan emphasized. See *Letters of Marshall McLuhan,* 505–6.

43 *Letters of Marshall McLuhan,* 354.

44 Ibid., 356–9, 362–3, 365–7. See also Mark Kingwell, 'Six Scenes of Separation: Confessions of a Post-Facto Trudeaumaniac in Pursuit of the Personality Cult,' in Andrew Cohen and J.L. Granatstein, eds., *Trudeau's Shadow:
The Life and Legacy of Pierre Elliott Trudeau* (Toronto: Random House,
1998), 86–7.

45 Trudeau's youthful flirtations with the ugly politics of 1930s fascism have
long been known, but the publication of Monique and Max Nemni, *Young
Trudeau: Son of Quebec, Father of Canada, 1919–1944* (Toronto: Douglas
Gibson Books, 2006), provided a fuller case and unleashed a barrage of
media commentary and journalistic reviews. More balanced is John English,
Citizen of the World: The Life of Pierre Elliott Trudeau, vol. 1, *1919–1968*
(Toronto: Knopf Canada, 2006), 45–106.

46 There are innumerable accounts of Trudeau's formative years. Overviews
include English, *Citizen of the World,* 1–203; Monique and Max Nemni, *Young
Trudeau;* Stephen Clarkson and Christina McCall, *Trudeau and Our Times,*
vol. 1, *The Magnificent Obsession* (Toronto: McClelland and Stewart, 1990),
23–51; Pierre Elliott Trudeau, *Memoirs* (Toronto: McClelland and Stewart,
1994), 3–62; Michel Vastel, *The Outsider: The Life of Pierre Elliott Trudeau*
(Toronto: Macmillan, 1990), 9–48.

47 English, *Citizen of the* World, 199–203; Clarkson and McCall, *Trudeau and
Our Times: The Magnificent Obsession,* 52–5; Trudeau, *Memoirs,* 62–3; Richard
Gwyn, *The Northern Magus: Pierre Trudeau and the Canadians* (Toronto:
McClelland and Stewart, 1980), 40–1; Trudeau, ed., *La grève de l'amiante:
Une étape de la révolution industrielle au Québec* (Montreal: Cité libre, 1956),
quote translated from 379. Ramsay Cook attributes his initial attraction to
Trudeau's reason and passion to a reading of Trudeau's 1956 writing on
Asbestos. See Cook, *The Teeth of Time: Remembering Pierre Elliott Trudeau*
(Kingston and Montreal: McGill-Queen's University Press, 2006), 10–11.
For a different appreciation of the Asbestos strike see Jacques Rouillard,
'La grève de l'amiante de 1949 et le projet de réforme de l'enterprise:
Comment le patronat a défendu son droit de gérance,' *Labour/Le Travail* 46
(Fall 2000): 307–42.

48 Trudeau, *Memoirs,* 65–9; Vastel, *Outsider,* 51–83. A succinct statement on
Trudeau's early role in *Cité libre* appears in English, *Citizen of the World,* 237–
40. For one statement on Trudeau's internationalism and the travels that
enriched it, see Pierre Trudeau and Jacques Hubert, *Two Innocents in Red
China* (Toronto: Oxford University Press, 1968). On Trudeau and religion

see John English, Richard Gwyn, and P. Whitney Lackenbauer, eds., *The Hidden Pierre Elliott Trudeau: The Faith behind the Politics* (Ottawa: Novalis, 2004).

49 See Gwyn, *Northern Magus*, 44–56; Clarkson and McCall, *Trudeau and Our Times: The Magnificent Obsession*, 52–75. For a useful collection of Trudeau's writings that contain *Cité libre* pieces from the period see Pierre Elliott Trudeau, *Against the Current: Selected Writings, 1939–1996*, edited by Gerard Pelletier (Toronto: McClelland and Stewart, 1996).

50 Gwyn, *Northern Magus*, 45–46; Clarkson and McCall, *Trudeau and Our Times: The Magnificent Obsession*, 76–84; Trudeau, 'The Identity Card Is Back,' *Against the Current*, 115.

51 Gwyn, *Northern Magus*, 45–46; Clarkson and McCall, *Trudeau and Our Times: The Magnificent Obsession*, 76–84; Pierre Elliott Trudeau, *The Essential Trudeau*, edited by Ron Graham (Toronto: McClelland and Stewart, 1998), 105–16; Vastel, *Outsider*, 92–101. Trudeau's key *Cité libre* articles of this period, 'Nationalist Alienation' and 'New Treason of the Intellectuals,' are reproduced in *Against the Current*, 143–81.

52 On the Conservative Party see Robert C. Coates, *Night of Knives* (Fredericton, NB: Brunswick Press, 1969); Peter C. Newman, *The Distemper of Our Times* (Winnipeg: Greywood, 1968), 91–176, while 185–223 detail Liberal Party gaffes.

53 Robert Bothwell, Ian Drummond, and John English, *Canada since 1945: Power, Politics, and Provincialism* (Toronto: University of Toronto Press, 1989), 271–6; Claude Morin, *Quebec vs. Ottawa: The Struggle for Self-Government* (Toronto: University of Toronto Press, 1976), 37; Trudeau, *Memoirs*, 77–88; Clarkson and McCall, *Trudeau and Our Times: The Magnificent Obsession*, 85–102; Newman, *The Distemper of Our Times*, 224–35; an acerbic account of 'the three wise men' is in Vastel, *Outsider*, 105–13. A useful discussion of de Gaulle is Olivier Courteaux, 'Canada's Foul-Weather Friend: How the War Disguised de Gaulle's Designs,' in Dimitry Anastakis, ed., *The Sixties: Passion, Politics, and Style* (Kingston and Montreal: McGill-Queen's University Press, 2008), 116–26.

54 Denis Smith, *Rogue Tory: The Life and Legend of John G. Diefenbaker* (Toronto: Mcfarlane, Walter and Ross, 1995), 549–59; Newman, *Distemper of Our Times*, 177–80; Donald Peacock, *Journey to Power: The Story of a Canadian Election* (Toronto: Ryerson Press, 1968), 12–109.

55 *Letters of Marshall McLuhan*, 354.

56 Diefenbaker was appalled by Trudeau's early dress in the House of Commons and made a rather large (and politically shrill) deal of it, claiming the member from Mount Royal showed a disregard for the dignities of Parliament. Asked by reporters what he proposed to do about this 'problem' of his

image, Trudeau looked at the press corps, shabbily attired as ever, and quipped: 'Get another tailor, I guess – but it won't be yours.' Gordon Donaldson, *Fifteen Men: Canada's Prime Ministers from Macdonald to Trudeau* (Toronto: Doubleday, 1969), 247; Nancy Southam, ed., *Pierre: Colleagues and Friends Talk about the Trudeau They Knew* (Toronto: McClelland and Stewart, 2005), 38, 199; Berton, *1967: The Last Good Year,* 359.

57 Cook, *Teeth of Time,* 44–5; English, *Citizen of the World,* 457–8; Peter Stursberg, *Lester Pearson and the Dream of Unity* (Toronto: Doubleday, 1978), 425; and on Trudeau's substantive views on federalism, Pierre Elliott Trudeau, 'We Need a Bill of Rights, Not a New Version of the BNA Act,' *Maclean's,* 8 February 1964, 24–5; Trudeau, 'Federalism, Nationalism, and Reason,' in P.A. Crepeau and C.B. Macpherson, eds., *The Future of Canadian Federalism/L'avenir du fédéralisme au Canada* (Toronto: University of Toronto Press, 1965), 16–35; Trudeau, *Federalism and the French Canadians* (Toronto: Macmillan, 1968).

58 Cook, *Teeth of Time,* 40–58; English, *Citizen of the World,* 445–63.

59 Gwyn, *Northern Magus,* 60. For a critical, even somewhat embittered, assessment of just this process see Walter Stewart, *Shrug: Trudeau in Power* (Toronto: New Press, 1971), 204–6. It is challenged by a more two-sided appreciation that animates the writing of Larry Zolf. See, for instance, Larry Zolf, 'Humble Arrogance: A Cautionary Tale of Trudeau and the Media,' in Andrew Cohen and J.L. Granatstein, eds., *Trudeau's Shadow: The Life and Legacy of Pierre Elliott Trudeau* (Toronto: Random House, 1998), 47–62, esp. 55–6.

60 'A Matter of Image,' *Maclean's,* March 1968, quoted in Paul Litt, 'Trudeaumania,' unpublished manuscript, December 2006. I am grateful to Professor Litt for providing me with a preliminary copy of his study of Trudeau and 1968, which meshes extremely well with my attempt to fit Trudeau and McLuhan together as figures of the 1960s. Litt's paper has subsequently appeared as 'Trudeaumania: Participatory Democracy in the Mass-Mediated Nation,' *Canadian Historical Review* 89 (March 2008): 27–54. The comment on African tribalism is quoted in Vastel, *Outsider,* 134. On Trudeau's statement on the state and the bedrooms of the nation see Peacock, *Journey to Power,* 177; John Saywell, 'Introduction,' Trudeau, *Federalism and the French Canadians,* xiii; Newman, *The Distemper of Our Times,* 401–2. Stewart, *Shrug,* refers to journalists using the term 'Camelot North' in their rush to embrace Trudeau (7) and to the significance and limitation of the bedrooms/nation line (12).

61 Litt, 'Trudeaumania,' first brought this to my attention, and Professor Litt pointed me in the direction of Clarkson and McCall, *Trudeau and Our Times: The Magnificent Obsession,* 108, which cites 'Unlocking the Locked Step of Law and Morality,' *Globe and Mail,* 12 December 1967.

62 For one contemporary comment on the apparently negligible importance of Trudeau's legal reforms for homosexuals, see Jack Batten, 'The Homosexual Life in Canada: Will Trudeau's Change in the Law Make Any Difference? An Answer from the Gay World,' *Saturday Night*, September 1969, 28–32.

63 For a discussion of the candidates see Judy LaMarsh, *Memoirs of a Bird in a Gilded Cage* (Toronto: McClelland and Stewart, 1969), 310–51; Newman, *The Distemper of Our Times*, 394–400.

64 Lester B. Pearson, *Mike: The Memoirs of the Right Honourable Lester B. Pearson*, vol. 3, *1957–1968* (Toronto: University of Toronto Press, 1975), 326.

65 The above paragraphs draw on a number of important newspaper articles on Trudeau, image, and the success of his non-candidacy style that appear in Rick Butler and Jean-Guy Carrier, eds., *The Trudeau Decade* (Toronto: Doubleday, 1979), 2–12, quoting Bain, Cook, and others. See, as well, Peacock, *Journey to Power*, 177–203, and the comments on Trudeaumania and women, 257–8; Gwyn, *Northern Magus*, 66–8; Clarkson and McCall, *Trudeau in Our Times: The Magnificent Obsession*, 110–12; Peter C. Newman, *A Nation Divided: Canada and the Coming of Pierre Trudeau* (New York: Knopf, 1969), 456; Newman, *Distemper of Our Times*, 403–4. Trudeau's sex appeal, not to be denied as a forceful attribute of Trudeaumania, is discussed in Larry Zolf, *Just Watch Me: Remembering Pierre Elliott Trudeau* (Toronto: James Lorimer, 1984), 17–28; Rick Salutin, 'Trudeau and the Left: Violence, Sex, Culture,' in Cohen and Granatstein, eds., *Trudeau's Shadow*, 177–94; and it figures in feminist views of his 'charm,' as in Judy Rebick, *Ten Thousand Roses: The Making of a Feminist Revolution* (Toronto: Penguin Canada, 2005), 7. On intellectuals and early support for Trudeau see Saywell, 'Introduction,' Trudeau, *Federalism and the French Canadians*, vii–xvii; Peter Newman, 'Opinion Makers Pick Their Man, Pierre Trudeau,' *Toronto Daily Star*, 13 January 1968. Ramsay Cook would later link Trudeau with what he stated succinctly was the defining mark of a political decade of importance: 'What has distinguished the 1960s from the previous decade in our political history is quite simply excitement.' Trudeau, and his capacity to excite, *was* admittedly a phenomenon in which style mattered, but it was a style that was substantive. Thus, when questioned in March 1968 as to whether 'he was all style and no content,' Trudeau, according to Cook, replied 'by quoting Buffon's famous remark that "le style, c'est l'homme meme."' But this quip, suggested Cook, went over too many heads: 'most people thought [Trudeau] meant his leather overcoat.' See Ramsay Cook, 'Federalism, Nationalism, and the Canadian Nation-State,' in Cook, *The Maple Leaf Forever: Essays on Nationalism and Politics in Canada* (Toronto: Macmillan, 1971), 23, 45; and, more retrospectively, Cook, *Teeth of Time*.

66 For a particularly early, hard-hitting, and perhaps overstated claim that Trudeaumania was little more than a right shift in the Liberal Party, a masking of the avoidance of a number of policy issues by raising shrill cries associated with the national question, Trudeau presenting himself as 'the knight who will slay the Quebec dragon,' see G. David Sheps, 'The Nature of Trudeaumania,' *Canadian Dimension* 5 (September-October 1968): 4–6.

67 The above paragraphs draw on Maurice Weston, 'The Trudeau of the Image Makers,' *Winnipeg Free Press*, 4 April 1968, in Butler and Carrier, eds., *The Trudeau Decade*, 13–14; Gwyn, *Northern Magus*, 60; Newman, *A Nation Divided*, 449–51; Pearson, *Mike: The Memoirs of the Right Honourable Lester B. Pearson*, 3: 32–327; Stewart, *Shrug*, 7, 12–13; Clarkson and McCall, *Trudeau and Our Times: The Magnificent Obsession*, 112; Gordon Donaldson, *Fifteen Men*, 238, 247; Marshall McLuhan, 'The Story of the Man in the Mask,' review of *Federalism and the French Canadians*, by Pierre Elliott Trudeau, *New York Times Book Review* (17 November 1968), 36–8; Marchand, *McLuhan*, 234; Bernard Dube, 'Trudeau – Pratfall and All,' *Montreal Gazette*, 9 April 1968, quoted in Clarkson and McCall, *Trudeau and Our Times: The Magnificent Obsession*, 111.

68 See Berton, *1967: The Last Good Year*, 256–367; Mark Kurlansky, *1968:The Year That Rocked the World* (New York: Ballantine, 2004), 351–2. For an interesting account of Trudeau's appeal to a New Leftist, antagonistic to much of his purpose, see Rick Salutin, 'Trudeau and the Left: Sex, Violence, Culture,' in Cohen and Granatstein, *Trudeau's Shadow*, 177–94. On Trudeau the gunslinger see Zolf, *Just Watch Me*.

69 The above paragraphs draw on: Newman, *A Nation Divided*, 459–69; Clarkson and McCall, *Trudeau and Our Times: The Magnificent Obsession*, 112–13; Berton, *1967: The Last Good Year*, 359; Gwyn, *Northern Magus*, 68–9, and on the future limitations of participatory democracy, 72–92, a point addressed as well in James Laxer and Robert Laxer, *The Liberal Idea of Canada: Pierre Trudeau and the Question of Canada's Survival* (Toronto: James Lorimer, 1977); Peacock, *Journey to Power*, 198–200; Stewart, *Shrug*, 206. On 'Just Society' see Piergiorgio Mazzocchi, 'Editorial: The Lame Policies of a "Just Society,"' *Le Devoir*, 26 October 1968, in Butler and Carrier, eds., *Trudeau Decade*, 74; Stewart, *Shrug*, 16–34; Peacock, *Journey to Power*, 334–6; John English, *The Life of Lester Pearson: The Worldly Years*, vol. 2, *1949–1972* (Toronto: Knopf, 1992), 381–93; and for an official representation, Pierre Elliott Trudeau, *Conversation with Canadians* (Toronto: University of Toronto Press, 1972); Thomas S. Axworthy and Pierre Elliott Trudeau, eds., *Towards a Just Society: The Trudeau Years* (Markham, ON: Viking, 1990).

70 Stewart, *Shrug*, 13; Gwyn, *Northern Magus*, 69–71; Peacock, *Journey to Power*, 325–83, with Lynch quoted at 345; Sheps, 'Nature of Trudeaumania,' 5; Donaldson, *Fifteen Men*, 237–8, 256. Privately, Trudeau was asking his friend Ramsay Cook if he had any ideas on how the United States might be prevailed upon to alter its stand 'even a little' on Vietnam. Cook, *Teeth of Time*, 37.

71 The above paragraphs draw on and quote from Southam, ed., *Pierre: Colleagues and Friends Talk about the Trudeau They Knew*, 75 (Keith Mitchell); Newman, *Distemper of Our Times*, 416; Carole de Vault with William Johnson, *The Informer: Confessions of an Ex-Terrorist* (Toronto: Fleet Books, 1982), 57–62. Ramsay Cook concluded that Trudeau's 24 June 1968 stand had been a measure of his physical toughness and intellectual courage. Cook, 'Federalism, Nationalism, and the Canadian Nation-State,' in *The Maple Leaf Forever*, 43–4.

72 Donaldson, *Fifteen Men*, 258.

73 For various editorials and articles following on Trudeau's victory see Butler and Carrier, eds., *The Trudeau Decade*, 42–59.

74 Quoted in Donaldson, *Fifteen Men*, 255. For discussions on Trudeau pro and con in a left magazine see Cy Gonick, 'Pierre Elliott Trudeau and "The New Politics,"' *Canadian Dimension* 5 (April-May 1968): 3–4; Richard Dahrin, 'The Media and the Rise of Pierre Elliott Trudeau,' *Canadian Dimension* 5 (June-July 1968): 5–6; and the symposium on 'Trudeau,' *Canadian Dimension* 5 (June-July 1968): 7–12.

75 Zolf, *The Dance of the Dialectic*, 24–30. On Expo as the necessary prerequisite to Trudeau and Trudeaumania see Gwyn, *Northern Magus*, 60–1; Editorial, *Peterborough Examiner*, 28 June 1968, in Butler and Carrier, eds., *Trudeau Decade*, 47; Berton, *1967: The Last Good Year*, 359.

76 Judy LaMarsh, *Bird in a Gilded Cage*, 228; Berton, *1967: The Last Good Year*, 367; Gwyn, *Northern Magus*, 71.

77 Zolf, *Just Watch Me*, 11–12.

78 Donaldson, *Fifteen Men*, 239, 258.

79 Richard Gwyn, 'Trudeau: The Idea of Canadianism,' in Cohen and Granatstein, eds., *Trudeau's Shadow*, 29, drawing on Clarkson and McCall, *Trudeau and Our Times: The Magnificent Obsession*, 9. As this book was being finished two different accounts of Trudeau appeared – one traditional biography, another memoir – that demonstrated the continuing interest in and appeal of Trudeau. See English, *Citizen of the World*, and Cook, *Teeth of Time*, and the reviews headed, 'I Must Become a Great Man,' in *Globe and Mail*, 14 October 2006, Books, Section D, 12–13.

80 Peacock, *Journey to Power*, 383.

6: Riotous Victorianism: From Youth Hooliganism to a Counterculture of Challenge

1 The above paragraph draws on and quotes sources cited in Craig Heron and Steve Penfold, *The Workers' Festival: A History of Labour Day in Canada* (Toronto: University of Toronto Press, 2005), esp. 27–30, 134–40; Nancy Bouchier, '"The 24th of May Is the Queen's Birthday": Civic Holidays and the Rise of Amateurism in Nineteenth-Century Towns,' *International Review of the History of Sport* 10 (August 1993): 164–85; Robert M. Stamp, 'Empire Day in the Schools of Ontario: The Training of Young Imperialists,' *Journal of Canadian Studies* 8 (August 1973): 32–42; H.V. Nelles, *The Art of Nation Building: Pageantry and Spectacle in Quebec's Tercentenary* (Toronto: University of Toronto Press, 1999), 241–4; 'Canada's Celebrations Both Noisy, Relaxing,' *Globe and Mail*, 24 May 1960; 'Newfoundland Awaits May 25 for Victoria Day,' *Peterborough Examiner*, 19 May 1970.

2 'Need New Name for Holiday,' *London Free Press*, 20 May 1968; '125 Fatalities Set Holiday Record,' *Peterborough Examiner*, 24 May 1966; 'Queen Victoria and All That,' *Peterborough Examiner*, 23 May 1967; 'Back Home Again – Bumper to Bumper' and 'At Least 110 Killed on Victoria Day Weekend,' *Globe and Mail*, 24 May 1966; 'Weekend Death Toll Reaches 85,' *Montreal Gazette*, 19 May 1964. I focus on the mid-1960s press commentary on the demise of Victoria Day. For a discussion of Victoria Day as a fading tradition based on newspaper coverage of the 1950s see José E. Igartua, *The Other Quiet Revolution: National Identities in English Canada, 1945–1971* (Vancouver: UBC Press, 2006), 107–9.

3 Dorothy Thompson, *Queen Victoria: Gender and Power* (London: Virago, 1990); Perry Anderson, 'Origins of the Present Crisis,' in Anderson, *English Questions* (London: Verso, 1992), 25.

4 For a general statement on how age-old Victorianism was waning in Canadian culture in the period from the First World War into the 1950s see Doug Owram, *Born at the Right Time: A History of the Baby Boom Generation* (Toronto: University of Toronto Press, 1996), esp. 19–20, 42, 259.

5 Alison L. Prentice and Susan E. Houston, eds., *Family, School, and Society in Nineteenth Century Canada* (Toronto: Oxford University Press, 1975), 270–90; Andrew Jones and Leonard Rutman, *In the Children's Aid: J.J. Kelso and Child Welfare in Ontario* (Toronto: University of Toronto Press, 1981); Jane Addams, *The Spirit of Youth and the City Streets* (New York: Macmillan, 1912); Emergy S. Bogardus, *The City Boy and His Problems: A Survey of Boy Life in Los Angeles* (Los Angeles: Rotary Club, 1926); Frederic Milton Thrasher, *The Gang: A Study of 1,313 Gangs in Chicago* (Chicago: University of Chicago Press, 1927). The

most accessible survey of juvenile delinquency in Canada is D. Owen
Carrigan, *Juvenile Delinquency in Canada: A History* (Concord, ON: Irwin,
1998). On the pivotal place of the 1920s in the first faint understandings of
modern youth and the designation of the teenager see Cynthia Comacchio,
*The Dominion of Youth: Adolescence and the Making of Modern Canada, 1920 to
1950* (Waterloo, ON: Wilfrid Laurier University Press, 2006).

6 Erik H. Erikson, *Childhood and Society* (New York: Norton, 1963; original
1950), esp. 401–2, 418–19; Erikson, *Identity, Youth, and Crisis* (New York:
Norton, 1968), esp. 74–90; Leerom Medovoi, *Rebels; Youth and the Cold War
Origins of Identity* (Durham and London: Duke University Press, 2005), 5–24;
Lawrence Freidman, *Identity's Architect: A Biography of Erik H. Erikson* (New
York: Scribner's, 1999). One attempt to wrestle with the continuities of
economic inequality and deprivation, alongside perceptions of changing
material circumstances, and the relation of this to the crisis of youth, is Paul
Goodman, *Growing Up Absurd: Problems of Youth in the Organized System* (New
York: Random House, 1960). Two Canadian studies, accenting youth in dif-
ferent ways, outlined the changing nature of concerns over the course of the
1940s and 1950s. See Kenneth H. Rogers, *Street Gangs in Toronto: A Study of
the Forgotten Boy* (Toronto: Ryerson Press, 1945); John R. Seeley, R. Alexander
Sim, and E.W. Looley, *Crestwood Heights: A Study of the Culture of Suburban Life*
(New York: Basic Books, 1956), 86–117.

7 Medovoi, *Rebels*, 24–30; Owram, *Born at the Right Time*, 136–158.

8 Medovoi, *Rebels*, 30–4; Robert Lindner, *Rebel without a Cause: The Hypnoanaly-
sis of a Criminal Psychopath* (New York: Grune and Stratton, 1944); Lindner,
Prescription for Rebellion (New York: Rinehart, 1952); Lindner, 'Raise Your
Child to Be a Rebel,' *McCall's*, February 1956, 31, 100–4.

9 Edgar Z. Friendenberg, *The Vanishing Adolescent* (New York: Dell, 1959), 32.

10 Ibid., 34–5.

11 Medovoi, 34–9; John Clare, 'The Scramble for the Teenage Dollar,'
Maclean's, 14 September 1957.

12 Benjamin Spock, *The Common Sense Book of Baby and Child Care* (New York
1946), 320, and 'Advertisement for Kiddicraft Toys,' *Maclean's*, 1 September
1953, 89, both quoted in Owram, *Born at the Right Time*, 84, 93.

13 Russell Jacoby, *The Last Intellectuals: American Culture in the Age of Academe*
(New York: Basic, 1987), 62–5; James Gilbert, *A Cycle of Outrage: America's
Reaction to the Juvenile Delinquent in the 1950s* (New York: Oxford University
Press, 1986).

14 Benjamin Fine, *1,000,000 Delinquents* (New York: World Publishing, 1955),
27–8, quoted in Jacoby, *Last Intellectuals*, 63. For similar concerns see Friedenberg, *The Vanishing Adolescent*, 122–4; and for Canada in the early 1960s,

David Lewis Stein, 'The "Have" Delinquents: Why Do They Go Wrong?' *Maclean's*, 25 January 1964.

15 Lawrence Lipton, *The Holy Barbarians* (New York: Julian Messner, 1959); Bryan D. Palmer, *Cultures of Darkness: Night Travels in the Histories of Transgression* (New York: Monthly Review, 2000), 370–86; Paul O'Neil, 'The Only Rebellion Around,' *Life Magazine* 1959, reprinted in Thomas Parkinson, ed., *A Casebook on the Beat* (New York: Crowell, 1961), 232, 235, quoted in Jacoby, *Last Intellectuals*, 66; Norman Mailer, 'The White Negro,' in Mailer, *Advertisements for Myself* (New York: Signet, 1960), 298–322, a much-criticized essay, as noted in Scott Saul, *Freedom Is, Freedom Ain't: Jazz and the Making of the Sixties* (Cambridge, MA: Harvard University Press, 2003), 68–70.

16 For a critique of the crime statistics as a meaningful indicator of trends see Daniel Bell, 'The Myth of the Crime Waves,' in Bell, *The End of Ideology* (New York: Free Press, 1962), 137–58.

17 For discussion of teenage girls, promiscuity, and juvenile delinquency see Joan Sangster, *Regulating Girls and Women: Sexuality, Family, and the Law in Ontario, 1920–1960* (Toronto: Oxford University Press, 2001); Sangster, *Girl Trouble: Female Delinquency in English Canada* (Toronto: Between the Lines, 2002). Note, as well, Sidney Katz, 'Going Steady: Is It Ruining Our Teenagers?' *Maclean's*, 3 January 1959. For the United States see Wini Breines, *Young, White, and Miserable: Growing Up Female in the Fifties* (Boston: Beacon Press, 1992).

18 Owram, *Born at the Right Time*, 142–4; 'Report of the Mayor's Conference Re Juvenile Delinquency and Associated Problems,' Board of Control Report No. 6, Adopted by City Council, 20 February 1950, City of Toronto Archives, series 100, 467004–4, Department of Public Welfare, Juvenile Delinquency and Youth Work, file 1355. (Hereafter, City of Toronto, Public Welfare, file #.)

19 Library and Archives of Canada, 'Crackdown on Comics, 1947–1966,' http://www.collectionscanada.ca/comics (accessed 2 February 2006); *Hansard*, 6 October 1949; 21 October 1949; 5 December, 1949; *Winnipeg Free Press*, 22 October 1949; Department of Justice Papers, Juvenile Delinquency Act, Public Archives of Canada, RG 13, vol. 2842, file 157471.

20 Carrigan, *Juvenile Delinquency in Canada*, 153; and for general commentary on the problem of crime statistics: John C. Weaver, *Crimes, Constables, and Courts: Order and Transgression in a Canadian City, 1816–1970* (Montreal and Kingston: McGill-Queen's University Press, 1995), 188–224; Helen Boritch and John Hagan, 'Crime and the Changing Forms of Class Control: Policing Public Order in "Toronto the Good," 1859–1955,' *Social Forces* 66 (December 1987): 307–35; Lynn Mcdonald, 'Crime and Punishment in Canada: A Statistical Test of the "Conventional Wisdom,"' *Canadian Review of Sociology*

and Anthropology 6 (1969): 212–36; Jane B. Sprott and Anthony N. Doob, 'Changing Models of Youth Justice in Canada,' *Crime and Justice: A Review of Research* 31 (2004): 185–242.

21 Carrigan, *Juvenile Delinquency in Canada,* 153; Mark Frank, *Poison for the Young: A Major Reason for Rising Juvenile Delinquency* (Toronto: Progress Books, 1962), 10.

22 Friedenberg, *The Vanishing Adolescent,* 176–7.

23 Ivor Brown, 'Teenagers a Problem in U.K.,' *Globe and Mail,* 18 May 1964; 'Highway Deaths and Teen-Age Battles Spoil Whitsun Holiday for Britons,' *Globe and Mail,* 19 May 1964; 'Police Hold 30 as Youth Gangs Clash in Britain,' *Globe and Mail,* 21 May 1964; 'Gang Wars Mar Holiday,' *Montreal Gazette,* 19 May 1964; 'Gang Warfare Stuns the British Conscience,' *Winnipeg Free Press,* 25 May 1964. For a brilliant discussion of youth cultures in 1960s Britain see Paul Willis, *Profane Culture* (London: Routledge and Kegan Paul, 1978).

24 *Juvenile Delinquency in Canada: The Report of the Department of Justice Committee on Juvenile Delinquency* (Ottawa: Queen's Printer, 1965).

25 Quotes, statements, and figures from Frank, *Poison for the Young,* and from Carrigan, *Juvenile Delinquency in Canada,* 158–64. See also Jane Becker, 'A Harvard Man's Life among Toronto's Young "Have-Nots,"' *Maclean's,* 25 January 1964.

26 David Lewis Stein, 'The "Have" Delinquents: Why Do They Go Wrong?' *Maclean's,* 25 January 1964.

27 Frank, *Poison for the Young.*

28 For an evocative and exciting treatment of the early 1960s in California see Mike Davis, 'Wild Streets: *American Graffiti* versus the Cold War,' *International Socialism Journal* (Summer 2001); Davis, 'As Bad as the H-Bomb,' *Dead Cities and Other Tales* (New York: New Press, 2002), 207–26, while a slightly later set of events is discussed by Davis in 'Riot Nights on Sunset Strip,' *Labour/Le Travail* 59 (Spring 2007): 199–214. A suggestive analytic account of the youth riot at the 1960 Newport Jazz Festival is in Saul, *Freedom Is, Freedom Ain't,* 99–122. Owram, *Born at the Right Time,* 144, suggests a similar process of historical development.

29 For discussions of Yorkville see Reginald G. Smart et al., *The Yorkville Subculture: A Study of the Life Styles and Interactions of Hippies and Non-Hippies* (Toronto: Addiction Research Foundation, 1969); Owram, *Born at the Right Time,* 210–15; Myrna Kostash, *Long Way from Home: The Story of the Sixties Generation in Canada* (Toronto: Lorimer, 1981), 107–44; Pierre Berton, *1967: The Last Good Year* (Toronto: Doubleday, 1997), 163–92. Most insightful is the presentation of Yorkville as a locale of alien performativity in the work of Stuart Henderson. See the excellent paper by Henderson,

'Toronto's Hippie Disease: The Yorkville Hepatitis Epidemic, August 1968,' presented to the Canadian Historical Association, York University, May 2006, published as Stuart Henderson, 'Toronto's Hippie Disease: End Days in the Yorkville Scene, August 1968,' *Journal of the Canadian Historical Association*, 17, n.s. (2006): 205–34. For a broad discussion relating to Quebec see Marcel Rioux, 'Youth in the Contemporary World and Quebec,' in W.E. Mann, ed., *Social and Cultural Change in Canada*, vol. 1 (Toronto: Copp Clark, 1970), 302–15.

30 'Need New Name for Holiday,' *London Free Press*, 20 May 1968.

31 'Canada's Celebrations Both Noisy, Relaxing,' *Globe and Mail*, 24 May 1960; 'Varied Celebrations Held,' *Peterborough Examiner*, 23 May 1961; 'Victoria Day Is Release for Canadian Contrasts,' *Peterborough Examiner*, 25 May 1965.

32 'Vandals Flood School,' and 'School Doors Broken,' *London Free Press*, 18 May 1964; 'Charge Children in School Blaze,' *Globe and Mail*, 18 May 1964.

33 'Firecrackers Blamed in Brant Airport Fire,' *London Free Press*, 22 May 1963; 'Fireworks Loss $400,000,' *London Free Press*, 23 May 1961; 'Provincial Curb on Fireworks Necessary,' *London Free Press*, 24 May 1961; 'Fire Chief Lauds Firecracker Law,' *London Free Press*, 22 May 1962; 'May Save Eye Injured by Cracker,' *London Free Press*, 18 May 1964; 'City's Firecracker ByLaw Praised by Police, Firemen,' *London Free Press*, 19 May 1962; 'Barn Burns, Cars Block Fire Trucks,' *Peterborough Examiner*, 23 May 1961; 'Fireworks: Improvement in Behavior,' *Peterborough Examiner*, 22 May 1962; 'Precautions Urged in Handling Holiday Fireworks,' *Peterborough Examiner*, 16 May 1964.

34 'Police, Firemen Harried on Holiday by Premature Fireworks Display,' and 'Mob Pelts Police with Fireworks,' *Hamilton Spectator*, 23 May 1961; 'Pointing the Finger at Alabama,' *Hamilton Spectator*, 24 May 1961; 'Hamilton Mob Ignites Store, Defies Police,' *London Free Press*, 23 May 1961; 'Youths Tossing Firecrackers Tie Up Traffic,' *Globe and Mail*, 23 May 1961.

35 'Mob of 400 Throws Firecrackers' *Hamilton Spectator*, 22 May 1962; 'Hundreds Rampage, Attack Police, Set Fires' and 'Jailed for Assault on Police,' *Hamilton Spectator*, 27 May 1963; David Carmichael, 'Police Clash with Mob in Hamilton,' *Globe and Mail*, 21 May1963; 'Victoria Day Picture Grim in Some Areas' and 'Firecracker Mob Dispersed by Police,' *Peterborough Examiner*, 21 May 1963.

36 'Police Head Off Holiday Violence by North End Mob' and 'Tact, Not Truncheons Nips James Street Row,' *Hamilton Spectator*, 19 May 1964; 'A Job Well Done,' *Hamilton Spectator*, 20 May 1964; 'Aided Police, Radio Scribe Commended,' 29 May 1964; City of Toronto, Public Welfare, file 1353.

37 'Barrage of Fireworks Ends Holiday with a Bang,' *Hamilton Spectator*, 24 May 1965; 'Downtown Fails to Explode,' *Hamilton Spectator*, 25 May 1965.

38 'Toronto Gang Attacks Firemen,' *Hamilton Spectator,* 25 May 1965; 'Firemen Attacked at Blaze,' *Globe and Mail,* 25 May 1965; 'Attack Firemen,' *London Free Press,* 25 May 1965.

39 Archives of Ontario, Ontario Housing Corporation Papers, RG 44-19-1, box 10, B1-7-2, file: Tenant Associations in Metro, Central Neighbourhood House, Grant Proposal from CNH to OHC, 22 September 1965 and Assessment of Youth Problems in Regent Park, June 1965; Frank Adams, 'Police Get Rumble Jitters, Teen-Agers Harassed,' *Globe and Mail,* 13 June 1964; 'Mrs. Campbell Assails Report, Says Delinquency Not Localized,' *Globe and Mail,* 20 May 1965; 'Statistics Misleading, Youth Officer Says,' *Globe and Mail,* 21 May 1965. My thanks to Sean Purdy for providing me with these documents. For a discussion of the Regent Park public housing complex see Robert Sean Purdy, 'From Place of Hope to Outcast Space: Territorial Regulation and Tenant Resistance in Regent Park Housing Project, 1949–2001,' PhD dissertation, Queen's University, 2003.

40 For general statements on drug use in the 1960s see Harold Kalant and Oriana Josseau Kalant, *Drugs, Society, and Personal Choice* (Toronto: Paperjacks, 1971); Greg Marquis, 'From Beverage to Drug: Alcohol and Other Drugs in 1960s and 1970s Canada,' *Journal of Canadian Studies* 39, no. 2 (2005): 57–80; Marcel Martel, *Not This Time: Canadians, Public Policy, and the Marijuana Question, 1961–1975* (Toronto: University of Toronto Press, 2006).

41 'Four Arrested after Disorder in Yorkville Area,' *Globe and Mail,* 18 May 1964; 'Motion Prohibits New Coffee Houses in Yorkville Area: Residents' Complaints Heard by Committee,' *Globe and Mail,* 27 May 1965.

42 For fuller discussion see Henderson, 'Toronto's Hippie Disease'; Reginald G. Smart and David Jackson, 'Yorkville Subculture,' in W.E. Mann, ed., *The Underside of Toronto* (Toronto: McClelland and Stewart, 1970), 109–22; J. Ruby, 'Hippies Love Balked as Cops Batter Sit-In,' *Workers Vanguard,* September 1967.

43 '50 Charged in "Bend" Liquor Raids,' *London Free Press,* 19 May 1964; Paul Gartlan, 'Police Win Opener at Bend,' *London Free Press,* 22 May 1967; 'No Room for the Wild Ones,' *Globe and Mail,* 20 May 1968. In 2007, the tradition of riotous Grand Bend Victorianism continued. The OPP boosted its Grand Bend detachment from 4 to 30 officers over the Victoria Day weekend and handed out 401 liquor violations. Rowdiness and underage drinking resulted in 89 evictions at the nearby Pinery campgrounds. See Pat Currie, 'Rowdy Vacationers Have OPP Scrambling,' *Globe and Mail,* 17 July 2007.

44 '9 Firemen Hurt in Rowdy Quebec Celebrations,' *London Free Press,* 24 May 1960; Dave Angus, 'Bonfires, Violence Mar Holiday Here,' *Montreal Gazette,* 24 May 1960; Bill Bantey, 'Police Order on Holiday Vandalism: "Get

Tough,"' *Montreal Gazette,* 29 May 1961; 'Police Cope with Fires, Mob Violence,' *Peterborough Examiner,* 24 May 1960.

45 Bill Bantey, 'Police Order on Holiday Vandalism: "Get Tough,"' *Montreal Gazette,* 20 May 1961.

46 'Police, Firemen Kept Busy; 35 Arrested but Damage Slight,' *Montreal Gazette,* 22 May 1961; Al Palmer and Jim Ferrabee, 'Hooligans Mostly Ignore "Get Tough Warning,"' *Montreal Gazette,* 23 May 1961.

47 Karl Marx, 'The Eighteenth Brumaire of Louis Bonaparte,' in Karl Marx and Frederick Engels, *Selected Works* (Moscow: Progress, 1968), 170.

48 First published as Frantz Fanon, *Les Damnés de la terre* (Paris: François Maspero, 1961), with a preface by Jean-Paul Sartre. Its influence is commented on extensively in Malcolm Reid, *The Shouting Signpainters: A Literary and Political Account of Quebec Revolutionary Nationalism* (Toronto: McClelland and Stewart, 1972).

49 As context see, among countless sources, Marcel Rioux, *Quebec in Question* (Toronto: James Lorimer, 1978), and the radical nationalist Leandré Bergeron, *The History of Quebec: A Patriot's Handbook* (Toronto: NC Press, 1971).

50 For a brief, accessible introduction only, see Reid, *The Shouting Signpainters,* 21–7; R. Comeau, D. Cooper, P. Vallières, eds., *FLQ: Un projet révolutionnaire* (Montreal: VLB Éditeur, 1990); Louis Fournier, *FLQ: The Anatomy of an Underground Movement* (Toronto: NC Press, 1984).

51 Carole de Vault with William Johnson, *The Informer: Confessions of an Ex-Terrorist* (Toronto: Fleet Books, 1982), 44–5; Kostash, *Long Way from Home,* 215; Gustave Morf, *Terror in Quebec: Case Studies of the FLQ* (Toronto: Clarke, Irwin, 1970), 1–8; James Stewart, *The FLQ: Seven Years of Terrorism* (Montreal: Montreal Star, 1970), 11. Spellings of the name Vincent Wilfrid O'Neill vary greatly in the literature. Here, and in chapter 10 below, I follow the spelling used by Morf.

52 See, for instance, Gerard Pelletier, 'Stage Two on the Road to Disaster,' *La Presse,* 18 May 1963; Leon Dion, 'Reflections on the FLQ,' *Le Devoir,* 21 June 1963, reprinted in *Canadian Forum* (August 1963), both appearing in Frank Scott and Michael Oliver, eds., *Quebec States Her Case* (Toronto: Macmillan, 1984), 88–100. The day after O'Neill's death, André Laurendeau, an influential liberal nationalist, authored an unambiguous denunciation of the FLQ, which he condemned as composed of criminals overcome by sickness, purveyors of 'the fireworks of hate.' He called for French Canadians to side with the victims of their bombings, making the Felquistes 'feel their isolation.' Quoted in Morf, *Terror in Quebec,* 6–7.

53 For the full text see 'The FLQ Manifesto,' in Scott and Oliver, eds., *Quebec States Her Case,* 83–7. There were actually three FLQ statements released in

April 1963. See their reproduction in Claude Savoie, *La Véritable Histoire du F.L.Q.* (Montreal: Éditions du Jour, 1963).

54 'New "Police Pool" Prepared to Meet Terrorist Attacks,' 'NATO Envoys under Guard after Threats,' 'Bomb Men Flown In,' 'FLQ Madness Draws Fire,' *Montreal Gazette*, 20 May 1963; 'Lesage Takes Lead in FLQ Hunt, Summons Forces, Offers $50,000,' 'Police, Army Squads Probe RCEME Rubble,' *Montreal Gazette*, 21 May 1963; Fournier, *FLQ*, 35–49. On 'Truncheon Saturday' see Fournier, *FLQ*, 72–3; Bergeron, *History of Quebec*, 219; Pierre Bourgault, *Écrits polémiques*, vol. 1 (Montreal: VLB Éditeur, 1982).

55 'Montreal Goons Join Separatists, Protest Victoria Day: 85 Arrests,' 'Ensign Burned by Students in Montreal,' *Globe and Mail*, 19 May 1964; 'Bomb Climaxes Wild Weekend,' *London Free Press*, 19 May 1964; 'Police on Horses Disperse Separatist Demonstration,' Paul Dubois, 'Traffic Snarled by Marchers on Several Main Streets,' *Montreal Gazette*, 19 May 1964; '27 Say "Not Guilty" Bail Boosted to $50,' *Montreal Gazette*, 20 May 1964; 'Unhappy Holidays,' *Montreal Gazette*, 20 May 1964; '250 Freed after Montreal Separatist Rallies,' *London Free Press*, 20 May 1964; '29 Have Cases Delayed to Fall,' *Montreal Gazette*, 1 June 1964. Later in the year, Montreal witnessed riots in protests of an actual visit by the Queen, the harsh repression of students chanting 'We are joyful, we are overflowing with joy' ending in a 'Saturday of the bludgeons.' See Bergeron, *Patriote's Handbook*, 216.

56 'Police Battle 2,000 "Hoodlums,"' *London Free Press*, 25 May 1965; 'Montreal Shows Danger of the Mob,' *London Free Press*, 26 May 1965.

57 The above paragraphs draw on Fournier, *FLQ*, 81; Paul Dubois and Grant Johnson, 'Young Separatists Plague Montreal's Holiday Weekend,' *Montreal Gazette*, 25 May 1965; 'Demonstration Aftermath' and 'Holiday Disorder,' *Montreal Gazette*, 26 May 1965; 'Troubles Forecast June 24,' *Montreal Gazette*, 4 June 1965; '"Not All Hooligans" Says Youth Leader,' *Montreal Gazette*, 5 June 1965; David Oancia, '100 Arrested in Montreal as Separatists Run Riot: Dynamiting Begins Day of Violence,' *Globe and Mail*, 25 May 1965; 'Will Apply Full Rigor of Law to Demonstrators, Wagner Says,' *Globe and Mail*, 26 May 1965; Tim Peters and Michael Blair, 'Montreal Demonstrators Jailed' and 'Victoria Day Is Release for Canadian Contrasts,' *Peterborough Examiner*, 25 May 1965; '200 Charges Laid in Demonstration,' *Peterborough Examiner*, 26 May 1965; '154 Face Charges in Montreal Riots,' *Hamilton Spectator*, 25 May 1965; '154 Montrealers Face Charges after Day of Separatist Rioting' and 'Police Battle 2,000 "Hoodlums,"' *London Free Press*, 25 May 1965; 'One Man Pleads Guilty, 88 Innocent in Aftermath of Montreal Rioting,' *London Free Press*, 26 May 1965.

58 Pierre Vallières, *White Niggers of America* (Toronto: McClelland and Stewart, 1971), 211; Fournier, *FLQ*, 77; Reid, *The Shouting Signpainters*, 44.

59 'Fire Warning Shots,' *London Free Press*, 25 May 1965; 'Monuments Defaced in Quebec,' *Montreal Gazette*, 25 May 1965.

60 'Montreal Police Break Up Hooligans' March,' *Globe and Mail*, 24 May 1966; John Dodd, 'Demonstrators Cause Havoc, Arrests Made' and 'Bombing, Marchers Cause Havoc in Montreal,' *Peterborough Examiner*, 24 May 1966; 'Five Youths Fined, 10 Awaiting Trial after Montreal Anti-Victoria Day Row,' *London Free Press*, 25 May 1966; Reid, *The Shouting Signpainters*, 45–7.

61 'Left-Wing Thinkers Hold Political Idea Exchange,' *Winnipeg Free Press*, 25 May 1964. For background on youthful alienation from conventional politics see Kay Kritzwiser, 'The Political Pulse on Canada's Campuses,' *Globe Magazine*, 19 May 1962.

62 'B.C. Bohemians Plot War for Peace,' *London Free Press*, 22 May 1965; 'Riots in Paris,' *Winnipeg Free Press*, 27 May 1968.

63 See Jim Cameron, '60 Hurt, 153 Arrested in New Columbia Battle,' *London Free Press*, 22 May 1968; and the editorials, 'Exploring Student Unrest,' *Peterborough Examiner*, 22 May 1968; 'The Unruly Student,' *Hamilton Spectator*, 4 May 1968. Note as well, 'Police Ponder Riot Dispersal Gas,' *Hamilton Spectator*, 22 May 1968.

64 As an introduction, accenting the repression of the paper, see Berton, *1967: The Last Good Year*, 186–97; Allan Engler, 'Underground Paper Suspended in BC,' *Workers Vanguard*, 16 October 1967.

65 For what is still the best account of this countercultural explosion in Canada see Kostash, *Long Way from Home*, 107–44. See also Owram, *Born at the Right Time*, 185–216; Jack Batten, 'The Dread Hippie Menace,' *Maclean's*, August 1967; and Ron Verzuh, *Underground Times: Canada's Flower-Child Revolutionaries* (Toronto: Deneau, 1989). The social explosion over drugs is perhaps best indicated by the August 1971 Gastown riots in Vancouver. One thousand protesters clashed with police in 'The Battle of Maple Tree Square,' angered by the actions of undercover police agents and their targeting of 'hippies' who advocated the legalization of marijuana. The cops arrested seventy-nine and charged thirty-eight with various offences. Mayor Tom Campbell went on an anti-hippie rampage, attempting to invoke the War Measures Act against the flower children, draft dodgers, and anti-war protesters, a number of whom led a symbolic invasion of the United States soon after the marijuana protests, surging into Blaine, Washington. A judicial inquiry into the Gastown events headed by Justice Thomas Dohm heard lurid police testimony of the role of 'professional revolutionaries' in orchestrating the events, a number of whom turned out to be local poets. Dohm concluded that the police had rioted and, in their indiscriminate beatings, use of riot batons, and unprecedented employment of horse-backed charges on crowds

of tourists and onlookers, had overstepped the bounds of their authority. For an introduction only, see Michael Barnholden, *Reading the Riot Act: A Short History of Riots in Vancouver* (Vancouver: Anvil Press, 2005).

66 San Francisco was the vanguard of such initiatives, with a number of hippie 'groups' uniting to declare a Council for the Summer of Love. See Margaret Wente, 'Summer of Love Was the Best of Times,' *Globe and Mail*, 4 August 2007.

67 Joe Wiesenfeld, 'Hippies Hold "Feed-in": 200 Attend Carnival in Memorial Park,' *Winnipeg Free Press*, 27 May 1968. I am grateful to Alvin Finkel for setting me straight on the non-existence of the Winnipeg Diggers and explaining how and why their creation in the press was a useful media fiction. On the Diggers elsewhere see Kostash, *Long Way from Home*, 125; 'A Founder of the Diggers Talks about What's Happening,' in Mitchell Goodman, compiler, *The Movement Toward a New America – The Beginnings of a Long Revolution – (A Collage) of What?* (Philadelphia: Pilgrim Press, 1970), 13–16.

68 '4,500 at Queen's Park But the Real Love-In Never Got Started' and 'More Watchers Than Watched at Love-In,' *Globe and Mail*, 23 May 1967; Richard J. Needham, 'Love Takes Many Strange Forms,' *Globe and Mail*, 24 May 1967. See also, for a Canadian comment on a similar New York event, Peter Gzowski, 'Revelations in a Sheep Meadow: A View of the Loving Generation,' *Saturday Night*, June 1967, 22–5, and for a photograph of a 1967 Regina 'love-in' at the Saskatchewan legislature, see Wente, 'Summer of Love.'

69 Smart and Jackson, 'Yorkville Subculture,' and June Callwood, 'Digger House,' in W.E. Mann, ed., *The Underside of Toronto*, 109–28; Callwood, 'The Right to Own Yourself,' *Canadian Dimension* 7 (August-September 1970), 4–5.

70 Pierre Berton, 'Allan Lamport Meets the Hippies,' in *The Smug Minority* (Toronto: McClelland and Stewart, 1968), 68–74.

71 J. Ruby, 'Hippies' Love Balked as Cops Batter Sit-In,' *Workers Vanguard*, September 1967; Berton, *1967: Last Good Year*, 163–72; and the discussion of Trailer and Grab Bag in Henderson, 'Toronto's Hippie Disease.'

72 For the promise and radicalism of the early Rochdale as an experiment in alternative education see Dennis Lee, 'Getting To Rochdale,' in Satu Repo, ed., *This Book Is about Schools* (New York: Pantheon, 1970), 354–80; Berton, *Smug Minority*, 38.

73 On Rochdale College see Barrie Zwicker, 'Rochdale: The Ultimate Freedom,' in Mann, ed., *Underside of Toronto*, 207–17; James Treat, *Around the Sacred Fire: Native Religious Activism in the Red Power Era – A Narrative Map of the Indian Ecumenical Conference* (New York: Palgrave Macmillan, 2003), 91–100; Kostash, *Long Way from Home*, 125–128; Ralph Osborne, *From Someplace Else: A Memoir* (Toronto: ECW Press, 2003); David Sharpe, *Rochdale: The Runaway*

College (Toronto: House of Anansi, 1987); 'Rochdale College: Organized Anarchy,' CBC Archives, http://archives.cbc.ca (accessed 13 July 2006).

74 Kostash, *Long Way from Home*, xv.

75 Expo 67 contributed to this process in its accent on youth. See Berton, *1967: The Last Good Year*, 272–300; Timothy Plumptre, 'First to Give Youth Its Own Showcase, Expo Provides a Club for Teeny Boppers,' *Globe and Mail*, 23 May 1967. I am not, of course, suggesting that youth *were* a class, as advocated in certain tracts of the times. See the comments in Kostash, *Long Way from Home*, 132–3; Pierre Guimond, 'The Youth Vote in Quebec,' in Dimitrios I. Roussopoulos, ed., *Quebec and Radical Social Change* (Montreal: Black Rose, 1974), 91–103; John and Margaret Rowntree, *The Political Economy of Youth (Youth as a Class)* (Ann Arbor, MI: Radical Education Project, c. 1968).

76 For one early statement on the counterculture see Peter Gzowski, 'Revelations in a Sheep Meadow: A View of the Loving Generation,' *Saturday Night*, June 1967, 22–6.

77 Wente, 'Summer of Love.'

78 Kostash, *Long Way from Home*, 117–21.

79 Ibid., 143.

7: Wildcat Workers: The Unruly Face of Class Struggle

1 See the compilation of articles in Douglas Hay and Paul Craven, eds., *Masters, Servants, and Magistrates in Britain and the Empire, 1562–1955* (Chapel Hill and London: University of North Carolina Press, 2004); Paul Craven, 'The Law of Master and Servant in Mid-Nineteenth Century Ontario,' in D.H. Flaherty, ed., *Essays in the History of Canadian Law*, vol. 1 (Toronto: Osgoode Society, 1981), 175–211.

2 Bryan D. Palmer, 'What's Law Got to Do With It? Historical Considerations on Class Struggle, Boundaries of Constraint, and Capitalist Authority,' *Osgoode Hall Law Journal* 41 (Summer-Fall 2003): 466–90.

3 Bob Russell, *Back to Work: Labour, State, and Industrial Relations in Canada* (Toronto: Nelson, 1990); Paul Craven, *An Impartial Umpire: Industrial Relations and the Canadian State, 1900–1911* (Toronto: University of Toronto Press, 1980); Judy Fudge and Eric Tucker, *Labour Before the Law: The Regulation of Workers' Collective Action in Canada, 1900–1948* (Toronto: Oxford University Press, 2001); Bryan D. Palmer, *Working-Class Experience: Rethinking the History of Canadian Labour, 1800–1991* (Toronto: McClelland and Stewart, 1992); Douglas Cruikshank and Gregory S. Kealey, 'Canadian Strike Statistics, 1891–1950,' *Labour/Le Travail* 20 (Fall 1987): 85–146.

4 Countless sources could be cited. See, for a sample only, Fudge and Tucker, *Labour Before the Law*, 153–315; Cruikshank and Kealey, 'Canadian Strike

Statistics, 1891–1950,' 117, 119–20; Stuart Marshall Jamieson, *Times of Trouble: Labour Unrest and Industrial Conflict in Canada, 1900–1966* (Ottawa: Information Canada, 1972), 214–343; H. Clare Pentland, *A Study of the Changing Social, Economic, and Political Background of the Canadian System of Industrial Relations: A Report Prepared for the Task Force on Labour Relations* (Ottawa: Supply and Services, 1968); Irving Martin Abella, *Nationalism, Communism, and Canadian Labour: The CIO, the Communist Party, and the Canadian Congress of Labour, 1935–1956* (Toronto: University of Toronto Press, 1973); Terry Copp, ed., *Industrial Unionism in Kitchener, 1937–1947* (Elora, ON: Cumnock Press, 1976); Cy Gonick, Paul Phillips, and Jesse Vorst, *Labour Gains, Labour Pains: Fifty Years of PC 1003* (Halifax: Garamond, 1995); Jerry Lembcke, *One Union in Wood: A Political History of the Internatinal Woodworkers of America* (New York: International, 1983); Laurel Sefton MacDowell, *Remember Kirkland Lake: The Gold Miners' Strike of 1941–1942* (Toronto: University of Toronto Press, 1983); Benjamin Isitt, 'Working Class Agency, the Cold War, and the Rise of a New Left: Political Change in British Columbia, 1948–1972,' preliminary draft of PhD presented to University of New Brunswick, 2007.

5 For the above paragraphs see Peter S. McInnis, *Harnessing Labour Confrontation: Shaping the Postwar Settlement in Canada, 1943–1950* (Toronto: University of Toronto Press, 2002); Ian McKay, *The Craft Transformed: An Essay on the Carpenters of Halifax, 1885–19985* (Halifax: Holdfast Press, 1985), 81–113; Leo Panitch and Donald Swartz, *The Assault on Trade Union Freedoms: From Wage Controls to Social Contract* (Halifax: Garamond, 1993), esp. 9–14; Peter J. Warrian, 'Labour Is Not a Commodity: A Study of the Rights of Labour in the Canadian Postwar Economy, 1944–1948,' PhD dissertation, University of Waterloo, 1986; David W.T. Mathieson, 'The Canadian Working Class and Industrial Legality, 1939–1949,' MA thesis, Queen's University, 1989; David Moulton, 'Ford Windsor 1945,' in Irving Abella, ed., *On Strike: Six Key Labour Struggles in Canada, 1919–1949* (Toronto: James Lorimer, 1975), 129–62; Herb Colling, *Ninety-Nine Days: The Ford Strike in Windsor in 1945* (Toronto: NC Press, 1995). Rand quotes from Justice Ivan C. Rand, 'Award on the Issue of Union Security in Ford Dispute,' *Labour Gazette* 46 (January 1946): 123–31.

6 Strong statements on the unambiguous value of the postwar settlement have been made by social democratic historians, as in Laurel Sefton MacDowell, *Renegade Lawyer: The Life of J.L. Cohen* (Toronto: University of Toronto Press, 2001); Desmond Morton, *Working People: An Illustrated History of Canadian Labour* (Ottawa: Deneau and Greenberg, 1980), 175–200; Kenneth McNaught, 'E.P. Thompson vs. Harold Logan: Writing about Labour and the Left in the 1970s,' *Canadian Historical Review* 62 (June 1981): 141–68.

7 Ed Finn, 'The New Militancy of Canadian Labour,' *Canadian Dimension* 3 (November–December 1965): 17.

8 For a brief statement on the Cold War in the unions see Palmer, *Working-Class Experience*, 245–52. The major statement, which does not question too closely or deeply the costs of anti-communist 'cleansing,' is Abella, *Nationalism, Communism and Canadian Labour*. Note, as well, Doug Smith, *Cold Warrior: C.S. Jackson and the United Electrical Workers* (St John's, NF: CCLH, 1997).

9 As an introduction to the unravelling of the postwar settlement and the contours of contemporary class struggle unfolding in its wake, see Panitch and Swartz, *The Assault on Trade Union Freedoms*; Yonatan Reshef and Sandra Rastin, *Unions in the Time of Revolution: Government Restructuring in Alberta and Ontario* (Toronto: University of Toronto Press, 2003); Bryan D. Palmer, 'System Failure: The Breakdown of the Postwar Settlement and the Politics of Labour in Our Time,' *Labour/Le Travail* 55 (Spring 2005): 334–46; Steven High, *Industrial Sunset: The Making of North America's Rust Belt, 1969–1984* (Toronto: University of Toronto Press, 2003).

10 For a preface to the class confrontation of the decade see G.F. MacDowell, *The Brandon Packers Strike: A Tragedy of Errors* (Toronto: McClelland and Stewart, 1971); Sam Gindin, *The Canadian Auto Workers: The Rise and Transformation of a Union* (Toronto: Lorimer, 1995), 139–66; Wayne Roberts, *Cracking the Canadian Formula: The Making of the Energy and Chemical Workers Union* (Toronto: Between the Lines, 1990), 91–104.

11 The following section draws directly on evidence and argument in Palmer, *Working-Class Experience*, 278–80. Much of the raw data is drawn from the 'Labour Force' tables in F.H. Leacy, ed., *Historical Statistics of Canada*, 2nd ed. (Ottawa: Statistics Canada, 1983). See, as well, Panitch and Swartz, *Assault on Trade Union Freedoms*, 14–16; Stuart Marshall Jamieson, *Times of Trouble: Labour Unrest and Industrial Conflict in Canada, 1900–1966* (Ottawa: Queen's Printer, 1968), 480–3; and for a more general discussion of youth and its influence in the 1960s, Doug Owram, *Born at the Right Time: A History of the Baby Boom Generation* (Toronto: University of Toronto Press, 1996), a book that nevertheless manages to skirt entirely issues of workers and trade unions.

12 Given the preliminary state of research into the wildcat wave of the mid-1960s, it is entirely possible that new research will turn up a number of women-led wildcats. Thus two wildcats involving forty-six members of the United Steelworkers and Aerocide Dispensers Limited took place in November 1964. The vast bulk of the wildcatters were women, many of them immigrants who supposedly had 'no facility in English.' They walked off their jobs protesting changes in work conditions, dissatisfaction with their union's inattention to their grievances, and resentment at a new eight-hour shift

schedule that left workers on the same job for a full day without the standard rotation of the past. The illegal walkouts resulted in the company discharging forty-three women, who then grieved and demanded reinstatement, which they secured through arbitration. See Central Ontario Industrial Relations Institute, *Labour Arbitration Cases*, vol. 16, 'Re United Steelworkers and Aerocide Dispensers Ltd.,' 15 April 1965, 57–72. My thanks to Joan Sangster for drawing my attention to this case.

13 As evidence from Paul Axelrod, *Scholars and Dollars: Politics, Economics, and the Universities of Ontario, 1945–1980* (Toronto: University of Toronto Press, 1982), esp. 141, suggests, while enrolment in and expenditure on higher education rose substantially from 1962 to 1968, it would not be until the later years of this period that such trends would register in relevance for working-class youth. See as well John Porter, *The Vertical Mosaic: An Analysis of Social Class and Power in Canada* (Toronto: University of Toronto Press, 1965), and, for numerical data for the mid-1960s, Dimitrios I. Roussopoulos, 'Towards a Revolutionary Youth Movement and an Extraparliamentary Opposition in Canada,' in Roussopoulos, ed., *The New Left in Canada* (Montreal: Our Generation Press, 1970), 136; Julyan Reid, 'Some Canadian Issues,' in Julyan Reid and Tim Reid, eds., *Student Power and the Canadian Campus* (Toronto: Peter Martin, 1969), 7.

14 Aside from the quantitative data drawn from *Historical Statistics of Canada*, note, as well, James W. Rinehart, *The Tyranny of Work* (Don Mills, ON: Academic Press, 1975), 4, 57, 70; Michael Humphries, 'The Insensitivity of the Union Movement to the Real Need of Union Members,' *Relations Industrielles / Industrial Relations* 23 (October 1968): 610; Gil Levine, 'The Coming Youth Revolt in Labour,' *Labour Gazette* 71 (November 1971): 722–32.

15 As introductions only, see Myrna Kostash, *Long Way from Home: The Story of the Sixties Generation in Canada* (Toronto: Lorimer, 1980), esp. 107–44; Kenneth Westhues, 'Inter-Generational Conflict in the Sixties,' in Samuel D. Clark, J.Paul Grayson, and Linda M. Grayson, eds., *Prophecy and Protest: Social Movements in Twentieth-Century Canada* (Toronto: Gage, 1975), esp. 394–8.

16 H.D. Woods, Chairman, *Canadian Industrial Relations: The Report of the Task Force on Labour Relations* (Ottawa: Privy Council Office, 1968), 99. Although from a slightly later period, note as well Levine, 'The Coming Youth Revolt in Labour,' 722–30.

17 For a particularly virulent attack on the superficial aspects of youth revolt see Peter Desbarats, 'The Most Forgettable Generation: A Sad Glance at the Exhausted New Wave of Revolutionary Youth,' *Saturday Night*, September 1969, 35–6.

18 Peter Townshend, recorded 13 October 1965, Pyle Studios, London, England. Towser Tunes, Inc./Fabulous Music, Ltd./ABKCO Music, Inc.

19 Finn, 'New Militancy and Canadian Labour,' 17. In the United States a number of journalistic commentators focused on the growing alienation of young workers in the late 1960s and the consequent eruption of 'blue-collar blues' and trade union rebelliousness. See Judson Gooding, 'Blue Collar Blues on the Assembly Line,' *Fortune Magazine*, July 1970; 'Strike Fever … and the Public Interest,' *Life Magazine*, 26 August 1966; Ken Weller, *The Lordstown Struggle and the Real Crisis in Production* (London: Solidarity, n.d. circa 1970); Bill Watson, *Counter-planning on the Shop Floor* (Somerville, MA: New England Free Press, 1971); Emma Rothschild, *Paradise Lost: The Decline of the Auto-Industrial Age* (New York: Random House, 1973). William Serrin, *The Company and the Union* (New York: Knopf, 1973), 39, notes that the number of official grievances at General Motors in the United States rose from 6,000 in 1960 to 256,000 in 1969. See as well James J. Matles, *The Young Worker Challenges the Union Establishment* (New York: United Electrical, Radio and Machine Workers of America, 1968).

20 'Trouble on the Line,' *Canadian Dimension* 9 (August-September 1973): 10–11.

21 'Wildcat Strike Poses Question: Are Leaders Out of Touch with Members?' *Globe and Mail*, 19 November 1965.

22 Finn, 'New Militancy of Canadian Labour,' 17.

23 Mungo James, 'Labour Lays It on the Line,' *Saturday Night*, December 1966, 27–8; Evelyn Dumas, 'The New Labour Left in Quebec,' in Dimitrios I. Roussopoulos, ed., *Quebec and Radical Social Change* (Montreal: Black Rose, 1974), 117. Note as well J.H.G. Crispo and H.W. Arthurs, 'Industrial Unrest in Canada: A Diagnosis of Recent Experience,' *Relations Industrielles / Industrial Relations* 23 (April 1968): 237–64; Levine, 'Coming Youth Revolt in Labour.'

24 Finn, 'New Militancy of Canadian Labour,' 17. See also comments by Dennis McDermott, quoted in Sam Gindin, *Canadian Auto Workers: The Birth and Transformation of a Union* (Toronto: Lorimer, 1995), 141, and for comment on workers' strikes and student protests in Paris 1968, Kirstin Ross, *May '68 and Its Afterlives* (Chicago: University of Chicago Press, 2002), esp. 32–3.

25 A.R. Carrothers, *Report of a Study on the Labour Injunction in Ontario*, vol. 2 (Toronto: Ontario Department of Labour, 1966), 396–7.

26 Woods, *Canadian Industrial Relations*, 98. See also Sam Gindin, *The Canadian Auto Workers: The Birth and Transformation of a Union* (Toronto: Lorimer, 1995), 143.

27 Louis Greenspan, 'Wages and Wildcats,' *Canadian Forum* (February 1967): 245.

28 Crispo and Arthurs, 'Industrial Unrest in Canada,' unpublished paper cited by Jamieson, *Times of Trouble*, 401; Greenspan, 'Wages and Wildcats,' 244–5;

James, 'Labour Lays It on the Line,' 26, quoting Harry Waisglass, *Towards Equitable Income Distribution.*

29 Standard statements on wildcat strikes can be found in Alvin W. Gouldner, *Wildcat Strike* (Yellow Springs, OH: Antioch Press, 1954); Martin Glaberman, *Wartime Strikes: The Struggle against the Non-strike Pledge in the UAW during World War II* (Detroit: Bewick/ed, 1980), 35–61; Rinehart, *Tyranny of Work*, 71–3; Maxwell Flood, 'The Growth of the Non-Institutional Response in the Canadian Industrial Sector,' *Relations Industrielles / Industrial Relations* 27 (1972): 603–15; Maxwell Flood, 'Some Reflections on Wildcat Strikes,' *Summation* 1 (June 1968): 1–14; Maxwell Flood, *Wildcat Strike in Lake City* (Ottawa: Queen's Printer, 1968).

30 'A Plague of Strikes,' *Globe and Mail*, 31 May 1966; 'The More Sensible Course,' *Globe and Mail*, 2 June 1966.

31 The above paragraphs draw on Palmer, *Working Class Experience*, 280, summarizing Jamieson's data; Jamieson, *Times of Trouble*, 371, 397; Joy McBride, 'The Wildcat Wave: Rank-and-File Rebellion in the Canadian Labour Movement, 1965–6,' unpublished paper, Queen's University, 17 August 1987, in possession of the author. On inflation and wage demands see James, 'Labour Lays It on the Line,' 25; Greenspan, 'Wages and Wildcats,' 244; Carrothers, *Study on the Labour Injunction*, 2: 399–408, 586; 'Construction Workers End Montreal Strike,' *Labour Gazette* 66 (July 1966): 349.

32 McBride, 'The Wildcat Wave'; Jamieson, *Times of Trouble*, 400–4; Woods, *Canadian Industrial Relations*, 131; Gindin, *Canadian Auto Workers*, 143.

33 On the opposition to injunctions see A.W.R. Carrothers, *Report of a Study on the Labour Injunction in Ontario*, vol. 1 (Toronto: October 1966); and the illuminating article by Joan Sangster, '"We No Longer Respect the Law": The Tilco Strike, Labour Injunctions, and the State,' *Labour/Le Travail* 53 (Spring 2004): 47–88. Carrothers, *Study on the Labour Injunction*, vol. 2, contains reprints of *Globe and Mail* articles from September 1965 to September 1966 relating to the 1965–6 labour upsurge. This collation of material was prepared for Carrothers by M.T. Mollison and is an extremely valuable source. Specific items relating to the *Oshawa Times*, Tilco, and other injunction-related strikes and actions are found on 313–56, 520–31. See also Donald C. MacDonald, Letter to the Editor, *Globe and Mail*, 2 August 1966; *Globe and Mail*, 12 February 1966; Ed Finn, 'The Lessons of Oshawa,' *Canadian Dimension* 3 (January-February 1965): 7–8; P. Kent, 'Ontario Unionists Defy Injunctions,' *Workers Vanguard*, March 1966. On the British Columbia context see Benjamin Isitt, 'Working Class Agency, the Cold War, and the Rise of a New Left: Political Change in British Columbia, 1948–1972,' preliminary draft of PhD dissertation, presented to University of New Brunswick, 2007, chap. 10.

34 *The Globe and Mail,* 21 June 1966; Carrothers, *Study on the Labour Injunction,* 2:
    409; Roberts, *Cracking the Canadian Formula,* 100; Paul Phillips, *No Power
    Greater: A Century of Labour in B.C.* (Vancouver: BC Federation of Labour,
    1967), 164; Ross Dowson, 'Urge General Strike as Judge Jails BC Leaders' and
    'BC Labor Debates Injunctions Policy,' *Workers Vanguard,* Mid-September
    1966; Mid-October 1966; and for background to the BC labour opposition to
    the injunction, A.W.R. Carrothers, *The Labour Injunction in British Columbia,
    1946–1955: With Particular Reference to the Law of Picketing* (Toronto and Mon-
    treal: CCH Canadian, Limited, 1956).

35 The above paragraphs draw on standard accounts of such battles in Jamieson,
    Times of Trouble, 422–46, which contains the report on Inco's wage offer (432);
    Flood, *Wildcat Strike in Lake City;* Bill Freeman, *1005: Political Life in a Union
    Local* (Toronto: James Lorimer, 1982), 99–116; Mr Justice Samuel Freedman,
    *Report of Industrial Inquiry Commission on Canadian Natinal Railways 'Run-
    Throughs'* (Ottawa: Queen's Printer, 1966), 69–80; Stephen G. Peitchinis,
    Labour–Management Relations in the Railway Industry (Ottawa: Queen's Printer,
    1971); Ed Finn, 'Why Canadian Workers Are Kicking,' *Canadian Dimension* 4
    (January-February 1967): 4–6; Stephen T. Wace, *The Longshoring Industry:
    Strikes and Their Impact* (Ottawa: Queen's Printer, 1968); 'Longshoremen's
    Strike Ends – With Reservations,' *Labour Gazette* 66 (September 1966): 497;
    Jean-Claude Parrot, *My Union, My Life: Jean-Claude Parrot and the Canadian
    Union of Postal Workers* (Halifax: Fernwood, 2005), 5–20. For the comment on
    postal workers' and union leadership see 'Wildcat Strike Poses Question: Are
    Leaders Out of Touch with Members?' *Globe and Mail,* 19 November 1965.
    Note as well Marvin Gandall, 'The Labour Movement: Two Decades Ago,'
    Canadian Dimension 18 (October-November 1984): 35–7.

36 A sense of the Teamster strike's volatility can be gleaned from press reports
    culled from the *Globe and Mail* and gathered in Carrothers, *Study on the
    Labour Injunction,* 2: 357–67, 383, 431. See, as well, Jamieson, *Times of Trou-
    ble,* 427–9; Arthur Kruger, 'Strike Wave – 1966,' *Canadian Forum* (July 1966):
    73–4; 'Brief Trucker Strike Sparked by Rebels,' *London Free Press,* 4 October
    1965; Graeme McKechnie, *The Trucking Industry* (Ottawa: Queen's Printer,
    1968); P. Kent, 'Ontario Teamster Lockout Projects Battle Cry – No Con-
    tract, No Work!' and 'Teamsters Solid, 40-hr. Week Now,' *Workers Vanguard,*
    Mid-January 1966; April 1966.

37 'Wildcat Strike Poses Question: Are Leaders Out of Touch with Members?'
    Globe and Mail, 19 November 1965.

38 James, 'Labour Lays It on the Line,' 28.

39 'Wildcat Strike Poses Question: Are Leaders Out of Touch with Members?'
    Globe and Mail, 19 November 1965.

40 Carrothers, *Study on the Labour Injunction,* 2: 452.
41 Maxwell Flood, 'The Wildcat Strike: Non-institutional Response in the Industrial Sector,' PhD dissertation, Michigan State University, 1971, 263, cited in McBride, 'The Wildcat Wave,' 20–1; *Globe and Mail* articles in Carrothers, *Study on the Labour Injunction,* 2: 367, 374.
42 See the brief discussion in McBride, 'The Wildcat Wave,' 20–2, citing, among other sources, 'Unions Stepping Up Battle against Injunctions,' *Toronto Daily Star,* 28 June 1966; 'Seek to Curb Violence at Strike-Bound Factory,' *Sarnia Observer,* 2 March 1967; 'Strikers Remanded on Intimidation Charges,' *St Catharines Standard,* 2 February 1967; 'Gates Stormed as Strike Starts with Night of Violence,' *Toronto Telegram,* 25 February 1965; '270 Men Stage Walkout,' *Winnipeg Free Press,* 22 June 1965; 'En Rebellion contre leurs chefs syndicaux, les employés du CN à Montréal demeurent en grève,' *Le Devoir,* 3 August 1966.
43 On the role of youth in the Stelco wildcat see Freeman, *1005,* 100–8; Flood, *Wildcat Strike in Lake City,* 9, 70–2; 'Vote to End Stelco Strike,' *Globe and Mail,* 8 August 1966, also in Carrothers, *Study on the Labour Injunction,* 2: 381.
44 James, 'Labour Lays It on the Line,' 26.
45 McBride, 'Wildcat Wave,' 26, 36, citing, among other sources, 'Warkworth Prison Dispute with Workmen Is Settled,' *Peterborough Examiner,* 13 December 1966; 'Union Action Defied by Electrical Workers,' *Globe and Mail,* 16 May 1966; 'Ford's Oakville Plant Lines Closed Down Over Night,' *Hamilton Spectator,* 26 January 1965. Also note Bryan D. Palmer, ed., *A Communist Life: Jack Scott and the Canadian Workers Movement, 1927–1985* (St John's, NF: CCLH, 1988), 176–83; Isitt, 'Working-Class Agency, the Cold War, and the Rise of a New Left,' 405–12; Carrothers, *Study on the Labour Injunction,* 2: 545–6; William E. Simkin, 'Refusals to Ratify Contracts,' *Industrial and Labor Relations Review* 4 (July 1968): 518–40.
46 Woods, *Canadian Industrial Relations,* 101.
47 Carrothers, *Study on the Labour Injunction,* 2: 373–5, 402, 516; Freeman, *1005,* 103; Flood, *Wildcat Srike in Lake City,* 12–19.
48 Finn, 'Why Canadian Workers Are Kicking,' 5.
49 Carrothers, *Study on the Labour Injunction,* 2: 426, 437–9, 443, 451, 532, 534.
50 Gindin, *Canadian Auto Workers,* 147.
51 Carrothers, *Study on the Labour Injunction,* 2: 385, 445, 539–40. For a managerial view of the tumultuous class relations on the Montreal waterfront in this period, see Alexander C. Pathy, *Waterfront Blues: Labour Strife at the Port of Montreal, 1960–1978* (Toronto: University of Toronto Press, 2004).
52 For a sense of this militant history see Mercedes Steedman, Peter Suschnnigg, and Dieter K. Buse, eds., *Hard Lessons: The Mine Mill Union in the Canadian*

Labour Movement (Toronto: Dundurn Press, 1995); M. Solski and J. Smaller, *Mine Mill: The History of the International Mine, Mill, and Smelter Workers in Canada since 1895* (Ottawa: Steel Rail, 1984); John Lang, 'A Lion in a Den of Daniels: A History of the International Union of Mine, Mill, and Smelter Workers, Sudbury, Ontario, 1942–1962,' MA thesis, University of Guelph, 1970.

53 On the Inco wildcat see especially Carrothers, *Study on the Labour Injunction*, 2: 367–78; Jamieson, *Times of Trouble*, 429–32; Flood, 'The Wildcat Strike,' 253, quoted in McBride, 'Wildcat Wave,' 43; Palmer, *Working-Class Experience*, 317.

54 The most detailed account is in Flood, *Wildcat Strike in Lake City*, which forms the evidence base for the discussion in Freeman, *1005*, 99–114. See also Carrothers, *Study on the Labour Injunction*, 2: 378–83; Jamieson, *Times of Trouble*, 433–5.

55 For official recognition of the problem of violence see Woods, *Canadian Industrial Relations*, 133.

56 Carrothers, *Study on the Labour Injunction*, 2: 482.

57 Ibid., 2: 434, 437, 532–3; 'Cars Blasted in Strike at School,' *Ottawa Journal*, 17 March 1966.

58 McBride, 'Wildcat Wave,' 26–7, citing among other sources, 'Violence-Torn Truckers Strike Keeps Rolling,' *Montreal Gazette*, 2 September 1966.

59 Jamieson, *Times of Trouble*, 440. See also Carrothers, *Study on the Labour Injunction*, 2: 515.

60 In this paragraph and below I draw on Joan Sangster's account of Ivan Rand, *Report of the Royal Commission Inquiry into Labour Disputes* (Toronto: Queen's Printer, 1968) in 'Tilco Strike,' 71–82. Sangster notes the Hiram Walker wildcat (73), citing *Toronto Telegram*, 23 March 1967.

61 Rand, *Report into Labour Disputes*, 6, 18, 29–30; also, Sangster, 'Tilco Strike,' 77–8.

62 My rough calculations from the tables in Rand, *Report into Labour Disputes*, 232–49; Douglas Fisher and Harry Crowe, *What Do You Know about the Rand Report?* (Don Mills, ON: Ontario Federation of Labour, 1968); Ed Finn, 'Labour: The Rand Report,' *Canadian Dimension* 5 (September-October 1968), 7–8.

63 Rand, *Report into Labour Disputes*, 18.

64 Carrothers, *Study on the Labour Injunction*, 2: 544; Black Rose Editorial Collective, *Quebec Labour: The Confederation of National Trade Unions Yesterday and Today* (Montreal: Black Rose, 1972), 21; Myrna Kostash, *Long Way from Home: The Story of the Sixties Generation in Canada* (Toronto: Lorimer, 1980), 216–17.

65 Louis Fournier, *FLQ: The Anatomy of an Underground Movement* (Toronto: NC Press, 1984), 81, 97–9.

66 Fournier, *FLQ*, 109; McBride, 'Wildcat Wave,' 27, citing 'Strikers Stone Employer Home,' *Sault Ste Marie Star*, 24 October 1966.

67 Black Rose Collective, *Quebec Labour*; Palmer, *Working-Class Experience*, 312–13; Ian McKay, *Rebels, Reds, Radicals: Rethinking Canada's Left History* (Toronto: Between the Lines, 2005), 185–8; Daniel Drache, ed., *Quebec: Only the Beginning: The Manifestoes of the Common Front* (Toronto: New Press, 1972); Bryan D. Palmer, '40 Years of Class Struggle,' *Canadian Dimension* 37 (November-December 2003): 37–8; Black Rose Books Editorial Collective, 'The Radicalization of Quebec Trade Unions,' *Radical America* 6 (March-April 1972): 51–76; and the entire issue of *Radical America* 6 (September-October 1972), esp. Peter Allnutt and Robert Chodos, 'Quebec into the Streets,' 29–52; Nick Auf de Mar, 'A Blue Collar October,' 68–79; and Richard Théorêt, 'The Struggle of the Common Front,' 93–101. The most thorough treatment of these developments is, to my knowledge, unpublished. See Sean William Mills, 'The Empire Within: Montreal, the Sixties, and the Forging of a Radical Imagination,' PhD dissertation, Queen's University, Kingston, 2007.

68 Pierre Vallières, *White Niggers of America: The Precocious Autobiography of a Quebec 'Terrorist'* (New York: Monthly Review Press, 1971), 208–9; Desmond Morton, *Working People: An Illustrated History of Canadian Labour* (Ottawa: Deneau and Greenberg, 1980), 267; Kostash, *Long Way from Home*, 217–19; Robert Chodos and Nick auf der Maur, eds., *Quebec: A Chronicle, 1968–1972* (Toronto: James, Lewis, and Samuel, 1972), 43; Fournier, *FLQ*, 151, 166, 191–2; Peter Allnutt and Robert Chodos, 'Quebec into the Streets,' *Last Post* 1 (December 1969): 20–8; Nic Auf der Maur, 'Montreal's Cabbies Fight City Hall,' *Last Post* 1 (April 1970): 19–25; Nic Auf der Maur, 'Les Gars de Lapalme,' *Last Post* 2 (October 1971): 32–40.

69 For a brief, popular introductory statement see Walter Stewart, *Strike!* (Toronto: McClelland and Stewart, 1977), 117–31.

70 Palmer, *Working-Class Experience*, 318; Rick Salutin, *Kent Rowley: The Organizer – A Canadian Union Life* (Toronto: Lorimer, 1980); Andrée Lévesque, ed., *Madeleine Parent: Activist* (Toronto: Sumach Press, 2005); Stephen Azzi, *Walter Gordon and the Rise of Canadian Nationalism* (Kingston and Montreal: McGill-Queen's University Press, 1999); Joy McBride, 'Wildcat Wave,' 30, quoting Flood, 'The Wildcat Strike,' 243.

71 'U.S. Unions Attacked by Lesage,' *Montreal Star*, 16 June 1965. This kind of state attack on international unionism was rare in English Canada, although it could be voiced in specific circumstances by politicians seeking office. See John Crispo, *International Unionism: A Study in Canadian–American Relations* (Toronto and New York: McGraw-Hill, 1967), 294, citing 'Home Rule Asked for Labour Unions,' *Globe and Mail*, 16 July 1964.

72 The standard account of international unionism in Canada in the mid-1960s
    is Crispo, *International Unionism.* For the figure on international union mem-
    bers as percentage of all Canadian unionists in 1975 see Stewart, *Strike!* 131.
73 See, for period-type critiques, Roger Howard and Jack Scott, 'International
    Unions and the Ideology of Class Collaboration,' and Charles Lipton, 'Cana-
    dian Unionism,' in Gary Teeple, ed., *Capitalism and the National Question in
    Canada* (Toronto: University of Toronto Press, 1972), 68–87, 102–19; Jack
    Scott, *Canadian Workers, American Unions: How the American Federation of
    Labour Took Over Canada's Unions* (Vancouver: New Star, 1978).
74 Lévesque, ed., *Parent,* 73; Freeman, *1005,* 97; Flood, *Wildcat Strike in Lake
    City,* 68–9.
75 Ed Finn, 'The Struggle for Canadian Labour Autonomy,' *Labour Gazette* 70
    (November 1970): 770, 774.
76 R.B. Morris, 'The Reverter Clause and Break-Aways in Canada,' in Teeple,
    ed., *Capitalism and the National Question in Canada,* 90–100; Ed Finn, 'The
    Struggle for Canadian Labour Autonomy,' *Labour Gazette* 70 (November
    1970): 766–74; Finn, 'Prospects of an Autonomous Labour Movement,'
    Canadian Dimension 5 (September-October 1968): 4; Palmer, *Working-Class
    Experience,* 320; Philip Resnick, 'The Breakaway Movement in Trail,' and
    Paul Knox, 'Breakaway Unionism in Kitimat,' in Paul Knox and Philip
    Resnick, eds., *Essays in BC Political Economy* (Vancouver: New Star Books,
    1974), 42–59; Palmer, ed., *A Communist Life,* 176–83; Alvin Finkel,
    'Winnipeg's CAIMAW: Business Unionism Replaces Business Unionism,'
    Canadian Dimension 8 (June 1971): 45–6; Philip Resnick, *The Land of Cain:
    Class and Nationalism in English Canada, 1945–1975* (Vancouver: New Star
    Books, 1977), 178–89, quote from 189; Isitt, 'Working-Class Agency,'
    375–423; Al King with Kae Braid, *Red Bait! Struggles of a Mine-Mill Local*
    (Vancouver: Kingbird, 1998).
77 Panitch and Swartz, *Assault on Trade Union Freedoms.*
78 James, 'Labour Lays It on the Line,' 28.

8: New Left Liberations: The Poetics, Praxis,
and Politics of Youth Radicalism

1   Peter Desbarats, 'The Most Forgettable Generation: A Sad Glance at the
    Exhausted New Wave of Revolutionary Youth,' *Saturday Night,* September
    1969, 35–6. For a general statement on the generational clash of the 1960s
    see Kenneth Westhues, 'Inter-Generational Conflict in the Sixties,' in S.D.
    Clark, J. Paul Grayson, and Linda M. Grayson, eds., *Prophecy and Protest: Social
    Movements in Twentieth-Century Canada* (Toronto: Gage, 1975), 387–408.

More positive is Evelyn Latowsky and Merrijoy Kelner, 'Youth: The New Tribal Group,' in D.I. Davies and Kathleen Herman, eds., *Social Space: Canadian Perspectives* (Toronto: New Press, 1971), 240–3; Marcel Rioux, 'Youth in the Contemporary World and Quebec,' in W.E. Mann, ed., *Social and Cultural Change in Canada*, vol. 1 (Toronto: Copp Clark, 1970), 302–15; 'CEGEPs, Charlebois, Chartrand: The Quebec Revolution Now – An Inter- view with Dimitri Roussopoulos,' in W.E. Mann, ed., *Social and Cultural Change in Canada*, vol. 2 (Toronto: Copp Clark, 1970), 200–10. In an unpublished paper Catherine Gidney problematizes and complicates the use of a generational analysis. See Gidney, 'War and the Concept of Genera- tion: The International Teach-Ins at the University of Toronto,' in posses- sion of the author.

2 June Callwood, 'Digger House,' in W.E. Mann, ed., *The Underside of Toronto* (Toronto: McClelland and Stewart, 1970), 123–8; 'Yorkville Revisited,' *Toronto Telegram*, 22 July 1969, quoted in Stuart Henderson, 'Toronto's Hippie Disease: The Yorkville Hepititis Epidemic, August 1968,' paper pre- sented to the Canadian Historical Association, York University, May 2006, published as 'Toronto's Hippie Disease: End Days in the Yorkville Scene, August 1968,' *Journal of the Canadian Historical Association* 17, n.s. (2006), 205–34.

3 Allen Ginsberg, 'Howl,' in Ginsberg, *Collected Poems, 1947–1980* (New York: Harper and Row, 1984), 126. The significance of 'Howl' is alluded to in Judith Clavir Albert and Stewart Edward Albert, eds., *The Sixties Papers: Docu- ments of a Rebellious Decade* (New York: Praeger, 1984), 68. On the Beats see, for an introduction only, Bryan D. Palmer, *Cultures of Darkness: Night Travels in the Histories of Transgression* (New York: Monthly Review, 2000), 370–86. The influence of jazz on the 1960s and its relationship to the New Left is brilliantly evoked in Scott Saul, *Freedom Is, Freedom Ain't: Jazz and the Making of the Sixties* (Cambridge, MA: Harvard University Press, 2003).

4 For accounts signalling the demise of aspects of 1960s New Leftism see, among many possible statements, the cluster of articles headed 'Cultural Revolution' in *Canadian Dimension* 7 (August-September 1970), 15–27: David Lewis Stein, 'Yippies/Defining a Revolutionary Life Style'; Alvin Finkel, 'Wither Commune - ism'; and Irwin Silber, 'Living the Revolution – and Living Off It,' quote from 26, or for more detail, Silber, *The Cultural Revolu- tion: A Marxist Analysis* (New York: Times Change, 1970). Note as well Jonah Raskin, *For the Hell of It: The Life and Times of Abbie Hoffman* (Berkeley: Univer- sity of California Press, 1996), and the books of Hoffman and Rubin: Abbie Hoffman, *Revolution for the Hell of It* (New York: Dial, 1968); *Woodstock Nation: A Talk-Rock Album* (New York: Random House, 1969); *Steal This Book* (New

York: Pirate Editions, 1971); Jerry Rubin, *Do It! Scenarios of the Revolution*
(New York: Simon and Schuster, 1970); *We Are Everywhere* (New York: Harper
and Row, 1971). See for the countercultural denouement, Myrna Kostash,
Long Way from Home: The Story of the Sixties Generation in Canada (Toronto:
Lorimer, 1980), 107–44, which cites an account of an unruly rock festival in
Toronto more subdued than Altamont but not markedly different in its
hucksterish facade. Note as well Larry Haiven, 'Festival Scene II,' *The Varsity*,
26 September 1969. Kent State headlined in *Globe and Mail*, 5 May 1970.
See also Martin Loney, 'Canada's New Left Still Needs a Biography,' *Canadian Dimension* 7 (December 1970): 75–6.

5 Kostash, *Long Way from Home*, xiii, 135, 260, 276. Kostash was perhaps less
subdued than a number of her counterparts, who were profiled in a journalistic account two years after her book appeared. But if these 1960s veterans
were not loud in voicing the continuity of their radicalism, few, if any, were
outright repenters. See Olivia Ward, 'The Sixties: Ideals Have Quietly Survived,' *Toronto Sunday Star*, 28 March 1982.

6 Thomas Walkom, '1968: It Was Spring and It Was a Time. And the Whole
World Exploded,' *Toronto Star*, 7 June 1998, quoting Kirzner. See also Kristin
Ross, *May '68 and Its Afterlives* (Chicago: University of Chicago Press, 2002).

7 Milton Acorn, *More Poems for People* (Toronto: NC Press, 1973), 86.

8 'Editorial: Sanitizing the Sixties,' *Canadian Dimension* 22 (November-
December 1988): 3. For discussion and evidence of the Canadian New Left's
collective commitment to a politics of revolutionary transformation see John
W. Cleveland, 'New Left, Not New Liberal: 1960s Movements in English
Canada and Quebec,' *Canadian Review of Sociology and Anthropology* 41
(February 2004): 67–84.

9 For broad international studies see, as a sampling only, Arthur Marwick, *The
Sixties: Cultural Revolution in Britain, France, Italy, and the United States, c.
1958–1974* (Oxford: Oxford University Press, 1998); David Caute, *The Year
of the Barricades: A Journey through 1968* (New York: Harper and Row, 1988);
Ronald Fraser et al., *1968: A Student Generation in Revolt* (New York: Knopf,
1988); Donald Sassoon, *One Hundred Years of Socialism: The West European Left
in the Twentieth Century* (New York: New Press, 1996), 275–440; Geoff Eley,
Forging Democracy: The History of the Left in Europe, 1850–2000 (Oxford:
Oxford University Press, 2002), 341–404. Most New Lefts had more complex origins in the Old Left than commentators have recognized. This was
most obvious in Britain and is evident in intellectual histories such as Lin
Chun, *The British New Left* (Edinburgh: Edinburgh University Press, 1993);
Michael Kenny, *The First New Left: British Intellectuals after Stalin* (London:
Lawrence and Wishart, 1995). But for the Old/New Left connections see as

well Maurice Isserman, *If I Had a Hammer: The Death of the Old Left and the Birth of the New Left* (New York: Basic, 1987), a useful study if one does not take its title's termination of Old Left organizations and ideas too seriously; and Paul Buhle, *History and the New Left: Madison, Wisconsin, 1950–1970* (Philadelphia: Temple University Press, 1990). Two British reminiscent treatments are Sheila Rowbotham, *Promise of a Dream: Remembering the Sixties* (London: Penguin, 2000); Tariq Ali, *Street Fighting Years: An Autobiography of the Sixties* (Glasgow: William Collins, 1987). The U.S. literature is immense and growing, but useful starting points are Todd Gitlin, *The Sixties: Years of Hope, Days of Rage* (New York: Bantam, 1987); Richard Flacks, *Making History: The American Left and the American Mind* (New York: Columbia University Press, 1988); David Farber, *Chicago '68* (Chicago: University of Chicago Press, 1988); Farber, ed., *The Sixties: From Memory to History* (Chapel Hill: University of North Carolina Press, 1994); James Miller, *Democracy in the Streets: From Port Huron to the Siege of Chicago* (Toronto: Simon and Schuster, 1987); Paul Buhle, *Marxism in the United States: Remapping the History of the American Left* (New York: Verso, 1991), 228–57. Seymour Martin Lipset and Sheldon S. Wolin, eds., *The Berkeley Student Revolt: Facts and Interpretations* (Garden City, NY: Doubleday, 1965), and Seymour Martin Lipset, *Rebellion in the University* (Boston: Little, Brown, 1971), were indications of early sociological interest in the student uprisings of the decade. For the right-wing assault on the New Left in the United States see Phillip Abbott Luce, *The New Left Today: America's Trojan Horse* (Washington: Capitol Hill Press, 1971). For documents of the rebellious 1960s that would have been read in Canada see Priscilla Long, *The New Left: A Collection of Essays* (Boston: Porter Sargeant Publisher, 1969); Mitchell Goodman, ed., *The Movement Toward a New America: The Beginning of a Long Revolution (A Collage) A What?* (Philadelphia: Pilgrim Press, 1970); Massimo Teodori, *The New Left: A Documentary History* (New York: Bobbs-Merrill, 1969); Judith Clavir Albert and Stewart Edward Albert, eds., *The Sixties Papers: Documents of a Rebellious Decade* (New York: Praeger, 1984). Particularly repressive was the killing of Mexico City protesters in 1968. See Elaine Carey, *Plaza of Sacrifices: Gender, Power, and Terror in 1968 Mexico* (Albuquerque: University of New Mexico Press, 2005).

10 Canada's New Left student movement is presented in international context in Cyril Levitt, *Children of Privilege: Student Revolt in the Sixties – A Study of Student Movements in Canada, the United States, and West Germany* (Toronto: University of Toronto Press, 1984). See also Doug Owram, *Born at the Right Time: A History of the Baby Boom Generation* (Toronto: University of Toronto Press, 1996), 159–316; Ron Verzuh, *Underground Times: Canada's Flower-Child Revolutionaries* (Toronto: Deneau, 1989); Kostash, *Long Way from Home*; Ian

McKay, *Rebels, Reds, and Radicals: Rethinking Canada's Left History* (Toronto: Between the Lines, 2005), 183–210; Bryan D. Palmer, ed., *A Communist Life: Jack Scott and the Canadian Workers Movement, 1927–1985* (St John's, NF: CCLH, 1988), 158–203; and the important early collection, Dimitrios I. Roussopoulos, ed., *The New Left in Canada* (Montreal: Black Rose, 1970). An unpublished study that I read after completing the writing of this book is an important contribution, detailing the particularity of developments in Montreal and providing a useful larger perspective as well. See Sean William Mills, 'The Empire Within: Montreal, the Sixties, and the Forging of a Radical Imagination,' PhD thesis, Queen's University, Kingston, 2007.

11 The above paragraphs draw on many sources, but see especially Kostash, *Long Way from Home*, 251–2; Max Elbaum, *Revolution in the Air: Sixties Radicals Turn to Lenin, Mao, and Che* (New York and London: Verso, 2002); Stokely Carmichael with Ekwueme Michael Thelwell, *Ready for Revolution: The Life and Struggles of Stokely Carmichael [Kwame Ture]* (New York: Scribner, 2003); Robin D G. Kelley, *Freedom Dreams: The Black Radical Imagination* (Boston: Beacon Press, 2002); Jeremy Varon, *Bringing the War Home: The Weather Underground, the Red Army Faction, and Revolutionary Violence in the Sixties and Seventies* (Berkeley: University of California Press, 2004). The *Guardian* was of course but one of many news outlets which came out as underground publications. For a sense of this contentious world of the U.S. alternative press in the 1960s see, for instance, Ray Mungo, *Famous Long Ago: My Life and Times with Liberation News Service* (Boston: Beacon Press, 1970); Ken Wachsberger, ed., *Voices from the Underground: A Directory of Resources and Sources on the Vietnam Era Underground Press* (Ann Arbor, MI: Azephony Press, 1993); Abe Peck, *Uncovering the Sixties: The Life and Times of the Underground Press* (New York: Pantheon, 1985).

12 Carl Oglesby, 'The Idea of the New Left,' in Obelsby, ed., *The New Left Reader* (New York: Grove Press, 1969), 13.

13 C. Wright Mills, 'Letter to the New Left,' *New Left Review* 5 (September-October 1960): 18–23. As the prod to Wright Mills's letter see E.P. Thompson, ed., *Out of Apathy* (London: Stevens and Sons, 1960). For a New Left reading of Mills see Tom Hayden, *Radical Nomad: C. Wright Mills and His Times* (Boulder and London: Paradigm Publishers, 2006).

14 Tom Hayden has recently provided an evocative introduction to the republication of *The Port Huron Statement: The Visionary Call of the 1960s Revolution* (New York: Thunder's Mouth Press, 2005), upon which this paragraph draws. See, for the fullest statement on the importance of the document, Miller, *Democracy in the Streets*.

15 See Herbert Marcuse, *An Essay on Liberation* (Harmondsworth: Penguin Books, 1969), esp. 33, 37, 82. Note as well the mimeographed radical

student bulletin, published at the University of Waterloo by the Federation of Students in 1968–9, *Praxis*. It struggled with questions that remain with the left today, as in Philip Resnick, 'Repressive Liberalism,' *Praxis* 2 (March 1969): 2–5. Callwood, 'Digger House,' 124, linked 'the Movement' of the 1960s with Marcuse, associating the 1966 hippies with 'the great refusal.'

16 See Lutz Niethammer, *Posthistoire: Has History Come to an End?* (New York and London: Verso, 1992); Francis Fukuyama, 'The End of History?' *The National Interest* (Summer 1989): 3–18; *The End of History and the Last Man* (New York: Maxwell Macmillan, 1992); and the impressive essay by Perry Anderson, 'The Ends of History,' in Anderson, *A Zone of Engagement* (New York and London: Verso, 1992), 279–375.

17 Mario Savio, 'An End to History,' *Humanity: An Arena of Critique and Commitment* 2 (December 1964), reprinted in Lipset and Wolin, eds., *The Berkeley Student Revolt*, 216–19.

18 Quotes from original New Left documents, cited in Kostash, *Long Way from Home*, 13–14.

19 See, for instance, Stanley Gray, 'The New Democratic Youth Convention,' *Canadian Dimension* 2 (September-October 1965): 23; Gray, 'New Left, Old Left,' *Canadian Dimension* 3 (November-December 1965): 11–13; James Harding, 'The NDP, the Regina Manifesto, and the New Left,' *Canadian Dimension* 4 (November-December 1966): 18–19; Gary Teeple, '"Liberals in a Hurry": Socialism and the CCF-NDP,' in Teeple, ed., *Capitalism and the National Question in Canada* (Toronto: University of Toronto Press, 1972), 229–50; Kostash, *Long Way from Home*, 249–50; Cy Gonick 'Students and Peace,' *Canadian Dimension* 2 (January-February 1965): 12; James Laxer and Arthur Pape, 'The New Left ... As It Sees Itself,' *Canadian Dimension* 3 (September-October 1966): 14–15. For a social democratic critical response to the New Left see Lloyd Stinson, 'Reply to the New Left,' *Canadian Dimension* 3 (March-April/May-June 1966), 56–7.

20 Gonick, 'Students and Peace,' 12; Kostash, *Long Way from Home*, 6.

21 Herbert Marcuse, 'On the New Left,' in Teodori, ed., *New Left*, 473.

22 Peter Gzowski, 'The Righteous Crusaders of the New Left,' *Maclean's*, 15 November 1965, 18–19, 39–42. See also Murray Bookchin, *Listen Marxist!* (New York: Times Change, 1971), reprinted in Bookchin, *Post-Scarcity Anarchism* (Berkeley: Ramparts Press, 1971), 173–220.

23 Philip Resnick, 'The New Left in Ontario,' in Roussopoulos, ed., *New Left in Canada*, 100.

24 James Harding, 'The New Left in British Columbia,' in Roussopoulos, ed., *New Left in Canada*, 39. For a later Harding statement see 'Still Thinking Globally since the Sixties,' *Canadian Dimension* 22 (November-December 1988), 16.

25 Dimitrios I. Roussopoulos, 'Towards a Revolutionary Youth Movement and an Extra-Parliamentary Opposition,' in Roussopoulos, ed., *New Left in Canada*, esp. 135-6, 141, 138. Roussopoulos borrowed a great deal from Bookchin's *Listen Marxist!*

26 For a contemporary critique of the Roussopoulos-edited *New Left in Canada*, see Martin Loney, 'Canada's New Left Still Needs a Biography,' 75-6.

27 Ruth Lisa Schechter, 'Translations of the Exile,' *Our Generation against Nuclear War* 3 (June 1964): 73.

28 Levitt, *Children of Privilege*, 40; Owram, *Born at the Right Time*, 218; Roussopoulos, ed., *New Left in Canada*, 8; Kostash, *Long Way from Home*, xxii; Catherine Gidney, 'Poisoning the Student Mind? The Student Christian Movement on the University of Toronto Campus, 1920-1965,' *Journal of the Canadian Historical Association* 8, n.s. (1997): 147-63.

29 The 3 November 1960 CUCND brief is quoted in Roussopoulos, ed., *New Left in Canada*, 9. On the religious motivation of CUCND see Levitt, *Children of Privilege*, 41-2; Owram, *Born at the Right Time*, 219.

30 Roussopoulos, ed., *New Left in Canada*, 8-9; Kostash, *Long Way from Home*, xxii-xxiii; Owram, *Born at the Right Time*, 165; Judy Rebick, *Ten Thousand Roses: The Making of a Feminist Revolution* (Toronto: Penguin, 2005), 3-5; Kay Macpherson and Meg Sears, 'The Voice of Women,' in Gwen Matheson, ed., *Women in the Canadian Mosaic* (Toronto: Peter Martin, 1976), 71-89; Kay Macpherson, 'The Seeds of the 70s,' *Canadian Dimension* 10 (June 1975): 39-41. Early issues of *Our Generation against Nuclear War* were edited by a large collective that included an impressive array of New Left and anti-disarmament figures from the United States, Great Britain, and Canada. With Dimitrios I. Roussopoulos a mainstay in Montreal, the quarterly journal was a considerable accomplishment and made many academic faculty sit up and take notice of the fledgling movement. For extensive discussion of unilateralism see the special issue of *Our Generation against Nuclear War* 3 (April 1965). On the influence on the NDP see 'New Party Declaration,' in Michael S. Cross, ed., *The Decline and Fall of a Good Idea: CCF-NDP Manifestoes, 1932 to 1969* (Toronto: New Hogtown Press, 1974), 41-2; *Policies of the New Democratic Party, 1961-1973* (Ottawa: NDP, 1974), 79-81.

31 The above paragraphs draw on Levitt, *Children of Privilege*, 159; Gonick, 'Students and Peace,' 12; Kostash, *Long Way from Home*, 5; Owram, *Born at the Right Time*, 220. On the Triple Revolution see W.H. Ferry et al., *The Triple Revolution* (Santa Barbara: The Ad Hoc Committee on the Triple Revolution, 1964), excerpts of which appear in Albert and Albert, eds., *Sixties Papers*, 197-208. The labour component of this Triple Revolution would, in the later 1960s, mesh well with a Gorzian strategy for labour that drew on much New Left

theorizing, especially that of Marcuse, as well as Old Left concerns of the 1950s that accented proletarian discontents (Harvey Swados), to insist that workers were being assailed by technology, deskilling, and immiseration. Gorz thus laid great stress on alienation, consumption, and the remaking of a working-class order dominated by marginalization and poverty. This 'new working class' thus coexisted with students rather well, precisely because university youth faced situations remarkably parallel to that of advanced capitalism's workers. See André Gorz, *Strategy for Labor: A Radical Proposal* (Boston: Beacon Press, 1967); Gorz, 'The Way Forward,' *New Left Review* 52 (November-December 1968): 47–66; Gorz, *Réforme et révolution* (Paris: Éditions du Seuil, 1969).

32 See C. George Benello and Dimitrios Roussopoulos, eds., *The Case for Participatory Democracy: Some Prospects for a Radical Society* (New York: Viking, 1971). For a critical questioning of participatory democracy as an American New Left initiative trapped in the cul-de-sac of a liberal tradition that could not 'perceive the necessity of evolving a political program that could engage the working class as a whole in revolutionary change,' see Krista Maeots, 'Some Problems in the Redefinition of Activism: The Rise and Fall of SUPA,' in D.I. Davies and Kathleen Herman, eds., *Social Space: Canadian Perspectives* (Toronto: New Press, 1971), 230–3.

33 That there were leaders whose ideas were known to the members, and were seen as carrying more weight, is indicated in some SUPA lines of verse referring to two key figures: Toronto's Art Pape and Montreal's Dimitri Roussopoulos. SUPA member Harvey L. Shepherd wrote: 'I know of all the problems of peasants and metropolis; / I know all that you need to know to organize the populace: / I know how to go limp so the policeman has to stop you less: / I know all the opinions of Art Pape and of Roussopoulos.' HLS, 'The Modern Radical,' *SUPA Newsletter* 1, no. 3, June 1965.

34 James Harding, 'An Ethical Movement in Search of an Analysis: The Student Union for Peace Action in Canada,' *Our Generation* 3 and 4 (May 1966): 20–9; Kostash, *Long Way from Home*, 5–9. For one early suggestion of problems in SUPA, which emphasized the need to transcend moralism, raised questions about non-violence, advocated building a larger mass organization, and pointed to the need for firmer lines of connection between systematic capitalist exploitation and war, see Andre Beckerman, 'A Critical View of SUPA,' *SUPA Newsletter* 1, no. 4, 23 June 1965. On decentralization, debates over it, and problems of SUPA's structure see S. Howard Gray, 'SUPA Federal Staff – Some Questions,' *SUPA Newsletter* 1, no. 6, 21 July 1965; Ken Drushka, 'Proposed Changes of the SUPA Structure,' 1, no. 7, 10 August 1965.

35 See Stanley Gray, 'Nationalism and Non-Alignment,' *Canadian Dimension* 3 (March-April/May-June 1966): 48–9.

36 Harding, 'Ethical Movement in Search of an Analysis,' 22; Dan Daniels, 'The Philosophy of Non-Violence,' *Canadian Dimension* 1 (September-October 1964): 14–15; John K. Rooke, 'The Use of Force,' *SUPA Newsletter* 1, no. 4, 23 June 1965.

37 On student syndicalism and its development in the New Left from 1965 to 1968, see Serge Joyal, *Student Syndicalism in Quebec* (Toronto: SUPA, 1965); Serge Joyal, 'Student Syndicalism in Quebec,' *Canadian Dimension* 2 (March-April 1965): 20–2; Carl Davidson, 'Student Syndicalism,' *Our Generation* 5 (May 1967): 102–11; Levitt, *Children of Privilege*, 171–6. On poverty and powerlessness see, for instance, *Our Generation* 4 (March 1967), which contains an editorial statement by Lucia Kowaluk, 'The Dimensions of Powerlessness' (5–7); Bryan M. Knight, 'On Poverty in Canada' (8–22); Todd Gitlin, 'Organizing the Poor in America' (22–9); and Nicholas Van Hoffman, 'Organizing the Ghetto' (30–40). On the earlier more moderate understandings of 1963–4 I benefited from hearing the presentation of Barbara Godard, 'Quebec, The National Question, and English-Canadian Student Activism in the 1960s' at the 'New World Coming: The Sixties and the Shaping of Global Consciousness' Conference at Queen's University, Kingston, 13–16 June 2007. Godard's talk accented the relations of student activists in Montreal and Toronto around questions of Quebec and Canada.

38 Kostash, *Long Way from Home*, 15.

39 See Dan Daniels, 'Why Civil Disobedience at La Macaza,' *Canadian Dimension* 1 (July-August 1964): 16.

40 Andre Cardinal, 'SUPA's Summer Projects,' *SUPA Newsletter* 1, no. 6, 21 July 1965.

41 Gitlin, 'Organizing the Poor in America'; Richard Rothstein, 'A Short History of ERAP,' *Our Generation* 3/4 (May 1966): 40–5; Eric Mann, 'New School for the Ghetto,' *Our Generation* 5 (September 1967): 67–73; Richard Rothstein, 'Evolution of the ERAP Organizers,' *Radical America* 2 (March-April 1968), reprinted in Priscilla Long, ed., *The New Left: A Collection of Essays* (Boston: Porter Sargeant, 1969), 272–88; Miller, *Democracy in the Streets*, 192–215, 262–4, 270–1; and the excellent collection of material in Teodori, ed., *New Left*, 128–49. As an endnote to Hayden's Newark project, see Tom Hayden, *Rebellion in Newark: Official Violence and Ghetto Response* (New York: Random House, 1967).

42 Levitt, *Children of Privilege*, 162–4; Kostash, *Long Way from Home*, 17–19; 'Students Win Where Others Lost,' *Toronto Daily Star*, 17 August 1965; Peggy Morton, 'Kingston Community Project,' *SUPA Newsletter* 1, no. 4, 23 June 1965; Don Carmichael, 'Kingston Community Project,' *SUPA Newsletter* 1, no. 6, 21 July 1965; Olivia Howell, 'Kingston Community Project,' *SUPA*

Newsletter 1, no. 5, 7 July 1965; Tony Tugwell, 'Kingston Report,' and 'Letter from Kingston,' *SUPA Newsletter* 1, no. 7, 10 August 1965.

43 Tugwell, 'Kingston Report'; Richard Harris, *Democracy in Kingston: A Social Movement in Urban Politics, 1965-1970* (Kingston and Montreal: McGill-Queen's University Press, 1988), 68-70; Maeots, 'The Rise and Fall of SUPA,' 230-1.

44 The above paragraphs draw on Kostash, *Long Way from Home*, 17-20; Dennis McDermott, 'Kingston Community Project,' *SUPA Newsletter* 1, no. 3, June 1965; McDermott, 'Graplo Spasms on a Poverty Project,' *SUPA Newsletter* 1, no. 6, 21 July 1965; Harris, *Democracy in Kingston*, contains much on Newman and Kingston activities, as does Margaret Daly, *The Revolution Game: The Short, Unhappy Life of the Company of Young Canadians* (Toronto: New Press, 1970), 15-25. For Spinks and the Trefann Court project see Graham Fraser, *Fighting Back: Urban Renewal in Trefann Court* (Toronto: Hakkert, 1972); Sarah Spinks, 'Urban Renewal: Toronto Community Union Project,' *Our Generation* 5 (September 1967): 102-5; Spinks, 'Trefann Court,' *SUPA Newsletter* 3, no. 3, January 1967; Spinks, 'Participatory Bureaucracy and the Hall-Dennis Report,' *This Magazine Is about Schools* 2 (Autumn 1968): 137-49. For *This Magazine* see the extremely useful collection of articles from its 1966-9 issues in Satu Repo, ed., *This Book Is about Schools* (New York: Pantheon, 1970), which contains a contribution by Marshall McLuhan to volume 1, number 1, 'Electronics and the Psychic Drop-Out' (383-9).

45 SUPA activist Liora Proctor would later note that she was told that in some northern Saskatchewan settings 'neestow' might well designate, particularly if drinking was involved, that a man was 'fooling around' with another man's wife. For Proctor this linguistic double-meaning, in which 'neestow' could mean both kin connection and cuckold, summed up the problems of student radicals assuming they could interact with Aboriginal cultures where the nuances and complexities of those cultures were actuallly foreign to them. See Proctor, 'The Student Neestow Project,' *Our Generation*, 4 (November 1966), 40, and the comment in Ian Milligan, '"No One Really Knows What SUPA Is": The English-Canadian New Left and Shifting Conceptions of Class, 1959-1968,' unpublished paper, 2008. I am grateful to Mr. Milligan for sending me his paper.

46 George Bain, 'The SUPA Affair,' *Globe and Mail*, no date, reprinted in *SUPA Newsletter* 1, no. 6, 21 July 1965, claimed that 'the student Neestow project will place 25 students among the Indians of Saskatchewan with a view to (among other things) instructing the Indians in how to use the weapon of public protest to secure their rights as citizens.' See also Levitt, *Children of Privilege*, 71-2. A useful discussion of the origins of the Neewstow Project,

and the place of Malcolm Norris, appears in Murray Dobbin, *The One-and-a-Half Men: The Story of Jim Brady and Malcolm Norris, Métis Patriots of the Twentieth Century* (Vancouver: New Star, 1981), 224–30, in which interviews with Harding and other SUPA figures are quoted.

47 Kostash, *Long Way from Home*, 15–16; Gzowski, 'The Righteous Crusaders of the New Left,' 40–1; Jill Annweiler, 'Student Neestow Partneship Project,' *SUPA Newsletter* 1, no. 3, June 1965; Dobbin, *One-and-a-Half Men*, esp. 228. For Pat Uhl's subsequent disillusionment with the Neestow Project see 'No Hope for Indians,' *Pro-tem: The Student Weekly of York University,* 3 December 1965.

48 The most accessible brief account of the Green Lake difficulties is in Dobbin, *One-and-a-Half Men*, 228–9. A four-part series in the *Saskatoon Star Phoenix* by the journalist Volkmar Richter outlined the government machinations as well as Malcolm Norris's militant rejoinders.

49 Liora Proctor, 'The Student Neestow Project,' and Clayton Ruby, 'Comments,' *Our Generation* 4 (November 1966): 40–8; Maeots, 'The Rise and Fall of SUPA,' 231, and for more on Proctor, Dobbin, *One-and-a-Half Men*, 234–5.

50 Kotash, *Long Way from Home*, 16–17; Lynne Butts, 'The Kootenay Project,' *SUPA Newsletter* 1, no. 4, 23 June 1965; Butts, 'The Beauty That Is Age,' *SUPA Newsletter* 1, no. 6, July 1965; Peter Boothroyd, 'Kootenays Project Report,' *SUPA Newsletter* 1, no. 8, 30 August 1965; Gzowski, 'The Righteous Crusaders of the New Left,' 41. Interest in the Doukhobors had been stimulated by Sima Holt's *Terror in the Name of God* (1964), which condemned the pacifist Sons of Freedom as fanatics and zealots. Among the New Left, Holt's book was regarded as a variant of 'hate literature.' See Kouozma J. Tarasoff, 'Zealots and Doukhobors,' *Canadian Dimension* 2 (March-April 1965): 23–4. For the reification of youth see John and Margaret Rowntree, 'Youth as a Class,' *Our Generation* 6 (May-July 1968): 155–89; James Laxer and Arthur Pape, 'Youth and Canadian Politics,' *Our Generation* 4 (November 1966): 15–21, which concluded: 'It is the Canadians under thirty years of age, who did not live through a period of accommodation to the "Great Society," and who have few vested interests in it, who will form the basis for an opposition movement.' Note, finally, the discussion of Doukhobors and the New Left in British Columbia in Benjamin Isitt, 'Working-Class Agency, the Cold War, and the Rise of a New Left: Political Change in British Columbia, 1948–1972,' preliminary draft of PhD dissertation, presented to the University of New Brunswick, 2007, 302–7.

51 Gzowski, 'The Righteous Crusaders of the New Left,' 41; Rocky Jones, 'Letter from Nova Scotia,' *SUPA Newsletter* 1, no. 8, 30 August 1965; Kostash, *Long Way from Home*, 12; Lynne Burrows, 'The Nova Scotia Project,' *SUPA*

Newsletter 3, no. 1, January 1967. On Africville see David Lewis Stein, 'The
Counterattack on Diehard Racism,' *Maclean's*, 20 October 1962; Sylvia
Fraser, 'The Slow and Welcome Death of Africville,' *Star Weekly*, 1 January
1966, 1–7; Donald H. Clairmont and Dennis William Magill, *Africville: The
Life and Death of a Canadian Black Community* (Toronto: Canadian Scholar's
Press, 1997).

52 Stan Gray, 'LaMacaza,' *SUPA Newsletter* 1, no. 3, June 1965; 'Project La Macaza,'
   1, no. 6, 21 July 1965; 'National Fund-Raising Trip for Project La Macaza,' 1,
   no. 8, 30 August 1965; Nancy Hannum, 'Peace and the Professions,' *SUPA
   Newsletter* 1, no. 3, June 1965; 1, no. 8, 30 August 1965. The Comox Project
   seemed in perpetual conflict with SUPA's Toronto office. See Linda Light,
   'Letter from Comox,' *SUPA Newsletter* 1, no. 4, 23 June 1965; 'Comox Project
   '65: The Comox Project Bulletin – A Review,' 1, no. 7, 10 August 1965; Peter
   Light, 'Comox Project '65 – The Report,' 1, no. 8, 30 August 1965; Light, 'An
   Answer to Tony Hyde,' 1, no. 8, 30 August 1965.

53 'School for Social Theory,' *SUPA Newsletter* 1, no. 6, 21 July 1965; 1, no. 8,
   30 August 1965; Matt Cohen, 'Hegel and the New Left: Report of a Meeting
   of Seminar of the School for Social Theory,' 1, no. 7, 10 August 1965; Miles
   Murray, 'An Afternoon with Darshan Singh: Report from the School for
   Social Theory,' 1, no. 7, 10 August 1965.

54 'School for Social Theory,' *SUPA Newsletter* 1, no. 8, 30 August 1965.

55 Levitt, *Children of Privilege*, 36.

56 Quoted in Owram, *Born at the Right Time*, 170.

57 Levitt, *Children of Privilege*, esp. 48, 209; George Clark, 'Students for a Democratic Society,' *Our Generation* 3 (May 1966): 30–9. For a somewhat mechanical nationalist critique of SUPA and the Canadian New Left as Americanized
   see James Laxer, 'The Americanization of the Canadian Student Movement,'
   in Ian Lumsden, ed., *Close the 49th Parallel: The Americanization of Canada*
   (Toronto: University of Toronto Press, 1970), 275–86. Cy Gonick thought
   the Canadian New Left little more than 'a pale reflection' of its U.S. counterpart. See Gonick, 'Strategies for Social Change,' *Canadian Dimension* 4
   (November-December 1966): 7. Hayden's connection to Toronto's SUPA
   leadership was close, and he offered advice, instruction, and inspiration, but
   he also used his Canadian connections as an escape from pressures in the
   United States. Thus one SUPA member told Myrna Kostash: 'SDS people
   used to come up to Toronto to rest. Tom Hayden came up and Carl Ogelsby.
   Tom stayed with Clay (Ruby) a week and didn't say a word. He was over-
   dosed, burned out; he came up to rest and never said one word to us.'
   Kostash, *Long Way from Home*, 26. For Hayden's influence on the highly dis-
   similar SUPA leaders, Pape and Roussopolous, see also James Laxer, 'The

Student Movement and Canadian Independence,' *Canadian Dimension* 6 (August–September 1969): 32.

58 Kostash, *Long Way from Home*, 9–10; 'The Sitdowners,' *Toronto Daily Star*, 20 March 1965; Harvey Shepherd, 'Men Must Speak,' *The Varsity*, 10 March 1965; 'A Guide to Forming a Friends of SNCC Group in Canada' (Toronto: Friends of SNCC, no date, c. 1964–5); Shepherd, 'SNCC Conference May 8–10: A Step Towards a Movement in Canada,' *SUPA Newsletter* 1, no. 3, June 1965; Shepherd, 'Mission to Mississippi,' *SUPA Newsletter* 1, no. 7, 10 August 1965; Shepherd, 'SNCC in Canada,' *SUPA Newsletter* 1, no. 8, 30 August 1965.

59 Writing on radical opposition to the Vietnam War is extensive. For an introduction to the subject see Miller, *Democracy in the Streets*; Varon, *Bringing the War Home*; and the extremely useful gathering of relevant material in Teodori, ed., *New Left*, 240–70; Albert and Albert, ed., *Sixties Papers*, 271–400. For the view of a Canadian New Leftist, Kostash, *Long Way from Home*, 31–54.

60 'Ending the War,' *Canadian Dimension* 2 (March-April 1965): 3; Cy Gonick, 'What Every Canadian Should Know about Vietnam,' and J.W. Warnock, 'Canadian Policy in Vietnam,' in *Canadian Dimension* 2 (May-June 1965): 3–7, 19–22; Gonick, 'What Every Canadian Should Know about Vietnam, Part II,' 'Debate on Vietnam: Douglas vs. Martin,' 'The Ugly Canadian,' and 'Open Letter,' *Canadian Dimension* 2 (July-August 1965): 3–5, 8–11, 29; Gonick, 'What Every Canadian Should Know about Vietnam, Part III,' and 'Norman Mailer on LBJ and Vietnam,' *Canadian Dimension* 2 (September-October 1965): 7–9, 10–12; W.E. Wilmott, 'Dominoes,' *Canadian Dimension* 3 (November-December 1965): 26–7; James Steele, 'Ottawa/Saigon Complicity,' *Our Generation* 4 (July 1966): 71–83; Philip Resnick, 'Canada, Vietnam, and the War Industries,' *Our Generation* 5 (November-December 1967): 16–30.

61 Richard Price, 'The New Left in Alberta,' in Roussopoulos, ed., *New Left in Canada*, 43.

62 'Conference on Vietnam, Carleton University, 12–13 June 1965,' *SUPA Newsletter* 1, no. 3, June 1965.

63 Liora Proctor, 'Teach-In,' *SUPA Newsletter* 1, no. 3, June 1965; Henry Tarvainen, 'International Teach-In for Toronto This Fall,' *SUPA Newsletter* 1, no. 4, 23 June 1965.

64 On the International Teach-Ins see Charles Hanly, *Revolution and Response* (Toronto: McClelland and Stewart, 1966); Gidney, 'War and the Concept of Generation'; and Jeffrey Rose and Michael Ignatieff, eds., *Religion and International Affairs: International Teach-In* (Toronto: Anansi, 1968). Extensive discussion/debate in *Canadian Forum* occurred around the 'Revolution and

Response' teach-in. See Charles Hanly, 'The Toronto Teach-In,' *Canadian Forum* 45 (September 1965): 130–1; and 'Symposium on the Teach-In,' *Canadian Forum* 45 (November 1965): 172–9, especially Art Pape's contribution, 'Teach-In as Institution,' 178. See also 'That Was a Teach-In That Was – Or Was It?' *Maclean's*, 15 November 1965.

65 'Open Letter to the 27th Parliament and the Government of Canada,' *Our Generation* 3 (May 1966): 90–5.

66 See Kostash, *Long Way from Home*, 44–62; Renee Goldsmith Kasinsky, *Refugees from Militarism* (New Brunswick, NJ: Transaction Books, 1976); Martin Satin, ed., *Manual for Draft-Age Immigrants to Canada* (Toronto: Anansi, 1970); Roger N. Williams, *The New Exiles: American War Resisters in Canada* (New York: Liveright, 1971); Kenneth Fred Emerick, *War Resisters in Canada: The World of the American Military-Political Refugees* (Knox, PA: Free Press, 1972); Jack Colhoun, 'The Exiles' Role in War Resistance,' *Monthly Review* 30 (March 1979): 27–43; John Hagan, *Northern Passage: American Vietnam War Resisters in Canada* (Cambridge, MA: Harvard University Press, 2001); Frank Kusch, *All American Boys: Draft Dodgers in Canada from the Vietnam War* (Westport, CT: Praeger, 2002); Pierre Berton, *1967: The Last Good Year* (Toronto: Doubleday, 1997), 197–203; David Churchill, 'An Ambiguous Welcome: Vietnam Draft Resistance, the Canadian State, and Cold War Containment,' *Histoire Sociale/Social History* 37 (May 2004): 1–26.

67 Maeots, 'The Rise and Fall of SUPA,' 231.

68 John S. Wagner, Secretary, University of Toronto CEWV, 'Draft Statement: Purposes and Structure,' Student Anti-War Conference Working Paper, no date, in possession of the author; Louis Fournier, *FLQ: The Anatomy of an Underground Movement* (Toronto: NC Press, 1984), 119.

69 Gzowski, 'The Righteous Crusaders of the New Left,' 19. See also, for an equally enthusiastic insider report, Stanley Gray, 'New Left, Old Left,' *Canadian Dimension* 3 (November-December 1965): 11–13.

70 The above paragraphs draw on Kostash, *Long Way from Home*, 21–4; Maeots, 'The Rise and Fall of SUPA,' 231; 'Question of the Issue,' *SUPA Newsletter* 1, no. 4, 23 June 1965.

71 The two standard works on the Company of Young Canadians are Daly, *The Revolution Game*, and Ian Hamilton, *The Children's Crusade: The Story of the Company of Young Canadians* (Toronto: Peter Martin, 1970). I draw as well on the brief discussion in Kostash, *Long Way from Home*, 19–28; Gzowski, 'The Righteous Crusaders of the New Left,' which contained an insert 'Why Activists Are Anti–Peace Corps,' 41, that maintained that most SUPA activists 'distrust the idea of the Company of Young Canadians.' See as well Martin Loney, 'A Political Economy of Citizen Participation,' in Leo Panitch, ed.,

The Canadian State: Political Economy and Political Power (Toronto: University of Toronto Press, 1977), 446–72; Levitt, *Children of Privilege*, 98; Berton, *1967: Last Good Year,* 172–86. On Goodings see Stewart Goodings, 'The Company of Young Canadians,' *SUPA Newsletter* 1, no. 8, 30 August 1965; Hamilton, *Children's Crusade*, 132–52.

72 Note Kostash, *Long Way from Home*, 21; Daly, *Revolution Game*, 132; 'CYC: The Bird That Cannot Even Fly,' *Our Generation* 6 (May-July 1968): 13–14.

73 Daly, *Revolution Game*, 31.

74 Hamilton, *Children's Crusade*, 46–58. For a SUPA statement on the anti-war rally see Donald McKelvey, 'That Vietnam Demonstration,' *SUPA Newsletter* 3, no. 3, January 1967, with the same issue containing a statement on 'The CYC and Social Change,' with a letter from Art Pape and Anthony Hyde of SUPA's Federal Council to Alan Clarke, Director of CYC.

75 Daly, *Revolution Game*, 101–33; 'CYC: The Bird That Cannot Even Fly,' 13–14; and comments in James Laxer, 'The Student Movement and Canadian Independence,' *Canadian Dimension* 6 (August-September 1969): 33–4; and in Maeots, 'The Rise and Fall of SUPA,' 232–3.

76 The above two paragraphs draw on Kostash, *Long Way from Home*, 20–8; Hamilton, *Children's Crusade*; Daly, *Revolution Game*, esp. 238; Loney, 'Citizen Participation,' 465–6; Jeremy Ashton, CYC Volunteer, 'Organizing Alberta Indians,' *SUPA Newsletter* 3, no. 3, January 1967; Melville Watkins, 'CYC,' *Canadian Dimension* 6 (February-March 1970): 5–6. For a representation of CYC in Quebec see Fournier, *FLQ*, 145–6, while a social democratic critique of CYC is Douglas Fisher, 'The New Left ... As Others See It,' *Canadian Dimension* 3 (September-October 1966): 15.

77 Cy Gonick, 'Strategies for Social Change,' *Canadian Dimension* 4 (November-December 1966): 8, 39–40. See also Maeots, 'The Rise and Fall of SUPA,' 233, which concludes: 'As the Canadian radical youth movement became increasingly socialist and anti-imperialist, it began to face up to the problems of corporate control of Canada and the challenges of the Canadian left tradition. The difficulties created by attempts to organize around the left liberalism of American populism were replaced by a new set of problems concerning the relationship of the socialist left with Canadian social democracy and with the country's social democratic labour tradition.'

78 For the final statement of denouement see Sue Helwig, 'SUPA Disbands,' *The Varsity,* 24 September 1967.

79 Kostash, *Long Way from Home*, 25; George Haggar, 'Wretched of the Earth (Frantz Fanon),' *Canadian Dimension* 3 (July-August 1966): 33–6; Roger O'Toole, *The Precipitous Path: Studies in Political Sects* (Toronto: Peter Martin, 1977), 33–56; 'The Role of the Left,' *SUPA Newsletter* 3, no. 4, January 1967;

Harvey Shepherd, 'Poetry,' *SUPA Newsletter* 3, no. 3, January 1967; Levitt, *Children of Privilege*. 102-3.

80 This New Left Committee statement is quoted in James Laxer, 'The Student Movement and Canadian Independence,' *Canadian Dimension* 4 (August-September 1969): 33. While the push to analyse Canadian society and its particular structure of modern capitalism often entailed utilizing the Marxist categories of political economy, such interpretive probes could also take anarchist directions, particularly if the subject was the state. See Dimitrios I. Roussopoulos, ed., *The Political Economy of the State* (Montreal: Black Rose, 1973).

81 Note the quotes and arguments developed in Owram, *Born at the Right Time*, 232; Levitt, *Children of Privilege*, 176; Roussopoulos, 'Towards a Revolutionary Youth Movement,' 143; Roussopoulos, 'What Is the New Radicalism?' *Our Generation* 6 (May-July 1968): 15-26; Roussopoulos, 'The Provos: Dutch Political Beatniks,' *Our Generation* 4 (July 1966): 67-70; Gerald Heard, 'LSD – The Way to Nirvana,' *Canadian Dimension* 1 (July-August 1964): 11-13; Abraham Hoffer, 'The Confrontation between the Psychedelic Experience and Society,' *Canadian Dimension* 4 (July-August 1967): 5-7. Note, as well, the debate over the article by C. George Benello, 'Wasteland Culture: Notes on Structure, Restructuring and Strategies for Social Change,' *Our Generation* 5 (September 1967): 19-47, continued in 'The New Movement and Its Organizational Theory,' by various authors, and Benello's rejoinder, 'Politics, Resistence, and Marxism,' *Our Generation* 5 (March-April 1968): 53-87; Christian Sivrel, 'The Big Fuss about Marihuana,' *SUPA Newsletter* 3, no. 3, January 1967.

82 For a regional account of developments in British Columbia see Isitt, 'Working-Class Agency,' 313-41.

83 See, as one contemporary survey, Andy Wernick, 'A Guide to the Student Left,' *The Varsity*, 24 September 1969, and for Wernick's rejection of vanguard organizations, Wernick, 'The Theory of the Vanguard Party and the Notion of Contradiction,' *Praxis* 1 (August 1968): 1-14 (pagination anew each article). Note as well, Varda Burstyn, 'Remember the Old Mole?' *Canadian Dimension* 22 (November-December 1988): 13.

84 Mel Watkins in *This Magazine* (November-December 1979): 42, quoted in Robert Hackett, 'Pie in the Sky: A History of the Ontario Waffle,' *Canadian Dimension* 15 (October-November 1980): 4. See from the socialist-feminist perspective the brief comment of Meg Luxton, 'Feminism as a Class Act: Working-Class Feminism and the Women's Movement in Canada,' *Labour/Le Travail* 48 (Fall 2001): 83-6.

85 Kostash, *Long Way from Home*, 25.

86 Jim Harding to Dear Cy, *Canadian Dimension* 7 (December 1970): 62.
87 Gray quoted in Levitt, *Children of Privilege*, 176; *SUPA Newsletter* 3, no. 7,
     9 May 1967; Stan Gray, 'The Greatest Canadian Shit Disturber,' *Canadian
     Dimension* 38 (November-December 2004), 13.
88 Stanley Gray, 'The New Student Radicalism: Is It an American Import?'
     Praxis, 1 (August 1968): 6–7.
89 On student syndicalism in this period, and the controversy surrounding the
     strategic orientation, see John Cleveland, *Student Syndicalism: A Program of
     Action* (Edmonton: Confrontations mimeograph, 1969); Andrew Wernick,
     'The Student Government Left, Syndicalism, and the Search for Strategy,'
     Praxis 2 (March 1969): 17–21.
90 On the Just Society Movement see Howard Buchbinder, 'The Just Society
     Movement,' in Brian Wharf, ed., *Community Work in Canada* (Toronto:
     McClelland and Stewart, 1979), 129–52; George Ford and Steven Langdon,
     'Just Society Movement: Toronto's Poor Organize,' *Canadian Dimension* 7
     (June-July 1970): 19–23. The Howard Buchbinder–led Praxis group strug-
     gled to keep alive the community-focused participatory democracy of SUPA,
     but its relations to bodies like the Just Society Movement, founded by single
     welfare mothers, were anything but smooth. See Margaret Hillyard Little,
     'Militant Mothers Fight Poverty: The Just Society Movement, 1968–1971,'
     Labour/Le Travail 59 (Spring 2007): 179–97. On the bridging of community
     and class struggle via the fusion of participatory democracy and workers'
     control see Gerry Hunnius, ed., *Participatory Democracy for Canada: Workers'
     Control and Community Control* (Montreal: Black Rose Press, 1971). Praxis had
     connections to the League for Social Reform and included figures such as
     Stephen Clarkson, Jane Jacobs, and Peter Russell. See Howard Buchbinder,
     'Guaranteed Annual Income: The Answer to Poverty for All But the Poor,'
     Canadian Dimension 7 (October-November 1970): 27–32; Buchbinder,
     'Participation, Control, and the EPO: A Consideration of Strategies,' *Our
     Generation* 7 (September 1971): 9–22; Buchbinder, 'Social Planning or
     Social Control: An Account of a Confrontation with the Social Welfare
     Establishment,' in Alan T.R. Powell, ed., *The City: Attacking Modern Myths*
     (Toronto: McClelland and Stewart, 1972), 131–60; Buchbinder, 'The
     Toronto Social Planning Council and the United Community Fund,' in
     Davies and Herman, eds., *Social Space*, 196–205. For New Left discussions of
     urban poverty and planning issues see James Lorimer and Myfanwy Phillips,
     Working People: Life in a Downtown City Neighbourhood (Toronto: J. Lewis and
     Samuel, 1971); Graham Fraser, *Fighting Back: Urban Renewal in Trefann Court*
     (Toronto: Hackett, 1972); and for the general context of state initiatives and
     popular mobilizations surrounding the period's 'war on poverty' see James

Struthers, *The Limits of Affluence: Welfare in Ontario, 1920–1970* (Toronto: University of Toronto Press, 1994), 211–30; Lawrence Felt, 'Militant Poor People and the Canadian State,' in Daniel Glenday, Hubert Guidon, and Allan Turowetz, eds., *Modernization and the Canadian State* (Toronto: Macmillan, 1978), 417–41.

91 Note Peter Warrian, 'The State of the Union, or Brothers and Sisters This Is Our Thing So Let It All Hang Out,' *Canadian Dimension* 5 (September–October 1968): 10–11.

92 Wernick, 'Blowin' in the Wind: CUS in Winnipeg,' *Canadian Forum* 48 (September 1968): 132–3.

93 On the League for Socialist Action see O'Toole, *Precipitous Path*, 12–32.

94 The above paragraphs draw on Resnick, 'The New Left in Ontario,' in Roussopoulos, ed., *New Left in Canada*, 98–103; Owram, *Born at the Right Time*, 289, 295–6; Melville H. Watkins, 'When the Kissing Had to Stop,' *Canadian Forum* 48 (September 1968): 134; Danny Drache, 'Canadian Students: Revolt and Apathy,' *Canadian Dimension* 5 (December–January 1967–8): 24–5; James Laxer, 'The Student Movement and Canadian Independence,' *Canadian Dimension* 6 (August–September 1969): 31; Caroline Brown, 'Student Protest in Canada,' in Davies and Herman, eds., *Social Space*, 234–9; John Cleveland, *Radical Youth and Alternatives for Action* (Edmonton: Confrontations mimeograph, 1969); Howard Zinn, *Dow Shall Not Kill* (Nashville, TN: Southern Student Organizing Committee, 1967); Stanley Aronowitz, 'Columbia: Turning Point for Radical Strategy,' *Guardian*, 1 June 1968; Tom Hayden, 'Two, Three, Many Columbias,' *Ramparts*, 15 June 1968, reprinted in *Our Generation* 6 (May–July 1968): 151–2; Eric Mann, 'The Columbia University Insurrection,' *Our Generation* 6 (May–July 1968): 101–20; Peter Lust, 'Red Rudi: The Dutschke Phenomenon,' *Canadian Dimension* 5 (April–May 1968): 10–11; Daniel Cohn-Bendit, *Obsolete Communism: The Left-Wing Alternative* (Harmondsworth: Penguin, 1969); 'Interview with Daniel Cohn–Bendit,' *Our Generation* 6 (May–July 1968): 95–100.

95 The best introduction to the Sir George Williams events is Dennis Forsythe, ed., *Let the Niggers Burn! The Sir George Williams University Affair and Its Caribbean Aftermath* (Montreal: Black Rose Books, 1971), which contains the poem by Rawle R. Frederick, 'Man Trap,' 75, quoted in this paragraph. For useful discussion of West Indian radicalism in Montreal in the mid-1960s, especially as it relates to the specific conferences organized in the 1966–8 years, see Alfie Roberts, *A View For Freedom: Alfie Roberts Speaks on the Caribbean, Cricket, Montreal, and C.L.R. James* (Montreal: Alfie Roberts Institute, 2005), esp. 65–88; David Austin, 'All Roads Lead to Montreal: Black Power, The Caribbean, and the Black Radical Tradition in Canada,' *Journal of*

African American History 92 (Fall 2007): 516–39; and there is brief mention of the conferences organized in this period in Carmichael [Kwame Ture], *Ready for Revolution*, 544, 581. Sean Mills has uncovered much on black Montreal in the 1960s. See Mills, 'The Empire Within,' 174–227.

96 The above paragraphs draw on a number of sources. As a journalistic description, Dorothy Eber's *The Computer Centre Party: Canada Meets Black Power* (Montreal: Tundra, 1969), is a reasonable, albeit depoliticized, account. For a more radical statement see the articles in Forsythe, ed., *Let the Niggers Burn!* See as well Owram, *Born at the Right Time*, 286–7; and for a discussion of newspaper reporting of the Sir George Williams events, Marcel Martel, '"Riots" at Sir George Williams: Construction of a Social Conflict in the Sixties,' paper presented to the Canadian Historical Association, York University, May 2006. The prosecutorial zeal and overkill is addressed in 'SGWU Blacks Get a Taste of Just Society,' *Last Post* 1 (April 1970): 5–7. Douglas and Cools, as well as the Sir George Williams events and other developments, are discussed in Roberts, *View for Freedom*, 65–88. Douglas would later, in 1971, be targeted by the RCMP, who had an agent-provocateur function as his bodyguard and chauffeur. Allegations were made that Douglas was involved in a plot to bomb Sir George Williams University, and he was arrested and eventually deported. See Fournier, *FLQ*, 318. Cools headed Toronto's Women in Transition counselling centre and was appointed to the Federal Parole Board in 1982, later to be a Trudeau appointment to the Canadian Senate. See Olivia Ward, 'The Sixties: Ideals Have Quietly Survived,' *Toronto Star*, 28 March 1982; Walkhom, '1968: It Was Spring.'

97 *Montreal Star*, 15 February 1969, quoted in Forsythe, ed., *Let the Niggers Burn!* 9. There was consistently hostile comment from segments of the left with respect to the nihilism of the Sir George Williams destruction. See, for instance, G. David Sheps, 'The Apocalyptic Fires at Sir George Williams University,' *Canadian Dimension* 5 (February 1969): 6–7, 52; Eugene D. Genovese, 'War on Two Fronts,' *Canadian Dimension* 6 (April-May 1969): 25–9; Charles Taylor, 'Marcuse's Authoritarian Utopia,' *Canadian Dimension* 7 (August-September 1970): 49–53. Neil Compton's, 'Sir George Williams Loses Its Innocence,' *Canadian Forum*, 49 (April 1969): 2–4, struggled to be balanced. For a decidedly more upbeat presentation of student revolt and its radical possibilities see the discussion of the 40,000-strong CEGEPs protest strikes in Quebec in October 1968 in 'CEGEPs, Charlebois, Chartrand,' in Mann, ed., *Social and Cultural Change*, 2: 200–10.

98 Kostash, *Long Way from Home*, 84, 95; Philip Rosen, 'The McGill Daily Incident,' *SUPA Newsletter* 3, no. 3, January 1967; Marlene Dixon, *Things Which Are Done in Secret* (Montreal: Black Rose Books, 1976), 28–55; 'Stan Gray:

Greatest Canadian Shit Disturber'; Stanley Gray, 'The Troubles at McGill,' *Canadian Dimension* 5 (January-March 1968): 35–9; and for Gray's movement into non-university struggles in Quebec, Gray, 'The Struggle for Quebec,' *Canadian Dimension* 6 (December-January 1969–70): 23–6; Fournier, *FLQ*. For a harsh critique of Gray from a student political figure see Julius Grey, 'The Paradox of Stanley Gray,' *Canadian Dimension* 6 (October-November 1969): 6–9.

99 See, for instance, John Braddock, 'Strife on Campus,' in Julyan Reid and Tim Reid, eds., *Student Power and the Canadian Campus* (Toronto: Peter Martin, 1969), 115–25; Kostash, *Long Way from Home*, 83–101; Alan Walker, 'The Revolt on Campus,' *Star Weekly Magazine*, 13 January 1968; Richard Wilbur, 'Go Away – The Strax Affair,' *Canadian Dimension* 6 (April-May 1970): 9–10, 54; James Pitsula, 'Cicero versus Socrates: The Liberal Arts Debate at the University of Saskatchewan, Regina Campus,' *Historical Studies in Education* 15 (Spring 2003): 101–29; Pitsula, 'Competing Ideals: Athletics and Student Radicalism at the University of Saskatachewan, Regina Campus, in the 1960s and 1970s,' *Sport History Review* 34 (May 2003): 60–79; Dennis Lee, 'Getting to Rochdale,' in Repo, ed., *This Book Is About Schools*, 354–80.

100 Kostash, *Long Way from Home*, 83–4, 93–4, 99–102; James Harding, 'What's Happening at Simon Fraser University,' *Our Generation* 6 (December-January 1969–70): 52–67; Kathleen Gough, 'The Struggle at Simon Fraser University,' *Monthly Review* 22 (May 1970): 31–45; Isitt, 'Working-Class Agency,' 358–66; Owram, *Born at the Right Time*, 242–7; 'Is Universal Accessibility Henceforth Only for the Rich?' *Peak*, 4 May 1966; Sharon Yandle, 'Post-Mortem on Strike Action,' *Peak*, 5 April 1967; Yandle, 'The End of PSA at Simon Fraser,' *Canadian Dimension* 6 (February-March 1970): 16–19; Mordecai Briemberg, 'Radical Campus – or Haunted House on the Hill?' *Canadian Dimension* 40 (March-April 2006): 57–8, a review of Hugh Johnson, *Radical Campus: Making Simon Fraser University* (Vancouver: Douglas and McIntyre, 2005). For the benevolent critique see Northrop Frye, 'Student Protest Has Shallow Roots,' *Toronto Daily Star*, 19 September 1968.

101 The term is borrowed from Glen Williams, 'Canada – The Case of the Wealthiest Colony,' *This Magazine* 10 (February-March 1976): 29–30.

102 A.W. Purdy, 'syllogism for theologians,' *Canadian Dimension* 5 (June-July 1968): 35.

103 See, for instance, Scott Gordon, 'Foreign Investment in Canada,' *Canadian Dimension* 1, nos. 1–2 (1963): 18–20; H.C. Pentland, 'Is Canada Possible? A Plan for a Canadian Owned Economy,' *Canadian Dimension* 1 (September-October 1964): 5–8.

104 C.J. Newman, '1966,' *Canadian Dimension* 3 (September-October 1966): 19.

105 Philip Resnick, *The Land of Cain: Class and Nationalism in English Canada, 1945–1975* (Vancouver: New Star, 1977); Stephen Azzi, *Walter Gordon and the Rise of Canadian Nationalism* (Montreal and Kingston: McGill-Queen's University Press, 1999). Indicative of the rising anti-Americanism of the period was Ian Lumsden, ed., *Close the 49th Parallel: The Americanization of Canada* (Toronto: University of Toronto Press, 1970). More subtle, but reflective of the nationalist impulses of the late 1960s, was Gary Teeple, ed., *Capitalism and the National Question in Canada.*

106 George Grant, 'Critique of the New Left,' *Our Generation* 3 (May 1966): 46–51; Grant, 'Tories, Socialists, and the Demise of Canada,' *Canadian Dimension* 3 (May-June 1965): 12–15; Grant, 'Canadian Fate and Imperialism,' *Canadian Dimension* 4 (March-April 1967): 21–5; Grant, *Lament for a Nation: The Defeat of Canadian Nationalism – 40th Anniversary Edition* (Montreal and Kingston: McGill-Queen's University Press, 2005); Gad Horowitz, 'Mosaics and Identity,' *Canadian Dimension* 3 (January-February 1966): 19; Horowitz, 'On the Fear of Nationalism – Nationalism and Socialism – A Sermon to the Moderates,' *Canadian Dimension* 4 (May-June 1967): 7–9; 'Horowitz and Grant Talk,' *Canadian Dimension* 6 (December-January 1969–70): 18–20.

107 See the review of Lumsden, ed., *Close the 49th Parallel* by Horowitz, 'Pigs and Cops: Reflections on Closing the 49th Parallel, Etc.,' *Canadian Dimension* 6 (April-May 1970): 34–5.

108 See, for instance, J.M. Freeman, 'Economic Continentalism,' *Our Generation* 4 (March 1967): 43–73; Frank W. Park, 'The Price of Independence,' *Canadian Dimension* 4 (March-April 1967): 26–8; Cy Gonick, 'The Political Economy of Canadian Independence,' *Canadian Dimension* 4 (May-June 1967): 12–19; 'The Task Force Report on Foreign Ownership,' *Canadian Dimension* 5 (April-May 1968): 15–20; Melville H. Watkins, *Foreign Ownership and the Structure of Canadian Industry: Report of the Task Force on the Structure of Canadian Industry* (Ottawa: Queen's Printer, 1968). The full fruit of this argumentation would appear in the early 1970s. See, for example, Kari Levitt, *Silent Surrender: The Multinational Corporation in Canada* (Toronto: Macmillan, 1970); Dave Godfrey, ed., *Gordon to Watkins to You, Documentary: The Battle for Control of Our Economy* (Toronto: New Press, 1970); Frank and Libbie Park, *Anatomy of Big Business* (Toronto: James Lewis and Samuel, 1973); Robert M. Laxer, ed., *Canada, Ltd.: The Political Economy of Dependency* (Toronto: McClelland and Stewart, 1973).

109 Resnick, *Land of Cain*, 187–8; Palmer, ed., *A Communist Life*, 167–8; Kostash, *Long Way from Home*, 28–30; Owram, *Born at the Right Time*, 300–1; Levitt, *Children of Privilege*, 84, 162.

110 'Do Canadians Really Want Independence? Yes! Toronto Star Poll,' *Canadian Dimension* 4 (March-April 1967): 18–19; 'An Open Letter to Canadian Nationalists,' *Canadian Dimension* 4 (May-June 1967): front cover.

111 Steve Moore and Debi Wells, *Imperialism and the National Question in Canada* (Toronto: Better Read Grapics, 1975).

112 James Laxer, 'The Student Movement and Canadian Independence,' *Canadian Dimension* 6 (August-September 1969): 27–34, 69. The positions taken in the Laxer article had in part been responded to in Stanley Gray, 'The New Student Radicalism: Is This an American Import Too?' *Praxis* 1 (August 1968): 1–8 (pagination anew each article).

113 John W. Warnock, 'Why I Am Anti-American,' *Canadian Dimension* 5 (November-December 1967): 11–12.

114 For a rather uncritical account of the Mathews–Steele endeavours see Jeffrey Cormier, *The Canadianization Movement: Emergence, Survival, and Success* (Toronto: University of Toronto Press, 2004). Note, as introductions only, James Steele and Robin Mathews, 'The Universities: Takeover of the Mind,' in Lumsden, ed., *Close the 49th Parallel*, 169–78; Mathews, 'Canadian Culture and the Liberal Ideology,' in Laxer, ed., *Canada, Ltd.*, 213–31; Melville H. Watkins, 'Education in the Branch Plant Economy,' *Canadian Dimension* 6 (October-November 1969): 37–9.

115 Robin Mathews, 'Opinion: On Draft Dodging and U.S. Imperialism in Canada,' *Canadian Dimension* 6 (February-March 1970): 10–11. Critical responses to Mathews's views appeared in later issues of *Canadian Dimension*.

116 For an evocative statement of Watkins's development see Mel Watkins, 'Learning to Move Left,' *This Magazine Is about Schools* 6 (Spring 1972): 68–92, which also contains much on the history of the Waffle prior to its expulsion by the NDP. Also, Mel Watkins, 'A Personal Dimension,' *Canadian Dimension* 40 (November-December 2006): 51–5.

117 Much of this would be evident in early-1970s labour struggles in Ontario such as strikes buttressed by Waffle and other left-wing picket support. As RCMP files for the autumn of 1971 reveal, battles such as those unfolding at the Brantford Texpack plant indicated how critical Waffle support was for militant labour, which also gained endorsement from various Maoist and Trotskyist groups. See National Archives of Canada, Royal Canadian Mounted Police Files, vol. 113, Waffle file, 2000/000182, with thanks to Joan Sangster for giving me her notes on these files. See also Joan Sangster, 'Remembering Texpack: Nationalism, Internationalism, and Militancy in Canadian Unions in the 1970s,' *Studies in Political Economy* 78 (Autumn 2006): 41–66.

118 For a discussion of the Waffle in BC, where future NDP premier David Barrett was an early, if uneasy, associate, see Isitt, 'Working-Class Agency,' 224–35.

119 Pat Smart recently offered a personal memoir in her presentation at the 'New World' conference: 'For an Independent Socialist Canada: Queen's University History Department and the Birth of the Waffle.'

120 One reflection of the differentiation of anti-imperialist, socialist, left nationalism from that of a rising economic nationalism in the ranks of the Liberal Party and mainstream New Democrats was the initiative taken by Gordon, economist Abraham Rotstein, and *Toronto Daily Star* editor Peter Newman, who formed the more middle-of-the-road Committee for an Independent Canada in September 1970 to counter the possibility that the Waffle would be seen as the voice of Canadian nationalist ideas. See Cy Gonick, 'Liberal-izing Continentalism,' *Canadian Dimension* 7 (October-November 1970): 4–5; Christina Newman, 'Growing Up Reluctantly,' *Maclean's*, August 1972, 58; Dave Godfrey, ed., *Gordon to Watkins to You.*

121 The above two paragraphs on the Waffle draw on John Bullen, 'The Ontario Waffle and the Struggle for an Independent Socialist Canada: Conflict within the NDP,' *Canadian Historical Review* 64 (June 1983): 188–215; Robert Hackett, 'Pie in the Sky: A History of the Ontario Waffle,' *Canadian Dimension* 15 (October-November 1980): 1–72; a symposium on 'The 20th Anniversary of the Waffle' appeared in two issues of *Studies in Political Economy* 32 (Summer 1990): 167–201; 33 (Autumn 1990): 161–92; Owram, *Born at the Right Time*, 301–3; Cy Gonick, 'The "Waffle" Manifesto,' *Canadian Dimension* 6 (October-November 1969): 4; Cy Gonick, 'The Lewises versus the Waffle,' *Canadian Dimension* 8 (June 1972): 4–6, 46–7; 'Wither Waffle,' *Canadian Dimension* 7 (April 1971): 24–6; 'Stephen Lewis's War with the Waffle: Double, Double, Toil and Trouble,' *Last Post* 2 (July 1972): 32–3. On labour and the Waffle see especially Varda Burstyn, 'The Waffle and the Women's Movement,' and Gil Levine, 'The Waffle and the Labour Movement,' *Studies in Political Economy* 33 (Autumn 1990): 180, 185–92. The Waffle Manifesto appears in Cross, ed., *The Decline and Fall of a Good Idea*, and for an account of the Waffle from an NDP mainstream loyalist see Desmond Morton, *NDP: The Dream of Power* (Toronto: Hakkert, 1974).

122 Cy Gonick, 'DeaD-en-Ded,' *Canadian Dimension* 8 (March-April 1972): 5.

123 'Saskatchewan Waffle Leaves NDP,' *Ontario Waffle News* 1 (November 1973): 1. Evidence of the Waffle stalling in lack of organization and programmatic coherence can be gleaned from reading various statements in a 1974 Ontario internal discussion bulletin, among them Treat Hull, 'Comment on the Waffle Election Programme,' Boyd Neil, 'Report on the CLC Convention,' and Corileen North, 'Fiscal Reform in the Waffle: An Opinion,' all in *Advance: For Independence and Socialism – Internal Discussion Journal of the Ontario Waffle* 2 (17 July 1974): 6–14.

124 See Burstyn, 'The Age of Women's Liberation,' *Canadian Dimension* 18 (October-November 1984): 21–6; Burstyn 'The Waffle and the Women's Movement,' 175–84, for suggestive opening statements, as well as Burstyn, 'Remember the Old Mole?' 13; and, most tellingly, Varda Kidd, 'Sexism Prevailed at the NDP Convention,' *Canadian Dimension* 8 (June 1971): 7–9. Fischer is quoted in what remains perhaps the best overall treatment of the Waffle, Hackett, 'Pie in the Sky,' 42–3. See as well Michael S. Cross, 'Third Class on the Titanic: The NDP Convention,' *Canadian Forum* (April-May 1971): 5. For an early materialist-feminist statement associated with the Waffle and published in the Movement for an Independent Socialist Canada's 'coming-out' statement see Christina Maria Hill, 'Women in the Canadian Economy,' in Robert M. Laxer, ed., *Canada, Ltd.,* 84–106. Note as well Krista Maeots, 'Organizing Woman,' in *Towards a Movement for an Independent Socialist Canada: A Proposal for the Ontario Waffle Conference, 19–20 August 1972,* a five-page statement in a mimeographed collection of short 'position papers' prepared as the Waffle faced the prospect of being drummed out of the NDP; and the important later contribution of the Kingston Waffle, 'Marxism, Feminism, and the Waffle,' *Advance: For Independence and Socialism – Internal Discussion Journal of the Ontario Waffle* 2 (17 July 1974): 1–5.

125 The above paragraphs draw on Margaret Benston, 'The Political Economy of Women's Liberation,' *Monthly Review* 21 (September 1969): 13–27; Margaret Benston and Pat Davitt, 'Women Invent Society,' *Canadian Dimension* 10 (June 1975): 69–79; Meg Luxton and Pat Armstrong, 'Margaret Lowe Benston, 1937–1991,' *Studies in Political Economy* 35 (Summer 1991): 6–11; 'Margaret Benston: A Tribute,' *Canadian Women Studies* 13 (Winter 1993): 6–36, which contains seven separate articles, including one by Marion Lowe. Benston's article was almost immediately responded to by Mickey and John Rowntree, 'More on the Political Economy of Women's Liberation,' *Monthly Review* 21 (January 1970): 26–32. For the Canadian research and writing of the 1970s and 1980s that grew out of Benston's discussion see, as examples only, Peggy Morton, 'Women's Work Is Never Done,' in *Women Unite! An Anthology of the Canadian Women's Movement* (Toronto: Canadian Women's Educational Press, 1972), 46–68; Dorothy Smith, 'Women, the Family, and Corporate Capitalism,' and Marylee Stephenson, 'Housewives in Women's Liberation,' in Stephenson, ed., *Women in Canada* (Don Mills, ON: General Publishing, 1977), 14–48, 109–25; Meg Luxton, *More Than a Labour of Love: Three Generations of Women's Work in the Home* (Toronto: Women's Educational Press, 1980); Bonnie Fox, ed., *Hidden in the Household: Women's Domestic Labour under Capitalism*

(Toronto: Women's Educational Press, 1980); Roberta Hamilton and
Michelle Barrett, eds., *The Politics of Diversity: Feminism, Marxism, and Nationalism* (London: Verso, 1986). For a fuller survey see Heather Jon Maroney
and Meg Luxton, eds., *Feminism and Political Economy: Women's Work,
Women's Struggles* (Toronto: Methuen, 1987), 17–19. Mariarosa Dall Costa
and Selma James, *The Power of Women and the Subversion of the Community*
(Bristol: Falling Wall Press, 1972); Juliet Mitchell, *Women: The Longest Revo-
lution* (New York: Pantheon, 1984). Among the long list of women's movement anthologies that republished Benston's article were *Liberation Now?,
Roles Women Play, Women in a Man-Made World*, and *Feminist Frameworks*. For
a recent collection that accents the historical importance of 'The Political
Economy of Women's Liberation,' see Rosemary Hennessy and Chrys
Ingraham, *Materialist Feminism: A Reader in Class, Difference, and Women's
Lives* (New York: Routledge, 1997).

126 This was remarkably *early* in the history of New Left feminism. In Britain,
for instance, the first major conference of New Left feminism was not conceived and organized until 1969–70.

127 On the context of the SUPA women's statement see Kostash, *Long Way from
Home*, 166–71; Owram, *Born at the Right Time*, 272–9. The major document
is Judy Bernstein, Peggy Morton, Linda Seese, Myrna Wood, 'Sisters,
Brothers, Lovers … Listen,' in *Women Unite! An Anthology of the Canadian
Women's Movement* (Toronto: Women's Educational Press, 1972), 31–9,
which originally appeared as a New England Free Press pamphlet, but see
as well Betty Burcher, '"Blue Meanies," Wheelies, Feelies, and Personalist
Bullshit,' *Praxis* 2 (March 1969): 15–16, 21. On the Royal Commission on
the Status of Women see Barbara M. Freeman, *The Satellite Sex: The Media
and Women's Issues in English Canada, 1966–1971* (Waterloo, ON: Wilfrid
Laurier University Press, 2001); Cerise Morris, '"Determination and
Thoroughness": The Movement for a Royal Commission on the Status of
Women,' *Atlantis* 5 (Spring 1980): 1–21. For the New Left/early women's
movement critique of the Royal Commission see Jackie Larkin, 'Status of
Women Report: Fundamental Questions Remain Unanswered,' *Canadian
Dimension* 7 (January-February 1971): 6–8.

128 Quoting Nancy Lubka, 'The Ins and Outs of Women's Liberation,' *Cana-
dian Dimension* 7 (June-July 1970): 24–9, quoted 25. Lubka drew heavily on
Margaret Benston's 1969 essay. For brief accounts of the development of a
New Left Women's Liberation Movement see Owram, *Born at the Right Time*,
277–9; Naiomi Black, 'The Canadian Women's Movement: The Second
Wave,' in Sandra Burt, Lorraine Code, and Lindsay Dorney, eds., *Changing
Patterns: Women in Canada* (Toronto: McClelland and Stewart, 1993), 154,

164–5, 172; Nancy Adamson, Linda Briskin, and Margaret McPhail, *Feminist Organizing for Change: The Contemporary Women's Movement in Canada* (Toronto: Oxford University Press, 1988), 42–4, 70; and Ian McKay, *Rebels, Reds, Radicals: Rethinking Canada's Left History* (Toronto: Between the Lines, 2005), 192–9.

129 As one woman involved in the McGill Student Movement and women's liberation recalled: 'When I entered university in 1966 I rapidly discovered a whole world of rebels and radicals. I early became interested in Marxism; in particular the 1844 manuscripts, the most humanist writings of Marx, had a profound effect on me.' Quoted in Adamson, Briskin, McPhail, *Feminist Organizing for Change*, 41.

130 See, especially, Laurel Limpus, 'Liberation of Women,' *This Magazine Is about Schools* 3 (Winter 1969): 61–74.

131 Naiomi Black, 'Canadian Women's Movement,' 154. See also the very helpful overview by Nancy Adamson, 'Feminists, Libbers, Lefties, and Radicals: The Emergence of the Women's Liberation Movement,' in Joy Parr, ed., *A Diversity of Women: Ontario, 1945–1980* (Toronto: University of Toronto Press, 1995), 252–80.

132 Marlene Dixon, 'Why Women's Liberation?' *Ramparts*, November 1969; Dixon, *Things That Are Done in Secret*, 101; Adamson, Briskin, McPhail, *Feminist Organizing for Change*, 43, 49; Chandler Davis, 'Hemisfair at Montreal,' *Canadian Forum* 48 (January 1969): 219–20; Mark Rudd, 'The Death of SDS,' in Dimitri Roussopoulos, ed., *The New Left: Legacy and Continuity* (Montreal: Black Rose, 2007), 84; Kostash, *Long Way from Home*, 184.

133 Adamson, 'Feminists, Libbers, Lefties, and Radicals,' 257.

134 See, for instance, 'Pie in the Sky: Royal Commission Recipe,' and 'Brief to the House of Commons,' *Women Unite!* 40–2, 114–20. Much is written on the Royal Commission on the Status of Women (RCSW), which began in 1967 and finally reported in 1970. Conventional understandings of the divergence of liberal and socialist feminists in their perspective on the RCSW have recently been problematized by Mary-Jo Nadeau, 'The Making and Unmaking of a "Parliament of Women": Nation, Race, and the Politics of the National Action Committee on the Status of Women (1972–1992),' PhD dissertation, York University, 2005.

135 Such actions in Toronto and Kingston are described in Adamson, 'Feminists, Libbers, Lefties, and Radicals,' 262–3.

136 Rebick, *Ten Thousand Roses*, 10–11.

137 The above paragraphs draw on Rebick, *Ten Thousand Roses*, 7–13, 35–46; Adamson, 'Feminists, Libbers, Lefties, and Radicals,' 263–4; Owram, *Born at the Right Time*, 278; Kostash, *Long Way from Home*, 171–4; Women's

Liberation News Services, 'University of Toronto Women Win Daycare,' *The Pedestal,* April 1970; Donna Cherniak and Allan Feingold, 'Birth Control Handbook,' in *Women Unite!* 109–13; Adamson, Briskin, McPhail, *Feminist Organizing for Change,* 45–7, 201–2; Frances Wasserlein, '"An Arrow Aimed at the Heart": The Vancouver Women's Caucus and the Abortion Campaign, 1969–1971,' MA thesis, Simon Fraser University, 1990; 'Abortion March Only a Start,' *Last Post* 1 (April 1970): 4–5. For an early statement on abortion and choice see Myrna Wood, 'Abortion and the Liberation of Women,' *Canadian Dimension* 5 (June-July 1967): 2. Two recent discussions are Ann Thompson, *Winning Choice on Abortion: How British Columbian and Canadian Feminists Won the Battles of the 1970s and 1980s* (Victoria: Trafford, 2004); and Christabel Sethna and Steve Hewitt, 'Staging Protest: The Abortion Caravan, Feminist Guerrilla Theatre and RCMP Spying on Women's Groups,' presented at 'New World.'

138 Kostash, *Long Way from Home,* 179–84; much of the material reprinted in *Women Unite!*; Luxton, 'Feminism as a Class Act'; Z. Farid and J. Kuyek, 'Who Speaks for Working-Class Women?' *Canadian Dimension* 10 (June 1975): 80–2; Myrna Wood, 'Whatever Happened to the Women's Movement?' *Canadian Dimension* 37 (September-October 2003): 23–4; Isitt, 'Working-Class Agency,' 273–9.

139 Adamson, Briskin, McPhail, *Feminist Organizing for Change,* 264–5; Kostash, *Long Way from Home,* 179; Bonnie Kreps, 'Radical Feminism,' *Women Unite!* 71–5.

140 See, for instance, Marlene Dixon, 'Women's Liberation: Opening Chapter Two,' *Canadian Dimension* 10 (June 1975): 56–68; Nadeau, 'The Making and Unmaking of a "Parliament of Women"';Wood, 'Whatever Happened to the Women's Movement?'

141 Kostash, *Long Way from Home,* 101–2; Owram, *Born at the Right Time,* 233–5, 297–8; Ralph Osborne, *From Someplace Else: A Memoir* (Toronto: ECW Press, 2003); Finkel, 'Wither Commune - ism,'; Steve Langdon, 'C.U.S.,' *Canadian Dimension* 6 (February-March 1970): 6–8.

142 See, for instance, Steve Hewitt, *Spying 101: The RCMP's Secret Activities at Canadian Universities, 1917–1997* (Toronto: University of Toronto Press, 2002), 119–70.

143 Howard Adelman, 'A Decade of Protest: Coroner's Report,' *Canadian Forum* 49 (February 1970): 258–60.

144 Irving Layton, 'Marxist,' *Canadian Forum* 49 (January 1970): 234.

145 On the limitations and development of gay and lesbian liberation in the 1960s and early 1970s see as introductions only Donald W. McLeod, *Lesbian and Gay Liberation in Canada: A Selected Annotated Chronology, 1964–*

1975 (Toronto: ECW Press, 1996); Becki L. Ross, *The House That Jill Built: A Lesbian Nation in Formation* (Toronto: University of Toronto Press, 1995); Adamson, Briskin, McPhail, *Feminist Organizing for Change*, 58–74; Gary Kinsman, *The Regulation of Desire: Homo and Hetero Sexualities* (Montreal: Black Rose Books, 1996), 288–93; Deborah Brock, '"Workers of the World Caress": An Interview with Gary Kinsman on Gay and Lesbian Organizing in the 1970s,' *Left History Online*, http://www.yorku.ca/lefthist/online/brock_kinsman.html (accessed 21 May 2006).

9: Quebec: Revolution Now!

1 For contemporary discussions see the liberally inclined Denis Smith, *Bleeding Hearts ... Bleeding Country: Canada and the Quebec Crisis* (Edmonton: Hurtig, 1971), and the more radical Dan Daniels, ed., *Quebec, Canada, and the October Crisis* (Montreal: Black Rose, 1973). See also the many, and often varying, contributions in Abraham Rotstein, ed., *Power Corrupted: The October Crisis and the Repression of Quebec* (Toronto: New Press, 1971). A recent liberal defence of the imposition of the War Measures Act is William Tetley, *The October Crisis, 1970: An Insider's View* (Montreal and Kingston: McGill-Queen's University Press, 2007).

2 'From Laurier,' *Canadian Dimension* 7 (December 1970): 2, 61. This issue of *Dimension*, a special number devoted to 'War Declared on Quebec,' carried with it an unusual disclaimer from the printer, Canadian Publishers Ltd., dis-associating the company from the opinions, articles, and contents of the magazine, which it stated were the sole responsibility of the publisher. Lapierre's writing of this period included Lapierre, 'Canada's Eldridge Cleaver and Malcolm X,' *New York Times Book Review,* 11 April 1971; Lapierre et al., eds., *Essays on the Left: Essays in Honour of T.C. Douglas* (Toronto: McClelland and Stewart, 1971).

3 A brief introductory statement is Ian McKay, *Rebels, Reds, and Radicals: Rethinking Canada's Left History* (Toronto: Between the Lines, 2005), 185–9. A recent unpublished dissertation contains a wealth of information on Montreal in this period. See Sean William Mills, 'The Empire Within: Montreal, the Sixties, and the Forging of a Radical Imagination,' PhD thesis, Queen's University, 2007. Mills's thesis was completed after I finished this book, but I have alluded lightly to some of its contents in what follows. For an account of post-1970 engagement of Quebec with English-Canadian pro-gressive intellectuals, an encounter in which the national question figures centrally, see Serge Denis, *Le Long Malentendu: Le Québec vu par les intellectuels progressistes au Canada anglais, 1970–1991* (Montreal: Boréal, 1992).

4 Consider, for instance, Pierre Elliott Trudeau, 'Some Obstacles to Democracy in Quebec,' *Canadian Journal of Economics and Political Science* 24 (August 1958): 297–311; or Trudeau, 'Quebec on the Eve of the Asbestos Strike,' in Ramsay Cook, ed., *French-Canadian Nationalism: An Anthology* (Toronto: Macmillan, 1971), 32–48. As a brief overview of the history of labour in Quebec see John Huot, 'The Quebec Background: The Character of Class Struggle in Quebec,' and (reprinted from *Solidaire*) 'A Short History of Trade Unions in Quebec,' both in *Radical America* 6 (September-October 1972): 3–22, 23–8.

5 Philip Resnick, *The Land of Cain: Class and Nationalism in English Canada, 1954–1975* (Vancouver: New Star, 1977), 192; NDP Socialist Caucus, *A Socialist Program for the New Democratic Party* (Toronto: Socialist Caucus, 1964); Alberta Socialist Caucus of the New Democratic Party, *A Socialist Manifesto for the New Democratic Party* (Edmonton: Alberta Socialist Caucus, NDP, 1966); Robert Hackett, 'Pie in the Sky: A History of the Ontario Waffle,' *Canadian Dimension* 15 (October-November 1980): 3, contextualizes the Waffle's significance in terms of Quebec and concludes that the Waffle's defeat 'marked the end of the NDP's flirtation with special status and self-determination for Quebec' (63); Gad Horowitz, 'On the Fear of Nationalism,' *Canadian Dimension* 4 (April 1967): 7–9; Horowitz, 'Trudeau vs. Trudeauism,' *Canadian Forum* 48 (May 1968): 29–30.

6 Al Purdy, 'The Peaceable Kingdom,' in Rotstein, *Power Corrupted*, 58–61.

7 As an introduction to the Union Nationale see Herbert Quinn, *The Union Nationale* (Toronto: University of Toronto Press, 1963); Richard Jones, *Duplessis and the Union Nationale Administration* (Ottawa: Canadian Historical Association Booklet #35, 1983); and the sympathetic biography, Conrad Black, *Duplessis* (Toronto: McClelland and Stewart, 1979).

8 For a detailed articulation of this understanding of Duplessis and the Union Nationale see Kenneth McRoberts and Dale Posgate, *Quebec: Social Change and Political Crisis* (Toronto: McClelland and Stewart, 1984), 60–93. On American capital's significance in the creation of Quebec as a colonial satellite see Sheilagh Hodgins Milner and Henry Milner, *The Decolonization of Quebec: An Analysis of Left-Wing Nationalism* (Toronto: McClelland and Stewart, 1973), 1–102.

9 See, for instance, Maurice Pinard, 'Working Class Politics: An Interpretation of the Quebec Case,' *Canadian Review of Sociology and Anthropology* 7 (1970): 87–109.

10 This and the following paragraphs draw heavily on the views first put forward in Bryan D. Palmer, *Working-Class Experience: The Rise and Reconstitution of Canadian Labour, 1800–1980* (Toronto: Butterworth, 1983), 257–63; Palmer, *Working-Class Experience: Rethinking the History of Canadian Labour,*

1800–1991 (Toronto: McClelland and Stewart, 1992), 307–13. For other perspectives see Jacques Rouillard, *Les Syndicats nationaux au Québec de 1900 à 1930* (Quebec: Les Presses de l'Université Laval, 1979); Rouillard, *Histoire de la CSN (1921–1981)* (Montreal: Confédération des syndicats nationaux, 1981); Rouillard, *Histoire du syndicalisme québécois: Des origins à nos jours* (Montreal: Boréal, 1989).

11 On 'the great darkness' see the chapter of this name in Pierre Vallières, *White Niggers of America* (Toronto: McClelland and Stewart, 1971), 121–68.

12 For an overview of these years, and one that places an important analytic accent on subtle divisions within intellectual currents, see Michael D. Behiels, *Prelude to Quebec's Quiet Revolution: Liberalism versus Neo-Nationalism, 1945–1960* (Kingston and Montreal: McGill-Queen's University Press, 1985).

13 See, for instance, Jacques Rouillard, 'Les Écrits d'Alfred Charpentier,' in Fernand Dumont, Jean Hamelin, and Jean-Pierre Montminy, eds., *Idéologies au Canada français, 1940–1976* (Quebec: Les Presses de l'Université Laval, 1981), 295–316.

14 For an introduction to this broad history see Irving M. Abella, *Nationalism, Communism, and Canadian Labour: The CIO, the Communist Party of Canada, and the Canadian Congress of Labour, 1935–1956* (Toronto: University of Toronto Press, 1973).

15 For an overview see Behiels, *Prelude to Quebec's Quiet Revolution*, 121–48.

16 Milner and Milner, *Decolonization of Quebec*, 148–50; Reginald Boisvert, 'La Grève et le mouvement ouvrier,' in Pierre Elliott Trudeau, ed., *La Grève d'amiante* (Montreal: Éditions Cité libre, 1956), 362; Mason Wade, *The French Canadians, 1760–1967*, vol. 2 (Toronto: Macmillan, 1968), 1019.

17 Jacques Rouillard, 'Major Changes in the Confédération des Travailleurs Catholiques du Canada, 1940–1960,' in Michael D. Behiels, ed., *Quebec Since 1945: Selected Readings* (Toronto: Copp Clark Pitman, 1987), 111–32.

18 Gerard Pelletier, 'La Grève et la presse,' in Trudeau, ed., *La Grève de l'amiante*, 278–9, translated and quoted in Milner and Milner, *Decolonization of Quebec*, 161.

19 Note the discussions in Benedict Anderson, *Imagined Communities: Reflections on the Origin and Spread of Nationalism* (London: Verso, 1983); E.J. Hobsbawm and Terence O. Ranger, eds., *The Invention of Tradition* (Cambridge: Cambridge University Press, 1983).

20 See Trudeau, ed., *La Grève de l'amiante*; Jacques Cousineau, SJ, 'La Grève de l'amiante,' *Relations* 103 (June 1949): 146; Jean C. Falardeau, *Bulletin des relations industrielles* 4 (March 1949): 68; Stuart Marshall Jamieson, 'Labour Unity in Quebec,' in Mason Wade, ed., *Canadian Dualism* (Toronto:

University of Toronto Press, 1960), 209; Fraser Isbester, 'Asbestos, 1949,' in
Irving Abella, ed., *On Strike: Six Key Labour Struggles in Canada, 1919–1949*
(Toronto: James Lorimer, 1975), 163–96, quote on 163. A recent revisionist
treatment of the Asbestos strike is Jacques Rouillard, 'La Grève de l'amiante
de 1949 et le projet de réforme de l'entreprise. Comment le patronat a
défendu son droit de gérace,' *Labour/Le Travail* 46 (Fall 2000): 307–42.

21 Vallières, *White Niggers of America*, 119; Léandre Bergeron, *The History of
Quebec: A Patriote's Handbook* (Toronto: NC Press, 1971), 194–7. With sales
approaching 100,000, Bergeron's book is arguably one of the best-selling of
modern Quebec texts, and one that put forward a view of Québécois history
very much in line with radical nationalist thought of the mid- to late 1960s.
See, for a more scholarly articulation of the meaning of Asbestos in terms of
the victory of the state and big business and the displacement of the Catholic Church, Hélène David, 'La Grève et le bon Dieu: La grève de l'amiante
au Québec,' *Sociologie et société* 1 (novembre 1969): 249–76. 'Roi nègre/
Negro King' was a term of common parlance among liberal and reform-
minded Québécois in the late 1950s and early 1960s, ostensibly coined by
André Laurendeau in a series of three editorials in *Le Devoir* over the course
of the summer and fall of 1958. Later this would be referred to as the admirable 'cannibal-king theory' by Pierre Elliott Trudeau, 'New Treason of the
Intellectuals,' in Trudeau, *Federalism and the French Canadians* (Toronto:
Macmillan, 1968), 163. In the original formulation of the concept, it was
directed at Duplessis and his servile relations with Anglo-American capital
and the federal Canadian state. But it would later be applied to any political
figure refusing to take up the cause of revolutionary Quebec nationalism.

22 Behiels, *Prelude to Quebec's Quiet Revolution*, contains extensive commentary
on the *Citélibristes*. Note, as well, Gérard Pelletier, *Years of Impatience, 1950–
1960* (Toronto: Methuen, 1985); Andrée Fortin, *Passage de la modernité: Les
intellectuals québécois et leurs revues* (Sainte-Foy: Les Presses de l'Université
Laval, 1993), 145–65.

23 A recent treatment of the Dupuis Frères strike is John Willis, 'Cette Manche
au syndicat – La grève chez Dupuis Frères en 1952,' *Labour/Le Travail* 57
(Spring 2006): 43–92.

24 For a succinct summary of the markers of oppression all too evident in
French Canada in the 1960s see Milner and Milner, *Decolonization of Quebec*,
31–68. I draw on the outline in Louis Fournier, *FLQ: The Anatomy of an
Underground Movement* (Toronto: NC Press, 1984), 17, an excellent source
upon which I rely extensively throughout this chapter.

25 Nicholas M. Regush, *Pierre Vallières: The Revolutionary Process in Quebec – A
Political Biography of the Author of 'White Niggers of America'* (Toronto: Fitzhenry

and Whiteside, 1973), 170–2. Note also the discussion of Montreal circa 1960 in Mills, 'The Empire Within,' 48–53.

26 For a brief outline of Chartrand's history up to the October Crisis of 1970 see 'Michel Chartrand's Thirty Year Conspiracy,' in Robert Chodos and Nick Auf der Maur, eds., *Quebec: A Chronicle, 1968–1972* (Toronto: James Lewis and Samuel, 1972), 77–90.

27 An important memoir, outlining the pioneering importance of the Ministry of Cultural Affairs, is Guy Fregault, *Chronique des années perdues* (Ottawa: Éditions Lemeac, 1976). Much on Hydro-Québec's significance, past and present, can be gleaned from the collection of statements and essays in Yves Belanger et Robert Comeau, eds., *Hydro-Québec: Autres temps, autres défies* (Sainte-Foy: Presses de l'Université du Québec, 1995), esp. Michel Belanger, 'Les Actions d'Hydro-Québec à vendre?' 89–96. Hydro-Québec helped launch René Lévesque as a voice of independence for Quebec. Lévesque's nationalism in this period was very much defined by economic priorities. See the interview with Lévesque by Jean-Marc Leger, *Le Devoir*, 5 July 1963, reprinted and translated in Frank Scott and Michael Oliver, eds., *Quebec States Her Case: Speeches and Articles from Quebec in the Years of Unrest* (Toronto: Macmillan, 1964), 132–45.

28 Quotes from Marcel Rioux, *Quebec in Question* (Toronto: James Lewis and Samuel, 1971), 75–6; Léon Dion, *Quebec: The Unfinished Revolution* (Montreal and Kingston: McGill-Queen's University Press, 1976), 23–4. For insights into the highly charged interpretive controversies associated with the Quiet Revolution see McRoberts and Posgate, *Quebec: Social Change and Political Crisis*, 94–154; Milner and Milner, *Decolonization of Quebec*, 167–94; Milner, *Politics in the New Quebec* (Toronto: McClelland and Stewart, 1978); Richard Jones, *Community in Crisis: French-Canadian Nationalism in Perspective* (Toronto: McClelland and Stewart, 1972); William Coleman, *The Independence Movement in Quebec, 1945–1980* (Toronto: University of Toronto Press, 1984); Coleman, 'The Class Bases of Language Policy in Quebec, 1949–1983,' in Alain G. Gagnon, ed., *Quebec: State and Society* (Toronto: Methuen, 1984), 388–409; Albert Breton, 'The Economics of Nationalism,' *Journal of Political Economy* 72 (August 1964): 376–86; Charles Taylor, 'Nationalism and the Political Intelligentsia: A Case Study,' *Queen's Quarterly* 72 (Spring 1965): 150–68; Daniel Latouche, 'La Vraie Nature de la révolution tranquille,' *Canadian Journal of Political Science* 7 (September 1974): 525–36; Vincent Lemieux, ed., *Quatre Élections provincials au Québec: 1956–1966* (Quebec: Les Presses de l'Université Laval, 1969); Michael D. Behiels, 'Quebec: Social Transformation and Ideological Renewal, 1940–1976,' and Marc Renaud, 'Quebec's New Middle Class in Search of Social Hegemony:

Causes and Political Consequences,' both in Behiels, *Quebec since 1945*, 21–79; Anne Legare, *Les Classes sociales au Québec* (Montreal: Presses de l'Université de Québec, 1977).

29 Richard Ares, *Nos Grandes Options politiques et constitutionelles* (Montreal: Bellarmin, 1967); Claude Morin, *Quebec vs. Ottawa* (Toronto: University of Toronto Press, 1976); Edward McWhinney, *Quebec and the Constitution, 1960–1978* (Toronto: University of Toronto Press, 1982). On the Royal Commission on Bilingualism and Biculturalism, set up in 1963, and co-chaired by Davidson Dunton and André Laurendeau, see Dion, *Quebec: The Unfinished Revolution*, 41–51; Coleman, *Independence Movement in Quebec*, 194–7; Donald James Horton, *André Laurendeau: French-Canadian Nationalist, 1912–1968* (Toronto: Oxford University Press, 1992); André Laurendeau, 'A Lesson in Separatism,' *Le Devoir*, 22 December 1962, reprinted and translated in Scott and Oliver, eds., *Quebec States Her Case*, 101–4.

30 On *survivance* see Ramsay Cook, '*La Survivance* French Canadian Style,' in Cook, *The Maple Leaf Forever: Essays on Nationalism and Politics in Canada* (Toronto: Macmillan, 1971), 114–40, and for an early balanced statement on religion's place in 1960s Quebec see Hubert Guindon, 'The Church in French-Canadian Society,' *Canadian Dimension* 4 (March 1967): 29–31. The fullest recent scholarly discussion is Michael Gauvreau, *The Catholic Origins of Quebec's Quiet Revolution, 1931–1970* (Montreal and Kingston: McGill-Queen's University Press, 2006). Recent attempts to suggest that 'the most radical Quebec nationalism of the 1960s' (the *indépendantiste* strain associated with the first-wave formation of the FLQ in the early 1960s) contained millennialist impulses that reveal continuities in the political influence of religious thought seem to me overstated and misguided. At root is a reduction of radical politics to a faith-based exercise in 'the fully mystical intensity' of a commitment to apocalyptic engagement, which in turn rests on a fundamentally pejorative view of 1960s radicalism as 'frenzied direct action.' See Eric Bédard, 'De la Quête millenariste à la thérapie du choc: La pensée felquiste jusqu'à la Crise d'octobre, 1970,' *Journal of Canadian Studies* 37 (Summer 2002): 33–46.

31 For a contemporary journalistic assessment see Peter Desbarats, *The State of Quebec: A Journalist's View of the Quiet Revolution* (Toronto: McClelland and Stewart, 1965), which has been expanded on from the French side in Pierre Godin, *La Revolution tranquille*, vols. 1 and 2 (Montreal: Boréal, 1991). Note, as well, the still-useful overview, Dale Thomson, *Jean Lesage and the Quiet Revolution* (Toronto: Macmillan, 1984), and the collection, Yves Belanger, Robert Comeau, et Céline Métivier, eds., *La Revolution tranquille 40 ans plus tard: Un bilan* (Montreal: VLB Éditeur, 2000).

32 For the final *Cité libre* statement see Pierre Elliott Trudeau, 'New Treason of
    the Intellectuals,' *Cité libre*, April 1962, reprinted along with other relevant
    articles and speeches on federalism in *Federalism and the French Canadians*,
    151–81.

33 For a brief account of Trudeau's trajectory see Cook, *Maple Leaf Forever*, 31–45.

34 Vallières, *White Niggers of America*, 178, 180.

35 For retrospective accounts of the failures of the Quiet Revolution see Dion,
    Quebec: The Unfinished Revolution; 'The Failure of the Quiet Revolution,' in
    Chodos and Auf der Maur, eds., *Quebec: A Chronicle*, 3–18; and Pierre Vallières,
    'The Unfruitful Reforms of the Quiet Revolution,' in Vallières, *The Impossible
    Quebec* (Montreal: Black Rose, 1980), 117–22, which concludes with the first
    quote above. The second quotation, also from Vallières, appears in Regush,
    Pierre Vallières, 84. Others, undoubtedly a majority and more moderate in
    their politics, concluded that the Quiet Revolution had indeed been a
    liberating, even revolutionary, departure from the limitations of the
    Duplessis period. André Laurendeau, for instance, denounced the FLQ in
    the pages of *Le Devoir* and retained a view that Quebec's Quiet Revolution
    had indeed broken very much with the past and its confinements. See
    Horton, *Laurendeau*.

36 On the political debt to Miron as an inspirational figure in Quebec's tumul-
    tuous 1960s see Vallières, *White Niggers of America*, 150–2, and Malcolm Reid,
    *The Shouting Signpainters: A Literary and Political Account of Quebec Revolution-
    ary Nationalism* (Toronto: McClelland and Stewart, 1972), esp. 183–93.
    Miron's poetic genius was largely unrecognized until at least the 1970s, but
    would certainly flower late in his life, in the 1980s. For an introduction only
    see Marc Plourde, ed., *The Agonized Life: Poems and Prose by Gaston Miron*
    (Montreal: Torchy Wharf Press, 1980), quoting 33, 37.

37 'Miron, the Anthropoet,' in *The Agonized Life*, 75–7.

38 As a brief overview of the profusion of literary and political journals devoted
    to revolutionary nationalism in the 1960s see Fortin, *Passage de la modernité*,
    167–91.

39 Although concentrating analysis on a later period of the RIN, see Gilles
    Dostaler, *Parti pris* 4 (janvier-février 1967): 26–27; Réjean Pelletier, *Les Mili-
    tants du R.I.N.* (Ottawa: Éditions de l'Université d'Ottawa, 1974).

40 The above paragraphs draw primarily on Reid, *The Shouting Signpainters*,
    197–202; Fournier, *FLQ*, 16–24; Marcel Chaput, *Pourquoi Je Suis séparatiste*
    (Montreal: Les Éditions du Jour, 1961); Andre D'Allemagne, *Le RIN et les
    débuts du mouvement indépendantise québécois* (Montreal: Éditions l'Étincelle,
    1974); Robert Major, 'Québécois ou Canadien français: Note sur l'identité
    québécoise et la fortune d'un vocable,' *Contemporary French Civilization* 2

(November 1977): 59–72; Vallières, *White Niggers of America*, 181, 280. A portrait of the Montreal bohemian milieu of the early 1960s from which many Felquistes would emerge is presented in Carole de Vault with William Johnson, *The Informer: Confessions of an Ex-Terrorist* (Toronto: Fleet Books, 1982), 35–46. The influence of Frantz Fanon, *Les Damnés de la terre* (Paris: François Maspero, 1961), within Quebec in the 1960s was extraordinary, as indeed it was in New Left circles worldwide. There is nevertheless little doubt that Fanon was first and perhaps most vigorously drawn upon in Quebec, at least when the influence is discussed in terms of Canada and the United States. Vallières says little about Fanon in *White Niggers of America* but does refer to himself as one of the 'wretched of the earth' (200). More extended commentary appears in Vallières, *Les Héritiers de Papineau: Itinéraire politique d'un 'nègre blanc' (1960–1985)* (Montreal: Québec/Amérique, 1986), 56, 66–7. A reflection of Fanon's later impact in English Canada is George S. Haggar, 'The Wretched of the Earth,' *Canadian Dimension* 3 (July-August 1966): 35–6. On Fanon see the important biography, David Macey, *Frantz Fanon: A Life* (London: Granta, 2000). Fanon's book had a preface by Jean-Paul Sartre, as did the psychological analysis of domination by Albert Memmi, *Portrait du colonisé* (Montreal: Éditions l'Étincelle, 1972), which, in its later republication, contained an appendix, 'Les Canadiens francais sont-ils colonisés?' For a fictional representation of this milieu see Herman Buller, *Days of Rage* (Montreal/Toronto: October Publications, 1974). Mills, 'The Empire Within,' presents the strongest statement of Fanon's influence in Montreal radical circles, orchestrating his discussion of 'the forging of a radical imagination' around the assimilation of Fanon's perspectives on decolonization.

41 Arguably the most accessible, succinct, and detailed portrait of the three early leaders of the FLQ is the admittedly hostile discussion in Gustave Morf, *Terror in Quebec: Case Studies of the FLQ* (Toronto: Clarke, Irwin, 1970), 20–33. See, as well, Fournier, *FLQ*, 28–41; James Stewart, *The FLQ: Seven Years of Terrorism* (Montreal: Montreal Star, 1970), 14–16.

42 The above paragraphs rely on Fournier, *FLQ*, 28–42; Claude Savoie, *La Véritable Histoire du F.L.Q.* (Montreal: Éditions du Jour, 1963); Regush, *Pierre Vallières*, 91–96; with the quote from the FLQ manifesto and other relevant discussion from Morf, *Terror in Quebec*, 2–15. See, as well, Bernard Smith, *Les Résistants du FLQ* (Montreal: Les Éditions Actualité, 1963). Largely ignored by the mainstream press, except for *Le Devoir*, which published a portion of Schoeters's 'Notice to the Population of Quebec,' the three 1963 Felquiste statements were later highlighted in Savoie, *La Véritable Histoire du F.L.Q.* See as well Scott and Oliver, eds., *Quebec States Her Case*, 83–7, from which the

quotations of Pelletier and Dion are drawn, 89, 100. Note, finally, Trudeau's assault on what he called counter-revolutionary separatism, which he pejoratively dubbed 'The Wigwam Complex' in Trudeau, 'Separatist Counter-Revolutionaries,' *Cité libre*, May 1964, reprinted in *Federalism and the French Canadians*, 204–12.

43 Morf, *Terror in Quebec*, 14–15; Fournier, *FLQ*, 19, 38, 41; Savoie, *La Véritable Histoire du F.L.Q.*, 49–53.

44 Dion, *Quebec: The Unfinished Revolution*, 26. Dion's book later (176) discusses the range of nationalist discourse evident in the early 1960s and extending into the 1970s, encompassing national aspirations cast in traditionalist conservative, liberal, social-democratic, and socialist expressions. Not all such nationalists would have seen the FLQ sympathetically, but it is possible that within *all* such nationalist formations there would have been expressions of understanding shading over to explicit support. Pelletier, writing originally in *La Presse*, 18 May 1963, is quoted in Frank and Oliver, eds., *Quebec States Her Case*, 90. Evidence of sympathy for the early FLQ was the widespread sale of Savoie's *La Véritable Histoire du F.L.Q.*, which quickly sold over 13,000 copies.

45 Quoted in Morf, *Terror in Quebec*, 31.

46 Fournier, *FLQ*, 49–50.

47 For a discussion of *joual* and its significance in Quebec in the 1960s see Michele Martin, 'Modulating Popular Culture: Cultural Critics on Tremblay's *Les Belles-Soeurs*,' *Labour/Le Travail* 25 (Fall 2003): 109–135.

48 Fournier, *FLQ*, 43–9, 69–71; Mort, *Terror in Quebec*, 36–8; Vallières, *Héritiers de Papineau*, 73, 83–8; Reid, *Shouting Signpainters*, which has extensive discussion of Maheu and *Parti pris*, but for the initial reaction to *Parti pris* see esp. 28–33. Vallières provides brief commentary differentiating *Parti pris* and *Révolution québécois*, as well as discussion of the MLP, in *White Niggers of America*, 206–11. Note also 'New Socialist Journals Reflect Quebec Ferment,' and 'New Possibilities for Unity of Quebec Left,' *Workers Vanguard* (Toronto), December 1964; June 1965; and John Huot, 'The Left in the Sixties: The Development of Socialist Ideology and Organization,' *Radical America* 6 (September-October 1972): 53–67. On *Parti pris* see as well André Cardinal, 'Quebec and the Intellectuals,' in Dimitrios I. Roussopoulos, ed., *Quebec and Radical Social Change* (Montreal: Black Rose, 1974), 70–1; 'Parti Pris Analyzes Quebec Struggles, Projects Socialist Solution,' and 'Quebec's Parti Pris Separatist, Socialist,' *Workers Vanguard*, October 1964; November 1964. The best accessible introduction to *La Cognée* is R. Comeau, D. Cooper, and P. Vallières, *FLQ: Un project révolutionnaire – Lettres et écrits felquistes, 1963–1982* (Outrement: VLB Éditeur, 1990), which contains an early essay by Vallières, 'Le FLQ existe-t-il?' 40–4, as well as a statement on the MLP, 'Le MLP et la

lutte de libération nationale,' 49–53. The issue of Quebec's national libera-
tion had been a thorn in the side of the PSQ since 1964. See 'Unionists
Strengthen Leadership, Result of PSQ Internal Dispute,' *Workers Vanguard,*
March 1964.

49 On Schirm and other developments outlined above see François Schirm,
Personne ne voudra savoir ton nom (Montreal: Éditions Quinze, 1982); Morf,
Terror in Quebec, 39–72; Fournier, *FLQ,* 56–68; 'French Intellectuals Protest
Hanging of Quebec Separatists,' *Workers Vanguard,* Mid-September 1965.

50 Hubert Aquin, *Prochain Épisode* (Toronto: McClelland and Stewart, 1967), 9,
124–5. See also Reid, *Shouting Signpainters,* 169–73, 179–80; Fournier, *FLQ,*
61–3; Aquin, *Blocs erratiques* (Montreal: Typo, 1998).

51 Among the many accounts that provide background are: Robert F. Williams,
Negroes with Guns (New York: Marzani and Munsell, 1962); Malcolm X with
Alex Haley, *The Autobiography of Malcolm X* (New York: Grove Press, 1965);
George Breitman, ed., *Malcolm X Speaks: Selected Speeches and Statements* (New
York: Grove Press, 1966); Stokely Carmichael and Charles V. Hamilton,
Black Power (New York: Vintage, 1967); Eldridge Cleaver, *Soul on Ice* (New
York: Dell, 1968); Robert L. Allen, *Black Awakening in Capitalist America*
(Garden City, NY: Doubleday, 1970); Eugene Victor Wolfenstein, *The Victims
of Democracy: Malcolm X and the Black Revolution* (Berkeley: University of
California Press, 1981); James A. Geschwender, *Class, Race, and Worker Insur-
gency: The League of Revolutionary Black Workers* (Cambridge: Cambridge Uni-
versity Press, 1977); Robert Carl Cohen, *Black Crusader: A Biography of Robert
Franklin Williams* (Secaucus, NJ: Lyle Stuart, 1972); Timothy B. Tyson, *Radio
Free Dixie: Robert F. Williams and the Roots of Black Power* (Raleigh: University of
North Carolina Press, 2000); Stokely Carmichael and Ekwueme Michael
Thelwell, *Ready for Revolution: The Life and Struggles of Stokely Carmichael
(Kwame Ture)* (New York: Scribner, 2003). Sean Mills points out in unpub-
lished work that Pierre Vallières had attempted to bring Malcolm X to
Montreal to speak before the black militant was assassinated. See Sean Mills,
'From *'Nègres Blancs'* to Black Power: Race and Politics in Sixties Montreal,'
paper presented to the Canadian Historical Association Annual Meetings,
York University, May 2006, citing *Révolution québécoise* 1 (novembre 1964):
52–7.

52 Vallières, *Héritiers de Papineau,* 73–8; 'QFL Threatens General Strike,' and
'Quebec Labour Attracts New Forces,' and 'Parti Pris Turns to Quebec Workers,' *Workers Vanguard,* Mid-April 1964; Mid-January 1965; Mid-August 1965.

53 Comeau, Cooper, Vallières, eds., *FLQ: Projet révolutionnaire,* 40–4, reprints
the Hebert/Vallières article, 'Le FLQ existe-t-il?'; Vallières, *Héritiers de
Papineau,* 88–92; Fournier, *FLQ,* 75–80, 89–92; Morf, *Terror in Quebec,* 77–84;

Stewart, *FLQ: Seven Years of Terrorism*, 28–30. Vallières and the FLQ were at this point sending their propaganda to contacts in Montevideo, Havana, Santiago, Buenos Aires, London, Paris, New York, Chicago, Philadelphia, and Berkeley. Regush, *Pierre Vallières*, 112. Legault's suicide became a rallying cry for dissidents of all stripes because there was prior indication that he was despondent and likely to harm himself, but the authorities did little to prevent him from taking his own life. Many therefore claimed that the state was responsible for his death. The security state surveillance of the FLQ in Quebec was, at least in the early to mid-1960s, hampered by the RCMP's inability to effectively penetrate the francophone milieu. It had nevertheless begun as early as 1963. See John Sawatsky, *Men in the Shadows: The Shocking Truth about the RCMP Security Service* (Toronto: Doubleday, 1980); Steve Hewitt, *Spying 101: The RCMP's Secret Activities at Canadian Universities, 1917–1997* (Toronto: University of Toronto Press, 2002), 162.

54 See, for instance, Vallières, *White Niggers of America*, 71–76; Vallières, *Héritiers de Papineau*, 101–11; Fournier, *FLQ*, 108–9. Copies of *Monthly Review* had been seized in the raid on the camp of the Schirm group in 1964. See Reid, *Shouting Signpainters*, 271.

55 Quoted in Fournier, *FLQ*, 98–9. There is an extensive discussion of both Vallières and Gagnon in Morf, *Terror in Quebec*, 80–118, but the discussion is highly prejudiced against the ideas and personalities of the two men.

56 Vallières, *White Niggers of America*, 214; Marc Laurendeau, *Les Québécois violents: Un ouvrage sur les causes et la rentabilité de la violence d'inspiration politique au Québec* (Sillery, PQ: Boréal, 1974), 49, quoted in Denis Monière, *Ideologies in Quebec: The Historical Development* (Toronto: University of Toronto Press, 1981), 269.

57 Stewart, *FLQ: Seven Years of Terrorism*, 30–2; Regush, *Pierre Vallières*, 118; Morf, *Terrorism in Quebec*, 80–93; Fournier, *FLQ*, 89–104; Reid, *Shouting Signpainters*, 267–79; Vallières, *Héritiers de Papineau*, 96–9; Comeau, Cooper, Vallières, eds., *FLQ: Projet révolutionnaire*, 149–59, reprints 'Grève de la Faim pour la reconnaissance "du crime politique" au Québec (Canada) et du statut de "prisonniers politiques" pour tous les partisans du FLQ.' At the time of the summer arrests of many members of the Vallières-Gagnon cell, the two leaders were in New York, building ties to the revolutionary left and preparing to publicize the ongoing repression in Quebec. Hearing of the arrest of their comrades, they returned to Montreal, drafted a statement of solidarity, and then went back to the United States, where they were later arrested. See Regush, *Pierre Vallières*, 4.

58 Note Lapierre's review, 'Canada's Eldridge Cleaver and Malcolm X,' which concludes: 'The F.L.Q. is not a Quebec phenomenon but a universal one.'

Vallières provides detailed comment on various Black Power movements and spokesmen in *White Niggers of America* (71–4), discusses internationalism (223–4), and talks about being jailed in 'The Tombs' (9–10). See also Vallières, *Héritiers de Papineau*, 117–19. Carmichael sent Vallières and Gagnon a telegram of solidarity as their trials began in Canada (Regush, *Pierre Vallières*, 5), and on Williams and Boggs see Williams, *Negroes with Guns*; James Lee Boggs, *The American Revolution: Pages from a Negro Worker's Notebook* (New York: Monthly Review, 1963).

59 On Vallières's retrospective comment on his title see Pierre Vallières, 'Préface: Écrire Début,' *Nègres blancs d'Amérique* (Montreal: Typo, 1994), 31. Léandre Bergeron also stressed that the struggle in Quebec was fundamentally about the internationalism of the nationalist forces. See Bergeron, 'The Nationalism of Internationalism,' *Canadian Dimension* 4 (November-December 1966): 45. For an excellent and broad-ranging discussion that situates Vallières's understanding of *négritude* as the consequence of imperialism see Mills, 'The Empire Within,' 127–72. Here and in the following paragraphs I reference directly the 1971 McClelland and Stewart edition of *White Niggers of America* with page numbers provided in parentheses in the text.

60 The above two paragraphs draw on many sources. On the issue of violence in 1960s radicalism see, for instance, Jeremy Varon, *Bringing the War Home: The Weather Underground, the Red Army Faction, and Revolutionary Violence in the Sixties and Seventies* (Berkeley: University of California Press, 2004); and the contemporary Québécois statement, Daniel Latouche, 'Political Violence in Perspective,' *Canadian Dimension* 7 (December 1970): 42–5. For a brief, insightful commentary on *White Niggers of America* see Ian McKay, 'For a New Kind of History: A Reconnaissance of 100 Years of Canadian Socialism,' *Labour/Le Travail* 46 (Fall 2000): 115–22. More conventionally dismissive is Reid, *Shouting Signpainters*, 281–8. Gagnon's criticisms were voiced *after* Vallières did an about-face in 1971, arguing that the FLQ no longer represented the way forward for French Quebeckers, whom he urged to turn instead to the Parti Québécois. See Pierre Vallières, *L'Urgence de choisir* (Montreal: Éditions Parti pris, 1971); and for Gagnon's response, Regush, *Pierre Vallières*, 46; Henry Milner, 'Pierre Vallières and Quebec Politics,' in Roussopoulos, ed., *Quebec and Radical Social Change*, 169–70. *White Niggers* can be read as a text concerned overwhelmingly with manhood because of its gender-specific language, its counterposed presentation of the sympathetic Vallières father and the unsympathetic Vallières mother, the confessed tortured personal relations of Vallières with women, and the conscious identification of males with struggle and women with passive accommodation. In its language of gender, *White Niggers* may not be as offensive as some of the African-American commentary on women's place

in revolutionary struggle, associated with Stokely Carmichael, H. Rap Brown, and others, but it should also be noted that some black nationalist writers at least struggled to address their relations with women. See Cleaver, *Soul on Ice*. Vallières, *White Niggers of America*, 20, ends his introduction to the book with the declaration: 'Let us learn the pride of being men.' Note, as well, Léandre Bergeron, 'In Response to Mr. Mappin on Nationalism,' *Canadian Dimension* 4 (May–June 1967): 41: 'But amongst the Quebecois there is another movement: an ardent desire to change this relationship so that the Quebecois can attain **manhood** as new Quebecois while at the same time participating in the world-wide struggle against **supranationalism**.' In FLQ circles of the late 1960s, it was not uncommon to denounce Trudeau publicly by naming him a 'fairy' or a 'faggot.' This hypermasculinity thus coded the politics of the FLQ. It would take Vallières at least four years from the publication of *White Niggers* to begin to address women's liberation. In the aftermath of the October Crisis he went underground and apparently read Kate Millet's *Sexual Politics* and Germaine Greer's *The Female Eunuch*, and, according to Regush, *Pierre Vallières*, 137–8, patriarchy now loomed large on Vallières's horizon of what had to be confronted and defeated in revolutionary struggle. Such views were not unrelated to a later shift in Vallières's sexual orientation. See Pierre Vallières, *Homosexualité et subversion* (Montreal 1994). Although De Vault's *The Informer* can hardly be treated as an entirely credible source, it being the statement of a paid agent of state infiltration and provocation, note as well her comments on the FLQ and sexuality (218). See also the comments on gender and violence in Paula Ruth Gilbert, *Violence and the Female Imagination: Quebec's Women Writers Re-Frame Gender in North American Cultures* (Montreal and Kingston: McGill-Queen's University Press, 2006), 87–8.

61 For the above paragraphs see McKay, '100 Years of Canadian Socialism,' 115–22; Reid, *Shouting Signpainters*, 281–2. On the writing of *White Niggers of America* see, for instance, Vallières, *Héritiers de Papineau*, 121–9, and for commentary on Vallières see as well Ron Haggart and Aubrey E. Golden, *Rumours of War* (Toronto: New Press, 1971), 119–34. One measure of *White Niggers'* importance is the extent to which sections of the book were reprinted in magazines of the left: 'From Working Class Slum to the FLQ: The Life Story of Pierre Vallières,' *Canadian Dimension* 7 (December 1970): 37–41; 'White Niggers of America,' *Last Post* 1 (November 1970): 26–34.

62 'White Negroes,' *The Last Post* 1 (December 1969): 7–8; Fournier, *FLQ*, 104–11, 122–3.

63 Fournier, *FLQ*, 117–24, and for a broad treatment of RCMP countersubversion on Canadian campuses, including details relating to the FLQ, see Hewitt, *Spying 101*, 156–70.

64 Fournier, *FLQ,* 112–14; Arthur Young, 'Nationalism in Quebec,' *Workers Vanguard,* 16 October 1967; Reid, *Shouting Signpainters,* 307.

65 The literature on 1968, and on Paris in May 1968, is immense. See, as an introduction only, David Caute, *The Year of the Barricades: A Journey through 1968* (New York: Harper and Rowe, 1988). A useful source on the Parisian events is Bernard E. Brown, *The French Revolt: May 1968* (New York: McCaleb-Seiler, 1970), while those seeking a sense of the New Left character of the period can gain much from a reading of Gabriel Cohn-Bendit and Daniel Cohn-Bendit, *Obsolete Communism: The Left-Wing Alternative* (London: Penguin, 1969), and Raymond Williams, ed., *May Day Manifesto 1968* (Harmondsworth: Penguin, 1968). I draw in the above paragraph on Bryan D. Palmer, *Cultures of Darkness: Night Travels in the Histories of Transgression* (New York: Monthly Review, 2000), 303–6, quoting Aron.

66 Comeau, Cooper, and Vallières, eds., *FLQ: Un Projet révolutionnaire,* 169–78; Fournier, *FLQ,* 127.

67 The most coherent and complete statement on these developments is Fournier, *FLQ.* For a snapshot presentation see Bergeron, *History of Quebec: A Patriote's Handbook,* 221–4. On Pépin and the CNTU see the useful collection of documents in Black Rose Collective, *Quebec Labour: The Confederation of National Trade Unions Yesterday and Today* (Montreal: Black Rose, 1972), quote from Pépin, 83.

68 Carole de Vault, *The Informer,* 57–62; *Le Lundi de la Matraque, 24 juin 1968* (Montreal: Parti pris, 1968); Fournier, *FLQ,* 130–1, 175–6.

69 Morf, *Terror in Quebec,* 130–4; Fournier, *FLQ,* 134–5, 139–41. For an account of the origins and development of the MLT, with much on Germain Archambault, see Nick Auf der Maur, 'Lessons on Fighting City Hall: A Study of Montreal's "Mouvement de Libération du Taxi,"' *Last Post* 1 (April 1970): 19–25, portions of which appear in 'Cabbies and Mail Truck Drivers,' in Chodos and Auf der Maur, eds., *Quebec: A Chronicle,* 19–47.

70 'CEGEPs, Charlebois, Chartrand: The Quebec Revolution Now: An Interview with Dimitri Roussopoulos,' in W.E.Mann, ed., *Social and Cultural Change in Canada,* vol. 2 (Toronto: Copp Clark, 1970), 200–10.

71 Bergeron, *History of Quebec: A Patriot's Handbook,* 223; Peter Allnutt and Robert Chodos, 'Quebec into the Streets,' *Last Post* 1 (December 1969): 20–8; Fournier, *FLQ,* 138–41; Dennis Forsythe, 'The Black Writers Conference: Days to Remember,' and L.R. Butcher, 'The Congress of Black Writers,' in Dennis Forsythe, ed., *Let the Niggers Burn! The Sir George Williams University Affair and Its Caribbean Aftermath* (Montreal: Black Rose Books, 1971), 57–74; David Austin, 'All Roads Lead to Montreal: Black Power, the Caribbean, and the Black Radical Tradition in Canada,' *Journal of African American*

History 92 (Fall 2007): 516–39; Chandler Davis, 'Hemisfair at Montreal,' *Canadian Forum* 48 (January 1969): 219–20; Morf, *Terror in Quebec*, 141; Hewitt, *Spying 101*, 150–4, 165–8; Stewart, *FLQ: Seven Years of Terrorism*, 44. Alfie Roberts, *A View for Freedom: Alfie Roberts Speaks on the Caribbean, Cricket, Montreal, and C.L.R. James* (Montreal: Alfie Roberts Institute, 2005), presents a view of black Montreal and the importance of West Indian influences, commenting on UHURU and anti-colonialism on p. 80. For a more elaborate discussion of UHURU see Mills, 'The Empire Within,' 201–20.

72 Morf, *Terror in Quebec*, 135–40; Fournier, *FLQ,* 149–53; Stewart, *FLQ: Seven Years of Terrorism*, 45–6.

73 Fournier, *FLQ,* 153–8; Marlene Dixon, *Things Which Are Done in Secret* (Montreal: Black Rose, 1976), quote from McGill VP, 49; Stewart, *FLQ: Seven Years of Terrorism*, 47–9; Allnutt and Chodos, 'Quebec into the Streets,' 20–8; Stanley Gray, 'The Struggle for Quebec,' *Canadian Dimension* 6 (December–January 1969–70): 23–6; Hewitt, *Spying 101*, 164–5.

74 Stewart, *FLQ: Seven Years of Terrorism*, 49–52; Allnutt and Chodos, 'Quebec into the Streets,' 25–8; Fournier, *FLQ,* 159–71. Mills presents detailed discussions of both Bill 63 and the Québécois language struggle and the emergence of women's liberation in Montreal in Mills, 'The Empire Within,' 219–327.

75 The above paragraphs present an overview of events and developments covered in Fournier, *FLQ,* 159–201; Stewart, *FLQ: Seven Years of Terrorism*, 49–55; Morf, *Terror in Quebec*, 143–51. Accounts that shed light on RCMP surveillance and John Starnes include Sawatsky, *Men in the Shadows*; Hewitt, *Spying 101*; Ian Adams, *S: Portrait of a Spy* (Toronto: Virgo, 1981); Carol de Vault, *The Informer.* For background on the Weather Underground and the Black Panthers see Varon, *Bringing the War Home*; Ron Jacobs, *The Way the Wind Blew: A History of the Weather Underground* (New York: Verso, 1997); Bill Ayers, *Fugitive Days: A Memoir* (Boston: Beacon Press, 2001); Susan Braudy, *Family Circle: The Boudins and the Aristocracy of the Left* (New York: Knopf, 2003); Philip S. Foner, *The Black Panthers Speak* (Philadelphia: J.B. Lippincott, 1970); Bobby Seale, *Seize the Time: The Story of the Black Panther Party and Huey P. Newton* (New York: Random House, 1970); Cleaver, *Soul on Ice*; H. Rap Brown, *Die Nigger Die!* (New York: Dell, 1969); Kathleen Cleaver and George Katsiaficas, eds., *Liberation, Imagination, and the Black Panther Party: A New Look at the Panthers and Their Legacy* (New York: Routledge, 2001). On Students for a Democratic Society see, among many possible sources, Tom Hayden, *The Port Huron Statement: The Visionary Call of the 1960s Revolution* (New York: Thunder's Mouth Press, 2005); James Miller, *Democracy in the Streets: From Port Huron to the Siege of Chicago* (New York: Simon and Schuster, 1987).

76 Fournier, *FLQ*, 195–210; Nick Auf der Maur, 'Les Gars de Lapalme,' *Last Post* 2 (October 1971): 35–40; Jean-Claude LeClerc, 'FRAP: Awakening the Powerless,' *Canadian Dimension* 7 (December 1970): 46–51; Peter Allnutt, 'Front d'Action Politique,' *Last Post* 1 (November 1970): 19–21.

77 Fournier, *FLQ*, 213–28, which contains the full text of the FLQ Manifesto, which also appears in Dan Daniels, ed., *Quebec/Canada and the October Crisis* (Montreal: Black Rose, 1973), 115–21; *Canadian Dimension* 7 (December 1970): 34–5. For FLQ documents see, as well, 'Revolutionary Strategy,' *Our Generation* 7, no. 3 (1970): 69–75. On the police response, the preparations for which had been in place for some time, see Pierre Vallières, *The Assassination of Pierre Laporte: Behind the October '70 Scenario* (Toronto: James Lorimer, 1977), 21–83; 'The Santo Domingo of Pierre Elliott Trudeau,' *Last Post* 1 (November 1970): 4–14; 'War Declared on Quebec,' *Canadian Dimension* 7 (December 1970): 4–18, 78.

78 'The Santo Domingo of Pierre Elliott Trudeau,' 7; Fournier, *FLQ*, 228–34; the important statement in Charles Taylor, 'Behind the Kidnappings: Alienation Too Profound for the System to Contain,' *Canadian Dimension* 7 (December 1970): 26–9; and Guy Rocher writing in *Québec-Presse*, 25 October 1970, quoted in John Saywell, *Quebec 70: A Documentary Narrative* (Toronto: University of Toronto Press, 1971), 149.

79 See, for instance, the statement of Fernand Dumont, *The Vigil of Quebec* (Toronto: University of Toronto Press, 1974).

80 The above paragraphs draw on Fournier, *FLQ*, 237–58. There are, of course, numerous accounts of the October Crisis. Full narratives appear in Saywell, *Quebec 70*; Jean-Claude Trait, *FLQ 70: Offensive d'automne* (Montreal: Les Éditions de L'Homme, 1970); and for the seventeen crucial days in October, Stewart, *FLQ: Seven Years of Terrorism*, 57–79. A snapshot of events appears in Bergeron, *History of Quebec: A Patriote's Handbook*, 230–4. Among the studies useful to consult: Vallières, *Assassination of Pierre Laporte*; Daniels, ed., *Quebec/Canada and the October Crisis*; Claude Ryan, *Le Devoir et la Crise d'Octobre 70* (Ottawa: Lemeac, 1971); Gerard Pelletier, *The October Crisis* (Toronto: McClelland and Stewart, 1971); Smith, *Bleeding Hearts, Bleeding Country*; Jean-François Cardin, *Comprendre Octobre 1970: Le FLQ, la crise et le syndicalisme* (Montreal: Méridien, 1990).

81 Fournier, *FLQ*, 257–72; Saywell, ed., *Quebec 70*, 111–35; Peter Katadotis, 'FRAP, FLQ, and Drapeau: Or How to Rig an Election,' in Daniels, ed., *Quebec/Canada and the October Crisis*, 76–80; De Vault, *The Informer*; Stewart, *FLQ: Seven Years of Terrorism*, 81–4; Malcolm Lewis and Christine Sylvester, *Crisis in Quebec* (Toronto: Ontario Institute for Studies in Education, 1973), 35–58.

82 Chartrand is quoted in Fournier, *FLQ,* 280; De Vault, *The Informer,* Hewitt, *Spying 101,* 168.

83 The above paragraphs draw on Regush, *Pierre Vallières,* 41–50; Pierre Vallières, *Choose!* (Toronto: New Press, 1972), esp. 36, 108–9; Vallières, *Héritiers de Papineau,* 173–273; Fournier, *FLQ,* 301, 314–16. McKay's statement that 'the ambiguously social-democratic Parti Québécois would win the allegiance of most of the cohort of 1968' is both undocumented and troubling in the ease with which it sidesteps the extent to which many socialist and *indépendantiste* advocates of the 1960s went into Trotskyist, Maoist, and other political formations in the 1970s. See McKay, '100 Years of Canadian Socialism,' 121. For a further critique of Vallières in this period see Henry Milner, 'Pierre Vallières and Quebec Politics,' in Roussopoulos, ed., *Quebec and Radical Social Change,* 165–73. Vallières would eventually come to find the PQ not entirely to his liking, authoring a critique of sovereignty-association and the 1976–80 years when Lévesque governed Quebec. See Vallières, *The Impossible Quebec: Illusions of Sovereignty-Association* (Montreal: Black Rose, 1980). Gagnon and Vallières increasingly differed on many questions, including the use of violence and the primacy of the national question. For Gagnon's evolving views see the collection of statements in 'The Political Journey of Charles Gagnon,' Socialist History Project, http://socialisthistory.ca/Remember/Profiles/GagnonCharles (accessed 20 December 2006).

84 Nick Auf der Maur, 'Labour Builds a Common Front,' *Last Post* 2 (December-January 1971–2): 8–18; Auf der Mar, 'The May Revolt Shakes Quebec,' and Malcolm Reid, 'Sept-Iles Revolt,' *Last Post* 2 (July 1972): 10–23, 26–8; also in Chodos and Auf der Maur, *Quebec: A Chronicle;* and the articles on Quebec's labour revolt gathered together in *Radical America* 6 (September-October 1972), some of which are reprinted from *Last Post.* See, as well, Daniel Drache, ed., *Quebec – Only the Beginning: The Manifestoes of the Common Front* (Toronto: New Press, 1972); Black Rose Books Editorial Collective, *Quebec Labour: The Confederation of National Trade Unions Yesterday and Today* (Montreal: Black Rose, 1975); Cardin, *Comprendre Octobre 1970,* for insight into the increasingly radical thought and militancy of Québécois syndicalism in this period. There is discussion of these events, finally, in Mills, 'The Empire Within,' 361–93.

85 Leo Panitch and Donald Swartz, *The Assault on Trade Union Freedoms: From Consent to Coercion Revisited* (Toronto: Garamond, 1988); Ralph Surette, 'The Year of the Manifestos,' *Last Post* 2 (July 1972): 28–31; Vallières, *Impossible Quebec.*

86 The sources that could be cited outlining such developments are numerous. Useful introductions to the changing contours of late capitalism's political

economy include: Ernest Mandel, *Late Capitalism* (London: Verso, 1978); David Harvey, *The Condition of Postmodernity: An Inquiry into the Origins of Cultural Change* (Oxford: Blackwell, 1989); Gary Teeple, *Globalization and the Decline of Social Reform: Into the Twenty-First Century* (Aurora, ON: Garamond, 2000); Henry Veltmeyer and James Petras, *Globalization Unmasked: Imperialism in the 21st Century* (Halifax: Fernwood, 2001); David Harvey, *A Brief History of Neoliberalism* (Oxford: Oxford University Press, 2005). For an incisive comment on the ideological terminus of this period see Perry Anderson, 'The Ends of History,' in Anderson, *A Zone of Engagement* (London: Verso, 1992), 279–375, which addresses a number of texts, including Francis Fukuyama, *The Ends of History and the Last Man* (New York: Free Press, 1992).

87 'Qu'est-ce qui le FLQ?' *Canadian Dimension* 7 (December 1970): 30–3. Vallières's *Choose!* is actually quite insightful in its discussion of the FLQ, especially if one is able to strip away the advocacy of the Parti Québécois. Also note McKay, '100 Years of Canadian Socialism,' 113–22.

88 Fournier, *FLQ,* 192. See also Sean Mills, 'From *"Nègres blancs"* to Black Power: Race and Politics in Sixties Montreal,' unpublished paper presented to the Canadian Historical Association Meetings, York University, Toronto, May 2006, citing Edmund Michael, 'Red Power in Canada,' *UHURU* 1 (29 September 1969). Vallières would later allude to the oppression of Inuit and Aboriginal peoples, but the reference was hardly well developed. See Vallières, *Choose!* 53.

10: The 'Discovery' of the 'Indian'

1 As an introduction to the rise of Red Power in Canada and the United States see the useful overview in Paul Chaat Smith and Robert Allen Warrior, *Like a Hurricane: The Indian Movement from Alcatraz to Wounded Knee* (New York: New Press, 1996).

2 Gerald R. [Taiaiake] Alfred, *Heeding the Voices of Our Ancestors: Kahnawake Mohawk Politics and the Rise of Native Nationalism* (Don Mills, ON: Oxford University Press, 1995); Taiaiake Alfred, *Peace, Power, Righteousness: An Indigenous Manifesto* (Don Mills, ON: Oxford University Press, 1999); Constance Backhouse, *Colour-Coded: A Legal History of Racism in Canada, 1900–1950* (Toronto: University of Toronto Press, 1999), 18–131; Ward Churchill, *Struggle for the Land: Indigenous Resistance to Genocide, Ecocide, and Expropriation in Contemporary North America* (Toronto: Between the Lines, 1992); M. Annette Jaimes, ed., *The State of Native America: Genocide, Colonization, and Resistance* (Boston: South End Press, 1992).

3 See, for instance, the collected essays, many of them written in the immediate aftermath of the rise of Red Power, in Vine Deloria, Jr, *For This Land: Writings*

on Religion in America (New York: Routledge, 1999); James Treat, *Around the Sacred Fire: Native Religious Activism in the Red Power Era – A Narrative Map of the Indian Ecumenical Conference* (New York: Palgrave Macmillan, 2003).

4 See Jeannette C. Armstrong, *Slash* (Penticton, BC: Theytus Books, 1990); Lee Maracle, *Bobbi Lee: Indian Rebel* (Toronto: Women's Press, 1990); Eden Robinson, *Monkey Beach* (Toronto: Knopf, 2000). See, as well, the collections of Native literature, Daniel David Moses and Terry Goldie, eds., *An Anthology of Canadian Native Literature in English* (Don Mills, ON: Oxford University Press, 2005), which contains Armstrong's essay, 'The Disempowerment of First North American Native Peoples and Empowerment through Their Writing,' 242–5; Joel T. Maki, *Let the Drums Be Your Heart: New Native Voices* (Vancouver and Toronto: Douglas and McIntyre, 1996).

5 Armstrong, *Slash*, 180–1. I have fused different paragraphs into one block statement.

6 Maracle, *Bobbi Lee*, esp 158–9, 208–9. Maracle's account presents a sustained discussion of the contacts between Red Power advocates and the ultra left in the 1960s. For a suggestion that it perhaps falls prey to some embellishment see Bryan D. Palmer, ed., *A Communist Life: Jack Scott and the Canadian Workers Movement, 1927–1985* (St John's, NF: CCLH, 1989), 171–2. I cite the accessible Lee Maracle 1990 edition of Bobbi Lee's life story, but it should not be forgotten that this book first appeared in 1975: Don Barnett and Rick Sterling, eds., *Bobbi Lee: Indian Rebel – Struggles of a Native Canadian Woman* (Richmond, BC: Liberation Support Movement Information Center, 1975).

7 See, for instance, Eric Wolf, *Europe and the People without History* (Berkeley: University of California Press, 1982).

8 For two British Columbia studies of insight see Hugh Brody, *Maps and Dreams: Indians and the British Columbia Frontier* (Harmondsworth: Penguin, 1983); Cole Harris, *Making Native Space: Colonialism, Resistance, and Reserves in British Columbia* (Vancouver: UBC Press, 2002).

9 An extensive literature exists. As a sample only, in which the experience of the North American land mass currently known as Canada is privileged, see E.E. Rich, 'Trade Habits and Economic Motivation among the Indians of North America,' *Canadian Journal of Economic and Political Science* 26 (February 1960): 35–53; L.F.S. Upton, 'The Extermination of the Beothuks of Newfoundland,' *Canadian Historical Review* 48 (June 1977): 133–53; A.G. Bailey, *The Conflict of European and Eastern Algonkian Cultures, 1504–1700* (Toronto: University of Toronto Press, 1969); Cornelius Jaenen, *Friend and Foe: Aspects of French-Amerindian Cultural Contact in the Sixteenth and Seventeenth Centuries* (Toronto: McClelland and Stewart, 1976); Bruce Trigger, *The Children of the Aataentsic: A History of the Huron People to 1660* (Montreal and Kingston: McGill-Queen's University Press, 1976); Calvin Martin, 'The

European Impact on the Culture of a Northeastern Algonquian Tribe: An Ecological Interpretation,' *William and Mary Quarterly* 31 (1974): 3–26; Karl H. Schlesier, 'Epidemics and Indian Middlemen: Rethinking the Wars of the Iroquois, 1609–1653,' *Ethnohistory* 23 (1976): 129–45; John L. Tobias, 'Canada's Subjugation of the Plains Cree, 1879–1885,' *Canadian Historical Review* 64 (December 1983): 519–48; Olive Patricia Dickason, *The Myth of the Savage and the Beginnings of French Colonialism in the Americas* (Edmonton: University of Alberta Press, 1984); Hugh Brody, *The People's Land: Inuit, Whites and the Eastern Arctic* (Vancouver: Douglas and McIntyre, 1991); Toby Morantz, *The White Man's Gonna Getcha: The Colonial Challenge to the Crees in Quebec* (Montreal and Kingston: McGill-Queen's University Press, 2002). Broad-ranging studies also include Ralph K. Andrist, *The Long Death: The Last Days of the Plains Indians* (New York: Collier, 1964); Ronald Wright, *Stolen Continents: The 'New World' through Indian Eyes* (Toronto: Penguin Books, 1992); Alfred W. Crosby, Jr, *The Columbia Exchange: Biological and Cultural Consequences of 1492* (Westport, CT: Greenwood, 1972); Crosby, Jr, *Ecological Imperialism: The Biological Expansion of Europe, 900–1900* (Cambridge: Cambridge University Press, 1986); William Cronon, *Changes in the Land: Indians, Colonists and the Ecology of New England* (New York: Hill and Wang, 1983); Richard Drinnon, *Facing West: The Metaphysics of Indian-Hating and Empire Building* (Minneapolis: University of Minnesota Press, 1980); Eduardo Galeano, *Open Veins of Latin America: Five Centuries of the Pillage of a Continent* (New York: Monthly Review Press, 1973).

10　On primitive accumulation see Karl Marx, *Capital*, vol. 1 (New York: International, 1967), 713–74; Michael Perelman, *The Invention of Capitalism: Classical Political Economy and the Secret of Primitive Accumulation* (Durham, NC: Duke University Press, 2000); Stephan Hymer, 'Robinson Crusoe and Primitive Accumulation,' *Monthly Review* 23 (September 1971): 11–36; Maurice Dobb, *Studies in the Development of Capitalism* (New York: International, 1947), 177–254, and for the conceptualization's application to Canadian Aboriginal experience, Vic Satzewich and Terry Wotherspoon, *First Nations: Race, Class, and Gender Relations* Scarborough, ON: Nelson, 1993), 18–28; Stanley Ryerson, *The Founding of Canada: Beginnings to 1815* (Toronto: Progress Books, 1960), 241. See also Michael Paul Rogin, *Fathers and Children: Andrew Jackson and the Subjugation of the American Indian* (New York: Vintage, 1976), 165–205.

11　Population estimates of Aboriginal decline are highly politicized and have varied over time. See Lenore A. Stiffarm and Phil Lane, Jr, 'The Demography of Native North America: A Question of American Indian Survival,' in Jaimes, ed., *State of Native America*, 23–54; Carole M. Gentry and Donald A.

Grinde, Jr, eds., *The Unheard Voices: American Indian Responses to the Columbian Quincentenary, 1492–1992* (Los Angeles: American Indian Studies Center, University of California, 1994), especially Gregory R. Campbell, 'The Politics of Counting: Critical Questions on the Depopulation Question of Native North America,' 101–7; Ward Churchill, 'American Indian Lands: The Native Ethic Amid Resource Development,' in Churchill, *Struggle for the Land*, 15–32; Churchill, *A Little Matter of Genocide: Holocaust Denial in the Americas, 1492 to the Present* (Winnipeg: Arbeiter Ring, 1998), esp. 1, 131–7; Russell Thornton, *American Indian Holocaust and Survival: A Population History since 1492* (Norman and London: Oklahoma University Press, 1987); David E. Stannard, *American Holocaust: The Conquest of the New World* (New York: Oxford University Press, 1992); William M. Denevan, ed., *The Native Population of the Americas in 1492* (Madison: University of Wisconsin Press, 1992); Alan C. Cairns, *Citizens Plus: Aboriginal Peoples and the Canadian State* (Vancouver: UBC Press, 2000), 35.

12 On the residential schools see J.R. Miller, *Shingwauk's Vision: A History of Native Residential Schools* (Toronto: University of Toronto Press, 1996); John S. Milloy, *A National Crime: The Canadian Government and the Residential School System, 1879 to 1986* (Winnipeg: University of Manitoba Press, 1999); Geoffrey York, *The Dispossessed: Life and Death in Native Canada* (London: Vintage UK), 22–53.

13 For one contemporary discussion see C.S. Brant, 'Canadians with Nothing to Celebrate: The Eskimos. Lessons from Greenland,' *Saturday Night*, June 1967, 29–31. See as well Peter J. Usher, *The Bankslanders: Economy and Ecology of a Frontier Trapping Community*, vol. 1, *History*; vol. 2, *Economy and Ecology*; and vol. 3, *The Community* (Ottawa: Information Canada, 1970).

14 In this chapter I use the terms Aboriginal, Native, and Indigenous interchangeably to refer to all peoples who have, for various reasons and at various times, been constructed by white colonizers and their states as human categories of the colonization process, labelling indigeneity. These categories, out of which the notion of status Indians emerged, are not only racialized but gendered, governed as they are by inherent prejudices against women and patriarchal assumptions about their place in social relations of property and identity. None of this is premised on the lived experience of a variety of Native peoples, let alone the co-mingling of colonizers and Indigenous people that resulted in another social construction, that of Métis. At this point, state-defined classifications of Native peoples have created difference and confusion, leading to divisions that of course serve the colonizing state and its interests. See Michael Kew, 'Making Indians,' in Rennie Warburton and David Coburn, eds., *Workers, Capital, and the State in British Columbia*

(Vancouver: UBC Press, 1988), 24–34; Bonita Lawrence, *'Real' Indians and Others: Mixed-Blood Urban Native Peoples and Indigenous Nationhood* (Vancouver: UBC Press, 2004); and for a brief discussion of the doubly disadvantaged plight of Native women, Canada, *Report of the Royal Commission on Aboriginal Peoples*, vol. 1, *Looking Forward, Looking Back* (Ottawa: Minister of Supply and Services, 1996), 300–7. There is a discussion of terminology in Alfred, *Peace, Power, Righteousness*, xxvi, that stakes out different ground, but I do not believe it is necessarily counterposed to the above.

15 For insights into primitive reductionism see Gerald M. Sider, *Lumbee Indian Histories: Race, Ethnicity, and Indian Identity in the Southern United States* (New York: Cambridge University Press, 1993), while the social construction of representations of Native peoples is dealt with in Daniel Francis, *The Imaginary Indian: The Image of the Indian in Canadian Culture* (Vancouver: Arsenal Pulp Press, 1992).

16 Note the recent statement in Gail D. MacLeitch, '"Red" Labor: Iroquois Participation in the Atlantic Economy,' *Labor: Studies in Working-Class History of the Americas* 1 (Winter 2004): 69–90.

17 This produced constraints related to agriculture as well. See Sarah Carter, *Lost Harvests: Prairie Indian Reserve Farmers and Government Policy* (Montreal and Kingston: McGill-Queen's University Press, 1990).

18 Robin Jarvis Brownlee, '"Living the same as the white people": Mohawk and Anishinabe Women's Labour in Southern Ontario, 1920–1940,' *Labour/Le Travail* 61 (Spring 2008): 41–68.

19 Quoted in Brownlee, 'Living the same as the white people,' 43.

20 See, for instance, Hugh Shewell, *'Enough to Keep Them Alive': Indian Welfare in Canada, 1873–1965* (Toronto: University of Toronto Press, 2004); *Poverty in Canada: Report of the Special Senate Committee on Poverty* (Ottawa: Information Canada, 1971), 34–5; Ian Adams et al., *The Real Poverty Report* (Edmonton: Hurtig, 1971), 68–74.

21 Among important statements on Aboriginal labour see Rolf Knight, *Indians at Work: An Informal History of Native Indian Labour in British Columbia* (Vancouver: New Star Books, 1978); Fred Wien, *Rebuilding the Economic Base of Indian Communities: The Mic Mac in Nova Scotia* (Montreal: Institute for Research on Public Policy, 1986); Frank Tough, *As Their Natural Resources Fail: Native Peoples and the Economic History of Northern Manitoba, 1870–1930* (Vancouver: UBC Press, 1996); John Lutz, 'After the Fur Trade: The Aboriginal Labouring Classes of British Columbia, 1849–1890,' *Journal of the Canadian Historical Association* 3, n.s. (1992): 69–94; Lutz, 'Work, Sex, and Death on the Great Thoroughfare: Annual Migrations of "Canadian Indians" to the American Pacific Northwest,' in John M. Findlay and Ken S. Coates, eds.,

Parallel Destinies: Canadian–American Relations West of the Rockies (Seattle: University of Washington Press, 2002), 80–103; Lutz, 'Gender and Work in Lekwammen Families, 1843–1970,' in Kathryn M. McPherson, Cecilia Louise Morgan, and Nancy Forestell, eds., *Gendered Pasts: Historical Essays in Femininity and Masculinity in Canada* (Don Mills, ON: Oxford University Press, 1999), 80–105; Steven High, 'Native Wage Labour and Independent Production During the "Era of Irrelevance,"' *Labour/Le Travail* 37 (Spring 1996): 243–64; Andrew Parnaby, '"The Best Men That Ever Worked the Lumber": Aboriginal Longshoremen on Burrard Inlet, BC, 1863–1939,' *Canadian Historical Review* 87 (2006): 53–71; Carol Williams, 'Between Doorstep Barter Economy and Industrial Wages: Mobility and Adaptability of Coast Salish Female Laborers in Coastal British Columbia, 1858–1890,' in Mark B. Spencer and Lucretia Scoufos, eds., *Native Being, Being Native: I dentity and Difference* (Durant: Southeastern Oklahoma State University Press, 2005), 16–27; Satzewich and Witherspoon, *First Nations*, esp. 450–2; Ron Laliberte and Vic Satzewich, 'Native Migrant Labour in the Southern Alberta Sugar-beet Industry: Coercion and Paternalism in the Recruitment of Labour,' *Canadian Review of Sociology and Anthropology* 26 (February 1999): 65–85. See also Colleen M. O'Neill, *Working the Navajo Way: Labor and Culture in the Twentieth Century* (Lawrence: University Press of Kansas, 2005); Paige Raibmon, *Authentic Indians: Episodes of Encounter from the Late Nineteenth-Century Northwest Coast* (Durham, NC: Duke University Press, 2006).

22 For an understated summary of much of this history of restriction see the discussion of the oppressive measures of the Indian Act in Canada, *Report of the Royal Commission on Aboriginal Peoples*, vol. 1, *Looking Forward, Looking Back*, esp. 281–307.

23 The literature on Indian acts, treaties, and the ideology of law and paternalist bureaucratic governance in Canadian Native–white relations is overwhelming. For a sampling of statements relevant to the above paragraphs see *Canadian Indian Treaties and Surrenders, from 1680–1890 in Two Volumes* (Ottawa: Brown, Chamberlin, 1891); *Canada Indian Treaties and Surrenders*, vol. 3 (Ottawa: C.H. Parmelee, 1912); Kew, 'Making Indians,' in Warburton and Coburn, eds., *Workers, Capital, and the State in British Columbia*, 24–34; Donald Purich, *Our Land: Native Rights in Canada* (Toronto: James Lorimer, 1986); Peter A. Cumming and Neil H. Mickenberg, eds., *Native Rights in Canada* (Toronto: Indian-Eskimo Association of Canada, 1980); E. Brian Titley, *A Narrow Vision: Duncan Campbell Scott and the Administration of Indian Affairs in Canada* (Vancouver: UBC Press, 1968); Douglas Cole and Ira Chaikin, *An Iron Hand upon the People: The Law against the Potlatch on the Northwest Coast* (Vancouver: Douglas and McIntyre, 1990); Dianne Newell, *Tangled*

Webs of History: Indians and the Law in Canada's Pacific Coast Fisheries (Toronto: University of Toronto Press, 1993); Bruce Clark, *Native Liberty, Crown Sovereignty: The Existing Aboriginal Right of Self-Government in Canada* (Montreal: McGill-Queen's University Press, 1990); Noel Dyck, *What Is the Indian 'Problem': Tutelage and Resistance in Canadian Indian Administration* (St John's, NF: Institute for Social and Economic Research, 1993); Backhouse, *Colour-Coded*, 18–131; Mary-Ellen Kelm, *Colonizing Bodies: Aboriginal Health and Healing in British Columbia, 1900–1950* (Vancouver: UBC Press, 1998); Robin J. Brownlee, *Fatherly Eye: Indian Agents, Government Power, and Aboriginal Resistance in Ontario, 1918–1939* (Don Mills, ON: Oxford University Press, 2003); Vic Satzewich, 'Indian Agents and the "Indian Problem" in Canada in 1946: Reconsidering the Theory of Coercive Tutelage,' *Canadian Journal of Native Studies* 17 (1997): 227–57.

24 The most influential statement was Robin Fisher, *Contact and Conflict: Indian–White Relations in British Columbia, 1774–1890* (Vancouver: UBC Press, 1977).

25 See, for instance, High, 'Native Wage Labour and Independent Production'; J.R. Miller, 'Owen Glendower, Hotspur, and Canadian Indian Policy,' in Miller, ed., *Sweet Promises: A Reader on Indian–White Relations in Canada* (Toronto: University of Toronto Press, 1991), 340–1.

26 Robin Brownlee and Mary-Ellen Kelm, 'Desperately Seeking Absolution: Native Agency as Colonialist Alibi,' *Canadian Historical Review* 75 (September 1994): 545.

27 See for instance Yale D. Belanger, 'Seeking a Seat at the Table: A Brief History of Indian Political Organizing in Canada, 1870–1951,' PhD dissertation, Trent University, 2006; Yale D. Belanger and David Newhouse, 'Emerging from the Shadows: The Pursuit of Aboriginal Self-Government to Promote Aboriginal Well-Being,' *Journal of Native Studies* 24 (2004): 129–222.

28 Within sectors of scholarship this condemnatory legacy of the 1960s certainly lives, especially among more radical scholarship of Indigenous peoples. See, for instance, Howard Adams, *A Tortured People: The Politics of Colonialism* (Penticton, BC: Theytus Books, 1995); Kiera L. Ladner, 'Negotiated Inferiority: The Royal Commission on Aboriginal People's Vision of a Renewed Relationship,' *American Review of Canadian Studies* 31 (Spring/ and Summer 2001): 241–64; Ladner, 'Rethinking the Past, Present, and Future of Aboriginal Governance,' in J. Brodie and L. Trimble, eds., *Reinventing Canada* (Toronto: Canadian Scholars Press, 2003). See as well Ward Churchill, *A Little Matter of Genocide*; Elizabeth Cook-Lynn, *Anti-Indianism in America: A Voice from Tatekeya's Earth* (Chicago: University of Illinois Press, 2001); Patricia Monture-Angus, *Journeying Forward: Dreaming First Nations'*

Independence (Halifax: Fernwood, 1997). But note Kerry Abel, 'Tangled, Lost and Bitter? Current Directions in the Writing of Native History,' *Acadiensis* 36 (Autumn 1996): 92–101.

29 Alfred, *Heeding the Voices of Our Ancestors*, esp. 1, 8, 77–82; Alfred, *Peace, Power, Righteousness*, 1–7; William N. Fenton and Elizabeth Tooker, 'Mohawk,' in Bruce Trigger, ed., *Handbook of North American Indians* (Washington, DC: Smithsonian, 1978), 466–80; Bruce E. Johansen, *Forgotten Founders: How the American Indian Helped Shape Democracy* (Boston: Harvard Commons Press, 1982).

30 See, for instance, Blair Stonechild and Bill Waiser, *Loyal Till Death: Indians and the North-West Rebellion* (Calgary: Fifth House, 1997).

31 Belanger, 'A Seat at the Table'; Peter Kulchyski, '"A Considerable Unrest": F.O. Loft and the League of Indians,' *Native Studies Review* 4 (1988): 95–117; E. Palmer Patterson, 'Andrew Paull and the Early History of British Columbia's Indian Organizations,' in Ian L.B. Getty and Donald B. Smith, eds., *'One Century Later': Western Canadian Reserve Indians Since Treaty 7* (Vancouver: UBC Press, 1978), 43–54; Hugh Shewell, 'Jules Sioui and Indian Political Radicalism in Canada, 1943–1944,' *Journal of Canadian Studies* 34 (Autumn 1999): 211–42; R. Scott Sheffield, *The Red Man's on the Warpath: The Image of the 'Indian' and the Second World War* (Vancouver: UBC Press, 2004); Benjamin Isitt, 'Working-Class Agency, the Cold War, and the Rise of a New Left: Political Change in British Columbia, 1948–1972,' preliminary draft of PhD dissertation, University of New Brunswick, 2007, 282–93.

32 See Murray Dobbin, *The One-and-a-Half Men: The Story of Jim Brady and Malcolm Norris, Métis Patriots of the Twentieth Century* (Vancouver: New Star, 1981).

33 Dobbin, *One-and-a-Half Men*, 183–200; Alfred, *Heeding the Voices of Our Ancestors*, esp. 67, 131, 158–61. In a later study, Alfred accents the factional fractures, dysfunctional debate, and violently self-destructive politics of the 1960s, which he attributes to colonization and control by whites. Yet the period was also 'a revolutionary time,' he acknowledges, and one that laid the basis for future developments. See *Peace, Power, Righteousness*, 6.

34 There are of course innumerable 'discoveries' of the 'Indian' predating the 1960s, and they might include those who early embraced the rights and struggles of Indians and Métis, such as William Henry Jackson/Honoré Joseph Jaxon, Helen Hunt Jackson, or the BC socialist James A. Teit; those who took on an Aboriginal identity, among the more famous being Grey Owl/Archie Belaney and Chief Buffalo Child Long Lance/Sylvester Long; or the response to literary figures such as E. Pauline Johnson (Tekahionwake). And white fascination with Aboriginal peoples, including the Inuit, is longstanding. Nonetheless, the particular cauldron of the 1960s produced a

politics of 'discovery' that was perhaps unique, especially in terms of the volatile mix of Aboriginal radicalism, state initiatives, and popular consciousness of Indigenous subordination. On the complexities of such continuities, see, among many writings: Donald B. Smith, 'Honoré Joseph Jaxon: A Lifelong Friend of Aboriginal Canada,' in Celia Haig-Brown and David A. Nock, eds., *With Good Intentions: Euro-Canadian and Aboriginal Relations in Colonial Canada* (Vancouver: UBC Press, 2006), 229–57; Helen Hunt Jackson, *A Century of Dishonor: The Early Crusade for Indian Reform*, ed. Andrew F. Rollo (New York: Harper, 1965; original 1881); Peter Campbell, '"Not as a White Man, Nor as a Sojourner": James A. Teit and the Fight for Native Rights in British Columbia, 1884–1922,' *Left History* 2 (1994): 37–57; Donald B. Smith, *From the Land of Shadows: The Making of Grey Owl* (Saskatoon: Western Producer Books, 1990); Smith, *Chief Buffalo Child Long Lance: The Glorious Imposter* (Red Deer, AB: Red Deer Press, 1999); Carole Gerson and Veronica Strong-Boag, *Paddling Her Own Canoe: The Times and Texts of E. Pauline Johnson (Tekahionwake)* (Toronto: University of Toronto Press, 2000); Julian W. Bilby, *Among Unknown Eskimo: An Account of Twelve Years Intimate Relations with the Primitive Eskimo of Ice-Bound Baffin Land, with a Description of Their Ways of Living, Hunting Customs and Beliefs* (Philadelphia: J.B. Lippincott, 1923). Peter Usher's *The Bankslanders*, published as a government report of the Department of Indian Affairs and Northern Development, indicated how the 1960s were different, striking as they did a new note of urgency with respect to the need to redress Aboriginal grievance.

35 Fred Gudmundson, 'Managing Our Own Lives: An Interview with George Erasamus,' *Canadian Dimension* 18 (October-November 1984): 27.

36 A succinct introduction is provided in Howard Adams, *A Tortured People: The Politics of Colonization* (Penticton, BC: Theytus Books, 1995), 75–92. On the concept of the Fourth World see George Manuel and Michael Posluns, 'The Fourth World,' in Robin Fisher and Kenneth Coates, eds., *Out of the Background: Readings on Native History* (Toronto: Copp Clark, 1988), 285–91, drawn from Manuel and Posluns, *The Fourth World: An Indian Reality* (Toronto: Collier-Macmillan, 1964). See also Tony Hall, *The American Empire and the Fourth World: The Bowl with One Spoon* (Montreal and Kingston: McGill-Queen's University Press, 2004).

37 Satzewich and Wotherspoon, *First Nations*, 229.

38 See Peter Kulchyski, '40 Years in Indian Country,' *Canadian Dimension* 37 (November-December 2003): 33–4; Philip Resnick, *The European Roots of Canadian Identity* (Peterborough, ON: Broadview, 2005), 34. See also J.W. Warnock, 'Red Power: An Interview with Howard Adams,' *Canadian Dimension* 5 (April-May 1968): 21–3.

39 Diamond Jenness, *The Indians of Canada* (Toronto: University of Toronto Press, 1977; original 1932). Jenness was articulating an old assumption embedded in the march of European empire. See Patrick Brantlinger, *Dark Vanishings: Discourse on the Extinction of Primitive Races, 1800–1930* (Ithaca, NY: Cornell University Press, 2003).

40 H.B. Hawthorn, ed., *A Survey of the Contemporary Indians of Canada: A Report on Economic, Political, Educational Needs and Policies,* vol. 1 (Ottawa: Indian Affairs Branch, 1966), 45.

41 Hawthorn, *Survey of the Contemporary Indians,* 45–6; Dick Fidler, *Red Power in Canada* (Toronto: Vanguard Publications, 1970), 3–4; Heather Robertson, *Reservations Are for Indians* (Toronto: James, Lewis, and Samuel, 1970), 27.

42 Robertson, *Reservations Are for Indians,* 15, 41, 138–9, 179, 181. For an update, in which it is difficult to see marked betterment, see York, *The Dispossessed,* 54–87. For reference to Manchester in the 1840s and contemporary shanty towns in the underdeveloped world see Frederick Engels, *The Condition of the Working Class in England in 1844* (London: George Allen and Unwin, 1943; original 1887); Mike Davis, *Planet of Slums* (New York: Verso, 2006).

43 As an example only note the case of *Guerin v. The Queen* in which it was revealed that in 1957 an Indian agent and former Anglican minister and principal of a residential school, Frank Anfield, had misrepresented the terms of a lease entered into by the Aboriginal Musqueam Band Council and the Shaughnessy Golf and Country Club involving 162 acres of reserve land. Anfield also pressured a government appraiser of the land to lower its stated value. In 1979 Chief Delbert Guerin and the Musqueam initially won compensation of $10 million plus post-judgment interest, but were forced by the federal government into the Federal Court of Appeal and, following its decision to overturn the original finding, into the Supreme Court of Canada. In 1984 Guerin and the Musqueam finally prevailed, at least on the legal front. See James Reynolds, *A Breach of Duty: Fiduciary Obligations and Aboriginal People* (Saskatoon: Purich Publishers, 2005). For an account of other legal struggles to redress significant material dispossession see Patricia Monture-Angus, *Journeying Forward: Dreaming First Nations' Independence* (Halifax: Fernwood, 1999).

44 Milloy, *A National Crime,* 211–15; Miller, *Shingwauk's Vision,* 400.

45 George Caldwell, *Indian Residential School Study* (Ottawa: Canadian Welfare Council for Department of Indian Affairs and Northern Development, 1967); Caldwell, 'An Island between Two Cultures: The Residential Indian School,' *Canadian Welfare* 43 (July-August 1967): 12–17; Beatrice Culleton, *In Search of April Raintree* (Winnipeg: Pemmican Publications, 1983); Maria Campbell, *Halfbreed* (Toronto: Seal, 1973).

46 Aboriginal Healing Foundation, *Final Report of the Aboriginal Healing Founda-tion*, vol. 1, *A Healing Journey: Reclaiming Wellness*; vol. 2, *Measuring Progress: Program Evaluation*; vol. 3, *Healing Practices in Aboriginal Communities* (Ottawa: Aboriginal Healing Foundation, 2006); Canada, *Report of the Royal Commis-sion on Aboriginal Peoples*, 1: 333–409.

47 The tragedy of the Grassy Narrows ordeal is vividly conveyed in Anastasia M. Shkilnyk, *A Poison Stronger Than Love: The Destruction of an Ojibwa Community* (New Haven and London: Yale University Press, 1985).

48 See for instance Frank James Testor and Peter Kulchyski, *Tammarniit (Mis-takes): Inuit Relocation in the Eastern Arctic, 1939–1963* (Vancouver: UBC Press, 1994); Ila Bussidor and Ustun Bilgen-Reinart, *Night Spirits: The Story of the Relocation of the Sayisi Dene* (Winnipeg: University of Manitoba Press, 1997).

49 For a brief overview only see Canada, *Report of the Royal Commission on Aborig-inal Peoples*, 1: 411–544.

50 Fidler, *Red Power*, 4; Patrick Johnston, *Native Children and the Child Welfare System* (Toronto: Lorimer, 1983), 23; Jeremy Hull, *Natives in a Class Society* (Saskatoon: One Sky, 1981), 22; Satzewich and Wotherspoon, *First Nations*, 90; Raymond Breton and Gail Grant, eds., *The Dynamics of Government Pro-grams for Urban Indians in the Prairie Provinces* (Montreal: Institute for Research on Public Policy, 1984), xxxv–xxxvi.

51 Hull, *Natives in a Class Society*, 19; Robertson, *Reservations Are for Indians*, 166–81; Kew, 'Making Indians,' 32. At Grassy Narrows, prior to the relocation of the reserve in 1963, 91 per cent of all deaths were attributable to natural causes. By the mid-1970s, 75 per cent of reserve deaths were due to alcohol or drug-induced violence, and included lethal stabbings, shootings, and expo-sure, as well as infanticide. In 1977–8 there were twenty-eight attempted sui-cides, with 12–16-year-olds dominating the statistics of those who attempted to take their lives. See Shkilnyk, *Poison Stronger than Love*, 11–49.

52 Breton and Grant, eds., *Dynamics of Government Programs*, 48; Satzewich and Wotherspoon, *First Nations*, 98; E. Dosman, *Indians: The Urban Dilemma* (Toronto: McClelland and Stewart, 1972); M. Nagler, *Indians in the City* (Ottawa: Canadian Research Centre for Anthropology, 1973; Hugh Brody, *Indians on Skid Row* (Ottawa: Northern Science Research Group, Depart-ment of Indian Affairs, 1971); David Ticoll and Stan Persky, 'Welcome to Ottawa! The Native People's Caravan,' *Canadian Dimension* 10 (January 1975): 14–31.

53 Morris C. Shumiatcher, 'Canadians with Nothing to Celebrate: The Plains Indians,' *Saturday Night*, June 1967, 29. While this statement may seem condescending to the Métis, it corresponds to Métis claims that in fact they

were far worse off than their 'Indian' brothers and sisters. See Duke Red-bird, *We Are Metis: A Metis View of the Development of a Native Canadian People* (Willowdale: Ontario Metis and Non Status Indian Association, 1980), esp. 32–3.

54 Peter Gzowski, 'Racism on the Prairies,' in Gzowski, *A Peter Gzowski Reader* (Toronto: McClelland and Stewart, 2001), 114.

55 Wilfred Pelletier, 'Childhood in an Indian Village,' in Satu Repo, ed., *This Book Is about Schools* (New York: Pantheon, 1970), 18–32.

56 Armstrong, *Slash*, 167.

57 Purich, *Our Land*, 183; Robertson, *Reservations Are for Indians*, 135; Satzewich and Wotherspoon, *First Nations*, 103; Pauline Comeau and Aldo Santin, *The First Canadians: A Profile of Native People Today* (Toronto: James Lorimer, 1995), 59.

58 James C. Scott, *Weapons of the Weak: Everyday Forms of Peasant Resistance* (New Haven: Yale University Press, 1985). For a discussion of Native people's prac-tices in relations to whites that is similar to Scott's suggestions about peasant behaviours towards lords see Niels Winther Braroe, *Indian and White: Self-Image and Interaction in a Canadian Plains Cree Community* (Stanford: Stanford University Press, 1975), 121–75.

59 Pelletier, 'Childhood,' 30.

60 See, for instance, Myrna Kostash, *Long Way From Home: The Story of the Sixties Generation in Canada* (Toronto: Lorimer, 1981), 147–65.

61 Robertson, *Reservations Are for Indians*, 135. Since the 1960s the deplorable conditions and social malaise on isolated reserves and in northern Inuit communities has continued, and periodic eruptions of journalistic outrage routinely detail the tragic legacies of a long-standing deterioration in Aboriginal Canada's well-being. For two recent examples, see Katherine Harding, 'In Nunavaut, an Epidemic of Violence and Despair,' *Globe and Mail*, 13 January 2007; Margaret Philp, 'A Slap in the Face of Every Cana-dian,' *Globe and Mail*, 3 February 2007.

62 For critical discussions of anthropology's influence see, among many possi-ble texts, Alan D. McMillan, *Native Peoples and Cultures of Canada: An Anthro-pological Overview* (Vancouver: Douglas and McIntyre, 1988), 7–18; Bernard McGrane, *Beyond Anthropology: Society and the Other* (New York: Columbia Uni-versity Press, 1989); Miller, *Skyscrapers Hide the Heavens*, 96–8; Noel Dyck, 'Cultures and Claims: Anthropology and Native Studies in Canada,' *Cana-dian Ethnic Studies* 22 (1990): 43–6. On Social Darwinism, see Richard Hofstadter, *Social Darwinism in American Thought* (New York: G. Braziller, 1959), and on artifacts and anthropologists, Douglas Cole, *Captured Heritage: The Scramble for Northwest Coast Artifacts* (Vancouver; Douglas and McIntyre,

1985). The Vine De Loria, Jr, quote is from *Custer Died for Your Sins: An Indian Manifesto* (New York: Macmillan, 1969), 78.

63　See, for instance, Brody, *Maps and Dreams*, and Braroe, *Indian and White*.

64　For discussion of Hawthorn and Price see Cairns, *Citizens Plus*, 52–65. For the continuity of the project of assimilation in the aftermath of the Second World War see as well Sheffield, *Red Man's on the Warpath*. Note for Jenness's significance, Peter Kulchyski, 'Anthropology in the Service of the State: Diamond Jenness and Canadian Indian Policy,' *Journal of Canadian Studies* 28 (Summer 1993): 21–40; Shewell, 'Jules Sioui and Indian Political Radicalism,' 215–19.

65　Cairns, *Citizens Plus*, 59, 161–2; H.B. Hawthorn, C.S. Belshaw, and Stuart Marshall Jamieson, *The Indians of British Columbia: A Study of Contemporary Social Adjustment* (Toronto: University of Toronto Press, 1958), 12, 39. On pages 478–9 of this 1958 report there is reference to Native peoples being a 'special class of Canadian citizens,' but this refers to specific taxation privileges and Cairns likely overestimates the significance of this passage.

66　For background and detail see Hugh Shewell, '"What Makes Indians Tick?": The Influence of Social Sciences on Canada's Indian Policy, 1947–1964,' *Histoire Sociale/Social History* 34 (May 2001): 133–67.

67　Hawthorn, *Survey of the Contemporary Indians of Canada*, 1: 13. Many histories and commentaries on Canadian Native peoples address the significance of the Hawthorn Report. For one account see Olive Patricia Dickason, *Canada's First Nations: A History of Founding Peoples from Earliest Times* (Toronto; McClelland and Stewart, 1994), 383–5.

68　Ian Adams, William Cameron, Brian Hill, and Peter Penz, *The Real Poverty Report* (Edmonton: Hurtig, 1971), 68–74; Jim Harding, 'Canada's Indians: A Powerless Minority,' in John Harp and John R. Hofley, eds., *Poverty in Canada* (Toronto: Prentice-Hall, 1971), esp. 240–3.

69　Miller, *Skyscrapers Hide the Heavens*, 223–4; Sally M. Weaver, *Making Canadian Indian Policy: The Hidden Agenda* (Toronto: University of Toronto Press, 1981).

70　Peter McFarlane, *Brotherhood to Nationhood: George Manuel and the Making of the Modern Indian Movement* (Toronto: Between the Lines, 1993), 89–90. Note the fuller account in Myra Rutherdale and Jim Miller, '"It's Our Country": First Nations' Participation in the Indian Pavilion at Expo 67,' *Journal of the Canadian Historical Association* 17, issue 2 (2006): 148–73.

71　For a radical Indigenous critique of Cairns see Dale Turner, *This Is Not a Peace Pipe: Towards a Critical Indigenous Philosophy* (Toronto: University of Toronto Press, 2006), esp. 38–56.

72　Robertson, *Reservations Are for Indians*, 303.

73 *Statement of the Government of Canada on Indian Policy, 1969* (Ottawa: Queen's
    Printer, Indian Affairs and Northern Development, 1969). For a thorough
    treatment of this period and its subsequent evolution see Weaver, *Making
    Canadian Indian Policy.* More radical is the discussion in James A. Duran,
    'The New Indian Policy: Lessons from the U.S.,' *Canadian Dimension* 6
    (December-January 1969–70): 21–3.
74 Miller, *Skysrapers Hide the Heavens,* 225.
75 There was of course support in Aboriginal circles for the White Paper,
    although it was definitely espoused by a distinct minority (estimated at about
    20 per cent of Indigenous leaders) and was vociferously opposed by most of
    the Native leadership, especially younger militants. For instance, one Native
    supporter of the White Paper, William I.C. Wuttunee, penned a critique of
    the new radicalism of Native youth and sided with Chrétien. See Wuttunee,
    Ruffled Feathers: Indians in Canadian Society (Calgary: Bell Books, 1971), but it
    earned him increasing marginalization in Aboriginal politics and he was
    barred from entering a number of reserves, including his Saskatchewan
    community, the Red Pheasant Reserve. For a militant repudiation of the pol-
    itics of Wuttunee, see Lloyd Roland Caibaiosai, 'The Politics of Patience,' in
    Waubageshig, ed., *The Only Good Indian: Essays by Canadian Indians* (Toronto:
    New Press, 1970), 153–4, which urges all Native people not to 'forget all the
    traitors who have been so brainwashed that they think what they are doing is
    right.' Mentioning Liberal politician Len Marchand and Wuttunee by name,
    Caibaiosai called on Aboriginal militants to 'remember them and every
    detail of their defection.' For broader discussion of pro-assimilationist
    thought among Natives see Cairns, *Citizens Plus,* 58–61; Dickason, *Canada's
    First Nations,* 387; Menno Boldt, 'Social Correlates of Nationalism: A Study
    of Native Indian Leaders in a Canadian Internal Colony,' *Comparative Politi-
    cal Studies* 14 (1981): 214–15; McFarlane, *Brotherhood to Nationhood,* 110–11.
76 For the record of liberalization see *Contemporary Indian Legislation, 1951–
    1978* (Ottawa: Treaties and Historical Research Centre, Corporate Policy,
    Department of Indian and Northern Affairs, 1981); Canada, *Looking
    Forward, Looking Back,* 307–19.
77 Kiera L. Ladner, 'Rethinking the Past, Present, and Future of Aboriginal
    Governance,' in J.Brodie and L. Trimble, eds., *Reinventing Canada* (Toronto:
    Canadian Scholars Press, 2003), 47; Belanger, 'Seeking a Seat at the Table,'
    152–61; Kulchyski, 'A Considerable Unrest,' 95–117; E. Brian Titley, 'The
    League of Indians of Canada: An Early Attempt to Create a National Native
    Organization,' *Saskatchewan Federated College Journal* 1 (1983): 53–63; Titley,
    A Narrow Vision, 102–9; Dobbin, *One-and-a-Half Men.* For a useful regional
    study see Paul Tennant, *Aboriginal Peoples and Politics: The Indian Land*

Question in British Columbia, 1849–1989 (Vancouver: UBC Press, 1990), esp. 84–113.

78 McFarlane, *Brotherhood to Nationhood*, 50.

79 Ibid., 45–72. See as well Tennant, *Aboriginal Peoples and Politics*, 125–38.

80 Alfred, *Heeding the Voices of Our Ancestors*, 160–1, with quotes on invasion and Conquest, and Laurence M. Hauptman, *The Iroquois Struggle for Survival: World War II to Red Power* (Syracuse, NY: Syracuse University Press, 1986), esp. 136–9, 150, 208, 225.

81 Purich, *Our Land*, 33; Mark Nagler, 'Patterns of Social Adjustment of Indians in the City,' in D.I. Davies and Kathleen Herman, eds., *Social Space: Canadian Perspectives* (Toronto: New Press, 1971), 126; Harold Cardinal, *The Unjust Society* (Vancouver: Douglas and McIntyre, 1999; original 1969), 88; Shewell, *Enough to Keep Them Alive*, 304–6.

82 Satzewich and Wotherspoon, *First Nations*, 229; J.S. Frideres, *Native Peoples in Canada: Contemporary Conflicts* (Scarborough, ON: Prentice-Hall, 1988), 268.

83 McFarlane, *Brotherhood to Nationhood*, 98; Satzewich and Wotherspoon, *First Nations*, 231.

84 McFarlane, *Brotherhood to Nationhood*, 70; *Peter Gzowski Reader*, 103–15, reprinting Gzowski, 'This Is Our Alabama,' *Maclean's*, 6 July 1963.

85 Dobbin, *One-and-a-Half Men*, 230–1. For conditions in northwestern Ontario towns such as Kenora see David H. Stymeist, *Ethnics and Indians: Social Relations in a Northwestern Ontario Town* (Toronto: Peter Martin, 1975).

86 Adams, *Tortured People*, 82–4; Dobbin, *One-and-a-Half Men*, 224–54.

87 McFarlane, *Brotherhood to Nationhood*, 97; Peter Matthiessen, *In the Spirit of Crazy Horse* (New York: Viking, 1983), 279; Steve Hewitt, *Spying 101: The RCMP's Secret Activities at Canadian Universities, 1917–1997* (Toronto: University of Toronto Press, 2002), 146, 156–8.

88 See especially the account of rising Aboriginal activism in the late 1960s and its connection to Black Power in Kostash, *Long Way from Home*, 147–65. For discussions of the importance of Fanon and theories of internal colonialism to Aboriginal militants see Waubageshig, 'The Comfortable Crisis,' in Waubageshig, ed., *The Only Good Indian*, 74–102; Maracle, *Bobbi Lee*, 194–5.

89 Kostash, *Long Way from Home*, 147–65; and on Alcatraz and Oakes there is much in Smith and Warrior, *Like a Hurricane*. But see as well Hauptman, *Iroquois Struggle for Survival*, 224–7; Richard Oakes, 'Alcatraz Is Not an Island,' *Ramparts* 11 (December 1969), esp. 35.

90 Andrew Nichols is quoted in 'New Brunswick Indians – Conservative Militants,' in Waubageshig, ed., *The Only Good Indian*, 50.

91 Cardinal, *The Unjust Society*, 90.

92 Redbird began writing poetry in his radical period of the late 1960s, much
    of it a condemnation of what white colonization had done to Native peoples.
    By 1977 he had mellowed somewhat and his best-known poem, 'I Am a
    Canadian,' was presented to Queen Elizabeth II during Silver Jubilee cele-
    brations. See Duke Redbird, 'I Am a Canadian,' in Moses and Goldie, eds.,
    Anthology of Native Literature, 114–15; and for Redbird's 1980 statement of
    Métis nationalism, see Redbird, *We Are Metis*.

93 Duke Redbird, 'I Am the Redman,' in Waubageshig, ed., *Only Good Indian*, 61.

94 Howard Adams, *Prison of Grass: Canada from the Native Point of View* (Toronto:
    General Publishing, 1975); Adams, *Tortured People*, 75; and the recently pub-
    lished Hartmut Lutz, ed., *Howard Adams: Otapawy! The Life of a Métis Leader in
    His Own Words and Those of His Contemporaries* (Saskatoon: Gabriel Dumont
    Institute, 2005). See also Fidler, *Red Power*, 15; Kostash, *Long Way from Home*,
    164–5. There is a brief discussion of the escalating militancy of Aboriginal
    politics and the development of Black Power sentiment in British Columbia
    in Isitt, 'Working-Class Agency, the Cold War, and the Rise of a New Left,'
    282–93, 307–10.

95 See among many possible general statements James Burke, *Paper Tomahawks:
    From Red Tape to Red Power* (Winnipeg: Queenston House, 1976); Tennant,
    Aboriginal Peoples and Politics, 139–64.

96 See Trudeau's full speech in Cumming and Mickenberg, eds., *Native Rights
    in Canada*, 331–2.

97 Cardinal, *The Unjust Society*.

98 See among many sources, Hauptman, *Iroquois Struggle for Survival*, 149–50,
    208, 222–7; Ernest Benedict, 'Indians and a Treaty,' in Waubageshig, *Only
    Good Indian*, 157–60; Oakes, 'Alcatraz Is Not an Island,' 35–40; Troy Johnson,
    'The Occupation of Alcatraz: Roots of American Indian Activism,' *Wicazo Sa
    Review* 10 (Autumn 1994): 63–79; Carolyn Strange and Tina Loo, 'Holding
    the Rock: The "Indianization" of Alcatraz Island, 1969–1999,' *The Public His-
    torian*, 23 (Winter 2001): 55–74; Smith and Warrior, *Like a Hurricane*; Treat,
    Around the Sacred Fire, 6–9, 32–3, which also addresses the importance of
    Vine DeLoria, Jr's *Custer Died for Your Sins* in its prediction of a revitalization
    of Aboriginal spirituality. Deloria, Jr, maintains that the protests of the 1960s
    were a continuation of older traditions and he argued that the media, in
    accenting the newness of Red Power, missed 'the entire meaning of the
    protest.' See Vine DeLoria, Jr, *Behind the Trail of Broken Treaties: An Indian
    Declaration of Independence* (New York: Dell, 1974), 4. While not wanting to
    understate continuity in Native protest, I would suggest that Red Power, like
    the New Left, needs to be considered both in its historical context and as
    something of a break from past protest traditions.

99   Cardinal, *The Unjust Society*; Fidler, *Red Power*, esp. 11, quoting *Globe and
     Mail*, 21 October 1967. Consider also the consequences of 'red' capitalism
     in terms of Native thought, evident in David Newhouse, 'Resistance Is
     Futile: Aboriginal Peoples Meet the Borg of Capitalism,' in John Douglas
     Bishop, ed., *Ethics and Capitalism* (Toronto: University of Toronto Press,
     2000), 141–55.

100 For a useful discussion of NARP see Maracle, *Bobbi Lee*. Also insightful is
     Armstrong, *Slash*, esp. 68–72, which suggests the emerging late-1960s con-
     nection of Red Power bodies like NARP and AIM. For a succinct and illu-
     minating statement of NARP's history and politics see Henry Jack, 'Native
     Alliance for Red Power,' in Waubageshig, ed., *Only Good Indian*, 162–78,
     and this book also contains a statement by NARP activist Gerry Gambill at a
     Conference on Human Rights at the Tobique Reserve in New Brunswick in
     August 1968 (179–80). The quote at the end of the paragraph comes from
     the same book, Lloyd Roland Caibaiosai, 'The Politics of Patience,' 149.

101 Fidler, *Red Power*, 8–9. On NARP see as well the brief comments in Isitt,
     'Working-Class Agency,' 291–3.

102 Maracle, *Bobbi Lee*, 218–19.

103 Cairns, *Citizens Plus*, 20. The Indian Chiefs of Alberta Red Paper, under the
     title 'Citizens Plus,' was reprinted in Waubageshig, ed., *Only Good Indian*,
     5–42.

104 Harold Cardinal, *The Rebirth of Canada's Indians* (Edmonton: Hurtig, 1977).

105 Cumming and Mickenberg, eds., *Native Rights in Canada*, 332.

106 Consider the discussion in Wayne Warry, *Unfinished Dreams: Community
     Healing and the Reality of Aboriginal Self-Government* (Toronto: University of
     Toronto Press, 1998).

107 Dee Brown, *Bury My Heart at Wounded Knee: An Indian History of the American
     West* (New York: Holt, Rinehart, and Winston, 1970); Smith and Warrior,
     Like a Hurricane; Dennis Banks with Richard Erdoes, *Ojibwa Warrior: Dennis
     Banks and the rise of the American Indian Movement* (Norman: University of
     Oklahoma Press, 2004); and for the best discussion of repression and the
     case of Peltier, Matthiessen, *In The Spirit of Crazy Horse*.

108 For a succinct overview see Peter Kulchyski, 'Forty Years in Indian Coun-
     try,' *Canadian Dimension* 37 (November-December 2003): 33–36. Specific
     struggles are discussed in Burke, *Paper Tomahawks*; John Gallagher and Cy
     Gonick, 'The Occupation of Anicinabe Park,' *Canadian Dimension* 10
     (November 1974): 21–40; David Ticoll and Stan Persky, 'Welcome to
     Ottawa: The Native People's Caravan,' *Canadian Dimension* 10 (January
     1975): 14–31; Vern Harper, *Following the Red Path: The Native People's Cara-
     van* (Toronto: NC Press, 1979); Morantz, *White Man's Gonna Getcha*; Boyce

Richardson, *Strangers Devour the Land: A Chronicle of the Assault upon the Last Coherent Hunting Culture in North America, the Cree Indians of Quebec, and Their Vast Primeval Homelands* (New York: Knopf, 1976); Richard F. Salisbury, *A Homeland for the Cree: Regional Development in James Bay, 1971–1981* (Montreal and Kingston: McGill-Queen's University Press, 1986); Mel Watkins, ed., *Dene Nation: The Colony Within* (Toronto: University of Toronto Press, 1977); Paul Driben and Robert S. Trudeau, *When Freedom Is Lost: The Dark Side of the Relationship between Government and the Fort Hope Band* (Toronto: University of Toronto Press, 1983). For different perspectives voiced at the time of the 2007 National Day of Action see Floyd Favel, 'Buckskin Revolution: A Cree Cultural Leader Speaks Out,' *Globe and Mail*, 12 June 2007; Collin Freeze, 'Mohawk Activist Resigned to Time behind Bars,' *Globe and Mail*, 2 July 2007.

109 For a scathing indictment of Aboriginal leaders' corruption and integration into the state and capitalism, one that draws very much on his experience in the Saskatchewan Métis politics of mobilization, see Adams, *Tortured People*, 177–95. Adams had alluded to this problem as early as 1968 in Warnock, 'Red Power: An Interview with Howard Adams,' 23. A Manitoba critique appears in Burke, *Paper Tomahawks*. Note, however, the more moderate Harold Cardinal, *The Rebirth of Canada's Indians*; Tennant's discussion of 'Big Money and Big Organizations' in the 1972–5 years in *Aboriginal Peoples and Politics*, 165–80; and Dyck's chapter on Native leaders and 1970s development initiatives in *What Is the Indian 'Problem,'* 119–38. On class differentiation in Native communities note as well Peter Usher, 'Northern Development, Impact Development, and Social Change,' in Noel Dyck and James B. Waldram, eds., *Anthropology, Public Policy and Native Peoples in Canada* (Montreal and Kingston: McGill-Queen's University Press, 1993), 98–130.

110 At this point it is recognized that Aboriginal peoples are not simply a disadvantaged 'racial minority,' but a collection of political entities seeking relations of autonomous and dignified coexistence with others in Canada. Such entities do not always seek the same solutions or structures of governance. See Rennie Warburton, 'Status, Class and the Politics of Canadian Aboriginal Peoples,' *Studies in Political Economy* 54 (Fall 1997): 119–41.

111 Adams, *Tortured People*, 83.

112 See Taiaiake Alfred, *Wasáse: Indigenous Pathways of Action and Freedom* (Peterborough, ON: Broadview Press, 2005).

113 On Harper see Dickason, *Canada's First Nations*, 420; Cairns, *Citizens Plus*, 146; Dyck, *What Is the Indian 'Problem,'* 160–1. Lee Maracle, *Sundogs* (Penticton, BC: Theytus Books, 1992), is a fictional account of Native

peoples' positive reaction to Harper, as well as their support for the Mohawk struggle to preserve their land in the armed standoff pitting Aboriginals against developers and the Quebec state in Oka over the period July–September 1990. A journalistic account of the significance of Harper, Oka, and the summer of 1990 is Richard Wagamese, *The Terrible Summer* (Toronto: Warwick, 1996). For more on the complexity of Oka see Gerald R. [Taiaiake] Alfred, 'From Bad to Worse: Internal Politics in the 1990 Oka Crisis at Kahnawake,' *Northeast Indian Quarterly* 8 (Spring 1991): 23–32. I am not suggesting that the 1960s illuminated the foundational place of Native peoples in Canadian identity for the first time. Such insights can be discerned much earlier in sensitive commentary on Canada, such as Harold Adams Innis's concluding remark in his 1930 major work, *The Fur Trade in Canada: An Introduction to Canadian Economic History* (Toronto: University of Toronto Press, 1962), 392: 'We have not yet realized that the Indian and his culture were fundamental to the growth of Canadian institutions.' Note as well Alexander John Watson, *Marginal Man: The Dark Vision of Harold Innis* (Toronto: University of Toronto Press, 2006), 46, 151. I think Gerald Friesen overemphasizes the centrality of Aboriginality to Canadian identity in a kind of transhistorical assertion of the development of the relationship by failing to appreciate the significant breakthroughs made in particular periods, one of which was the 1960s. See Friesen, *Citizens and Nation: An Essay on History, Communication, and Canada* (Toronto: University of Toronto Press, 2000), 52–4; Resnick, *European Roots of Canadian Identity*, 34.

11: Ironic Canadianism: National Identity and the 1960s

1 See Blair Fraser, *The Search for Identity: Canada – Postwar to Present* (Toronto: Doubleday, 1967), esp. 119–20, 248. Also Leslie Wright, compiler, *The War Years in the Oshawa Region: A Collection of Interviews, Newspaper Clippings, and Other Related Material* (Oshawa: Oshawa Public Library Board, 1975), 307–17. I am indebted to Christine McLaughlin for bringing this source to my attention. For a discussion of the curriculum of British-Canadian identity in the schools see José E. Igartua, *The Other Quiet Revolution: National Identitites in English Canada, 1945–71* (Vancouver: University of British Columbia Press, 2006), 63–88.

2 George Grant, *Lament for a Nation: The Defeat of Canadian Nationalism, 40th Anniversary Edition* (Montreal and Kingston: McGill-Queen's University Press, 2005); Fraser, *Search for Identity*, 311.

3 Fraser, *Search for Identity*, 315.

4 I am grateful to Neil S. Forkey for calling my attention to MacLennan's views. See, for a fuller discussion, Forkey, '"Thinking Like a River": The Making of Hugh MacLennan's Environmental Consciousness,' *Journal of Canadian Studies* 41 (Spring 2007): 42–65. Also, Hugh MacLennan, 'Thinking Like a River,' *Rivers of Canada* (Toronto: Macmillan, 1974), esp. 12.

5 MacLennan, 'Thinking Like a River,' 7–12.

6 Pierre Berton, *The Comfortable Pew: A Critical Look at the Church in the New Age* (Toronto: McClelland and Stewart, 1965); Berton, *The Smug Minority* (Toronto: McLelland and Stewart, 1968); John Porter, *The Vertical Mosaic: An Analysis of Social Class and Power in Canada* (Toronto: University of Toronto Press, 1965).

7 MacLennan, 'Thinking Like a River,' 7–12; Berton, *Smug Minority*, 74; Karl Marx and Friedrich Engels, *Manifesto of the Communist Party* (New York: Arrow Editions, 1933; original 1848), 7.

8 J.L. Granatstein, *Canada, 1957–1967: The Years of Uncertainty and Innovation* (Toronto: McClelland and Stewart, 1986), 308.

9 Pierre Berton, *1967: The Last Good Year* (Toronto: Doubleday, 1997), 367, contrasted with *The Smug Minority*, esp. 26–9, 39–44; Judy LaMarsh, *Memoirs of a Bird in a Gilded Cage* (Toronto: McClelland and Stewart, 1969), 228.

10 Betty Friedan, *The Feminine Mystique* (New York: Norton, 1963). For statements which complicate our understandings of the suburbs and the 1950s see Veronica Strong-Boag, '"Their Side of the Story": Women's Voices from Ontario, 1954–60,' in Joy Parr, ed., *A Diversity of Women: Ontario, 1945–1980* (Toronto: University of Toronto Press, 1995), 46–74; Valerie Joyce Korinek, *Roughing It in the Suburbs: Reading 'Chatelaine' Magazine in the Fifties and Sixties* (Toronto: University of Toronto Press, 2000).

11 Fraser, *Search for Identity*, 113–21; Franca Iacovetta, *Gatekeepers: Reshaping Immigrant Lives in Cold War Canada* (Toronto: Between the Lines, 2006), esp. 1–19; Igartua, *Other Quiet Revolution*, 16–62, with the *Ottawa Journal*, 'Young Men in a Hurry,' 16 April 1946, quoted on 25–6.

12 See, for instance, Barlow Cumberland, *History of the Union Jack and Flags of the Empire* (Toronto: McClelland, Goodchild and Stewart, 1914), esp. lines of verse from 'The Union Jack,' 11; John Ross Matheson, *Canada's Flag: A Search for a Country* (Belleville, ON: Mika, 1986), 1–64; Rick Archbold, *I Stand for Canada: The Story of the Maple Leaf Flag* (Toronto: Macfarlane, Walter, and Ross, 2002), 6.

13 Mabel Harbour, *Does Canada Need a New Flag? Some Facts Which All Loyal Canadians Should Know* (Toronto: British-Israel-World Federation, no date), no pagination.

14 Igartua, *Other Quiet Revolution*, 171–7.

15 Quoted in Fraser, *Search for Identity*, 242.

16 The 'Pearson Pennant' is pictured in Archbold, *I Stand for Canada*, 97, and its origins are commented on in Matheson, *Canada's Flag*, 128–9, where Whitton is quoted, 88, a text that explores the debate over the flag fully, 65–187. See also Granatstein, *Canada, 1957–1967*, 201–5; Igartua, *Other Quiet Revoltuion*, 171–92.

17 Igartua, *Other Quiet Revolution*, 188; Fraser, *Search for an Identity*, 247; Granatstein, *Canada, 1957–1967*, 205.

18 Quoted in Matheson, *Canada's Flag*, 184.

19 For comment on Expo 67 see Berton, *1967*, 256–99; Granatstein, *Canada, 1957–1967*, 302–4; Gary R. Miedema, *For Canada's Sake: Public Religion, Centennial Celebrations, and the Re-making of Canada in the 1960s* (Montreal and Kingston: McGill-Queen's University Press, 2005), 114–36.

20 Berton, *1967*, 256, 275; Granatstein, *Canada, 1957–1967*, 303.

21 See Meidema, *For Canada's Sake*, 121–2.

22 Berton, *1967*, 273.

23 Ibid., 359.

24 Barry Lord, 'A Visit to Expo '67,' *Canadian Dimension* 4 (September-October 1967): 30–2.

Index

internationalism, 14, 365

Internationalists, The, 281

International Mine, Mill, and Smelter Workers Union, 231, 239

International Molders and Allied Workers Union, 239

International Monetary Fund (IMF), 28, 32–3, 34, 38, 41, 44

International Nickel Company. *See* Inco

International Teach-In, 271–2

International Union of Operating Engineers, 239

internment camps, 10

Inuit peoples, 372, 384, 409

Inuit Tapirisat of Canada, 409

Ireland, 356

irony, 5–9, 13, 14, 20, 21, 145, 148, 150, 174, 176, 185, 197, 214, 241, 262, 276, 295, 307, 313, 331, 415–30; of Chuvalo–Ali fight, 127–37; of Diefenbaker 'interregnum,' 71–3; of sex appeal, 105–9

Iroquois confederacy, 377; *Kaienerekowa* (Great Law of Peace), 377

Iroquois Declaration of Independence, 404

Iroquois peoples, 397–8

Irvine, Russell, 228

Irwin, Arthur, 17

Isbester, Fraser, 318

Israel, 334

Italy, 158; student revolts in, 283; women's movement in, 298

Jack, Henry, 406

Jackson, Helen Hunt, 561n34

Jackson, William Henry, 561n34

Jacobs, Jane, 526n90

James, C.L.R., 111

James, Mungo, 219

James, Selma, 298

James Bay hydro-electric development, 409

Jameson, Fredric, 23, 434n19

Jamieson, Stuart Marshall, 222–3, 389

Jaxon, Honoré Joseph, 561n34

Jefferson Airplane, 204

Jeffries, Jim, 117–18

Jenness, Diamond, 379, 389

Jewish immigrant groups, 114

Johannson, Ingemar, 122

Johnson, Daniel, 164, 172

Johnson, E. Pauline, 561n34

Johnson, Jack, 117–20

Johnson, Lyndon B., 270, 428

Joli, Henri W., 226

Jones, Rocky, 267, 285

Joplin, Janis, 247

joual, 331

Juba, Steve, 133

Junction, The (Toronto), 113–16

Juneau, Pierre, 320

'Just Society,' 171, 176, 380, 403

Just Society Movement, 282, 526n90

juvenile delinquency. *See* delinquency

Juzda, Bill, 133

Kahnawake Mohawks, 377–8, 397

Kanesatake (Quebec), 409–10

Karl, Harry, 85

KCP. *See* Kingston Community Project

Kearney, Jim, 129–30

Keeler, Christine, 97–8

Kelso, J.J., 183

Kennedy, John F., 39, 44, 59–63, 66, 125

Kenora (Ontario), 399

Kent State University, 247